# International Handbook of Rural Demography

# International Handbooks of Population

## Volume 3

**Series Editor**

Dudley L. Poston, Jr.
Professor of Sociology, George T. & Gladys H. Abell Professor of Liberal Arts
Director, Asian Studies Program
Texas A&M University
ACAD Bldg. 425B (office)
College Station, Texas 77843-4351, USA

The *International Handbooks of Population* offer up-to-date scholarly summaries and sources of information on the major subject areas and issues of demography and population. Each handbook examines its particular subject area in depth, providing timely, accessible coverage of its full scale and scope, discusses substantive contributions for deeper understanding, and provides reliable guidance on the direction of future developments.

Volumes will explore topics of vital interest: Population Aging, Poverty, Mortality, Family Demography, Migration, Race and Ethnic Demography and more. Each volume will provide a state-of-the-art treatment of its respective area. The series will quickly prove useful to a broad audience including demographers, practitioners and scholars across a range of disciplines.

For further volumes:
http://www.springer.com/series/8111

László J. Kulcsár · Katherine J. Curtis
Editors

# International Handbook of Rural Demography

*Editors*
László J. Kulcsár
Kansas State University
Sociology, Anthropology and Social Work
Waters Hall 202D
Manhattan, KS 66506
USA
kulcsar@ksu.edu

Katherine J. Curtis
University of Wisconsin-Madison
Community and Environmental Sociology
1450 Linden Drive
Madison, WI 53706
USA
kcurtis@ssc.wisc.edu

ISSN 1877-9204
ISBN 978-94-007-1841-8          e-ISBN 978-94-007-1842-5
DOI 10.1007/978-94-007-1842-5
Springer Dordrecht Heidelberg London New York

Library of Congress Control Number: 2011937704

© Springer Science+Business Media B.V. 2012
No part of this work may be reproduced, stored in a retrieval system, or transmitted in any form or by any means, electronic, mechanical, photocopying, microfilming, recording or otherwise, without written permission from the Publisher, with the exception of any material supplied specifically for the purpose of being entered and executed on a computer system, for exclusive use by the purchaser of the work.

Printed on acid-free paper

Springer is part of Springer Science+Business Media (www.springer.com)

# Acknowledgements

This handbook would not have been possible without our colleagues in the W–2001 – Population Dynamics and Change: Aging, Ethnicity and Land Use Change in Rural Communities working group under the USDA CSREES. This community of rural demographers from various academic fields has been the conceptual nucleus behind this project. We wish to thank Dudley L. Poston for his confidence and support throughout the whole process as well as David L. Brown and Joachim Singelmann for their continuous advice and encouragement.

We would like to acknowledge the Kansas Agricultural Experiment Station at Kansas State University and the Wisconsin Agricultural Experiment Station at the University of Wisconsin-Madison for supporting the production of the handbook. We would also like to thank Rozalynn Klaas in the Applied Population Laboratory at the University of Wisconsin-Madison for her copyediting the handbook with infinite energy and patience.

This handbook is dedicated to all rural demographers, members of a relatively small but unique and devoted community who understand the links between the land and the people, and who carry on this scholarship for the benefit of all. We also dedicate this handbook to the people comprising the world's often unrecognized rural population.

# Contents

1 **Why Does Rural Demography Still Matter?** .............. 1
László J. Kulcsár and Katherine J. Curtis

**Part 1 Fundamental Issues and Trends in Rural Demography**

2 **Challenges in the Analysis of Rural Populations in the United States** .............. 7
Steve H. Murdock, Michael Cline, and Mary Zey

3 **Rural Natural Increase in the New Century: America's Third Demographic Transition** .............. 17
Kenneth M. Johnson and Daniel T. Lichter

4 **Migration and Rural Population Change: Comparative Views in More Developed Nations** .............. 35
David L. Brown

5 **World Urbanization: Destiny and Reconceptualization** .............. 49
Avery M. Guest

6 **Rural Aging in International Context** .............. 67
E. Helen Berry

**Part 2 Regional and Country Case Studies in Rural Demography**

7 **Europe's Rural Demography** .............. 81
Anthony Champion

8 **The Demography of Rural Latin America: The Case of Chile** .............. 95
Leif Jensen and David Ader

9 **Rural Demography in Asia and the Pacific Rim** .............. 111
Gavin Jones and Premchand Dommaraju

10 **Demographic Change and Rural-Urban Inequality in Sub-Saharan Africa: Theory and Trends** .............. 125
Parfait M. Eloundou-Enyegue and Sarah C. Giroux

| 11 | **Demographic Structure and Process in Rural China** . . . . . . . . . . | 137 |
|---|---|---|
| | Dudley L. Poston, Mary Ann Davis, and Danielle Xiaodan Deng | |
| 12 | **Rural Population Trends in Mexico: Demographic and Labor Changes** . . . . . . . . . . . . . . . . . . . . . . . . . . . . . . . | 155 |
| | Landy Sanchez and Edith Pacheco | |
| 13 | **Rural Demography of India** . . . . . . . . . . . . . . . . . . . . . . . | 169 |
| | T.V. Sekher | |
| 14 | **The Aboriginal People of Canada: A Rural Perspective** . . . . . . . . | 191 |
| | Gustave Goldmann | |

**Part 3 Social, Economic, and Environmental Dynamics in Rural Demography**

| 15 | **Rural Race and Ethnicity** . . . . . . . . . . . . . . . . . . . . . . . . | 207 |
|---|---|---|
| | Rogelio Sáenz | |
| 16 | **Family Matters: Gender, Work Arrangements, and the Rural Myth** . . . . . . . . . . . . . . . . . . . . . . . . . . . . . . . | 225 |
| | Leann M. Tigges and Hae Yeon Choo | |
| 17 | **Rural Families in Transition** . . . . . . . . . . . . . . . . . . . . . . | 239 |
| | Kristin E. Smith and Marybeth J. Mattingly | |
| 18 | **Rural Health Disparities** . . . . . . . . . . . . . . . . . . . . . . . . . | 255 |
| | P. Johnelle Sparks | |
| 19 | **Perspectives on U.S. Rural Labor Markets in the First Decade of the Twenty-First Century** . . . . . . . . . . . . . . . . . . | 273 |
| | Alexander C. Vias | |
| 20 | **Race and Place: Determinants of Poverty in the Texas Borderland and the Lower Mississippi Delta** . . . . . . . . . . . . . . | 293 |
| | Joachim Singelmann, Tim Slack, and Kayla Fontenot | |
| 21 | **Rural Jobs: Making a Living in the Countryside** . . . . . . . . . . . | 307 |
| | Gary Paul Green | |
| 22 | **The Spatial Heterogeneity and Geographic Extent of Population Deconcentration: Measurement and Policy Implications** . . . . . . . . . . . . . . . . . . . . . . . . . . . | 319 |
| | Joanna P. Ganning and Benjamin D. McCall | |
| 23 | **Integrating Ecology and Demography to Understand the Interrelationship Between Environmental Issues and Rural Populations** . . . . . . . . . . . . . . . . . . . . . . . . . . | 333 |
| | Christopher A. Lepczyk, Marc Linderman, and Roger B. Hammer | |
| 24 | **Boom or Bust? Population Dynamics in Natural Resource-Dependent Counties** . . . . . . . . . . . . . . . . . . . . . . | 349 |
| | Richelle Winkler, Cheng Cheng, and Shaun Golding | |

## Part 4 Broad Perspectives for Future Rural Demography

**25 Neoliberal Democratization and Public Health Inequalities in Sub-Saharan Africa: A Proposed Conceptual and Empirical Design** .................... 369
Moshi Optat Herman

**26 Diverse Ruralities in the 21st Century: From Effacement to (Re-)Invention** .................... 387
Keith Halfacree

**Index** .................... 401

# Contributors

**David Ader** Department of Agricultural Economics and Rural Sociology and the Population Research Institute, Pennsylvania State University, University Park, PA 16802, USA, dra145@psu.edu

**E. Helen Berry** Department of Sociology, Social Work and Anthropology, Utah State University, Logan, UT 84322-0730, USA, Eddy.Berry@usu.edu

**David L. Brown** Department of Development Sociology, Cornell University, Ithaca, NY 14850, USA, Dlb17@cornell.edu

**Anthony Champion** School of Geography, Politics and Sociology, University of Newcastle, Newcastle upon Tyne NE1 7RU, UK, tony.champion@newcastle.ac.uk

**Cheng Cheng** Applied Population Laboratory, Department of Community and Environmental Sociology, University of Wisconsin-Madison, Madison, WI 53706, USA, cheng25@wisc.edu

**Hae Yeon Choo** Department of Sociology, University of Wisconsin-Madison, Madison, WI 53706, USA, hychoo@ssc.wisc.edu

**Michael Cline** Department of Sociology, Rice University, Houston, TX 77005-1827, USA, Mec6@rice.edu

**Katherine J. Curtis** Department of Community and Environmental Sociology, University of Wisconsin-Madison, Madison, WI 53706, USA, kcurtis@ssc.wisc.edu

**Mary Ann Davis** Department of Sociology, Sam Houston State University, Huntsville, TX 77341-2446, USA, mad011@shsu.edu

**Danielle Xiaodan Deng** Department of Sociology, Texas A&M University, College Station, TX 77843-4351, USA, danielle523@gmail.com

**Premchand Dommaraju** Division of Sociology, School of Humanities and Social Sciences, Nanyang Technological University, 637332 Singapore, premchand@ntu.edu.sg

**Parfait M. Eloundou-Enyegue** Department of Development Sociology, Cornell University, Ithaca, NY 14853, USA, pme7@cornell.edu

**Kayla Fontenot** Department of Sociology, Louisiana State University, Baton Rouge, LA 70803, USA, kfonte8@tigers.lsu.edu

**Joanna P. Ganning** Department of Public Policy Studies, Saint Louis University, Saint Louis, MO 63103, USA, jganning@slu.edu

**Sarah C. Giroux** Department of Development Sociology, Cornell University, Ithaca, NY 14853, USA, sh104@cornell.edu

**Shaun Golding** Department of Community and Environmental Sociology, University of Wisconsin-Madison, Madison, WI 53706, USA, sgolding@ssc.wisc.edu

**Gustave Goldmann** University of Ottawa, Ottawa, ON, K1N 6N5, Canada; Carleton University, Ottawa, ON, K1S 5B6, Canada, ggoldman@uottawa.ca

**Gary Paul Green** Department of Community and Environmental Sociology, University of Wisconsin-Madison, Madison, WI 53706, USA, gpgreen@wisc.edu

**Avery M. Guest** Department of Sociology, University of Washington, Seattle, WA 98195-3340, USA, averyguest@gmail.com

**Keith Halfacree** Department of Geography, School of the Environment and Society, Swansea University, Swansea SA2 8PP, UK, k.h.halfacree@swansea.ac.uk

**Roger B. Hammer** Department of Sociology, Oregon State University, Corvallis, OR 97331, USA, rhammer@oregonstate.edu

**Moshi Optat Herman** Department of Sociology, Brown University, Providence, RI 02912, USA, optat_tengia@brown.edu

**Leif Jensen** Department of Agricultural Economics and Rural Sociology and the Population Research Institute, Pennsylvania State University, University Park, PA 16802, USA, lij1@psu.edu

**Kenneth M. Johnson** Department of Sociology and Carsey Institute, University of New Hampshire, Durham, NH 03824, USA, Ken.Johnson@unh.edu

**Gavin Jones** Asia Research Institute, National University of Singapore, 259770, Singapore, arigwj@nus.edu.sg

**László J. Kulcsár** Department of Sociology, Anthropology and Social Work, Kansas State University, Manhattan, KS 66506, USA, kulcsar@ksu.edu

**Christopher A. Lepczyk** Department of Natural Resources and Environmental Management, University of Hawai'i at Mānoa, Honolulu, HI 96822, USA, lepczyk@hawaii.edu

**Daniel T. Lichter** Departments of Policy Analysis and Management and Sociology, Cornell University, Ithaca, NY 14853, USA, DTL28@cornell.edu

**Marc Linderman** Department of Geography, The University of Iowa, Iowa City, IA 52242, USA, marc-linderman@uiowa.edu

**Marybeth J. Mattingly** The Carsey Institute and Department of Sociology, University of New Hampshire, Durham, NH 03824, USA, beth.mattingly@unh.edu

**Benjamin D. McCall** Department of Public Policy Studies, Saint Louis University, Saint Louis, MO 63103, USA, bmccall3@slu.edu

**Steve H. Murdock** Department of Sociology, Rice University, Houston, TX 77005-1827, USA, Shm3@rice.edu

**Edith Pacheco** El Colegio de México, A.C. Center for Demographic, Urban, and Environmental Studies, C.P.10740, México, D.F., México, mpacheco@colmex.mx

**Dudley L. Poston, Jr.** Department of Sociology, Texas A&M University, College Station, TX 77843-4351, USA, d-poston@tamu.edu

**Rogelio Sáenz** College of Public Policy, University of Texas at San Antonio, San Antonio, TX 78207, USA, Rogelio.Saenz@utsa.edu

**Landy Sanchez** El Colegio de México, A.C. Center for Demographic, Urban, and Environmental Studies, C.P.10740, México, D.F., México, lsanchez@colmex.mx

**T.V. Sekher** Department of Population Policies and Programmes, International Institute for Population Sciences (IIPS), Deonar, Mumbai 400 088, India, tvsekher@gmail.com

**Joachim Singelmann** Department of Demography, The University of Texas at San Antonio, 501 W. Durango Blvd., San Antonio, TX 78207, USA; Wissenschaftszentrum Berlin (WZB), Berlin, Germany, Joachim.Singelmann@utsa.edu

**Tim Slack** Department of Sociology, Louisiana State University, Baton Rouge, LA 70803, USA, slack@lsu.edu

**Kristin E. Smith** The Carsey Institute and Department of Sociology, University of New Hampshire, Durham, NH 03824, USA, kristin.smith@unh.edu

**P. Johnelle Sparks** Department of Demography, University of Texas at San Antonio, San Antonio, TX 78207, USA, johnelle.sparks@utsa.edu

**Leann M. Tigges** Department of Community and Environmental Sociology, University of Wisconsin-Madison, Madison, WI 53706, USA, lmtigges@wisc.edu

**Alexander C. Vias**[†] Geography Department, University of Connecticut, Storrs, CT 06269-4148, USA, alexander.vias@uconn.edu

**Richelle Winkler** Department of Social Sciences, Michigan Technological University, Houghton, MI 49931, USA; Applied Population Laboratory, Department of Community and Environmental Sociology, University of Wisconsin-Madison, Madison, WI 53706, USA, rwinkler@mtu.edu

**Mary Zey** Departments of Demography and Organization Studies, The University of Texas at San Antonio, San Antonio, TX 78249, USA, Mary.zey@utsa.edu

# Why Does Rural Demography Still Matter?

László J. Kulcsár and Katherine J. Curtis

## The Importance of Rural Demography

By the late 1970s, agricultural collectivization had ended in Hungary. The urban industrialization agenda of state socialism induced mass rural out-migration. The older generations who were left behind had started farming before the collectivization began, and were very much attached to the land they were allowed to keep. Of course, this is not something that one notices as a child when visiting grandparents in villages like Hernád was at that time. As a demographer looking back to those days, it is not impossible to identify the roots of those population trends that pose significant challenges in rural Hungary today. The mental image of rurality for a child was that of strong family traditions, harvest celebrations and weekend trips. For the grandparents it was the way of life, riddled with the struggle to make a living under a policy regime with a strong pro-urban development agenda. And for the parents it was a dual image, a place they left for the bright lights of the city but also the place where their roots remained.

Meanwhile, halfway across the world in the high plains of Montana, rural-to-urban out-migration had long been underway. During this period, rural America as a whole was experiencing population ebbs and flows known to demographers as the "population turnaround" and "rural renaissance." But in this isolated rural community on the Hi-Line, hundreds of miles from the nearest metropolitan area or national treasure, population mostly ebbed as descendants of homesteaders encouraged their own offspring to seek greater fortunes elsewhere. Agricultural policy, global markets, and environmental conditions were tied up in individual and household decisions about whether to stay, when to marry, who should work, and what education meant. Rurality meant negotiating between economic preservation and identity. Such negotiations were complicated by gender and ethnicity, as attachments to place and access to the world beyond the small town were not equally experienced by or available to everyone in the community.

As these two personal impressions from the authors intimate, over the course of history, rural places have been seen as population reserves for urbanization and industrialization. Rurality was often synonymous with backwardness, and modernization in many countries was conceptualized and understood as a shrinking proportion of the population living in rural areas. Policy measures more often promoted urban expansion than rural development, and in some cases rural areas were deliberately left undeveloped. As a result, in most countries, rural areas are economically disadvantaged and rural populations are more likely to live in poverty. Such disadvantages are often related to demographic trends and composition causing significant challenges for policy makers today. It is particularly important for the international community of scholars and policy makers to understand rural demographic trends to best assess and prepare for future changes and challenges that will confront rural populations.

The most common perception of rurality stems from a dichotomous view of what is urban and rural which, subsequently, assumes that rural areas are

L.J. Kulcsár (✉)
Department of Sociology, Anthropology and Social Work,
Kansas State University, Manhattan, KS 66506, USA
e-mail: kulcsar@ksu.edu

homogeneous. This assumption is far from being true. Scholars in recent years have advocated for settlement morphology beyond this dichotomy (Champion & Hugo, 2004). This could and should be developed at the national level, similarly to how the term "urban" is defined. Although this may hinder international comparisons, it is still the best way to address the significant cultural, social, economic, administrative and political differences across countries.

Trends in developed countries show that rural areas are increasingly diverse in economic structure; in fact, the presence of certain amenities, historical development patterns or cultural conditions can reverse long-term rural depopulation and can lead to the reevaluation of rurality. Rural is no longer synonymous with agricultural since many communities have developed multifunctional economic structures together with complex local societies and a diverse demographic composition.

The growing complexity of rural society is partly a product of significant international variation in rural demographic trends. About 90% of the rural population lives in less developed countries (UN, 2010). There are dramatic regional differences in the resources, policy regimes, cultural conditions, and development challenges that rural communities confront. Although it is important to identify common themes in rural demography, it is also crucial to examine regional variations of rural population composition and change. Regional variation is evident; from the idyllic British countryside, across the American Great Plains and China's rural hinterland to areas in Africa still dominated by subsistence agriculture, rural areas bear different natural resources, cultural values, social norms, and economic opportunities.

Similarly, within-country differences are significant as well. Taking the United States as an example, the amenity-rich rural areas of Colorado show little resemblance to the agricultural communities of Iowa, just as the African-American communities of the South are different from the High Plains of the Texas panhandle. In each of those places, local histories and traditions are intertwined with the social fabric of the communities, producing various outcomes for even generally uniform demographic trends such as population aging.

The implication of this recent diversification is that the future development trajectory of rural communities will differ too, increasingly based on local characteristics, including population composition. Some will remain or become sustainable places to live, while others will struggle with rapid depopulation. Therefore, rural demography as a field will not lose its importance. Rather, the field will become ever more important to assess the drivers and impacts of the increasingly complex rural society. In order to successfully address growth disparities, policy makers need to understand how demographic dynamics are related to the economic, social, and environmental characteristics of rural areas. The interactions between the changing demographic composition (e.g., aging, outmigration) and economic capacity (e.g., tax revenues, labor force composition) influence the sustainability potential of rural communities.

Researchers also need to understand the unique aspects of the rural context to produce meaningful results that will continue to advance policy and scholarship. Although rural places are diverse, several of the challenges that rural areas face are more or less uniform trends. Managing natural resources, addressing the local impacts of the global economy or reconceptualizing what "rural" means in a rapidly changing world are tasks facing most if not all rural communities in all nations.

## Rurality and Global Rural Demographic Trends

Although scholars have spent considerable time and effort discussing and measuring urbanization, trying to identify universal trends and characteristics (see for example Burgess, 1925; Tisdale, 1942; Tilly, 1974; Castells, 1977; de Vries, 1984; Berry & Wheeler, 2005), rurality was neglected by this discourse. It remained so during the study of suburbanization (Jackson, 1985; Teaford, 2008), and for most of the discourse about counterurbanization, a new demographic trend in postindustrial countries (Berry, 1976; Vining & Kontuly, 1978; Fielding, 1982; Champion, 1989; Kontuly, 1998).

In recent years, however, the interest in better understanding urban complexity as well as rurality has increased, and culminated in the edited volume by Tony Champion and Graeme Hugo (2004). Beyond the rich conceptual and empirical discussion, it also featured the two major arguments for rural complexity. The first is the theme of rural being diverse, building on the traditions of human ecology. Brown and Cromartie (2004) argued that rurality is a multidimensional concept and the movement away from a dichotomous urban-rural definition should acknowledge the complexity within the rural category as well. In other words, it is not enough to refine our understanding of what urban is because that still leaves rural as the residual, but scholars should study the diversity of rural places too, based on four major dimensions: ecological, economic, institutional, and sociocultural attributes of places.

The second major theme contesting the simplified definition of rural was elaborated by Halfacree (2004). This theme takes a more conceptual perspective, emphasizing the social construction of rurality. It captures rural diversity by focusing less on material or functional indicators and more on the conceptual link between the actual rural places and their social representation. Rural diversity is acknowledged by contesting the quest for essential features and universal measurements, and by emphasizing the strong contextual nature of rurality.

Both themes, together with the recent scholarship arguing for more complexity in definitions state that urban and rural are closely connected. Once we move away from the dichotomy, the scale can be reconstructed as everything being urban (or rural), and the differences are simply in the degrees. This conceptualization works well within an ecological approach. However, it is less useful for addressing value-based identities connected to urban titles. In such cases, the scale represents political identities or values as opposed to clear statistical categories or neutral mental constructs. Rurality is often burdened with the image of development deficiencies, the backwater, and becomes part of a political game of titles, strengthening a simplified, dichotomous view (Kulcsár & Brown, 2011). Here, a constructivist approach could help reconceptualize rurality and, in turn, result in a new operationalization for statistical measurement.

But what makes the issue of rurality and rural population trends more than just a theoretical exercise? According to the 2009 revision of the World Urbanization Prospects, some time during 2008 the proportion of rural population dropped below 50% for the first time in human history (UN, 2010). This is a trend which is unlikely to reverse. Indeed, the global rural population is expected to reach a maximum of 3.5 billion in 2020 and to decline slowly thereafter. By 2050, the world will have half a billion less rural residents than today (UN, 2010).

In 1950, only six of the thirty most populous countries had urban populations above 50%. By 2009, this number increased to 16. If the UN projections hold, in 2050 all but one of the thirty most populous countries will have more urban than rural residents (UN, 2010). At the same time, the list will also change considerably given uneven patterns of population growth across the globe.

Urbanization occurs unevenly across world regions (see Tables 1.1 and 1.2, and also Chapter 5 in this volume). Europe and North America were already predominantly urban in 1950. Latin America turned mostly urban in the mid-1960s. Despite the recent global crossover, Africa still has 200 million more rural residents than city dwellers. The difference in Asia is more than 600 million people (UN, 2010). The combined *surplus* of rural population in Africa and Asia equals the total population of Europe. These regional differences indicate that the global rural population is increasingly concentrated in less developed regions. Most of the rural population growth in the future will occur in Asia and Africa, until rural populations peak in those regions too, in about ten and thirty years respectively. For example, compared to 1950, Africa's

**Table 1.1** Rural populations by selected world regions (millions)

|  | 1950 | 1960 | 1970 | 1980 | 1990 | 2000 | 2010 | 2020 | 2030 | 2040 | 2050 |
| --- | --- | --- | --- | --- | --- | --- | --- | --- | --- | --- | --- |
| World | 1,800 | 2,026 | 2,356 | 2,710 | 3,036 | 3,278 | 3,422 | 3,499 | 3,409 | 3,182 | 2,864 |
| More developed regions | 385 | 377 | 356 | 343 | 336 | 326 | 307 | 280 | 245 | 209 | 176 |
| Less developed regions | 1,415 | 1,649 | 2,000 | 2,368 | 2,700 | 2,952 | 3,115 | 3,218 | 3,164 | 2,973 | 2,689 |
| Africa | 195 | 232 | 280 | 348 | 434 | 525 | 620 | 707 | 763 | 783 | 768 |
| Asia | 1,174 | 1,356 | 1,642 | 1,934 | 2,176 | 2,337 | 2,409 | 2,427 | 2,318 | 2,111 | 1,849 |
| Europe | 267 | 260 | 244 | 227 | 218 | 212 | 199 | 180 | 156 | 131 | 109 |
| Northern America | 62 | 61 | 61 | 66 | 69 | 66 | 63 | 59 | 55 | 50 | 44 |
| Latin America | 98 | 111 | 123 | 129 | 131 | 128 | 120 | 112 | 104 | 94 | 82 |

*Source*: UN (2010).

**Table 1.2** Rural populations by selected world regions as percent of the 1950 population

| | 1960 | 1970 | 1980 | 1990 | 2000 | 2010 | 2020 | 2030 | 2040 | 2050 |
|---|---|---|---|---|---|---|---|---|---|---|
| World | 113 | 131 | 151 | 169 | 182 | 190 | 194 | 189 | 177 | 159 |
| More developed regions | 98 | 92 | 89 | 87 | 85 | 80 | 73 | 64 | 54 | 46 |
| Less developed regions | 117 | 141 | 167 | 191 | 209 | 220 | 227 | 224 | 210 | 190 |
| Africa | 119 | 144 | 179 | 223 | 270 | 319 | 364 | 392 | 403 | 395 |
| Asia | 116 | 140 | 165 | 185 | 199 | 205 | 207 | 198 | 180 | 158 |
| Europe | 97 | 91 | 85 | 82 | 80 | 75 | 68 | 58 | 49 | 41 |
| Northern America | 99 | 98 | 107 | 112 | 107 | 101 | 95 | 88 | 80 | 71 |
| Latin America | 113 | 125 | 132 | 134 | 130 | 122 | 115 | 106 | 96 | 83 |

*Source*: UN (2010).

rural population tripled by today, and is expected to grow until around 2040 when it peaks at a number four times as large as it was in 1950 (Table 1.2). If one were to construct a mental image of rural life today, it is increasingly likely to be that of rurality in Africa or Asia.

Thus, despite the general decline in the relative size of the rural population, rural communities will remain the home to a large proportion of the global population in the foreseeable future. At the same time, the regional distribution of rural population will change significantly. However, apart from these facts, there are further important reasons why it is crucial to understand contemporary rural demographic trends.

Natural and social systems are inherently linked, therefore a discourse on natural resources and the environment cannot neglect humans who live in rural areas that supply most of the natural resources and absorb most of the environmental impact. Rural areas will continue to cover most of the land surface and will provide most of the natural resources to sustain the global population. The discourse on population change and the use of natural resources dates back to Malthus' time, and had several variants over the past two hundred years, usually seen from the perspective of urban populations, simply identifying the needs of urban places that were supposedly the drivers of modernization and societal progress.

In recent years, considerable attention was given to the links between demographic trends, land use, and environmental impacts. Despite the rapid urbanization and farmland conversion, the vast majority of the land and the natural resources underneath it are and will remain in rural areas. Rural areas provide resources that have been traditionally exported and transformed into higher value products in other locations. Today, lower populated, resource-rich areas face the challenge of managing natural resources for community sustainability in terms of economic and population growth. In certain cases, economic and population growth are separated, and economically successful production systems co-exist with long-term depopulation (White, 2008). Economic structures with particularly specialized and short-term perspectives, such as hyperextraction regimes like farming and mining, are good examples for production booms related to nonsustainable demographic structures.

To ensure the sustainable use of natural resources it is important to have sustainable social systems in place. As a field, demography is particularly well positioned to inform policy makers and scholars about broad structural trends that affect rural populations, as well as to assess the community development impact of population trends. The time of grand population policies and demographic engineering is largely over, but carefully selected incentives must be in place to balance economic growth and social equity in the context of demographic sustainability.

## The Structure of the Handbook

This is the first book written on rural demography from an international perspective. Books on rural development seldom have cross-national or cross-regional comparisons, and do not discuss the demographic determinants in detail. Books on general demographic themes usually do not focus on the rural aspect of population dynamics, apart from a few examples on rural depopulation mostly taken as a byproduct of urbanization and modernization. This handbook fills a tremendous gap by investigating rural population trends from an international perspective and deconstructing the processes that drive rural demography. The content and organization of the handbook reflects the diversity of rural places as well as the fundamental rural demographic trends and their interaction with development patterns.

Chapters 2–6 address fundamental issues and trends, starting with the challenges of rural demographic analysis using the United States as the example. This relates to the point about rurality being complex enough to require a multifaceted analytical approach. The subsequent four chapters discuss within the international context natural increase and migration, the two fundamental components of demographic change, as well as urbanization and aging, basic trends that are affecting rural population composition and change.

Chapters 7–14 are regional or country case studies. The first four chapters discuss Europe, Latin America, Asia, and Africa, focusing on rural trends and differences across the rural-urban spectrum. Next to follow are chapters detailing specific dynamics operating within selected countries: China, Mexico, India, and Canada. These eight case studies address the similarities and differences of rural demographic trends across countries.

The chapters immediately following the case studies discuss social and economic dynamics related to demographic trends in the context of the rural United States. Chapters 15–18 address social components, including race and ethnicity, gender, family, and health. Chapters 19–22 focus on economic trends, analyzing labor markets, poverty, and the economic impact of population deconcentration at the urban fringe.

In Chapters 23 and 24 the Handbook reaches back to the theme of environment and natural resources, providing impetus for future research linking natural and social systems. Chapter 23 discusses the link between ecology and demography from a conceptual perspective, while Chapter 24 provides an applied outlook on demography and natural resource dependence.

The last two chapters of the Handbook revisit the broad perspectives on studying rurality. Chapter 25 discusses the impact of the current neoliberal economic development paradigm on rural-urban inequalities, offering a conceptual framework for political demography. Finally, Chapter 26 reaches back to the second theme arguing for rural complexity by discussing the social construction of diverse ruralities. Although not a formal synthesis of the myriad issues addressed in the preceding chapters, the final chapter ends where future demographic research on rural populations might begin. Demographic research and policy would be best served by analyses that consider the social, political, economic and environmental contexts—whether unique to or shared by several countries—and the associated implications for the meaning and measurement of rural. Just as rural populations and places continue to evolve in their demographic characteristics and processes in the 21st century, so too must the approaches of those who study them.

## References

Berry, B. (1976). The counterurbanization process: Urban America since 1970. In B. J. L. Berry (Ed.), *Urbanization and counterurbanization* (pp. 111–143). Beverly Hills, CA: Sage.

Berry, B., & Wheeler, J. (Eds.). (2005). *Urban geography in America, 1950–2000. Paradigms and personalities.* New York: Routledge.

Brown, D., & Cromartie, J. (2004). The nature of rurality in postindustrial society. In T. Champion & G. Hugo (Eds.), *New forms of urbanization: Beyond the urban-rural dichotomy* (pp. 269–284). Aldershot, England: Ashgate.

Burgess, E. W. (1967) [1925]. The growth of the city: An introduction to a research project. In E. W. Burgess & R. D. McKenzie (Eds.), *The city* (pp. 47–62). Chicago: University of Chicago Press.

Castells, M. (1977). *The urban question.* London: Edward Arnold.

Champion, A. G. (Ed.). (1989). *Counterurbanization. The changing pace and nature of population deconcentration.* London: Edward Arnold.

Champion, A. G., & Hugo, G. (Eds.). (2004). *New forms of urbanization: Beyond the urban-rural dichotomy.* Aldershot, England: Ashgate.

de Vries, J. (1984). *European urbanization 1500–1800.* Cambridge: Harvard University Press.

Fielding, A. J. (1982). Counterurbanization in Western Europe. *Progress in Planning, 17,* 1–52.

Halfacree, K. (2004). Rethinking 'rurality'. In T. Champion & G. Hugo (Eds.), *New forms of urbanization: Beyond the urban-rural dichotomy* (pp. 285–304). Aldershot, England: Ashgate.

Jackson, K. (1985). *Crabgrass frontier: The suburbanization of the United States.* New York: Oxford University Press.

Kontuly, T. (1998). Contrasting the counterurbanisation experience in European nations. In P. Boyle & K. Halfacree (Eds.), *Migration into rural areas* (pp. 61–78). *Theories and issues.* Chichester: Wiley.

Kulcsár, L. J., & Brown, D. L. (2011). The political economy of urban reclassification in post-socialist Hungary. *Regional Studies, 45*, 479–490.

Teaford, J. C. (2008). *The American suburb*. New York: Routledge.

Tilly, C. (Ed.). (1974). *Urban world*. Boston: Little Brown.

Tisdale, H. (1942). The process of urbanization. *Social Forces, 20*, 311–316.

United Nations (UN). (2010). *World urbanization prospects, the 2009 revision*. New York: United Nations (UN).

Vining, D. R., & Kontuly, T. (1978). Population dispersal and major metropolitan regions: An international comparison. *International Regional Science Review, 3*, 49–73.

White, K. J. C. (2008). Population change and farm dependence: Temporal and spatial variation in the U.S. great plains, 1900–2000. *Demography, 45*, 363–386.

# Challenges in the Analysis of Rural Populations in the United States

Steve H. Murdock, Michael Cline, and Mary Zey

## Defining Rural in Rural Demography

### Defining the Concept of Rural

Rural demography is, in some ways, a misnomer because it is really just demography in which the population of interest resides in an area defined as rural. As will be demonstrated below, it is not a discipline that analyzes distinct populations using a distinct form of demographic analysis. Whatever the appropriate label however, there is little doubt that rural demographers face unique conceptual and methodological challenges because of the small number of persons in the areal locations of their populations of interest. They are often forced to analyze data for areas which are simply defined as residual (to urban) geographic areas that may or may not be true functioning areas in which population patterns can, in fact, be attributed to their "rural" characteristics (for excellent discussions of this dilemma see Hugo, Champion, & Lattes, 2003; Isserman, 2005; Farmer, 2008).

Defining what is rural is thus a key part of rural demography. What can and should be done to define "rural" areas has received substantial conceptual and empirical examination. The definition of "rural" as applied to rural areas such as communities has been a major topic of debate in areas such as rural sociology and rural geography since the inception of these disciplines (for discussions of these roots see Murdock and Sutton, 1974; Bunce, 1982; Wilkinson, 1991; Farmer, 2008). Discussions of what delineates an urban community, and hence by omission defines a rural community, have a similarly long tradition in demography as well (see for example, Hawley, 1950, 1986). Assertions that rural is defined by how people make a living in a given geographic area and attempts to delineate rural areas by using the predominance (usually in terms of the percent employed) of employment in "rural" industries such as agriculture, forestry, mining and other extractive industries in an area are often insufficient to identify what many believe is the social uniqueness of rural areas (see for example, Duncan & Reiss, 1956; Brown & Swanson, 2003). Similarly, conceptions of rural areas as defined by the frequency and form of interactions among residents are extremely difficult to implement for comparative studies of a large number of areas (see Bernard, 1955; Kaufman, 1959). More prevalent but equally difficult are the attempts to define rural as place or space (see for example, Warren, 1972; Kraenzel, 1980) because they often involve delineations based entirely on density or distance from a large urban center when in fact what is dense and at what distances rural and urban areas maintain key linkages is highly dependent on geography and culture, factors that are defined and appear to operate differently from East to West and from North to South in the United States with even wider variation internationally. To date there is no clear resolution of these problems.

The resolution of issues surrounding what is rural may seem to some of the pragmatic adherents of the discipline of demography as of limited importance to their analysis. However, the dilemma for the rural demographer (who may be impatient about such

S.H. Murdock (✉)
Department of Sociology, Rice University, Houston,
TX 77005-1827, USA
e-mail: Shm3@rice.edu

definitional tasks that may delay attempts to analyze demographic patterns in "rural" areas) is that it is difficult to argue that demographic change in rural areas is unique and important if one does not know what defines such an area and what it is about such areas that causes their demographic phenomena to be unique. Although this is not the place for a further elaboration of the conceptual basis of rurality, of what is meant by rural and thus of how it should be defined, rural demographers clearly have a stake in what other rural scholars determine as the essence of rurality.

## Identifying the Geography of Rural Areas: The Problem of the Residual

Regardless of how rural is viewed conceptually, the delineation of rural areas has long been a major concern of those who collect and use data for sparsely settled areas (for example, see the effects of changing definitions on the size of the populations of rural areas over time in U.S. Bureau of the Census, Current Population Reports P-23, number 1, 1949). Unfortunately, in many cases, rural areas have been largely defined as the residual areas remaining after "urbanized areas" and "urban clusters" (in the most recent decennial censuses) land areas and populations have been subtracted from the total areas and populations of the United States (see Federal Register 67-51, March 15, 2002 for the most recent delineation of urban area criteria and see McKibben & Faust, 2004 for an excellent review of rural and urban definitions in the United States and internationally). Repeated major changes in the definitions of rural areas (most notably in 1950, 1970, and 2000) have occurred with each leading to definitional reductions in the number of persons in rural areas. The change in definition in 2000 was particularly problematic because it allowed for territory to be delineated as urban if it were in areas in close proximity (as a result of a "hop" or "jump" [used in identifying urban territory], see the Federal Register citation noted above) to a larger urban concentration and made it nearly impossible to argue that the remaining rural areas were areas with sufficient geographic and demographic integrity to be analyzed as distinct, socially meaningful, groupings.

As a result, analysts of rural areas in the United States have increasingly used sets of counties delineated as nonmetropolitan. Nonmetropolitan counties simply being those counties remaining after metropolitan and—in 2000 and after—micropolitan counties as defined by the U.S. Office of Management and Budget were subtracted from all counties in the United States (see US Office of Management and Budget [OMB], Federal Register for December 27, 2000 for a delineation of the standards used). As defined by OMB, metropolitan and micropolitan areas consist of groups of counties with places (or groups of related places) of 50,000 or more and 10,000 or more persons, respectively, and related (via commuting) counties. The remaining residual counties defined by omission as nonmetropolitan have required substantial additional development in order to provide useful groupings for the analysis of rural population patterns.

In fact, since the first use of Standard Metropolitan Statistical Areas and/or Metropolitan Statistical Areas several widely devised delineations of nonmetropolitan or rural areas, created by Calvin Beale and others at the United States Department of Agriculture, have come to dominate the literature on rural population change. Three have had particularly widespread use. These are the Rural-Urban Continuum codes (see Butler & Beale, 1994, 2003), the Urban Influence Codes (see Ghelfi & Parker, 1997, 2003) and the Economic Research Service County Typology (Cook & Mizer, 1994, 2003; US Economic Research Service, 2003). The Rural-Urban Continuum codes combine metropolitan and nonmetropolitan status together with proximity and population size as a means of delineating ten relatively unique types of metropolitan and nonmetropolitan areas. The Urban influence codes similarly combine metropolitan and non-metropolitan counties into nine codes (US Economic Research Service, 2004). The county typology combines counties in six county nonmetropolitan economic types (farming-dependent, mining-dependent, manufacturing-dependent, government-dependent, services-dependent, and nonspecialized) based on percentages of persons employed in such economic activities and in seven policy types (retirement-destination, persistent poverty, housing stress, low education, low employment, population loss, and nonmetro recreation) based on employment, income, housing, and demographic characteristics to delineate what are seen as—and have been proven to be—nonmetropolitan county types with significantly unique population patterns particularly as related to migration origins and destinations (Beale, 1975;

Frey, 1987; Fuguitt, Brown, & Beale, 1989; Beale & Johnson, 1998; Johnson & Fuguitt, 2000; Lichter & Johnson, 2006).

Despite their utility the metropolitan and nonmetropolitan counties, as Isserman (2005) clearly shows, are far from definitive relative to their unique identification of urban or rural areas or their populations. Examining data from the 2000 Census, he finds that,

> In fact 30 million people live in rural areas within metropolitan counties. Thus the majority of rural residents are in metropolitan counties…half the rural population lives in territory that is economically and socially integrated with cities (literally within urbanized areas ranging from 59,000 to 18 million population). Another quarter of the rural population lives in territory integrated with cities or towns as small as 10,000 and the final quarter lives in rural areas not integrated with towns of that size (at least not when measured by the 25 percent commuting integration criterion) (Isserman, 2005, 470).

The need for a redefinition of rural is shared by numerous others (see for example Hugo et al., 2003; Woods, 2009). Although useful, Isserman's argument for a new categorization drawing on data from three separate federal agencies may require more interagency cooperation and prioritization than is currently possible. In sum, although widely used, such typologies only partially capture the populations in the areas of interest.

In addition to the use of aggregate data, another currently and widely used means of analyzing rural population patterns or the effects of rurality on populations in rural areas is the use of data from national representative sample surveys. However, because of the sample size of many national representative sample surveys, rural demographers who do analyses based on them, and who wish to make generalizations about specific phenomena in rural areas, must often assume that persons who reside in such diverse rural areas as New England, the Great Plains, the Rural South, and those living in the Mountain West are exposed to similar determinants of behavior and experience because of their rurality. The sample sizes in such surveys often simply do not allow one to reliably estimate regional differences in rural patterns so that causative factors unique to regions can be controlled. In fact, the generalizability of such data to rural areas is ultimately dependent on the extent to which such surveys have included rural criteria in their sampling strata. As a result, the analysis and identification of the causative effects of "rural" characteristics on population patterns may be particularly difficult and problematic in such surveys. The need for larger representative samples that oversample rural areas such as those being collected in the Community and Environment in Rural America (CERA) surveys conducted by the Carsey Institute is apparent (Carsey Institute, 2010). Until such surveys are more prevalent, the use of national random sample surveys for rural demographic analysis will remain challenging.

Additional difficulties will be introduced into the analysis of rural areas by the substitution of the American Community Survey (ACS) in the 2010 census for the long-form data on socioeconomic characteristics provided by decennial population censuses through 2000 (U.S. Bureau of the Census, 2009). Although this survey has a number of advantages over the old long-form data providing recurrent and more current (including annual) data than that provided by the old long form, its sample sizes, and the sampling procedures used in its final survey completion processes lead to larger sampling error than those used in the decennial long-form. The increases in sample size currently being sought by the census would clearly help alleviate this problem but, in the absence of substantial increases, those doing rural research will need to be aware of the size of sampling errors and the breadth of confidence intervals for such data when using them for analyses in rural areas.

Overall, researchers have increasingly come to rely on the typologies (with their clear limitations) to define what is rural and to provide the context in which rural population issues are analyzed. What this means is that rural population change comes to be defined as what happens in rural areas as typologized. Data that allow for more refined definitions related to rural areas that reflect a complex of economic and land-use characteristics or that cannot be delineated by county boundaries or for which data are simply not available on a uniform basis get ignored and data for the typologized areas substituted for them. However, one often cannot determine what it is about agriculturally dependent areas that led to a specific set of demographic patterns versus those in mining-dependent areas because there are likely to be more differences among such areas than simply their employment in selected industries. Clearly, attention must be given to developing more complex and increasingly diverse criteria for such typologies.

In sum, it may be argued that rural demographic research has suffered both from a lack of agreement about the conceptual basis of rurality and from having its geographic basis for the analysis of rural effects defined residually (Isserman, 2005; Voss, 2007). In fact, rural demographers, geographers and others have, for some time (see for example, Fuguitt, Heaton, & Lichter, 1988; Ford, 1999; Isserman, 2005; Porter & Howell, 2008; White, 2008; Woods, 2009) argued that the use of residual categories and the changes in areal units classification categories make it difficult to identify the dimensions of rurality that are most critical in determining demographic and social behavior (Fuguitt et al., 1988). The definitional and categorical challenges faced by the analyst of rural populations in the United States are thus substantial.

## Defining Rural Areas Internationally

Internationally, as in the United States, rural is primarily defined residually, as that which is not urban. However, the Demographic Yearbook of the United Nations for 2007 (United Nations, 2009) indicates a wide variety of numerical and purely declaratory definitions of urban and resultant rural residuals. Numerically this source indicates that in two nations rural was any place with less than 50,000 persons; two nations defined rural as areas with fewer than 20,000 persons; six nations designated places and regions with less than 10,000 persons as rural; seven defined nations fewer than 5,000 persons as rural; one used 3,000, seven used less than 2,500, eleven used places less than 2,000, four nations designated town and cities less than 1,500 as rural, eight nations less than 1,000 and 51 designated certain areas as urban as a result of density, nonagrarian economic pursuits or used multiple criteria to define urban with the remainder of their countries being rural. This diversity of definition indicates both how difficult nations have found it to define urban and the rural residual; but, at the same time, how tied all of them are to the need to delineate those areas with fewer people, agrarian occupations, and less dense settlement (see Voss, 2000; McKibben & Faust, 2004). The problems that confront rural demographers in the United States are those which also impact international demographers interested in population phenomena in other less densely settled areas around the world.

## Examples of Difficulties in the Use of Rural Population Data in Analyses of Important Areas of Rural Life

The difficulties resulting from small population size and the distributions of population over spaces that are central concerns of rural demographers are manifested in numerous examples of how these issues practically affect what rural demographers are able to do in addressing key conceptual and empirical questions. In this section, we examine several examples of these. The ones examined are not inclusive of all, or perhaps even the most important, of such analyses but provide examples of additional difficulties that the rural researcher faces because of the size and distributions of the populations in which they are interested.

## Measuring the Effects of Rural Areal Characteristics on Demographic Processes

Analysts of rural fertility (Johnson & Keppel, 1986; Tolnay, 1987; Heaton, Lichter, & Amoateng, 1989; Arcury, Williams, & Kryscio, 1990; Albrecht & Albrecht, 2004), mortality (Woods, 2003; Hayward & Gorman, 2004) and migration (Beale, 1975; Long & DeAre, 1988; Heaton et al., 1989; Fuguitt & Brown, 1990; Taylor & Martin, 1997; Johnson & Fuguitt, 2000; Lichter & Johnson, 2000; Lichter & Johnson, 2006) have faced a myriad of problems related to having a sufficient number of cases to ensure the validity of generalizations about demographic processes in rural areas. This is clear in the studies of rates of fertility, mortality, and migration in rural areas noted above.

Although standard demographic methods (see Shyrock & Siegel, 1976; Murdock & Ellis, 1991; Siegel, 2002; Siegel & Swanson, 2004; Murdock & Swanson, 2008) generally recommend the pooling of years of vital statistics data on births and deaths over time, even such pooling may fail to provide the number of cases necessary to have confidence in the differences in levels of occurrence between areas with small populations. In the smallest of areas, however, even this procedure often leaves the rural researcher with a dilemma. Does he/she pool a sufficient number of years of data to ensure that the rates are indicative of the population cohort while largely ignoring the temporal changes that may have occurred during the period of accumulation or does he/she attempt to substitute rates for larger population areas or other areas that are demographically similar to the area of interest? Although it is a dilemma for which there is no ideal solution (see Siegel & Swanson, 2004 for discussions of this) there is always a danger in using either too few or too many years in the rates related to such applications. In fact, even the most sophisticated techniques often face severe limitations in the face of limited data (see Smith & Shahidullah, 1995).

Another solution to the problem of an insufficient number of cases which is often employed (Smith & Shahidullah, 1995; Smith, Tayman, & Swanson, 2001; Murdock, Kelley, Jordan, Pecotte, & Luedke, 2006; Murdock & Swanson, 2008) is to use data for similar areas' patterns which are deemed to be indicative of the area of interest. This often leads to the use of rural area or population subgroup averages or the simple substitution of state or rural averages for specific cohorts in specific rural locations. The problem of discerning the truly comparable areas which can be used as the bases for adaptations to other areas is challenging. The rural demographer is often faced with the reality of not only dealing with the typical analytical challenges of all demographic analysis but also managing the additional problems entailed in using data on vital events that may not be representative of the demographic processes of interest in the study area.

The problems noted above are even greater in the analysis of migration in rural areas (Johnson, Voss, Hammer, Fuguitt, & McNiven, 2005) because internal migration in the United States must either be determined residually or use data sets for which sample sizes are often limited, and hence often unreliable. As is well known residual measures are highly affected by errors in fertility and mortality and these processes are difficult to measure for rural areas. The problems in these measures are therefore visited upon migration. In addition, such direct measures as those found in SF3 (US Census Bureau Summary File 3), ACS data, and IRS (Internal Revenue Service) data suffer from high levels of sampling error because of their small samples for rural areas. Net migration estimates, particularly for the smallest of rural areas, are thus often unstable and potentially fallacious. Again, the risks for rural analysts are accentuated because of small population numbers.

## Estimates and Projections of Rural Populations

The difficulties entailed in the estimation and projection of rural populations is, in part, the same as those discussed in the determination of fertility, mortality and migration rates. The small number of vital events is a problem not only for establishing rates for rural areas but also for estimating them and projecting them (see Murdock & Ellis, 1991; Smith et al., 2001; Siegel & Swanson, 2004; Murdock et al., 2006). However, extending or extrapolating rates into current or future periods creates yet additional challenges. Because of the paucity of data on the rates for fertility, mortality, and migration phenomena in many small rural areas, there are often also no discernable past patterns of change over time which can serve as a basis of estimation of current patterns or for projecting future patterns. As difficult as it is to discern what comparable areas should be used as the basis for establishing rates for current periods, it is even more difficult to identify areas with future trajectories that one is willing to use as models for small population areas. Because the areas with more complete historical records of vital events and discernable patterns of change over time nearly always have larger populations, the result is that one must often select future trajectories based on areas that are not directly comparable to those for the rural areas for which one wishes to make projections. Although assessments of the utility of various projection assumptions and methods are critically important (see Murdock, Hamm, Voss, Fannin, & Pecotte, 1991; Smith et al., 2001; Murdock et al., 2006) in only a few cases (see however Smith & Shahidullah, 1995) have attempts been made to determine how the trajectories often substituted for small rural areas impact projection accuracy.

Difficulties also arise in the use of other estimation and projection procedures. For example, one commonly used estimation method (see Smith et al., 2001; Murdock et al., 2006) that does not directly utilize birth, death, and net migration data is the housing unit method in which changes in the number of housing units are used to estimate population change. In general, data from building and completion permits are used to measure housing change but permits may not even be required in some rural areas and, in other areas, bodies approving construction do not necessarily keep the type of completion data necessary to estimate population change. In addition, housing unit count-related data may be misleading in periods of recession when multiple families and households may be forced to live in single-family units. In fact, in nearly all symptomatic methods that use change in some factor other than population to estimate population such symptoms (electric meters, school enrollment, etc.) either are not available for rural areas or are for geographic areas that do not correspond with the area for which an estimate is desired. In sum, demographers completing estimates or projections for small rural areas often make projections of future vital events and of migration or use other indicators largely on the basis of little more than faith in their ability to pick appropriate comparison areas and indicators of patterns of population change.

## Examples from the Analysis of Health Conditions in Rural Areas

Other examples of the difficulties often encountered in the analysis of population-based phenomena in rural areas can be seen in the area of rural health (see Pol & Thomas, 1992; Murdock, Hoque, Johnson, & McGehee, 2003; McGehee, Hall, & Murdock, 2004; Lamb & Siegel, 2004; Murdock, Hoque, & McGehee, 2005; Hoque, McCusker, Murdock, & Perez, 2010, also Chapter 18 in this volume). Here the difficulties entailed are those of attempting to discern prevalence and incidence of specific types of diseases or disorders in rural locations where the number of cases is often so small that it is difficult to establish how prevalent a particular disease may be and how its incidence has changed over time. It is again usually a case of having a small number of observations and discerning whether the rates one can derive are valid and reliable. In many cases, in fact, one might argue that the use of rate substitution from larger areas or areas with similar populations but different types of geographic, economic, and social contexts is so extensive that the health statuses and trends attributed to specific rural areas may be truly synthetic.

Other problems in the analyses of rural health occur when population characteristics are added to basic data on prevalence and incidence. For example, racial and ethnic data are often critical to understanding health-related demographic change in many rural areas (see McGehee et al., 2004). Inclusions of multiple demographic characteristics place—additional demands on data acquisition and, in the absence of data sets of sufficient size, requires additional data simulations and substitutions. Analyses of rural health conditions are often stressed beyond the levels supported by the available data.

## Examples from Population and the Environment: Assessing the Demographic Impacts of Environmental Change

The difficulty of linking population factors to specific pieces of geography is clearly illustrated in the analyses of the socioeconomic (including demographic) impacts of various types of natural resource and industrial developments (Murdock & Leistritz, 1979; Leistritz & Murdock, 1981; Murdock et al., 1999). In such analysis, the difficulties entailed include not only those related to the small number of demographic and other events in rural areas but also to how demographic events in one type of geography can be traced to natural resource or industrial developments that occur in other geographic areas. For example, it is common for such a development to attract workers who work directly at the project but who commute from widely dispersed geographic areas. In this case, to which area's socioeconomic, demographic, and environmental factors do you attribute the differences in impacts among persons with different demographic characteristics? The number of workers may be dictated by the project in one location but how workers from other areas are impacted will depend on the conditions in the areas in which they live as well as the areas in which they work. However, with the methods most commonly used in the area of socioeconomic impact analysis it is often simply assumed that the changes occurring in a population in an aerially defined impact area can be identified by examining demographic (such as migration patterns) and other socioeconomic changes occurring among those directly or indirectly impacted (via working at the facility or living in areas where the facility is located) by the project and that other differences in the specific geographic areas in which they live are not determinative. This problem of linking affected populations to relevant geography was discussed above but work in this area shows an accentuation of the problems entailed because it becomes especially difficult in impact analyses to ensure that the population being affected is adequately linked to the impacted geography.

## Toward the Integration of Rural and Rural Space in Rural Demography

In this chapter we have examined issues related to the definition of "rural" and of the alignment of population and space within rural areas and we provided examples of the challenges faced by rural demographers because of small populations in rural areas and the misalignment of populations being affected by spatially delimited events. We noted that analysis by Isserman (2005), Porter and Howell (2008), and Woods (2009) and others reveal that there is a lack of a clear delineation of rural and urban space such that many rural residents live in areas defined as metropolitan or urban and many urban residents live in areas that are often defined as rural. As Porter and Howell (2008) further suggest, there is evidence of extensive rural activities in areas defined as urban and, as Isserman (2005) and Woods (2009) suggest, there are apparent urban activities in spatial areas defined as rural. We also noted that the most used operational definitions of rural space are residual definitions; that is, what is not urban or metropolitan is rural or nonmetropolitan.

The problem of defining one areal unit is not, of course, unique to rural scholars. Urban scholars face a similar problem. Thus the obvious counterpart to Isserman's (2005), Porter and Howell's (2008), and Woods' (2009) assessments is that those mixed areas of rural and urban areas are just as problematic for the urban as for the rural scholar. The major difference, however, is that urban scholars are less likely to be faced with problems related to an insufficient number of cases for their analyses. The problems of areal delineation combined with the problem of scarcity of observations in the areal units identified is a set of problems more directly visited upon rural than upon urban scholars.

Given such issues, we argue that the use of the null category as the definition of rural should not, and need not, be continued given current technology. There are several reasons for suggesting that the time for conceptual clarification and related spatial delineation may be at hand.

First, despite disagreements about the extent to which specific economic activities or functions, forms of interaction, use and density of use of space form the appropriate dimensions of any definition of rurality (see Warren, 1972; Wilkinson, 1991 and others) we believe it is possible to delineate a set of elements of rural (including these and others) for which there is sufficient agreement to allow for at least tentative definitions of the elements of rural to be formulated elements that are superior to the current residual categories used to operationalize rural. There may be no perfect or totally agreed upon definition; but, there is likely to be more agreement on conceptual terms than has been possible to delimit operationally to date.

Second, residual definitions have prevailed in empirical analyses because it was essential to use current geographical areas delineated for other purposes and with criteria related to such purposes as approximations for the rural areas with rural populations that rural demographers wish to study. This was the case because it was not possible to systematically analyze small units of geography and to control for key features of the characteristics of populations in that geography so as to delineate the determinative factors in that space that affect population change and characteristics. As Voss (2007) eloquently suggests and as Hugo et al. (2003) have delineated, current forms of geographic information system technology and spatial analysis methods may allow rural demographers to take small levels of census geography and control for the effects of specific characteristics and thus to better identify the "rural" characteristics that truly determine differences in fertility, mortality, migration, and other rural demographic phenomena.

If this could be done the conceptual definitions of rural and its operational definitions in space could be substantially reconciled compared to current practices. Although there are still likely to be incongruities between space as defined by the Census Bureau and other official data agencies and rural space and populations as defined conceptually, we believe the "distance" between them can be reduced. As noted in the introduction, steps toward such reconciliation are essential because, until rural demographers are able to delineate their conception of rural in space, they are unlikely to be able to truly establish what it is within rurality that is determinative of demographic phenomena.

# References

Albrecht, D. E., & Albrecht, C. M. (2004). Metro/nonmetro residence, nonmarital conception, and conception outcomes. *Rural Sociology, 69*(3), 430–452.

Arcury, T. A., Williams, B. J., & Kryscio, R. J. (1990). Birth seasonality in a rural county, 1911–1979. *American Journal of Human Biology, 2*, 675–689.

Beale, C. L. (1975). *The revival of widespread population growth in nonmetropolitan America*. Washington, DC: Economic Research Service, US Department of Agriculture.

Beale, C. L., & Johnson, K. M. (1998). The identification of recreational counties in nonmetropolitan areas of the United States. *Population Research and Policy Review, 17*, 37–53.

Bernard, J. (1955). Social psychological aspects of community study. *British Journal of Sociology, 2*(March), 12–30.

Brown, D., & Swanson, L. (2003). *Challenges for rural America in the twenty-first century*. University Park: Pennsylvania State University.

Bunce, M. (1982). *Rural settlement in an urban world*. New York: St. Martin's Press.

Butler, M., & Beale, C. (1994 and revised 2003). *Rural-urban continuum codes for metro and nonmetro counties*. Washington, DC: U.S. Economic Research Service.

Carsey Institute. (2010). *Community and environment in rural America (CERA) survey*. Durham, NH: Author.

Cook, P., & Mizer, K. (1994 and revised 2003). *The revised EPS county typology: An overview*. Washington, DC: U.S. Economic Research Service.

Duncan, O. D., & Reiss, A. J., Jr. (1956). *Social characteristics of urban and rural communities*. New York: Wiley.

Farmer, F. L. (2008). The definition of rural. In G. Goreham (Ed.), *Encyclopedia of rural America* (2nd ed., pp. 833–835). Millerton, NY: Greyhouse Publishing.

Ford, T. (1999). Understanding population growth in the peri-urban region. *International Journal of Population Geography, 5*, 197–311.

Frey, W. H. (1987). Migration and depopulation of the metropolis: Regional restructuring or rural renaissance? *American Sociological Review, 52*(2), 240–257.

Fuguitt, G. V., & Brown, D. L. (1990). Residential preferences and population redistribution: 1972–1988. *Demography, 27*(4), 589–600.

Fuguitt, G. V., Brown, D. L., & Beale, C. L. (1989). *Rural and small town America*. New York: Russell Sage Foundation.

Fuguitt, G. V., Heaton, T. B., & Lichter, D. T. (1988). Monitoring the metropolization process. *Demography, 25*(1), 115–128.

Ghelfi, L., & Parker, T. (1997). A county level measurement of urban influence. *Rural Development Perspectives, 12*(2).

Ghelfi, L., & Parker, T. (2003). *Measuring rurality: Urban influence codes* (pp. 32–40). Washington, DC: U.S. Economic Research Service.

Hawley, A. H. (1950). *Human ecology: A theory of community structure*. New York: Ronald Press.

Hawley, A. H. (1986). *Human ecology: A theoretical essay*. Chicago: University of Chicago Press.

Hayward, M. D., & Gorman, B. K. (2004). The long arm of childhood: The influence of early-life social conditions on men's mortality. *Demography, 41*(1), 87–107.

Heaton, T. B., Lichter, D. T., & Amoateng, A. (1989). The timing of family formation: Rural-urban differentials in first intercourse, childbirth, and marriage. *Rural Sociology, 54*(1), 1–16.

Hoque, N., McCusker, M. E., Murdock, S. H., & Perez, D. (2010). The implications of change in population size, distribution, and composition on the number of overweight and obese adults and the direct and indirect cost associated with overweight and obese adults in Texas through 2040. *Population Research and Policy Review, 29*(2), 173–191.

Hugo, G., Champion, A., & Lattes, A. (2003). Toward a new conceptualization of settlements for demography. *Population and Development Review, 29*(2), 277–297.

Isserman, A. M. (2005). In the national interest: Defining rural and urban correctly in research and public policy. *International Regional Science Review, 28*(4), 465–499.

Johnson, K. M., & Fuguitt, G. V. (2000). Continuity and change in rural migration patterns, 1950–1995. *Rural Sociology, 65*(1), 27–49.

Johnson, K. M., Voss, P. R., Hammer, R. B., Fuguitt, G. V., & McNiven, S. (2005). Temporal and spatial variation in age-specific net migration in the United States. *Demography, 42*(4), 791–812.

Johnson, N. E., & Keppel, K. G. (1986). The effect of fertility on migration. *Rural Sociology, 51*(2), 212–221.

Kaufman, H. (1959). Toward an interactional conception of community. *Social Forces, 38*(October), 9–17.

Kraenzel, C. (1980). *The social cost of space in Yonland*. Bozeman, MT: Big Sky Press.

Lamb, V. L., & Siegel, J. S. (2004). Health demography. In J. S. Siegel & D. A. Swanson (Eds.), *The methods and materials of demography* (pp. 341–370). Boston: Elsevier Science.

Leistritz, F. L., & Murdock, S. H. (1981). *The socioeconomic impacts of resource development: Methods for assessment*. Boulder, CO: Westview Press.

Lichter, D. T., & Johnson, K. M. (2000). Continuity and change in rural migration patterns, 1950–1995. *Rural Sociology, 65*(1), 27–49.

Lichter, D. T., & Johnson, K. M. (2006). Emerging rural settlement patterns and the geographic redistribution of America's new immigrants. *Rural Sociology, 71*(1), 109–131.

Long, L., & DeAre, D. (1988). US population redistribution: A perspective on the nonmetropolitan turnaround. *Population and Development Review, 14*(3), 433–450.

McGehee, M. A., Hall, S. D., & Murdock, S. H. (2004). Rural and urban death rates by race/ethnicity and gender, Texas: 1990–2000. *The Journal of Multicultural Nursing and Health, 10*(2), 13–22.

McKibben, J. N., & Faust, K. A. (2004). Population distribution: Classification of residence. In J. S. Siegel & D. A. Swanson (Eds.), *The methods and materials of demography* (2nd ed., p. 819). Amsterdam: Elsevier Academic Press.

Murdock, S., & Ellis, D. R. (1991). *Applied demography: An introduction to basic concepts, methods, and data*. Boulder, CO: Westview Press.

Murdock, S., Hamm, R. R., Voss, P. R., Fannin, D., & Pecotte, B. (1991). Evaluating small-area population projections. *Journal of the American Planning Association, 57*, 432–443.

Murdock, S., Hoque, M. N., Johnson, K., & McGehee, M. (2003). Racial/ethnic diversification in metropolitan and nonmetropolitan population change in the United States:

Implications for health care provision in rural America. *The Journal of Rural Health, 19*(4), 425–432.

Murdock, S., Hoque, M. N., & McGehee, M. (2005). Population change in the United States: Implications of an aging and diversifying population for health care in the 21st century. In T. Miles & A. Forino (Eds.), *Annual review of gerontology and geriatrics: Aging healthcare workforce issues* (Vol. 25, pp. 19–63). New York: Springer.

Murdock, S., Kelley, C., Jordan, J., Pecotte, B., & Luedke, A. (2006). *Demographics: A guide to methods and data sources for media, Business, and government.* Boulder, CO: Paradigm Publishers.

Murdock, S., Krannich, R. S., Leistritz, F. L., Spies, S., Wulfhorst, J. D., Wrigley, K., et al. (1999). *Hazardous wastes in rural America: Impacts, implications and options for rural communities.* Boulder, CO: Rowman and Littlefield Publishers.

Murdock, S., & Leistritz, F. L. (1979). *Energy development in the western United States: Impact on rural areas.* New York: Praeger Publishers.

Murdock, S., & Sutton, W., Jr. (1974). The new ecology and community theory: Similarities, differences, and convergencies. *Rural Sociology, 39*(3), 319–333.

Murdock, S., & Swanson, D. A. (Eds.). (2008). *Applied demography in the twenty-first century.* Berlin: Springer.

Pol, L. G., & Thomas, R. K. (1992). *The demography of health and health care.* New York: Plenum Press.

Porter, J. R., & Howell, F. M. (2008). On the 'urbanness' of metropolitan areas: Testing the homogeneity assumption, 1970–2000. *Population Research and Policy Review, 28,* 589–613.

Shyrock, H. S., & Siegel, J. S. (1976). *The methods and materials of demography.* New York: Academic.

Siegel, J. (2002). *Applied demography: Applications to business, government, law, and public policy.* San Diego, CA: Academic.

Siegel, J., & Swanson, D. (2004). *The methods and materials of demography* (2nd ed.). Amsterdam: Elsevier Academic Press.

Smith, S., & Shahidullah, M. (1995). An evaluation of population projection errors for Census tracts. *Journal of the American Statistical Association, 90,* 64–71.

Smith, S., Tayman, J., & Swanson, D. (2001). *State and local population projections: Methods and analysis.* Amsterdam: Kluwer Academic/Plenum Publishers.

Taylor, J. E., & Martin, P. L. (1997). The immigrant subsidy in US agriculture: Farm employment, poverty, and welfare. *Population and Development Review, 23*(4), 855–874.

Tolnay, S. E. (1987). The decline of black marital fertility in the rural South: 1910–1940. *American Sociological Review, 52*(April), 211–217.

United Nations. (2009). *Demographic yearbook: 2007.* New York: United Nations Press.

U.S. Census Bureau. (1949). *The development of the urban-rural classification system in the United States: 1874–1949.* Series P23-1. Washington, DC: U.S. Bureau of the Census.

U.S. Census Bureau. (2002). Urban area criteria for Census 2000. *Federal Register, 67*(51), 11663–11670.

U.S. Census Bureau. (2009). *American Community Survey: Design and methodology.* Washington, DC: U.S. Bureau of the Census.

U.S. Economic Research Service. (2003). *Rural-urban continuum codes.* United Sates Department of Agriculture. Retrieved April 8, 2010, from www.ers.usda.gov/briefing/ruralurbancontinuumcodes/

U.S. Economic Research Service. (2004). *Measuring rurality: 2004 county typology codes.* United Sates Department of Agriculture. Retrieved April 8, 2010, from www.ers.usda.gov/briefing/rurality/typology

U.S. Office of Management and Budget. (2000). Standards for defining metropolitan and micropolitan statistical areas. *Federal Register, 65*(249), 82228–82238.

Voss, P. (2000). Rural areas. In M. Anderson (Ed.), *The encyclopedia of the United States census* (pp. 320–322). Washington, DC: Congressional Quarterly Press.

Voss, P. (2007). Demography as a spatial social science. *Population Research and Policy Review, 26*(5), 457–476.

Warren, R. (1972). *The community in America.* Chicago: Rand McNally.

White, K. J. C. (2008). Population change and farm dependence: Temporal and spatial variation in the U.S. Great Plains, 1900–2000. *Demography, 45*(2), 363–386.

Wilkinson, K. P. (1991). The rural-urban variable in community research. In K. P. Wilkinson (Ed.), *The community in rural America* (pp. 37–59). Middleton, WS: Social Ecology Press.

Woods, M. (2009). Rural geography: Blurring boundaries and making connections. *Progress in Human Geography, 33*(6), 849–858.

Woods, R. (2003). Urban-rural mortality differentials: An unresolved debate. *Population and Development Review, 29*(1), 29–46.

# Rural Natural Increase in the New Century: America's Third Demographic Transition

Kenneth M. Johnson and Daniel T. Lichter

## Rural Natural Increase in the New Century: America's Third Demographic Transition?

The United States, like most industrial nations in Europe and East Asia, is aging rapidly (Lutz, Sanderson, & Scherbov, 2008). Increases in the absolute size of the elderly population reflect past fertility – the aging of the baby boom populations – and increasing longevity at older ages. Declines in fertility, especially in developed countries, have also placed upward demographic pressure on the percentage of elderly. Increasing shares of elderly in Japan and throughout Europe have resulted largely from below-replacement levels of fertility (Morgan, 2003; Jóźwiak & Kotowska, 2008). Much of the developed world has entered a new period of incipient population decline borne of natural decrease – the excess of death over births (Reher, 2007; Howse, 2006). Coleman (2006) calls this the "Third Demographic Transition."[1] Most European countries now face the prospect of easing longstanding restrictions on minority or ethnic immigration in order to accommodate growing labor shortages due to population aging.

The long-term demographic forecast in the United States is much different from Europe's. Indeed, the U.S. total fertility rate in 2008 was only slightly below replacement levels – 2,085.5 births per 1,000 women of reproductive age (Hamilton, Martin, & Ventura, 2010). The U.S. also has imported roughly 1 million legal immigrants annually over the past decade or so (Martin & Midgley, 2010). National or overall patterns, however, mask substantial geographic variation. In America's rural areas, for example, emerging patterns of natural decrease – born of population aging and chronically low fertility rate – suggest incipient population declines that largely mimic patterns in much of Europe. This chapter has several specific objectives. First, we describe county patterns of natural decrease and identify the demographic sources of change (i.e., shifts in the balance of fertility and mortality) over the 1950–2005 period. Second, we identify spatial variation in patterns of natural increase and decrease, and identify the large role of Hispanic in-migration in slowing or even offsetting the pace of population change in many parts of rural America. Third, we show how racial diversity has accelerated as a result of population aging (of a largely white population) and new in-migration of racial minorities, especially of Hispanics, who are typically of reproductive age and have fertility rates well above replacement levels. The aging process in rural America, like current patterns in many low-fertility countries (Coleman,

---

K.M. Johnson (✉)
Department of Sociology and Carsey Institute, University of New Hampshire, Durham, NH 03824, USA
e-mail: Ken.Johnson@unh.edu

[1] The "Third Demographic Transition" contrasts with the (first) demographic transition which is characterized by societal transitions from high fertility and mortality to low fertility and mortality rates, and the "Second Demographic Transition," which usually refers to the growing disconnection between marriage and childbearing (i.e., rising nonmarital fertility) and to rapidly changing family structure that results from delayed marriage, rising cohabitation, and high rates of divorce (e.g., Lesthaeghe, 1995).

2006), suggests that racial minorities may be transforming the original (largely white) population into an increasingly minority population.

## Natural Increase and Decrease in Rural America

Population growth in rural America reflects a balancing act between natural increase (i.e., births minus deaths) and net migration (in- minus out-migration). Early in the nation's history, net in-migration fueled most rural growth as vast new frontiers of the country were opened to homesteading and commercial development (e.g., forestry and mining) (Fuguitt, Brown, & Beale, 1989; Fischer & Hout, 2006). Soon after settlement, natural increase began to contribute heavily to population growth, due to high rural fertility rates among a growing rural population of reproductive age. A youthful age structure also brought unusually low crude death rates, which exacerbated the demographic effects of high fertility rates. By the 1920s, however, people began leaving rural America, attracted by the economic and social opportunities in the nation's booming big cities, while the mechanization and consolidation of agricultural production led to a growing surplus of farm workers unable to find work (Greenwood, 1975; Easterlin, 1976). The magnitude of rural net out-migration varied from decade to decade and from place to place, but the general pattern was unchanging: more people left rural areas than came. Of course, there were exceptions to this trend in some industrializing regions, such as the Northeast, and at the urban fringe, where rural communities and the open countryside would eventually be gobbled up by the rapid outward population and economic expansion of metropolitan areas. Still, more than half of the nation's rural counties lost population between 1920 and 1970 (Johnson, 1985, 2006).

By the mid-20th century, rural net out-migration meant that the modest rural population gains were fueled entirely by natural increase (Johnson, 2006). High rural fertility – helped along by the post-WWII baby boom – brought a surplus of births over deaths which offset the overall migration losses to urban areas. Rural population gains nevertheless dwindled in much of the agricultural heartland. With the waning of the Baby Boom in the late-1960s, the historically large surplus of births over deaths that sustained modest nonmetropolitan population growth had ended. Continuing net out-migration of young adults, along with aging-in-place, contributed heavily to the aging of the rural population (Lichter, Fuguitt, Heaton, & Clifford, 1981). Rural-urban fertility also converged with modernization and rural development, and net migration came to play a dominant role in population growth and decline processes in nonmetropolitan areas.

The diminishing demographic influence of natural increase in nonmetropolitan America was most clearly revealed in the remarkable demographic turnaround of the 1970s. For the first time in at least 150 years, population gains in nonmetropolitan areas exceeded those in metropolitan areas; indeed, nonmetro areas grew at the expense of metropolitan areas, as more people left metropolitan areas than arrived from rural areas (Fuguitt, 1985). Widespread net migration gains in rural counties were fueled by rural restructuring – job growth associated with rural retirement migration, natural resources (e.g., coal and gas), and recreational development – changing residential preferences (Brown & Wardwell, 1980; Fuguitt, 1985). The rural-urban turnaround was short-lived. Rural population growth slowed in the 1980s with the return of widespread net out-migration from rural areas. But just as unexpectedly, rural population growth rebounded in the 1990s as migration to rural areas accelerated (Johnson & Beale, 1994). However, as the 1990s came to an end, there was evidence that nonmetropolitan population gains were slowing (Cromartie, 2001; Beale, 2000; Johnson & Cromartie, 2006). Thus, at the dawn of the 21st century the demographic implications of natural increase and net migration for the future of rural America are once again in question.

Natural increase and net migration are frequently characterized and reported as two distinctly different demographic processes when, in fact, they are intertwined. Migration tends to be age selective; young adults are typically over-represented in migration streams. This has significant second-order effects on fertility and natural increase. Age-specific migration typically diminishes the numbers of young adults in counties experiencing outmigration and increases their numbers in receiving counties. Net out-migration thus tends to diminish natural increase through reductions in fertility and increases in mortality as populations age. As we shall see, natural increase – and natural decrease in some cases – now plays an important but often unappreciated demographic role in reshaping America's settlement patterns. New rural immigration also is emerging as a powerful demographic force in nonmetropolitan America (Lichter & Johnson, 2009). High rates of fertility give demographic impetus to a large second-order effect of rural Hispanic immigration, not unlike patterns observed on the rural frontier a century ago (Johnson & Lichter, 2008). Our purpose here is to update our understanding of nonmetropolitan trends in natural increase/decrease in the first decade of the 21st century.

## Data and Methods

Counties are the unit of analysis. They have historically stable boundaries and are a basic unit for reporting fertility, mortality, and census data by the federal government. Counties are also appropriate units of analysis because metropolitan areas are built up from them (county-equivalents are used for New England). Counties are designated as metropolitan or nonmetropolitan using criteria developed by the U.S. Office of Management and Budget. We use a constant 2004 metropolitan-nonmetropolitan classification. Using a fixed definition of nonmetropolitan and metropolitan removes the effect of reclassification from the calculation of longitudinal population change. Metro areas include counties containing an urban core of 50,000 or more population (or central city), along with adjacent counties that are highly integrated with the core county as measured by commuting patterns. There are 1,090 metro counties. The remaining 2,051 counties are classified as nonmetro. For ease of exposition, we use the terms metro and urban (and nonmetro and rural) interchangeably. We have further identified large metro core counties as those counties that contain the central city of metropolitan areas of 1 million or more, and consider them separately from all other metropolitan counties.

Counties are also classified using a typology developed by the Economic Research Service of the U.S. Department of Agriculture which classifies nonmetropolitan counties along economic and policy dimensions (Economic Research Service, 2004). The county classification developed by Johnson and Beale (2002) also identifies nonmetropolitan counties where recreation is a major factor in the local economy.

County population data comes from the decennial Census of population and from the Federal-State Cooperative Population Estimates program. This FSCPE program estimates the population on an annual basis as of July 1st; here we consider the period from April 1, 1990 through July 1, 2009. The FSCPE also provides data on the number of births and deaths in each year. The estimates of net migration used here were derived by the residual method whereby net migration is what is left when natural increase (births minus deaths) is subtracted from total population change. For some analyses, we also report net international migration and net domestic migration as reported in the FSCPE, these elements do not sum to net migration because of residuals and differences in coverage in the various censuses. The National Center for Health Statistics (NCHS) provided us with special tabulations of births and deaths by county by Hispanic origin for 2000–2005.[2]

For our analysis of natural decrease, we use historical data from a number of sources. Calvin Beale provided data on the incidence of natural decrease from 1950 through 1966. Published data on births and deaths are used to determine the incidence of natural decrease in 1967 and 1968. Births and deaths from 1969 through 1989 are from a special tabulation by the Estimates and Projections Branch of the Bureau of the Census. Data on births and deaths from 1990 through July of 2009 are from the Federal-State Cooperative Population Estimates series.

We also use Census Bureau annual estimates of the population by age, sex, race and Hispanic origin from April of 2000 to July of 2008 released in May of 2009 (U.S. Census Bureau, 2009) to examine contemporary

---

[2] In a small number of counties, NCHS suppressed the number of Hispanic births for confidentiality purposes. We used estimation procedures to allocate these suppressed births to specific counties. NCHS suppressed Hispanic births in a specific county in a specific year, if the number of Hispanic births was small. All counties in a given state with suppressed births were flagged as having suppressed data and the total number of Hispanic births in the state that were suppressed was reported. We used historical data (Hispanic births in a given county during another year) or estimated what proportion of all children that were Hispanic and resided in suppressed counties resided in this specific county to allocate suppressed Hispanic births in a given year to a specific suppressed county. Although this introduces an unknown but small degree of error in our estimates, we are confident that at the level of aggregation at which we present our results, it has no material impact on our overall conclusions.

patterns of change for children and youth. In addition, data from the 1990 and 2000 Decennial Census have been adjusted for under-enumeration by age, race and Hispanic origin.

To insure compatibility with the 1990 census data, the self-identified multiracial population in 2000 is reallocated to single racial categories (see Johnson, Voss, Hammer, Fuguitt, & McNiven, 2005 for a full description). We identify four ethnoracial groups: (1) Hispanics of any race, (2) non-Hispanic whites, (3) non-Hispanic blacks, and (4) all other non-Hispanics, including those who reported two or more races. Asians are the largest racial group included in this "other" category. They constitute 51% of the 19 and under group in the other category. To examine the uneven spatial distribution of different racial and ethnic populations, we estimate the number and percentage of *majority-minority counties* – those having at least half their young people from minority groups in 2008 – and *near majority-minority counties* – those having between 40 and 50% minority populations. Throughout the discussion of results, we refer to persons aged 19 or younger as "young" or the youth population.

## Analysis

### Recent Demographic Change in Nonmetropolitan and Metropolitan Areas

The role of natural increase in the growth of rural America declined over the last half of the 20th century but re-emerged as a prominent demographic force in the modest growth of rural America in the early 21st century. Nonmetropolitan population growth slowed precipitously after 2000. Between 2000 and 2009, rural counties gained 1.4 million residents (2.9%) to reach a population of 50.2 million in July of 2009.

As shown in Table 3.1, most rural population growth came from natural increase. In all, the gain of 1,082,000 from natural increase represents 77% of the total nonmetropolitan population gain during the period. In nonadjacent nonmetropolitan counties – those remote from metropolitan areas – natural increase of 381,000 accounts for the entire population increase, offsetting losses from net out-migration. In adjacent nonmetropolitan counties, those contiguous to metropolitan counties, natural increase accounted for 702,000 or 56% of the population gain.

Natural increase also continued to be important in the nation's urban areas. It produced nearly two-thirds of the population gain in metropolitan counties between 2000 and 2009. Of the metropolitan population gain of 24,176,000, nearly two-thirds (61.9%) came from natural increase. The excess of births over deaths was particularly important to population gains in the large urban cores, where it partially offset substantial domestic outmigration (data not shown).

The reemergence of natural population change (i.e., either natural decrease or increase) as the primary driver of population growth in rural areas reflects the diminishing influence of net migration. Since 2000, migration to rural areas has slowed. Overall, the non-metropolitan migration gain of 325,000 is less than 13% of what it was during the 1990s (Table 3.1). Nonmetropolitan counties that were not adjacent to a metropolitan area experienced a net migration loss of –227,000 (–1.3%) between 2000 and 2009. In the faster growing adjacent counties, migration contributed an additional 552,000 residents. This was a significant part of the overall gain, but was still less than growth from natural increase. Moreover, any population gains from migration were fueled primarily by immigration. Without immigration, nonmetropolitan counties would have experienced net out-migration between 2000 and 2009. As we shall see, new Hispanic immigration has important second-order effects on rural fertility.

The large demographic role of natural increase contrasts sharply with the situation during the rural rebound period of the 1990s, when net in-migration accounted for most of the rural population growth. During the 1990s, the rural population grew by 4.1 million (Table 3.1). Thus, the annualized population growth rate in rural America since 2000 is only one-third of what it was during the 1990s. A comparison of nonmetropolitan net migration in the 1990s with the post-2000 period explains much of this difference. In the 1990s, migration accounted for nearly two-thirds of the entire nonmetropolitan population gain, but after 2000 it represented less than one-half of the population gain. Nonmetropolitan counties gained 2.7 million residents from migration during the 1990s, but only 325,000 between 2000 and 2009.

Natural increase clearly has become a much more prominent factor in the overall growth or decline in rural areas. This is not because natural increase has

# 3 Rural Natural Increase in the New Century: America's Third Demographic Transition

**Table 3.1** Demographic change in metropolitan and nonmetropolitan United States, 2000–2009

| | Counties | 2000 Population | Population change 2000–2009 | | | Natural increase 2000–2009 | | | Net migration 2000–2009 | | | | |
|---|---|---|---|---|---|---|---|---|---|---|---|---|---|
| | | | Absolute Change | Percent Change | Percent Growing | Absolute Change | Percent Change | Percent Growing | Absolute Change | Percent Change | Percent Growing | Domestic Migration | Immigration |
| Metropolitan total | 1,090 | 232,582,941 | 24,175,770 | 10.4 | 81.9 | 14,792,394 | 6.4 | 91.1 | 9,383,376 | 4.0 | 67.1 | 1,237,474 | 8,145,902 |
| Nonmetro – adjacent | 1,058 | 31,911,883 | 1,254,118 | 3.9 | 51.4 | 701,766 | 2.2 | 69.3 | 552,352 | 1.7 | 42.7 | 232,271 | 320,081 |
| Nonmetro – not adjacent | 992 | 16,913,508 | 153,803 | 0.9 | 34.0 | 380,721 | 2.3 | 56.5 | −226,918 | −1.3 | 25.2 | −385,776 | 158,858 |
| Nonmetropolitan total | 2,050 | 48,825,391 | 1,407,921 | 2.9 | 43.0 | 1,082,487 | 2.2 | 63.1 | 325,434 | 0.7 | 34.2 | −153,505 | 478,939 |
| Total United States | 3,140 | 281,408,332 | 25,583,691 | 9.1 | 56.5 | 15,874,881 | 5.6 | 72.8 | 9,708,810 | 3.5 | 45.6 | 1,083,969 | 8,624,841 |

U.S. Census Bureau Population Estimates, March 2010.

surged. Rather, the share of overall population growth due to natural increase increased because of sharp reductions in rural net migration. In fact, the volume of natural increase has diminished in rural America. It was already slowing dramatically by the 1990s, when it supplied 1.4 million new residents to nonmetropolitan areas. At current rates, natural increase in the first decade of the new century is likely to produce fewer than 1.2 million new residents.

## Demographic Change in County Types

Rural America is a diverse place. With 75% of the land area and 50 million residents, it is not surprising that the patterns of natural increase vary across this vast region.

Farming and mining no longer monopolize the overall rural economy, but these industries nevertheless remain important in many parts of nonmetropolitan America. Table 3.2 shows the demographic trends in these traditional rural regions. Farming still dominates the local economy of some 403 rural counties. Mining (which includes oil and gas extraction) is a major force in another 113 counties. Between 2000 and 2008, the population of farming-dependent counties diminished by 2.3%. The overall natural increase gain in such counties was 2.7%, slightly above the nonmetropolitan average of 2.2%. But even with natural increase, the farm county population declined because it was insufficient to offset a net migration loss of 4.7%. In contrast, such areas grew during the 1990s because both natural increase and migration contributed to population gains. Mining counties also suffered a net migration loss, but these losses were offset by natural increase, producing a minimal population gain. In all, 83% of farming counties and 66% of mining counties lost population between 2000 and 2009. In these most traditional of rural counties, natural increase fueled what growth there was and cushioned the impact of migration losses.

Small population gains or outright decline in farming and mining counties are well known, while manufacturing counties have traditionally been one of the bright spots of rural demographic change. In fact, rural development strategies have traditionally focused on expanding the manufacturing base. Manufacturing counties enjoyed significant population and migration gains during the 1990s, but growth slowed dramatically thereafter. The net population gain was 1.7% between 2000 and 2009 and most manufacturing counties lost population. Natural increase continued in the vast majority of nonmetropolitan manufacturing counties, but net migration losses became widespread. The natural increase of nearly 397,000 was sufficient to offset the migration loss of 89,000, but growth rates slowed dramatically from the 1990s. The globalization of manufacturing coupled with the recent economic downturn negatively impacted the rural manufacturing sector, which includes low technology, low wage jobs that are increasingly shifted offshore (Johnson & Cromartie, 2006; Johnson, 2006). The result was net outmigration. Other counties with substantial population losses included those with histories of persistently high poverty rates (e.g., over 20%). Here, natural increase was substantial, but insufficient to offset significant net migration losses.

There is a striking contrast between the counties discussed above, which focus on traditional rural activities and those with natural amenities, recreational opportunities, or quality of life advantages. Researchers have used different methods to identify high-amenity areas, but there is widespread agreement that major concentrations of these counties exist in the mountain and coastal regions of the West, in the upper Great Lakes, in coastal and scenic areas of New England and upstate New York, in the foothills of the Appalachians and Ozarks and in coastal regions from Virginia to Florida (Johnson & Beale, 2002; McGranahan, 1999; Economic Research Service, 2004). Recreation and retirement counties have consistently been the fastest growing counties in rural America – though the rate of growth has slowed recently. Retirement counties grew by more than 11.7% between 2000 and 2009. Recreational counties grew by 8.8% during the period. For these counties, migration has fueled virtually all of the growth. Each county type does have modest natural increase, but it is below the nonmetropolitan average.

Rates of natural increase are especially low in retirement destination counties. In part this is because of in-migration of older people into such counties. Indeed, by definition, retirement destination counties receive substantial net inflows of older adults (their population 60 and over must have grown by at least 15% between 1990 and 2000 to be classified as retirement destinations). Although the elderly are not the only ones attracted to these counties,

**Table 3.2** Demographic change in the nonmetropolitan United States by county type, 2000–2009

| | Counties | 2000 Population | Population change 2000–2009 | | | Natural increase 2000–2009 | | | Net migration 2000–2009 | | | Domestic Migration | Immigration |
|---|---|---|---|---|---|---|---|---|---|---|---|---|---|
| | | | Absolute Change | Percent Change | Percent Growing | Absolute Change | Percent Change | Percent Growing | Absolute Change | Percent Change | Percent Growing | | |
| Farming | 403 | 3,001,985 | −64,130 | −2.1 | 18.4 | 81,738 | 2.7 | 50.6 | −145,868 | −4.9 | 10.7 | 59,683 | −205,551 |
| Mining | 113 | 2,055,033 | 15,607 | 0.8 | 33.6 | 51,831 | 2.5 | 65.5 | −36,224 | −1.8 | 23.0 | 12,465 | −48,689 |
| Manufacturing | 584 | 18,448,694 | 307,787 | 1.7 | 47.1 | 397,113 | 2.2 | 72.9 | −89,326 | −0.5 | 36.8 | 177,712 | −267,038 |
| Federal/State | 221 | 6,228,805 | 334,100 | 5.4 | 59.3 | 241,488 | 3.9 | 70.6 | 92,612 | 1.5 | 44.3 | 57,531 | 35,081 |
| Service | 114 | 4,364,437 | 501,095 | 11.5 | 77.2 | 61,249 | 1.4 | 57.9 | 439,846 | 10.1 | 77.2 | 54,056 | 385,790 |
| Persistent Poverty | 340 | 6,658,825 | −33,098 | −0.5 | 36.5 | 252,986 | 3.8 | 80.6 | −286,084 | −4.3 | 17.6 | 58,004 | −344,088 |
| Recreation | 299 | 7,423,219 | 656,314 | 8.8 | 63.1 | 137,719 | 1.9 | 57.4 | 518,595 | 7.0 | 58.7 | 86,075 | 432,520 |
| Retirement | 277 | 7,855,521 | 915,744 | 11.7 | 80.9 | 107,591 | 1.4 | 53.1 | 808,153 | 10.3 | 78.7 | 91,292 | 716,861 |
| Nonmetropolitan Total | 2,050 | 48,825,391 | 1,407,921 | 2.9 | 43.0 | 1,082,487 | 2.2 | 63.1 | 325,434 | 0.7 | 34.2 | 478,939 | −153,505 |

U.S. Census Bureau Population Estimates, March 2010.

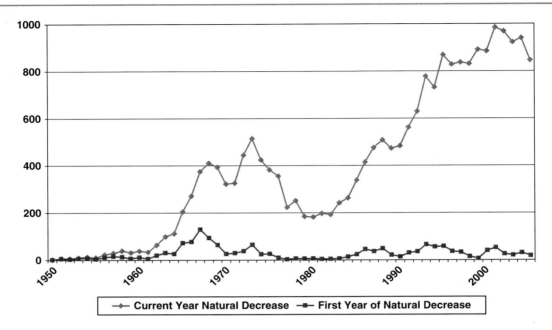

**Fig. 3.1** Incidence of natural decrease in U.S. counties, 1950–2005

they comprise a disproportionate share of in-migrants. Older populations obviously suffer higher mortality than younger populations, who also contribute to population growth through fertility. It is not surprising that natural increase in retirement destination counties is very low. In fact, nearly 47% of them had more deaths than births. Only farm-dependent counties had a smaller proportion of counties with natural increase during the 2000s.

## Natural Decrease in Rural America

Natural decrease occurs when deaths exceed births in a population. Historically, natural decrease has been unusual in the American experience, with few instances of county-level natural decrease reported prior to the middle of the 20th century.[3] Near the end of the Great Depression, natural decrease occurred in a few counties (Dorn, 1939), but it was short-lived. A few instances of natural decrease also occurred during the 1950s (Beale, 1964, 1969), but overall this demographic phenomenon was rare during the baby boom period of high fertility (Fig. 3.1). Natural decrease became more common during the 1960s, particularly near the end of the decade, as fertility levels fell, and then became considerably more widespread geographically during the 1970s (Johnson & Purdy, 1980). The longitudinal pattern during the 1970s was quite different from that of the 1950s and 1960s. After a brief respite in 1970 and 1971, the incidence of natural decrease rapidly rose to a peak in 1973 and then subsided. Natural decrease remained at this low ebb through 1982 (Fuguitt et al., 1989). However, by 1989, the number of natural decrease counties was again on the rise (Johnson, 1993; Johnson & Beale, 2002). Natural decrease accelerated rapidly after 1990 and by the end of the decade had nearly doubled. The number of natural decrease counties continued to rise until 2004. After this natural decrease subsided somewhat from these record levels, but continued to remain high by historical standards.

Natural decrease is particularly relevant for rural areas because more than 90% of U.S. counties with episodes of natural decrease are classified as nonmetropolitan. Between 2000 and 2008, 750

---

[3] The geographic scale of analysis is particularly relevant to the study of natural decrease in the United States. Although natural decrease has probably occurred in small geographic areas (towns, villages) intermittently for some time, it was extremely rare at the county level until the 1960s (Beale, 1969). The first statewide incidence of natural decrease occurred in West Virginia in the late 1990s.

nonmetropolitan counties (36%) experienced overall natural decrease. This is up from approximately 29% in the 1990s. The incidence and severity of natural decrease is influenced by proximity to metropolitan areas. Nearly 45% of remote nonmetropolitan counties – those not adjacent to a metropolitan area – had natural decrease between 2000 and 2009. In contrast, only 30% counties adjacent to metropolitan counties experienced natural decrease.

Natural decrease counties are regionally concentrated. The earliest occurrences of natural decrease were in agricultural areas of the Great Plains, Western and Southern Corn Belt, and East and Central Texas as well as in the Ozark-Ouachita Uplands. Natural decrease also was observed early in some mining and timber-dependent rural counties of the Upper Great Lakes and in Florida counties that were among the first to receive retirement migrants (Fig. 3.2). Later, natural decrease spread to other rural areas of the South, New York and Pennsylvania, the Upper Great Lakes, parts of the West in the 1990s and eventually to Indiana and Ohio.

The heavy concentrations of natural decrease counties on the Great Plains and in the Corn Belt reflect the linkage between dependence on agriculture and persistent out-migration and low fertility. Farming counties are the most likely to suffer natural decrease: nearly 50% experienced natural decrease between 2000 and 2009. Many agricultural counties have sustained decades of outmigration by young adults, leaving behind fewer young families of childbearing age (Johnson et al., 2005; Johnson & Fuguitt, 2000; Fuguitt et al., 1989). Natural decrease also is observed in 47% of the nonmetropolitan counties classified as retirement destinations by USDA (United States Department of Agriculture). Retirement counties have received a substantial net inflow of older adults for many years. Older migrants push up mortality rates, while obviously contributing nothing to the number of births in counties. The retirement counties of Florida are the best examples of this, but similar clusters exist in the Upper Great Lakes, in the Southeast, Ozarks and portions of the West.

Past research offers two explanations for how variation in demographic components manifests itself in

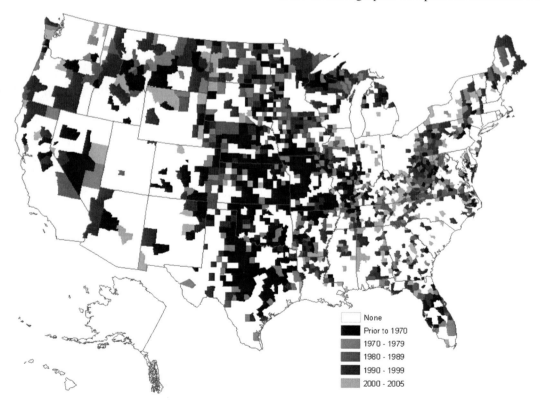

**Fig. 3.2** First year of natural decrease, 1950–2005

natural decrease. First, natural decrease may result from low fertility (Dorn, 1939). Age structure distortions caused by protracted age-specific migration is the second explanation offered for natural decrease (Beale, 1969). Most research supports Beale's findings regarding the importance of age structure shifts in accounting for postwar natural decrease (Adamchak, 1981; Chang, 1974; Johnson, 1993, 2011; Johnson & Beale, 1992; Johnson & Purdy, 1980).

Areas with a deficit of young adults and a surplus of older adults are at greater risk of natural decrease. Eventually, even with fertility rates at the national average, diminishing numbers of young adults cannot produce sufficient births to offset the rising number of deaths to the larger, older cohorts (Beale, 1969; Johnson, 1993; Johnson & Beale, 1992). Nonmetropolitan natural decrease counties have significantly fewer 20–50-year olds than the U.S. as a whole. The greatest shortfall is always among those 20–29. In contrast, natural decrease counties are populated by a disproportionate share aged 50 and over. Because age-specific mortality rates are much higher for older adults, their disproportionate concentration in these counties accelerates natural decrease by increasing the number of deaths.

Prolonged age-specific migration patterns produced the age structure shifts evident in nonmetropolitan natural decrease areas. For decades, migration drained young adults from these areas, while the older population remained (or grew through migration). The exodus of young adults and retention of older adults is not unique to natural decrease areas; in fact, it is common in much of nonmetropolitan America (Fuguitt & Heaton, 1995; Johnson et al., 2005; Johnson & Fuguitt, 2000, also Chapter 6 in this volume). What differs is its magnitude. In natural decrease areas, the outflow of young adults (20–29) was more substantial. The demographic impact of out-migration among young adults is magnified by the aging in place and by an influx of older migrants in some areas. Thus, for several generations the older population grew while the young left.[4]

Dorn (1939) argued that low fertility caused the initial outbreak of natural decrease in the 1930s. However, the relationship between natural decrease and fertility is complex. The high fertility of the baby boom era postponed the onset of natural decrease in many counties, while the rapid fertility decline in the early 1970s contributed to its rising incidence at the time. The ebb and flow of natural decrease roughly approximates nationwide trends in fertility from 1950–1980 (data not shown). However, natural decrease rose sharply after 1980 despite an upward trajectory in births in the nation as a whole.

Why have births diminished so rapidly in nonmetropolitan natural decrease areas in the past several decades? It is not because women in such areas are having fewer children than their counterparts elsewhere in the U.S. Although the gap between fertility levels in natural decrease counties and the U.S. have diminished in recent decades, such counties still had total fertility rates near the national average in 2000 (Johnson, 2011). However, a general decline in nonmetropolitan age-specific fertility rates contributed to the diminished number of births in natural decrease areas after 1980. Fuguitt, Beale, and Reibel (1991) reported a substantial decline in nonmetropolitan age-specific fertility rates in the 1980s. The traditionally higher birth rates of nonmetropolitan women had been converging with those of urban women for some time and by 1990, the overall fertility rates for these two groups were virtually equivalent (Long & Nucci, 1997). So, both temporal variations and normative changes in family size contributed to the changing incidence of natural decrease.

Not all natural decrease areas face a bleak future. Although natural decrease will likely continue in some areas, this is not a demographic certainty in light of the recent influx of immigrants into nonmetropolitan areas (Kandel & Cromartie, 2004; Lichter & Johnson, 2006). New immigration has brought significant increases in the number of Hispanic births, which also is impacting on rural natural increase (Lichter & Johnson, 2006; Johnson & Lichter, 2008). As we shall see, the influx of rural immigrants and new minority groups to rural

---

[4] Though it would be extremely valuable to have post-2000 age-specific migration data, it is calculated as a residual. The residual method, which calculates age-specific net migration as the difference between an expected and actual population in a county, requires extremely detailed and accurate counts of the population by age, race, and sex. Only the decennial Census enumerations provide the accurate beginning and end of period data required for calculating age-specific net migration.

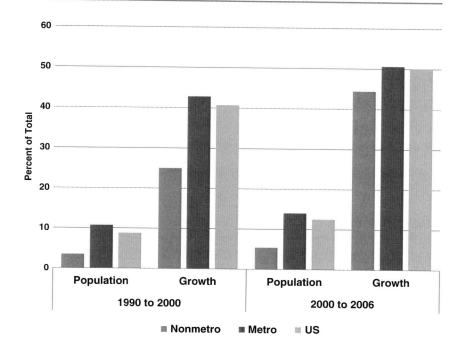

**Fig. 3.3** Hispanic percentage of population and population growth by metropolitan status, 1990–2000 and 2000–2006 *Source*: Johnson and Lichter (2008).

America is having a profound impact on rural natural increase and the age structure of rural populations.

## The Impact of Hispanic and Minority Population Change on Rural Natural Increase

Any analysis of demographic trends in rural America must acknowledge the growing demographic impact of new Hispanic immigrants. Indeed, America's Hispanic population – both native- and foreign-born – is rapidly diffusing spatially, especially into smaller metropolitan cities (Singer, 2004) and less densely settled small towns and rural areas in the South and Midwest (Lichter & Johnson, 2006). New Hispanic migrants have large secondary demographic effects on fertility and natural increase in new rural Hispanic destinations. The growing number of births to new Hispanic residents has dampened or even offset recent white natural decrease and population declines.[5]

Indeed, the demographic impact of Hispanic population dynamics is perhaps best reflected in the demographic components of change that account for overall U.S. population growth (not Hispanic growth alone). Hispanics have accounted for a rapidly accelerating share of U.S. population growth over the past two decades. During the 1990s, for example, the U.S. population grew by 32.7 million persons – the largest population increase in U.S. history. Hispanics accounted for 13.3 million, or nearly 41%, of this population growth (see Fig. 3.3). The Hispanic population grew by 58% during the 1990s, while the overall U.S. population grew by only 13%. For 2000–2006, the U.S. population grew by 18 million. Hispanics accounted for 50% of this gain, even though they represented only 12.5% of the population in 2000.

Despite recent nonmetropolitan growth, Hispanics remain spatially concentrated in metropolitan areas: Over 90% resided in metropolitan areas in 2000. Hispanics represented 14% of the metropolitan population, but accounted for over half (50.6%) of its growth between 2000 and 2006. In nonmetropolitan areas, the demographic impact of Hispanics also is

---

[5] Of course, these secondary effects of natural increase will presumably dissipate with cultural and economic incorporation of Hispanics and aging-in-place. Fertility rates among native-born Hispanics are substantially lower than rates among foreign-born Hispanics, although age at first birth is much earlier among native-born than foreign-born Hispanics. Like other immigrant populations, fertility rates among Hispanics also tend to decline over successive generations; first-generation Hispanics have much higher fertility rates or parities than second- or third-generation Hispanics (Carter, 2000).

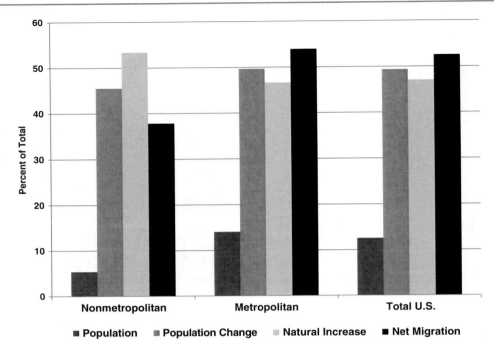

**Fig. 3.4** Hispanic contribution to population and demographic change 2000–2005
*Source*: Johnson and Lichter (2008).

large and rarely acknowledged. There, Hispanics represented only 3.5% of the rural population in 1990, but they accounted for nearly 26% of population growth over the ensuing decade. The demographic impact was even larger between 2000 and 2006, when Hispanics accounted for 44.4% of nonmetro population growth. The large demographic footprint belies the small size of the rural Hispanic population. Hispanics represented only 5.4% of the nonmetro population.[6]

Growth of the Hispanic population has been fueled by both natural increase and net migration (see Chapter 15 in this volume). Net migration provided the bulk of the Hispanic population gain during the 1990s. In metro areas, for example, migration accounted for 57% of the overall Hispanic gain. The gains due to net migration were even larger in nonmetro areas: 67% of the Hispanic population gain of 1,044,000 came from migration. Much of this migration gain was due to immigration.[7]

After 2000, the growing demographic importance of Hispanic natural increase is clearly evident. Between 2000 and 2005, most Hispanic population growth came from natural increase rather than net migration, both in metro and nonmetro areas. More than 58% of the nonmetro Hispanic increase and 55% of the metro Hispanic population gain was due to the excess of births over deaths (Fig. 3.4). In short, natural increase rather than immigration is now the primary engine of Hispanic population growth.

---

[6] Hispanic population increases were not restricted to locations proximate to metropolitan areas. The overall nonmetro Hispanic population gain from 1990–2000 was 65.7%. The gain was larger in nonmetro counties adjacent to a metropolitan area (73.4%) than in nonadjacent counties (54.2%). In all, nonmetro counties gained just over a million Hispanic residents during the 1990s. The metro percentage gain was slightly smaller than that in nonmetro areas (60.2%), though it was considerably larger in absolute terms at 12, 272,000. Between 2000 and 2005, the nonmetro Hispanic population grew by 18.9% adding another 497,000 residents with the gains in adjacent areas again exceeding those in nonadjacent counties. The metro population also continued to gain Hispanics, with a 21.1% gain of 6,885,000.

[7] But recent research suggests that some of the net Hispanic migration gain in rural areas also resulted from movement out of traditional Hispanic settlement areas in the Southwest and elsewhere (Lichter & Johnson, 2006; Donato, Tolbert, Nucci, & Kawano, 2007). The foreign-born population represents only 30% of the nonmetro Hispanic population, although a growing share of Hispanic in-migrants to rural areas appears to be arriving directly from Latin America countries (Kandel & Cromartie, 2004).

The growing demographic impact of natural increase results from extremely high Hispanic birth-to-death ratios. Between 2000 and 2005, there were 5.7 births for every death in the Hispanic population in nonmetro areas. This ratio was even higher in metro areas – 7.8 births per death. This ratio contrasts sharply with the overall birth-to-death ratio of 1.2 in nonmetro areas and 1.8 in metro areas (Johnson & Lichter, 2008). The pronounced difference between Hispanic and overall birth-to-death ratios reflects three interrelated factors. First, the Hispanic population is much younger than the U.S. population (median age of Hispanics is 27 compared to 40 for non-Hispanic whites) resulting in proportionately more women of childbearing age. Second, age-specific fertility levels are higher for Hispanic women at every age from 15–29. Finally, the youthfulness of the Hispanic population produces a paucity of deaths because proportionately fewer Hispanics are in age groups at high risk of mortality. Clearly, a large secondary effect associated with rapid in-migration of Hispanics is now revealed in fertility and natural increase.

Hispanics are rapidly dispersing geographically and natural increase is fueling the demographic and economic transformation of new destination communities. Our previous research revealed that about one-half of the nonmetro Hispanic population now resides outside of traditional Hispanic settlements in the rural Southwest (Johnson & Lichter, 2008). Hispanic resettlement patterns have been instrumental in offsetting non-Hispanic white population declines, especially in the Great Plains. Over 200 nonmetro counties – double the number observed for the 1990s (Kandel & Cromartie, 2004) – would have experienced population decline during 2000–2005 without Hispanic migrants and natural increase.

Our results paint a compelling new demographic portrait of rural America, one showing a growing number of areas being transformed demographically by high rates of in-migration and natural increase of Hispanics. Rural scholars have lamented for decades the decline of small towns, a result of persistent rural out-migration and economic stagnation in much of nonmetro America (see Johnson & Fuguitt, 2000). Our new research suggests that Hispanic natural increase and migration gains are fueling new growth in hundreds of rural counties.

## Natural Increase and Population Diversity

The first evidence of the impact of the growing Hispanic population on rural America is reflected in recent data on the racial/ethnic structure of the rural child population. Nationwide, minority children represented 43% of the U.S. population under the age of 20 (Johnson & Lichter, 2010). In contrast, only 31% of the adult population is minority. Last year, 48.6% of the babies born in the U.S. were minority: the highest percentage in U.S. history. Hispanics represent the largest share of this minority youth population. More than 21% of the population under the age of 20 was Hispanic in 2008 (Johnson & Lichter, 2010). Though high levels of Hispanic natural increase make it the fastest growing component of the nonmetropolitan population, it is important to recognize that it isn't the only minority population in rural America.

Two factors are driving the rapid increase in the number of minority births in the U.S. in both rural and urban areas. The racial mix in the number of women of childbearing age has changed significantly. Between 1990 and 2008, the number of non-Hispanic white women of prime childbearing age diminished by 5.6 million (19%). In contrast, there were 4.5 million (40%) more minority women in their prime childbearing years. Of these, 3.1 million (68%) were Hispanic. As a result, the proportion of all women in their prime childbearing years who were non-Hispanic white diminished from 73% in 1990 to 61% in 2008 (Johnson & Lichter, 2010).

Differential fertility rates are another important driver of the changing proportion of young people who are minority. High Hispanic fertility rates combined with the rapid growth of Hispanic women of childbearing age have produced the exceptionally large numbers of Hispanic births. Indeed, if current fertility patterns persist, Hispanic women will have 2.99 children during their lifetimes. In contrast, if current fertility rates are sustained non-Hispanic white women are likely to have 1.87 children. African-American fertility rates are higher than those for whites, but declined from 2.5 children per woman in 1990 to 2.13 in 2007. This has contributed to the reduction in black young people. The groups that compose most of our "other" minority category (Asians and Native Americans) also have relatively low total fertility (2.04 and 1.86, respectively), so recent youth gains in these groups are due to the rising numbers of women of childbearing age (mostly because of Asian immigration) rather than to high fertility rates. In sum, low non-Hispanic white fertility clearly exacerbates the demographic impact of the growing number of minority women and their higher fertility on America's racial and ethnic mix.

The conventional wisdom is that growing diversity is largely a big-city phenomenon. But our analyses reveal that the new growth of minority children is particularly pronounced in rural areas. Minority children still constitute a considerably smaller proportion of all nonmetropolitan children (26%) than they do of metropolitan children (46%). The rural youth population actually declined by 6.5% after 2000 (Fig. 3.5). Nonmetropolitan areas actually had fewer young people in 2008 than 2000 – roughly 900,000 fewer – because there were a million (–10.3%) fewer non-Hispanic white youth in 2008 than in 2000. The population loss among black young people was nearly as large as whites in percentage terms (–8.3%). Only the significant growth of the rural Hispanic youth population kept rural child population losses from being even greater. The number of young Hispanics grew by 278,000 between 2000 and 2008. However, even such significant gains in Hispanic young people (26.5%) were insufficient to offset the substantial youth population losses of whites and blacks in rural areas.

Nor were rural areas the only places to gain Hispanic young people. This is reflected in disproportionately large absolute and percentage gains *outside* the urban core counties of metropolitan areas with more than one million residents. Indeed, the suburban and smaller metropolitan counties, where minority gains are now most heavily concentrated, are home to 44.6 million (54%) of the nation's 82.6 million young people. A significant majority are non-Hispanic white (63%), despite a decline of more than a million (–3.7%) since 2000. In contrast, each minority population of children and youths grew rapidly here. The number of Hispanics has swelled by 2.1 million (37%) since 2000; this is the largest gain of any minority population in any area during this period.

In the large urban cores, where minority populations have traditionally clustered, 63% of the 25.2 million children and youth are minority. Minority populations continued to grow in these areas, despite declines among blacks and whites. The black population loss is actually larger on a percentage basis than the loss for non-Hispanic whites. These declines have been largely offset by large Hispanic population gains. When combined with other minorities, the population of children and youth increased by more than a million.

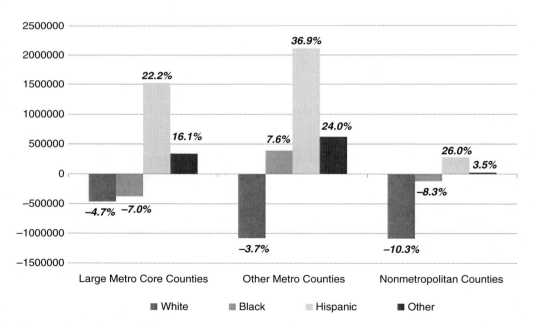

**Fig. 3.5** Population change for children by race/Hispanic origin, 2000–2008
*Source*: Johnson and Lichter (2010).
*Note*: Children under 20 years of age.

Evidence of the geographic implications of current fertility patterns is also evident in the spatial distribution of minority children in the U.S. Indeed, 504 counties now have a majority of minority young people (i.e., majority-minority counties) and another 286 are "near" majority-minority, with between 40 and 50% minority youth populations (Fig. 3.6). Of these, 321 majority-minority youth counties are nonmetropolitan as are 170 of the near majority-minority counties. These patterns among young people clearly are a harbinger of future racial change and diversity in America, especially as deaths among the older largely white population are replaced disproportionately by minority births. In 2008, many more counties had majority-minority youth populations than had overall majority-minority populations (504 vs. 309).

## Discussion and Conclusion

Recent demographic trends in Europe – especially the emergence of below-replacement fertility – have been much different from those in the United States. The "Third Demographic Transition," is well underway in much of Europe. It has been characterized by population aging, borne of declining fertility, and a rapidly changing ethnic composition, borne of rapid new immigration of ethnic minorities (Coleman, 2006). As we have shown in this chapter, aspects of the "Third Demographic Transition" observed in Europe also now seem to be underway in a large number of remote rural counties in the United States. Persistent out-migration, natural decrease, and new immigration are rapidly changing the social and economic fabric of many parts of America.

The purpose of this chapter is modest: To examine nonmetropolitan demographic trends in the first decade of the 21st century, with a particular focus on natural increase. Demographic growth and change in rural America results from both natural increase and net migration. Natural increase and migration represent distinctly different but intimately interrelated demographic processes. But migration alone has received the lion's share of attention. Because county in- and

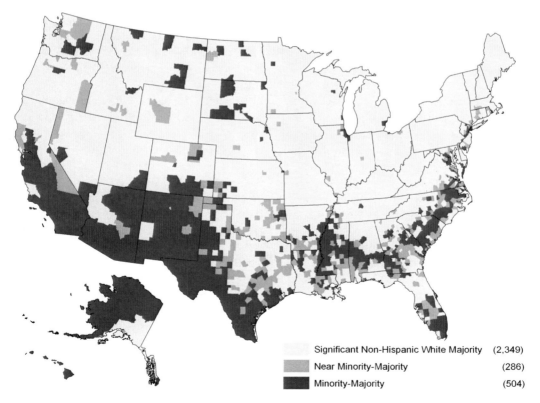

**Fig. 3.6** Distribution of minority and non-Hispanic white population under age 20, 2008
*Source:* Johnson and Lichter (2010).

out-migration are highly age selective it has important secondary effects on both fertility and mortality, leading to natural increase in some areas and natural decrease in others. Immigration has also had a powerful influence on natural increase in nonmetropolitan America, adding another twist to an unfolding demographic story. Our research documents how the symbiotic interaction between natural increase and migration has played out differently over the geographic region that encompasses rural America.

Our results clearly show that natural increase has re-emerged as a prominent demographic force in the growth of rural America in the first decade of the 21st century. Nearly 77% of the rural population growth since 2000 is due to natural increase. In fact, in remote rural areas, natural increase has fueled all the growth. Natural increase was also important in the traditional rural areas – those highly dependent on farming and mining. In contrast, migration rather than natural increase fueled much of the growth in recreational and retirement areas. This is a striking contrast to the patterns of the rural rebound of the 1990s when migration accounted for most nonmetropolitan growth.

Perhaps paradoxically, natural increase has become more important demographically even as the volume of natural increase has declined. In other nonmetro counties, natural decrease has been on the rise. That natural decrease could rise so sharply in an era when annual births nationwide are now at levels not seen since the baby boom underscores the complex set of factors that influence the demographic structure of rural America. Natural decrease is a consequence of protracted outmigration of generation after generation of young adults from rural areas. Currently, low fertility rates and population aging make natural decrease an on-going concern. The spatial clustering of rural natural decrease has implications for rural economic development efforts that face the prospect of a rapid population aging and incipient decline.

The growing presence of Hispanics introduces a new element into the demographic calculus of nonmetropolitan America. Indeed, Hispanics represent a new source of demographic vigor in many parts of rural America, especially in the Midwest and Southeast. Our results revealed that about one-half of the nonmetro Hispanic population now resides outside of traditional Hispanic settlements in the rural Southwest. Moreover, a substantial and growing number of nonmetro counties experienced non-Hispanic white population declines, but nevertheless experienced Hispanic population gains. Hispanics are transforming the social and economic fabric of many small towns, while raising important policy questions about their successful incorporation into American society (Massey, 2008). The early 2000s have highlighted a new spatial patterning of racial and ethnic diversity in America.

The rapid growth of the Hispanic population – fueled increasingly by natural increase rather than in-migration – also underscores the changing racial and ethnic mix of America's young people. Two powerful demographic forces place young people in the vanguard of America's new diversity. The first is the rapid increase in the number of minority children – with Hispanics accounting for 80% of U.S. population growth. The second equally dramatic but less widely recognized force is absolute declines in the population of non-Hispanic white youth. Together, these two trends have increased the proportion of minority youth from 38.5% of the U.S. total in 2000 to 43% in 2008. In rural areas, the recent growth of the minority child population has offset significant declines in the number of young non-Hispanics. This is a direct reflection of the rising levels of Hispanic births in rural areas. At the same time, broad rural regions remain where interaction between young people from different backgrounds is limited.

In conclusion, our research contributes to policy discussions by delineating the rapidity and geographic scale at which rural America is changing. It does so by emphasizing the critical demographic role that natural increase/decrease is playing in this transition. America will continue to become an increasingly diverse place, beginning with children and youth. Natural increase – through fertility – is an important force reshaping the racial and ethnic mix of the countryside just as it did during earlier immigration waves of America's history. The relative influence of natural increase and migration in nonmetropolitan areas has waxed and waned in recent decades. Although not often recognized as such, recent demographic trends in rural America have clear parallels to patterns in Europe associated with population aging, below-replacement fertility, and increasing racial and ethnic diversity. The so-called "Third Demographic Transition" arguably now has a demographic foothold in rural America.

# References

Adamchak, D. J. (1981). Population decrease and change in nonmetropolitan Kansas. *Transactions of the Kansas Academy of Science, 84*(1), 15–31.

Beale, C. L. (1964). Rural depopulation in the United States: Some demographic consequences of agricultural adjustments. *Demography, 1*, 264–272.

Beale, C. L. (1969). Natural decrease of population: The current and prospective status of an emergent American phenomenon. *Demography, 6*, 91–99.

Beale, C. L. (2000). Nonmetro population growth recedes in a time of unprecedented national prosperity. *Rural Conditions and Trends, 11*, 27–31.

Brown, D. L., & Wardwell, J. M. (1980). *New directions in urban-rural migration*. New York: Academic.

Carter, M. (2000). Fertility of Mexican immigrant women in the U.S.: A closer look. *Social Science Quarterly, 81*, 1073–1086.

Chang, H. C. (1974). Natural population decrease in Iowa counties. *Demography, 11*, 657–672.

Coleman, D. (2006). Immigration and ethnic change in low-fertility countries: A third demographic transition. *Population and Development Review, 32*, 401–446.

Cromartie, J. B. (2001). Nonmetro outmigration exceeds inmigration for the first time in a decade. *Rural America, 16*, 35–37.

Donato, K. M., Tolbert, C., Nucci, A., & Kawano, Y. (2007). Recent immigrant settlement in the nonmetro United States: Evidence from internal census data. *Rural Sociology, 72*, 537–559.

Dorn, H. E. (1939). The natural decrease of population in certain American counties. *Journal of the American Statistical Association, 34*, 106–109.

Easterlin, R. (1976). Population change and farm settlement in the Northern United States. *Journal of Economic History, 36*, 45–75.

Economic Research Service. (2004). *Measuring rurality: 2004 County typology codes methods, data sources, and documentation*. Retrieved July 15, 2010, from http://www.ers.usda.gov/Briefing/Rurality/Typology/Methods

Fischer, C. S., & Hout, M. (2006). *Century of difference: How America changed in the last one hundred years*. New York: Russell Sage Foundation.

Fuguitt, G. V. (1985). The nonmetropolitan population turnaround. *Annual Review of Sociology, 11*, 259–280.

Fuguitt, G. V., Beale, C. L., & Reibel, M. (1991). Recent trends in metropolitan-nonmetropolitan fertility. *Rural Sociology, 56*(3), 475–486.

Fuguitt, G. V., Brown, D. L., & Beale, C. L. (1989). *Rural and small town America*. New York: Russell Sage Foundation.

Fuguitt, G. V., & Heaton, T. B. (1995). The impact of migration on the nonmetropolitan population age structure, 1960–1990. *Population Research and Policy Review, 14*, 215–232.

Greenwood, M. J. (1975). Research on internal migration in the United States: A survey. *Journal of Economic Literature, 13*, 397–433.

Hamilton, B. E., Martin, J. A., & Ventura, S. J. (2010, April 6). Births: Preliminary data for 2008. *National Vital Statistical Reports, 58*(16), 2010.

Howse, K. (2006). The benefits of migration for an ageing Europe. *Ageing Horizons, 4*, 12–18.

Johnson, K. M. (1985). *The impact of population change on business activity in rural America*. Boulder, CO: Westview Press.

Johnson, K. M. (1993). When deaths exceed births: Natural decrease in the United States. *International Regional Science Review, 15*, 179–198.

Johnson, K. M. (2006). Demographic trends in rural and small town America. *Reports on America, 1*(1), 1–35. Carsey Institute, University of New Hampshire.

Johnson, K. M. (2011). The continuing incidence of natural decrease in American counties. *Rural Sociology, 76*, 74–100.

Johnson, K. M., & Beale, C. L. (1992). Natural population decrease in the United States. *Rural Development Perspectives, 8*, 8–15.

Johnson, K. M., & Beale, C. L. (1994). The recent revival of widespread population growth in nonmetropolitan areas of the United States. *Rural Sociology, 59*(4), 655–667.

Johnson, K. M., & Beale, C. L. (2002). Nonmetro recreation counties: Their identification and rapid growth. *Rural America, 17*(4), 12–19.

Johnson, K. M., & Cromartie, J. B. (2006). The rural rebound and its aftermath: Changing demographic dynamics and regional contrasts. In W. Kandel & D. L. Brown (Eds.), *Population change and rural society* (pp. 25–49). Dordrecht, Netherlands: Springer.

Johnson, K. M., & Fuguitt, G. V. (2000). Continuity and change in rural migration patterns, 1950–1995. *Rural Sociology, 65*, 27–49.

Johnson, K. M., & Lichter, D. T. (2008). Natural increase: A new source of population in emerging Hispanic destinations in the United States. *Population and Development Review, 34*, 327–346.

Johnson, K. M., & Lichter, D. T. (2010). The growing diversity of America's children and youth: Spatial and temporal dimensions. *Population and Development Review, 31*(1), 151–176.

Johnson, K. M., & Purdy, R. L. (1980). Recent nonmetropolitan population change in fifty year perspective. *Demography, 17*, 57–80.

Johnson, K. M., Voss, P. R., Hammer, R. B., Fuguitt, G. V., & McNiven, S. (2005). Temporal and spatial variation in age-specific net migration in the United States. *Demography, 42*(4), 791–812.

Jóźwiak, J., & Kotowska, I. E. (2008). Decreasing birth rates in Europe: Reasons and remedies. *European View, 7*, 225–236.

Kandel, W., & Cromartie, J. (2004). *New patterns of Hispanic settlement in rural America*. Rural Development Research Report 99. Washington, DC: Economic Research Service, USDA.

Lesthaeghe, R. (1995). The second demographic transition in Western countries: An interpretation. In K. O. Mason & A.-M. Jensen (Eds.), *Gender and family change in industrialized countries* (pp. 17–62). Oxford, England: Oxford University Press.

Lichter, D. T., Fuguitt, G. V., Heaton, T. B., & Clifford, W. B. (1981). Components of change in the residential concentration of the elderly population: 1950 1975. *Journal of Gerontology, 36*(September), 480–489.

Lichter, D. T., & Johnson, K. M. (2006). Emerging rural settlement patterns and the geographic redistribution of America's new immigrants. *Rural Sociology, 71*, 109–131.

Lichter, D. T., & Johnson, K. M. (2009). Immigrant gateways and Hispanic migration to new destinations. *International Migration Review, 43*, 496–518.

Long, L., & Nucci, A. (1997). The "clean break" revisited. Is U.S. population again deconcentrating? *Environment and Planning A, 29*, 1355–1366.

Lutz, W., Sanderson, W., & Scherbov, S. (2008). The coming acceleration of global population ageing. *Nature, 451*, 716–719.

Martin, P., & Midgley, E. (2010). *Immigration in America 2010.* Washington, DC: Population Reference Bureau.

Massey, D. S. (2008) *New faces in new places: The changing geography of American immigration.* New York: Russell Sage.

McGranahan, D. A. (1999). *Natural amenities drive population change.* Agricultural Economics Report No. 718. Washington, DC: Economic Research Service, U. S. Department of Agriculture.

Morgan, S. P. (2003). Is low fertility a twenty-first-century demographic crisis? *Demography, 40*, 589–603.

Reher, D. S. (2007). Towards long-term population decline: A discussion of relevant issues. *European Journal of Population, 23*, 189–207.

Singer, A. (2004). *The rise of new immigrant gateways.* The living cities census series. Washington, DC: Brookings Institution.

U.S. Census Bureau. (2009). *Annual county resident population estimates by age, sex, race, and Hispanic origin: April 1, 2000 to July 1, 2008.* Retrieved May 29, 2009, from http://www.census.gov/popest/counties/asrh/files/CC-EST2008-ALLDATA

# Migration and Rural Population Change: Comparative Views in More Developed Nations

David L. Brown

## Introduction

The distribution of population among urban and rural places is of particular interest to researchers and policy analysts because of the intimate link between urbanization and socioeconomic development. Given this link, it is unsurprising that the level of urbanization is higher in more developed countries while less developed countries have higher rates of urbanization.[1] The study of urbanization has moved beyond the urban-rural dichotomy (Champion & Hugo, 2004), but urban-rural population redistribution remains an important focus of research and policy analysis especially as it affects the prospects for economic development, access to opportunities and the quality of community life. Although the focus of such studies is mainly on urban places and environments, by its very nature population redistribution also affects rural communities through the transfer of people and economic activities, by emerging social and economic dependencies that develop over space (Woods, 2009; Lichter & Brown, 2011), and by the declining rural share of population, economy, and social and political influence that accompany urbanization. The rural implications of urbanization merit attention, hence, this chapter examines migration's contribution to internal population redistribution with a particular emphasis on the way in which it affects rural population change.

This chapter focuses on the rural implications of urbanization in *more developed* countries. This may seem counterintuitive because as indicated earlier developed nations are already highly urbanized,[2] and their rates of increase of urbanization are far lower than in less developed nations (United Nations, 2008). Hence, it would seem that most of the important contemporary aspects of urbanization would be found in less developed, rapidly urbanizing contexts. In many respects this is true (Keiner, Koll-Schretzenmayr, & Schmid, 2005), but research during the last quarter century in the US, Europe and other OECD countries has demonstrated that urbanization and development are not necessarily directly related to each other. In other words, they can become unlinked. What was once thought to be an uninterruptable and continuous positive relationship between urbanization and the level of development has been shown to reverse under certain situations (Zelinsky, 1971; Brown & Wardwell, 1980; Champion, 1989; Geyer & Kontuly, 1993, see also Chapter 5 in this volume). It is unsurprising that the *rate* of urbanization would slow as a nation becomes increasingly urbanized (and developed) because at high levels of urbanization each additional percent urban is increasingly difficult to produce. However, counter-urbanization, an inverse relationship between population size and the rate of population growth (Fielding, 1982), is not predicted

---

D.L. Brown (✉)
Department of Development Sociology, Cornell University, Ithaca, NY 14850, USA
e-mail: Dlb17@cornell.edu

[1] The rate of urbanization is considerably higher in less developed nations. In fact, according to the UN, the percent urban in the less developed regions, 42 percent in 2003, will rise to 57% by 2030 (United Nations, 2008).

[2] The percent urban in more developed nations is projected to increase to 82% by 2030 (United Nations, 2008).

by standard regional economic development theory (Mitchell, 2004). It is this fluctuation in the *direction* of urbanization that justifies attention to rural-urban population redistribution in more developed countries, and especially how rural-urban population transfers affect the size and composition of rural populations of more developed nations.

It is well known that natural increase declines as an accompaniment of social and economic development. Less well known is that spatial variability in natural increase diminishes as well. High fertility that characterized rural and agricultural regions declines as rural economies are transformed from agriculture to goods and service production, and as technology displaces labor thereby diminishing the need for unpaid household help on farms. In the US for example, the number of children under 5 per 1,000 rural women age 20–44 was about 1,325 in 1800 while the ratio of children to urban women was about 850. In 1980, in contrast, the rural ratio was about 500 children per 1,000 women of childbearing age, and about 375 for urban women. Hence, the rural-urban gap in fertility fell from 475 children per 1,000 women in 1800 to only 100 in 1980 (Fuguitt, Brown, & Beale, 1989). In other words, rural fertility declined much more rapidly than urban fertility as the nation moved through its demographic transition. In the absence of substantial spatial differences in mortality and longevity[3] this means that natural increase ceases to differ significantly across places, and hence ceases to contribute much to spatial variability in rates of population change. Accordingly, migration becomes the major reason for differential population growth across space in more developed nations, and hence, will be this chapter's major focus.

## The Demographic Approach to Examining Urbanization and Population Redistribution

Urbanization and counter-urbanization are two main aspects of population redistribution experienced by many of today's most highly developed nations. Urbanization involves a broad-scale social change where societies are transformed from localized, small-scale, homogeneous activities to large-scale, differentiated, coordinated activities. As a result, urban communities and economies come to dominate societies because geographic concentration of differentiated and coordinated activities is efficient. Economies of scale are realized, and productivity enhanced when complementary functions are integrated in complex, high-density divisions of labor. As the level of urbanization advances, so does the strength and extensiveness of social, economic and political relationships binding cities with their hinterlands.[4] City and periphery, rather than being independent social and economic spaces, are transformed into integrated social and economic systems. City-hinterland interdependence becomes a defining characteristic of highly urbanized societies.[5]

Counter-urbanization, in contrast to urbanization, is more likely to involve residential redistribution while having much less effect on the location of economic activities (Champion, Coombes, & Brown, 2009). In other words, even as counter-urbanization affects various aspects of community organization, it does *not* involve a fundamental restructuring of the urban-based territorial division of labor. Neither does counter-urbanization signal the dismantling of the urban residential concentration. In England, for example, where rural areas have grown faster than their urban counterparts for many decades, the level of urbanization was essentially the same in 2001 than a decade before even though rural populations grew much more rapidly during the decade (Rural Evidence Research Centre, 2005).[6]

Although scholars generally acknowledge the essential politico-economic nature of urbanization

---

[3] Age-adjusted all-cause mortality tends to be somewhat higher in rural areas (Cosby et al., 2008), but the difference is not sufficient to have a major impact on natural increase.

[4] Tilly (1974), Duncan, Scott, Lieberson, Duncan, and Winsboro (1960), and others.

[5] In the contemporary world, large metropolises extend far beyond their national boundaries to become world cities that dominate hinterlands that are often global in scope. Doreen Massey (2007), Saskia Sassen (2006) and others have observed that world cities are now the major nodes through which global economic relations are managed and controlled. As Sassen (2006, p. 122) has written, "...cities are strategic places that concentrate command functions, global markets, and...production sites for the advanced corporate service industries."

[6] England uses at least two rural-urban definitions. Using the "district level" measure, England would be approximately 2/3 urban in 1991 and 2000. Percent urban would be considerably higher in both of these years by alternative measures.

(Smith & Borocz, 1995), the measurement of urbanization tends to focus mainly on population redistribution. This practice is heavily influenced by Hope Tisdale's (1942) strictly demographic conceptualization of urbanization as a process of population concentration—a process that builds cities. According to Tisdale, cities are defined by two demographic characteristics—population size and population density. Accordingly, urbanization proceeds through multiplication of the number of cities and through population growth of existing cities. Hence, nations urbanize when the share of their population living in urban places increases, and the share living in rural areas declines, for example when urban rates of population growth exceed rural rates. However, as Charles Tilly (1974) and others have pointed out, urbanization does not mean that rural populations are necessarily declining or even growing slowly. It simply means that the rate of urban population growth exceeds that of its rural counterparts. This demographic perspective has influenced the ways in which official statistical agencies delineate urban and rural populations and measure the *level* and *rate* of urbanization. Even when suitable data are available to examine urban and rural areas in a more fully theorized, multidimensional manner, the costs of doing so are typically prohibitive (Brown & Cromartie, 2004). In this chapter I will employ the demographic perspective and examine migration's contribution to urbanization and counter-urbanization in various parts of the more developed world.

## Critique of the Demographic Approach

Before proceeding, it is necessary to acknowledge legitimate critiques of this demographic "accounting" approach to examining the level and rate of urbanization. First, as observed above, urbanization involves more than population concentration. In addition, even if one agrees, as I do, that population concentration is a valid indicator of the level of urbanization, the dichotomization of urban and rural populations is controversial for at least three reasons. First, thresholds of population size and density are somewhat arbitrary. What may seem large for some purposes, for determining the location of major trauma hospitals for example, may far exceed the necessary threshold for determining the optimal location of automobile dealerships or dry cleaners. Disagreement on appropriate and scientifically accurate thresholds of population size and density for differentiating urban and rural populations is reflected in the wide variety of statistical practice employed throughout the world. In Europe alone, the minimum urban size threshold ranges from 1,500 (Ireland) to 20,000 (Switzerland) (United Nations, 2008).

Second, the process of urbanization should be conceptualized and measured as a variable characteristic of places not as a set of discrete categories. Accordingly, although places can be arrayed on a continuum that ranges from clearly rural locations, for example those identified as "non-core based places" in the U.S statistical system, to global mega cities such as New York, London, Paris, Mexico City or Beijing, places located in between these extremes are not unambiguously urban or rural. These intermediate locales are of particular interest because they tend to be where growth and change are occurring, and where decisions over land use, the proper scale and content of education and other community issues are particularly contentious. Moreover, these areas are often located at the urbanizing periphery of expanding metropolitan areas, and hence are experiencing dramatic transformations of their social and economic lives (Cromartie, 2006).

Third, all measurement systems, including those in social science, seek to maximize differences between categories while minimizing within-category variability. In other words, social science categories, such as those designed to measure the level and pace of urbanization, are not unitary or homogeneous. In the US, for example, the metropolitan category ranges from 50,000 to over 19 million population while the non-metropolitan category includes counties with small cities of 20,000 or greater population and counties that lack even one place with 2,500 residents.

It also merits noting that some scholars reject a materialistic concept of urban and urbanization such as that utilized by demographers and other quantitative social scientists, preferring instead a cognitive or representational alternative. As Halfacre (2004, p. 288) observed, "The rural is thus shifted from a material sphere of the locality to the dematerialized realm of mental space: it becomes a virtual structure." This is important because as Halfacre noted (1993, p. 29), "The world is organized, understood and mediated through these basic cognitive units." I acknowledge that the ideational concept of "the rural" is interesting

## Demographic Dynamics of Urbanization and Population Redistribution

### Migration's Contribution to Urbanization and Counter-Urbanization

As shown by many scholars, migration's contribution to urbanization varies over time and across nations (Billsborow, 1998; Chen, Valente, & Zlotnick, 1998; White & Lindstrom, 2006). Migration is the principal source of urbanization prior to a nation's entering the demographic transition because natural increase is low or negative in both urban and rural areas. In fact, prior to the demographic transition, net rural-urban migration is typically needed to simply replace urban natural decrease. However, once a nation enters the demographic transition, natural increase begins to play a more important role in national [and urban] population growth, and this contribution increases as natural increase climbs to high levels. For example, in Africa during the late 1990s, natural increase contributed 75% of urban population growth.[8] However, as nations bring their birth rates under control in the context of lowered mortality, thereby moving through their demographic transitions, natural increase begins to contribute less to urban growth and migration contributes more. For example, across Asia which has experienced significant declines in total fertility rates since the 1970s, natural increase only accounted for about half of urban population growth between 2000 and 2005 (without China) ranging from 30% in East Asia to 48% in Southeast Asia (Cohen, 2004; United Nations, 2006). Similarly, in Latin America where fertility and mortality rates have been relatively low for at least three decades, rural to urban migration accounted for over 100% of urbanization between 1950 and 2000 (Lattes, Rodriguez, & Villa, 2004).[9]

## Migration and Rural Population Change in More Developed Nations

Similar to the case in Latin America, migration is the major determinant of rural-urban population redistribution in North America, Europe, and other highly developed regions of the world. However, as indicated earlier, the direction of population redistribution in these regions is not always toward increased concentration. In this section, I examine migration's role in recent rural population growth in England, the US and Hungary, three highly developed, but distinctly different countries. Not only do these countries have differing sociopolitical and demographic histories, they also have differing institutional and socioeconomic structures. So although all three countries are highly urbanized, the historical trajectory of urbanization and migration's role in urbanization are importantly different. For example, England and the US were both over 80% urban by the turn of the 21st century, but England had already exceeded 50% urban by 1851 (Champion & Brown, 2012a) while the US only reached this milestone around 1930 (Fuguitt et al., 1989). In both instances, because industrialization tends to be accompanied by population concentration in large, dense places, the high level of urbanization reflects a history of capitalist industrial development. The US's slower pace is simply associated with its later development and the persistence of a huge agrarian sector prior to the Second World War. In Hungary, in contrast, state policy interfered with the relationship between economic transformation and population concentration (Szelenyi, 1996). This resulted in dramatic rural depopulation, the location of heavy industry in politically favored locations and "under-urbanization," a mismatch between the location of industrial jobs in large cities and the supply of housing and public services in such places.

In this section I first describe rural-urban population redistribution in England where counter-urbanization was first noted, and where it has continued unabated since at least the 1930s (Champion & Brown, 2012a). This will be followed by an analysis of migration and urbanization and counter-urbanization in the US where the direction of rural-urban internal migration

---

[7] Except that ideational representations of the "rural idyll" may contribute to residential preferences and migration decision making.

[8] Reclassification of rural areas to urban areas can also play an important role in urbanization.

[9] Latin American countries differ widely in this respect. In fact, migration was a negative factor in urbanization in Mexico between 1990 and 2000 because much rural-urban migration had international destinations.

has shifted from decade to decade. The third case is Hungary where counter-urbanization appeared in 1990, and *seems to be* a result of the transformation from state socialism to market capitalism.

## Measurement of Urban and Rural Is Not Comparable Between the US, England, and Hungary

Before examining these case studies, however, it should be emphasized that the statistical delineation of urban and rural populations differs markedly across these three countries so the following analysis is not strictly comparable in a statistical sense.[10] Rather, I am placing the experiences of these three countries in parallel so that fundamental similarities and differences in migration and population redistribution can be noted.

*England*: Building a coherent and usable definition of rural for England is challenging because there are many perceptions and interpretations of the term.[11] Accordingly, the urban-rural delineation is less uniform in England compared with the US.[12] Because this chapter focuses on urban-rural migration and population redistribution, I will briefly discuss how urban and rural areas are distinguished in conventional statistical practice. England (and Wales) uses two principal methods of defining rural, both of which were developed by the Office of National Statistics (ONS, 2009; Commission on Rural Communities, 2010). The main distinction between these two urban-rural categorizations is that one was built up from very small building blocks while the other is for large administrative units averaging 120,000 population. The first categorization might be characterized as the "urban through hamlets" schema. Using data from the 2001 census, the ONS delineated eight different classes of urban and rural places based on population size and density. Urban areas have populations of 10,000 or more while rural areas have less than 10,000 inhabitants. Both urban and rural areas are then subdivided according to population density (sparse vs. less sparse) and then the rural categories are further divided according to whether settlements are hamlets or isolated dwellings, villages, or towns and the urban fringe.

The second delineation of urban and rural areas includes six categories of local authority districts and unitary authorities that range from predominately urban to predominately rural. Three of the six categories are urban with the remaining three being rural. At one end of the scale, major urban areas have either 100,000 people or 50% of their populations in urban areas of 750,000 or more. At the other end of the spectrum, local authorities characterized as "rural 80" have at least 80% of their population in rural settlements and larger market towns. This classification scheme is widely used by the Department of Environment, Food and Rural Affairs (DEFRA) and other government bodies.

*The US*: The US utilizes a highly transparent methodology for differentiating rural and urban areas. Briefly, the US has two parallel systems: (a) urban and rural and (b) metropolitan and nonmetropolitan (Brown, Cromartie, & Kulcsár, 2004). The metropolitan-nonmetropolitan delineation is compiled from county-level data as determined by the Office of Management and Budget. However, the US Census Bureau and most other federal government agencies use the metropolitan-nonmetropolitan delineation for data display and analysis. The urban-rural distinction focuses on the presence and size of "nodal" population concentrations while the metropolitan-nonmetropolitan distinction is a regional economic concept involving a large city (urbanized area) and its interdependent hinterland. The metropolitan delineation aggregates entire counties whereas the urban-rural distinction is generally determined by the amount and density of population residing within (often municipal) place boundaries.[13] Social scientists typically use county data aggregated by metropolitan-nonmetropolitan status to study long-term trends of urbanization and

---

[10] For a concise discussion of the statistical measurement of urban and rural in England and US see Champion and Brown (2012b). For a discussion of the measurement of urban and rural in Hungary, see Brown et al. (2005).

[11] I examine England in this chapter because of the availability of long-term historical data series and resulting analysis. England (and Wales) use the same method of differentiating urban and rural populations while Scotland and Northern Ireland use different criteria.

[12] In addition, statistical practice differs between England and Wales compared with Northern Ireland and Scotland.

[13] This is not always true since "unincorporated" places can be urban or rural depending on the number of persons living there.

counter-urbanization.[14] The metropolitan system's advantages for statistical analysis are that county boundaries tend to be stable over time and a wide range of socioeconomic data, in addition to population dynamics, are available at the county level. The main disadvantage is that counties can be rather socially distant from the actual communities where people live and work. In addition, a county's metropolitan/nonmetropolitan status can shift over time which can affect the relative rates of population growth and net migration between metropolitan and nonmetropolitan categories (Fuguitt, Heaton, & Lichter, 1988).

In both England and the US, the delineation of population according to urban-rural residence is operationally transparent, conforming to at least two official classification systems. Moreover, the two main US systems are closely linked to each other since metropolitan central counties are defined as having an urbanized area or urban cluster of minimum population size and density. In England and Wales, in contrast, the two ONS classifications are not closely linked in an operational sense. It should also be noted that although both countries use official classification systems for displaying census data, various government agencies in both countries are free to use other geographic schema for targeting and administering programs, and to determine program eligibility (Cromartie & Bucholtz, 2008).

*Hungary*: The Hungarian system involves a simple trichotomy between Budapest, the capital, towns (urban places) and villages (rural places). Like other developed countries, the vast majority of the nation's settlements continue to be rural (89%) while most people live in urban areas (69%). In contrast, to England and the US, the Hungarian system for examining urban-rural migration and population redistribution is *not* transparent. The Hungarian system is influenced by a socialist legacy that favored urban places as the location of economic activity. As a result, there is strong political pressure for places to obtain the urban ["town"] title. Ironically, between 1974 and the regime change in 1989 urban reclassification was regulated by a clear set of rules, even though there is evidence that villages sometimes merged simply to meet the population and service provision thresholds.[15] In contrast, since the regime change in 1989, urban reclassification has become a nontransparent political game. Empirical research clearly demonstrates that "in many instances urban reclassification is neither a consequence of prior development nor an objectively planned tool for regional development" (Kulcsár & Brown, 2011, p. 10). The authors of this study conclude that urban reclassification is a one time opportunity for the central government to build political capital in particular regions. As a result, Hungary has a substantial number of places with urban titles, but which lack urban functions.

## Continuous Counter-Urbanization in England

The industrial revolution is thought to have begun in England, so it is unsurprising that England was one of the first nations to experience mass urbanization. If one simply examines the distribution of population between urban and rural areas, three quarters of England's population already lived in urban environments by the turn of the twentieth century. However, if one uses a "differential urbanization" approach (Geyer & Kontuly, 1993), thereby examining the changing distribution of population between different sizes of urban places, Britain was still undergoing a process of urbanization in the 1950s (Hall & Hay, 1980). Since then, however, England has experienced uninterrupted counter-urbanization, with the rural category having the highest rate of population growth of any type of local labor market area in both the 1970s and 1980s (Champion, 2003). Champion (1989, p. 89) showed that counter-urbanization during the 1970s was a "widespread process of deconcentration across national space" rather than a result of relatively short distance spillover from metropolitan central areas to suburbs and/or nearby rural areas. He noted, counter-urbanization during the 1970s cannot be explained by a single factor. Rather, a complex mix

---

[14] These two systems, of course, are not independent of each other because metropolitan central counties are determined by the presence of an urbanized area having at least 50,000 population.

[15] Between 1974 and 1989, urban places were the location of communal services and had to meet a population threshold of 8,000.

of economic transformations and government policies can be identified (Champion, 1989). He observed that economic growth and prosperity during the 1960s fueled counter-urbanization in the 1970s when the trend reached its peak. Employment deconcentration mirrored population shifts as did house building. Many manufacturing firms located branch plants in provincial locations and channeled new investment and office development to areas that had been adversely affected by deindustrialization and the decline of mining and extractive activities. From a policy standpoint, the clearing of substandard housing from inner city areas displaced large populations[16] while the *New and Expanded Towns Program* provided residential opportunities beyond urban green belts. As a result of the postwar baby boom, the number of school age children reached its peak in the early 1970s thereby contributing to housing pressure throughout the urban system, especially in lower density areas. Additionally, the expansion of controlled access highways and trunk roads increased the locational flexibility of both businesses and households.

Since 1991, rural areas have continued to grow faster than urban areas and England as a whole, with most of this growth concentrated in the urban-rural fringe. However, as Champion and Brown (2012a) showed, using a district level measure of urban and rural for England, the gap between urban and rural growth rates has narrowed since 1991 because urban growth has accelerated while rural rates have been stagnant. This narrowing of the rural advantage is especially influenced by the relatively slow growth rates experienced by the "rural extremes." In contrast, the rate of growth in urban-rural fringe areas has increased between 1991 and 2008 even as the percentage point difference between fringe and urban districts declined from 0.44 in 1991–2001 to 0.31 during 2001–2008 (Champion & Brown, 2012a). As a result of this long-term rural growth advantage, the rural population has increased slightly as a percentage of England's total population.

## Migration's Role in England's Counter-Urbanization During Recent Decades

Rural population growth since 1991 in England has been driven almost entirely by migration (see Table 4.1). In contrast, rural natural increase has been very low during this time, in fact negative for most rural areas. This is undoubtedly a result of older age composition with relatively few persons of child-bearing age residing in many rural areas (Champion & Shepherd, 2006). Champion and Brown (2012a) showed that natural increase has been virtually zero since 2001 while net migration increased from 0.60% per year during 1991–1995 to 0.79% in 2003–2008. Moreover, as can be seen in Table 4.1, positive rural net migration originated from elsewhere in England as well as from abroad.[17] Net in-migration from urban areas in England is a long established contributor to the UK's counter-urbanization while positive net international migration to rural areas is a recent phenomenon. About 86% of the rural migration gain originated in England and elsewhere in the UK, especially from major urban areas. This migration gain is mainly motivated by rural amenities and perceived quality of life considerations, and is selective of persons between ages 30–59, and children under age 16 who accompanied their parents to new rural locations (Champion & Shepherd, 2006). Research shows that many working-age in-movers to rural communities commuted back to their urban jobs (Champion et al., 2009). Pre-retirement-age movers comprised an important component of the rural migration stream, and can be expected to age in place after retirement.

As shown in Table 4.1, rural areas also received almost 123,000 immigrants from abroad during 2001–2008. Although small in relative terms, immigration to rural areas is unprecedented in British history. Even during 2000–2004, few international migrants moved to rural England. However, in 2004 eight Eastern European and Baltic countries joined the EU, and England was one of only three existing EU members to permit unrestricted immigration from these "A-8" countries.[18] Hence, this new international migration

---

[16] A policy shift in the 1970s changed the emphasis from slum removal to improvement of older dwellings. To some extent this resulted in gentrification, but improved housing opportunities for lower income families as well.

[17] In fact, elsewhere throughout the UK, not just in England.

[18] Most other EU countries opted for 7-year transitional arrangements that did allow some limited A-8 immigration.

**Table 4.1** Components of population change, England, 2001–2008

| District, type[a] | Population Change | Natural Increase/Decrease | Migration | | |
|---|---|---|---|---|---|
| | | | Total | Within[b] UK | International |
| England | 1977.5 | 891.1 | 1086.4 | −142.9 | 1229.3 |
| Urban | 1044.5 | 863.2 | 182.3 | −924.4 | 1106.7 |
| Rural of which: | 932.0 | 27.9 | 904.1 | 781.5 | 122.6 |
| Significantly Rural | 314.1 | 66.2 | 247.9 | 172.6 | 75.3 |
| 50 Percent Rural | 275.1 | −7.9 | 283.0 | 265.3 | 17.7 |
| 80 Percent Rural | 342.7 | −30.5 | 373.2 | 343.6 | 29.6 |

[a] DEFRA District Types (Dept. of Environment, Farming and Rural Affairs).
[b] Within-England migration plus migration between England and Wales, Northern Ireland and Scotland.
*Source*: Champion and Brown (2012a). Compiled from ONS data. Crown copyright.

stream largely originated in A-8 nations. Research by Green, De Hoyos, Jones, and Owen (2009) showed that the number of foreigners living in rural districts who registered for National Insurance Numbers more than doubled between 2002–03 and 2005–06.[19] As a result the rural share of international registrants increased from 12 to 19%.

## Counter-Urbanization in the US, But Only Sometimes

Rather than experiencing a continuous process of urbanization or counter-urbanization like England, the U.S. has had four major reversals in the direction of rural-urban migration since 1970 (Johnson & Cromartie, 2006).[20] Prior to the 1970s, the nation's level of urbanization increased regularly with each succeeding census. Although the *pace* of urbanization had slowed by 1970, the trend was still toward increasing urban concentration. Then, in the 1970s, for the first time in recorded history, rural areas grew faster than their urban counterparts. Moreover, like in England, rural population growth was mostly the result of *net in-migration* from urban to rural counties.

The reasons for the rural population turnaround of the 1970s involved four interrelated factors: deconcentration of employment, modernization of rural life, population aging, and preferences for rural living. After decades of urban industrial concentration, manufacturing establishments began to locate and/or expand in rural areas searching for lower wage workers, fewer and weaker regulations, less unionization and compliant local governments that were willing to subsidize industrial re-locations and expansions. In addition, the 1970s saw rural areas gain parity with respect to electrification, all-weather roads, and telephone service. These two structural transformations, jobs and community infrastructure, meant that persons who preferred rural living could now actualize their residential preferences with a minimum of economic and life style sacrifice (Brown, Fuguitt, Heaton, & Waseem, 1997). In addition, an increasing number of American workers were retiring earlier with more secure incomes. Some of these older persons chose to relocate in rural retirement destinations that featured outdoor amenities and other community attributes conducive to retirement living (Brown & Glasgow, 2008).

In contrast to England, the 1970s rural turnaround in the US did not usher in a stable pattern of rural population growth and net in-migration exceeding that of urban areas (see Table 4.2). By the 1980s, the urban sector had regained its growth advantage, and the net flow of migration was from rural areas into cities once again. In fact, research shows that retirement destinations were the only type of rural community to maintain a strong record of population growth and in-migration during this decade. The early 1990s saw the relative rate of growth and net in-migration swing back to favor rural areas once again. Rural areas were doing a better job of retaining their population than during the

---

[19] The number tripled in districts that are 80% rural and doubled in areas that are 50% rural.
[20] The rural-urban analysis in this section is based on data for metropolitan (urban) vs. nonmetropolitan (rural) counties.

**Table 4.2** Components of population change by metropolitan status and adjacency 1970–2009

|  | Population change | | Net migration | | Natural increase | |
| --- | --- | --- | --- | --- | --- | --- |
|  | Absolute Change | Percent Change | Absolute Change | Percent Change | Absolute Change | Percent Change |
| **1970–1980:** | | | | | | |
| All nonmetropolitan | 5,868 | 13.5 | 3,159 | 7.3 | 2,631 | 6.1 |
| Nonadjacent | 2,540 | 12.7 | 1,223 | 6.1 | 1,249 | 6.2 |
| Adjacent | 3,328 | 14.1 | 1,936 | 8.2 | 1,381 | 6.3 |
| Metropolitan | 17,280 | 10.8 | 5,948 | 3.7 | 11,198 | 7.0 |
| Total | 23,147 | 11.4 | 9,107 | 4.5 | 13,829 | 6.8 |
| **1980–1990:** | | | | | | |
| All nonmetropolitan | 1,296 | 2.6 | −1,379 | −2.8 | 2,675 | 5.4 |
| Nonadjacent | 110 | 0.5 | −1,184 | −5.2 | 1,294 | 5.7 |
| Adjacent | 1,186 | 4.4 | −195 | −0.7 | 1,381 | 5.1 |
| Metropolitan | 20,871 | 11.8 | 6,585 | 3.7 | 14,286 | 8.1 |
| Total | 22,168 | 9.8 | 5,206 | 2.3 | 16,962 | 7.5 |
| **1990–2000:** | | | | | | |
| All nonmetropolitan | 5,262 | 10.4 | 3,535 | 7.0 | 1,727 | 3.4 |
| Nonadjacent | 1,853 | 8.2 | 1,092 | 4.8 | 762 | 3.4 |
| Adjacent | 3,409 | 12.1 | 2,443 | 8.7 | 966 | 3.4 |
| Metropolitan | 27,456 | 13.9 | 12,124 | 6.1 | 15,332 | 7.7 |
| Total | 32,716 | 13.2 | 15,659 | 6.3 | 17,059 | 6.9 |
| **2000–2009:** | | | | | | |
| All nonmetropolitan | 1,408 | 2.9 | 325 | 0.7 | 1,082 | 2.2 |
| Nonadjacent | 154 | 0.9 | −227 | −1.3 | 381 | 2.3 |
| Adjacent | 1,254 | 3.9 | 552 | 1.7 | 702 | 2.2 |
| Metropolitan | 24,176 | 10.4 | 9,383 | 4.0 | 14,792 | 6.4 |
| Total | 25,584 | 9.1 | 9,709 | 3.5 | 15,875 | 5.6 |

*Notes*: 1993 Metropolitan Status used for all periods. Change reported in '000s.
*Source*: Kenneth M. Johnson, using data from U.S. Census Bureau.

1980s, but the advantage proved to be short lived. In fact, by the end of the decade, urban areas had regained their growth and migration advantage.

Data for the most recent nine years are displayed in Table 4.2 and Fig. 4.1. These data show that metropolitan areas are growing far more rapidly than their nonmetropolitan counterparts (10.4 vs. 2.9%), and most of this difference is because of migration. As shown in the bottom panel of Table 4.2, about two thirds of metropolitan population growth is attributable to net migration while over three quarters of nonmetropolitan growth is migration related. Not only did nonmetropolitan areas have a substantially lower migration rate than their metropolitan counterparts, but migration was actually negative in nonmetropolitan counties not adjacent to metropolitan areas while adjacent nonmetropolitan counties gained migrants. Accordingly, in the US case, using a "differential urbanization approach" shows that migration can either contribute to counter-urbanization (adjacent counties) or it can be a force of continued urbanization (nonadjacent counties). In other words, both processes are occurring simultaneously at different settlement levels in the same nation.

As was true in England, rural migration in the US originated from elsewhere in the US and from

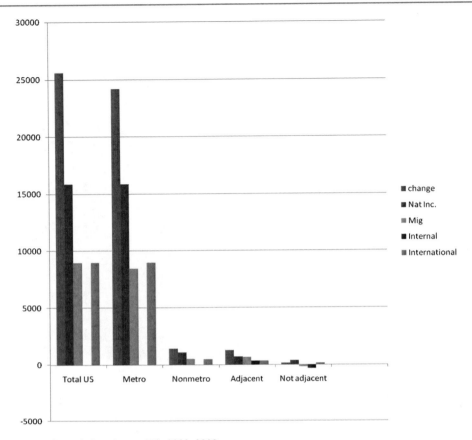

**Fig. 4.1** Components of population change, US, 2000–2009
*Source*: USDA-ERS/Compiled by Tim Parker.

abroad. The data in Fig. 4.1 show that metropolitan areas gained over 8 million migrants from abroad while losing 27,000 persons to nonmetropolitan areas. Nonmetropolitan areas gained about a half-million international migrants and about 27,000 internal migrants from metropolitan areas. Accordingly, the majority of international migration continues to be focused on metropolitan destinations while the internal migration interchange between metropolitan and nonmetropolitan areas favors nonmetro areas, but only slightly. The picture is quite different if one disaggregates nonmetropolitan areas by whether they are adjacent to a metropolitan area or not. This distinction shows that adjacent counties had both positive international and internal migration during 2000–2009, while nonadjacent counties gained international migrants and lost over 163,000 internal migrants, some to metropolitan areas in the US and others to nonmetropolitan counties adjacent to metropolitan areas.

International migration to rural destinations in the US is predominately from Mexico (Kritz & Gurak, 2004), and is strongly associated with the presence of industries such as meat packing and construction where low-wage jobs are plentiful.[21] Mexican migration has been transformed from a narrow movement focused mainly on the Southwest to a nationwide phenomenon. This is true in both metropolitan and nonmetropolitan areas. Kandel and Parrado (2006) showed that Mexican immigration is having its strongest impact on rural population growth outside of the traditional southwestern locations, and in industries outside of agriculture. In rural America, new Hispanic communities are concentrated in the Southeast, the Ozark Mountains, and the upper Midwest.

---

[21] While these jobs are low wage in the US context, they pay superior wages than could be expected in Mexico.

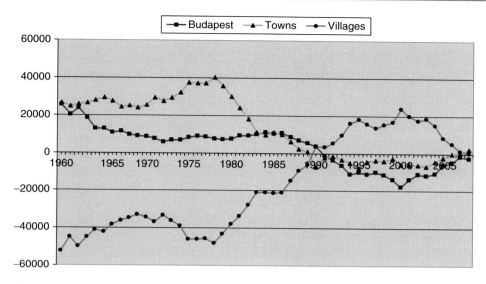

**Fig. 4.2** Net migration by urban-rural residence, Hungary, 1960–2008
*Source*: Hungarian Central Statistical Office: T-Star data base.

## The Hungarian Case

Similar to the long-term trend of continuous population deconcentration experienced by England, smaller places outgrew larger places in Hungary from around 1990 through 2005. However, relative rates of population growth and net migration have now converged at very low or negative rates, and virtually no population redistribution is occurring in Hungary at the present time. Research by Brown, Kulcsár, Kulcsár, and Obadovics (2005), showed that Hungary's transition from population concentration to deconcentration began around 1978, even though the crossover from rural decline to rural growth occurred a decade later. In other words, the 1989 crossover was simply a coincidence and unrelated to the regime change that occurred in that year. The trend toward eventual deconcentration was set in motion in 1978. Prior to 1978, the socialist state targeted economic development toward larger cities and towns and away from rural villages. In fact, during most of this time Hungary had an explicit policy of rural depopulation (Andrusz, Harloe, & Szelenyi, 1996). Targeted urban economic development resulted in dramatic population shifts from villages into the towns and cities where employment was centered, or where daily commuting to employment in larger places was possible. The year 1978 is a turning point not because of a change in the ideology of centrally planned urban-industrial growth, but because the poor performance of the Hungarian economy meant that the state was unable to continue funding targeted urban development. During the late 1970s, village out-migration, a direct result of the state's de facto rural depopulation policies, moderated and urban migration gains diminished (see Fig. 4.2). Hence, the shift from negative to positive rural migration that occurred in 1989 is only coincidentally associated with the regime change from state socialism. Rather, it is the continuation of a gradual process set in motion by policy changes instituted in the late 1970s. In contrast, neither the US nor England has ever intervened in the location of economic activity in such a direct manner.

During the 1990s, net in-migration to rural places in Hungary mainly occurred in the suburbs of large cities, and in towns and villages located close enough to large cities to facilitate daily job commuting. In contrast, Budapest, and other large cities, many of which had been targeted as growth centers during socialism, experienced substantial net out-migration.[22] Since 2000, Hungary has lost population, mainly because of negative natural increase and a lack of international migration. Moreover, the data in Table 4.3

---

[22] Outmigration was also marked in towns located outside of the commuting range of a large city. Far villages, in contrast did not experience net out migration during this time.

**Table 4.3** Population growth rates by urban-rural residence, Hungary, 2000–2008

| Category | Number of places | Rate of population change |
|---|---|---|
| Budapest | 1 | −0.004 |
| Budapest Suburbs | 78 | 0.026 |
| County rank towns | 23 | −0.003 |
| Towns (ex county rank) | 265 | −0.001 |
| Villages | 2,846 | −0.003 |

*Source*: Hungarian Central Statistical Office: T-Star data base.

show that the country experienced virtually no population redistribution during this decade. Budapest's suburbs are the only category of places to experience any growth, and growth here was extremely low. The data in Fig. 4.2 show that *net* internal migration was virtually nonexistent in towns, villages, or in the capital. Unfortunately, migration data for 2000–2008 for villages and towns cannot be disaggregated into those located in Budapest's suburban ring, nor can county-rank towns be identified separately. However, this disaggregation can be done for 2007–2008. Unsurprisingly, these data show that residential mobility was very low in that year. Budapest's suburbs experienced a very small net gain while other categories of places had small losses or were stagnant. Reduced internal migration is unsurprising given the dampening effects of the 2008 recession. Even in the US, the world's most mobile population, internal migration rates declined dramatically during the recent recession (Frey, 2009).

## Conclusions

In this chapter, I have focused on the impact of urban-rural migration for rural population change in the developed world. I have presented data for three highly developed yet quite different nations that show that migration is the dominant determinant of population redistribution. Although migration drives population redistribution in all instances, the direction of redistribution differs across the three cases. In England, migrants are moving from more to less dense locales and population has been deconcentrating consistently for over 50 years. In addition, as Champion (2003) observed, counter-urbanization is a nationwide phenomenon in England that brings population growth to the full range of rural places. Migration also drives population redistribution and rural population change in the US, but in this instance the direction of migration streams has fluctuated between urban and rural destinations during the past half century. In contrast to the consistent counter-urbanization trends described for England, the US has experienced a rural population turnaround, a reversal of the turnaround, and a rural rebound. Since 1995, urban areas have once again gained a significant growth advantage over their rural counterparts, but in this case the urban advantage is fueled by international migration, most of which is destined for metropolitan areas. In contrast, the internal population interchange between metropolitan areas and the next tier of nonmetropolitan counties favors the adjacent counties even as more remote nonmetropolitan counties continue to send more migrants to cities than they receive in exchange.

Hungary also experienced counter-urbanization from around 1990 through 2000, but in this instance net in-migration was only experienced by suburbs and settlements within commuting range of large cities. More remote rural locales did not gain migrants from more highly urbanized places. Since 2005, internal migration has virtually ceased in Hungary, and with it population redistribution. Hungary's overall population has declined while the rural-urban redistribution of population has ceased. This is in direct contrast with the late 1990s and early 2000s when most analysts predicted continued population deconcentration as a result of internal migration to suburbs and rural places within commuting range of larger places. Perhaps this pattern will reassert itself after the recession has recovered and foreign capitalists resume investing in so called "leading regions" (Brown, Greskovits, & Kulcsár, 2007).

Accordingly, these three cases, which seem to have much in common, actually show how complex migration and population redistribution is beneath the surface. Clearly, one size does *not* fit all when it comes to explaining the associations between migration, urbanization and rural population change in the developed world. Several decades ago Wilber Zelinsky (1971) proposed the *theory of mobility transition* in which countries tend to experience similar mobility processes at comparable levels of social and economic development. The three cases compared in this chapter show that hypothesizing about development trajectories that characterize multiple nations is a risky business. With respect to migration and population redistribution, one is on solid ground contending that migration is the principal determinant of population redistribution in more developed nations, but the ground is much shakier when one attempts to predict the direction of redistribution accompanying social and economic transformations that occur in the world's most highly developed regions.

## References

Andrusz, G., Harloe, M., & Szelenyi, I. (1996). *Cities under socialism*. Cambridge, MA: Blackwell.

Billsborow, R. (1998). *Migration, urbanization and development: New directions and issues*. Norwell, MA and New York: Kluwer Publishers and United Nations Population Fund.

Brown, D. L., & Cromartie, J. (2004). The nature of rurality in post-industrial society. In T. Champion & G. Hugo (Eds.), *New forms of urbanization: Beyond the urban-rural dichotomy* (pp. 269–284). Aldershot: Ashgate.

Brown, D. L., Cromartie, J., & Kulcsár, L. J. (2004). Micropolitan areas and the measurement of American urbanization. *Population Research and Policy Review, 23*(4), 399–418.

Brown, D. L., Fuguitt, G., Heaton, T., & Waseem, S. (1997). Continuities in size of place preferences in the United States, 1972–92. *Rural Sociology, 62*(4), 408–428.

Brown, D. L., & Glasgow, N. (2008). *Rural retirement migration*. Dordrecht: Springer.

Brown, D. L., Greskovits, B., & Kulcsár, L. J. (2007). Leading sectors and leading regions: Economic restructuring and regional inequality in Hungary since 1990. *International Journal of Urban and Regional Research, 31*(3), 522–542.

Brown, D. L., Kulcsár, L. J., Kulcsár, L., & Obadovics, C. (2005). Post-socialist restructuring and population redistribution in Hungary. *Rural Sociology, 70*(3), 336–359.

Brown, D. L., & Wardwell, J. (Eds.). (1980). *New directions in urban-rural migration*. New York: Academic.

Champion, T. (1989). *Counter-urbanization*. London: Edward Arnold.

Champion, T. (Ed.). (2003). Testing the differential urbanization model in Great Britain, 1901–91. *Tidjschrift voor Economische en Sociale Geografie, 94*(1), 11–22.

Champion, T., & Brown, D. L. (2011a). Migration and urban-rural population redistribution in the UK and US. In M. Shucksmith, D. L. Brown, S. Shortall, M. Warner, & J. Vergunst (Eds.), *Rural transformations and rural policies in the UK and US* (Chapter 3). New York: Routledge.

Champion, T., & Brown, D. L. (2011b). The statistical measurement of urban and rural residence in the UK and US. In M. Shucksmith, D.L. Brown, S. Shortall, M. Warner, & J. Vergunst (Eds.), *Rural transformations and rural policies in the UK and US* (Annex.). New York: Routledge.

Champion, T., Coombes, M., & Brown, D. L. (2009). Migration and longer distance commuting in rural England. *Regional Studies, 43*(10), 1245–1259.

Champion, T., & Hugo, G. (2004). *New forms of urbanization: Beyond the urban-rural dichotomy*. Aldershot: Ashgate.

Champion, T., & Shepherd, J. (2006). Demographic change in rural England. In P. Lowe & L. Speakman (Eds.), *The ageing countryside: The growing older population of rural England* (pp. 29–50). London: Age Concern.

Chen, N., Valente, P., & Zlotnick, H. (1998). What do we know about urbanization? In R. Billsboro (Ed.), *Migration, urbanization and development: New directions and issues* (pp. 59–88). Norwell, MA and New York: Kluwer Publishers and United Nations Population Fund.

Cohen, B. (2004). Urban growth in developing countries: A review of current trends. *World Development, 32*(1), 23–51.

Commission for Rural Communities. (2010). *The state of the countryside, 2010*. Cheltenham: Commission for Rural Communities.

Cosby, A. T., Neeves, R., Crossman, J., Crossman, W., James, N., Feierabend, D. (2008). Preliminary evidence for and emerging nonmetropolitan mortality penalty in the United States. *American Journal of Public Health, 98*(8), 1470–1472.

Cromartie, J. (2006). Metro expansion and nonmetro change in the South. In W. Kandel & D. L. Brown (Eds.), *Population change and rural society* (pp. 233–252). Dordrecht: Springer.

Cromartie, J., & Bucholtz, S. (2008). *Defining rural in rural America*. Amber Waves. Retrieved December 10, 2010, from http://www.ers.usda.gov/AmberWaves/June08/Features/RuralAmerica.htm

Duncan, O., Scott, W., Lieberson, S., Duncan, B., & Winsboro, H. (1960). *Metropolis and region*. Baltimore, MD: Resources for the Future.

Fielding, A. (1982). Counter-urbanization in Western Europe. *Progress in Planning, 17*(1), 1–52.

Frey, W. (2009). *The great American migration slowdown*. Washington, DC: Brookings Institution.

Fuguitt, G., Brown, D. L., & Beale, C. (1989). *Rural and small town America*. New York: Russell Sage Foundation.

Fuguitt, G., Heaton, T., & Lichter, D. (1988). Monitoring the metropolitanization process. *Demography, 25*(1), 115–128.

Geyer, H., & Kontuly, T. (1993). A theoretical foundation for the concept of differential urbanization. *International Regional Science Review, 15*(2), 157–177.

Green, A., De Hoyos, M., Jones, P., & Owen, D. (2009). Rural development and labour supply challenges in the UK: The role of non-UK migrants. *Regional Studies, 43*(10), 1261–1274.

Halfacre, K. (1993). Locality and social representation: Space, discourse, and alternative definitions of the rural. *Journal of Rural Studies, 9*(1), 23–37.

Halfacre, K. (2004). Rethinking rurality. In T. Champion & G. Hugo (Eds.), *New forms of urbanization: Beyond the urban-rural dichotomy* (pp. 285–304). Aldershot: Ashgate.

Hall, P., & Hay, D. (1980). *Growth centres in the European urban system*. London: Heinemann.

Johnson, K., & Cromartie, J. (2006). The rural rebound and its aftermath: Changing demographic dynamics and regional contrasts. In W. Kandel & D. L. Brown (Eds.), *Population change and rural society* (pp. 25–50). Dordrecht: Springer.

Kandel, W., & Parrado, E. (2006). Rural Hispanic population growth: Public policy impacts in nonmetro counties. In W. Kandel & D. L. Brown (Eds.), *Population change and rural society* (pp. 155–176). Dordrecht: Springer.

Keiner, M., Koll-Schretzenmayr, M., & Schmid, W. (Eds.). (2005). *Managing urban futures: Sustainability and urban growth in developing countries*. Aldershot: Ashgate.

Kritz, M., & Gurak, D. (2004). *Immigration and a changing America*. New York: Russell Sage Foundation.

Kulcsár, L. J., & Brown, D. L. (2011). The political economy of urban reclassification in post-socialist Hungary. *Regional Studies, 45*(4), 479–490.

Lattes, A., Rodriguez, J., & Villa, M. (2004). Population dynamics and urbanization in Latin America: Concepts and limitations. In T. Champion & G. Hugo (Eds.), *New forms of urbanization: Beyond the urban-rural dichotomy* (pp. 89–112). Aldershot: Ashgate.

Lichter, D., & Brown, D. L. (2011). Rural America in an urban society: Changing spatial and social boundaries. *Annual Review of Sociology, 37*, 565–592.

Massey, D. (2007). *World city*. Cambridge: Polity Press.

Mitchell, C. (2004). Making sense of counterurbanization. *Journal of Rural Studies, 20*(1), 15–34.

Office of National Statistics. (2009). *Rural Urban definition: England and Wales*. Retrieved December 8, 2010, from http://www.ons.gov.uk/about-statistics/geography/products/area-classifications/rural-urban-definition-and-la-classification/rural-urban-definition/index.html

Rural Evidence Research Centre. (2005). *Rural England: Demographic change and projections, 1991–2028*. London: Birkbeck College, University of London.

Sassen, S. (2006) *Cities in the world economy*. Thousand Oaks, CA: Pine Forge Press.

Smith, D., & Borocz, J. (Eds.). (1995). *A new world order? Global transformations in the late twentieth century*. Westport, CT: Greenwood Press.

Szelenyi, I. (1996). Cities under socialism—and after. In G. Andrusz, M. Harlow, & I. Szelenyi (Eds.), *Cities after socialism* (pp. 286–317). Oxford: Blackwell.

Tilly, C. (1974). *An urban world*. Boston: Little Brown.

Tisdale, H. (1942). The process of urbanization. *Social Forces, 20*, 311–316.

United Nations. (2006). *World development indicators*. New York: UN ESCAP.

United Nations. (2008). *World urbanization prospects: The 2007 revision*. New York: United Nations Population Division.

White, M., & Lindstrom, D. (2006). Internal migration. In D. Poston & M. Micklin (Eds.), *Handbook of population* (pp. 311–346). New York: Springer.

Woods, M. (2009). Rural geography: Blurring boundaries and making connections. *Progress in Human Geography, 33*(6), 849–858.

Zelinsky, W. (1971). The hypothesis of the mobility transition. *Geographical Review, 61*(2), 219–249.

# World Urbanization: Destiny and Reconceptualization

Avery M. Guest

## Urban Definitions

In a classic paper, Tisdale (1942) defined a city as a place with a large population living at high density or concentration. From this perspective, urbanization became the process of increasing numbers and concentrations at high densities. Tisdale's definition has the virtue of conceptual simplicity, but, more importantly, it permits study of basic patterns of urbanization over most of human history. Unfortunately, these definitions are so abstract that they do not lead to easy statistical measurement, and, as a result, data collecting agencies such as the United Nations have accepted the variable urban definitions that are used by its constituent members. By this conceptualization, rural becomes the residual from urban.

The country-specific definitions (United Nations, 2008a) are based often on size or density thresholds to identify urban populations, but the criteria show some variation across countries. For instance, only 200 or more inhabitants in an Icelandic locality are necessary for an urban place, while 50,000 are required in Japan. In the United States, the basic urban-rural definition is based on 2,500 residents. Fortunately for comparative purposes, the great majority of countries use definitions that encompass populations of 2,000–10,000. Because the practical range of specific definitions is somewhat limited, we can use United Nations data with some caution to compare across countries. In addition, other criteria of cities and urbanization are often used such as the nature of administrative/political districts and the type of employment activity (most typically, manufacturing).

In this essay, I find Tisdale's conceptualization and the United Nations measurement both useful, and will use them to study trends and variations in urbanization. But they admittedly do not capture very well the trends that I note above, such as the increasingly low levels of spread density among urbanites (even relative to rural areas) and the increasingly ambiguous boundary between urban and rural. I comment further on related issues at the end of this essay.

## Two Urban Revolutions

For most of human history, populations lived in small hunting/gathering groups due to their lack of skills in producing food through settled agriculture. Most groups spent their time in collecting food products and had little surplus to support members who engaged in other activities. The total population of the world grew quite slowly and was small by today's standards due to the relative balance of typically high mortality and fertility rates. Until 10,000 BC (give or take a few thousand years), permanents settlements were either lacking or had only a few huts.

The first cities that appeared, by almost any definition, emerged in the Middle East a few thousand years before the birth of Jesus (Massey, 2005, 100–136; Sjoberg, 1960). They were a product of improvements in agricultural productivity such as the use of simple digging tools and harvested plant seeds that produced enough surplus so that some people could live in

A.M. Guest (✉)
Department of Sociology, University of Washington, Seattle, WA 98195-3340, USA
e-mail: averyguest@gmail.com

villages. Rarely having populations above a few thousand, the resulting settlements were heavily oriented to the trade and security protection of surrounding farm communities. The cities often appeared in river valleys where the water nutrients produced agricultural surpluses and traders established markets to sell goods.

The economy of cities depended heavily on agriculture, and many cities could survive only by importation of agricultural products through exploitation (often military) of their hinterlands. The existence and size of the early cities was generally tenuous because their populations lacked the technological and organizational skills to control well the surrounding environments. Surpluses were often so meager that little food could be stored to feed communities in more dire times. Slow transportation by foot, cart, or primitive ships produced difficulties in gathering food from extensive surrounding territories.

Regardless of how one defines an urban community, less than 2% of the world lived in cities before 1800. The technology and social organization of human society were not static over the many centuries after the first cities appeared, but they had little pronounced effect on urbanization. Grauman (1976) argues that, until 1800, the percentage of urban dwellers changed hardly at all over many centuries.

The Industrial Revolution, the key turning point in urbanization, appeared definitively in the late 1700s, primarily in the countries of Northern Europe (such as England) and in areas of overseas European settlement in North America (such as the United States). As Hawley (1971) points out, a key feature of the Industrial Revolution was the development of specialization. A factory system emerged with large-scale work sites where various sets of employees produced large amounts of finished products through specialized sets of skills in the productive process. Different types of workplaces grew interdependent by providing inputs and outputs to other types of workplaces (as exemplified by the interdependence of tire, steel, and car body companies). Geographic areas became interdependent by specializing in various types of manufactured products that could be traded with other regions.

Although specialization was key to industrialization and urbanization, one should not neglect a multitude of other technological and organizational changes that were taking place. Improvements in transportation after the early 1800s such as the railroad and steam-driven ships facilitated trade around the world, creating a need for ports and financial centers. Cities emerged as major focal points of growing national governments that were coordinating the lives of citizenry.

The short period of 150 years from 1800 to 1950 saw the development of sustained, significant urbanization in what we know as the European world. Davis (1955, 433) estimates that the percentage of the world's population living in cities of at least 20,000 roughly doubled every 50 years, increasing from 2.4% in 1800 to 20.9% in 1950. The largest cities developed populations of several hundred thousand, and a few cities appeared with populations over 1 million.

The Industrial Revolution gradually spread in one form or another to most of the world. Parts of the world continued to differ greatly in their degree of industrialization but almost all parts were involved in various roles such as supplying raw materials and producing finished material products. Thus, Europe, areas of overseas European settlement, and Japan dominated the industrial system while much of the world's southern hemisphere served in more subsidiary roles. Variations in industrialization over countries became clearly associated with variations in other national characteristics such as per capita income, educational attainment, the role of the mass media, health conditions, and the concentration of population in cities (Schnore, 1962). In essence, economic development and urbanization became closely related across parts of the world.

Urbanization in the industrial revolution was also tied to the significant leap in population growth after 1800. Before 1800, global levels of mortality and fertility were imbalanced to only a slight degree. But the industrial revolution also brought a steep decline in mortality, followed by a slower decline in fertility, in the most industrialized parts of the world. Many factors were undoubtedly key to the mortality decline. For instance, the gradual revolution in agriculture led to a bigger and more varied diet for many individuals, increasing their nutrition and ability to ward off diseases. By the early 1900s, our abominable knowledge of effective medical care began to change, altering even more the life expectancy and producing even more population growth (McNeill, 1976).

Characterizing urbanization in terms of the percentage living in cities is useful, but one should not rely completely on it to understand urbanization. As an aspect of the growth of total populations, both urban and rural areas have often grown rapidly. Even in societies with small changes in their percentage urban, the numbers living in cities have increased dramatically.

## Since 1950

By 1950, most of the world could be divided largely into a developed European-based world with significant urbanization and a less-developed non-white world with relatively low levels of urbanization. There were only a few exceptions to this pattern such as Japan which had waged war in the 1930s and early 1940s to control Asian economies and thwart the power of developed European countries.

After 1950 (known as the post-World War II period), this dichotomy in urbanization began to change, especially in the eastern part of Asia where countries such as China, Malaysia, South Korea, and Thailand sustained vigorous economic development and urbanization. Furthermore, the growth of the percentage of the world's population living in cities (often termed the "population implosion") grew more generally from 29.1% in 1950 to 48.6% in 2005. The United Nations projects it will reach 50% in 2010 (United Nations, 2008c, Table A.2).

The world's total population size (the "population explosion") expanded even more dramatically than the growth of the percentage of the world's population living in cities, from approximately 2.52 billion in 1950 to 6.52 billion in 2000, with growth especially occurring in the least developed parts of the world (United Nations, 2008a, Table 5.1). The major factor behind the unparalleled growth in world population size was the amazing decline in mortality throughout the great bulk of countries (Schultz, 1993). This mortality decline reflected a variety of factors, but almost all agree now that unprecedented advances in medical and public health technology have been crucial.

The growth of the world's population had affected the growth rate of urban populations in the early stages of the Industrial Revolution, but the impact was dramatic in the post-1950 period, especially in developing parts of the world that have experienced the greatest

**Table 5.1** The 20 largest urban agglomerations: 1950 and 2007

| Rank | 2007 | Population millions | 1950 | Population millions |
|---|---|---|---|---|
| 1 | Tokyo, Japan | 35.7 | New York-Newark, USA | 12.3 |
| 2 | New York-Newark, USA | 19.0 | Tokyo, Japan | 11.3 |
| 3 | Mexico City, Mexico | 19.0 | London, United Kingdom | 8.4 |
| 4 | Mumbai (Bombay), India | 19.0 | Paris, France | 5.4 |
| 5 | São Paulo, Brazil | 18.8 | Moscow, Russia | 5.4 |
| 6 | Delhi, India | 15.9 | Shanghai, China | 5.3 |
| 7 | Shanghai, China | 15.0 | Rhein-Ruhr North, Germany | 5.3 |
| 8 | Kolkata (Calcutta), India | 14.8 | Buenos Aires, Argentina | 5.0 |
| 9 | Dhaka, Bangladesh | 13.5 | Chicago, USA | 5.0 |
| 10 | Buenos Aires, Argentina | 12.8 | Kolkata (Calcutta), India | 4.4 |
| 11 | Los Angeles, USA | 12.5 | Osaka-Kobe, Japan | 4.1 |
| 12 | Karachi, Pakistan | 12.1 | Los Angeles, USA | 4.0 |
| 13 | Al-Qahirah (Cairo), Egypt | 11.9 | Beijing, China | 3.9 |
| 14 | Rio de Janeiro, Brazil | 11.7 | Milan, Italy | 3.6 |
| 15 | Osaka-Kobe, Japan | 11.3 | Berlin, Germany | 3.3 |
| 16 | Beijing, China | 11.1 | Philadelphia, USA | 3.1 |
| 17 | Manila, Philippines | 11.1 | Mumbai (Bombay), India | 3.0 |
| 18 | Moscow, Russia | 10.5 | Rio de Janeiro, Brazil | 2.9 |
| 19 | Istanbul, Turkey | 10.1 | St. Petersburg, Russia | 2.9 |
| 20 | Paris, France | 9.9 | Mexico City, Mexico | 2.9 |

declines in mortality. Even in societies with relatively small increases in percentage urban, the size of the total urban population rose dramatically as an offshoot of population growth.

An important issue in the study of the massive urban development in recent decades is the relative role of natural population growth versus rural to urban migration (Todaro, 1980); both are important, but it is extremely difficult to obtain reliable data on both for a large sample of countries (United Nations, 2008a). In comparing British urban growth in the 19th century with developing countries in recent decades, Williamson (1988) argues that migration to cities was relatively more important in the British experience. However, as British population growth increased in the 19th century, the relative role of migration allegedly decreased.

The rapid growth of urban populations in the past few decades has produced sustained pressure on the provision of adequate services for urban residents in areas such as transportation, health, education, and recreational opportunities (Brockerhoff & Brennan, 1998). These pressures undoubtedly were great in the so-called European industrial period, but the growth rates of cities were nowhere near as great. Fortunately, for all their problems, rapidly growing urban agglomerations sometimes have access to advanced technology in areas such as transportation and public health that may help alleviate some difficulties.

Since 1950, further dramatic technological and organizational changes have occurred in human society, with clear implications today for population concentration. The productivity of agriculture has become so great that most of the developed societies employ less than 5% of their workers as farmers. In the United States, 1.9% of the population in 1991 lived on farms compared to 15.3% in 1950 (Carter et al., 2006, Table Da1-13). About 40% of the world's labor force continues to be employed in agriculture, but the share in individual countries seems to drop dramatically to less than 10% when the gross domestic product reaches $10,000 per capita (Gollin, 2010).

## Spread Urbanization

During most urban history, cities were quite limited in their geographic size and were probably characterized by fairly discrete boundaries with rural territories. The extreme but common case was the walled city where the several thousand inhabitants erected high, sturdy walls around themselves, primarily to protect themselves from invaders (Hawley, 1971, 21–22). Even in very large cities before 1800, the geographic diameters of cities were usually only a handful of miles in length. Some activities such as market trading were conducted outside the wall, but agricultural production quickly became dominant a short distance from the walls.

In the Industrial Revolution, the wall declined greatly in importance. Technological advances in weapons made possible long-distance and air-borne shelling of people behind the walls, essentially making them "sitting ducks."

Nevertheless, the relatively slow means of transportation and communication in the early industrial period forced residents to live closely together so that they could conduct daily businesses. As today, most urbanites were probably willing to travel a half-hour or so daily between home and workplaces, but most transportation within urban centers was limited to walking for the majority and the use of the horse or animal-drawn cart for others, generally the well-to-do. Interestingly, for much of the 19th century, travel between cities was probably more effective than travel within cities. Where waterways such as rivers and lakes existed, people and goods could often move with some speed between urban points. The development of the steam-driven railway also facilitated inter-urban travel (Hawley, 1978).

Cities with high population growth in the early industrial revolution probably expanded some in geographic size, but a major response had to be increasing congestion at the center by cramming more people into the finite space. Because methods of construction rarely permitted very tall buildings, central congestion was probably universally high, providing little respite from intense interaction with others. In the United States, central congestion in major cities seemed to increase until the early 1900s (Gardner, n.d.; Winsborough, 1963).

In highly developed societies, the effects of transportation improvements on the geographic size of cities probably became important in the late 1800s (Hawley, 1978; Ward, 1971). One major development was the electric streetcar which, among its virtues, had a relatively low effect on air quality in comparison to the steam-driven railroads (Warner, 1972). The electric streetcar had a somewhat paradoxical effect. On the one hand, since it generally emanated on fixed lines from the center of the city, it tended to increase the value of the center that was now accessible from many points, but on the other hand, the electric streetcar through its relatively rapid speed for the time also enhanced the possibilities of moving outward. The streetcar almost certainly had the effect of increasing the specialization of land uses (such as workplaces relative to residences, rich relative to poor residences, etc.) because there was now more space for development and activities did not require such a close physical proximity given the increased speed of travel.

Later (mainly starting in the 1920s), the mass purchase of the motor vehicle led to even faster travel outward (Guest, 1984; Tobin, 1976). In addition, the motor vehicle could easily travel to a variety of points, reducing the orientation of urbanites to the center of their community. Sizable amounts of suburbanization began, and what we call the metropolitan community emerged. Urban agglomerations began to have central cities that had been the major historical points of sizable growth, suburban rings with numerous political jurisdictions, and even more peripheral areas (sometimes known as exurbia or the urban-rural fringe) where a mixture of traditional urban and rural activities met and intermixed (Mori, 1998).

In the 1950s, the development of limited access, multiple-lane highways increased even more the possible dispersal of the population. The rising use of the motor vehicle probably reduced dramatically the demand for specific geographic locations within urban places. Decreasingly, work and residential activities depended on close physical proximity (Guest & Cluett, 1974).

The greatest virtue of the centers in traditional urban agglomerations was their ability to provide needed physical access. Without this need, it is hardly surprising that many urban centers throughout the world have experienced dramatic absolute losses in residents and workplaces (Guest, 1975; Hawley, 1972; Sternlieb, 1971; Summers, Cheshire, & Senn, 1999). The population has spread out at long distances from the traditional centers, producing suburbanization as perhaps the major aspect of urbanization in developed societies in recent years (Guest & Brown, 2005). Yet, these changes in the crucial importance of physical proximity have not meant that all activities locate in a formless pattern. Thus, many downtowns of major urban concentrations remain the locale of activities that still depend on physical proximity (witness employment agencies, bank headquarters, branches of government, and lawyers and judges).

The development and expansion of high-quality highways produced ribbon-like patterns around major urban centers, with business and residential ventures locating on the strips that shot outward. Much of this development occurred in previously rural, even agricultural territory. There were too many farmers, given the productivity of American agriculture, and farmers could sometimes sell their lands for urban-type development. The urban and the rural became increasingly intermixed (Champion & Hugo, 2004). The people living in these strips may be called rural because they lack the numbers and density to be urban, but much diversity exists among the rural population (Brown & Cromartie, 2004). They are a far cry from the perhaps overly imagined rural "oafs" of a few centuries ago.

Although my description is primarily based on the experience of highly developed societies, the outward spread of population is occurring all over the world (Hackenberg, 1980), constrained to some extent by the already existing structure of urban places and by the degree to which technology and communications can "liberate" individuals from fixed points around the center. Even some of the poorest countries in the world have developed spread urban centers at low density. In a visit during the late 1990s to Malawi, one of the world's poorest countries, I found that the major city (Blantyre) was heavily composed of a number of hut-type villages that were loosely connected. But there was also little development of a dense center, and the community spread over a large area.

Now, we are engaged in a continuing revolution in electronic communication with undoubted but still a bit obscure implications for spread urbanization. The development of computers has facilitated the location of some activities at substantial distances from each other. As an example, retired seniors, often supported by social security and sometimes generous pensions, may head to the rural areas for a variety of reasons, including a desire to commune with nature and the low cost of living (Wardwell, 1980). Even in classic rural areas, they can enjoy recent Hollywood movies and read the New York Times on their home computers in somewhat isolated homes.

The effects of communication advances may be striking partly because new types of employment are especially oriented to this technology. Although manufacturing still remains an important productive tool, "service" work that involves contact between individuals rather than contact between individuals and the material goods that they process has become the driving force of many economies (Schettkat & Yocarini, 2006). Service work involves diverse specific industries, including government service, health, education, recreation and travel, finance/banks, advertising and business services.

On the surface, the focus on interpersonal contact in many work organizations would seem to necessitate even more clustering together of populations. In addition, because services generally do not depend on location near raw natural resources (such as iron and coal), they are even more compatible (in some ways) than manufacturing with an urban world.

But the need for people to meet face-to-face is often balanced with the possibility of people interacting electronically at distances that are thousands of miles away. We know that major U.S. credit card operations are located in relatively rural states such as the Dakotas. Sophisticated professional workers such as lawyers, scientists, and government planners can often take their work to officially designated rural areas and communicate electronically with home offices, clients, or other colleagues. Medical doctors and their patients can meet in the same examining room or consult with each other through televisions and computer screens that are literally thousands of miles apart. At least theoretically, workplaces and residences could be located at very low densities that extend outward for miles and miles, into what we conventionally consider rural areas.

Nevertheless, one should not make far-fetched claims about the spread of the urban field. Studies of Americans (Fuguitt & Brown, 1990) have shown that, given a somewhat open-ended choice, traditional urban centers would decline even more in population, surrendering large numbers to the urban and rural periphery. However, the unmet desire for location on the urban periphery seems to be accompanied by a desire to live fairly near a traditional urban center.

A probable correlate of spread urbanization is the development of "metropolitan dominance," the idea that the size and location of the metropolis influences gradients of activities around it, even in rural areas that are many miles away. In a classic, early test of the theory, Bogue (1950) used 1940 census data to show that, as one moved away from central cities as far as 200 miles, population residential densities, the importance of wholesaling and retailing, and income decreased in regular gradients. Others (Berry & Horton, 1970, 46–47) have also found similar patterns.

But we need new studies of how metropolitan dominance has changed over time. It is possible that gradients of metropolitan dominance could be declining if physical proximity to related activities no longer matters much. In support of this, Guest and Brown (2005) found that suburbs in proximity to central cities grew somewhat slower than those located on the periphery in the 1970s, but the pattern was much more ambiguous in the 1990s. Frey (2004) claims that characteristics such as social status are increasingly similar between central cities and their suburban rings and between metropolitan and nonmetropolitan areas.

## How Does Urbanization Occur?

We need to know more about how cities develop and urbanization occurs across a variety of societies. Are there general patterns across societies, or do individual countries behave in what appear to be idiosyncratic ways? The United Nations has made a laudable effort to collect data, often estimates, on patterns since 1950. With some intellectual trepidation, I turn to these data to sketch how urbanization patterns occur. My trepidation stems from the certainty that clear-cut urban and rural definitions are difficult to sustain in many countries, and that the meaning of the definitions may vary somewhat.

In analyzing urbanization, as I have indicated, one needs to distinguish between increases in the percentage urban and increases in the total numbers of urban dwellers. I discuss first how changes in percentage urban seem to occur across societies. Then, I turn more briefly to patterns of absolute urban and rural population growth.

On the basis of United Nations data (2008c), Fig. 5.1 shows the relationship between percent urban in 1950 and in 2005 for 160 recognized national units. The analysis includes national units with at least 100,000 residents in 2005, thus removing a number of "special" situations (such as principalities in Europe and small island entities). I have also eliminated from the analysis three units that are essentially city states, Hong Kong, Singapore, and Macao.

A general pattern is quite evident in the figure. Most noteworthy is the fact that urbanization seems to be an

# 5 World Urbanization: Destiny and Reconceptualization

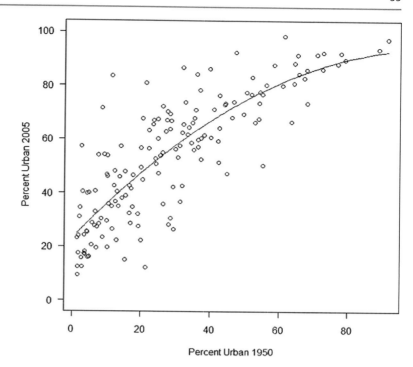

**Fig. 5.1** Temporal relationship between levels of urbanization

unalterable process. Note that a very high percentage of points fall in the upper part of the graph, indicating that their levels of urbanization in 2005 are higher than in 1950. No country experienced significant loss in percentage urban.

Urbanization levels are clearly correlated over time. Previous urbanization has a strong positive effect on subsequent urbanization. The general pattern is described by a quadratic regression equation, as shown in Fig. 5.1. The line initially climbs rapidly, but then the speed of urbanization slows down at high levels. Using the regression line, the average country with 20% urban in 1950 would have 47.4% in 2005, a substantial gain of 27.4 percentage points. However, a typical country with 80% urban in 1950 would have 89.7% in 2005, a smaller gain of 9.7 percentage points. The pattern among highly urban countries is partially a statistical artifact; as a society becomes urban, it is difficult for the percentage to increase much.

Although the average patterns are instructive, we also need to recognize that countries differ greatly in their levels of 2005 urbanization in relationship to their 1950 urbanization, especially in the "middle" ranges of 1950 urbanization. Note that countries with very low levels of urbanization (say less than 20% in 1950) tend to cluster together on the graph, indicating that they show relatively similar patterns of change. In countries with over 60% urban in 1950, there is also a similar clustering of 2005 levels. Among countries in the middle range of urbanization (between 20 and 60% in 1950), there are some striking variations in 2005 levels. Thus, as some examples, let us take Venezuela, Latvia, and Turkmenistan. In 1950, they had very similar levels of percent urban (47.3, 46.4, and 45.0, respectively). In 2005, their respective urban percentages were 92.3, 68.0, and 49.5. It appears that variability in national experience primarily occurs in the take-off for high urbanization so that countries in the middle ranges show quite different patterns.

Figure 5.2 shows another useful country-specific pattern, the relationship between urban levels and a United Nations statistical measure of social well-being, the Human Development Index (HDI), based on levels of income, educational development, and life expectancy. The HDI, varying from 0.00 to 1.00, may be considered a crude but useful measure of national development (Sagar & Najam, 1998). As might be expected, a clear positive relationship ($r = 0.739$) exists between the variables, but a substantial range in urbanization exists within broadly defined levels of the HDI. This is especially true at mid-levels of the HDI, as some of the countries with roughly similar HDI

**Fig. 5.2** Relationship between HDI and urbanization

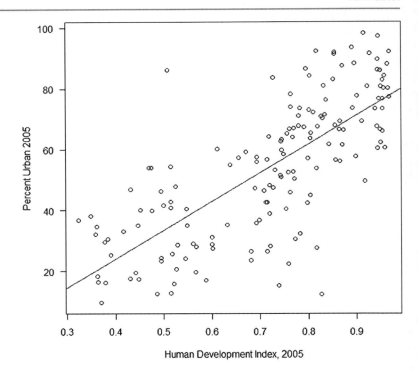

scores have sharply different levels of urbanization; some of these mid-level countries may be in transitional stages of the development process where levels of urbanization are in some disequilibrium.

Also noteworthy are the patterns for urbanization among what might be considered highly developed countries, those arbitrarily characterized by HDI scores above 0.83. Among, these countries, urbanization levels are always above 50%, indicating that substantial urbanization is an almost inevitable correlate of high levels of development. Yet, the graph also shows that scores above 0.83 are hardly associated with a pattern of further advances in levels of urbanization. In short, highly developed countries are almost inevitably urban but the exact level of urbanization is quite variable among them.

Undoubtedly, some of the variation in urbanization at high levels of economic development reflects the varying definitions across UN units, but it may also indicate a "real" pattern, that societies may be economically healthy with various mixes of urban and rural populations. It would be useful to know more about why variations in urbanization occur across highly developed societies. Another interesting aspect of the figure is the fact that hardly any societies are almost completely urban in 2005. Although the world is headed with some rush toward urbanization, it is apparently not about to become a completely urban world.

How well is urbanization in 2005 predicted by the variables that we have considered, urbanization level in 1950 and economic productivity in 2005? Given that definitions of urban differ some across countries, one would never expect that all variation would be explained. The curvilinear quadratic regression in Fig. 5.1 explains 67.6% of the variance in 2005 urbanization. The 2005 HDI level (used in Fig. 5.2) explains 54.7% of the variance. When level of social development is included in the equation with the curvilinear form of urbanization in 1950, some 69.3% of the variance in urbanization 2005 is explained. The fact that the HDI score explains so little additional variance $(69.3 - 67.6 = 1.7)$ may be interpreted by some as indicating that development has little relationship to recent urbanization, but previous urbanization and development probably relate in complex ways. Given what I have already said about the long-term history of urbanization, few readers should be surprised that the independent, predictive variables do well in explaining 2005 urbanization.

In recent years, some scholars have studied whether urbanization levels may actually decrease in societies, what is called counterurbanization. Evidence of some counterurbanization has been suggested for European countries (Champion, 1989). Counterurbanization may reflect a real decline in what most folks would consider as a city or it may simply represent an expansion of the urban field into what are officially called rural territories. Consistent with European observations, demographers report that nonmetropolitan areas in the United States have periodically since the 1970s grown faster than metropolitan areas (Johnson & Cromartie, 2006). The reasons for this are not entirely clear but probably relate to a variety of definitional factors and the changing nature of urbanization.

In the recent past, a number of hypotheses have been proposed to further explain cross-national urbanization levels, related to such factors as conditions in agricultural areas (Firebaugh, 1979; Shandra, London, & Williamson, 2003). Bradshaw (1987) posits that countries with low economic investment in the rural sector will have unusual rates of urbanization and that high foreign investment will be used to replace labor-intensive agricultural workers with machinery, further stimulating urbanization.

Kasarda and Crenshaw (1991) review many of the empirical studies on this topic that were done in the last part of the 20th century. They find many of the studies unconvincing for a variety of reasons including the lack of comparable data across countries and the fact that empirical measures of important cross-national variables may have ambiguous sociological interpretations as to their meaning. Many cross-national indicators are also highly intercorrelated, creating statistical problems in determining which variable is really the "true" cause of urbanization. Scholars such as Firebaugh and Bradshaw were limited in their studies by the small number of empirical observations, a problem that is decreasing with improvement in the collection of relevant data.

An intriguing issue in the study of urbanization is whether some countries are over-urbanized, which is generally interpreted to mean that their levels of economic development are inadequate to support the proportion of the population that lives in cities (Kasarda & Crenshaw, 1991; Preston, 1979). This issue is frequently applied to countries that are usually considered impoverished or developing at relatively slow rates, especially in Africa, Asia, and Latin America. Advocates of this view (Berry, 1981, 75) seem to assume that there is some normal equilibrium relationship between development, especially the importance of manufacturing, and urbanization. It does seem that there is a strong empirical relationship between the two, as I have just demonstrated, but it is unclear whether countries with high levels of urbanization relative to levels of development are so because of some pathological condition or simply failure to consider other technological and organizational variables that might explain urbanization.

The over-urbanization issue is related to a continuing scholarly debate about whether urban in-migrants in many developing countries are being pushed there by the terrible economic conditions in rural areas or by the economic opportunities in cities. The conventional wisdom is that urban migrants in the early stages of the Industrial Revolution were primarily pulled by economic opportunities, but some have argued that the pull of cities also dominates in recent urban growth of low to moderate income countries (Kelley & Williamson, 1984; Todaro, 1980).

Because scholars overwhelmingly agree that development indicators should be related to urbanization, some useful analysis might proceed inductively by classifying specific countries that seem to have unusually high or low levels of urbanization, even after accounting for previous urbanization and economic development. Using the same regression as described above, I determined the ten countries that had the most urbanization in 2005 relative to what might be predicted on the basis of 1950 urbanization and 1980 HDI score. The greatest excess urbanization was found in Gabon (found in West Africa) which had 83.6% urban while its predicted level was 41.8%, a giant difference of 41.4%. The other nine in order of "excess" percent urbanization level were: Djibouti, 29.2; Oman, 29.0; Saudi Arabia, 27.9; Lebanon, 26.6; Botswana, 25.4; South Korea, 25.0; Angola, 23.0; Laos, 23.0; Venezuela, 21.5. I was immediately struck by the fact that six of these countries are major exporters of oil (Gabon, Djibouti, Oman, Saudi Arabia, Angola, and Venezuela). Botswana also emphasizes export of raw materials, in this case, diamonds. Four of the countries were characterized by extensive internal civil violence in the second half of the 20th century that probably led to great disruption of rural life (Lebanon, South Korea, Angola, and Laos). According to the over-urbanization perspective, these ten countries have "pathological" levels of urbanization, given their levels of previous urbanization and development. Yet, it also seems possible that other explanations might be constructed out of their industrial structures and domestic histories.

## Growth Rates Versus Percentage Change

The growth of world cities needs to be understood as not just a shift in population from rural areas to cities. Actually, due to the tremendous rates of total population growth in many countries, both urban and rural population sizes grow absolutely.

Indeed, the United Nations data show that urban and rural absolute population growth rates are strongly correlated positively across societies, indicating that percentage increases in urbanization need not be related to absolute declines in the rural population. To determine this, I use another measure of absolute growth than the commonly considered percentage growth rate over a time period. Focusing on percentage growth rate patterns leads to a few countries with rather extreme rates. To produce a more normally distributed variable, I have calculated, separately by urban and rural sector, the ratio of 1950 population size to 2005 population size. In order to measure growth by a positive number, I have subtracted the ratios from 1. The maximum value is 1.0, in which case the sector had no population in 1950 but at least some population in 2005. The two growth ratios are clearly correlated in a positive direction ($r = 0.63$) across the countries. Therefore, changes in urban percent in countries generally reflect the fact that the urban population is growing faster than the rural population, not that the rural population is necessarily declining in absolute numbers.

Figure 5.3 shows the relationship between 1980 HDI scores and growth rates of urban and rural populations between 1950 and 2005. While 1980 development occurs after population growth in some years, using data for other years shows similar patterns. The choice of 1980 is useful because the year is a good intermediate choice over the large number of years between 1950 and 2005. On the figure, different symbols are used for the rural and urban growth rates, and each country appears twice (for separate urban and rural growth). I have also shown the separate linear regression lines when the HDI score is used to predict urban and rural growth.

The figure shows negative relationships of economic development with both urban and rural growth

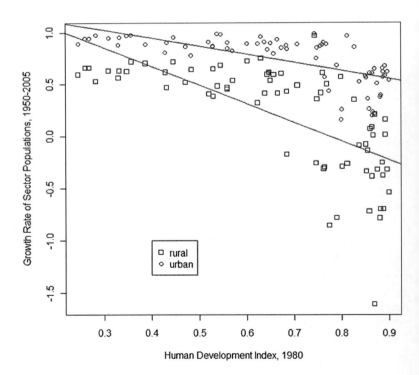

**Fig. 5.3** Urban and rural growth by HDI, 1950–2005

in contrast to the positive relationship with urban percent in 2005. The least developed countries have the greatest rates of urban and rural growth, undoubtedly a reflection of their typically large declines in death rates without concomitant declines in birth rates.

Furthermore, development seems to have a stronger relationship with rural than urban growth. The regression line for the urban rates, shown at the top of the figure, declines more slowly than the line for rural rates. Another way of summarizing is by noting that absolute rural growth is high at low levels of development but actually negative in many cases at high levels of development. However, the figure shows that highly developed countries have widely varying patterns of rural growth, partly an artifact of how the rural sector is measured across countries but also probably a substantive finding that indicates highly developed societies can accommodate a wide range of urban-rural mixes.

Even though urban growth is greatest in the least developed societies, it is positive in almost all the societies. The rates of urban growth in some of the least developed societies are strikingly high. For instance, Viet Nam (in East Asia) and Mali (in Africa) were among the lowest per capita product countries in the world in 1975. According to the data set, the proportion urban in Viet Nam in 1950 was only 0.14 relative to the number in 2005 (or the 1950 urban populations was only about one-seventh the 2005 urban population). In Mali, the proportion was even more striking, the proportion urban in Mali in 1950 was only 0.08 relative to the number in 2005. Yet, the growth of the rural populations in these countries was also striking (but less than the urban growth). The rural population in Viet Nam in 1950 was only 0.39 relative to the proportion in 2005. The analogous figure for Mali was 0.38. The staggering figures on urban growth for some countries indicate that that urban growth rates are basically out-of-control, leading to serious problems in supplying basic services for populations. But rural growth rates have also been incredibly high.

In recent years, world population growth has begun to decline in percentage rates from its very high levels of 2% about 1970, primarily because many countries now have faster fertility than mortality declines. This trend will slow down some the percentage urban and rural growth rates in many countries. However, given the increasingly large total population in the world, high absolute rates of urban and rural growth rates will continue, especially in low and middle income countries.

## Regional Patterns

Some of the above findings are useful for understanding the aggregate patterns between 1950 and 2005 by major geographic regions. In the subsequent figure, the urbanization patterns are based on aggregating the population figures for each region. The regions have been collapsed using United Nations criteria, but I have also made a few alterations on the basis of history of economic development and cultural similarity. In my analysis, Canada and the United States are included with Europe because the North American countries were essentially settled as colonies and participated in the same general emergence of industrialization. I have created a category of Mediterranean Basin countries that includes primarily Arab/Moslem parts (Algeria, Egypt, Libya, Morocco, and Tunisia) of North Africa and the UN category of Western Asia. Thus, the Africa category primarily includes what is known as sub-Sahara Africa.

Figure 5.4 shows that the European world and Oceania (primarily composed of the relatively developed societies of Australia and New Zealand) generally have the highest percentage urban at each point in time, consistent with their typical status as highly developed societies. The two least developed parts of the world, Africa and South Central Asia (including countries such as Bangladesh, India, and Pakistan) have the lowest levels of urbanization at each time point. All regions of the world (except Oceania) have steep, relatively continuous increases in their urban percentages. At the end of the period, the regions are ranked in the same order as in the legend.

The steepest increases are found for America, East Asia, and the Mediterranean Basin regions; countries in these parts of the world have generally shown the largest improvements in economic development during the late 20th century. In the mid-20th century, parts of America already had some moderately developed countries (such as Argentina and Chile), consistent with their relatively high levels of urbanization at the time. East Asia (including such countries as China, the Republic of Korea, and Taiwan) has the most rapid gains in percentage urban, consistent with reports that many of these countries were the great economic success story of the post-1950 period. This region started in 1950 with generally low levels of economic development, but then became characterized by several

**Fig. 5.4** Trend in urban percent by region, 1950–2005

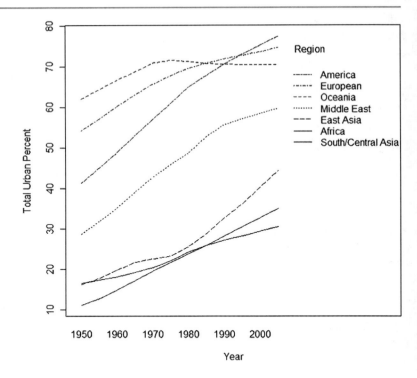

countries that were called "The Asian Tigers," due to their aggressive economic development (Chia et al., 2007).

As implied earlier for countries, a simple analysis of percentage urban may be somewhat deceptive for categorizing the relative patterns of absolute urban and rural population change. Consistent with Fig. 5.4, the UN data (not shown) indicate that all regions of the world except for Oceania are characterized by rapid increases in their urban populations. Indeed, over five-year periods from 1950 to 2005, the rapidity of urban change seems generally to be accelerating over time. The regions, just as the total sample of countries, differ more in rural than urban growth rates.

The most interesting regional patterns are found for East Asia and South Central Asia where both urban and rural growth have occurred quite rapidly, although rural growth seems to have slowed down in East Asia. These patterns indicate that East Asia is undergoing the most rapid urbanization because fast urban growth is outpacing significantly the fast rural growth. China is a key country in population numbers within Asia. For many years after the communists assumed control in China (1948), urban growth was artificially constrained by a system that limited the number of permits to live in cities. In the past two decades, that system broke down as the urban economy expanded, creating tremendous growth rates in recent years for many urban agglomerations (Chan, 2001; Zhu, 2004). South Central Asia presents a less extreme pattern than East Asia, as the relative balance of high urban and rural growth is more equal, leading to a slower rate of urbanization.

## Rise of Megacities

Urban communities are linked together in what is often called "systems of cities" (Alderson & Beckfield, 2004; Duncan, Duncan, Lieberson, Scott, & Winsborough, 1960; Meyer, 2003; Sassen, 1994), both within countries and internationally. Links may be measured by such indicators as air passenger travel, the location of central and peripheral offices of corporations, migration patterns, banking transactions, and the diffusion of dress styles. Some urban concentrations can be viewed as more important or powerful than others. Thus, everyone would undoubtedly agree that New York City is at the top of the system of cities in the United States, but then one could get in some interesting discussion on where places such as Chicago, Houston, and Los Angeles stand in relationship to New York, themselves, and to other urban centers.

Most societies have an uneven distribution of urban agglomerations by size of place. Almost inevitably, there are a very small number of extremely large places, and then the number of places in lower size classes increases as one descends the size hierarchy. The reasons for this are varied. One factor may be derived from what is called central place theory (Berry & Pred, 1961). Very large places often have very specialized service and retailing activities that require large hinterlands, while small places often serve very general functions (such as pumping gas and selling food) that require only small hinterlands. As a consequence, a few large cities will dominate their hinterlands while a much larger number of small cities will influence limited territories. But other factors may be involved. Relatively large places may further enhance their attraction because employers that exchange goods, ideas, and services with other employers may try to concentrate in a few places where they have extensive accessibility. Large places may also attract employers because there are large potential markets to buy their products. In addition, as large places emerge in a society, they may use their political power to obtain even more resources that would attract even more population (Aiken & Alford, 1970).

Given the tremendous absolute increases in urban population sizes, the evident growth of very large individual cities would be anticipated. Indeed, this is so, as indicated by Table 5.1 that shows the 20 largest urban agglomerations in 1950 and in 2007 (United Nations, 2008b). Note that the largest urban agglomerations are much larger in 2007 than 1950, often by multiples. In addition, the geographic location of these agglomerations has shifted from the so-called European world to other regions, especially Asia (which has the highest overall absolute urban growth). In 1950, 11 of the 20 largest were in Europe or the United States; in 2007, only three were.

Recently, scholars have developed the term Megacity to describe urban agglomerations of at least 10 million. Using this standard, all the top 20 in 2007 were Megacities in comparison to two in 1950. A key reason for the growth of the Megacities is the overall population growth of most cities. Small and large concentrations have both grown in the face of societal population growth, but we especially notice the very large ones.

The emergence of Megacities is very real, but undoubtedly the ability to measure this phenomenon has decreased over time. The development of spread urbanization has made it increasingly difficult to tell where the urban population ends and the rural territory begins. On a recent trip to China, I was especially aware of this. For instance, Table 5.1 shows that the UN population of Shanghai is 15.0 million, but from personal observations I could see that the "urban" region of Shanghai encompasses a much larger area, involving many millions more people.

Scholars have discovered that, across societies, the sheer dominance of very large cities relative to small cities often varies. In some countries, the largest urban agglomeration is a "primate" or is multiple times the size of any other place (usually more than twice as large). Another manifestation of this occurs when a society has one large place that has an unusually high proportion of all urban dwellers. Short and Pinet-Peralta (2009) have found that primacy is disproportionately characteristic of Latin America and Africa. Yet, primacy is found in a wide variety of societies: for instance, London in England and Paris in France, among highly developed societies; Buenos Aires in Argentina and Jakarta in Indonesia, among less developed societies. This indicates that the social causes of primacy may reflect a variety of social and environmental factors.

Undoubtedly the major correlate of urban primacy is the population/geographic size of the society. When a society has a large population, sizable urban centers are likely to develop in various parts to serve the needs of the population living there. When a society is small, one large urban concentration can arise to serve the population.

Some scholars have wondered whether primacy may also be a pathological characteristic of some societies (Berry, 1981, 95–99), found in situations where development is "distorted." For instance, a number of societies that were once European colonies had very large cities developed as administrative, military, and trading places to serve the interests of the colonizers. In the contemporary world, some have alleged, that urban elites try to maximize the best jobs and economic opportunities in their home towns, thereby increasing the incentive for individuals to live there (Bradshaw, 1987). A more general societal correlate of primacy may be its level of economic development, because poor countries often have histories as colonies of dominant European powers. Furthermore, it seems possible that poor countries, given their low levels of democracy relative to rich countries, may have urban elites who exert disproportionate influence to maximize growth in the largest place.

One can see support for both societal size and development effects in Fig. 5.5 that shows the relationship of a country's total population size in 2005 to the proportion of its urban population living in the largest concentration in 2007. One measure of primacy is the ratio of the population of the largest urban concentration to the population of the second largest. However, the United Nations data at my disposal (2008b) presents populations of the second largest places only when they have at least 100,000 residents. My alternative measure of primacy, easy-to-calculate, is the proportion of a society's urban population that lives in the largest place. I have also labeled the countries by three levels of their HDI score in 2005 to determine whether poor countries have higher levels (United Nations, 2010). If development stage matters, the relatively poor countries should be above the regression line that predicts urban concentration from the population size of the society. In other words, relatively poor societies should have more urban concentration than predicted by the regression line.

As Fig. 5.5 shows, there is a high tendency for the countries with low HDI scores to be above the line while the developed countries have a somewhat higher chance to fall below the line. This means that, independent of population size, low levels of development are associated with high primacy. In a regression equation, I predicted the concentration of the urban population in the largest city, controlling for the country's population size in natural logarithms. The average country in the lowest HDI group was characterized by a concentration 8.1 percentage points higher than the high HDI countries, once the effect of population size was statistically controlled. The average moderate HDI country had a concentration 2.1% higher than the high countries.

These patterns may have some implications for thinking about "spread urbanization" and metropolitan dominance. Small, poor countries are likely to have one dominant metropolis that exerts a strong influence on other urban and rural patterns throughout the country. In large, wealthy countries, small places and rural

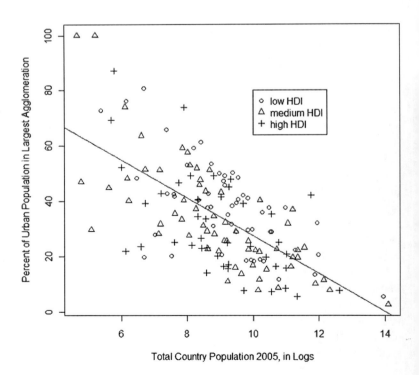

**Fig. 5.5** Relationship of size, HDI to urban primacy

areas are likely to have orientations to multiple large urban agglomerations.

## Conclusion

How will we think in the future about defining urban and rural? As a demographer, I like approaches that focus on relatively simple measures of population size and concentration. At least potentially, these may be measured across time (historical periods) and national boundaries. From these measures, the potential exists to develop fairly universal theories of the causes and consequences of urbanization.

Others (Lampard, 1961; Tacoli, 1998) have tried to focus more on definitions of urban that emphasize type of employment (usually nonagriculture) and behavioral ways of life (typically urban populations are believed to be rationalistic and impersonal). Type of employment may be useful for some definitional purposes, but it limits us to very specific situations because employment structures have changed historically and still vary noticeably across contemporary societies that, by most standards, have large cities. Behavioral traits may be an important consequence of urbanization, but are difficult to measure with much reliability. In additions, our ability to reconstruct the past in terms of urban behavior is difficult due to a lack of data.

The basic demographic measurement of urban and rural in terms of basic size and density thresholds (as used by the United Nations and emphasized in this paper's data analysis) has much to recommend it (Fuguitt, 2004), especially in terms of the availability of data. In addition, it stills helps in differentiating social and economic characteristics of populations. However, it will increasingly be limited in value as population agglomerations become larger and more variable in size, as density declines in some geographic areas while increasing in others, and as the physical boundaries of high density areas become more ambiguous. The distinction of urban vs. rural may become less tenable than distinguishing among urban and rural types.

Realistically, I cannot discuss seriously all the specific possibilities of measuring urban and rural in this one general essay. There is an emerging extensive literature on this topic (du Plessis, Beshiri, & Bollman, 2002; John, 2008, see also Chapter 2 in this volume). Nevertheless, the scholarly community needs to devote more attention to developing a variety of measures that can be employed for comparative purposes to understand the evolving world urbanization.

## References

Aiken, M., & Alford, R. R. (1970). Community structure and innovation: The case of urban renewal. *American Sociological Review, 35*, 650–665.

Alderson, A. S., & Beckfield, J. (2004). Power and position in the world city system. *American Journal of Sociology, 109*, 811–851.

Berry, B. J. L. (1981). *Comparative urbanization: Divergent paths in the twentieth century*. New York: St. Martin's Press.

Berry, B. J. L., & Horton, F. (1970). *Geographic perspectives on urban systems*. Englewood Cliffs, NJ: Prentice-Hall.

Berry, B. J. L., & Pred, A. (1961). *Central place studies: A bibliography of theory and applications*. Philadelphia, PA: Regional Science Research Institute.

Bogue, Don J. (1950). *The structure of the metropolitan community: A study of dominance and subdominance*. Ann Arbor, MI: Rackman School of Graduate Studies, University of Michigan.

Bradshaw, Y. (1987). Urbanization and underdevelopment: A global study of modernization, urban bias, and economic dependency. *American Sociological Review, 52*, 224–239.

Brockerhoff, M., & Brennan, E. (1998). The poverty of cities in developing regions. *Population and Development Review, 24*, 75–113.

Brown, D. L., & Cromartie, J. B. (2004). The nature of rurality in post-industrial society. In A. G. Champion & G. Hugo (Eds.), *New forms of urbanization: Beyond the urban-rural dichotomy* (pp. 269–283). Burlington, VT: Ashgate Publishing.

Carter, S. B., Gartner, S. S., Haines, M. R., Olmstead, A. L., Sutch, R., & Wright, G. (2006). *Historical statistics of the United States* (Vol. 4). New York: Cambridge University Press.

Champion, A. G. (1989). *Counterurbanization: The changing pace of and nature of population deconcentration*. London: Edward Arnold.

Champion, A. G., & Hugo, G. (2004). Introduction: Moving beyond the urban-rural dichotomy. In A. G. Champion & G. Hugo (Eds.), *New forms of urbanization: Beyond the urban-rural dichotomy* (pp. 3–24). Burlington, VT: Ashgate Publishing.

Chan, K. W. (2001). Recent migration in China: Patterns, trends, and policies. *Asian Perspectives, 25*(4), 127–155.

Chia, H.-B., Egri, C., Ralston, D., Fu, P., Kuo, M.-H., Lee, C.-H., et al. (2007). Four tigers and the dragon: Values differences, similarities, and consensus. *Asia Pacific Journal of Management, 24*, 305–320.

Davis, K. (1955). The origin and growth of urbanization in the world. *American Journal of Sociology, 60*(5), 429–437.

Duncan, O. D., Duncan, B., Lieberson, S., Scott, W. R., & Winsborough, H. H. (1960). *Metropolis and region*. Baltimore, MD: Johns Hopkins Press.

du Plessis, V., Beshiri, R., & Bollman, R. D. (2002). *Definitions of "rural"*. Ottawa, ON: Statistics Canada, Agriculture Division.

Firebaugh, G. (1979). Structural determinants of urbanization in Asia and Latin America, 1950–1970. *American Sociological Review, 44*, 199–215.

Frey, W. H. (2004). The fading of city-suburb and metro-nonmetro distinctions in the United States. In A. G. Champion & G. Hugo (Eds.), *New forms of urbanization: Beyond the urban-rural dichotomy* (pp. 67–88). Burlington, VT: Ashgate Publishing.

Fuguitt, G. V. (2004). Some demographic aspects of rurality. *Research in Social Stratification and Mobility, 22*, 73–90.

Fuguitt, G. V., & Brown, D. L. (1990). Residential preferences and population redistribution: 1972–1988. *Demography, 27*, 589–600.

Gardner, T. (n.d.). New York (Manhattan) wards: Population & density 1800–1910. *Demographia*. Retrieved March 9, 2010, from www.demographia.com/db-nyc-ward1800.htm.

Gollin, D. (2010). Agricultural productivity and economic growth. In P. Pingali & R. Evenson (Eds.), *Handbook of agricultural economics* (Vol. 4, pp. 3826–3866). New York: Elsevier.

Grauman, J. V. (1976). Orders of magnitude of the world's urban population in history. *Population Bulletin of the United Nations, 8*, 16–33.

Guest, A. M. (1975). Population suburbanization in American metropolitan areas, 1940–1970. *Geographical Analysis, 7*, 267–283.

Guest, A. M. (1984). The city. In M. Micklin & H. Choldin (Eds.), *Sociological human ecology: Contemporary issues and applications* (pp. 277–322). Boulder, CO: Westview Press.

Guest, A. M., & Brown, S. K. (2005). Population distribution and suburbanization. In D. L. Poston & M. Micklin (Eds.), *Handbook of population* (pp. 57–84). New York: Springer.

Guest, A. M., & Cluett, C. (1974). Metropolitan retail nucleation. *Demography, 11*, 493–507.

Hackenberg, R. (1980). New patterns of urbanization in Southeast Asia: An assessment. *Population and Development Review, 6*, 391–419.

Hawley, A. (1971). *Urban society: An ecological approach*. New York: Ronald Press.

Hawley, A. (1972). Population density and the city. *Demography, 9*, 521–529.

Hawley, A. (1978). Urbanization as process. In D. Street (Ed.), *Handbook of contemporary urban life* (pp. 3–26). San Francisco: Jossey-Bass.

John, P. L. (2008). *What is rural?* Beltsville, MD: USDA, National Agricultural Library, Rural Information Center.

Johnson, K., & Cromartie, J. (2006). The rural rebound and its aftermath. In W. Kandel & D. Brown (Eds.), *The population of rural America: Demographic research for a new century* (pp. 25–49). New York: Kluwer.

Kasarda, J. D., & Crenshaw, E. M. (1991). Third world urbanization: Dimensions, theories, and determinants. *Annual Review of Sociology, 17*, 467–501.

Kelley, A. C., & Williamson, J. G. (1984). Population growth, industrial revolutions, and the urban transition. *Population and Development Review, 10*, 419–441.

Lampard, E. E. (1961). American historians and the study of urbanization. *American Historical Review, 67*, 49–61.

Massey, D. S. (2005). *Strangers in a strange land: Humans in an urbanizing world*. New York: W.W. Norton & Co.

McNeill, W. H. (1976). *Plagues and peoples*. Garden City, NY: Anchor Press/Doubleday.

Meyer, D. R. (2003). The challenge of research on the global network of cities. *Urban Geography, 24*, 301–313.

Mori, H. (1998). Land conversion at the urban fringe: A comparative study of Japan, Britain and the Netherlands. *Urban Studies, 35*, 1541–1558.

Preston, S. H. (1979). Urban growth in developing countries: A demographic reappraisal. *Population and Development Review, 5*, 195–215.

Sagar, A. D., & Najam, A. (1998). The human development index: A critical review. *Ecological Economics, 25*, 249–264.

Sassen, S. (1994). *Cities in a world economy*. Thousand Oaks, CA: Pine Forge Press.

Schettkat, R., & Yocarini, L. (2006). The shift to services employment: A review of the literature. *Structural Change and Economic Dynamics, 17*, 127–147.

Schnore, L. F. (1962). Social problems in an urban-industrial context. *Social Problems, 9*(3), 228–240.

Schultz, T. P. (1993). Mortality decline in the low-income world: Causes and consequences. *American Economic Review, 83*, 337–342.

Shandra, J. M., London, B., & Williamson, J. B. (2003). Environmental degradation, environmental sustainability, and overurbanization in the developing world: A quantitative, cross-national analysis. *Sociological Perspectives, 46*(3), 309–329.

Short, J. R., & Pinet-Peralta, L. M. (2009). Urban primacy: Reopening the debate. *Geography Compass, 3*(3), 1245–1266.

Sjoberg, G. (1960). *The pre-industrial city: Past and present*. New York: Free Press.

Sternlieb, G. (1971). The city as sandbox. *Public Interest, 25*, 14–21.

Summers, A. A., Cheshire, P. C., & Senn, L. (Eds.). (1999). *Urban change in the United States and Western Europe: Comparative analysis and policy*. Washington, DC: Urban Institute Press.

Tacoli, C. (1998). Rural-urban interactions: A guide to the literature. *Environment and Urbanization, 10*, 147–166.

Tisdale, H. (1942). The process of urbanization. *Social Forces, 20*(3), 311–316.

Tobin, G. A. (1976). Suburbanization and the development of motor transportation: Transportation technology and the suburbanization process. In B. Schwartz (Ed.), *The changing faces of the suburbs* (pp. 95–111). Chicago: University of Chicago Press.

Todaro, M. P. (1980). Urbanization in developing nations: Trends, prospects, and policies. *Journal of Geography, 79*(5), 164–174.

United Nations. (2008a). *Demographic yearbook, 2005*. New York: Department of Economic and Social Affairs, Statistical Office, United Nations.

United Nations. (2008b). *Urban agglomerations, 2007*. Department of Economic and Social Affairs, Statistical Office, United Nations. Retrieved February 9, 2010, from http://www.un.org/esa/population/publications/wup2007/2007_urban_agglomerations_chart.pdf

United Nations. (2008c). *World urbanization prospects: The 2007 revision population database*. Department of Economic and Social Affairs, Statistical Office, United Nations. Retrieved February 9, 2010, from http://esa.un.org/unup.

United Nations. (2010). *National accounts*. Department of Economic and Social Affairs, Statistical Office, United Nations. Retrieved February 9, 2010, from http://unstats.un.org/unsd/nationalaccount/default.asp

Ward, D. (1971). *Cities and immigrants*. New York: Oxford University Press.

Wardwell, J. M. (1980). Toward a theory of urban-rural migration in the developed world. In D. L. Brown & J. M. Wardwell (Eds.), *New directions in urban-rural migration: The population turnaround in rural America* (pp. 71–114). New York: Academic.

Warner, S. B. (1972). *The urban wilderness: A history of the American city*. New York: Harper & Row.

Williamson, J. G. (1988). Migration selectivity, urbanization, and industrial revolutions. *Population and Development Review, 14*, 287–314.

Winsborough, H. H. (1963). An ecological approach to the theory of suburbanization. *American Journal of Sociology, 68*, 565–570.

Zhu, Y. (2004). Changing urbanization processes and in situ rural-urban transformation: Reflections on China's settlement definitions. In A. G. Champion & G. Hugo (Eds.), *New forms of urbanization: Beyond the urban-rural dichotomy* (pp. 207–228). Burlington, VT: Ashgate Publishing.

# Rural Aging in International Context

E. Helen Berry

## Introduction

No discussion of population patterns, rural or urban, can fail to address population aging. As the United Nations in its volume on World Population Aging (2007) makes clear, population aging has been an established phenomenon in the developed regions of the world and an increasingly important one in developing regions of the world since 1950. The worldwide proportion of persons age 65 and over has tripled since 1950 and is anticipated to triple again between 2000 and 2050 (United Nations, 2007). The rapid change from primarily youthful societies to a more evenly balanced proportion of age groups in developing countries and to a distribution of ages skewed older in developed nations has had profound impacts on social systems and economies. Of greater import is that the changes in age structures have a greater influence in rural places: any small change in rural populations is magnified because rural places are already less densely populated with longer distances between households and towns and have fewer economic resources to support services.

The term aging has different meanings, depending on whether one discusses aging on an individual or a societal level. On the individual scale, aging includes the physiological changes that come with the passage of time from birth to death. The meaning of *population aging* is quite different than for the individual. When a population ages the changes are in the ratio of young people to elderly. A decrease in fertility rates results in a relatively larger proportion of persons in older age groups to those younger. Thus, a decline in the proportion of persons at younger ages relative to an increase in the proportion of persons in older age is the effective definition of population aging.

For rural places, percentage older or younger is less important than is the actual number of persons within a geographic region. The real issue for most rural elders is not median age or a proportion at retirement age or even old-age dependency ratios. Rather, the key is the actual number of elders in a given space. The reason that numbers are of most relevance is that it is the density of population relative to resources and geographic size of region that limits or enhances the ability to support services, health care, retirement homes, senior centers, or transportation services for older populations. The problem in rural places is, and always has been, that the density of population across the landscape tends to make the support for services less consistent and less available. Even the tax base necessary to provide critical mass for senior centers and retirement homes or basic transportation or infrastructure, whether for elders or for the general population, may be hard to come by making access difficult to impossible.

## How Is Aging Measured?

Several methods have been used to measure aging and its related variables. The two most common measures are the median age of the population and the

---

E.H. Berry (✉)
Department of Sociology, Social Work and Anthropology, Utah State University, Logan, UT 84322-0730, USA
e-mail: Eddy.Berry@usu.edu

percentage of the population older than age 65. Percent over age 65 is commonly utilized because it is an intuitive measure although some authors and institutions use different start points for the beginning of old age. The United Nations (2009) uses percentage over age 60, not age 65, as do Lutz, Sanderson, and Scherbov (2008) because age 65 is an arbitrary choice and does not take into account longer or shorter life expectancies that can be found in various regions of the world (83 in Japan; 45 in sub-Saharan Africa) (United Nations, 2009).

Using U.S. Census Bureau figures (2007), the U.S. percentage over age 65 in 1980 had reached 11.3%; 12.5% in 1990 and 12.4% in 2000. The percentage over age 65 declined slightly after 1990 although the actual number rose from 25,550,000 in 1980 to 34,992,000 by 2000. As a result, the percentage over 65 can be somewhat misleading as it does not take into account proportionate changes in other parts of the population or the absolute increase in size of the population. With 2010 Census data not yet available, the American Community Survey (ACS) reported 12.6% of Americans over age 65 (2010). These percentages are 12.4% for urban and 13.3% for rural places as can be seen in Table 6.1. For those living in the more urban places, also called metropolitan and micropolitan places, the percentages dropped as low as 11.4% for those in principal cities of metropolitan places but in nonmetropolitan and nonmicropolitan (non-metro/nonmicropolitan) statistical areas the percent over age 65 is 16.5% (ACS, 2010).

Utilizing median age of a population to measure aging provides a different method of describing population aging, one that takes into account the relative size of both older and younger populations. The median age describes the point at which half of the population is older and half of that population is younger. In the U.S., overall, the median age of the population increased from 30 in 1980 to 32.8 in 1990 and 35.3 in 2000 (U.S. Census Bureau, 2007, Table 7).

In 2009, the differential between rural and urban areas was more than four years with urban places

**Table 6.1** U.S. median age; percent by age 65 and 85 and over; and ethnicity by geographic status

|  | Median age | Percent age 65 and over | Percent age 85 and over | Percent white | Percent African American | Percent native American |
|---|---|---|---|---|---|---|
| United States | 36.5 | 12.6 | 1.7 | 74.5 | 12.4 | 0.8 |
| URBAN and RURAL |  |  |  |  |  |  |
| Urban | 35.6 | 12.4 | 1.8 | 70.7 | 14.1 | 0.6 |
| Rural | 39.7 | 13.3 | 1.4 | 87.1 | 6.4 | 1.4 |
| *Inside and outside metropolitan and micropolitan statistical area* |  |  |  |  |  |  |
| In metropolitan or micropolitan |  |  |  |  |  |  |
| Statistical area | 36.2 | 12.3 | 1.7 | 73.7 | 12.6 | 0.7 |
| In metropolitan |  |  |  |  |  |  |
| Statistical area | 36.0 | 12.0 | 1.6 | 72.5 | 13.1 | 0.6 |
| In principal city | 33.7 | 11.4 | 1.7 | 62.1 | 19.2 | 0.6 |
| Not in principal city | 37.5 | 12.5 | 1.6 | 79.3 | 9.1 | 0.6 |
| In micropolitan |  |  |  |  |  |  |
| Statistical area | 38.5 | 14.8 | 2.0 | 84.1 | 8.5 | 1.6 |
| In principal city | 34.7 | 14.8 | 2.5 | 78.8 | 12.2 | 1.2 |
| Not in principal city | 40.1 | 14.8 | 1.7 | 86.7 | 6.7 | 1.7 |
| Not in metropolitan or micropolitan |  |  |  |  |  |  |
| Statistical area | 41.0 | 16.5 | 2.2 | 85.4 | 8.3 | 2.4 |

*Source*: American Community Survey (2010) (Tables GCT0101, GCT0103, GCT0104, GCT0201, GCT0202, and GCT0204).

**Table 6.2** Summary characteristics: fertility rate, percent age groups, dependency ratio, and life expectancy

| Year | Total fertility rate | Percent age 0–14 | Percent age 15–64 | Percent age 65+ | Old age dependency | Life expectancy at birth |
|---|---|---|---|---|---|---|
| 1950 | 5.0 | 34.3 | 60.5 | 5.2 | 0.1 | 46.6 |
| 2000 | 2.8 | 30.1 | 63.0 | 6.9 | 0.1 | 65.5 |
| 2050 | 2.0 | 20.1 | 64.0 | 15.9 | 0.2 | 74.3 |
| 2070 | 1.9 | 16.4 | 59.2 | 24.4 | 0.4 | 78.0 |

*Source*: United Nations (2007).

having a median age of 35.6 and rural ones a median of 39.7 (ACS, 2010). When the ACS makes the finer geographical distinctions between principal cities of metropolitan statistical areas and nonmetro/nonmicropolitan geographical areas, as seen in Table 6.1 the median age in the most urban places is 33.7 vs. 40.1 in the nonmetro/nonmicropolitan places (ACS, 2010). In other words, the farther from large urban places the older the population.

Two other population measures are the total dependency ratio and the old-age dependency ratio. The total dependency ratio is the sum of those ages 0–14 plus those 65 and older in ratio to the working-age population. The old age dependency ratio is the ratio of those over age 64 to the working population, age 15–64. The advantage to these two ratios is that they provide a sense of the relative size of generations.

The old-age dependency ratio is often used to illustrate reasons for concern relative to labor force participation or social security issues and is reported at the world level in Table 6.2. The ratio is extensively discussed by Bongaarts (2004) and takes into account the ratio of persons over age 65 to those in the working population, defined as those ages 15–64. The bias in this measure is that there is an assumed retirement age of 65 which is not always realistic in either developing nations, where people cannot always retire, or in developed ones. As Bongaarts (2004) points out, there are wide differentials between countries in dates of access to public pensions, with Italy using age 55; the U.S using 62; and Canada Germany, and Japan providing access at 60. The French and British, rather famously, have spent the fall of 2010 protesting over an increase in their retirement age to 62. For most regions, good data on dependency ratios are available for rural and urban places, but the data often do not take into account differentials in retirement ages, nor take data account of those who are already taking pensions relative to those who are not.

## How and Why Does Population Aging Occur?

Generally, population aging is more due to declining birth rates than to increasing life expectancy. Changes in life expectancy are important and relevant but the effects of longer lifespans are more subtle and have had less dramatic influences on population aging than other factors until recently.

The demographic transition, described by Thompson, refers to a steady decline in mortality especially in Europe and North America in the 17th through 19th centuries accompanied by a decline in birth rates (1929). Although both changes in fertility and mortality occurred over similar periods of time, at the beginning of the transition the rates of deaths among infants and children had been higher than that of adults. Thus the demographic transition from high to low death and birth rates resulted in increases in life expectancy at birth but the increase in life expectancy was particularly noticeable among the young (Petersen, 1975). As infants began to survive past age five, then past age 14 or 15, the proportion of young people in the population increased radically (Goldstein, 2010) and produced *proportionate* declines in the older population even as the *number* in the older population increased. Not until birth rates dropped to low levels with respect to death rates did the population in older ages increase enough for there to be a proportionate change relative to the population in younger ages.

To exemplify this, consider the U.S. decline in birth rates since 1800. Greenwood, Seshadri, and Vandenbroucke (2005) document that the U.S. experienced a long-term decline in birth rates between

1800 and 1940, with a short recovery between 1940 and 1964 (the baby boom) followed by a continuing decline in birth rates thereafter. White women in 1800, as an example, had, on average, seven children,[1] life expectancy was approximately 32 years at birth; and median age was 16 years. Percentage of persons over age 65 was not reported for 1800 but one can deduce that if median age was 16, the proportion in the older ages was not high.

In 1890, average family size had dropped to 3.9 children per woman, life expectancy at birth had reached nearly 40; and median age had increased to 22. In 1890 only 3.9% of the population was reported to be over age 65. By comparison, in 2009, the birth rate for U.S. women hovered near 2: non-Hispanic white and Asian American women had 1.9 children on average; African American women had 2.15 children, and Hispanic women bore 2.96 children on average (Greenwood et al., 2005; Jacobson & Mather, 2010). The percentage over 65 had increased to 12.1 and life expectancy reached 78 years (U.S. Census Bureau, 2007). The decline in birth rates resulted in a decreasing proportion of the population in the younger ages. Because more Americans were surviving to older ages, the portion of the population over age 65 by comparison to those younger had resulted in an older population.

At the same time that the fertility rate was declining, the U.S. was urbanizing. In 1800, 6% of the U.S. population was urban (U.S. Census Bureau, 1975). By 1890, the urban population was 36% and in 1940 the population had exceeded 57% urban (U.S. Census Bureau, 1975). The rural population is now estimated to be only about 20% and is not expected to have changed much since the 2000 census, the last date when figures were available (U.S. Census Bureau, 2007).

The relationship between the decline in the fertility rate and the increase in the proportion urban is not necessarily a causal one. A variety of authors have placed the reasons for each change elsewhere (e.g. Van de Walle & Knodel, 1980). At the same time, both variables have been shown to be associated with economic and social change and both are known to be associated with overall improvements in life expectancy and lifespan. As a region or country becomes more developed with better public health, economic, technological and other infrastructural improvements population life expectancy increases. As a result human longevity has increased as much as six hours per day since the 1850s in developed countries thereby exacerbating population aging (Vaupel, 2010). When life expectancy increases there is some impact on the proportion of elders to youth. In the situation where fertility is falling and life expectancy is increasing, population aging will occur more rapidly and become particularly noticeable.

## The Role of Migration

A third variable can alter the rate of population aging, particularly in rural places: migration. The movement of youth out of rural places and the in-migration of middle-aged and older adults into rural places impacts both the pace and magnitude of rural aging. The out-migration of rural youth is a long-standing phenomenon in developed and developing countries whether to fulfill job aspirations, find employment (Brooks, Toney, Berry, & Lim, 2010; Harris & Todaro, 1970; Mabogunje, 1970), or as a result of push factors such as loss of economic resources at place of origin relative to place of destination (Garasky, 2002; Johnson, 2006; Johnson, Voss, Hammer, Fuguitt, & McNiven, 2005) increasing the ratio of elders to the remaining young people in rural places and is a phenomenon that has long been modeled by demographers.

Migration of older persons into rural places is also important. Litwak and Longino (1987) suggest that there are three migrations made by elders and that these moves are made upon retirement or close to retirement ages. The first is made by younger retirees to a place to enjoy retirement; the second move is toward family; and the third move is by the oldest old to a place where care can be provided. In the U.S., the movement of retirees into rural places is a reverse migration phenomenon that has been documented only relatively recently (Beale, 1975). The reverse migration may be to seek amenities as suggested by Litwak and Longino and documented in the U.S. and England (McGranahan, 1999; Brown, Glasgow with

---

[1] The fertility rate is measured here by the total fertility rate. The total fertility rate is the sum of the age-specific fertility rates for all women currently in the childbearing years. As such, the TFR is not an actual estimate of family size, but an amalgamation of the fertility behavior of women in a number of cohorts. However, the TFR is a good approximation of what is happening to women at a given point in time.

Kulcsar, Bolender, & Arguillas, 2008; Raymer, Abel, & Smith, 2007). A variety of rural places have become retirement destinations for healthy and relatively well-off retirees including Maine, Michigan, Arizona, and other amenity-rich destinations (Brown et al., 2008). Conversely, as shown in China and elsewhere (Zimmer & Korinek, 2010) migration to rural places may occur to seek care from family members in the case of illness or advanced age, as according to the later stages of the developmental typology (Litwak & Longino, 1987).

Thus, for rural places, the reasons that population aging is more dramatic are multivariate but heavily associated with migration. Still the primary reason for population aging has been the decline in fertility rates. A glance at Fig. 6.1 shows that the total fertility rate has been in decline in more urbanized regions for some time and is anticipated to continue doing so. The resulting impact will be that the ratio of older to younger persons has been and will continue to increase worldwide. The impact of declining birth rates has and will differ by region, with much older populations in the most urbanized and developed regions and countries, like Europe or Japan. In regions where fertility is declining relatively slowly, such as sub-Saharan Africa or the Indian subcontinent, the proportion of the aged to the younger population remains lower. The latter regions have tended to be poorer and, even where developing rapidly, are more agricultural and less urbanized, as can be seen in Table 6.3. This bifurcation between low fertility and high proportions of elderly in comparison to high fertility and lower proportions of elderly can also be seen in subgroups within nations and is likely to remain well into the 21st century.

## Where are the Oldest Old?

Given the breadth of this question, the answer depends on whether one is in Africa or Latin America, or in Europe, North America, or Japan. To simplify the topic, our focus will stay primarily on the U.S. In the U.S, distance from urban places is positively correlated with aging. Referring to Table 6.1, the central cities of the largest U.S. metropolitan areas have a median age of 33.7, but outside their principal city the median age is 37.5. The smaller, micropolitan places have principal cities with median ages of 34.7; outside primary micropolitan cities the median age is 40.1 and in nonmetropolitan areas median age is 41. Percentages over age 65 in metropolitan places follow approximately similar patterns with those in the principal cities having the lowest percentages at 11.4% but those in nonmetro/nonmicropolitan areas having 16.5% over age 65. In other words, the more rural one is, the more surrounded by elders one is.

When it comes to the U.S. oldest old, those over 85, the aging of the countryside is more subtle. Table 6.1 reports that the principal cities of metropolitan and micropolitan places have higher percentages in the

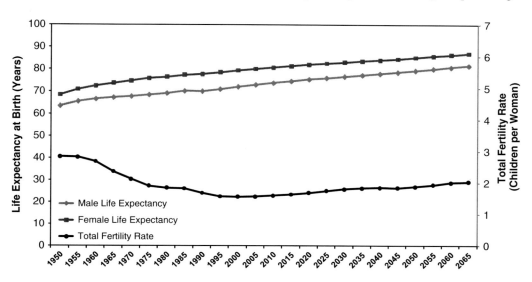

**Fig. 6.1** Total fertility rate and life expectancy at birth more developed regions, 1950–2065
*Source*: United Nations (2010).

**Table 6.3** Countries with the largest percentage of population over age 65 and under age 15 and life expectancy of each

| Countries with oldest populations | Percent age 65 and over, 2007 | Life expectancy, 2007 | Percent rural, 2010 | Countries with youngest populations | Percent age 15 and under, 2007 | Life expectancy, 2007 | Percent rural, 2010 |
|---|---|---|---|---|---|---|---|
| Japan | 22.6 | 83 | 34 | Niger | 50.1 | 48 | 84 |
| Germany | 20.5 | 80 | 26 | Uganda | 48.7 | 52 | 98 |
| Italy | 20.4 | 82 | 32 | Burkina Faso | 46.5 | 53 | 84 |
| Sweden | 18.3 | 81 | 16 | Dem. Rep. Congo | 46.4 | 46 | 66 |
| Greece | 18.3 | 80 | 39 | Zambia | 46.2 | 42 | – |
| Portugal | 17.9 | 79 | 41 | Malawi | 45.9 | 49 | 81 |
| Bulgaria | 17.6 | 73 | 29 | Afghanistan | 45.9 | 44 | 76 |
| Austria | 17.6 | 80 | 33 | Chad | 45.6 | 49 | 73 |
| Latvia | 17.4 | 73 | 32 | Somalia | 44.9 | 49 | 63 |
| Belgium | 17.4 | 80 | 3 | Tanzania | 44.7 | 55 | 75 |

*Source*: Adapted from Population Reference Bureau (2010) and United Nations (2007).

over age 85 group, 1.7% and 2.5% respectively, but outside of those principal cities, the percentages are 1.6% and 1.7%, respectively, implying that once upon reaching this oldest of ages, elders either move to more urban places for access to services or are found their because that is where more nursing and retirement homes are located. However, 2.2% of the oldest old are still to be found in nonmetropolitan areas.

## Aging and Population Composition

Another piece of what makes rural aging different from aging in urban places is often diversity. Using patterns of ethnicity as an example, historical patterns of migration have often resulted in relatively dramatic differences in racial and ethnic composition between the aged in rural and the aged in urban places although again these patterns may be subtle. Again following the U.S. example, the more rural the place, the more likely to be part of the dominant racial/ethnic group. Although overall the U.S is 74.5% white (Table 6.1), rural areas are 87.1% so. Metropolitan places are less so at 72.5% overall, but smaller micropolitan places reach 84.1% and nonmetro/nonmicropolitan places are 85.4% white. In the reverse of this pattern, the percent African Americans in urban areas is 14.1% and plunges to 6.4% in rural areas. When residence for Blacks is broken down by residence in principal cities of metropolitan or micropolitan places, percentages are higher – 19.2% in metro and 12.2% in micro; but in nonmetro places the percentage drops to 8.3%. Similar patterns are found for other racial/ethnic groups with the primary exception being Native Americans although their percentage in nonmetro/micropolitan areas is 2.4% as compared to the U.S. total of 0.8% overall and 0.7% in metro and micropolitan places combined (ACS, 2010).

In other words, patterns of ethnicity and rurality vary depending on the nature of any region's cultural, social, and economic history. In the U.S. the elderly in rural places are more generally white than not. Such a factor is unimportant if race is unimportant which is culturally rare but is also not the topic of this chapter. The key factor here is that diversity tends to be most concentrated in cities and that rural places are less diverse.

One aspect of aging that should be clear, from looking at Figs. 6.1 and 6.2 is that life expectancy for females is somewhat higher than for males. At every age and in almost every country in the world, women outlive men (Population Reference Bureau, 2010). The implication for rural areas is that if rural areas are older than urban ones, then rural areas should have higher percentages of older women than older men. To begin, women's life expectancy is longer than men's thanks to the improvements in public health and childbearing practices that began in the 1600s and helped to create the demographic transition (Kammeyer & Ginn, 1986). The U.S. number of men per 100 women, called the sex

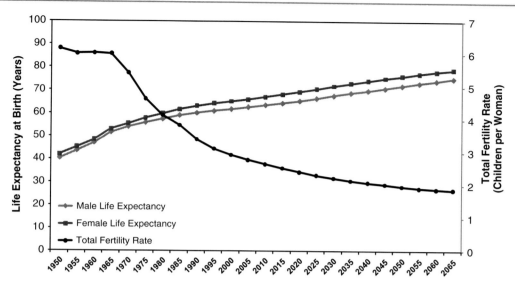

**Fig. 6.2** Total fertility rate and life expectancy at birth less developed regions, 1950–2065
*Source*: United Nations (2010).

ratio, declines from over 107 men per 100 women, to a one-to-one ratio by age 50. Beyond age 85 there are fewer than 48 men for every 100 women in the same age group (ACS, 2010).

International differences suggest that culture is key to whether being single or a woman in a rural area is important or not. An example is documented by Chapman and Peace (2008) in the Canadian cowboy attitude that the rural west is "no place for a woman." Men are characterized as best suited to life on the frontier and women are seen as helpmeets to husbands, making women virtually invisible in rural Canada (Chapman & Peace, 2008). Yet just south of the Canadian Rockies Marquart-Pyatt and Petrzelka (2008) found that when it comes to public affairs, community involvement, community development and tourism rural, older women play critical roles in economic development and tourism in rural areas in the western U.S. although they too note that women's role tends to be unsung.

Regardless of culture, gender has implications for rural women that it does not have for men. For one thing, women's longer life expectancy means that older rural women are more often living without a partner than older rural or urban men or older urban women, even when living within some form of extended family (Gratton & Guttman, 2010). For another, because older women come from cohorts in that they were less likely to work or, if they were employed, they were employed in jobs that earned less and established less retirement income than men, elderly rural women are more likely to be poor (Glasgow & Brown, 1998).

What is unusual in U.S. rural areas is that the proportions married in rural areas, particularly at younger ages, show a strong bias toward females being married and males being unmarried. Examining Table 6.4, the sex ratio for age 15–44 who are unmarried is substantially higher in rural areas than in urban ones – 124.7 to 110.2. Data on marriage for older age groups is not currently available. However, looking at column two of the same table, it can be seen that 61% of those in rural places are married while only 46 some percent in urban areas are. Columns 3 and 4 of the table also indicate that while males seem to be more likely to have never married in general, showing higher percentages across all geographic categories, the percent of men who have never married to the percentage of women who have never married continues to remain higher in rural areas, even in the most rural places.

The sex ratio discrepancy in rural places has been explained by a lack of service sector jobs in rural places; the greater numbers of jobs that are dominated by men, such as agriculture and extraction; and the placement of prisons which are themselves more often male than female (Kirschner, Berry, & Glasgow, 2006; Vias & Nelson, 2006). Still, given the longer life expectancy of women, whether in rural or urban places, the sex ratio imbalance among the married

**Table 6.4** Sex ratios for unmarried and married households as available

|  | Sex ratio, unmarried men per 100 unmarried women, age 15–44 | Percent married couple households | Percent men age 15 and over, never married | Percent women age 15 and over, never married |
|---|---|---|---|---|
|  | (1) | (2) | (3) | (4) |
| United States | 112.7 | 49.7 | 34.1 | 27.7 |
| Urban and rural |  |  |  |  |
| Urban | 110.2 | 46.3 | 36.6 | 30.0 |
| Rural | 124.7 | 61.0 | 26.2 | 19.6 |
| *Inside and outside metropolitan and micropolitan statistical area* |  |  |  |  |
| In Metropolitan or micropolitan |  |  |  |  |
| Statistical area | 111.9 | 49.4 | 34.6 | 28.2 |
| In Metropolitan |  |  |  |  |
| Statistical area | 111.2 | 49.1 | 35.0 | 28.8 |
| In principal city | 108.2 | 40.0 | 41.5 | 34.8 |
| Not in principal city | 113.8 | 55.4 | 30.8 | 24.8 |

*Source*: American Community Survey (2010) (Tables GCT1203, GCT1101, GCT1201, and GCT1202).

and unmarried in rural and nonmetro places is of interest. Obviously, women in rural places are either married or they leave, whether poor or not. Older men in rural places, even when unmarried, tend to stay there.

## Implications of Aging for Rural Populations

### Aging and the Workforce

Discussion of the sex ratio differential might be a good place to begin discussing the implications of rural population aging for societies. Perhaps the easiest way to examine these implications is to look at the country that is currently the "oldest" and has been dealing with the challenges of aging and rural aging for the longest. Japan made dramatic changes from high to low fertility, has the highest life expectancy, and, in terms of the rural experience, is among the most urbanized of societies, but as a result has been dealing with rural population aging for some time already.

Japan experienced a very rapid decline in fertility rates from a rate of 5 children per woman (TFR) in 1920 to 1.5 by 1980. The country has the oldest life expectancy in the world, age 82, with 30% of the population over 60 and 20% over age 80 (United Nations, 2009, Table 2 reports that for those over 60, 44% are male; for those over 80, only 1/3 are male [Dyck, 2010; Onishi, 2008]). As in the U.S., the Japanese preponderance of females in the older age categories is due to women's longer life expectancy, approximately 88 years to men's 82 years (Population Reference Bureau, 2006). Immigration to Japan is not common and less than 2% of the population are immigrants. The population of Japan has been declining since 2005 (Tabuchi, 2009).

The aging of Japan has occurred at the same time as the rapid industrialization and change to an information economy since WWII. The socioeconomic changes have simultaneously influenced household structure in that 42% of older Japanese live with their children, a proportion that is down from 70% in 1980 (Population Reference Bureau, 2006). In 2010 40% of older Japanese are expected to be living with a spouse and 13% living alone, up from 18% and 8%, respectively, in 1970 (Population Reference Bureau, 2006). The changed household pattern seems to be increasingly common in other developed countries. The move to independent living has occurred primarily since the 1950s and is associated with an increasing desire by elders to live independently (Ruggles, 2009).

More importantly, the population aging in congruence with the change from an agricultural to an industrial and information economy has resulted in a farm crisis. Japanese food production has long been based on small-scale agriculture relying on large numbers of farmers. The loss of farmers means the loss of farms and a resulting need for imports (Dyck, 2010). To reduce the impact, Japan agreed to guest worker programs that hired Brazilians of Japanese descent, and Chinese and Filipino guest workers in a country where there is much hesitation about foreigners (Onishi, 2008). The guest worker programs have been controversial and somewhat resented. By the time of the 2008 recession the guest workers from Latin America were being paid to return home in spite of labor shortages in farming and fishing towns (Tabuchi, 2009).

The challenge of a declining work force compared to increasing proportions of retirees is not confined to Japan. The European Union (EU) has a number of older countries. Twenty-two percent of the United Kingdom was over age 60 in 2009 as was 25% of Sweden; 26% of both Italy and Germany; and 23% of each Switzerland and Portugal (Goll, 2010). The percentages, which of course differ from those reported in Table 6.3 for those over age 65, make it clear that the aged population will continue to increase rapidly. As reported by Goll (2010), each country's rural areas had older populations than urban places, although the proportion of the elder population was increasing more quickly in urban places. The effect of the aging of the EU has been that guest worker programs have been necessary in both rural and urban places and as the 2008 recession has drawn on, the EU has become less welcoming to immigrants, even from member states (Povoledo, 2008).

Having an elderly population, then, has implications for rural economies. Siegel (1980) recognized that the elderly require different kinds of services than do younger people and as there are larger cadres of elderly there will be greater demand in rural places for those services, including transportation, health-care services, retirement homes, or cleaning services. These requirements are often linked to specific needs for housing and often to migration.

Translating Siegel's insight directly to Litwak and Longino's (1987) developmental sequencing of retirement migration referenced earlier, the first of Litwak and Longino's migrations, that of youthful elderly migrating, coincides with retirement amenity migration (Cromartie & Nelson, 2009). Rural amenity retirees are increasingly well documented and bode well for the places to which they move. Brown et al. (2008) call them "gray gold" as these elders bring monetary resources and human capital to rural places thereby creating and ultimately building infrastructure. Brown and Glasgow also show that many of these retirees are moving to areas where they already have family so that the amenity migrants often skip Litwak and Longino's second step, the move toward caregivers.

However, Litwak and Longino's third step appears to be well supported by the statistics in Table 6.1 on the U.S. oldest old: a higher proportion of the 85 and older population live in urban places than rural ones. Apparently, older people live in rural places until a lack of resources there forces them to move. The resources may be retirement homes or the resources may be caregivers or relatives, but the suggestion in the statistics is that the oldest old have moved toward care because care does not seem to be available in rural places.

Obviously, a lack of resources would be more than just a U.S. phenomenon: as an example, Zimmer and Korinek (2010) establish that family members in China return to rural places from the booming cities to care for older relatives as necessary and that older relatives return to rural places to gain care, as needed, from younger relatives. Internationally, then, there is obvious economic development and related employment opportunities in rural places for those who are able to provide care to the oldest old.

## Preferences in Care Taking and the Elderly

Granted, historically families serve as a social security system for elders, so that a relative increase in the number and proportion of elders affects families. Although the nature of families differs worldwide, there is a relatively well-documented preference for nuclear families in the older countries, particularly those of northwestern Europe. Elsewhere there is a greater reliance on more complex family structures that include higher percentages of elderly residing with kin.

Ruggles (2009) reports that east and south-east European countries followed by northwest Europe and the United States have the lowest proportions of elderly residing with relatives. Middle Eastern countries, followed by Sub-Saharan African; then Latin American countries have the highest percentages of elderly residing with family, especially descendants (Ruggles, 2009). However, as the interest here is in whether or not this is more or less dramatic in rural places, the results for agricultural areas or those that are less developed are of greater importance. Ruggles (2009) and Goody (1996) show that percentage agricultural employment in a country was closely associated with proportion living with kin. Each author shows that with economic development and presumed concomitant urbanization the proportion of elders not living with kin increases. In other words, the more developed a country, the more likely to be urban and the less likely elders will be to be living in extended families regardless of culture.

In countries where traditionally elders live with family, it is often assumed that families will maintain the financial and nonfinancial costs of caring for infirm elderly. The assumption is part of the traditional return on investment that parents make in children; a part of a mutual intergenerational transfer of wealth that includes both wealth invested in children, but later, wealth being utilized to care for parents. To return again to the Chinese example, Zimmer and Korinek (2010) confirm the tradition of co-residence of the elderly with children, appears to continue in China even though Chinese traditional society is changing very rapidly. They report the tradition continues at the same time that the Chinese government has put in place some security assistance for elders in rural places who have daughters or who have no children upon whom to rely (Ebenstein & Leung, 2010).

In more developed countries of the world, including those dominated by immigrants from northwestern Europe like the U.S., state-sponsored social security systems have become normative and are assumed to be necessary as a result of the greater likelihood of nuclear family systems and of the lesser preference for and likelihood of living near kin in rural places (Gratton & Guttman, 2010). The problem with reliance on state-sponsored support systems is that, as the old age dependency ratio shows for more developed countries (Table 6.2) as higher proportions of the elderly rely on smaller proportions of workers there is an economic burden on the working-age population that in turn places greater pressure on older populations to continue working or to establish other, nongovernmental support (Bongaarts, 2004).

The reason for concern for caregiving in the nonmetropolitan U.S. is that the nonmetropolitan population reports poorer health as measured by physical limitations than do metropolitan residents, 12 compared to 9% (Kusmin, 2009). Nonmetropolitan persons reported more activity limitations (16 vs. 11%) and problems with home management (Kusmin, 2006). In 2007 15% of all individuals had no health care in nonmetropolitan areas, including two percent of the elderly population (Jones, Parker, Ahearn, Mishra, & Variyam, 2009).

Rural residents indicated that they were more likely to seek health-care services in urban than rural places, at least in part because of the lack of delivery services in rural areas (Kusmin, 2006). Where the old age dependency ratio is lower, as in less developed countries of the world (see again Table 6.2), the economic burden of elders on workers is not so high but a child-worker dependency ratio is more the problem and the need is greater for schools. As Table 6.3 showed, often these younger countries are in Africa and in HIV/AIDS-impacted areas.

In the reverse of the developed nation family structures described above, in rural Africa, including South Africa and Kenya, as well as in Thailand and other settings where the HIV/AIDS epidemic has impacted family relationships, a variety of research has documented that elders have become caretakers for grandchildren whose parents have died or become ill. In these cases, households become the unit that cares for both youth and elders, in rural places. The households of these rural elders, almost universally, exhibit more poverty and are more likely to be headed by women (see Murphy, 2008; Knodel, Kespichayawattana, Saengtienchai, & Wiwatwanich, 2010; Hosegood & Timaeus, 2005 for examples.) Knodel et al. (2010) has shown, in areas hit hardest by the HIV/AIDS epidemic, elders and most often rural elders have become a form of back up social security system for when young adults become ill or die and leave young children behind.

But to claim that this is an entirely Asian or African phenomenon would be inaccurate as Table 6.4 illustrates. The percentage of grandparents and grandchildren living together is substantially higher in rural and in nonmetro/nonmicropolitan geographic areas than in the urban and metro places. The ACS (2010) reports that these grandparents are responsible for the grandchildren making elders a form of back-up social security or at least a form of childcare in the U.S. as well as in Africa.

## The Take Home

The rapid growth of the population of persons over the age of 65 in combination with continuing declines in fertility is resulting in one of the most demographically dramatic events of the past century. Not since Thompson (1929) documented the beginnings of demographic transition has a demographic event been so dramatic. The impact of the large cohorts in the older ages, relative to the smaller cohorts in younger ages is influencing families and labor force issues worldwide.

Rural places are aging more rapidly in some places than others. In developed countries where fertility rates had dropped earliest and which are now the older countries of the world, demand for labor has already resulted in large influxes of labor from countries where fertility rates have not dropped until more recently and where young laborers are, therefore, more plentiful. Guest worker programs and legal or illegal immigration throughout Europe, North and South America, Japan, and other older countries have resulted in political tensions particularly as the 2008 recession has stretched on. Even in China, the floating rural labor population has resulted in illegal immigration to the cities that has left rural elders behind to care for the grandchildren and to do the farming while also resulting in tensions in Chinese boom cities like Beijing and Shanghai (Berry, 2009; Sando, 1986). Because the populations of rural places are small, the presence of guest workers or the lack of any but older workers will always be felt more dramatically there.

Rural aging has been accompanied by changes in household and family structures. The movement of young adults to cities leaves elders behind, exacerbating any labor force shortages in rural places but also often resulting in or at least being accompanied by an increase in nuclear family households. Researchers have been observing an increased preference for nuclear family households in some cultures. However, where there is a strong cultural preference for shared households by families and elders multigenerational households remain common (Ruggles, 2009).

Lastly, by the time the current youngest countries in the world experience the boom in their elder populations, the oldest countries in the world will have moved beyond this stage. The current oldest countries will have either learned to cope with semipermanent labor shortages or with immigration. Whether immigration will "solve" the problem of labor shortages or will reduce the populations in the youngest countries remains to be seen.

## References

American Community Survey. (2010). *2005–2009 American community survey 5-year estimates, geographic comparison tables*. American Factfinder. http://factfinder.census.gov/servlet/GCTSubjectShowTablesServlet?_ts=311961242315. Accessed 17 December 2010.

Beale, C. L. (1975). *The revival of widespread population growth in nonmetropolitan America*. Washington, DC: Economic Research Service, U.S. Department of Agriculture. ERS-605.

Berry, E H. (2009). Comparative understanding of rural-urban migration and migrant integration: China and U.S./Mexico migration in comparison. *Proceedings of the 2009 Shanghai Forum*, Fudan University, Shanghai.

Bongaarts, J. (2004). Population aging and the rising cost of public pensions. *Population and Development Review, 30*(1), 1–23.

Brooks, T., Toney, M. B., Berry, E. H., & Lim, S. L. (2010). Aspirations of rural youth as predictors of migration. *Journal of Rural and Community Development, 5*(3), 19–36.

Brown, D. L., Glasgow, N., Kulcsar, L. J., Bolender, B. C., & Arguillas, M.-J. (2008). *Rural retirement migration*. Dordrecht: Springer.

Chapman, S. A., & Peace, S. (2008). Rurality and ageing well: 'a long time here'. In N. Keating (Ed.), *Rural ageing: A good place to grow old* (pp. 21–32). United Kingdom: Policy Press.

Cromartie, J., & Nelson, P. (2009). *Baby boom migration and its impact on rural America* (36 pp). Economic Research Report No. (ERR-79). Washington, DC: Economic Research Service, USDA.

Dyck, J. (2010). *Japan: Issues and Analysis*. Briefing Rooms. Retrieved August 2, 2010, from ERS USDA http://www.ers.usda.gov/Briefing/japan/issuesandanalysis.htm#demographic

Ebenstein, A., & Leung, S. (2010). Son preference and access to social insurance in rural China: Evidence from China's rural pension program. *Population and Development Review, 36*(1), 47–70.

Garasky, S. (2002). Where are they going? A comparison of Urban and rural youths' locational choices after leaving the parental home. *Social Science Research, 31*(3), 409–431.

Glasgow, N., & Brown, D. A. (1998). Older, rural and poor. In R. T. Coward & J. A. Krout (Eds.), *Aging in rural settings: Life circumstances & distinctive features* (pp. 187–207). Dordrecht: Springer.

Goldstein, J. R. (2010). How populations age. In R. Uhlenberg (Ed.), *International handbook of population aging* (pp. 7–18). Dordrecht: Springer.

Goll, M. (2010). *Ageing in the European Union: Where exactly? Rural areas are losing the young generation quicker than urban areas*. Eurostat. Retrieved June 10, 2010, from http://ec.europa.eu/eurostat

Goody, J. (1996). Comparing family systems in Europe and Asia: Are there different sets of rules? *Population and Development Review, 22*, 1–20.

Gratton, B., & Guttman, M. P. (2010). Emptying the nest: Older men in the United States, 1880–2000. *Population and Development Review, 36*(2), 331–356.

Greenwood, J., Seshadri, A., & Vandenbroucke, G. (2005). The baby boom and baby bust. *The American Economic Review, 95*(1), 183–207.

Harris, J. R., & Todaro, M. P. (1970). Migration, unemployment and development. *American Economic Review, 60*, 126–142.

Hosegood, V., & Timaeus, I. (2005). The impact of adult mortality on the living arrangements of older people in rural South Africa. *Ageing & Society, 25*(3), 435–444.

Jacobson, L. A., & Mather, M. (2010). U.S. economic and social trends since 2000. *Population Bulletin, 65*(1), 1–18.

Johnson, K. M. (2006). *Rural America undergoing a diversity of demographic change. Population reference bureau*. Retrieved June 4, 2010, from http://www.prb.org/Articles/2006/RuralAmericaUndergoingaDiversityofDemographicChange.aspx

Johnson, K. M., Voss, P. R., Hammer, R. B., Fuguitt, G. V., & McNiven, S. (2005). Temporal and spatial variation in age-specific net migration in the United States. *Demography, 42*, 791–812.

Jones, C. A., Parker, T. S., Ahearn, M., Mishra, A. K., & Variyam, J. N. (2009). *Health status and health care access of farm and rural populations*. ERS Report Summary Economic Research Service. Retrieved July 4, 2010, from

Kammeyer, K. C. W., & Ginn, H. (1986) *An introduction to population*. Chicago: The Dorsey Press.

Kirschner, A., Berry, E. H., & Glasgow, N. (2006). The changing faces of rural America. In W. A. Kandel & D. L. Brown (Eds.), *Population change and rural society* (pp. 53–74). Dordrecht, Netherlands: Springer.

Knodel, J., Kespichayawattana, J., Saengtienchai, C., & Wiwatwanich, S. (2010). How left behind are rural parents of migrant children? Evidence from Thailand. *Ageing and Society, 30*(5), 811–841.

Kusmin, L. D. (2006). *Rural America at a Glance, 2006 Edition*. Economic Information Bulletin Number 18. Washington, DC: Economic Research Service, U.S.D.A.

Kusmin, L. (2009). *Rural America at a Glance, 2009*. Economic Information Bulletin No. (EIB-59). Washington, DC: Economic Research Service, U.S.D.A

Litwak, E., & Longino, C. (1987). Migration patterns among the elderly: A developmental perspective. *The Gerontologist, 27*, 266–272.

Lutz, W., Sanderson, W., & Scherbov, S. (2008). The coming acceleration of global population ageing. *Nature, 451*(8), 716–719.

Mabogunje, A. L. (1970). Systems approach to a theory of rural-urban migration. *Geographical Analysis, 2*(1), 1–18.

Marquart-Pyatt, S. T., & Petrzelka, P. (2008). Trust, the democratic process and involvement in a rural community. *Rural Sociology, 73*(2), 250–274.

McGranahan, D. A. (1999). *Natural Amenities Drive Rural Population Change*. Agricultural Economic Report No. (AER781). Washington, DC: Economic Research Service, U.S.D.A.

Murphy, L. (2008). AIDS and kitchen gardens: Insights from a village in Western Kenya. *Population & Environment, 29*(3–5), 133–161.

Onishi, N. (2008, August 15). As its work force ages, Japan needs and fears Chinese labor. *The New York Times*, p. A5.

Petersen, W. (1975) *Population* (3rd ed.). New York: MacMillan.

Population Reference Bureau. (2006). *2006 world population data sheet*. Washington, DC: Population Reference Bureau.

Population Reference Bureau. (2010). *2010 world population data sheet*. Washington, DC: Population Reference Bureau.

Povoledo, E. (2008). Italy struggles with immigration and aging. *New York Times*. Retrieved July 22, 2010, from http://www.nytimes.com/2008/06/22/world/europe/22iht-migrants.1.13879021.html?_r=1&ref=elisabettapovoledo&pagewanted=all

Raymer, J., Abel, G., & Smith, P. W. F. (2007). Combining census and registration data to estimate detailed elderly migration flows in England and Wales. *Journal of the Royal Statistical Society: Series A, 170*(4), 891–908.

Ruggles, S. (2009). Reconsidering the northwest European Family System: Living arrangements of the aged in comparative historical perspective. *Population and Development Review, 35*(2), 249–273.

Sando, R. (1986). Doing the work of two generations: The impact of out-migration on the elderly in rural Taiwan. *Journal of Cross-Cultural Gerontology, 1*(2), 163–175.

Siegel, J. (1980). On the demography of aging. *Demography, 17*(4), 345–364.

Tabuchi, H. (2009, April 23). Japan Pays Foreign Workers to go Home. *The New York Times*, p. B1.

Thompson, W. S. (1929). Population. *American Journal of Sociology, 34*(6), 959–975.

United Nations. (2007). *World population aging 2009*. Department of Economic and Social Affairs Population Division. New York: United Nations.

United Nations. (2009). *World population prospects: The 2008 revision*. Population Newsletter. Department of Economic and Social Affairs Population Division. New York: United Nations.

U.S. Census Bureau. (1975). *Historical statistics of the United States: Colonial times to 1970*. Washington, DC: U.S. Government Printing Office.

U.S. Census Bureau. (2007). *Statistical abstract of the United States: 2008* (127th ed.). Washington, DC: U.S. Census Bureau.

Van De Walle, E., & Knodel, J. (1980). Europe's fertility transition: New evidence and lessons for today's developing world. *Population Bulletin, 34*(6), 3–44.

Vaupel, J. W. (2010). Biodemography of human ageing. *Nature*. doi: 10.1038/nature08984. Published online 24 March 2010.

Vias, A., & Nelson, P. (2006). Changing livelihoods in rural America. In W. A. Kandel & D. L. Brown (Eds.), *Population change and rural society* (pp. 75–102). Dordrecht: Springer.

Zimmer, Z., & Korinek, K. (2010). Shifting coresidence near the end of life: Comparing decedents and survivors of a follow-up study in China. *Demography, 47*(3), 537–554.

# Europe's Rural Demography

Anthony Champion

Europe was the cradle of mass urbanization, even if it was the Middle East that saw humankind taking the first significant steps towards urban life. In particular, England was the first country to record more than half its population living in urban agglomerations, this being achieved by the time of its 1851 census – the position reached by the whole world only in 2008 according to the latest official estimates (UN, 2010). Conversely, today Europe is by no means the least rural continent: its 27% of population classified as rural in 2010 is higher than for three other major regions of the world (see next section). Moreover, according to Antrop's (2004) tracing of European urbanization from 500 BC, even now built-over land comprises barely 1% of the continent's land surface. Even the sources which classify territory on the basis of larger statistical units than individual parcels of land confirm the predominance of rural areas, though varying considerably on what they give as the size of the rural share (cf. European Union, 2009; Schmied, 2005a). While the rural population share continues to decline in Europe as across the world, this continent still contains a substantial body of population and especially territory that is deemed rural.

Before proceeding further, it is important to recognize that the statistical analysis of Europe's rural demography is anything but straightforward. In particular, there are two sets of definitional issues upon which there seems to be little agreement between sources, helping to account for the differences in the size and importance of the "rural" just alluded to. The first of these is what comprises Europe, notably its eastern boundary, with the definition always based on whole countries for statistical convenience. The most international of official sources, the UN, follows the conventional approach of using the Ural Mountains, but this means including the whole of the Russian Federation amongst its 48 European countries. By contrast, the continent's main official sources revolve around the European Union through its agency, Eurostat. While the latter's coverage has grown substantially over the years as the EU has accepted more member states (with its current 27 including Cyprus which the UN regards as part of Asia), besides Russia it also excludes the former Soviet Union republics of Belarus, Moldova and Ukraine, as well as Albania, much of former Yugoslavia, Iceland, Norway and Switzerland, plus a number of very small states such as Andorra, Liechtenstein and Monaco. The other, equally fundamental, definitional issue concerns how to distinguish rural from urban areas: each country has developed its own criteria and, indeed, few if any national statistical agencies apply the same definition for all purposes. For example, more than 30 different definitions are used by the UK's government departments alone, with reports of similar complexity elsewhere (see, for instance, Champion & Brown, 2012; Champion & Hugo, 2004).

The following account of Europe's rural demography cuts through this statistical morass in two ways. One is that, when statistics on the rural population are presented, the text specifies what are their national coverage and the territorial classification on which they are based. The other is a selective focus on the

A. Champion (✉)
School of Geography, Politics and Sociology, University of Newcastle, Newcastle upon Tyne NE1 7RU, UK
e-mail: tony.champion@newcastle.ac.uk

principal dimensions of rural population change across Europe, with these being exemplified by case studies where pan-European statistics do not exist. The first of these dimensions, covered in the next section, uses UN data to document Europe's declining share of the world's rural (and total) population and highlight the substantial range in rural population shares between the its four regions and 48 countries. The following section uses both floating and fixed definitions of rural areas to calculate rates of overall population change for rural Europe, with the latter approach in particular demonstrating the important influences on these rates of the degree of remoteness from large cities and whether in the east or west of the continent. The direct drivers of these patterns are then probed in the next section, which breaks them down into their change components. This shows that, while natural-change differences help to explain the weakness associated with both remoteness and a post-socialist context, it is migration that forms the dominant driver of regional diversity across rural Europe, both directly and also through the way in which its impact on regional age structures affects the numbers of births and deaths. The following two sections therefore deal respectively with rural out-migration, with particular attention being given to the exodus of young adults, and rural in-migration, including the contribution of retirees, the non-elderly and international labour migrants. The concluding section discusses the policy implications and suggests an agenda for future research.

## Rural Europe in the Wider World

The biennial editions of the United Nations' *World Urbanization Prospects* provide the best way of setting rural Europe in its world context, not least because of this source's global coverage and the efforts which it makes to achieve international consistency through using an agglomeration-based definition for distinguishing urban from rural areas. According to its most recent "Revision" (UN, 2010), Europe's rural population totalled 201 million in 2009, giving it a 5.9% share of the world's rural total of 3.4 billion. This compares with the continent's 15.5% share of the global urban population (531 million out of 3.4 billion) and its 10.7% share of the planet's total population. Europe's share of the world's rural population has been falling steadily, down from 14.8% in 1950 to 9.2% in 1975, but the pace of its shrinkage has been slowing as its remaining rural numbers have shrunk and the world's rural population growth rate has slowed. It is projected that between 2009 and 2050 the continent's share will have fallen by just 2 further percentage points to 3.8%. At that point, its rural population will have declined to 106 million out of a world total that by then is down to under 2.9 million.

On this basis, though Europe is still among the least rural parts of the world, the distinctive position which it inherited from the early onset of mass urbanization has steadily been eroded by the progress of the urban transition across the rest of the world. By 1950, less than half – 48.7% – of the population of Europe (as defined on the basis of the UN's current 48 countries) remained rural, but already Northern America and Australia/New Zealand had lower proportions. Europe's rural proportion continued to fall steadily, but in the 1970s its pace of decline slowed significantly amidst fairly widespread observations of "counter-urbanization" tendencies (Champion, 1989). By 1990 the overall rural level for Latin America and the Caribbean had also fallen below Europe's, meaning that by then all three major elements of the New World had become more urbanized than the main source region of their settlers. In the past two decades, despite some signs of an urban resurgence in Europe (Turok & Mykhnenko, 2007), its 27% rural proportion in 2010 – while still less than half the 58–60% levels of Africa and Asia – is significantly above the 18–20% levels of the two Americas and especially the 11% of Australia/New Zealand.

At the same time, there is considerable variation within the continent. In terms of the UN's four regional divisions of Europe, there remains a major contrast between the South and East on the one hand and the North and West on the other (UN, 2010). In 1950 the latter's 30 and 36% rural proportions, respectively, were well below those of 55 and 60% for the South and East. The gap has narrowed considerably over the last six decades, but still in 2010 the 31–32% rural levels of the South and East were half as much again as the 20–21% levels of the North and West. National differences are much larger, as would be expected, and have not narrowed quite as much over time. Focusing on just the 35 larger countries (those with at least 1 million people in 2010), the range of rural proportions fell from almost 80 percentage points in 1950 – between Belgium's 8.5% and Bosnia's 86% – to around 50 in 2010, ranging from Belgium's 2.6% to Moldova's 53%. Even though part of the diversity apparent from the published statistics will – despite the UN's best efforts – no doubt be due to the lack of consistency in urban/rural definition between countries, substantial differences still exist in the magnitude of rural across Europe.

## Rural Population Change in Europe

It is in relation to measuring changes over time in the size of Europe's rural populations that the definitional and methodological issues cause most difficulty. Besides the options concerning the continent's coverage and the way in which "rural" is defined (see above), the picture resulting from such calculations will differ according to whether the territorial delineation is fixed or allowed to vary. In particular, a major contrast can be expected between approaches based on the continuous updating of the territory that is left after urban agglomerations are identified, on the one hand, and the use of statistical regions that are classified on socio-economic criteria and held constant for the time period under analysis, on the other.

The former approach is well exemplified by the UN's estimates of urban and rural population numbers, which in their latest Revision (UN, 2010) run from 1950 with projections through to 2050. Using essentially a floating definition of urban and rural settlement, this source shows that Europe's rural population has not only been declining as a proportion of the continent's total population but has also been contracting in absolute terms, down by an average of 0.5% a year in both 1950–1975 and 1975–2010. Moreover, such a population decline is found for virtually all of its 48 countries, even those which at times have been reported as experiencing counterurbanization (see below). This is because it is not only natural change and migration than can produce change in the rural total but also the reclassification of territory between rural and urban. Thus, if a settlement starting with a population below the urban threshold grows steadily as a result of net in-migration from the surrounding countryside or an influx from a larger city, it will eventually be reclassified as urban.

By contrast, the use of a fixed territorial classification yields a much more varied picture of population change – one of growth as well as decline – across rural Europe. A number of studies primarily focused on the current 27 member states of the EU reveal two principal dimensions of variability, namely remoteness from large cities and West versus East. In relation to the former, Dijkstra and Poelman (2008) reveal that, while the "predominantly rural" regions of the EU-27 hardly changed their overall number of residents between 1995 and 2004, those classified as "close to a city" grew by an average of 0.10% a year, whereas the remoter ones averaged –0.18%. A follow-up study by Johansson and Kupiszewski (2009), which covered 31 countries (the EU27 plus Liechtenstein, Norway, Switzerland and Turkey), revealed a similar contraction, though using the alternative metric shown in Fig. 7.1. Whereas 56% of the 2000 population of the regions classified as "Predominantly Rural, close to a City" (PRC) were living in regions which were growing in population (types 1–3 in the bolder shading), the figure was only 44% for the "Predominantly Rural, Remote" (PRR) regions. Accessibility to a city also yielded a premium for the Intermediate Regions, but even the level for this IRC category fell short of the 83% for the Predominantly Urban (PU) regions (Fig. 7.1).

Bengs and Schmidt-Thomé (2006), analyzing population change for 1995–1999, found that the remoteness factor applies much more to the 15 pre-2004 EU members and Switzerland than to the more recently joining countries of central and eastern Europe plus Cyprus and Malta (the 12 Accession states or "A12"). For the former's regions with a low degree of urban influence, there was a regular decline in growth rate with increasing remoteness (as measured by an index of human intervention based on the artificial, agricultural and residual shares of land cover). For the A12, by contrast, only the regions with a medium level of remoteness grew over this period, while those with high and low levels both recorded substantial depopulation. Along with the results for the A12's more urbanized regions indicating population growth for the regions of medium and high remoteness but sharp loss for the most built-up regions, this was interpreted as evidence of "a kind of suburbanization" prevailing in eastern Europe at this time (Bengs & Schmidt-Thomé, 2006, 173).

Conversely, a regionally disaggregated study of population change between 2001 and 2005 (ESPON, 2008) reveals considerable variety among the remoter regions of Europe. Indeed, overall there was almost

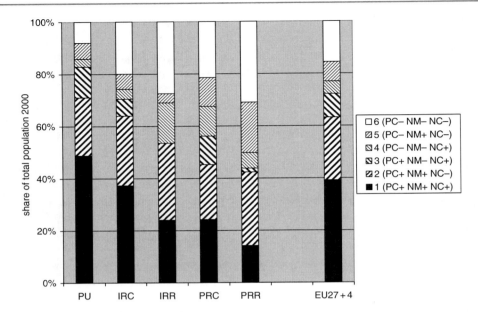

**Fig. 7.1** The distribution of the 2000 population across six demographic types for an urban-rural classification of regions in 31 European countries
*Source*: based on Johansson and Kupiszewski (2009), Table 3.3. See text for country coverage and key to the urban-rural categories.

exactly a 50:50 split between the remote regions that grew over this period and those that saw population shrinkage. Again, however, a broad regional contrast was evident. Almost all the remote regions in the three Baltic states and the other eastern members of the A12 experienced depopulation over this period, but so also did the large remote regions of Finland and Sweden and parts of Greece, suggesting a real geographical divide rather than just a political one. Meanwhile, the growing ones were to be found mainly in the western half of Europe, notably Spain, France, Ireland, the UK and Norway, but excluding Portugal where its own remoter eastern regions registered "negative demographic development" (ESPON, 2008, 12).

A case study of Britain, based on a finer-grained set of statistical areas, confirms the penalty imposed by remoteness as well as the existence of positive demographic development in rural territory (Champion & Brown, 2012). Local government districts classified as "rural extremes" averaged 0.57% growth a year between 2001 and 2008, which was below the 0.71% annual rate for the main agricultural districts which was again lower than the 0.81% rate for the districts fringing the main urban areas. Impressively, even the rate for the most remote category outpaced urban Britain's overall rate of 0.50% a year, as had also been the pattern in the previous two decades. This suggests a continuation of urban-to-rural population movement or "counter-urbanization" in this country.

## Direct Drivers of Population Change Across Rural Europe

In explaining patterns and trends in population change, the conventional approach is to first disaggregate them into the main components of change and only then to seek component-specific understanding. The most fundamental distinction is between natural change and migration, with the former comprising the difference between births and deaths and the most important distinction in the latter being between within-country and international migration, though each of these can be further divided up into their gross inflows and outflows for particular types of area as well as into particular types of migration stream like students, labour migrants, retirees and refugees.

By way of an example, Champion and Brown (2012) have applied this approach to England for 2001–2008 (see Chapter 4 in this volume). Their results show that the natural change component plays almost no part in the strong population growth recorded over this period by the more rural parts. Over these 7 years, rural England's surplus of births

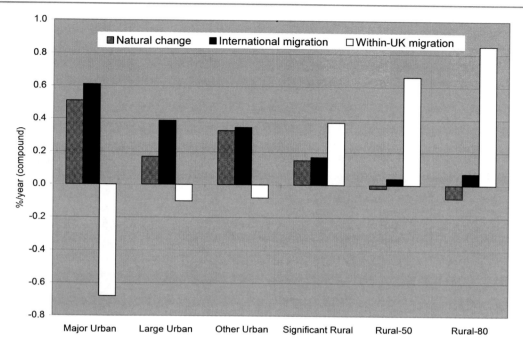

**Fig. 7.2** Components of the annual rate of population change, 2001–2008, for an urban-rural classification of England's local government districts
*Source*: based on Champion and Brown (2012), Table 3.2.

over deaths amounted only 28,000, compared with an urban surplus of 863,000. Moreover, as shown in Fig. 7.2, the rural surplus was confined to areas fringing urban England, as denoted by the "Significant Rural" category of districts, with natural decrease occurring in the two most rural types. As regards the migration component, rural England has been gaining from both an urban exodus and from net immigration from overseas, but while the latter has become more important in recent years, it can be seen that the within-UK population movement remains the primary driver. Between 2001 and 2008 rural England made a net gain of over 780,000 residents from within-UK migration compared to one of just 123,000 from international migration. Moreover, as shown in Fig. 7.2, the former exhibits a very clear "counter-urbanization" pattern: all three types of urban districts record net losses to the rest of the UK and each of the three rural district types gains, with the rate of gain being strongest for the most rural type.

No similar analysis by urban-rural type appears to have been undertaken for Europe as a whole. The nearest equivalent appears to be the study of 31 countries by Johansson and Kupiszewski (2009) which, as already mentioned, used a five-fold classification of regions based on degrees of rurality and remoteness. Although this did not give actual change rates, it differentiated regions according to whether their overall population growth, natural change and migration balance were positive or negative. As is clear from Fig. 7.1 above, it is the remote rural regions (PRR type) that appear the weakest: compared to the other four types, these have the smallest population share living in regions with positive change in both migration and natural change (black shading) and the largest share in regions with negative change on both components (white shading), whilst also having the largest shares living in other regions registering natural decrease, whether associated with migration gains or losses (the two categories shown with upward line shading). In all, 78% of the PRR's population was living in regions experiencing natural decrease, compared with 53% for the more accessible rural regions (PRC), 60% for the remote intermediate regions (IRR), 52% for the more accessible intermediates (IRC) and 36% for the predominantly urban (PU) regions. Unfortunately, the international and internal components of the migration balance are not separated out in this analysis, but it is notable that 62% of the PRR population was living in regions with a positive overall balance, exceeding the

57% levels found for both the PRC and IRR regions. This is suggestive of a degree of counter-urban migration within countries, given that the higher proportions for the IRC and PU types (70 and 77% respectively) are no doubt swelled by international migration, as in the UK example.

One other report (European Union, 2009) is helpful in providing country-level detail on the migration component for most of the EU-27 (omitting Denmark and the UK due to data problems), though it uses the original OECD classification of regions (i.e. without the remoteness dimension) and the NUTS2 regions rather than the finer-grained NUTS3 ones. Particularly revealing is the comparison between the aggregates for the "old" EU and the 12 accession (A12) states. Whereas for the EU as a whole the net migration rate in 2005 was highest for the PU regions and fell progressively for the IR and PR ones, the A12 countries were found to be driving this "urbanization" pattern, with a net migratory loss of 1.3 per 1,000 for their PR regions and gains of 0.6 and 2.6 for their IR and PU regions, respectively. By contrast, for the 13 "old" members included in the study, the strongest migratory gain was for their PR regions. In addition, the study's data on change since 2000 suggests that this contrast has emerged only recently: in the A12 all three types of region had been experiencing fairly uniform rates of net migration loss 5 years before, and in the "old" EU it was the PR and IR regions that recorded the biggest acceleration in net in-migration rates between 2000 and 2005.

This apparent emergence of demographic differences between the eastern and western parts of the continent since the start of the 21st century no doubt reflects the economic challenges posed for the A12 countries by the opening of their borders. The resultant increase in international competition has been accompanied not only by reduced natural increase (mainly through a fall in fertility but in some cases also due to rising mortality rates) but, even more importantly, also by major changes in migration flows (including increased rural-to-urban migration within these states and especially an unprecedentedly large exodus to the rest of the EU from both their rural and urban areas). The "old EU" and the other countries in western Europe have not only been on the receiving end of this post-socialist diaspora, but have also been experiencing high levels of net immigration from the rest of the world. As described in more detail below, the latter has taken many forms including labour migrants, students, spouses or other forms of family reunification, refugees and asylum-seekers. Nevertheless, both these and the A12 migrants have tended to be quite similar in at least one respect, with the vast majority of arrivals being 20–40 years old. As a result, along with migration providing a direct population gain for western Europe, this has also generated something of a boost to natural increase rates there. Although urban areas tend to predominate as destinations of these inflows to western Europe, recent immigration seems to have impacted more on rural areas than was the case previously, with especially important implications for those more peripheral and remote parts of countries which have traditionally experienced youth out-migration to the cities and have seen their natural change become negative.

## Rural Out-Migration

Although the above-mentioned existence of rural regions with negative migration balances provides the most obvious evidence of rural out-migration in Europe, the latter is a process that affects all areas in gross terms to some extent and is one that has been happening for decades in most countries. Even where this exodus is more than offset by the number of in-migrants, it has a significant effect on rural demography because the out-migrants normally differ from in-migrants in a number of respects, most notably age. Across Europe, as indeed in most countries of the more and less developed world alike, the outflow is dominated by young adults seeking further education, more and better jobs, and/or easier access to the types of services that offer a higher quality of life. Besides these, older working-age people can form a sizeable proportion of the exodus from rural areas undergoing a rapid contraction in traditional sources of employment, while the elderly may also participate as they become increasingly infirm and make "defensive" moves towards less remote locations. Some of this movement takes place over relatively short distances, as people move from the countryside into local towns, but much, especially among the adult youth, involves longer-distance moves to the most urbanized regions and their large cities.

The UK provides a good example in that, despite overall net migration gains for almost all its rural districts, most of them also experience a net exodus of young adults (Champion & Brown, 2012). The rate of migration loss is greatest for 15–19 year olds, but is nearly as high for the 20–24s, with the most remote areas being the worst affected. According to a study of England (Champion & Shepherd, 2006), it is the smallest settlements of the most sparsely populated areas that suffer most, with a net loss of around 10% a year for both these age groups in 2000–2001. A case study of the Scottish Borders (Jones & Jamieson, 1997) found that only one in three of those in school at age 16 were still living in the survey area three years later. Moving for educational purposes is a major driver of this process, boosted by the official goal of raising higher-education participation rates to 50%. For instance, in a case study set in the Scottish Western Isles, almost three-quarters of out-migrants were found to have moved in order to continue education (Stockdale, 2002). Meanwhile, among those not going beyond secondary schooling, departures for employment reasons dominate, either because of the total lack of jobs or in search of work with better pay or career prospects (Green, 2005), but housing and social reasons have also been reported as rural workers move to nearby towns to access affordable accommodation or to escape the claustrophobic atmosphere of village life (Houston & Lever, 2001; Rugg & Jones, 1999; Stockdale, 2002).

Similar conclusions are presented by Bien, Lappe, and Rathgeber (2005) in their summary of the results of an EU-funded study of the living conditions of young rural people in five countries. In Finland the experience of many young people is that the countryside does not have much to offer, so they want to leave, the girls even more so than boys. For two thirds of the young people surveyed, the main drawbacks were the restricted job opportunities and the comparatively low wages. In all, 56% gave better job opportunities in cities as the reason for wanting to move there, while 38% mentioned educational objectives and 29% better entertainment. In northern Sweden young people face higher than average unemployment rates and the streamlining of social services, while in Calabria in southern Italy the unemployment rate for men aged under 25 was 47% and was even higher for young women, at 66%. Young adults in eastern Germany have been facing particular problems due to the painful transition from the centrally planned economy of the former GDR, with economic restructuring reducing the value of their qualifications, lowering their pay and destabilizing their job prospects. In Estonia, too, objective as well as subjective data clearly show that material conditions are significantly better in urban than rural areas, with income per household 20–30% lower in the latter. Indeed the youth exodus is so ingrained across rural Europe that a "culture" of out-migration appears to exist, such that not to engage in it may be considered a sign of underachievement (Horváth, 2008; Stockdale, 2004).

The demographic impact of the youth exodus is substantial and takes at least three forms. There is not only the direct loss of the people involved but also the fact that the babies that they would otherwise have produced in rural areas are now born in urban areas. Along with the fact that the young adults who remain in Europe's rural areas no longer have much higher fertility rates than urban dwellers, this helps to explain why so much of rural Europe is now experiencing natural decrease (see above). Also fuelling the latter is the indirect effect of both these impacts in contributing to the process of rural population ageing and the resultant raising of crude death rates. Although there is some evidence of the out-migrants returning to their home area, the total numbers tend to be relatively small. Moreover, those who do return are not normally moving back at the most productive stages of their working lives because of the shortage of more skilled jobs in the countryside, but only later in their lives when their help is needed to support elderly relatives or they inherit family property, by which stage they may well be "empty nester" households because of their own children having already left home. Indeed, the return process may serve more to accelerate than abate the rural ageing impact.

## Rural In-Migration

Although all rural areas can be expected to experience some degree of gross in-migration even if only through people moving quite locally between one rural area and another close by, the focus here is on net migration streams that increase the total population of the rural parts of a whole country or larger continental region. On this basis, there are two main categories of population movement, both of relatively recent origin. One of these is urban-to-rural migration, sometimes referred to as "urban exodus" or "counter-urbanization", which takes place mainly within countries and has been the subject of a great deal of European research since the 1970s. Secondly is international migration which has traditionally been a cause of rural depopulation in Europe (see above) but in the last couple of decades has become a significant source of rural growth in some parts of the continent.

The "urban exodus" phenomenon has a long history, but it has varied considerably in its nature and scale over time (Champion, 1989, 2001a). In the pre-industrial era it was a seasonal or periodic feature of life for the governing class of wealthy land owners who escaped from their town houses in the heat of the summer or when epidemics threatened. More recently this behaviour was paralleled by the building of rural mansions by successful industrialists and entrepreneurs who similarly wished to avoid the squalor and disease of the fast-growing towns but also in some cases wanted to be accepted into the social world of the aristocracy and rural gentry. The main part of the exodus at this time, however, took the form of suburban extensions which then spread even wider with the improvements in rail and motorized transport. Not until the 1970s was it recognized – initially in the USA (Beale, 1975; Berry, 1976) but soon afterwards also in Europe and elsewhere (e.g. Vining & Kontuly, 1978; Fielding, 1982) – that the exodus was causing a population turnaround in rural areas which were relatively remote from cities. This led to much speculation about the dawning of a new "post-industrial" pattern of population distribution in which the dominant process would be "counter-urbanization" rather than urbanization, this being underpinned by transport and other infrastructural improvements allowing the dispersal of economic activity to lower-cost locations and permitting more people to exercise their preference for a higher quality and lower cost of living than the metropolitan norm (Champion, 1989).

Subsequent research has led to the "backdating" of the counter-urbanization tendency (e.g. Champion, 2003; Kontuly & Geyer, 2003). Indeed, quite soon it became clear that the process had already been pioneered by retired urbanites that no longer had any need for easy access to metropolitan jobs and could generate spare capital by selling their family home and buying a smaller property in a low-price rural area. Although seaside and spa towns were the main beneficiaries of retirement migration in the early days, rural destinations had become increasingly popular by the 1960s, partly reflecting a shift in the location of holiday-making activity earlier in their lives. However, the main change in the 1970s was the adoption of this migration behaviour by a much wider section of society. The latter comprised not only people in their immediate pre-retirement phase but also people in their 30s and 40s, including those setting up businesses themselves as well as workers taking advantage of a more general urban-rural shift in economic activity (Bosworth, 2008). Moreover, while research has tended to stress the prosperity of the rural incomers, by no means all of them can be considered "gentrifiers", even in the UK (Stockdale, 2010). Some are "reluctant commuters" having to endure long commutes in order to access cheaper housing (Gkartzios & Scott, 2010), while others are returners, going back home to care for ageing parents or to fall back on family support during an economic downturn (Brown, Kulcsár, Kulcsár, & Obadovics, 2005; Jauhiainen, 2009; Milbourne, 2007; Ni Laoire, 2007). Also among their number are people on portable unemployment benefits and those seeking an alternative "back to the land" lifestyle (Halfacree, 1994; Schmied, 2005b).

Yet, as seen earlier, the spatial impact of this urban exodus has so far turned out to be uneven. The attraction of the "rural idyll" appears longest established and most powerful in western Europe, being particularly well documented in the UK, Ireland and the Netherlands (Cawley, 2005; Champion, Atkins, Coombes, & Fotheringham, 1998; Champion, 2001b; Dam, Heins, & Elberson, 2002; Heins, 2004; Mahon, 2007; Matthews, Taylor, Sherwood, Tucker, & Limb, 2000). In parts of Europe, perhaps most commonly in the Nordic countries but also elsewhere including Ireland (Norris & Winston, 2009), a significant part of this pull has been in the form of seasonal movement and second-home ownership (Gallent, Mace, & Tewdewr-Jones, 2005). Where this is the case, however, it would probably not have been reflected in the population statistics as these usually refer to usual residents only. Conversely, second homes and holiday lettings can impact indirectly on rural demography, if they cause the displacement of the less wealthy through the pressure they place on the local housing stock or if secondary residences eventually become their owners' principal homes.

The emergence of international migration as a contributor to population growth in rural Europe is of even more recent origin than counter-urbanization, with rural areas having traditionally been a large net supplier of migrants to the New World and with the international movement of "guest workers" within Europe in the third quarter of the 20th century being dominated by moves from the more rural parts of Mediterranean Europe to city-based manufacturing jobs in France and Germany. Much of this between-country movement follows an urban-to-rural pattern (Halfacree, 2008). Just as for within-country counter-urbanization, this was pioneered by retirees. Indeed, this was very much the same phenomenon that could occur within the boundaries of the USA between "snow-belt" and "sun-belt", and it was facilitated by the creation and expansion of the EU and the associated agreements on health-care rights and the portability of pensions and welfare benefits across national borders. There is now a rich literature on the nature and spatial incidence of this international retirement migration, along with that on the sun-bound tourism that formed the precursor of this more permanent settlement (see, for instance, Casado-Diaz, Kaiser, & Warnes, 2004; Hoggart & Buller, 1995; King, Warnes, & Williams, 2000; Niedomysl, 2005; Warnes & Williams, 2006; Williams & Hall, 2001; Williams, King, & Warnes, 1997). Moreover, the destinations continue to evolve, notably with central and eastern parts of Europe becoming more popular as costs have increased in the Mediterranean zone and cheaper options have opened up in the new Accession states (see, for instance, Illes, 2005, on Hungary).

As with within-country counter-urbanization, this international rural influx has also come to include people of working age. One of the best documented examples is that of UK nationals settling in rural France and starting businesses (Buller & Hoggart, 1994; Hoggart & Buller, 1995). Such "enterprising expatriates" have also been identified more widely across rural southern Europe (Stone & Stubbs, 2007) and it can be expected that this process will now be spreading into central and east European countries with their newly available opportunities and cheaper operating costs. Numerically, however, the majority of this new flow is in the form of people taking jobs with individual rural employers or engaged by agencies used by them. Since the late 1980s non-European migrants have been playing an increasingly important role in rural southern Europe, including the case of Africans working in Spanish agriculture (Hoggart & Mendoza, 1999). At the same time, there have been substantial movements of workers within Europe. In particular, the last two decades have seen a substantial flow of Albanians to Greece and Italy to work on the land (Kasimis, 2008; Labrianidis & Sykas, 2009). Fonseca (2008) documents the new waves of immigration to the small towns and rural areas of Portugal from Moldova, Romania, Russia and the Ukraine. The biggest single movement in recent years has been the westward movement of labour migrants from the EU Accession countries, most notably to the three countries that did not impose transition arrangements in 2004: the UK, Ireland and Sweden. Although the majority of these workers were destined for the cities, rural regions attracted a much higher proportion than has been the norm for immigration streams (Cawley, 2010; Coombes, Champion, & Raybould, 2007; Doyle, Hughes, & Wadensjo, 2006; Gilpin, Henty, Lemos, Portes, & Bullen, 2006).

## Rural Population Impacts

This review has shown that, despite being the hearth of mass industrialization and urbanization, Europe still possesses a substantial rural population, irrespective of whether the latter is measured on the basis of non-urban settlements or in terms of the characteristics of larger statistical areas. Indeed, on the latter definition, there are many parts of rural Europe that have been gaining population in recent years, notably areas in the western half of the continent and areas situated closer to major metropolitan centres but also with many exceptions that produce a rather complex mosaic of growth and decline. In its turn, this testifies to the variety of drivers that are contributing to rural population change across Europe, making it difficult to gauge their separate impacts and anticipate what the future may have in store.

It is migration that is the major reason for the differences in rural population change both between areas and over time, not just directly but also through its impact on natural change. In fact, though the evidence base is sketchy, it would seem that variations in family size and life expectancy are generally much smaller than in the past, both in urban-rural differentials and those within rural Europe. Much more important now in determining whether or not births exceed deaths in an area is the composition of its population, notably by age. In particular, natural decrease is associated with areas experiencing the greatest exodus of youth as well as those that have proved the most attractive destinations for retirement migration. The counter-urbanization process has increasingly been involving working-age people, even to more remote rural areas, but many have had their children before moving and will eventually age in place there after these have moved back to urban areas for educational, work or other reasons. International labour migration, in taking on a less urban-focused pattern in recent years, has also contributed to a rejuvenation of many rural areas in terms of both numbers and age structure, as well as boosting birth rates in some cases and introducing new cultural and sometimes also ethnic and racial elements to Europe's countryside. In some cases, the arrival of labour migrants has allowed farmers to continue in business rather than having to abandon the countryside (see, for instance, Kasimis, 2008; Labrianidis & Sykas, 2009; TUC, 2004). Conversely, this labour migration can be quite transient, with studies showing that many soon return to their home countries or else move on to the cities in their destination country in search of better-paid and more skilled work (see, for instance, Hierro & Maza, 2010).

At the same time, to some extent these migration-induced changes can be seen as merely accentuating changes in Europe's rural demography that have already been occurring as a result of more general societal transformations. In particular, the term "second demographic transition" was coined specifically with respect to population trends in Europe, which took off in its northern and western countries in the 1960s and have subsequently spread right across the continent and beyond (European Commission, 2007; Lesthaeghe, 2010). Although some of its main features have been most pronounced in more urban areas, such as lone parenting and ethnic diversification, others have been more widespread and indeed rural Europe is leading the way in population ageing (Davoudi, Wishardt, & Strange, 2010; Scharf, Wenger, Thissen, & Burholt, 2005). This is very clear in England, where for the most rural district type it is projected that by 2028 those aged 50 years and over will account for almost 50% of the population, compared to just under 40% in 2003 and compared to a 2028 projection of just 35% for the major cities (Champion & Shepherd, 2006). Similarly, across Europe, the ESPON (2008) baseline scenario's projection for 2030 shows a median age of around 50 or more for substantial swathes of the more rural parts of Europe, most notably southern Portugal, northern Spain, Sardinia, Corsica, northern Italy and eastern Finland. Longer-term projections to 2050 by DEMIFER (2010) point to the central and eastern regions of Europe as facing the steepest rises in old-age and very-old-age dependency ratios, irrespective of which of its four scenarios is used. Along with the ageing of the farming population, these demographic developments suggest that challenging times lie ahead for many parts of rural Europe.

In terms of policy interventions, it is important that these recognize the sheer diversity of situations that exists across rural Europe. Johansson and Kupiszewski's (2009) discussion of policy options revolves around the 6-fold typology of demographic types shown in Fig. 7.1. In effect, they argue for the conventional approach of "triage". The type 1 regions of rural Europe, namely those gaining population from both natural increase and migration, "do not require any policy intervention" because "their demographic future is sustainable" (p. 37). At the other extreme, the type 6 regions with natural decrease and net out-migration "should not be targeted with demographic policy measures" as "such support will not be economic", though these regions will continue to need the funding of social services while there are people still living there (p. 38). Finally, "the main battlefield in terms of policy measures should be the regions in between with a mixture of positive and negative components" (p. 38). For types 2 and 5 with natural decrease, measures should be adopted to support families as well as increase job availability for women, while quite similarly job generation and improved access to services are seen as the key to reducing the net migration losses of types 3 and 4.

Conversely, the bluntness of this assessment, especially in relation to the type 6 regions, is somewhat at odds with the more nuanced and politically sensitive stance of the EU and national governments. As laid out by the European Commission (2008), building on principles set out in the Lisbon and Gothenburg Agendas and the framework for Territorial Cohesion enshrined in the Treaty of Lisbon, this involves reducing spatial economic differences and pursuing balanced regional development through enabling all regions to develop to their full potential and "turning territorial diversity into strength" (the report's subtitle). It is to be achieved by introducing new themes of policy action, new sets of relationships binding EU territories at different levels and new forms of cooperation, coordination and partnership. The most important areas for intervention are those with the largest budgets, namely Cohesion Policy and the EU Rural Development Policy, but others with significant territorial impact should not be neglected, including Transport Policy, the Sustainable Development Strategy, Integrated Maritime Policy, the Environmental Action Programme, Research and Innovation Policy, Neighbourhood Policy, Cultural Policy, Employment and Social Affairs Policy and – last but not least though not explicitly mentioned in the Territorial Agenda – Pillar 1 of the Common Agricultural Policy. Through all these mechanisms the key priorities are to overcome the sectoral bias and associated silo mentality of these thematic programmes and instead achieve a holistic territorially based approach, particularly one based on the recognition of the interdependence between rural and urban areas at regional and local levels. Two years on, however, in an age of economic recession and public-sector deficits, there must be some uncertainty about how enthusiastically these plans for rebalancing rural Europe can be pursued.

Finally, both the scale of the challenge and the variety of potential interventions impose the need for a good knowledge of the dimensions and dynamics of Europe's rural demography. The successive programmes run by ESPON and all the other studies documented in this review (restricted though it is to those published in English) have significantly increased our understanding, but a substantial research agenda remains. Given how much change seems to have occurred over the past decade, most notably arising from EU expansion, one fundamental priority is the fuller and more consistent monitoring and analysis of population trends across Europe, allied to the release of more data specifically on rural areas. In this context, immediate attention needs to be given to the differential spatial impacts of recession since 2008 on both the market economy and government spending. Already, there is at least anecdotal evidence of a slowdown in migration flows and the returning home of A12 labour migrants, which are helping to alter the context for economic recovery. Equally urgent in some views, though with a much longer time horizon, is the need for research on the implications of climate change for the rural economy. While EDORA (2010) discusses the 2030 situations arising from four alternative scenarios that vary the pace of climate change and level of economic regulation, it admits that its own funding is insufficient for undertaking a full review of the threats and opportunities arising from this source, including alternative energy, changes to farming practice and migration, with the latter including the effects of change outside Europe. There is also a continuing EU concern with governance issues, including how best to harness institutional capital at the local level, develop greater connectivity between the various territorial levels of government and frame support mechanisms that can match the diversity of rural areas across the continent.

## References

Antrop, M. (2004). Landscape change and the urbanization process in Europe. *Landscape and Urban Planning, 67*, 9–26.

Beale, C. (1975). *The revival of population growth in nonmetropolitan America*. ERS Report 605. Washington, DC: USDA-ERS.

Bengs, C., & Schmidt-Thomé, K. (2006). *Urban-rural relations in Europe: EPSON 1.1.2 Final Report*. Brussels: ESPON Monitoring Committee.

Berry, B. J. L. (Ed.). (1976). *Urbanization and counterurbanization*. Beverly Hills, CA: Sage.

Bien, W., Lappe, L., & Rathgeber, R. (2005). The situation of young people in rural areas. In D. Schmied (Ed.), *Winning and losing: The changing geography of Europe's rural areas* (pp. 141–166). Aldershot: Ashgate.

Bosworth, G. (2008). Entrepreneurial in-migrants and economic development in rural England. *International Journal of Entrepreneurship and Small Business, 6*(3), 355–369.

Brown, D. L., Kulcsár, L. J., Kulcsár, L., & Obadovics, C. S. (2005). Post-socialist restructuring and population redistribution in Hungary. *Rural Sociology, 70*, 336–359.

Buller, H., & Hoggart, K. (1994). *International counterurbanization: British migrants to rural France*. Aldershot: Avebury.

Casado-Diaz, M., Kaiser, C., & Warnes, A. (2004). Northern European retired residents in nine southern European areas: Characteristics, motivations and adjustment. *Ageing and Society, 24*, 353–381.

Cawley, M. (2005). A booming country – a booming countryside? The Celtic Tiger phenomenon and the consequences for rural areas. In D. Schmied (Ed.), *Winning and losing: The changing geography of Europe's rural areas* (pp. 233–246). Aldershot: Ashgate.

Cawley, M. (2010). *Labour in-migration to small towns and rural areas: Polish and Lithuanian migrants in Ireland*. Paper presented at 'Contemporary Labour Migration: National and International Perspectives' Conference, Galway, Ireland, 12–13 May 2010.

Champion, A. G. (Ed.). (1989). *Counterurbanization: The changing pace and nature of population deconcentration*. London: Edward Arnold.

Champion, T. (2001a). Urbanization, suburbanization, counterurbanization, reurbanization. In R. Paddison (Ed.), *Handbook of urban studies* (pp. 143–161). London: Sage.

Champion, T. (2001b). The continuing urban-rural population movement in Britain: Trends, patterns, significance. *Éspace, Populations, Sociétés, 2001-1-2*, 37–51.

Champion, T. (2003). Testing the differential urbanization model in Great Britain, 1901–91. *Tijdschrift voor Economische en Sociale Geografie, 94*(1), 11–22.

Champion, T., Atkins, D., Coombes, M., & Fotheringham, S. (1998). *Urban Exodus*. London: Council for the Protection of Rural England.

Champion, T., & Brown, D. L. (2012). Migration and urban-rural population redistribution in the UK and US. In M. Shucksmith, D. L. Brown, S. Shortall, J. Vergunst, & M. Warner (Eds.), *Rural transformations and rural polices in the UK and US*. London: Routledge.

Champion, T., & Hugo, G. (Eds.). (2004). *New forms of urbanization: Beyond the urban/rural dichotomy*. Aldershot: Ashgate.

Champion, T., & Shepherd, J. (2006). Demographic change in rural England. In P. Lowe & L. Speakman (Eds.), *The ageing countryside: The growing older population of rural England* (pp. 29–50). London: Age Concern England.

Coombes, M., Champion, T., & Raybould, S. (2007). Did the early A8 in-migrants to England go to areas of labour shortage? *Local Economy, 22*(4), 335–348.

Dam, F. van, Heins, S., & Elberson, B. S. (2002). Lay discourses of the rural and stated and revealed preferences for rural living. Some evidence of the existence of a rural idyll in the Netherlands. *Journal of Rural Studies, 18*, 461–476.

Davoudi, S., Wishardt, M., & Strange, I. (2010). The ageing of Europe: Demographic scenarios of Europe's future. *Futures*. doi: 10.1016/j.futures.2010.04.11.

DEMIFER. (2010). *Demographic and migratory flows affecting European regions and cities*. ESPON Applied Research Project 2013/1/3, Draft Final Report. Luxembourg and The Hague: ESPON and NIDI.

Dijkstra, L., & Poelman, H. (2008). Remote rural regions: How proximity to a city influences the performance of rural regions. *Regional Focus*. doi: 01/2008, 1–8.

Doyle, N., Hughes, G., & Wadensjo, E. (2006). *Freedom of movement for workers from Central and Eastern Europe: Experiences in Ireland and Sweden*. Report 2006/5. Stockholm: Swedish Institute for European Policy Studies.

EDORA. (2010). s*European development opportunities in rural areas: Draft final report*. ESPON Applied Research Project 2013/1/2. Luxembourg: ESPON.

ESPON. (2008). Territorial dynamics in Europe: Trends in population development. Territorial Observation No.1. Luxembourg: ESPON.

European Commission. (2007). *Europe's demographic future: Facts and figures on challenges and opportunities*. Luxembourg: Office for Official Publications of the European Communities.

European Commission. (2008). *Green paper on territorial cohesion. Turning territorial diversity into strength*. COM(2008) 616 Final. Brussels: European Commission.

European Union. (2009). *Rural development in the European Union: Statistical and economic information*. Report 2009. Brussels: European Union Directorate-General for Agriculture and Rural Development.

Fielding, A. J. (1982). Counterurbanization in Western Europe. *Progress in Planning, 17*, 1–52.

Fonseca, M. L. (2008). New waves of immigration to small towns and rural areas in Portugal. *Population, Space and Place, 14*(6), 525–536.

Gallent, N., Mace, A., & Tewdewr-Jones, M. (2005). *Second homes: European perspectives and UK policies*. Aldershot: Ashgate.

Gilpin, N., Henty, M., Lemos, S., Portes, J., & Bullen, C. (2006). *The impact of free movement of workers from Central and Eastern Europe on the UK labour market*. London: HMSO.

Gkartzios, M., & Scott, M. (2010). Residential mobilities and house building in rural Ireland: Evidence from three case studies. *Sociologia Ruralis, 50*(1), 64–84.

Green, A. (2005). Employment restructuring in rural areas. In D. Schmied (Ed.), *Winning and losing: The changing geography of Europe's rural areas* (pp. 21–33). Aldershot: Ashgate.

Halfacree, K. (1994). The importance of the 'rural' in the constitution of counterurbanization: Evidence from England in the 1980s. *Sociologia Ruralis, 34*, 164–189.

Halfacree, K. (2008). To revitalise counterurbanization research? Recognising an international and fuller picture. *Population, Space and Place, 14*(6), 479–496.

Heins, S. (2004). Rural living in city and countryside: Demand and supply in the Netherlands. *Journal of Housing and the Built Environment, 19*, 391–408.

Hierro, M., & Maza, A. (2010). Per capita income convergence and internal migration in Spain: Are foreign-born migrants playing an important role? *Papers in Regional Science, 89*(1), 89–107.

Hoggart, K., & Buller, H. (1995) Retired British home owners in rural France. *Ageing and Society, 15*, 325–353.

Hoggart, K., & Mendoza, C. (1999). African immigrant workers in Spanish agriculture. *Sociologia Ruralis, 39*, 538–562.

Horváth, I. (2008). The culture of migration of rural Romanian youth. *Journal of Ethnic and Migration Studies, 34*(5), 771–786.

Houston, D., & Lever, W. (2001). *Migration within and from rural areas in England*. Cheltenham: Countryside Agency.

Illes, S. (2005). Elderly immigration to Hungary. *Migration Letters, 2*(2), 164–169.

Jauhiainen, I. S. (2009). Will the retiring baby boomers return to rural periphery? *Journal of Rural Studies, 25*, 25–34.

Johansson, M., & Kupiszewski, M. (2009). Demography. Working Paper 1, EDORA (European Development Opportunities for Rural Areas) Applied Research Project 2013/1/2. Luxembourg: ESPON.

Jones, G., & Jamieson, L. (1997). Young people in rural Scotland: Getting out and staying on. *CES Briefing* No 13, Edinburgh University.

Kasimis, C. (2008). Survival and expansion: Migrants in Greek rural regions. *Population, Space and Place, 14*(6), 511–524.

King, R., Warnes, T., & Williams, A. (2000). *Sunset lives. British retirement migration to the Mediterranean*. Oxford: Berg Publishers.

Kontuly, T., & Geyer, H. S. (2003). Lessons learnt from testing the differential urbanization model. *Tijdschrift voor Economische en Sociale Geografie, 94*(1), 124–128.

Labrianidis, L., & Sykas, T. (2009). Migrants, economic mobility and socio-economic change in rural areas: The case of Greece. *European Urban and Regional Studies, 16*(3), 237–256.

Lesthaeghe, R. (2010). The unfolding story of the second demographic transition. *Population and Development Review, 36*(2), 211–251.

Mahon, M. (2007). New populations; shifting expectations: The changing experience of Irish rural space and place. *Journal of Rural Studies, 23*, 345–356.

Matthews, H., Taylor, M., Sherwood, K., Tucker, F., & Limb, M. (2000). Growing up in the countryside: Children and the rural idyll. *Journal of Rural Studies, 16*, 141–153.

Milbourne, P. (2007). Re-populating rural studies: Migrations, movements and mobilities. *Journal of Rural Studies, 23*, 381–386.

Niedomysl, T. (2005). Tourism and interregional migration in Sweden: An explorative approach. *Population, Space and Place, 11*(3), 187–204.

Ni Laoire, C. (2007). The 'green green grass of home'? Return migration to rural Ireland. *Journal of Rural Studies, 23*, 332–344.

Norris, M., & Winston, N. (2009). Rising second home numbers in rural Ireland: Distribution, drivers and implications. *European Planning Studies, 17*(9), 1303–1322.

Rugg, J., & Jones, A. (1999). *Getting a job, finding a home: Rural youth transitions*. Bristol: Policy Press.

Scharf, T., Wenger, G. C., Thissen, F., & Burholt, V. (2005). Older people in rural Europe: A comparative analysis. In D. Schmied (Ed.), *Winning and losing: The changing geography of Europe's rural areas* (pp. 187–202). Aldershot: Ashgate.

Schmied, D. (Ed.). (2005a) *Winning and losing: The changing geography of Europe's rural areas*. Aldershot: Ashgate.

Schmied, D. (2005b). Incomers and locals in the European countryside. In D. Schmied (Ed.), *Winning and losing: The changing geography of Europe's rural areas* (pp. 21–33). Aldershot: Ashgate.

Stockdale, A. (2002). Out-migration from rural Scotland: The importance of family and social networks. *Sociologia Ruralis, 42*(1), 41–64.

Stockdale, A. (2004). Rural out-migration: Community consequences and individual migrant experiences. *Sociologia Ruralis, 44*(2), 149–176.

Stockdale, A. (2010). The diverse geographies of rural gentrification in Scotland. *Journal of Rural Studies, 26*(1), 31–40.

Stone, I., & Stubbs, C. (2007). Enterprising expatriates: Lifestyle migration and entrepreneurship in rural southern Europe. *Entrepreneurship and Regional Development, 19*, 433–450.

TUC (2004). *Migrant workers from the New Europe. Propping up rural and small town Britain*. London: Trades Union Congress.

Turok, I., & Mykhnenko, V. (2007). The trajectories of European cities, 1960–2005. *Cities, 24*(3), 165–182.

UN. (2010). *World urbanization prospects, 2009 revision*. New York: United Nations.

Vining, D. R., & Kontuly, T. (1978). Population dispersal from major metropolitan regions: An international comparison. *International Regional Science Review, 3*, 49–73.

Warnes, A., & Williams, A. (2006). Older migrants in Europe: A new focus for migration studies. *Journal of Ethnic and Migration Studies, 32*, 1257–1281.

Williams, A., & Hall, C. (2001). Tourism and migration: New relationships between production and consumption. *Tourism Geography, 2*, 5–27.

Williams, A., King, R., & Warnes, T. (1997). A place in the sun: International retirement migration from northern to southern Europe. *European Urban and regional Studies, 4*, 115–134.

# The Demography of Rural Latin America: The Case of Chile

Leif Jensen and David Ader

## Introduction

Early in 1960 U.S. President Dwight D. Eisenhower toured South America with stops in Brazil, Argentina, Chile, and Uruguay. Peering down from his Pan Am 707 he likely would have viewed a scene not dissimilar to that of today. A virtual low-altitude flyover of Latin America using Google Maps reveals a landscape that is overwhelmingly rural. From Tijuana, Mexico south to Tierra del Fuego, from Ecuador east to northern Brazil, and across the Caribbean, the human geography is one of relatively far flung but immense primate cities and smaller regional cities separated by utterly vast stretches of land with sparsely distributed human populations. These people live in the many thousands of small municipalities that dot the countryside, in isolated jungle settlements or the open country, amongst plantations and other agricultural areas, in rugged mountain towns and indigenous villages, and in other unquestionably rural places.

But on the ground and in demographic terms, things were changing fast in Latin America at around the time of Eisenhower's tour. In the decades straddling 1960, the population of Latin America increased by two-thirds, from 218.3 million in 1950 to 361.4 million in 1970 (Brea, 2003). The period also was one of marked urbanization – driven largely by rural-to-urban migration but also immigration from abroad – that continues to this day (Portes & Walton, 1976; Portes & Roberts, 2005). Today about 77% of Latin America's 580 million people are urban (Population Reference Bureau, 2009). Our concern in this chapter is with the 133 million rural inhabitants of Latin America and, in particular, with their demographic and socioeconomic characteristics.

Although we provide some information about rural Latin America as a whole, for illustrative purposes we focus on the rural demography of just one country, Chile. In the pages that follow we describe salient demographic conditions and trends in Latin America generally, with as much attention to rural-urban differences in this regard as possible. We then offer a demographic portrait of rural Chile through original analysis of nationally representative household survey data. We summarize and discuss our results in a concluding section.

## The Demography of Latin America: A Thumbnail Sketch

Jorge Brea (2003) provides a useful review of recent population dynamics in Latin America. He divides the region's demographic history into four eras: one of population decline owing to the decimation of the indigenous population from initial contact with

---

L. Jensen (✉)
Department of Agricultural Economics and Rural Sociology and the Population Research Institute, Pennsylvania State University, University Park, PA 16802, USA
e-mail: lij1@psu.edu

The authors are, respectively, Professor of Rural Sociology and Demography and Ph.D. candidate in Rural Sociology and Demography in the Department of Agricultural Economics and Rural Sociology and the Population Research Institute, The Pennsylvania State University, University Park, PA, USA.

Europeans and the brutality of colonization (1492–1650), a second period of slow growth due to high mortality and very modest European settlement (1650–1850), a third era of more moderate growth when European immigration – notably from Portugal, Spain and Italy – increased, bringing with it a demand for labor satisfied partly through the African slave trade and labor immigration from East Asia (1850–1950), and finally a period of rapid growth as, one by one, Latin American countries underwent the demographic transition and the spike in natural increase that entails (1950–2000). Brea (2003) notes diversity across Latin American countries in this regard, with some still in the midst of the transition, and others fully through it with relatively low birth and death rates. But overall this era of demographic transition has given rise to a relatively youthful age structure, which promises continued high population growth in the years ahead through the forces of population momentum.

Some aspects of these eras of demographic change in Latin America have special relevance for its rural demography. The first era of indigenous population decline draws attention to the important pre-European history of the region, the flourishing of several indigenous civilizations, and their subsequent subjugation and decline during the periods of colonization and immigration. The story is a familiar one. To this day indigenous groups contribute importantly to the race/ethnic diversity of Latin America, are more likely to reside in rural areas, and they often endure rates of poverty and hardship much above those of European-origin people (de Alcantara, 2008; Psacharopoulos & Patrinos, 1994).

The most recent era of demographic transition and rapid growth during the latter half of the 20th century bears special emphasis. First, while high fertility and low mortality gave rise to rapid growth, fertility was particularly high in rural areas of Latin America and remains so today. Also, the rural-urban fertility difference is greater in those countries still undergoing the transition (e.g., Honduras) and is less pronounced though still apparent in those countries that have already advanced through it (e.g., Chile) (Brea, 2003). Second, the era of rapid growth coincided with one of intense urbanization. Indeed, the region went from about 90% rural in 1900 to only about 25% rural a century later (Brea, 2003). High rural fertility and labor-saving advancements in agricultural techniques certainly were push factors. But rural residents were being pulled as well. From 1930 through the 1970s the prevailing approach to economic development in Latin America was import substitution industrialization (ISI) which involved heavy investment in urban industrial infrastructure (to the neglect of rural areas) and resulted in massive rural-to-urban migration flows (Portes & Roberts, 2005). Migrants were drawn not only by manufacturing jobs themselves, but also growing ancillary and supporting industries, both formal and informal (Portes & Roberts, 2005). Not surprisingly, those who migrated tended to be better educated and prime-aged adults. This brain drain would have left behind a rural population with higher age dependency ratios who depended on limited rural employment, subsistence agriculture, and occasional remittances from those who sojourned to the city.

It is no coincidence that Eisenhower visited in 1960. Cold War competition between the First and Second Worlds for influence over Latin America – with its rapid population and economic growth – was intense (McMichael, 2008). The past half century or more of Latin American history is characterized by significant and seismic shifts in political-economic approaches to development and rates of economic growth. The shift from ISI strategies in many countries to neo-liberal approaches in keeping with the Washington Consensus (Portes & Roberts, 2005) is emblematic of these transitions. It seems natural, therefore, to speculate about the interplay between economic swings and demographic outcomes. Palloni, Hill, and Aguirre (1996) undertook just such an assessment with time-series data for several Latin American countries spanning the early to late 1900s. Although they find some expected evidence that economic shocks result in delayed marriages, lower fertility, and higher morbidity and mortality, the effects are not uniformly strong or in the expected direction.

In short, Latin America experienced rapid population growth and urbanization during the 1900s, but remains a vast and diverse region with rural places and populations that are vitally important. With this brief sketch as background, we begin to explore the rural demography of Latin America more deeply by examining the case of Chile. As a point of departure, we place the country in sociopolitical and demographic context.

## Chile: Demographic Status and Change

Chile is an upper middle income country (World Bank, 2010) with a 2009 Human Development Index that places it 44th worldwide and in the "high human development" category (UNDP, 2010). Not only is Chile thus one of Latin America's most prosperous countries, it is one of the most demographically advanced as well. Its low fertility, mortality and natural increase place it in Brea's (2003) "advanced [demographic] transition" category, a distinction Chile shares with Cuba, Argentina, and Uruguay. Moreover, Chile's infant mortality rate (7.6 per thousand) is South America's lowest (with only Cuba and Guadeloupe having lower rates in all of Latin America), and its life expectancy at birth (78) is likewise South America's highest (with only a handful of Caribbean and Central American countries having life expectancies as high or slightly higher) (Population Reference Bureau, 2009). Chile's currently advanced demographic status culminates a demographic transition that was in full swing in the mid-20th century; mortality was in decline since the early 1900s yet fertility was only beginning to decline (Cabello, 1956). The Latin American and Caribbean Demographic Center (CELADE) (2003) provides data for the period 1950–2050 indicating that Chile's growth rate peaked at 2.39% during the 1960–65 period. The total fertility rate peaked at 5.33 children per woman during the 1955–60 period and is expected to dip below replacement level by 2025.

Like other Latin American nations, Chile's rapid mid- to late-1900s population growth was accompanied by substantial urbanization fueled demographically by rural-to-urban migration (Portes & Roberts, 2005). Up to 1973 Chile followed a strong ISI approach emphasizing industrial development in urban centers that drew migrants from surrounding rural communities, particularly those less isolated places with stronger links to national institutions (Conning, 1972). The military dictatorship of Augusto Pinochet ushered in an export-oriented industrialization strategy and strict adherence to the neoliberal principles embodied in the Washington Consensus. McMichael (2008, p. 158) observes that "Chile was structurally adjusted before structural adjustment became fashionable." Portes and Roberts (2005) indicate that the new free market approach changed the nature of urbanization away from one of urban primacy by allowing for economic and population growth in secondary urban centers. Moreover, Chile's neoliberal experiment also stressed the export of primary goods – copper, lumber and wood products, fruit, wine, and fish – which are more likely to be located in rural areas. The possibility then is that the rate of urbanization also may have declined in the last decades of the Century.

Historical demographic data confirm both the rapid mid-Century growth of the Chilean population and the steady increase in the percentage of Chileans residing in urban areas. Drawing on data reported by Weeks (1970) and CELADE (2003), Table 8.1 shows that from 1907 through 2000, the Chilean population increased fivefold (from 3.2 to 15.2 million) and the percentage living in urban areas doubled from 43.2 to 85.7. In the subsequent quarter-century, Chile's population is projected to increase to 19.5 million with 90.3% of them living in urban areas. Although the data seem to indicate some slow-down in the pace of urbanization, this may partly reflect ceiling effects since the overall percentage urban is already so high.

**Table 8.1** Population size and percent urban in Chile, 1865–2025

| Year | Population (in millions) | Percent urban |
| --- | --- | --- |
| 1865 | 1.8 | 28.6 |
| 1875 | 2.1 | 35.0 |
| 1885 | 2.5 | 41.7 |
| 1895 | 2.7 | 45.4 |
| 1907 | 3.2 | 43.2 |
| 1920 | 3.7 | 46.4 |
| 1930 | 4.3 | 49.4 |
| 1940 | 5.0 | 52.5 |
| 1952 | 5.9 | 60.2 |
| 1960 | 7.4 | 66.5 |
| 1970 | NA | 73.0 |
| 1975 | 10.3 | NA |
| 1990 | NA | 82.8 |
| 2000 | 15.2 | 85.7 |
| 2010 | NA | 87.9 |
| 2025 | 19.5 | 90.3 |

*Sources*: 1865–1960 (Weeks, 1970); 1970–2025 (CELADE, 2003).

Given that Chile is a demographically advanced country in which a scant 10% are expected to live in rural areas by 2025, one might question the need for a study of the demography of rural Chile. Several reasons justify the focus. First, with all due caution regarding linear or stage approaches to development, the very fact that the nation *is* demographically advanced suggests it may provide insight into what other Latin American nations, still undergoing the demographic transition, can expect.

Second, being a slender country but already highly urbanized, the stresses of urbanization and, by implication, the need for meaningful rural development, are apt to be particularly acute. Romero and Ordenes (2004) report significant environmental degradation caused by the sprawl of Santiago and other Andean cities. Changes in land cover and use have caused decreased soil moisture, vegetation productivity, air and water quality and other environmental problems in erstwhile rural areas. While Romero and Ordenes (2004) call for greater environmental awareness in the area of urban planning, we would argue that such problems might be alleviated if not averted altogether by policies to promote environmentally sustainable development in *rural* Chile.

A third reason pertains to population aging. That Chile underwent its demographic transition in the mid-20th century and has now advanced through it, means that it will be one of the first Latin American nations to contend with problems associated with an aging population, as those born during the country's spike in natural increase advance into their elder years. Chile is in fact expected to experience a rapid rise in its elderly population in the years ahead. From 1950 to 2000 the proportion of the Chilean population aged 60 years or older increased from 12.1 to 16.6%. By 2050 the proportion is projected to soar to 41.8%. This, along with a projected 31.7% aged 0–14, means that in 2050 Chile will have an age dependency rate of 73.6% (CELADE, 2003). That Chile's period of rapid population growth was accompanied by heavy rural-to-urban migration of prime-aged adults, suggests that the graying of the population may be a particularly acute challenge for rural communities in Chile (Brea, 2003). Indeed, by 2025 the percent elderly is expected to be 30.0 and 35.8 in urban and rural Chile, respectively, with the corresponding overall age dependency rates being 66.7 and 77.0% (CELADE, 2003). A relative lack of prime-aged adults looms for Chile, especially in the countryside.

Fourth, Chile's geographic diversity makes it an inherently interesting research setting. The country's rural areas range from deserts in the north, to mountain communities in the Andes, to rich and fertile valleys, to coastal fishing villages, to fjords in the frigid south. The diversity prompts Madaleno and Gurovich (2004, p. 517) to conclude "the country is a geography and geology class." Accordingly, in our analysis below we pay attention to regional diversity within Chile. Finally, Chile's national data systems are highly developed and advanced such that the data needed to compare rural and urban Chile are readily available.

## Data

The broad goal of this chapter is to provide a demographic portrait of rural Chile. To do so, we analyze data from a nationally representative household survey. This household survey – The National Socioeconomic Characterization Survey (CASEN) – is conducted by the Chilean Ministry of Planning and Cooperation (MIDEPLAN) in conjunction with the University of Chile. The CASEN is the only regularly conducted national survey containing such broad range of socioeconomic and demographic characteristics of Chilean households (Pizzolitto, 2005). The CASEN is a repeated cross-sectional survey of over 70,000 households conducted biannually since 1990. It is based on a multistage random sampling design that relies on data from the 2002 Chilean Population Census and is stratified by region and rural/urban residence. Our analyses are weighted accordingly. The CASEN is representative of the entire population in urban as well as rural areas (Pizzolitto, 2005; MIDEPLAN, 2006).[1]

Comparative statistics on percent of population that is urban and rural are readily found, though they must be regarded cautiously given country-to-country variation in definitions. Indeed, one such source, the Population Reference Bureau (2009: 18) notes, "[c]ountries define urban in many different ways, from population centers of 100 or more dwellings to only

---

[1] We considered using the Chilean Census itself for this analysis. The Census is conducted every ten years by the *Instituto Nacional de Estadísticas* (National Statistics Institute) in years ending in 2. As 2002 was the most recent census and the CASEN has a somewhat wider range of variables available, we chose to analyze the CASEN.

the population living in national and provincial capitals." Even within countries definitions will vary, and Chile is no exception. In regard to historical data he compiled, Weeks (1970, p. 72) writes, "[t]he definition of 'urban' in Chile has no minimum size limit but rather is administratively defined. It is comprised of all provincial capitals plus other places which have an 'urban' character, such as street (sic), water supply, etc." In his studies of rural-urban migration in Chile, Conning (1971, 1972) drew on the concept of community differentiation or the strength of ties to the national system through educational, economic, or other national institutions to essentially define as rural those isolated Chilean communities that lacked these ties. Still others call into question the validity of the "urban versus rural" distinction in Chile. In a study that unfortunately conflates rural and agriculture, Madaleno and Gurovich (2004) highlight the significant agricultural activity occurring in peri-urban Santiago – thus blurring the rural-urban distinction, in their view.

Here we rely on the ecological definition of urban and rural used in the CASEN survey. The official definition of urban places is determined by the National Institute of Statistics. It defines urban places as those with more than 2000 inhabitants or with 1001–2000 inhabitants and 50% or more being economically active in secondary or tertiary sectors. The only exceptions to this definition are places dedicated to tourism and recreation. For these to be considered urban they need more than 250 dwellings concentrated together regardless of whether or not they meet the necessary population requirements. All other places that do not meet these criteria – and their inhabitants – are defined as rural.

## Rural Chile: A Sociodemographic Portrait

As noted, Chile is ecologically diverse. The north is home to the driest desert in the world. Rainfall is scarce and land less arable, so people concentrate in areas where the ecology is capable of sustaining larger populations (i.e., along rivers or coasts). In contrast the southern part of Chile contains fertile valleys with many lakes and mountain streams fed by high annual precipitation. Agriculture and fishing have been able to support large populations, but these inhabitants are able to survive in smaller more dispersed groups. The central part of the country is more urban and is home to the so-called "metropolitan region" (i.e., Santiago and Valparaiso). In recognition of this regional diversity, in the tables that follow we present data for rural and urban Chile as a whole and for rural and urban places by the three distinct regions: North, Central, and South.

## Basic Demographic Characteristics

We begin by discussing basic demographic differences between rural and urban areas. According to the 2006 CASEN, in Chile 13% of the total population lives in rural areas. This overall percentage masks sizable differences by region. Only about 10% in the North and 9% in the Central regions are rural. However, over 26% of those in the South live in rural areas. In addition to the ecological reasons noted above, there are historical considerations as well. The South was and continues to be inhabited by indigenous populations who have maintained a more agrarian and rural lifestyle. The south was the last region to be colonized by Europeans and, as such, has had less time for the population to congregate in urban areas (Clapp, 1998). Finally, with regard to the distribution of the Chilean population across regions, the majority (62%) live in the Central Region, followed by the South (26%) and North (12%).[2]

Chile is rooted historically in a Catholic tradition that stresses the centrality of marriage and family to society (Langton & Rapoport, 1976; Sigmund, 1986). Indeed, it was not until 2006 that Chile legalized divorce making it the last Western Hemisphere country to do so. Previous legislation did allow the annulment of a marriage through a legal procedure in court, although this was costly. The lack of divorce legislation is often attributed to the conservative parliament that has been strongly influenced by the guidelines of the Roman Catholic Church. Because divorce was not legal and annulment was difficult, many marriages ended de facto in separation. Also, cohabitation is common. Table 8.2 shows the civil (marital) status of the total population aged 18 and older. At a national

---

[2] Because of space limitations, these and other results from our analysis of the CASEN data could not appear within the tables presented in this chapter. However, all CASEN results are available in tabular form from the authors upon request.

**Table 8.2** Civil status of those 18+ years, by rural urban, Chile 2006 (percent)

| | National | | | North | | | Central | | | South | | |
|---|---|---|---|---|---|---|---|---|---|---|---|---|
| | Total | Rural | Urban | Total | Rural | Urban | Total | Rural | Urban | Total | Rural | Urban |
| Married | 43.9 | 47.1 | 43.4 | 38.3 | 37.7 | 38.4 | 44.2 | 48.1 | 43.8 | 45.5 | 48 | 44.7 |
| Cohabiting | 13.6 | 13.7 | 13.6 | 18.8 | 22.4 | 18.4 | 13.4 | 12.8 | 13.5 | 11.9 | 12.9 | 11.7 |
| Annulled | 0.2 | 0.1 | 0.2 | 0.1 | 0.0 | 0.1 | 0.3 | 0.1 | 0.3 | 0.2 | 0.1 | 0.2 |
| Separated | 6.1 | 3.4 | 6.5 | 6.7 | 4.2 | 6.9 | 6.4 | 3.5 | 6.7 | 4.9 | 3.1 | 5.5 |
| Divorced | 0.2 | 0.1 | 0.2 | 0.2 | 0.2 | 0.2 | 0.2 | 0.1 | 0.2 | 0.2 | 0.1 | 0.2 |
| Widowed | 5.8 | 5.9 | 5.7 | 5.5 | 5.1 | 5.6 | 5.5 | 5.5 | 5.5 | 6.4 | 6.4 | 6.4 |
| Single | 30.3 | 29.7 | 30.4 | 30.5 | 30.3 | 30.5 | 30 | 29.9 | 30.1 | 30.9 | 29.4 | 31.4 |

*Source*: National Socioeconomic Characterization Survey, MIDEPLAN (2006).

level 43.9% of adults are married. However, in rural areas the percentage married is higher, at 47.1%. This seems reasonable since rural areas in Chile tend to be more conservative and marriage may be considered an important step in the lifecycle. That separation is roughly half as likely in rural areas (3.4 versus 6.5%, respectively) also aligns with this rural adherence to marriage. Given the challenges of rural living it may be more expedient for rural couples to remain in the relationship for the sake of economic survival, rather than to go it alone. For example, in urban areas there is housing available for rent, but this is less so in rural areas making separation less of an option for those who lack access to land or housing (Rojas & Greene, 1995; Sabatini & Salcedo, 2007). The presence of children may also complicate the process of separation.

Perhaps contrary to the image of a rural commitment to marriage, the prevalence of single, never-married adults is only slightly higher in rural areas, and cohabitation is actually the slightest bit more prevalent there. It is noteworthy that almost one in seven Chilean adults is cohabiting, a likely vestige of the historical unavailability of divorce. Until only very recently, when separated people formed new relationships they could not remarry and are thus counted as cohabiting. With regard to regional differences, the Central and South regions conform to the overall pattern. In the North, however, marriage is less common and cohabitation more common among adults. Also in the North rural folks are slightly less likely to be married but notably more likely to cohabit, relative to their urban counterparts. This regional pattern may be attributed, in part, to the marriage process in Chile. In order to legally marry, the couple must either go to a civil registry, or have a legal representative come to their wedding. With rural places in the North being more spatially dispersed, this legal requirement may be harder to achieve, resulting in a greater prevalence of cohabitation.

Table 8.3 shows the age distribution of the Chilean population. Overall the data suggest a youthful age structure but not overwhelmingly so, with about one in four Chileans being under age 16. At the national level there is little rural/urban difference in the proportion of the population aged 0–15. Within regions the data suggest that in the North and Central regions the prevalence of children (those under 16) is actually slightly higher in urban than rural areas. This may reflect migration patterns that attract the young – including children and those who bear them – to urban locales. The opposite is seen in the South where children are slightly more prevalent in rural areas. Rural

**Table 8.3** Age distribution, Chile 2006 (percent)

| Age | National | | | North | | | Central | | | South | | |
|---|---|---|---|---|---|---|---|---|---|---|---|---|
| | Total | Rural | Urban | Total | Rural | Urban | Total | Rural | Urban | Total | Rural | Urban |
| 0–5 | 8.3 | 8.1 | 8.3 | 9.2 | 9.0 | 9.3 | 8.2 | 7.9 | 8.3 | 8.1 | 8.2 | 8.0 |
| 6–15 | 17.0 | 17.1 | 16.9 | 17.2 | 17.2 | 17.2 | 16.8 | 16.6 | 16.8 | 17.2 | 17.6 | 17.1 |
| 16–64 | 65.5 | 63.1 | 65.9 | 64.8 | 62.6 | 65.1 | 66.0 | 64.3 | 66.1 | 64.7 | 62.1 | 65.5 |
| 65+ | 9.2 | 11.7 | 8.9 | 8.7 | 11.2 | 8.4 | 9.0 | 11.2 | 8.8 | 10.0 | 12.2 | 9.4 |

*Source*: National Socioeconomic Characterization Survey, MIDEPLAN (2006).

families in the South are apt to be agricultural and therefore in need of the labor that children can provide. It may also indicate the concentration of indigenous groups (notably the Mapuche) in the rural South.

When we look at the older ages some interesting residential differences emerge. There is a greater prevalence of prime-aged adults (16–64) in urban than rural areas at the national-level and within each region. This makes sense as this age group is economically active. Where jobs are often scarce in rural areas, people migrate to cities to find work or receive training (Bergquist, 1986). Marriage partners may also be scarce in rural areas, so those at that stage in their lives may find more opportunities for marriage in the city. The implication is that rural populations are old, or at least older. Indeed, while about 9% is 65 or older in Chile overall, in rural areas elders comprise about 12% of the population. This graying of rural more than urban Chile is seen in each region of the country and is an issue with which policy makers will have to contend as the Chilean population continues to become older.

We also examined household size differences between rural and urban areas.[3] At the national level the median household size is about four people. Over 75% of the total Chilean population lives in households with between three and six people. Although conventional wisdom holds that rural households have more members, the distributions are remarkably similar. If anything, rural individuals are more likely to live in households with fewer (1–4) members, a difference that is particularly apparent in the North. Although a number of factors might account for these patterns, noteworthy among them is rural-urban migration which naturally depresses household size in rural areas.

As noted, indigenous people existed in what is now Chile long before European colonization, and today they comprise a sizable minority – about 7% of the total population. As in other regions of the world, Chile's indigenous population is also disproportionately rural.[4] Indeed, the prevalence of indigenous people is three times greater in rural than urban areas – 15 versus 5%, respectively. Here again there is striking regional diversity. In the North, home to descendants of the Inca Empire, over 12% of the rural population is indigenous compared to only about 7% of urban areas. In the South – where the Mapuche people concentrate and where the percent indigenous is highest – the rural-urban difference is even greater. There, about 30% of the population in rural areas identify as indigenous compared to only about 9% in urban areas. The prevalence of indigenous people is far lower in the more metropolitan Central region where they comprise a greater share of the urban than rural population.

**Economic Circumstances**

Since the demise of the military dictatorship of Augusto Pinochet and the return to democracy in the early 1980s, an abiding concern of successive administrations has been poverty alleviation. The CASEN data indicate that, using the nation's official definitions of poverty and extreme poverty, 13.7% of the population is either poor or extremely poor.[5] The corresponding figures for rural and urban residents are 12.3 and 14.0, respectively. The region-specific numbers suggest higher prevalence of poverty in the South, but otherwise tell the same story with regard to rural-urban differences. Rural folks are *not* worse off, ostensibly. It should be noted, however, that the official definition of poverty in Chile is an income-based measure that equates household income to a poverty threshold, and that these thresholds are decidedly lower in rural areas. Although this reflects the reasonable assumption that costs of living are lower and self-provisioning higher in rural Chile, it does suggest the need to consider additional measures of well-being.

Table 8.4 shows the distribution of the population across income quintiles – determined at the national level – by rural-urban residence and region. At the national level, about 23% of the population falls into the lowest income quintile whereas only about 17% are in the highest.[6] While the distribution for urban individuals suggests that 20% are in the lowest quintile and

---

[3] Results not shown but are available in tabular form upon request.

[4] Results not shown but are available in tabular form upon request.

[5] Results not shown but are available in tabular form upon request.

[6] That the overall distribution diverges from a uniform 20% in each category reflects the fact that household size is greater among poorer households, such that, for example, the poorest quintile accounts for a greater than 20% share of all individuals.

**Table 8.4** Income quintiles by rural urban and region, Chile 2006 (percent)

|  | National | | | North | | | Central | | | South | | |
| --- | --- | --- | --- | --- | --- | --- | --- | --- | --- | --- | --- | --- |
|  | Total | Rural | Urban | Total | Rural | Urban | Total | Rural | Urban | Total | Rural | Urban |
| First (lowest) | 22.6 | 39.2 | 20.1 | 21.0 | 36.7 | 19.3 | 19.3 | 33.0 | 17.9 | 31.1 | 45.3 | 26.7 |
| Second | 22.0 | 26.4 | 21.3 | 21.9 | 23.6 | 21.7 | 21.2 | 28.9 | 20.5 | 23.7 | 24.6 | 23.5 |
| Third | 20.0 | 17.3 | 20.4 | 22.1 | 17.0 | 22.6 | 20.6 | 19.9 | 20.6 | 17.6 | 14.9 | 18.4 |
| Fourth | 18.9 | 10.3 | 20.2 | 21.1 | 12.6 | 22.0 | 19.9 | 11.0 | 20.7 | 15.7 | 9.2 | 17.7 |
| Fifth | 16.6 | 6.8 | 18.0 | 14.0 | 10.1 | 14.4 | 19.0 | 7.1 | 20.2 | 11.9 | 5.9 | 13.7 |

*Source*: National Socioeconomic Characterization Survey, MIDEPLAN (2006).

18% in the highest, the rural population is drastically less well off with about 40 and 7% in the lowest and highest quintiles, respectively. This rural disadvantage is found in all three regions. The rural South is worst off, with about 45% of all residents living in households with incomes below the 20th percentile for the nation, and only 6% in the highest quintile.

## Literacy and Education

A well-known correlate of economic well-being is human capital. Through formal education and work experience, individuals develop a bundle of skills that they trade for wages and salaries. Those with greater human capital are more likely to work and to command higher incomes. A most fundamental skill in today's world is literacy. Table 8.5 shows the illiteracy of the Chilean population broken down by age. Overall, the prevalence of illiteracy is greater among rural than urban adults (10.9 and 2.9%, respectively). Not surprisingly, there also is a striking age gradation such that older individuals – people who often never attended school – have the highest percentages that cannot read or write. One might surmise that the rural disadvantage is due to its older age distribution. However, in every age category rural areas have a higher prevalence of illiteracy though, to be sure, the gap increases with age. In the youngest age group there is only a 0.4 percentage point difference in illiteracy between rural and urban adults which compares to a 23.2 percentage point difference among those aged 70 or more. This rural disadvantage holds across all regions. Simply put, rural adults in Chile are less apt to be literate compared to urban residents.

Typically, literacy is gained through formal schooling. With such wide rural-urban disparities in literacy it makes sense to examine differences in educational attainment. Although rates of literacy and school attendance are quite high in Chile, access to education is not always equally distributed (Post, 2001), and there are distinct rural disadvantages in this regard. Indeed, while adults in urban Chile have completed over 10 years of formal schooling on average, rural

**Table 8.5** Illiteracy and educational achievement, people aged 15 and over, Chile, 2006 (percent)

|  | National | | | North | | | Central | | | South | | |
| --- | --- | --- | --- | --- | --- | --- | --- | --- | --- | --- | --- | --- |
|  | Total | Rural | Urban | Total | Rural | Urban | Total | Rural | Urban | Total | Rural | Urban |
| Percent illiterate | 3.9 | 10.9 | 2.9 | 2.6 | 8.1 | 2.0 | 3.2 | 10.4 | 2.5 | 6.0 | 11.8 | 4.2 |
| No formal education | 3.1 | 7.2 | 2.5 | 2.9 | 7.0 | 2.5 | 2.8 | 7.2 | 2.3 | 4.2 | 7.4 | 3.2 |
| Incomplete primary | 15.5 | 33.7 | 12.8 | 13.1 | 28.7 | 11.4 | 13.9 | 30.8 | 12.2 | 20.4 | 37.3 | 15.2 |
| Complete primary | 11.8 | 17.8 | 10.9 | 11.6 | 16.3 | 11.1 | 11.3 | 17.6 | 10.6 | 13.0 | 18.3 | 11.4 |
| Incomplete secondary | 21.3 | 17.6 | 21.8 | 23.7 | 20.2 | 24.1 | 21.1 | 17.5 | 21.5 | 20.4 | 17.2 | 21.4 |
| Complete secondary | 28.1 | 17.6 | 29.6 | 31.0 | 19.2 | 32.3 | 28.7 | 19.6 | 29.6 | 25.3 | 15.4 | 28.3 |
| Incomplete university | 9.2 | 2.9 | 10.1 | 9.2 | 3.7 | 9.8 | 9.7 | 3.5 | 10.3 | 8.0 | 2.3 | 9.8 |
| Complete university | 11.0 | 3.1 | 12.2 | 8.5 | 4.9 | 8.9 | 12.5 | 3.7 | 13.4 | 8.7 | 2.2 | 10.6 |

*Source*: National Socioeconomic Characterization Survey, MIDEPLAN (2006).

**Table 8.6** Labor force participation, Chile, 2006 (percent)

| | National | | | North | | | Central | | | South | | |
|---|---|---|---|---|---|---|---|---|---|---|---|---|
| | Total | Rural | Urban | Total | Rural | Urban | Total | Rural | Urban | Total | Rural | Urban |
| Labor force participation rate | 53.1 | 47.0 | 54.0 | 51.7 | 49.4 | 51.9 | 55.3 | 50.6 | 55.8 | 48.6 | 43.2 | 50.2 |
| Male | 68.3 | 67.8 | 68.4 | 67.5 | 68.9 | 67.3 | 69.9 | 70.6 | 69.8 | 64.8 | 65.0 | 64.7 |
| Female | 39.2 | 25.6 | 41.1 | 36.6 | 30.0 | 37.3 | 42.0 | 29.9 | 43.2 | 33.6 | 20.8 | 37.2 |
| Unemployment rate | 4.2 | 2.5 | 4.4 | 4.0 | 2.2 | 4.2 | 4.2 | 2.4 | 4.4 | 4.2 | 2.7 | 4.6 |
| Male | 4.4 | 2.9 | 4.6 | 4.4 | 2.7 | 4.6 | 4.3 | 2.3 | 4.5 | 4.5 | 3.4 | 4.8 |
| Female | 4.0 | 2.1 | 4.3 | 3.7 | 1.7 | 3.9 | 4.2 | 2.4 | 4.3 | 3.9 | 2.0 | 4.5 |
| Inactive in labor market | 42.7 | 50.5 | 41.6 | 44.3 | 48.4 | 43.9 | 40.5 | 47.1 | 39.8 | 47.2 | 54.1 | 45.2 |
| Male | 27.4 | 29.4 | 27.1 | 28.1 | 28.4 | 28.1 | 25.8 | 27.1 | 25.7 | 30.8 | 31.6 | 30.5 |
| Female | 56.7 | 72.3 | 54.6 | 59.7 | 68.3 | 58.8 | 53.8 | 67.8 | 52.5 | 62.5 | 77.3 | 58.3 |

*Source*: National Socioeconomic Characterization Survey, MIDEPLAN (2006).

adults have completed fewer than eight.[7] Mean years of schooling is lowest in the South, the rural South in particular. In addition to simple years of schooling, the completion of sequential levels of education and the credentialing this entails also is important for signaling skill sets to prospective employers. Table 8.5 also shows the distribution of Chilean adults across categories of educational attainment. Nationally only about 3% of adults have never attended school. However, this prevalence jumps to over 7% among rural adults. Indeed, rural areas – at the national level and within regions – have a larger percentage of adults who have never attended school, did not complete primary education or only completed primary school, than urban areas. At the other end of the education spectrum, while 11% of all adults and 12% of urban adults have completed a university degree, only 3% of rural adults have done so. Again, these patterns hold across regions and attainment is particularly low among those living in the South.

## Employment Characteristics

Education imparts knowledge, skills, and experiences that enhance the employability of individuals. Table 8.6 presents information on labor force status of Chilean adults. Overall, participation in the labor market is lower in rural areas, both at the national level and within regions, which certainly reflects the comparative lack of employment opportunities relative to urban locations. It is not that rural adults are therefore more likely to be unemployed – defined as being out of work and looking. Indeed, unemployment rates were relatively low in Chile in 2006 (around 4%), and were lower still in rural areas nationally and within regions (roughly 2.5%). Rather, rural adults are more likely to be out of the labor force altogether. While 41.6% of urban adults are inactive in the labor market, the rate is closer to half (50.5%) among rural adults. This group would include elders, homemakers, those working in the informal economy, and others. Both nationally and within each region, the comparatively high rate of labor force inactivity in rural areas is due importantly to the fact that rural women are much less likely to be working in the formal labor market than are urban women. Nationally 72.3% of rural women are inactive (i.e., 27.7 are in the labor force, whether employed or unemployed), versus only 54.6% of urban women. Residential differences among men are much less stark.

Table 8.7 shows, for those adults who are employed, their distribution across industry of employment. That employment in agriculture is more common in rural Chile is hardly surprising, but the large share of all rural workers in agriculture and the magnitude of the rural-urban difference are quite striking. Close to 60% of rural workers are in agriculture, which compares to a scant 7% of urban workers. This pattern is seen nationally and within each region, and reflects the tremendous importance of agriculture for both the

---
[7] Results not shown but are available in tabular form upon request.

**Table 8.7** Employment industry by rural urban, Chile, 2006 (percent)

| | National | | | North | | | Central | | | South | | |
|---|---|---|---|---|---|---|---|---|---|---|---|---|
| | Total | Rural | Urban | Total | Rural | Urban | Total | Rural | Urban | Total | Rural | Urban |
| Agriculture | 12.5 | 59.2 | 6.5 | 11.6 | 53.7 | 7.3 | 9.9 | 59.2 | 5.5 | 19.8 | 60.4 | 9.2 |
| Mining | 1.7 | 1.2 | 1.8 | 8.6 | 7.6 | 8.7 | 0.9 | 0.7 | 1.0 | 0.4 | 0.3 | 0.4 |
| Manufacturing | 13.5 | 7.9 | 14.2 | 9.1 | 4.3 | 9.6 | 14.2 | 7.9 | 14.8 | 13.7 | 8.7 | 15.0 |
| Construction | 9.3 | 5.3 | 9.8 | 8.9 | 4.8 | 9.3 | 9.3 | 5.0 | 9.7 | 9.4 | 5.8 | 10.4 |
| Utilities | 0.5 | 0.6 | 0.5 | 0.4 | 1.2 | 0.3 | 0.6 | 0.6 | 0.5 | 0.5 | 0.5 | 0.5 |
| Commerce | 19.7 | 8.3 | 21.1 | 20.5 | 10.0 | 21.6 | 20.2 | 8.4 | 21.3 | 17.7 | 7.9 | 20.3 |
| Transportation | 7.7 | 3.4 | 8.2 | 9.6 | 3.7 | 10.2 | 7.6 | 3.6 | 8.0 | 7.9 | 3.0 | 6.9 |
| Finances | 7.3 | 1.6 | 8.0 | 5.2 | 2.2 | 5.5 | 8.6 | 1.8 | 9.2 | 4.6 | 1.2 | 5.5 |
| Services | 26.9 | 12.1 | 28.8 | 24.9 | 12.4 | 26.2 | 27.3 | 12.3 | 28.7 | 26.5 | 11.9 | 30.3 |
| Other | 1.1 | 0.4 | 1.1 | 1.2 | 0.2 | 1.3 | 1.3 | 0.5 | 1.3 | 0.4 | 0.3 | 0.5 |

*Source*: National Socioeconomic Characterization Survey, MIDEPLAN (2006).

rural and national economies. Chile has long followed an export-oriented approach to economic development that has, in recent decades, emphasized the export of agricultural products (e.g., fruits, wine). Previously exports consisted largely of copper and other metals procured through mining. The percentages in Table 8.7 show that mining activity is located predominantly in the North. At the national level, only about 2% of workers are employed in mining. However, about 9% of workers in the North are so employed, compared to less than 1% in the Central and South regions. With the exception of agriculture, virtually all other key industries are more prevalent in urban areas. These include manufacturing, construction, sales and service industries, which provide opportunities for skilled and unskilled workers alike. Although this industrial structure typifies countries in all parts of the world, it underscores a disadvantage for rural people that is all too apparent in the case of Chile.

Another way positions in the labor market differ is by type of employment or what is sometimes termed "class of worker." The CASEN data indicate that a sizable majority of all workers are employees in the private sector (60.3% of all workers nationally).[8] Those who are self-employed (and who do not formally employ others) comprise about 20% of workers. Those who run their own businesses that employ others, government workers, workers for public companies, and other workers comprise smaller shares of the Chilean workforce. With regard to rural-urban differences it is noteworthy that self-employment is more common in rural areas. While about 20% of all Chilean workers are self-employed, 27% of rural workers are. This may reflect the importance of agriculture in rural areas and, in particular, the presence of small farmers. The greater prevalence of the self-employed in rural areas is seen in the North and South, but not the Central region. This too might reflect the lower percentage of workers in agriculture in that region. Rural central Chile sticks out also for having a relatively high proportion of workers in the private sector (about 72%). This reflects the close proximity to industries and multiple urban centers. People living in rural areas in the Central region may not have to travel far to find work in urban areas and many can commute via public and informal transportation systems. People from other regions, in order to find work or achieve higher education, may need to migrate to do so. Reflecting the tendency for government jobs to be located in towns and cities, rural workers are less likely than their urban counterparts to be employed by the government.

## Migration

Compared to other demographic processes, migration often has the greatest and certainly the most immediate impact on the demographic composition of localities.

---

[8] Results not shown but are available in tabular form upon request.

**Table 8.8** Migration by rural urban, Chile 2006 (percent)

|  | National | | | North | | | Central | | | South | | |
| --- | --- | --- | --- | --- | --- | --- | --- | --- | --- | --- | --- | --- |
|  | Total | Rural | Urban | Total | Rural | Urban | Total | Rural | Urban | Total | Rural | Urban |
| Where living at birth | | | | | | | | | | | | |
| Born in same community | 54.0 | 71.7 | 51.4 | 63.0 | 69.6 | 62.3 | 47.9 | 69.8 | 45.7 | 64.6 | 73.9 | 61.7 |
| Born in different community | 44.3 | 27.3 | 46.8 | 34.7 | 28.5 | 35.3 | 50.4 | 29.1 | 52.5 | 34.4 | 25.4 | 37.2 |
| Born in different country | 1.0 | 0.4 | 1.0 | 1.1 | 1.4 | 1.0 | 1.1 | 0.4 | 1.2 | 0.5 | 0.3 | 0.5 |
| Where living 5 years ago | | | | | | | | | | | | |
| Lived in same community | 90.6 | 94.4 | 90.0 | 92.1 | 94.3 | 91.8 | 89.3 | 94.6 | 88.8 | 92.9 | 94.3 | 92.4 |
| Lived in different community | 8.4 | 5.1 | 8.9 | 6.6 | 5.1 | 6.8 | 9.4 | 4.9 | 9.9 | 6.7 | 5.4 | 7.1 |
| Lived in different country | 0.4 | 0.2 | 0.5 | 0.3 | 0.5 | 0.3 | 0.6 | 0.2 | 0.6 | 0.2 | 0.1 | 0.2 |

*Source*: National Socioeconomic Characterization Survey, MIDEPLAN (2006).

People migrate for many reasons, often to find jobs or gain access to education. Consistent with historical trends in Chile and Latin America in general, much of the internal migration is from rural areas to urban areas. Table 8.8 shows that nationally about 54% of people lived in the same community (in 2006) in which they were born. However, whereas about half (51%) of urban residents still lived where they were born, the figure is closer to 70% among rural Chileans suggesting less mobility among them. This pattern holds for each region.

Focusing in on migration during the five years prior to the survey, the second panel of Table 8.8 indicates that recent migration (as compared to migrant since birth) is understandably less common. Overall about 91% of Chileans lived in the same community as they did five years prior to the survey. Here again, however, urban residents appear somewhat more mobile. About 90% of the urban population lived in the same community five years prior, while the corresponding figure for rural residents stood at 94%. These patterns hold across all regions.

## Household Amenities and Resources

Migration is influenced by push and pull factors that are driven by characteristics of places of residence. Infrastructure and social services, like access to clean water and electricity, are often scarce in rural areas, arguably making life more challenging. Table 8.9 shows residential variation in access to a range of utilities. In urban Chile, about 93% of the population has access to a public water system which compares to only about 48% of rural residents. Many people in rural areas have wells but some still have to collect water from springs or rivers. Almost all urban people have access to water inside their homes (about 99%) but only about 78% of rural people do. Once the water is used up in urban homes, for at least 93% of them it is drained away by a public sewer system. Only about 11% of rural residents enjoy this public utility. About 34% of rural people use an outhouse compared to only about 1% of urban residents. When we compare access to electricity, only one tenth of 1% of urban residents does not have access to electricity compared to about 3% of rural residents. These patterns hold across regions of Chile and are certainly consistent with what we know about rural infrastructures the world over.

This rural disadvantage may account for some of the motivation for migration to urban areas, but other differences are also salient. In today's globalizing world, many people enjoy the benefits of technology. Many no longer have to wash clothes by hand, or heat water over a fire. People can travel faster, and stay connected with phones and the internet as well as receive news via television. But these benefits are not distributed equally across space. As seen in Table 8.10 the rural population has fewer vehicles, washing machines, refrigerators, water heaters, and telephones. They also have less cable TV, fewer computers and less internet access, suggesting an important dimension of the digital divide. Indeed, it is noteworthy that not having internet service available is the single most important

**Table 8.9** Source of household utilities by rural urban, Chile 2006 (percent)

| | National | | | North | | | Central | | | South | | |
|---|---|---|---|---|---|---|---|---|---|---|---|---|
| | Total | Rural | Urban | Total | Rural | Urban | Total | Rural | Urban | Total | Rural | Urban |
| Water | | | | | | | | | | | | |
| Public with meter | 86.9 | 47.7 | 92.7 | 91.9 | 66.3 | 94.7 | 90.0 | 66.2 | 92.3 | 77.4 | 27.4 | 92.7 |
| Public with shared meter | 5.6 | 4.3 | 5.8 | 4.0 | 3.2 | 4.1 | 6.3 | 7.7 | 6.2 | 4.5 | 1.5 | 5.4 |
| Public no meter | 0.8 | 1.8 | 0.7 | 0.7 | 2.9 | 0.5 | 0.6 | 0.8 | 0.6 | 1.3 | 2.4 | 1.0 |
| Well | 4.3 | 31.1 | 0.4 | 1.4 | 11.4 | 0.3 | 2.1 | 19.8 | 0.4 | 10.9 | 45.0 | 0.5 |
| River or spring | 1.6 | 12.4 | 0.0 | 0.8 | 8.5 | 0.0 | 0.3 | 3.2 | 0.0 | 5.0 | 21.3 | 0.1 |
| Other | 0.7 | 2.7 | 0.4 | 1.1 | 7.7 | 0.4 | 0.6 | 2.1 | 0.4 | 0.8 | 2.3 | 0.3 |
| Access to water | | | | | | | | | | | | |
| Inside house | 95.9 | 78.0 | 98.5 | 96.2 | 70.8 | 99.0 | 97.0 | 82.7 | 98.4 | 93.0 | 75.2 | 98.5 |
| Outside house | 2.3 | 10.1 | 1.1 | 1.6 | 11.3 | 0.5 | 2.1 | 11.0 | 1.2 | 2.9 | 9.0 | 1.0 |
| Carry it to the house | 1.9 | 11.8 | 0.4 | 2.2 | 18.0 | 0.5 | 0.9 | 6.2 | 0.3 | 4.0 | 15.7 | 0.5 |
| Waste disposal (sewage) | | | | | | | | | | | | |
| Public sewer | 82.8 | 11.1 | 93.4 | 89.7 | 22.4 | 96.9 | 86.5 | 13.2 | 93.7 | 71.0 | 7.0 | 90.5 |
| Septic | 8.7 | 44.1 | 3.5 | 4.8 | 37.2 | 1.3 | 7.8 | 53.4 | 3.3 | 12.7 | 36.9 | 5.4 |
| Toilet connected to hole | 1.7 | 9.1 | 0.6 | 1.4 | 10.3 | 0.5 | 1.2 | 7.7 | 0.6 | 2.9 | 10.1 | 0.7 |
| Outhouse | 5.3 | 33.5 | 1.1 | 3.4 | 26.5 | 1.0 | 2.8 | 23.1 | 0.8 | 12.0 | 44.3 | 2.2 |
| Outhouse over canal | 0.1 | 0.2 | 0.0 | 0.0 | 0.1 | 0.0 | 0.1 | 0.2 | 0.1 | 0.1 | 0.2 | 0.0 |
| None | 1.3 | 1.9 | 1.3 | 0.7 | 3.5 | 0.4 | 1.5 | 2.0 | 1.5 | 1.2 | 1.4 | 1.2 |
| Electricity | | | | | | | | | | | | |
| Public with meter | 92.5 | 82.0 | 94.0 | 93.2 | 74.9 | 95.2 | 93.3 | 84.6 | 94.1 | 90.2 | 80.9 | 93.1 |
| Public with shared meter | 5.9 | 11.2 | 5.1 | 4.4 | 8.3 | 4.0 | 5.8 | 12.7 | 5.1 | 6.6 | 10.4 | 5.4 |
| Public no meter | 0.9 | 2.0 | 0.7 | 0.7 | 3.1 | 0.4 | 0.7 | 1.3 | 0.6 | 1.5 | 2.4 | 1.2 |
| Generator | 0.2 | 1.4 | 0.0 | 0.5 | 4.1 | 0.1 | 0.1 | 0.5 | 0.0 | 0.4 | 1.7 | 0.0 |
| Solar Panel | 0.0 | 0.3 | 0.0 | 0.3 | 3.2 | 0.0 | 0.0 | 0.0 | 0.0 | 0.0 | 0.1 | 0.0 |
| Other | 0.1 | 0.3 | 0.0 | 0.8 | 0.5 | 0.0 | 0.0 | 0.1 | 0.0 | 0.1 | 0.3 | 0.0 |
| None | 0.5 | 2.8 | 0.1 | 0.8 | 5.9 | 0.3 | 0.1 | 0.8 | 0.1 | 1.2 | 4.1 | 0.3 |

*Source*: National Socioeconomic Characterization Survey, MIDEPLAN (2006).

reason why rural residents say they are not "on-line." To the extent that this rural disadvantage is viewed as detrimental, then the poverty and deprivation of individuals, households, and the places they live need to be addressed.

Education and work experience comprise key components of human capital. Also important for success is, arguably, cultural capital. The CASEN also includes data on attendance at cultural events and numbers of books read. Rural residents are consistently disadvantaged in these respects.[9] For example, while about 83% of the urban population had not been to a museum in the past year, about 95% of rural residents have not done so. About 82% of the urban population has not been to the movies in the last year, which compares to 96% of the rural population. This rural disadvantage in cultural capital obtains in all regions of Chile.

---

[9] Results not shown but are available in tabular form upon request.

**Table 8.10** Household resources by rural urban, Chile 2006 (percent)

| | National | | | North | | | Central | | | South | | |
|---|---|---|---|---|---|---|---|---|---|---|---|---|
| | Total | Rural | Urban | Total | Rural | Urban | Total | Rural | Urban | Total | Rural | Urban |
| Personal vehicle work | 21.8 | 17.7 | 22.4 | 20.6 | 17.7 | 20.9 | 23.0 | 19.6 | 23.4 | 19.4 | 16.0 | 20.5 |
| Vehicle washing | 6.7 | 6.8 | 6.6 | 7.6 | 7.7 | 7.5 | 6.9 | 8.3 | 6.8 | 5.6 | 5.3 | 5.6 |
| Machine | 55.9 | 33.3 | 59.2 | 49.0 | 29.0 | 51.3 | 59.1 | 36.7 | 61.2 | 51.4 | 31.1 | 57.5 |
| Refrigerator | 74.2 | 66.0 | 75.3 | 69.3 | 58.7 | 70.5 | 76.9 | 74.1 | 77.1 | 69.8 | 60.1 | 72.8 |
| Water Heater | 52.8 | 23.6 | 57.0 | 41.9 | 22.9 | 44.1 | 62.6 | 37.4 | 65.0 | 34.4 | 11.4 | 41.3 |
| Land line telephone | 39.4 | 7.2 | 44.1 | 35.3 | 9.6 | 38.2 | 44.4 | 9.9 | 47.7 | 29.4 | 4.3 | 37.0 |
| Cell phone | | | | | | | | | | | | |
| Yes prepaid | 43.7 | 39.1 | 44.4 | 47.0 | 34.8 | 48.3 | 43.1 | 43.0 | 43.1 | 43.7 | 36.3 | 46.0 |
| Yes contract | 10.3 | 4.1 | 11.2 | 7.6 | 6.4 | 7.7 | 12.0 | 5.0 | 12.7 | 7.6 | 2.9 | 9.1 |
| Do not have | 46.0 | 56.8 | 44.4 | 45.5 | 58.8 | 44.0 | 44.9 | 52.0 | 44.2 | 48.7 | 60.8 | 45.0 |
| Television with cable | 22.2 | 5.3 | 24.7 | 24.8 | 8.9 | 26.6 | 23.2 | 6.6 | 24.8 | 18.6 | 3.3 | 23.2 |
| Computer | 28.6 | 8.8 | 31.5 | 27.0 | 9.8 | 28.9 | 31.4 | 11.2 | 33.4 | 22.7 | 6.6 | 27.5 |
| Internet | | | | | | | | | | | | |
| Yes dial-up | 12.9 | 9.6 | 13.0 | 12.9 | 14.9 | 12.8 | 13.0 | 9.2 | 13.1 | 12.5 | 8.8 | 12.8 |
| Yes broadband | 44.1 | 19.1 | 45.0 | 41.7 | 27.7 | 42.2 | 47.7 | 23.7 | 48.1 | 34.4 | 9.4 | 36.1 |
| No connection | 42.4 | 70.9 | 41.3 | 44.5 | 57.4 | 44.0 | 39.1 | 66.5 | 38.2 | 52.4 | 81.4 | 50.4 |
| Reason for no internet | | | | | | | | | | | | |
| Not interested | 18.4 | 10.2 | 19.0 | 19.6 | 10.7 | 20.0 | 18.1 | 10.7 | 18.5 | 18.6 | 9.4 | 19.6 |
| Too expensive | 53.8 | 34.6 | 55.1 | 52.8 | 26.8 | 54.1 | 53.4 | 36.8 | 54.2 | 55.5 | 33.7 | 57.9 |
| No service Available | 8.7 | 46.5 | 6.2 | 10.9 | 55.4 | 8.7 | 7.8 | 43.9 | 5.8 | 9.9 | 47.6 | 5.7 |
| Other | 19.1 | 8.8 | 19.8 | 16.7 | 7.1 | 17.2 | 20.8 | 8.6 | 21.4 | 16.0 | 9.4 | 16.8 |

*Source*: National Socioeconomic Characterization Survey, MIDEPLAN (2006).

## Summary and Discussion

As in other world regions the Twentieth Century brought profound demographic change to Latin America. The demographic transition resulted in sharp population increases, and economic transformations were manifest in rapid industrial growth and urbanization. While the landscapes remain largely rural, the populations no longer are. The decline from 90 to 25% rural, itself a product of urban-oriented development and massive rural-to-urban migration flows, cannot but have changed the circumstances of rural populations and rendered them comparatively vulnerable. Our purpose here was to provide an entrée into the rural demography of Latin America by focusing on one of the region's more demographically advanced, urban and prosperous nations, Chile. Being further along, Chile may offer clues about what lay ahead for other Latin American nations. It certainly is an ecologically diverse nation where the stresses of urbanization and the need for rural development are clear.

Analyzing nationally representative survey data from 2006, we document that the Chilean population is overwhelmingly urban, with only 13% of Chileans living in rural areas. A rural-urban comparison across basic demographic characteristics revealed that rural adults are more likely to be married and to cohabit, and rural folks are more likely to be elderly and residentially stable. Other patterns conform even more strongly to conventional wisdom. The prevalence of indigenous people is much greater in the countryside, for example. Yet other differences run counter to general expectation. Notably, if anything rural folks live in households with fewer members, not larger households.

In general the more glaring rural-urban contrasts are found for measures of socioeconomic well-being, and these almost uniformly point to a rural disadvantage. Rural residents have much lower incomes; albeit low, they suffer from much higher rates of illiteracy; they have lower educational attainment measured either in years or levels completed; they are less likely to be formally employed (owing largely to the much lower labor force participation rates among rural than urban women); when employed they are much less likely to be working in anything other than the agricultural sector; they are much less likely to have access to public utilities (e.g., water and sewer); they have fewer material possessions including access to the internet; and they score worse on measures of cultural capital.

It is the nature of descriptive demographic portraits that they raise questions about why observed patterns and trends exist, and point the way to further research. By way of conclusion, we synthesize the various speculations we have made in this chapter to identify three broad and interrelated areas of inquiry that could be pursued. These are rural economic disadvantage, rural-to-urban migration, and rural marriage and family.

A rich research agenda could be built around the causes, consequences and policy implications of the kinds of rural economic disadvantage we document here in the case of Chile. Certainly the industrial base of the rural economy that relies heavily on agriculture and other natural resource-based industries needs to be fully explored. It is well known that lack of industrial diversity is detrimental. It is an empirical question, however, whether family and local dependence on natural resource industries necessarily entails socioeconomic disadvantage. Jensen, Yang, and Muñoz (2011), for example, find that in Chile dependence on agriculture, forestry, and fishing (but not mining) reduces the likelihood that children in families and in places dependent on these industries will be attending school. Conversely, López and Anríquez (2004) found that in the 1990s agricultural growth was in and of itself strongly associated with declines in headcount poverty in Chile.

Agriculture, forestry, fishing, and mining are likely to remain central to Chile's economic growth in the years ahead and will necessarily remain located in rural areas. Combined with our finding of the greater prevalence of self-employment in rural areas, all this suggests that research is needed to determine whether efforts to promote rural economic development via entrepreneurship hold promise in addressing the economic disadvantages of rural residence. More generally, research on rural economic well-being and livelihood strategies should be directed toward understanding whether the much lower incomes reported by rural households is offset by informal economic activities, self-provisioning, lower cost of living, and other compensating factors. Such research would help determine whether the lower poverty thresholds that officially apply in rural Chile are justified, and might allow such adjustments to be fine tuned. Research also is needed on the double jeopardy faced by rural indigenous peoples living in Chile and elsewhere in Latin America. This work might usefully focus in on *their* unique livelihood strategies, the determinants and consequences of integration with mainstream society, the impact of targeted ameliorative social policies, and related areas.

A second promising area of future research concerns rural-to-urban migration. The more elderly age structure of rural areas and the greater likelihood that urban residents are migrants, and recent migrants in particular, are consistent with a prevailing rural-to-urban internal migration flow in Chile. However, definitive evidence would require more detailed data on migration histories. Other issues to be explored relate to the characteristics of migrants and nonmigrants. To what extent do education and skill levels differ, and what are the implications of these differences for human capital stocks in places of origin and destination? If rural-to-urban migrants are younger, what are the implications for rural age structures and for the well-being of elders who are aging in place in the countryside? What is the nature and extent of remittance flows from erstwhile rural residents living in the city, and what is the impact of remittances on rural household well-being and the economic circumstances of rural communities more generally? What are the motivations for rural-to-urban migration and what might be done to retain young adults in rural areas? After all, genuine rural development in new industrial pursuits that are more ecologically sensitive and sustainable likewise holds promise in attracting urban residents – or averting rural-to-urban migration in the first place – thus reducing the detrimental impacts of urbanization.

A third worthwhile area of inquiry would be to examine patterns of marriage and family formation in rural and urban areas. Our analysis suggested only mild rural-urban differences in civil status, but did indicate a higher prevalence of marriage and lower prevalence of separation in rural areas. To what extent can these differences be attributed to residential variation in familism, to the greater difficulty in ending a marriage in rural areas, or to other factors? Research is also needed on the implications of Chile's 2006 divorce law for rates of marriage formation and dissolution and whether there are rural-urban differences in this respect.

Regardless of whether future research focuses on rural economic deprivation, rural-to-urban migration, rural marriage and family formation, or other aspects of rural demography, research also is needed that takes a much broader regional perspective and that draws comparisons between the highly diverse range of countries in Latin America. We have argued that because Chile is demographically advanced – it is only one of a handful of Latin American countries that has moved so far through the demographic transition – it may presage forthcoming demographic changes to be experienced by other Latin American countries. Even this assumption may be mere conjecture and open to debate, further underscoring the need for cross-country analysis. It would be a massive undertaking to assemble nationally representative survey or census data for a large number of – not to mention all – Latin American countries that would all have geographic identifiers for rural residence, some reach back in time, and demographic variables that could be made optimally comparable.[10] Such an effort is needed however, not least to keep Latin America's rural people and their prospects and vulnerabilities from fading further from view.

**Acknowledgements** Infrastructural support was provided by the Population Research Institute, The Pennsylvania State University, which has core support from the National Institute on Child Health and Human Development (2 R24 HD041025-06). The authors are responsible for any substantive or analytic errors.

## References

Bergquist, C. W. (1986). *Labor in Latin America: Comparative essays on Chile, Argentina, Venezuela, and Colombia*. Stanford, CA: Stanford University Press.

Brea, J. A. (2003). Population dynamics in Latin America. *Population Bulletin, 58*(1), 1–36.

Cabello, O. (1956). The demography of Chile. *Population Studies, 9*(3), 237–250.

CELADE (2003). *Latin America and the Caribbean: Population ageing*. Demographic Bulletin. Santiago, Chile: Latin American and Caribbean Demographic Centre.

Clapp, R. A. (1998). Regions of refuge and the agrarian question: Peasant agriculture and plantation forestry in Chilean araucania. *World Development, 26*(4), 571–589.

Conning, A. M. (1971). Rural community differentiation and the rate of rural-urban migration in Chile. *Rural Sociology, 36*(3), 296–314.

Conning, A. M. (1972). Rural urban destinations of migrants and community differentiation in a rural region of Chile. *International Migration Review, 6*(2), 148–157.

de Alcantara, C. H. (2008). Indigenous peoples, poverty and human development in Latin America. *Development and Change, 39*(1), 189–191.

Jensen, L., Yang, T., & Muñoz, P. (2011). Natural resource dependence: Implications for children's schooling and work in Chile. *Society and Natural Resources, 24*(9).

Langton, K. P., & Rapoport, R. (1976). Religion and leftist mobilization in Chile. *Comparative Political Studies, 9*(3), 277–308.

López, R., & Anríquez, G. (2004). Poverty and agricultural growth: Chile in the 1990s. *eJADE: electronic Journal of Agricultural and Development Economics, 1*(1), 6–24.

Madaleno, I. M., & Gurovich, A. (2004). "Urban versus rural" no longer matches reality: An early public agro-residential development in periurban Santiago, Chile. *Cities, 21*(6), 513–526.

McMichael, P. (2008). *Development and social change: A global perspective* (4th ed.). Los Angeles, CA: Pine Forge Press.

MIDEPLAN. (2006). *Manual de Usario Base de Datos. Ministerio de Planificación y Cooperación*. Santiago, Chile: Gobierno de Chile.

Palloni, A., Hill, K., & Aguirre, G. P. (1996). Economic swings and demographic changes in the history of Latin America. *Population Studies, 50*(1), 105–132.

Pizzolitto, G. (2005). *Poverty and inequality in Chile: Methodological issues and a literature review*. CEDLAS Working Paper 20, Universidad Nacional de La Plata.

Population Reference Bureau. (2009). *World Population Data Sheet, 2009*. Washington, DC: Population Reference Bureau.

Portes, A., & Roberts, B. R. (2005). The free-market city: Latin American urbanization in the years of the

---

[10] Researchers would have a head start in this endeavor by consulting and capitalizing on data provided by the Integrated Public Use Microdata Series (IPUMS) International project at the University of Minnesota. Here researchers can download census data from about a dozen of Latin America's 38 countries. The great benefit of IPUMS International data for researchers is the effort that goes into harmonizing the variables in the data sets to make them maximally comparable across countries. We did not pursue this option here both because of the tremendous variation across countries in the definition of rural (sometimes defined administratively, sometimes according to various cutoffs for population size of place) and because of the greater breadth of variables available in the CASEN.

neo-liberal experiment. *Studies in Comparative International Development, 40*(1), 43–82.

Portes, A., & Walton, J. (1976). *Urban Latin America: The political condition from above and below*. Austin, TX: University of Texas Press.

Post, D. (2001). *Children's work, schooling, and welfare in Latin America*. Boulder, CO: Westview Press.

Psacharopoulos, G., & Patrinos, H. A. (Eds.). (1994). *Indigenous people and poverty in Latin America: An empirical analysis*. Washington, DC: The World Bank.

Rojas, E., & Greene, M. (1995). Reaching the poor: Lessons from the Chilean housing experience. *Environment and Urbanization, 7*(2), 31–50.

Romero, H., & Ordenes, F. (2004). Emerging urbanization and the southern Andes: Environmental impacts of urban sprawl in Santiago de Chile and the Andean Piedmont. *Mountain Research and Development, 24*(3), 197–201.

Sabatini, F., & Salcedo, R. (2007). Gated communities and the poor in Santiago, Chile: Functional and symbolic integration in a context of aggressive capitalist colonization of lower-class areas. *Housing Policy Debate, 18*(3), 577–606.

Sigmund, P. E. (1986). Revolution, counterrevolution, and the catholic church in Chile. *The ANNALS of the American Academy of Political and Social Science, 483*(1), 25–35.

UNDP. (2010). *Human Development Report 2009 – HDI rankings*. Retrieved June 1, 2010, from http://hdr.undp.org/en/statistics/

Weeks, J. R. (1970). Urban and rural natural increase in Chile. *The Milbank Memorial Fund Quarterly, 48*(1), 71–89.

World Bank. (2010). *Country classification, data and statistics*. Retrieved June 1, 2010, from http://data.worldbank.org/country/chile

# Rural Demography in Asia and the Pacific Rim

Gavin Jones and Premchand Dommaraju

## Introduction

In preparing this chapter, we are very conscious of the controversy over the appropriateness of the binary division of population into its urban and rural segments. As long ago as 1969, John Grauman, in a United Nations report on the growth of the world's urban and rural populations, noted that "with the increase in number of urban attributes and their wider diffusion, it is doubtful whether the historic twofold 'urban' and 'rural' distinction will retain its relevance much longer" (United Nations, 1969, 3). More recently, an IUSSP committee published a report entitled *New Forms of Urbanization: Beyond the Urban-Rural Dichotomy* (Champion & Hugo, 2004), which emphasized the need to break away from the traditional urban-rural dichotomy. Ideas which were debated in this book included the introduction of a third category intermediate between urban and rural; the treatment of the settlement system as a continuum that can, if necessary, be split into many categories; and recognition that human settlement is multidimensional (Champion & Hugo, 2004, 12). As for those populations designated rural by the definitions employed in different countries, it was noted that they could be subdivided by some measure of degree of rurality, or by some kind of functional criteria, or in terms of level of accessibility to large metropolitan centres (Champion & Hugo, 2004, 376).

G. Jones (✉)
Asia Research Institute, National University of Singapore, 259770 Singapore
e-mail: arigwj@nus.edu.sg

The blurring of the urban-rural division in Asian countries shares many of the "counterurbanization" features that make rural residence both attractive and feasible for many urbanites in Western countries (e.g. the broadening of locational options for many activities, see Champion, 1989). However, there are some other distinctive reasons in the case of some Asian countries, such as the desire to escape the dangers of crime and civil unrest in large cities.

Most of the data available by kind of settlement pattern still follows the simple urban-rural classification. Unfortunately, what is considered rural differs widely between Asian countries, thus complicating inter-country comparisons of the characteristics of rural populations. Thus, what is considered rural in Thailand, Malaysia or, probably, India includes more people living in quasi-urban environments than is the case in the Philippines (Jones, 2004, 115–121).

Another point stressed in a number of studies is the increasing "urbanity" of life in many rural areas, and the blurring of the previously sharp rural-urban distinctions in ways of living resulting from electrification, the communications and transportation revolution, and rising educational levels. In Southeast Asia at least, the extent to which "urban" amenities and modes of communication have permeated rural areas over the past 40 years has been astonishing, as the forces of modernization "impinge on formerly isolated, inward-looking, self-sufficient and agriculturally-based communities" (Rigg, 1997, 157).

In the 1960s ... in areas such as Thailand's northeast, most of Indochina, and most of rural Philippines and Indonesia, roads were few, and often impassable in the wet season. Lack of roads and the poverty of villagers meant that public transportation was embryonic at best. Radios were rare and TV was unknown. Villagers' main source of information about the outside world was the newspapers that occasionally found their way into the village. In Java, by the 1990s, there remained major differences between rural villages close to major cities and those more isolated in mountainous areas or in some of the poor limestone areas of the south coast. But the true isolation of the 1960s had vanished. Road access had improved, public transportation had been revolutionized by ubiquitous minibuses which ply between towns and rural areas, and radio and TV communications had brought villagers in touch with the same programmes watched by their city compatriots. The expansion of education had brought literacy and heightened aspirations to the most isolated rural areas (Jones, 1997, 239).

In one case study of change over three decades in a Javanese village up to 1985 by a highly perceptive demographer (Keyfitz, 1985), the extent of change was carefully documented, and was indeed massive. This case could be multiplied many times over throughout the region. In recent times, increasing possession of cell phones by rural households has dramatically changed the ability to keep in touch with absent family members. In Thailand, the percent owing a cell phone among rural households with an elderly member rose from below 15% in 1994 to about 71% in 2007 (National Statistics Office, 2007).

The accessibility of rural areas to towns or larger cities is an important factor differentiating rural areas from each other. One proposed operational definition of rurality is based on population density and distance to large cities (Chomitz, Buys, & Thomas, 2005). They argue that

> these criteria are important gradients along which economic behavior [sic] and appropriate development interventions vary substantially. Where population densities are low, markets of all kinds are thin, and the unit cost of delivering most social services and many kinds of infrastructure is high. Where large urban areas are distant, farm-gate or factory-gate prices of outputs will be low and input prices will be high, and it will be difficult to recruit skilled people to public service or private enterprise. Thus, low population density and remoteness together define a set of rural areas that face special development challenges (World Bank, 2010, 157).

However, it should be noted that distance is not identical to accessibility, as much depends on efficiency of transport networks.

## Time Trends in Size of Rural Populations

In this chapter, we do not include discussion of India and China, as they are covered elsewhere in this book (see Chapters 11 and 13 in this volume). However, aggregate figures for Eastern and South-Central Asia in Fig. 9.1 do include India and China.

The rural population in Asia is expected to reach a peak of 2.4 billion around 2015 and to decline steadily thereafter (Fig. 9.1). Trends in the rural population of Asia are determined by two things: the rate of natural increase of the rural population and the net migration balance. Rates of natural increase are positive, though declining, but are offset wholly or partially by net outmigration. The resultant trends in size of rural populations differ considerably across Asia. The growth in the rural population of Asia is driven mainly by growth in South-Central Asia, where birth rates, though falling, remain much higher than in East and Southeast Asia. Whereas the rural population in Eastern Asia began to decline in the mid-1990s, the rural populations in South-Central Asia and South-East Asia are expected to grow until 2025 and 2020, respectively. The rural population of South-Central Asia is expected to reach a maximum of 1.3 billion by 2025, which is only slightly less than the entire rural population of Asia in 1960. All regions of Asia, however, are expected to have smaller rural populations in 2050 than today.

The point at which the rural population began, or will begin, to decline in absolute numbers is important for any country. This point was reached in Japan in 1955, in South Korea in 1965, in China and Iran in 1990, in Indonesia in 1995 and in Malaysia in 2000 (see United Nations, 2009). Other Asian countries are yet to reach this point. It is important to note that these declines in rural population began well before rates of natural increase in rural areas turned negative (indeed, up to this point, they have only turned negative in Japan). This underlines the importance of population loss to rural areas through rural-urban migration, in the transition from rural population growth to rural population decline.[1]

---

[1] It should be added that replacement level fertility was reached in these countries well before rates of natural increase turned negative, because of the effect of "population momentum" (generation of many births by the high proportion of the population

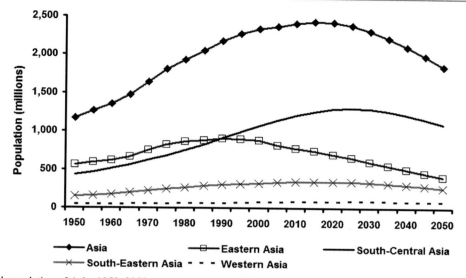

**Fig. 9.1** Rural population of Asia, 1950–2050
*Source*: United Nations Population Division (2009).
*Notes*: Eastern Asia: China; China, Hong Kong SAR; China, Macao SAR; Dem. People's Republic of Korea; Japan; Mongolia; Republic of Korea. South-Central Asia: Afghanistan; Bangladesh; Bhutan; India; Iran; Kazakhstan; Kyrgyzstan; Maldives; Nepal; Pakistan; Sri Lanka; Tajikistan; Turkmenistan; Uzbekistan. South-Eastern Asia: Brunei Darussalam; Cambodia; Indonesia; Lao People's Democratic Republic; Malaysia; Myanmar; Philippines; Singapore; Thailand; Timor-Leste; Viet Nam. Western Asia: Armenia; Azerbaijan; Bahrain; Cyprus; Georgia; Iraq; Israel; Jordan; Kuwait; Lebanon; Occupied Palestinian Territory; Oman; Qatar; Saudi Arabia; Syrian Arab Republic; Turkey; United Arab Emirates; Yemen.

By mid-century, most of the rural population in Asia will be concentrated in South-Central Asia (about 60%) followed by Eastern Asia (about 22%). Eastern Asia had the highest number of rural inhabitants in the 1950s, but by the mid-1980s, the rural population of South-Central Asia began to outnumber Eastern Asia, where by this time rural population was on the decline.

In 1950, about 70–85% of populations in the four regions of Asia were rural (Table 9.1). By mid-century, all major regions in Asia will have less than half of the population living in rural areas. In 2010, South-Central Asia was the least urbanized (68% rural) followed by South-Eastern Asia (about 58% rural). In many countries in Asia, the rural population will constitute less than one-third of the total population by 2050. The Republic of Korea, Malaysia and Saudi Arabia will be less than 12% rural by 2050; all three countries had about 78% of population living in rural areas in 1950. Only two major Asian countries, Sri Lanka and Cambodia, will have more than half of their population living in rural areas by 2050.

Sri Lanka is the only country in the region to have witnessed an increase in percent of rural population over the last half century. Sri Lanka, like many other Asian countries, observed an increase in urbanization in the 1950s, 1960s and up to the mid-1970s. This trend reversed, however, with the rural percentage of the population increasing beginning in the late 1970s and stabilizing at around 85%. One reason for this high level of rural population is the strict definition employed by the Sri Lankan censuses to define urban areas. In the 2001 census, urban areas were defined as comprising all Municipal and Urban Council areas. While the definition of urban regions was different in earlier censuses, the data presented here for the earlier censuses have been adjusted by the UN to match the 2001 definition. This strict definition of what constitutes an urban region may, as noted by the Department of Census and Statistics (2006), lead to an "underestimate of the true picture of the urban sector". Besides the definitional issue, government policies to promote rural development and low levels of investment in industry and other sectors in the urban areas dampened urban growth (Sri Lanka Country Report, 2002).

---

in the reproductive ages). This has been a factor lengthening the lead time between the onset of a decline in rural population and the onset of negative rates of natural increase of the rural population.

**Table 9.1** Percent rural, selected countries and periods, 1950–2050

|  | 1950 | 1975 | 2000 | 2010 | 2025 | 2050 |
|---|---|---|---|---|---|---|
| **Asia** | 83.7 | 76.0 | 63.2 | 57.8 | 50.1 | 35.3 |
| **Eastern Asia** | 84.5 | 76.6 | 59.6 | 49.8 | 39.3 | 25.7 |
| Japan | 65.1 | 43.2 | 34.8 | 33.2 | 28.9 | 19.9 |
| Republic of Korea | 78.6 | 52.0 | 20.4 | 17.0 | 13.3 | 9.2 |
| **South-Central Asia** | 83.6 | 77.8 | 70.5 | 67.9 | 61.2 | 44.0 |
| Bangladesh | 95.7 | 90.2 | 76.4 | 71.9 | 62.6 | 43.6 |
| Iran | 72.5 | 54.3 | 35.8 | 29.2 | 22.0 | 14.5 |
| Pakistan | 82.5 | 73.7 | 66.9 | 64.1 | 57.5 | 40.6 |
| Sri Lanka | 84.7 | 77.9 | 84.2 | 85.7 | 82.8 | 68.7 |
| **South-Eastern Asia** | 84.5 | 76.7 | 61.8 | 58.2 | 50.3 | 34.6 |
| Cambodia | 89.8 | 95.6 | 83.1 | 79.9 | 73.7 | 56.2 |
| Indonesia | 87.6 | 80.7 | 58.0 | 55.7 | 49.3 | 34.1 |
| Lao PDR | 92.8 | 88.9 | 78.0 | 66.8 | 51.0 | 32.0 |
| Malaysia | 79.6 | 62.3 | 38.0 | 27.8 | 19.5 | 12.1 |
| Philippines | 72.9 | 64.4 | 52.0 | 51.1 | 44.6 | 30.6 |
| Thailand | 83.5 | 76.2 | 68.9 | 66.0 | 57.8 | 40.0 |
| Viet Nam | 88.4 | 81.2 | 75.5 | 69.6 | 59.5 | 41.0 |
| **Western Asia** | 71.4 | 51.3 | 36.2 | 33.5 | 29.1 | 20.5 |
| Iraq | 64.9 | 38.6 | 32.2 | 33.8 | 32.3 | 23.1 |
| Saudi Arabia | 78.7 | 41.7 | 20.2 | 17.9 | 14.8 | 10.3 |
| Turkey | 75.2 | 58.4 | 35.3 | 30.4 | 24.1 | 16.0 |
| Yemen | 94.2 | 85.2 | 73.7 | 68.2 | 58.3 | 39.8 |

*Source*: United Nations Population Division (2009).
*Notes*: Definition of regions same as in Fig. 9.1. The estimates for regions include data from all countries in the region including those not shown in this table.

There are currently major differences in the growth of rural population between the major regions of Asia. The rural population will continue to grow by more than 0.5% annually over the next 15 years in South-Central Asia and Western Asia (Table 9.2). However, the rural population in South-Eastern Asia will not see any growth and the rural population in Eastern Asia will decline by more than 1% annually between 2010 and 2025. In the last 35 years (1975–2010), while the Republic of Korea had the fastest rate of decline in rural population (2.2% annually), Pakistan and Iraq had the highest rate of growth of rural population (about 2.3% annually).

With the exception of Sri Lanka, in all major countries in Asia the percentage of population living in rural areas has been declining since 1975. For Asia as a whole, percent rural population declined by about 0.78% every year between 1975 and 2010 and this trend is expected to intensify in the coming decades. In Malaysia the proportion of the population residing in rural areas declined by more than 2% annually over the last 35 years and this trend is expected to continue over the next 15 years.

# Migration

In Southeast Asia, when populations were less dense and much unopened land remained available, rural-rural migration was the major form of migration. This was certainly true of Thailand before the 1980s (Goldstein & Goldstein, 1986, Table 10) and of

**Table 9.2** Growth rates in rural population and percent rural, selected countries and periods

| | Average annual rate of change in rural population (percentage) | | | | Average annual rate of change in percent rural (percentage) | | | |
|---|---|---|---|---|---|---|---|---|
| | 1950–1975 | 1975–2010 | 2010–2025 | 2025–2050 | 1950–1975 | 1975–2010 | 2010–2025 | 2025–2050 |
| **Asia** | 1.73 | 0.82 | −0.06 | −1.03 | −0.39 | −0.78 | −0.96 | −1.39 |
| **Eastern Asia** | 1.58 | −0.17 | −1.18 | −1.86 | −0.39 | −1.23 | −1.57 | −1.71 |
| Japan | −0.45 | −0.38 | −1.25 | −2.18 | −1.65 | −0.75 | −0.92 | −1.49 |
| Republic of Korea | 0.71 | −2.23 | −1.53 | −1.95 | −1.66 | −3.19 | −1.66 | −1.48 |
| **South-Central Asia** | 1.85 | 1.63 | 0.52 | −0.70 | −0.29 | −0.39 | −0.70 | −1.32 |
| Bangladesh | 2.14 | 1.45 | 0.22 | −0.92 | −0.24 | −0.65 | −0.92 | −1.45 |
| Iran | 1.56 | 0.55 | −0.91 | −1.24 | −1.16 | −1.77 | −1.90 | −1.67 |
| Pakistan | 1.74 | 2.33 | 1.19 | −0.15 | −0.45 | −0.40 | −0.73 | −1.39 |
| Sri Lanka | 1.73 | 1.39 | 0.28 | −0.81 | −0.33 | 0.27 | −0.23 | −0.75 |
| **South-Eastern Asia** | 1.99 | 0.96 | 0.00 | −1.04 | −0.39 | −0.79 | −0.97 | −1.50 |
| Cambodia | 2.21 | 1.64 | 1.01 | −0.18 | 0.25 | −0.51 | −0.53 | −1.09 |
| Indonesia | 1.80 | 0.57 | 0.02 | −1.12 | −0.33 | −1.06 | −0.81 | −1.48 |
| Lao PDR | 2.25 | 1.32 | −0.12 | −0.83 | −0.17 | −0.82 | −1.80 | −1.87 |
| Malaysia | 1.81 | 0.05 | −1.10 | −1.25 | −0.98 | −2.30 | −2.37 | −1.89 |
| Philippines | 2.48 | 1.62 | 0.60 | −0.62 | −0.49 | −0.66 | −0.90 | −1.50 |
| Thailand | 2.51 | 0.96 | −0.47 | −1.42 | −0.36 | −0.41 | −0.89 | −1.47 |
| Viet Nam | 1.91 | 1.33 | −0.14 | −1.13 | −0.34 | −0.44 | −1.05 | −1.49 |
| **Western Asia** | 1.38 | 1.16 | 0.61 | −0.45 | −1.32 | −1.22 | −0.94 | −1.40 |
| Iraq | 0.89 | 2.37 | 2.04 | 0.10 | −2.07 | −0.38 | −0.30 | −1.34 |
| Saudi Arabia | 0.73 | 1.27 | 0.46 | −0.46 | −2.55 | −2.41 | −1.30 | −1.44 |
| Turkey | 1.59 | −0.13 | −0.58 | −1.20 | −1.01 | −1.87 | −1.54 | −1.64 |
| Yemen | 1.58 | 2.88 | 1.50 | 0.13 | −0.40 | −0.63 | −1.04 | −1.52 |

*Source*: Computed based on data from United Nations Population Division (2009).

Malaysia before the 1970s (ESCAP, 1982, 58). In Thailand, people were moving from the central plain and lower north regions to less-populated *changwats* (provinces) toward the border with Thailand and Laos. However, as urban populations built up and the rural land frontier closed, rural-rural migration decreased in relative importance and the focus of migration from rural areas became increasingly to urban areas. In Thailand, this resulted in rural-rural flows and rural-urban flows becoming equal in size by 1995–2000. In the Philippines, in the 1950s and 1960s, two general patterns of migration could be observed: "a dominant rural-to-urban stream from the Visayas and some parts of Luzon towards Manila and its vicinity, and a rural-to-rural flow of migrants towards frontier Mindanao" (Carino, 1976, 255). In more recent times, rural-rural migration has diminished with the closing of the land frontier. In Indonesia, the official transmigration program, which moved landless and poor rural dwellers from Java and Bali to the outer islands, resulted in large volumes of rural-rural migration, particularly in the late 1970s and 1980s. However, numbers dwindled after that, as the transmigration program contracted drastically, and even before the transmigration program lost importance, there was already considerable movement into urban areas of Java from the outer islands (Hugo, 1997, Table 5.7), and rural-urban migration taking place within Java and within other parts of Indonesia.

Rural-urban migration is now the key movement from rural areas, throughout East and Southeast Asia. This is demonstrated by recent data from Malaysia,

Vietnam and Indonesia, which show that migrants leaving rural areas are now focused heavily on urban destinations.[2] Young, unmarried people are predominant in this rural-urban migration, and there is also a female predominance among these young migrants, which is particularly marked in migration to the largest cities of Indonesia, Thailand and the Philippines – Jakarta, Bangkok and Manila. This appears to relate to the employment opportunities for young females in the cities in manufacturing, clerical activities, in domestic service and in the sex industry. The patterns in East and Southeast Asia resemble those in Latin America, but differ markedly from those in South Asia, where female migration is much more restricted, and dominated by short-distance marriage migration.

While studies of mobility usually concentrate on long-term or permanent migration, there is a great deal of variation in patterns of mobility. Major patterns of seasonal and circular migration have been recorded for Thailand (especially from the north-eastern provinces to Bangkok and the South: see Porpora & Lim, 1987) and Java (Hugo, 1982). Such patterns enable rural dwellers to avail themselves of urban work opportunities during times of slack conditions in agriculture, and so increase the income of their rural-based families.

## Characteristics of Rural Populations

We stressed in the introductory section that the urban-rural distinction in Asia is becoming increasingly blurred. Nevertheless, those classified as rural dwellers in Asia according to national definitions do differ substantially from those classified as urban dwellers, both in terms of some of their demographic characteristics and when related to a number of indicators of development. The difference in development indicators appears to be almost always to the detriment of the rural dwellers. This section will elaborate on some of these differences.

## Demographic Structure

Rural populations typically have higher mortality and higher fertility than urban populations and both rural and urban populations have been affected by patterns of migration. On balance, this is likely to result in a different age and sex structure for rural and urban populations, though the possible range of differences resulting from these different patterns is infinite. Are there any generalizations that can be made about typical patterns of differences?

One generalization that might be ventured is that where fertility rates are higher in rural areas, the proportion of children in the population is likely to be higher than in urban areas. Another is that where net outmigration from rural areas is high, rural areas will have a relative shortage of young working-age population, since the age pattern of outmigration is dominated by this age group. While this feature may be true of rural areas as a whole, it is likely that it will be particularly characteristic of certain regions, where outmigration is highest.

To examine the net outcome of some of these factors in the case of four Southeast Asian countries, Table 9.3 shows the broad age structure of rural and urban populations in various parts of Indonesia, Malaysia and Thailand in 2000, and the Philippines in 1990. In both rural and urban areas of Thailand, the proportion of children is lower than in Indonesia or Malaysia, and in the Philippines it is much higher, reflecting the lower levels of fertility in Thailand and the high levels in the Philippines. But more important in the context of a study of rural-urban differences is the fact that in all four countries there is a distinct excess in proportion of children in rural areas, a deficiency in the proportion aged 15–29 and to a lesser extent at ages 30–49, and an excess in proportion of population at ages over 50. Data (not shown) for earlier years show that this pattern has held over time. It is likely that it holds quite generally in Asian countries.

## Education and Health

The rural population of Asia is less educated than the urban population and this is especially pronounced in poorer countries in the region and for women (Table 9.4). The most extreme example is Pakistan, where women in urban areas are about four times

---

[2] For example, in Malaysia, rural-urban migrants account for 13% of all recent migrants, compared with only 5% for rural-rural migrants. Because of Malaysia's high level of urbanization, urban-urban migrants dominate migration flows (69%). In Vietnam, where urbanization is much lower, rural-urban migrants are a larger share, with rural-rural flows well behind.

**Table 9.3** Proportion of population in broad age groups, rural and urban areas, Indonesia, Malaysia and Thailand, 2000, Philippines 1990

| Country and age group | Rural | Urban | Ratio, rural/urban |
|---|---|---|---|
| **Indonesia** | | | |
| 0–14 | 32.1 | 28.2 | 1.13 |
| 15–29 | 27.1 | 32.3 | 0.83 |
| 30–49 | 26.0 | 27.3 | 0.95 |
| 50+ | 14.8 | 12.2 | 1.21 |
| **Malaysia** | | | |
| 0–14 | 36.8 | 31.1 | 1.18 |
| 15–29 | 25.0 | 28.8 | 0.87 |
| 30–49 | 23.6 | 26.2 | 0.90 |
| 50+ | 14.6 | 13.9 | 1.05 |
| **Thailand** | | | |
| 0–14 | 25.9 | 20.2 | 1.28 |
| 15–29 | 24.4 | 28.2 | 0.87 |
| 30–49 | 31.5 | 34.1 | 0.92 |
| 50+ | 18.2 | 17.5 | 1.04 |
| **Philippines** | | | |
| 0–14 | 42.2 | 36.9 | 1.14 |
| 15–29 | 27.2 | 30.2 | 0.90 |
| 30–49 | 19.5 | 22.4 | 0.87 |
| 50+ | 11.1 | 10.5 | 1.06 |

*Source*: Calculated from population census reports for each country.

**Table 9.4** Education and health characteristics, selected countries

| | Percent of women completing secondary school or higher: urban/rural | Infant mortality rate: rural/urban |
|---|---|---|
| **South-Central Asia** | | |
| Bangladesh, 2007 | 1.47 | 1.17 |
| Pakistan, 2006–7 | 3.94 | 1.23 |
| **South-Eastern Asia** | | |
| Cambodia, 2005 | 2.05 | 1.42 |
| Indonesia, 2007 | 1.81 | 1.46 |
| Philippines, 2008 | 1.26 | 1.73 |
| Viet Nam, 2002 | – | 2.22 |

*Source*: Data from the Demographic Health Surveys (DHS, 2010) accessed from the MEASURE DHS STAT compiler tool www.measuredhs.com.

**Table 9.5** Indonesia: Percent attending school by age group, 2005

| Age group | Urban | Rural |
|---|---|---|
| 5–6 | 29.0 | 6.7 |
| 7–12 | 93.1 | 90.3 |
| 13–15 | 83.6 | 71.8 |
| 16–18 | 56.0 | 37.1 |
| 19–24 | 15.8 | 4.8 |

*Source*: Badan Pusat Statistik (2006), Tables 14 and 19.

more likely to complete secondary school than women in rural areas. This perhaps reflects lack of access to schools nearby in rural areas whereas it is much easier to find good schools nearby in urban areas. In a culture where purdah[3] is practiced, lack of nearby schools poses particular problems for girls' education in Pakistan. But it is true generally throughout the region that parents tend to be more concerned for their daughters' safety when they have to travel (on foot, bicycle or bus) long distances to school (e.g. on Indonesia, see Oey-Gardiner, 1991). As seen in Indonesia (Table 9.5), children in rural areas start school late. However, school enrolment among children age 7–12 does not differ markedly compared to the differences seen at later ages.

It is at the higher levels of education that the rural-urban differences become more marked. For example, while about 16% of urban youth in Indonesia were enrolled in school/college only 5% of rural youth were in school/college (see Table 9.5). These figures may be slightly misleading, because rural children wishing to pursue higher education will normally have to move to urban areas to do so. Therefore, some of those attending higher education institutions in urban areas will really be from a rural background.

School enrolments tell us only part of the story of urban-rural differences in access to education. A more telling indicator is the proportion of pupils who begin in primary school who graduate from that level of education within the specified time period. Another indicator would be the quality of rural schools. This could be ascertained if information were available on the quality of teachers in rural and urban schools, teacher absenteeism, quality of school buildings, availability of teaching materials, and the pedagogical processes

---
[3] Purdah is the practice of seclusion of women, either by keeping them at home or ensuring that they are veiled when they venture outside the house.

adopted by teachers. In the less developed countries of the region in particular, strong rural-urban discrepancies can be found in these indicators, along the lines of those documented in a study of the quality of primary schools in a number of developing countries (Carron & Chau, 1996). As stated by Coombs (1985, 223) "Surveys and direct observation in many different developing countries have confirmed that schools in the hinterland have insufficient textbooks and other training materials and equipment and a disproportionate share of untrained and unqualified primary teachers. They often have high pupil and teacher absentee rates and operate fewer days per year than many urban schools".

There is clear rural disadvantage when it comes to health. In all the countries included in Table 9.4, rural Infant Mortality Rate (IMR) is higher (ranging from 17 to 122% higher) in rural areas than in urban areas. In comparing rural and urban areas, it is necessary to take into account the heterogeneity within urban areas. Although rural IMR is higher than urban IMR, in some countries rural IMR is lower compared to that of the urban slum population (National Research Council, 2003, 284–286). Higher IMR in rural areas reflects the disadvantage in household factors including access to clear drinking water and sanitation facilities. Rural households could also have difficulty in accessing health facilities. The lower education of women in rural areas could also contribute to the poorer health conditions, as it has been shown that education of mothers is an important factor in child survival (Desai & Alva, 1998). Children in urban slums suffer from not only inadequate water and sanitation, but also live in overcrowded and unhealthy living conditions which help explain higher child mortality rates (UNFPA, 2007). Besides infant mortality, there are certain rural-urban differences in health profiles and the epidemiological transition (National Research Council, 2003).

## Income (Poverty)

Poverty in Asia has often been characterized as an overwhelmingly rural problem. Much of the poverty in the developing countries in the region is concentrated in rural areas. Percent of population living under the poverty line is higher by at least 50% or more in rural areas than in urban areas (Table 9.6).

**Table 9.6** Population in poverty, percent, selected countries

| | Urban | Rural | Poverty ratio: rural/urban |
|---|---|---|---|
| **South-Central Asia** | | | |
| Bangladesh, 2005 | 28.4 | 43.8 | 1.54 |
| Nepal, 2003–4 | 9.6 | 34.6 | 3.60 |
| Pakistan, 2004 | 14.9 | 28.1 | 1.88 |
| Sri Lanka, 2002 | 7.9 | 24.7 | 3.12 |
| **South-Eastern Asia** | | | |
| Cambodia, 2004 | 18 | 38 | 2.11 |
| Indonesia, 2004 | 12.1 | 20 | 1.65 |
| Malaysia, 2002 | 2 | 11.4 | 5.70 |
| Thailand, 2002 | 4 | 12.6 | 3.15 |
| Vietnam, 2002 | 6.6 | 35.6 | 5.39 |

*Source*: Nepal, Cambodia and Vietnam from World Bank (2008). Data for other countries from Asian Development Bank (ADB), Key Indicators, 2007. (Table 1: Poverty, Inequality, and Human Development).

The poverty estimates presented in Table 9.6 are based on countries' poverty lines (thresholds) and these poverty lines are not uniform across countries in the region. This should not be a concern for the present chapter as we are interested in rural-urban poverty and not in comparison of poverty across countries in the region. Even comparing poverty across rural and urban areas in the same country is not without difficulty. There are various approaches to calculate poverty thresholds (based on income or consumption, including only food items or including both food and non-food items, calorie intake etc., to name just a few considerations). There are additional considerations when it comes to defining rural and urban poverty lines. In most countries poverty thresholds are calculated separately for rural and urban areas to take into account the differences in consumption patterns and cost of goods, among other things. For instance, in the Philippines, food menus for rural and urban areas are constructed separately by considering local consumption pattern, and the price for buying these food items are evaluated at local prices to derive poverty thresholds for rural and urban areas separately. Under these criteria, about 12% of the urban population and 37% of the rural population lived below the poverty line in 1997 in the Philippines (Balisacan, 2003).

Regardless of the methodology used for calculating poverty lines, for most countries in the region the rural poverty threshold is lower than the urban poverty threshold, reflecting both lower costs in rural areas and differences in consumption patterns. And larger proportions of rural households fall below the poverty threshold than do urban households. In the case of Vietnam, it is estimated that households in urban areas need to spend at least 1,342,000 dong to be out of poverty, but in rural areas just 1,054,000 dong (Duong & Trinh, 1999). However, as seen in Table 9.6, a far higher proportion of people were living in poverty in rural areas compared to urban areas in Vietnam (35.6 vs. 6.6%).

Growth in GDP per capita has coincided with the decline in the share of GDP from agriculture (Dercon, 2009). Although the growth in GDP has the potential to reduce poverty rates, its benefits are unevenly distributed with urban areas gaining more than rural areas. This has perpetuated concentration of the poor in rural areas in many countries in the region. Lower productivity and lower growth in the agricultural sector, coupled with outmigration of young people to cities has contributed to the persistence of poverty in rural areas (Jones, 2009). Rural poor also are more likely to be chronically poor given the limited opportunity for escape from poverty in the rural areas (Hazell & Rosegrant, 2000). Though rural poverty rates are higher than urban poverty rates in much of Asia, in many countries of the region rural poverty has been declining. Growth in smallholder agriculture in Indonesia, Malaysia, and Taiwan in the 1960s and 1970s, and Green Revolution in many countries in the region during the same period led to declines in rural poverty (International Fund for Agricultural Development, 2002). The rapid agricultural growth has been instrumental for major declines in rural poverty in the region.

The rural poor in Asia are mainly the landless, marginal and subsistence farmers, and indigenous people (International Fund for Agricultural Development, 2002). Among the rural poor in Asia who owned agricultural land, the size of landholding was much smaller and less irrigated than the land owned by the non-poor (Hazell & Rosegrant, 2000), thus limiting the potential for productivity growth. For many rural poor in Asia besides income from agricultural activities, an important source of income is from non-farm activities. These non-farm activities include income through seasonal employment in urban areas and income from non-agricultural work in rural areas (United Nations, 2007).

## Employment Structure

The share of employment in agriculture[4] has been declining throughout Asia. This is closely linked to trends in urbanization, since most agricultural sector employment is in rural areas, and a fairly high proportion of rural employment is in the agricultural sector. Rural-urban mobility – not only permanent migration, but also seasonal migration and commuting – has been the key demographic mechanism in the shift in the employment structure away from agriculture.

There are large inter-country variations in the number of persons employed in agriculture, ranging from about 78% in Lao PDR to 4% in Japan in 2007 (Table 9.7). Even during the 12-year period between 1995 and 2007 all countries listed in Table 9.7 clearly show a decline in employment in the agriculture sector (though the decline in Indonesia was, surprisingly, slight), and this trend is expected to continue.[5] Despite the declines in the agriculture sector, the sector provides more than one-third of employment in most countries in Asia, except in Eastern Asia and in Malaysia.

Throughout East Asia, the share of the agriculture sector in total employment has declined sharply. In East Asia (excluding China), it fell from 35% in 1950 to 14% in 1980; in Southeast Asia, it fell less sharply from 72% in 1950 to 56% in 1980. Declines in the agricultural sector's share have continued since then; for example, in Java, it fell from 61% of employment in 1971 to 40% in 2000.

Although most agricultural employment is in rural areas and agriculture is the predominant employment sector in rural areas, agriculture tends to provide a declining proportion of rural employment over time

---

[4] For the sake of brevity, the term "agriculture" in this paper refers to the industrial sector generally defined as "agriculture, forestry, hunting and fishing". In most cases, agriculture provides by far the largest share of employment in this sector.

[5] It must be noted that the classification of employment by industry in censuses and labour force surveys can be misleading because only one activity is reported, despite the multiple activities characterizing the work patterns of many rural dwellers.

**Table 9.7** Employment in agriculture (percent of total employment), selected countries, 1995 and 2007

|  | 1995 | 2007 |
|---|---|---|
| **Eastern Asia** | | |
| Japan | 5.7 | 4.2 |
| Republic of Korea | 11.8 | 7.4 |
| **South-Central Asia** | | |
| Bangladesh[a] | 48.9 | 48.1 |
| Pakistan | 46.8 | 43.7 |
| Sri Lanka | 36.7 | 31.3 |
| **South-Eastern Asia** | | |
| Cambodia | 81.4 | 59.1 |
| Indonesia | 44.0 | 43.7 |
| Lao PDR[a] | – | 78.5 |
| Malaysia | 20.0 | 14.8 |
| Philippines | 43.4 | 36.1 |
| Thailand | 46.7 | 39.5 |
| Viet Nam | 71.3 | 53.8 |

[a] Data for Bangladesh are from 1996 and 2006. Data for Lao PDR from 2005.
*Source*: Asian Development Bank (ADB), Key Indicators for Asia and the Pacific, 2009.

(United Nations, 1980, Table 9). The rural labour force does not simply passively release agricultural workers for non-agricultural employment in the towns, but it can itself undergo major modifications in occupational structure over the course of economic development. For example, non-agricultural employment provided 35% of total employment in rural areas of East Java in 1985 (Jones, 1993, 81–2), and this proportion is one that can change over time – albeit, much influenced by changes in the definitions of urban areas employed in the country concerned, and by definitions of migration, which can result in inclusion in the rural workforce of rural-based workers who are in the city as circular migrants at the time of a census or labour force survey, but are not intending to stay for more than six months.

A key development in all the successful countries of East Asia was the diversification of rural labour markets over time. Oshima stresses the seasonality of labour demand in agriculture in what he refers to as "monsoon Asia" (Oshima, 1988). As a general notion of why East Asian countries grew spectacularly in the three decades after 1950, followed by a group of Southeast Asian countries since the 1970s, but not South Asian countries, he argues that the process of growth was "started by keeping labour in agriculture, providing more and better productive activities during the slack months through multicropping, and diversification with fruit and vegetable growing, root crops, poultry and other animal products, and fishery, together with greater off-farm employment from labour-intensive industrial production. The more plentiful work opportunities for farm family members during the slack months contribute to higher annual incomes and an expanding domestic market for industries and services, eventually leading to a fully employed labour force. With a tighter labour market, real wages start to accelerate and mechanization spreads to the vast majority of farms and firms, and the substitution of labour by small machines begins to raise total factor productivity and GDP per capita" (Oshima, 1988, 10–11). He also sees agriculture-based, labour-intensive industrialization as having been favourable for keeping income disparities low, and lowering fertility rates. Japan was the pacesetter, but other East Asian countries were soon to follow in its footsteps (Oshima, 1988, 110–116).

Table 9.8 shows the change in the employment structure in rural areas of Indonesia over time. According to the census data (in the first four columns), the share of agriculture has fallen, though not drastically. This is not surprising, since one of the criteria for deciding whether a village is urban or rural is the percentage of families whose main source of income is agriculture. However, the table also illustrates the kinds of difficulties encountered in tracing employment trends over time in many countries of Asia. Definitions of industry in Indonesia were changed in the 2000 census, making comparisons with earlier censuses hazardous. Using data from Sakernas (the labour force survey) leaves many questions unanswered, because this includes only labourers and employees, and not employers, self-employed and unpaid family workers. Many of those working in agriculture, and also in trade, fall in the categories excluded from the survey, and this no doubt explains why the proportion of the rural labour force in agriculture and trade appears much lower using the Sakernas data, and the proportions in manufacturing, construction and services much higher.

The densely populated island of Java provides a useful case study of some of the employment trends affecting densely populated parts of East and Southeast Asia. Java's population has risen from 76 million in

## 9 Rural Demography in Asia and the Pacific Rim

**Table 9.8** Indonesia: industrial structure of employment in rural areas (percent)

| Sector | Census data | | | | Sakernas data | |
|---|---|---|---|---|---|---|
| | 1971 | 1980 | 1990 | 2000 | 2000 | 2008 |
| Agriculture | 76.3 | 67.2 | 65.4 | 67.8 | 35.9 | 41.1 |
| Mining | 0.1 | 0.7 | 1.0 | –[a] | –[a] | 2.4 |
| Manufacturing | 6.1 | 8.0 | 9.2 | 4.5 | 21.6 | 15.0 |
| Construction | 1.2 | 2.7 | 3.3 | –[a] | 11.6 | 12.5 |
| Trade | 8.4 | 10.2 | 10.7 | 8.3 | 5.0 | 5.5 |
| Transportation | 1.3 | 1.8 | 2.4 | 1.6 | 3.9 | 4.2 |
| Services | 6.7 | 9.4 | 7.9 | 9.3 | 21.2 | 19.0 |
| Other | 0.0 | 0.1 | 0.1 | 8.5[a] | 0.8 | 0.3 |
| **Total** | **100** | **100** | **100** | **100** | **100** | **100** |

[a] Included in "other". In the 2000 Census, "other" included mining and quarrying, construction, and electricity, gas and water.
*Source*: Population censuses; the final two columns are calculated from Sakernas (labour force survey) data (Badan Pusat Statistik, various year), which cover only labourers and employees. In the case of 2008, the two rounds (February and August) are averaged.

1971 to 137 million in 2010 and overall population density from 560 per sq. km. in 1971 to 1,010 per sq. km. in 2010. The island contains Indonesia's three largest cities – Jakarta, Surabaya and Bandung, and many other smaller cities with intricate linkages to surrounding rural areas. Although almost half of Java's population lives in urban areas, the population density in rural areas is very high.

In Java, Manning (1998, 141) notes three developments in rural labour markets: integration of rural labour markets across activities; more intense urban and rural labour market linkages; and corresponding changes in wage institutions and contracts. The 1970s were a period of labour market stress in Java, with rural population and labour force continuing to increase, high levels of landlessness, and considerable poverty. Rural wage rates stagnated, and labour was displaced in the harvesting and processing of rice through new harvesting technology and altered hiring arrangements and systems of payment (Collier, 1981). Rural-urban migration, much of it in the form of commuting and circular migration, increased (Hugo, 1978). Survival strategies of poor households involved low-return farm labour, and whatever other employment or income-earning activity was on offer, often outside the village (Hart, 1986).

The situation began to change in the late 1970s as the oil boom intensified, many traditional labour-intensive industries found it hard to compete with new industries in urban and peri-urban locations, and job opportunities increased with greater spending on rural public works programs and sustained rice production growth. Many rural households, both landowning and landless households, began to derive most of their income from non-agricultural sources (White, 1991; see also Shand, 1986 for broader Asian patterns). By the early 1980s, rising educational levels in rural areas made more young people disinclined to work in agriculture. At the same time, opportunities for agricultural work were more limited, as a result of mechanization and widespread use of herbicides, and both non-agricultural employment opportunities in rural areas and employment opportunities in the towns were increasing. Rural-urban linkages were strengthening, as a result of improved transportation and communications, and even working abroad (in the Middle East and Malaysia) was becoming more common (Manning, 1998, Chapter 6). These trends have continued since then.

### Effect of Proximity to Cities

Studies in Indonesia on the effect on employment structure of proximity of rural areas to large cities in the 1970s and 1980s show very clearly that the percentage of non-agricultural employment in the rural areas of various *kabupaten* (regencies) of Java tended to be highest in the kabupaten close to the large cities, especially Jakarta, Bandung, Surabaya, and Yogyakarta-Surakarta, and lowest in those that are more isolated from large cities (Jones, Nurhidayati, Simandjuntak, & Prakosa, 1984). Figure 9.2 shows the situation for males in 1980. There may be a number of reasons. One

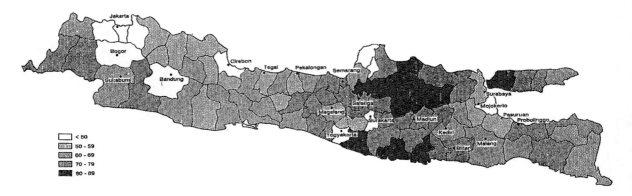

**Fig. 9.2** Java: percentage of employed males in agriculture, rural areas of Kabupaten, 1980

is that some cities had spilled over their boundaries, so that some of what was being recorded as rural population was really suburban. Another is that factories and service sector establishments built in rural areas were more likely to be located in areas close to the large cities than in areas further away. Another is that rural dwellers in areas close to the large cities could avail themselves of the opportunities to commute to urban jobs. One study indicated that "a high proportion of workers in villages within a radius of 60 kilometres from cities and industrial centres had moved out of agriculture altogether by 1993. Labour shortages were widely reported in many of these now peri-urban villages, and real wage rates had increased substantially in rice equivalents since 1980" (Manning, 1998, 146, citing Collier, Santoso, Soentoro, & Wibowo, 1993).

Recent analyses of the employment structure of rural areas in Indonesia according to their proximity to cities are not available. However, it is reasonable to expect that the field of influence of the cities on employment structure in surrounding rural areas has widened, with the improvement of the transportation infrastructure and the greater availability of means of transportation. One study, conducted in association with the 2000 Population Census, indicated that just over one million commuters travelled into Jakarta daily from surrounding areas of Bogor, Depok, Tangerang and Bekasi. The number would have been even higher if the study had included those coming from even further afield. These commuters were relatively highly educated, and about half of them spent as long as one to two hours getting to their workplace (Mamas & Komalasari, 2008, 132–134). Although the majority of them were probably living in areas designated as urban, a significant proportion would have been commuting from rural areas.

How comparable is the recent experience of Java with that of countries such as Taiwan and Korea (and earlier, Japan) in terms of the role of diversification of rural income-earning opportunities in holding the rural labour force in rural areas? In Taiwan and Japan (though less so in Korea) agricultural diversification and intensification proceeded hand-in-hand with commuting to urban jobs and establishment of factories in rural areas. Agricultural diversification and intensification and increasing off-farm employment opportunities enabled farm family real incomes to be substantially increased, and thus limited the incentive for relocation to the cities, as well as increasing the size of the rural market for manufactured goods and services. This fortunate outcome was based on high overall rates of economic growth and intensive efforts to raise farm productivity (Oshima, 1983). Trends in Java share some common features with the East Asian countries, but others are distinctive. Despite extreme population densities in rural Java, Javanese agriculture has managed to absorb labour beyond the expectations of many analysts, partly because of development of new, labour-intensive activities such as upland vegetable farming, citrus fruits and apples, and labour-intensive dairy farming and chicken farming. At the same time, the number of agricultural wage workers has declined steadily, as many were absorbed into informal sector work in urban areas, either permanently or through commuting or circular migration, and transport and construction work in rural areas (Manning, 1998, 91).

## Conclusions

The rural population of Asia will begin to decline steadily after 2015, though the timing of onset of this decline differs by many decades between the different countries of Asia. But what is involved in being a rural dweller has changed significantly in recent decades. In general, the earlier sharp distinctions between urban and rural residence in terms of access to electricity, television, and communications facilities have blurred greatly. Road transportation has developed remarkably, especially in the middle-income countries of the region such as Thailand and rapidly growing economies such as Indonesia, placing formerly isolated villages within much readier reach of larger towns, thus opening hitherto unthinkable possibilities for commuting and circular migration. Rural populations do, however, remain disadvantaged in many ways, as indicated by sharp rural-urban differentials in educational, health and income indicators. Rural income sources were always more diversified than revealed by employment survey data, which prioritized one occupation or industry whereas multiple activities were the common pattern for many rural dwellers. But they have become even more diverse, especially in rural areas within commuting distance of major cities.

Some of the more pressing issues for research into the changing demography of rural Asia include the implications of the changing family structures consequent on declining fertility, population ageing and patterns of migration to urban areas. In Thailand, studies have shown that the absent children of rural elderly are able to provide financial and emotional support, particularly now that cell-phones are almost ubiquitous, but that the care of frail and disabled elderly requires physical proximity (Knodel & Chayovan, 2008). Issues of eldercare are pressing for all ageing populations in the region, but have particular nuances for rural populations.

## References

ADB. (2007). *Key indicators 2007: Inequality in Asia*. Manila: Asian Development Bank.
ADB. (2009). *Key indicators for Asia and the Pacific 2009*. Manila: Asian Development Bank.
Badan Pusat Statistik (BPS). (2006). *Population of Indonesia: Results of the Intercensal Population Survey 2005, Series S1*. Jakarta: BPS.
Badan Pusat Statistik (BPS). (various years). *Labor force situation in Indonesia*. Jakarta: BPS.
Balisacan, A. M. (2003). Poverty comparison in the Philippines: Is what we know about the poor robust? In C. Edmonds (Ed.), *Reducing poverty in Asia: Emerging issues in growth, targeting, and measurement* (pp. 197–219). Cheltenham, UK: Edward Elgar.
Carino, B. V. (1976). Managing migration streams and population redistribution: Alternative strategies and research needs. In R. A. Bulatao (Ed.), *Philippine population research*. Makati, Rizal: Population Center Foundation.
Carron, G., & Chau, T. N. (1996). *The quality of primary schools in different development contexts*. Paris: International Institute for Educational Planning.
Champion, A. G. (Ed.). (1989). *Counterurbanization: The changing pace and nature of population deconcentration*. London: Edward Arnold.
Champion, T., & Hugo, G. (Eds.). (2004). *New forms of urbanization: Beyond the urban-rural dichotomy*. Aldershot, England: Ashgate.
Chomitz, K. M., Buys, P., & Thomas, T. S. (2005). *Quantifying the rural-urban gradient in Latin America and the Caribbean*. World Bank Policy Research Working Paper (WPS3634).
Collier, W. L. (1981). Agricultural evolution in Java. In G. E. Hansen (Ed.), *Agricultural and rural development in Indonesia* (pp. 147–173). Boulder, CO: Westview Press.
Collier, W. L., Santoso, K., Soentoro, & Wibowo, R. (1993). *A new approach to rural development in Java: Twenty five years of village studies*. Unpublished paper, Jakarta.
Coombs, P. H. (1985). *The world crises in education: The view from the eighties*. New York: Oxford University Press.
Department of Census and Statistics. (2006). *Brief analysis of population and housing characteristics*. Colombo: Sri Lanka. http://www.statistics.gov.lk/PopHouSat/index.asp.
Dercon, S. (2009). Rural poverty: Old challenges in new contexts. *The World Bank Research Observer, 24*(1), 1–28.
Desai, S., & Alva, S. (1998). Maternal education and child health: Is there a strong causal relationship? *Demography, 35*(1), 71–81.
DHS. (2010). *MEASURE DHS STAT compiler tool*. www.measuredhs.com
Duong, N. B., & Trinh, D. T. (1999). Identification of poverty in Vietnam. In D. Haughton, J. Haughton, S. Bales, T. T. K. Chuyen, & N. N. Nga (Eds.), *Health and wealth in Vietnam: An analysis of household living standards* (pp. 139–152). Singapore: Institute of Southeast Asian Studies Press.
ESCAP. (1982). *Migration, urbanization and development in Malaysia*. Country Report, Comparative Study on Migration, Urbanization and Development in the ESCAP Region.
Goldstein, S., & Goldstein, A. (1986). *Migration in Thailand: A twenty-five-year review*. Papers of the East-West Population Institute, No. 100. Honolulu, Hawaii.
Hart, G. (1986). *Power, labor and livelihood: Processes of change in rural Java*. Berkeley, CA: University of California Press.
Hazell, P., & Rosegrant, M. (2000). *Transforming the rural Asian economy: The unfinished revolution*. New York: Oxford University Press.
Hugo, G. (1978). *Population mobility in west Java*. Yogyakarta: Gadjah Mada University Press.

Hugo, G. (1982). Circular migration in Indonesia. *Population and Development Review, 8*(1), 59–83.

Hugo, G. (1997). Changing patterns and processes of population mobility. In G. W. Jones & T. H. Hull (Eds.), *Indonesia assessment: Population and human resources* (pp. 68–100). Singapore: Institute of Southeast Asian Studies.

International Fund for Agricultural Development. (2002). *Assessment of rural poverty in Asia and the Pacific*. Rome: IFAD.

Jones, G. W. (1993). East Java: Educational change and changing employment structure. In H. Dick, J. J. Fox, & J. Mackie (Eds.), *Balanced development: East Java in the new order* (pp. 75–100). Singapore: Oxford University Press.

Jones, G. W. (1997). The thoroughgoing urbanization of East and Southeast Asia. *Asia Pacific Viewpoint, 38*(3), 237–250.

Jones, G. W. (2004). Urbanization trends in Asia: The conceptual and definitional challenges. In T. Champion & G. Hugo (Eds.), *New forms of urbanization* (pp. 113–132). Aldershot, Hants: Ashgate Publishing Limited.

Jones, G. W. (2009). Population and poverty: The situation in Asia and the Pacific. A*sia-Pacific Population Journal, 24*(1), 65–86.

Jones, G. W., Nurhidayati, F., Simandjuntak, E., & Prakosa, D. (1984). *Urbanization and structure change in employment in Indonesia: Evidence from province and Kabupaten level analysis of 1971–1980 census data*. Report T1.4/C2. Jakarta: National Urban Development Strategy Project.

Keyfitz, N. (1985). An East Javanese village in 1953 and 1985: Observations on development. *Population and Development Review, 11*(4), 695–719.

Knodel, J., & Chayovan, N. (2008). *Population Ageing and the well-being of older persons in Thailand: Past trends, current situation and future challenges*. Papers in Population Ageing No. 5. Bangkok: UNFPA.

Mamas, S. G. M., & Komalasari, R. (2008). Jakarta – dynamics of change and livability. In G. W. Jones & M. Douglass (Eds.), *Mega-urban regions in Pacific Asia: Urban dynamics in a global era* (pp. 109–149). Singapore: NUS Press.

Manning, C. (1998). *Indonesian labour in transition: An East Asian success story?* Cambridge: Cambridge University Press.

National Research Council. (2003). *Cities transformed: Demographic change and its implications in the developing world*. Washington, DC: National Academies Press.

National Statistics Office. (2007). *Survey of older persons*. Bangkok: NSO.

Oey-Gardiner, M. (1991). Gender differences in schooling in Indonesia. *Bulletin of Indonesian Economic Studies, 27*(1), 57–80.

Oshima, H. (1983). *Off-farm employment and incomes in post-war East Asia*. Paper prepared for the Conference on Off-farm Employment in the Development of Rural Asia, Chiangmai, Thailand.

Oshima, H. T. (1988). *Economic growth of monsoon Asia: A comparative survey*. Tokyo: University of Tokyo Press.

Porpora, D., & Lim, M. H. (1987). The political economic factors of migration to Bangkok. *Journal of Contemporary Asia, 17*(1), 76–89.

Rigg, J. (1997). *Southeast Asia: The human landscape of modernization and development*. London: Routledge.

Shand, R. T. (Ed.). (1986). *Off-farm employment in the development of rural Asia*. Canberra: National Centre for Development Studies, Australian National University.

Sri Lanka Country Report. (2002). *Population division, ministry of health nutrition and welfare*. Report submitted for the Fifth Asian and Pacific Population Conference. UNESCAP: Bangkok, Thailand.

UNFPA. (2007). *State of world population 2007: Unleashing the potential of urban growth*. New York: UNFPA.

United Nations. (1969). *Growth of the world's urban and rural population, 1920–2000, Population Studies No. 44*. New York: United Nations.

United Nations. (1980). *Patterns of rural and urban population growth, Population Studies No. 68*. New York: Unites Nations.

United Nations. (2007). *Persistent and emerging issues in rural poverty reduction*. Bangkok: UN Economic and Social Commission for Asia and the Pacific.

United Nations Population Division. (2009). *World urbanization prospects: The 2009 Revision*. New York: United Nations.

White, B. (1991). Economic diversification and agrarian change in rural Java, 1900–1990. In P. Alexander, P. Boomgaard, & B. White (Eds.), *In the shadow of agriculture: Non-farm activities in the Javanese economy, past and present* (pp. 41–69). Amsterdam: Royal Tropical Institute.

World Bank. (2008). *Poverty data: A supplement to world development indicators 2008*. Washington, DC: World Bank.

World Bank. (2010). *2010 World development indicators*. Washington, DC: The World Bank.

# Demographic Change and Rural-Urban Inequality in Sub-Saharan Africa: Theory and Trends

Parfait M. Eloundou-Enyegue and Sarah C. Giroux

**Abbreviations**

DHS   Demographic and Health Surveys
HIV   Human Immunodeficiency Virus
MLD   Mean Logarithmic Deviation
NRC   National Research Council (US)
UN    United Nations
UNICEF United Nations' Children Fund
UNDP  United Nations Development Program
TFR   Total Fertility Rate

## Introduction

In theory, demographic change can spur socioeconomic change, and a rich body of literature has reviewed the many arguments why trends in the growth and structure of national populations might affect such outcomes as economic growth, savings, poverty rates, child schooling, or health for instance (Birdsall, Kelley, & Sinding, 2001; Bloom, Canning, & Sevilla, 2003; Greene & Merrick, 2005; Mason & Lee, 2004). While the early literature had mostly focused on aggregate relationships between *national* demographic rates and *national* economic outcomes, recent studies have begun to explore internal inequality in these processes, whether this inequality is deployed across socioeconomic or rural-urban lines. Under this more disaggregated perspective, the second demographic transition in progress within industrial nations is expected to create *"divergent destinies"* for middle and lower-income families (McLanahan, 2004). Studies in developing nations likewise show great unevenness in the pace or depth of their early demographic transitions. In the specific case of sub-Saharan Africa, the region's fertility transitions, which began in the 1990s and brought the region's fertility levels from 6.3 to nearly 5 today, appear to follow a three-stage pattern "with fertility initially declining in urban areas while remaining stable in rural areas, then fertility falling in both settings but more rapidly among urban dwellers, and finally with fertility declining more in rural than in urban areas" (Shapiro & Tambashe, 2001, p. 111). Insofar as fertility influences socioeconomic outcomes, such uneven declines might worsen the economic inequality between rural and urban communities in Africa, a region in the world where the extent of rural poverty is already quite high. Because 80% of the poor in Africa live in rural areas (World Bank, 2000), how Africa's rural-urban gap responds to demographic change is an important question. Unfortunately, few studies have fully articulated, let alone monitor the links between demographic change and rural-urban inequality (World Bank, 2000). The time is apposite for such review, as African countries are now in the midst of their demographic transitions. For the region as a whole, national birth rates fell on average by 20% in the last two decades; youth age dependency (in relation to the working age population) has likewise fallen from a peak of 88% in the mid 1980s to 78% today; and the share of urban population has more than doubled since independence in the 1960s (from 15 to about 37% today), despite higher rural than urban fertility.

The purpose of this article is twofold. Its first, theoretical, objective is to propose a simple argument

P.M. Eloundou-Enyegue (✉)
Department of Development Sociology, Cornell University,
Ithaca, NY 14853, USA
e-mail: pme7@cornell.edu

linking demographic change to rural-urban inequality. A second, empirical, objective is to review recent demographic trends, with an eye to making indirect inferences about prospects for rural-urban inequality. Our central postulate is that Africa's demographic transitions shape rural-urban inequality through proximate processes of demographic *differentiation* and demographic *exchange*. Demographic differentiation refers to the growing inequality in demographic outcomes linked to socioeconomic wellbeing. Such outcomes include fertility, age structure, or the educational composition of the population (Lam, 1986; Lam & Levison, 1992; Mare, 1997; De La Croix & Doepke, 2003). Conversely, demographic exchange refers to the redistribution of population between urban and rural communities in patterns that mitigate rural-urban inequality in wellbeing. Beyond the rural-to-urban migration of adult workers in response to wage disparities (DeJong & Gardner, 1981), processes of demographic exchange include the fosterage of children (Isiugo-Abanihe, 1985). Fosterage is the practice of sending one's children to live with relatives or friends for extended periods of time. Contrary to adoption, fosterage is a temporary, partial, and informal transfer of guardianship: the children's primary loyalty remains to biological parents; guardianship can be terminated if any of the parties becomes dissatisfied with the arrangement; and the cost burden of rearing foster children may be shared, with the biological parents often bearing some of the schooling or health expenses. Fosterage is pervasive in Africa and much of it flows from rural to urban areas. In some countries, as many as one third of children live with someone other than their biological mother (Caldwell & Caldwell, 1987; Isiugo-Abanihe, 1985; Mensch, Bruce, & Greene, 1998). Importantly, fosterage has been shown to enhance the education and employment opportunities of rural children and, as such, it is often viewed as a potent buffer against rural-urban inequality (Mahieu, 1989; Akresh, 2005).

Processes of demographic differentiation and exchange can thus combine to shape trends in rural-urban inequality in sub-Saharan Africa. While demographic differentiation would exacerbate economic inequality, processes of demographic exchange (especially fosterage) would buffer it. Accordingly, the overall trend in rural-urban inequality would reflect these two opposite influences. By monitoring demographic trends, one can indirectly make tentative inferences about the harder-to-document trends in economic inequality between rural and urban communities.

## Why Rural-Urban Inequality Matters

Rural-urban inequality matters for both intrinsic and extrinsic reasons. One might intrinsically be concerned about the welfare of rural populations, seen as a vulnerable group in the context of urban bias or selective globalization, and many studies have indeed shown large rural-urban differences in wages and social infrastructure (Gugler & Flanagan, 1978; Lipton, 1977; Giroux, 2008; Sahn & Stifel, 2003). The emerging concern, however, is whether these inequalities continue to grow under the influence of globalization. In 1975, fewer than 3 out of 1,000 Africans owned a television set. This number has multiplied by nearly 20, reaching 52 per 1,000 in 1998, and it further quadrupled to reach about 210 per 1,000 in the mid-2000s. Similar expansion occurred in the number of phone lines, mobile phones, and Internet access. While in 1970 only 1 out of 100 Africans had access to a telephone, this number skyrocketed to 35 by 2008 (World Bank, 2010). The region had virtually no internet users in 1990, but 6.5% of its population was connected by 2008 (World Bank, 2010). This expansion unfortunately remains asymmetric, reaching the urban middle class more than rural poor. With only a few exceptions, the urban/rural ratios in access exceed 10:1 and 5:1 for television and telephone, respectively (Christy, 2004). While urban Africa increasingly plugs into global society, most rural communities remain disconnected from global communication. Insofar as globalization carries economic opportunity, this selective "glurbanization" might fuel inequality between rural and urban communities of Africa. Compounding this digital divide is unequal access in more traditional resources and services: only 5% of rural Africans have electricity (versus 88% of residents of large cities) (Hewitt & Montgomery, 2001). Most (90%) rural households lack access to electricity, running water, flush toilets, and access to health care. In the Central African Republic, for instance, "maternal child services congregated in cities and operated erratically in rural areas" (Hewitt & Montgomery, 2001). Angola likewise had only 13% of the government health staff working in rural areas, while housing 65% of the population (United Nations Development Programme, 2003). More broadly, Sahn and Stifel (2003) found that the standards of living in rural areas of sub-Saharan Africa almost universally trail far behind those in urban areas. Again, a concern is that selective globalization would widen the rural-urban gap in Africa, even as it brings some of the urban labor force in greater contact with the rest of the world.

One might also be extrinsically interested in rural-urban inequality as a component of global inequality. Global inequality is the sum of between-country and within-country inequality, and although inequality between countries seems to be declining on a global scale,[1] the global inequality could still be rising depending on trends within countries. Although studies recognize the importance of intracountry inequalities, they typically lack the detailed data to monitor these inequalities, whether across regional, ethnic, or class lines (Firebaugh & Goesling, 2004). Rural-urban inequality is particularly relevant at a time when the world is achieving parity in the size of its rural versus urban populations (United Nations, 2009). With this parity in population weights, rural-urban differentials will likely drive national and global inequality more decisively than has historically been the case. The weight of rural populations, and its importance in driving national inequality, has certainly increased in sub-Saharan Africa where the region's share of rural population has declined from 85% in the 1960s to about 63% today (United Nations, 2009). Again, research on global inequality is hampered by a paucity of historical data on internal inequality, including along rural-urban lines. Given such lack of direct evidence, we propose an indirect approach focused on proximate demographic drivers of rural-urban inequality, as discussed below.

## Demographic Correlates of Rural-Urban Inequality

Given the lack of direct evidence on trends in rural-urban inequality, demography is used here as a proxy. The idea is to monitor demographic processes proximately related to rural-urban inequality. Key processes explored here include both *demographic differentiation* and *demographic exchange*.

## Demographic Differentiation

Several demographic outcomes are expected to affect economic wellbeing. At the microlevel, high fertility has been argued to dilute human capital investments in individual children: Large progenies compete for parental resources, and each additional child is seen as reducing the resources available to siblings (Blake, 1989). Accordingly, rural-urban differences in fertility would portend inequality in human capital and productivity. Since fertility behavior is conversely shaped by economic conditions, a vicious cycle between high fertility and adverse economic conditions becomes plausible in theory. Empirically, how much children's sibsize affects their schooling and life chances has been found to vary greatly across contexts (Lloyd, 1994). Effects tend to be weak where fertility is uniformly high or education uniformly low, or where public subsidization of education is available to poor and large families. They strengthen when national birth rates fall, as is the case in many African countries today. Although sibsize is known to affect schooling, the ultimate implications for employment are unclear in Africa's current context of low graduate employment (Demographic and Health Surveys, 2010).

At the macrolevel, the size, age structure, and educational composition of national populations might also shape inequality. Some of these influences are purely mechanical: For instance, the relative size of populations is often factored as a weighing variable in classic computations of national and global inequality (Firebaugh & Goesling, 2004). Age structure is likewise treated as a mechanical influence, in macroeconomic projections of savings, investments, or economic growth that assume constancy in age-specific behavior (Bloom et al., 2003). Beyond such mechanical influences, more substantive effects might

---

[1] Between 1980 and 1998 for instance, the between-nation income inequality (as measured by the Mean Logarithmic Deviation) has declined from about 0.63 to 0.49 (Firebaugh & Goesling, 2004). Importantly, similar convergence is not visible across African countries. Instead, GDP inequality (as measured by the squared coefficient of variation) doubled from about 0.75 in the early 1960s to about 1.6 at the turn of the century (Kandiwa, 2007). Africa thus stands as an exception to the convergence noted for world countries as a whole. This differentiation extends to children's schooling and mortality, raising concerns about future inequality (UNICEF, 2008; Eloundou-Enyegue & Rehman, 2009).

be considered. For instance, the size and growth of national population might increase the pressure on farmland, schooling, or employment. Population density may spur productivity, slower population growth may raise output per worker, or changes in age structure may likewise affect productivity (Boserup, 1996; NRC, 1986). Given the lack of consensus on these substantive influences (National Research Council, 1986), this paper focuses on mechanical effects, specifically those of the relative size, age structure, and education composition of populations.

## Demographic Exchange

The demographic exchanges considered in this analysis include processes – such as migration and child fosterage – that move populations between rural and urban communities in ways that could mitigate inequality in opportunity and wellbeing. In theory, rural-urban migration has been linked to wage imbalances between the rural and urban sectors, even as this migration often continues in the face of high urban unemployment (DeJong & Gardner, 1981). Even as the role of current wage differentials has increasingly been downplayed in more nuanced explanations that emphasize longer term and family strategies as well as cumulative causation (Massey, 1990), migration and subsequent remittances continue to feature prominently as a potential source of economic redistribution. Return migration – whether in response to high urban unemployment or retirement – can also foster social change in rural areas in ways that ultimately bridge the rural urban divide (Courade, 1994). Although these various influences are plausible in theory, the limited historical data on migration flows complicates empirical analysis. Moreover, recent work by Potts (2009) suggests that urbanization levels are declining or stagnating in many sub-Saharan countries including Zambia, Cote D'Ivoire, Mali, Benin, Mozambique, Senegal, Zimbabwe, Mauritania, Burkina Faso, and Niger. While the situation is more mixed in east Africa, this evidence suggests that, as a result of declining economic opportunities available in many urban areas, rural-to-urban migration may not persist as a viable buffer of rural-urban inequality.

Our analyses thus focus on fosterage. Fosterage, the practice of granting temporary guardianship of children to relatives, is pervasive in Africa. As many as one third of children live with someone other than their biological mother (Demographic and Health Surveys, 2010), and much of the fostering flows from rural to urban areas. Fosterage "enables parents to escape some of the costs of schooling that might otherwise... make it necessary that fertility be reduced if the children are to be property educated" (Montgomery, Kouame, & Oliver, 1995, p. 15). African children spend a substantial portion of their childhood years living away from their mothers, roughly 18% in Ghana, 16% in Senegal, and 12% in Mali (Lloyd & Desai, 1992). Between 1998 and 2000, 27% of households in rural Burkina Faso either sent or received a foster child, and these fostered children spent an average of 2.75 years away from their parents (Akresh, 2005). These transfers are central to the economic mobility of children from rural families seeking access to urban schooling and employment opportunities. Because they channel the mobility of rural children and because they enable the representation of rural constituencies among the urban elite, these kinship networks have been argued to deflect class conflict along rural-urban lines (Mahieu, 1989). Insofar as fosterage redistributes children across households, it has the potential to reduce inequality, including across rural-urban lines. The question however, is whether mere physical/geographic redistribution is enough, and whether fosterage could turn out to be exploitative rather than ameliorative. Some studies find assistance to foster children to be selectively contingent on kinship ties (Case, Paxson, & Ableidinger, 2004). Others raise concern that urban families are increasingly strained in their capacity to accommodate foster children (Lloyd & Gage-Brandon, 1994; McDaniel & Zulu, 1994). Whether fosterage continues to buffer rural-urban inequality requires evidence about both the volume and the direction of fosterage flows. In other words, buffering is strongest if many children are fostered, and they are mostly fostered from large, poor, and rural into smaller, wealthier, and urban families. In sum, where one lacks direct historical evidence on economic inequality between rural and urban areas, we propose monitoring, as a substitute, the trends in demographic differentiation and demographic exchange between rural and urban communities.

## Data

To examine recent trends in these proximate processes, we use data from Demographic Health Surveys (DHS). The DHS are a series of national representative surveys fielded over the last two decades in over 75 developing countries of Africa, Asia, and Latin America. Started in 1984, these surveys have collected information on topics such as fertility, family planning, maternal and child health, gender, HIV/AIDS, malaria, and nutrition. The surveys include core data on fertility and health, but also include information on household wealth, schooling, and residence, thus permitting detailed analyses of the relationship between demographic forces and inequality (Demographic and Health Surveys, 2010). The DHS website facilitates easy tabulation of summary information that can be disaggregated by residence. The unit of analysis is a country-period and our sample of country-periods covers data from 97 surveys in 39 sub-Saharan countries over a time span roughly from 1990 to 2008. Of the 39 countries covered, four (Senegal, Ghana, Kenya, and Nigeria) were surveyed five times, seven were surveyed four times, seven were surveyed three times, seven twice, and the rest (14) once. Our analyses mostly rely on simple statistical correlation/regression of demographic outcomes of rural and urban populations. The idea is to compare, for each country-period, urban and rural outcomes, i.e., examine the rural-urban gap and its trend. We scatter plot the magnitude of this gap and its dependency on time or context, focusing particularly on a country's stage in demographic transition. Data show great variability in the sampled countries. In particular, national fertility rates averaged 5.6 births per women but ranged between 2.9 and 7.4, thus covering the full range between pretransitional to near-replacement fertility levels. The percentage of adults in the national population ranged from 41 to 51%; the percentage of adults with some high school education ranged from 4 to 46%! And the percentage of rural children out-fostered similar spanned a wide range, from 5 to 40%!

The regressions do not control for covariates and, as such, results must not suggest causation. Rather, they are mere correlations showing rural-urban differentiation as countries progress through various transitions. For instance, when studying the fertility differentiation, one can scatter plot the rural-to-urban ratio (Y-axis) against the urban or national fertility level (X-axis). Differentiation is said to occur if the gap widens as urban fertility declines. To describe the trend, we use the $b$ and $R^2$ values associated with the scatter plot. The $b$ value indicates the marginal widening of the gap for each unit advance in the fertility transition; the $R^2$ value represents the strength of association between the rural-urban gap and the stage in fertility transition. It is worth noting, as another weakness, that we use a static correlation to study what is intrinsically a historical process. One would ideally prefer tracking actual demographic *change* within each country, and using countries – not country-periods – as units of analysis. Unfortunately, doing so would reduce the analysis to the few countries that had fielded multiple surveys. On the basis of past comparisons of these two analytical strategies in studying inequality and demographic transitions in sub-Saharan Africa (Giroux, Eloundou-Enyegue, & Lichter, 2008), findings should be similar.

## Findings

### Demographic Differentiation

This section shows evidence on the extent of demographic differentiation between rural and urban communities of Africa, as they advance through their demographic transitions. The analyses examine differentiation in fertility, age structure, and educational composition, respectively.

### Fertility

Figure 10.1 plots the cross-sectional relationship between total fertility rate (TFR, on the X-axis) and rural-to-urban ratios in TFRs (Y-axis). On the Y-axis, values above 1 imply higher rural, than urban, fertility. As the chart shows, the ratios increase as fertility declines, suggesting a widening gap between rural and urban fertility during the fertility transition. On the basis of the estimated predictive equation, rural fertility is estimated to be 36% higher than urban fertility when the national TFR is 7 births per woman, but the corresponding figure rises to 73% when the national TFR falls to 3. Contrary to the more detailed and historical findings in Shapiro and Tambashe (2002),

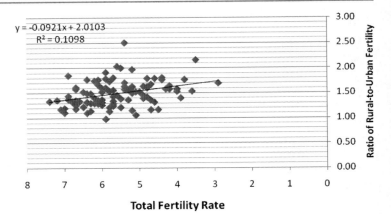

**Fig. 10.1** Trends in the rural-urban ratio in fertility through the fertility transition

our data show no curvilinearity or reversal. The cross-sectional nature of our data precludes strong conclusions, but these findings are consistent with the idea that rural-urban inequality does widen during the course of fertility transitions. One can speculate about the sources of this differentiation, i.e., whether they reflect growing differences in fertility demand or access to contraception. If fertility desires are increasingly diverging, and if these desires reflect differences in economic opportunities, then the conditions are met for a vicious cycle that would reproduce rural-urban inequality in the coming years. As the gap in sibsize grows between rural and urban children, so will the gap in educational attainment and possibly school quality, given the likely effects of sibsize on schooling.

The burden of large sibsize compounds other structural disadvantages faced by rural children, whether in family poverty, distance to schools, understaffing, poorer infrastructure, and other intangibles. Such compounding means that rural children will likely find themselves at an increasing disadvantage in the competition for educational opportunities.

## Age Structure

Figure 10.2 shows the relationship between age structure in urban areas (specifically the percentage of people between the ages of 15–64) and the gap in age structure between urban and rural communities

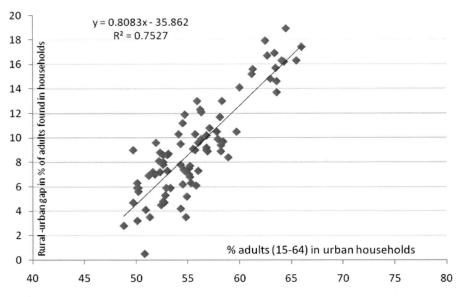

**Fig. 10.2** Trends in the rural-urban gap in age structure through the aging transition

(Y-axis). It reveals a steep and positive relationship. As the percentage of adults grows in urban areas, the gap with rural areas rises sharply ($b = 0.8$; $R^2 = 0.75$). The predictive equation on the chart implies that when the percentage of adults among the urban population is 50%, the rural percentage averages about 45.5%; when the urban percentage rises to 65% for instance, the rural percentage only increases to roughly 48%. In other words, the rural urban gap increases from 4.5 to nearly 17 percentage points, indicating an uneven transition in age structure. During these early transition phases, rural communities increasingly lag behind urban populations in the decline in age dependency. Combined with the earlier results on fertility, these findings imply growing demographic inequality between rural and urban areas.

How this differentiation in age structure affects economic inequality must be considered. In theory, age structure affects age dependency which in turn shapes savings, investments and, ultimately, economic growth. However, some of the links in this chain – in particular between age dependency and savings – are fairly weak in many sub-Saharan countries. Strong correlations are found between age structure and real age dependency[2] and between savings and economic growth.[3] Such findings reduce concern over the material implications of a widening gap in age dependency between rural and urban communities. As long as reductions in dependency burden do not improve savings and economic growth, rural communities suffer little penalty from lagging behind urban communities in their age transition. This concern is further allayed if one considers differences in the very meaning of age structure, as rural and urban sectors differ in their normative life cycle, notably the duration of schooling, the prevalence of child labor, life expectancy, and the age at retirement. The normative age boundaries for dependency may vary markedly for urban and rural communities.

**Educational Composition**

Economic inequality between rural and urban populations also depends upon changes in population composition, notably by education. The earnings premium on education in Africa remains high among those employed in the formal sector of the economy, even as graduate unemployment itself has risen (Demographic and Health Surveys, 2010; Psacharopoulos & Patrinos, 2002). Educated workers might also compete better in the informal economy or in international labor markets. Figure 10.3 shows how the rural-urban gap in schooling changes as the levels of urban education increase. For both males and females, there is a sharp increase in rural-urban gaps. In countries where only 20% of males have some high-school education, this gap is smaller than it is when over 50% of urban males have some high school education. Although the fitted regression line in Fig. 10.3 suggests a linear relationship, a fuller analysis (results not shown) indicates that this relationship is in fact curvilinear. The current divergence will eventually slow down and some convergence will occur. For now however, rural populations are increasingly lagging behind urban households in educational attainment.

**Demographic Exchange**

Although the rural-urban differentiation shown in the previous section raises concern for future economic inequality, this inequality could potentially be buffered by processes of demographic exchanges such as child fosterage. Table 10.1 shows the recent changes in fosterage among urban and rural households. The changes are examined within each country, between the first and last survey year. Although the time span between these surveys varies anywhere from 5 to 16 years, this period was generally characterized by economic or health hardship, as mounting rates of AIDS

---

[2] With some allowance for normative patterns of child labor and adult employment, a 10% decline in youth-adult ratio translated into an 8.4% decline in youth age dependency, and the association between the two variables was quite close (92% of all variation in youth age dependency was associated with changes in youth adult ratio) (Eloundou-Enyegue & Makki, 2010).

[3] For instance, a 10% increase in savings translated on average into a 2% increase in growth (and savings accounted for about 14% of variation in economic growth). Conversely, the crucial middle link between age dependency and savings was weak. Only a very small percentage (1%) of the total change in savings was tied to reduced age dependency. Perhaps generalized poverty, inequality, foreign debt servicing, capital flight, and rising consumerism all helped erode the potential benefits from reduced age dependency. Only in a handful of countries (Angola, Chad, Senegal, Comoros, and the Republic of Congo) could one see a substantial link between reduced age dependency and savings during the study period.

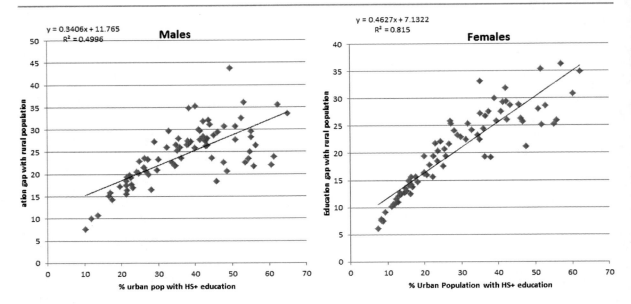

**Fig. 10.3** Trends in rural-urban gap in education through the urban educational transition

**Table 10.1** Recent changes in the levels of child fosterage living in surveyed families, among urban and rural populations

| Country and survey year | | | | Rural families | | | Urban families | | | Rural + urban families | | |
|---|---|---|---|---|---|---|---|---|---|---|---|---|
| Country | Subregion | Last | First | Final year | Initial year | Change | Final year | Initial year | Change | Final year | Initial year | Change |
| Ethiopia | East/South | 2005 | 2000 | 7.9 | 9.6 | −1.7 | 15.6 | 14.4 | 1.2 | 8.6 | 10.1 | −1.5 |
| Rwanda | East/South | 2005 | 2000 | 11.5 | 12.9 | −1.4 | 11.5 | 19.5 | −8 | 11.5 | 13.8 | −2.3 |
| Mozambique | East/South | 2003 | 1997 | 12.5 | 12.5 | 0 | 14.6 | 13.6 | 1 | 13.1 | 12.8 | 0.3 |
| Eritrea | East/South | 2002 | 1995 | 4.8 | 5 | −0.2 | 6.8 | 6.6 | 0.2 | 5.6 | 5.4 | 0.2 |
| Kenya | East/South | 2003 | 1993 | 10.8 | 9.4 | 1.4 | 9.1 | 9 | 0.1 | 10.5 | 9.3 | 1.2 |
| Uganda | East/South | 2006 | 1995 | 17.5 | 16.5 | 1 | 18.8 | 20.7 | −1.9 | 17.6 | 16.9 | 0.7 |
| Zimbabwe | East/South | 2005 | 1994 | 27.7 | 19.3 | 8.4 | 17.8 | 11 | 6.8 | 25.3 | 17.6 | 7.7 |
| Malawi | East/South | 2004 | 1992 | 17.7 | 13.5 | 4.2 | 18.6 | 15.8 | 2.8 | 17.7 | 13.8 | 3.9 |
| Tanzania | East/South | 2004 | 1991 | 11.8 | 11.9 | −0.1 | 16.2 | 3.4 | 12.8 | 12.7 | 12.4 | 0.3 |
| Namibia | East/South | 2006 | 1992 | 40.1 | 32.4 | 7.7 | 18.6 | 16.5 | 2.1 | 32.7 | 28.6 | 4.1 |
| Zambia | East/South | 2007 | 1992 | 15.8 | 15.1 | 0.7 | 17.9 | 12.8 | 5.1 | 16.4 | 14.1 | 2.3 |
| Madagascar | East/South | 2008 | 1992 | 11.6 | 10.2 | 1.4 | 14.7 | 11.2 | 3.5 | 11.9 | 10.3 | 1.6 |
| Guinea | West/Cent | 2005 | 1999 | 11.5 | 12.2 | −0.7 | 18 | 18.5 | −0.5 | 13.3 | 14 | −0.7 |
| Chad | West/Cent | 2004 | 1996 | 8.6 | 9.1 | −0.5 | 12.7 | 12.4 | 0.3 | 9.5 | 9.9 | −0.4 |
| Nigeria | West/Cent | 2008 | 1999 | 8.5 | 8.5 | 0 | 9.7 | 9.5 | 0.2 | 8.8 | 8.9 | −0.1 |
| Benin | West/Cent | 2006 | 1996 | 10 | 11.6 | −1.6 | 13.5 | 18.7 | −5.2 | 11.3 | 14.1 | −2.8 |
| Burkina | West/Cent | 2003 | 1993 | 7.5 | 9.3 | −1.8 | 14.4 | 14.4 | 0 | 8.4 | 10.1 | −1.7 |
| Mali | West/Cent | 2006 | 1995 | 7.6 | 7.3 | 0.3 | 13.4 | 11.9 | 1.5 | 9.1 | 8.7 | 0.4 |
| Cameroon | West/Cent | 2004 | 1991 | 13.2 | 13.2 | 0 | 16.1 | 12 | 4.1 | 14.6 | 12.8 | 1.8 |
| Senegal | West/Cent | 2005 | 1992 | 13.2 | 11.8 | 1.4 | 12.3 | 11.1 | 1.2 | 12.9 | 11.7 | 1.2 |
| Niger | West/Cent | 2006 | 1992 | 9.8 | 12.7 | −2.9 | 11.2 | 12.6 | −1.4 | 9.9 | 12.8 | −2.9 |
| Ghana | West/Cent | 2008 | 1993 | 14.6 | 13.9 | 0.7 | 18.2 | 16 | 2.2 | 16.1 | 14.5 | 1.6 |

mortality and economic difficulties were straining the extended family solidarity. In that context, a number of observers anticipated a decline in the practice of fosterage (Courade, 1994; Eloundou-Enyegue & Stokes, 2002).

The results in Table 10.1 belie these expectations, as most countries in East and Southern Africa maintained or even raised their fosterage rates; declines were more frequent in Central and West Africa, but the magnitude of decline was typically quite small. Only in two cases (Niger and Benin) did the decline exceed 2 percentage points. In short, there is little evidence of a substantial retreat from the practice of fosterage. To be sure, a full analysis must go beyond mere counts and consider additional factors such as qualitative changes in the direction of fosterage flows, the types of fosterage (i.e., whether orphans displace nonorphans), or the care afforded foster children when they settle in the host household. On the basis of the evidence presented here however, there is little indication of change in the overall volume of fosterage. The tentative conclusion, therefore, is that the buffering of inequality through processes of demographic exchange – here child fosterage – has not eroded even as African countries undergo their fertility transitions, care for increasing numbers of orphans, and experience globalization.

## Conclusion

Insofar as demography affects socioeconomic outcomes, national patterns of demographic change can foretell possible changes in economic inequality within countries. Trends in rural-urban inequality, in particular, will likely be shaped by both demographic differentiation of rural versus urban areas – in terms of sibsize, age structure, or educational composition – and the continued demographic exchanges between rural and urban families. Building on this premise and using evidence from 97 surveys fielded in 39 sub-Saharan countries between 1980 and 2008, we examine recent demographic change in sub-Saharan Africa and its implications for rural-urban inequality. We find a clear demographic differentiation: The rural-urban ratio in fertility rises during the course of national fertility transitions, from 1.36 when the national birth rate stands at 7, to 1.73 when this birth rate falls to 3 births per woman. If higher fertility dilutes family resources, such differentiation places rural children at an increasing disadvantage. Rural-urban inequality in educational composition is also widening, as countries advance in their educational transitions. So is the rural-urban gap in age structure, which rises from 4.5 percentage points in early stages of the transition to 17 percentage points in countries that are most advanced in this transition. Together, these three findings warrant concern about growing economic inequality between rural and urban communities. Conversely, demographic exchange – specifically child fosterage – does not appear to be declining, and this could in theory buffer the potential growth in rural-urban inequality. It is unclear, however, whether these steady trends in fosterage will suffice to withstand the disequalizing influences from the ongoing demographic differentiation. Even if the number of children fostered is not declining, the support granted these children may erode in response to difficult economic conditions, the strain from orphan populations, or the growing competition for costly educational opportunities. In that light, and despite the resilience of demographic exchange systems, there are grounds to worry about widening economic inequality between rural and urban families.

The limitations of our analyses must be underscored. We rely on simple statistical correlations that only support tentative claims about these relationships. We use cross-sectional evidence to infer historical change, a practice that could be misleading if countries in the region follow distinct historical trajectories. Finally, our analyses of the buffering from fosterage do not include fine-grained information about the direction of fosterage flows or the level of support received by foster children. Additionally, we don't consider the role that migration might play as a buffer. With these caveats, our findings draw attention to the prospects of growing rural-urban inequality. Given the systematic differentiation in the demographic outlook of rural and urban communities, some economic differentiation seems quite plausible. Clearly, demography is not destiny. Nor is the meaning of demography the same for rural and urban communities. For instance, the cost-burden of large sibsize and age dependency need not be the same for rural and urban families. Still, in an era of globalization when rural and urban children increasingly compete in the same labor market, these vast differences in family and community opportunities may yet lead to the similarly "divergent destinies" posited in industrial nations during the second demographic transition.

# References

Akresh, R. (2005). *Risk, network quality, and family structure: Child fostering decisions in Burkina Faso*. Economic Growth Center, Yale University.

Birdsall, N., Kelley, A., & Sinding, S. (2001). *Population matters. Demographic change, economic growth, and poverty in the developing world*. New York: Oxford University Press.

Blake, J. (1989). *Family size and achievement*. Berkeley, CA: University of California Press.

Bloom, D. E., Canning, D., & Sevilla, J. (2003). *The demographic dividend: A new perspective on the economic consequences of population change*. Rand Corp.

Boserup, E. (1996). Development theory: An analytical framework and selected application. *Population and Development Review, 22*(3), 505–515.

Caldwell, J. C., & Caldwell, P. (1987). The cultural context of high fertility in sub-Saharan Africa. *Population and Development Review, 13*, 409–437.

Case, A., Paxson, C., & Ableidinger, J. (2004). Orphans in Africa: Parental death, poverty, and school enrollment. *Demography, 41*, 483–508.

Christy, R. D. (2004). *Achieving sustainable communities in a global economy: Alternative private strategies and public policies*. Singapore: World Scientific Publishing.

Courade, G. (1994). *Le village camerounais à l'heure de l'ajustement*. Paris: Karthala.

DeJong, G., & Gardner, R. W. (1981). *Migration decision making*. New York: Pergamon Press.

De La Croix, D., & Doepke, M. (2003). Inequality and growth: Why differential fertility matters. *The American Economic Review, 93*, 1091–1113.

Demographic and Health Surveys (DHS). (2006/2010). *Statcompiler, ORC Macro*. Retrieved January 1, 2006, from http://www.statcompiler.com

Eloundou-Enyegue, P. M., & Makki, F. (2010). Virtuous or vicious? Revisiting the population development nexus in the MDG Era. *XavierIMB International Journal of Development and Social Research, 1*(1), 66–84.

Eloundou-Enyegue, P. M., & Rehman, A. (2009). Growing up global and equal? Recent trends in inequality among world children. *Journal of Children and Poverty, 15*(2), 95–118.

Eloundou-Enyegue, P. M., & Stokes, C. S. (2002). Will economic crises in Africa weaken rural-urban ties? Evidence from child fosterage trends in Cameroon. *Rural Sociology, 67*(2), 278–298.

Firebaugh, G., & Goesling, B. (2004). Accounting for the recent decline in global income inequality. *American Journal of Sociology, 110*, 283–312.

Giroux, S. C. (2008). Rural parentage and labor market disadvantage in a sub-Saharan setting: Sources and trends. *Rural Sociology, 73*, 339–369.

Giroux, S., Eloundou-Enyegue, P. M., & Lichter, D. (2008). Recent trends in fertility inequality in sub-Saharan Africa: Differentials versus overall inequality. *Studies in Family Planning, 39*(3), 187–198.

Greene, M., & Merrick, T. (2005). *Poverty reduction: Does reproductive health matter?* Health Nutrition and Population (HNP) Discussion Paper. Washington, DC: World Bank.

Gugler, J., & Flanagan, W. G. (1978). *Urbanization and social change in West Africa*. Cambridge: Cambridge University Press.

Hewitt, P., & Montgomery, M. R. (2001). *Poverty and public services in developing country cities*. Population Council Working Paper.

Isiugo-Abanihe, U. C. (1985). Child fosterage in West Africa. *Population and Development Review, 11*, 53–73.

Kandiwa, V. (2007). *Hegemony and homogeneity: The socio-economic differentiation of African countries since the 1960s*. Unpublished masters thesis, Cornell University, Ithaca, NY.

Lam, D. (1986). The dynamics of population growth, differential fertility, and inequality. *The American Economic Review, 76*, 1103–1116.

Lam, D., & Levison, D. (1992). Age, experience, and schooling: Decomposing earnings inequality in the United States and Brazil. *Sociological Inquiry, 62*, 220–245.

Lipton, M. (1977). *Why poor people stay poor: Urban bias in world development*. Cambridge: Harvard University Press.

Lloyd, C. B. (1994). *Investing in the next generation: The implications of high fertility at the level of the family*. Research Division Working Papers No. 63. New York: The Population Council.

Lloyd, C. B., & Desai, S. (1992). Children's living arrangements in developing countries. *Population Research and Policy Review, 11*, 193–216.

Lloyd, C. B., & Gage-Brandon, A. J. (1994). High fertility and children's schooling in Ghana: Sex differences in parental contributions and educational outcomes. *Population Studies, 48*, 293–306.

Mahieu, F. R. (1989). Transfers et communauté africaine. *Stateco, June*, 107–136.

Mare, R. D. (1997). Differential fertility, intergenerational educational mobility, and racial inequality. *Social Science Research, 26*, 263–291.

Mason, A., & Lee, S. H. (2004). The demographic dividend and poverty reduction. *Proceedings of the United Nations Seminar on the Relevance of Population Aspects for the Achievement of the Millennium Development Goals, New York, 17–19 November 2004*.

Massey, D. (1990). Social structure, household strategies, and the cumulative causation of migration. *Population Index, 56*(1), 3–26.

McDaniel, A., & Zulu, E. (1994). *Mothers, fathers and children: Regional patterns in child-parent residence in sub-Saharan Africa*. Paper presented at the Annual Meeting of the Population Association of America, Miami, 5–7 May.

McLanahan, S. (2004). Diverging destinies: How children are faring under the second demographic transition. *Demography, 41*, 607–627.

Mensch, B. S., Bruce, J., & Greene, M. E. (1998). *The unchartered passage: Girls' adolescence in the developing world*. New York: Population Council.

Montgomery, M., Kouame, A., & Oliver, R. (1995). *The tradeoff between number of children and child schooling: Evidence from Côte d'Ivoire and Ghana*. World Bank Publications.

National Research Council (NRC). (1986). *Population growth and economic development: Policy questions*. Washington, DC: National Academy Press.

Potts, D. (2009). The slowing of sub-Saharan Africa's urbanization: Evidence and implications for urban livelihoods. *Environment and Urbanization, 21*, 253–259.

Psacharopoulos, G., & Patrinos, H. (2002). *Returns to investment in education: A further update*. World Bank Policy Research Working Paper No. 2881. Washington, DC: World Bank.

Sahn, D. E., & Stifel, D. C. (2003). Urban–rural inequality in living standards in Africa. *Journal of African Economies, 12*, 564–597.

Shapiro, D., & Tambashe, B. O. (2001). Gender, poverty, family structure, and investments in children's education in Kinshasa, Congo. *Economics of Education Review, 20*, 359–375.

Shapiro, D. & Tambashe, B. O. (2002). Fertility transitions in urban and rural sub-Saharan Africa: Preliminary evidence of a three-stage process. *Journal of African Population Studies, 8*(2 and 3), 103–127.

United Nations (UN). (2009). *World urbanization prospects: The 2009 revision*. New York: United Nations.

United Nations Children's Fund (UNICEF). (2008). *The state of African children 2008*. New York: United Nations.

United Nations Development Programme (UNDP). (2003). *Human development report*. New York: Oxford University Press.

World Bank. (2000). *Can Africa claim the 20th century*. Washington, DC: The World Bank.

World Bank. (2010). *World development indicators online*. Washington, DC: The World Bank.

# Demographic Structure and Process in Rural China

## 11

Dudley L. Poston, Mary Ann Davis, and Danielle Xiaodan Deng

## Introduction

This chapter focuses on rural demography in the People's Republic of China. To provide some perspective for our coverage of China's rural demographic structures and processes, we first present a brief overview of China, its history and recent emergence as a world power, followed by a short demographic overview. We then introduce the issue of the definition in China of rurality, followed by a discussion of the changing nature of the rural-urban population distribution in China since the founding of the People's Republic of China in 1949. We next consider socioeconomic disparities in rural and urban China. Then we turn to an examination of the age and sex structures of rural and urban China, and next to a brief consideration of marital status. Next, we discuss the demographic processes in rural and urban China. We finally address the situation of the minority nationalities in rural China.

## Contemporary China: An Overview

China is the most populated nation globally, with an estimated population size in 2007 of just under 1.322 billion, which is about 20% of the world's population (Central Intelligence Agency, 2007). China has a relatively low population density of 138 persons/km$^2$,

situated in an overall land area of almost 9,597 km$^2$ (Central Intelligence Agency, 2007). Geographically, China is the fourth largest country in the world, after Russia, Canada, and the United States (the U.S. at almost 9,827 km$^2$ is just slightly larger than China).

Up until the past few centuries, population growth and decline in China over several thousand years have been relatively stable, with slight increases in population size during times of dynastic prosperity, and decreases during dynastic declines, wars, and famine (see Fig. 11.1). Two thousand years of Chinese records and archives show that for all the centuries prior to the 17th century, China's population size increased and decreased slightly, but generally stayed at around 50–60 million. Indeed at the start of the Ming Dynasty (in 1368) the size of China's population was not much larger than it was at the time of Christ. For all the dynasties up until China's last dynasty, the Qing, China's population swayed roughly with the rise and fall of a dynasty (most dynasties ruled for about 200–300 years). The population grew at the initial years of the dynasty, but rarely exceeded 80 million. Population size would then fall so that one-third or sometimes one-half of the original population was decimated. Mortality then was too high to allow much of an increase in population (Poston & Duan, 2000; Poston, Gu, & Luo, 2004).

To illustrate, from 1400 to 1500 the size of the Chinese population did not change appreciably, growing only by 25 million. It grew by another 50 million from 1500 to 1600 (see Fig. 11.1). But since the mid-1700s, after the establishment of the Qing Dynasty, there were ever so slight reductions in mortality so that the population kept growing beyond the old limit of about 80 million. Indeed the Qing was the first dynasty

---

D.L. Poston (✉)
Department of Sociology, Texas A&M University, College Station, TX 77843-4351, USA
e-mail: d-poston@tamu.edu

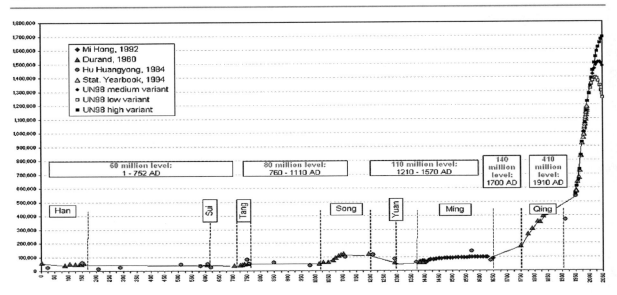

**Fig. 11.1** China's population growth, AD 0–2050
*Source*: Heilig (1999).

to have and sustain a population size above 100 million. By 1850 there were over 420 million people in the country, six to eight times the traditional level (of 60–80 million) that was the demographic norm 200 years or so previously (Fig. 11.1). The Qing was the only dynasty to live up to the perpetual Chinese ideal of "numerous descendants." It is indeed ironic that by achieving this ideal, not only was the Qing wiped out, but China's dynastic system of almost four thousand years was eradicated. Previously, declines in population resulted in the collapse of the dynasties. The Qing fell in 1911 as the population became too large, not too small.

China is one of the earliest civilizations in the world, with its beginnings dating back nearly five thousand years. It was once the strongest and most powerful country in the world (Fairbank & Goldman, 2006). China was known historically for its urban centers and has one of the longest urban traditions of any country in the world. Cities first made their appearance in China more than two thousand years ago. By the year 100 AD the city of Luoyang had reached a population size of 650,000, a number equal at the time to that of Rome (United Nations, 1980, p. 6). Chang'an (present day Xi'an), the capital of China during the Tang Dynasty (618–907 AD), attained a population size of one million residents in 700 AD, the first million-plus city in all of Asia (Chandler & Fox, 1974, p. 291; Chandler, 1987). Chang'an was the center of trade and culture in the world, and measured 5 by 6 miles in area. "Between 600 and 900 AD, no Western capital could compete [with Chang'an] in size and grandeur" (Fairbank & Goldman, 2006, p. 8). But like most civilizations centuries ago, the bulk of China's population was rural.

It was during the Tang Dynasty that China may have first reached its global prominence, significantly influencing at that time all the other known countries of the world, politically, economically, and culturally. But by the end of the Qing Dynasty (1644–1911 AD), China was no longer an influential world power, but an ineffective country, as reflected in its weakened military domination, less developed ways of production, and moribund political system. In 1911 the last ruler of the Qing Dynasty was overthrown.

The Republic of China was formed in early 1912 and was headed by Sun Yat-sen, the first President. During the next few decades there was political and social unrest due to the civil war between the Nationalists and the Communists, and the invasion of China by Japan just prior to World War II.

In 1949 Mao Zedong and the Chinese Communist Party assumed control of the country and established a new government, the People's Republic of China; the country was then free of external oppression. The Communists redistributed rural land on an almost equal basis among the many residents of the countryside, and as we will see below, the country became more urban. About ten years after the founding of the People's Republic, the "Great Leap Forward" occurred along with a resulting famine and tremendous social and economic setbacks. The economic problems and famine were due to both natural disasters such as floods, plant diseases, and drought, as well as to bureaucratic inefficiency and improper management by Mao and other leaders. Between 30 and 45 million Chinese perished during these few years (Ashton, Hill, Piazza, & Zeitz, 1984; Becker, 1998; Dikotter, 2010). The economy began to recover in the early 1960s, but the country soon once again experienced extensive internal strife during the Cultural Revolution, which began in 1966 and did not formally end until Mao's death in 1976.

In the late 1970s when Deng Xiao Ping assumed control of the country, market-based economic reforms were first introduced, and there were further increases in the size of the urban population. Living standards in both urban and rural areas improved significantly, although more so among the urban residents. By 2010, China had become the world's largest exporter, the third largest importer, and the largest producer of most commodities. China has also made significant advances in science, technology, and education. The country's importance is now also reflected by its permanent membership on the United Nations Security Council, as well as in several other international organizations.

When Mao Zedong and the Chinese Communists took over the country in 1949, the population numbered about 550 million, a figure 30% higher than 100 years earlier (Fig. 11.1). This 550 million was about 10 times larger than China's historical equilibrium population of around 60 million.

As a socialist regime, the People's Republic of China was founded on the premise that the past years of chaos, civil war, and political instability were now over. This resulted in a fresh impetus for population growth, especially in the rural areas, which led to levels of natural increase of a very high scale. Between 1950 and 1980, China added another 433 million people to its population (see Fig. 11.1). The population size of over 1.3 billion in 2007 is almost 10 times the size of the mid-17th century population of around 130 million.

In the 300 years from 1650 to 1950, the average annual increase of China's population was around 1.5–1.6 million; this is 80–100 times greater than the annual increases in China before 1650. Since 1949, the average annual increase in population climbed to around 14 million per year. In the 1960s – the high growth years – the average annual increase was as high as 22 million. Even with the reduction of the birth rate in the 1970s, the average annual population increases have been around 10 million.

In ancient China, an increase of 14–22 million people took 700–1000 years. In the 1960s, 1970s, and 1980s a population increase of 14–22 million occurred almost every year (Poston et al., 2004).

## The Definition in China of Rurality, and the Changing Rural-Urban Population Distribution

We turn now to a discussion of the definition of rurality in China. There are many ways to define rurality, for example with respect to population density, culture, occupational structure, public service, geographic location, and amenity disparity, to mention a few approaches (see Chapter 2 in this volume). We rely in this chapter on the definitions of rurality as presented in the Censuses of China, even though these have changed and/or have been modified in past decades. Let us consider some of these definitions by focusing on specific censuses.

China has a long and rich urban history. For most of the thousand years between 800 and 1800, China was unsurpassed in both the number and size distribution of its cities. However, since about 1800, urbanization in China has not paralleled the scale achieved in the West. Although Asia's first million-plus city was a Chinese city appearing more than twelve centuries ago, China had only two cities in 1922 with populations exceeding one million, namely, Shanghai and Guangzhou (Poston, Tian, & Jia, 1990). China's recent history has been much more typified by very large rural populations in both absolute and relative terms. We show below that according to the 1953 census, 87% of the population of China resided in rural areas.

There have been six national censuses in the People's Republic of China since its founding in 1949. The first was conducted in 1953 shortly after Mao Zedong and the Chinese Communist Party assumed control of the country. The second was conducted in 1964, two years prior to the start of the Great Proletarian Cultural Revolution that lasted until 1976.

The third census, thought by many to be China's first truly modern census (Poston, 1992), was conducted in 1982 with significant assistance from the United Nations. The country's 4th and 5th censuses were conducted in 1990 and in 2000 (Banister & Hill, 2004; Tien, 1991, p. 7). Although the 6th census was conducted in 2010, as of the time of the writing of this chapter, data have not yet been released from the 2010 census.

The definitions of urban and rural have not been consistent in the various censuses of China. The 1953 census actually lacked consensus on a definition of rurality and accordingly provided very little specific information on cities, towns and nonurban, i.e., rural areas. Because of the lack of agreement with regard to what was urban and what was rural, the Chinese State Council in 1955 created specific urban and rural criteria. Urban areas were defined as counties or higher level administrative centers with populations of 2,000 or more, and with three-fourths or more of the residents in nonagricultural employment (Hsu, 1985, p. 243). Everything else was rural.

In 1963 Chinese officials stipulated that for an area to be urban it must have "a population of 2,500 to 3,000, of whom 85% or more were nonagricultural" (Banister, 1987, p. 328). This eliminated many earlier towns from their urban status, and, concomitantly, led to a decline in urban places between 1953 and 1982, from 5,402 places to 2,900 places. The definitions from these earlier Chinese censuses (prior to 1982) also restricted the urban population to the permanent resident population, thus excluding from the urban counts the temporary residents, contract employees, and other unofficial residents, an enumeration practice contrary to the international standard of inclusion (Banister, 1987).

Modifications in the definition were later made for the 1982 census and for the 1990 census, and these were based largely on a person's household registration, known as the person's *hukou*. Heilig (2003) noted, "the hukou system reports the *legal* status of a Chinese citizen: [if] a person ... [is] registered with a village committee, then he or she automatically belongs to the rural population; [if] ... a person [is] registered with a street (or block) committee in a town or city, then the person is an urban inhabitant" (Heilig, 2003, p. 5).

Heilig then asked "how large, actually, is China's rural population," and answered his question as "the short answer is that no one really knows" (Heilig, 2003, p. 4) because there are so many definitions of urban and rural. Depending on which rural definition was being used, the percentage of the 1990 population of China classified as rural would range from 47 to 74 to 82% (Heilig, 2003, Table 1). Thus, current rural data are not consistent with earlier rural data issued by Chinese officials, owing to the changes in definitions (Goldstein, 1990).

Because the censuses have used varying definitions of rural and urban, the State Statistical Bureau reconstructed and standardized the data using common definitions so that the data from the censuses and other surveys could be compared. Strictly speaking, an urban area is now defined as an urban district, city and town with a population density higher than 1,500/km$^2$; in remote, sparsely populated areas, towns with lower densities and populations that provide administrative functions may be designated as urban; only the population living in streets, town sites, and adjacent villages are counted as urban. The residual areas are rural.

We use these reconstructed census data from various *China Statistical Yearbooks* for a review of the changing rural-urban population distribution in China (see Table 11.1). In our analysis, we have combined the census categories of city and town to form the urban population. Throughout this chapter we use official data, and follow the practice of combining the categories of city and town into a single urban category.

In the 1953 census, 86.7% of the population of China, or 505.3 million of the country's total population of 582.6 million, were rural residents. By 2000 the rural percentage had decreased to 63.8%, representing 807.4 million of China's total population of 1.27 billion. This represents a fair reduction from the 834 million in 1990.

Table 11.2 combines reconstructed rural and urban percentage data for China in five-year categories from 1950 through 2004, along with corresponding rural and urban percentages for the more developed, less developed, and least developed countries of the world. Generally speaking, the more developed countries include the countries of Europe, North America, and Australia/Oceania, along with Russia and Japan; the least developed countries are mainly those in sub-Saharan Africa, and the less developed countries are all others.

**Table 11.1** Reconstructed rural and urban populations (in ten-thousands): China, 1953–2000

|  | 1953 | 1964 | 1982 | 1990 | 2000 |
|---|---|---|---|---|---|
| Urban population | 7,726 | 12,710 | 21,082 | 29,971 | 45,844 |
| Percent | 13.26 | 18.30 | 20.91 | 26.44 | 36.22 |
| (City) | – | – | 14,525 | 21,122 | 29,263 |
| (Town) | 7,726 | 9,455 | 6,106 | 8,492 | 16,614 |
| Rural population | 50,534 | 56,748 | 79,736 | 83,397 | 80,739 |
| Percent | 86.74 | 81.70 | 79.09 | 73.56 | 63.78 |
| Total population | 58,260 | 69,458 | 100,818 | 113,368 | 126,583 |

*Notes*: Military population is included in the urban counts. Data exclude Hong Kong, Macao, and Taiwan.
*Source*: 2007 China Statistical Yearbook.

**Table 11.2** Percentages of the rural and urban populations of China, and of the more developed, less developed, and least developed countries of the world, 1950–2004

| Year | China | | More developed | | Less developed | | Least developed | |
|---|---|---|---|---|---|---|---|---|
|  | Percent Urban | Percent Rural | Percent Urban | Percent Rural | Percent Urban | Percent Rural | Percent Urban | Percent Rural |
| 1950 | 11.2 | 88.8 | 52.5 | 47.5 | 18.0 | 82.0 | 7.3 | 92.7 |
| 1955 | 13.5 | 86.5 | 55.6 | 44.4 | 19.7 | 80.3 | 8.3 | 91.7 |
| 1960 | 19.8 | 80.2 | 58.7 | 41.3 | 21.7 | 78.3 | 9.5 | 90.5 |
| 1965 | 18.0 | 82.0 | 61.7 | 38.3 | 23.7 | 76.3 | 11.1 | 88.9 |
| 1970 | 17.4 | 82.6 | 64.6 | 35.4 | 25.3 | 74.7 | 13.1 | 86.9 |
| 1975 | 17.3 | 82.7 | 67.0 | 33.0 | 27.0 | 73.0 | 14.8 | 85.2 |
| 1980 | 19.4 | 80.6 | 68.8 | 31.2 | 29.6 | 70.4 | 17.3 | 82.7 |
| 1985 | 23.7 | 76.3 | 70.0 | 30.0 | 32.3 | 67.7 | 19.1 | 80.9 |
| 1990 | 26.4 | 73.6 | 71.2 | 28.8 | 35.1 | 64.9 | 21.0 | 79.0 |
| 1995 | 29.0 | 71.0 | 72.2 | 27.8 | 37.6 | 62.4 | 22.9 | 77.1 |
| 2000 | 36.2 | 63.8 | 73.1 | 26.9 | 40.2 | 59.8 | 24.8 | 75.2 |
| 2004 | 41.8 | 58.2 | 74.0 | 26.0 | 42.7 | 57.3 | 27.0 | 73.0 |

*Notes*: Military population in China included in urban. Data exclude Hong Kong, Macao, and Taiwan.
*Source*: China: 1949–1978, China Statistical Database, 1998. China: 1978–2004, China Statistical Yearbook, 2005. Global: United Nations, World Urbanization Prospects, 2007.

Notably, although there we see an increase in China's rural percentage during the years of the Great Leap Forward (late 1950s to early 1960s) and the years of the Cultural Revolution (mid-1960s to mid-1970s), there has been a steady decrease in the relative size of China's rural population since the 1980s. Overall, the percentage rural has decreased from a high of 88.8% in 1950 to 58.2% in 2004.

As noted, Table 11.2 also includes rural percentage data for countries according to the United Nations criteria of more developed, less developed, and least developed. There are some obvious limitations in using United Nations data for rural comparisons because the data are provided by multiple nations, and rurality is sometimes defined differentially. However, the generally agreed upon definition for a rural designation is that the area has less than 2,500 population (United Nations, 2007).

In 1950 China's rural population of 88.8% was close to the rural population percentage of the least developed regions, 92.7%, compared to a relative number of 47.5% for the most developed populations, a percentage by the way which is lower than China's rural percentage in 2004. By 2004 China's rural percentage was more closely comparable to that of the less developed countries. We turn next to a consideration of socioeconomic disparities in rural and urban China.

## Socioeconomic Disparities Between Rural and Urban Areas

The major dimension of inequality in China is the rural-urban divide. This is largely a result of the household registration system used by the Chinese government since 1958. At birth, individuals are broadly divided into two categories, agricultural or nonagricultural, which essentially represent a distinction between "rural" and "urban." This basically ascriptive designation is based on the person's place of birth, and the occupation, livelihood and other attributes of the person's parents (You & Poston, 2004). Changing from an agricultural, i.e., rural *hukou*, to a nonagricultural, i.e., urban *hukou*, in past years was very difficult because it was tightly and strictly regulated by the government (Chan & Buckingham, 2008).

Since China has always had a large rural population (see Tables 11.1 and 11.2 above) comprised mainly of poor farm workers, the *hukou* system served to limit the mass migration of poor peasants from rural to urban areas, ensuring a certain degree of structural stability, and preventing potential disruptions of China's economic and social order. Hence the system enabled the maintenance of rural-urban differences. Between the 1950s and the 1980s, this was important because China's planned economy focused on the development of agriculture in the rural areas and the development of industry in the urban areas (Farris, He, Iwinska-Nowak, & Poston, forthcoming).

During China's rapid industrialization, state economic development has centered on urban industrial progress. This development has tended to strengthen the infrastructure of services in urban areas at the expense of rural areas. Agricultural prices were often lowered in order to divert state economic support for urban and industrial development. China, like many developing nations, has a continuing governmental economic support structure providing an advantage for urban over rural areas.

> (In China) the share of government expenditures in the rural sector remains relatively low. In 2000, for example, nearly 65% of China's population resided in rural areas; however, rural investment accounted for only 20% of total government expenditures. Moreover, almost 50% of national GDP was produced by the rural sector (agriculture and rural township and village enterprises) in 2000 (Fan et al., 2005, p. 24).

Table 11.3 uses *China Statistical Yearbook* (2007) data to contextualize rural and urban disparities from 1990 and 2006. The first and most notable difference is in income. Rural incomes have grown between 1990 and 2006, from 683 Yuan per capita to 3,587 Yuan per capita, indicating some attention by the government to raise rural incomes. But the changes in urban annual incomes have been much more dramatic. In 1990, urban per capita income was 1,510 Yuan, over twice that of rural income. This disparity has continued so that by 2006 urban per capita income was 11,759 Yuan compared to rural per capita income of but 3,587 Yuan.

**Table 11.3** Urban and rural differences in living condition amenities in China: 1990 through 2006

|  |  | 1990 | 2000 | 2005 | 2006 |
|---|---|---|---|---|---|
| Per capita annual income (yuan) | Urban | 1,510 | 6,380 | 10,493 | 11,759 |
|  | Rural | 683 | 2,253 | 3,255 | 3,587 |
| Color TVs per 100 households | Urban | 59 | 116.6 | 134.8 | 137.4 |
|  | Rural | 4.7 | 48.7 | 84.1 | 89.4 |
| Percent of income spent on health care | Urban | 2 | 6.4 | 7.6 | 7.1 |
|  | Rural | 3.3 | 5.2 | 6.6 | 6.8 |

*Source*: 2007 China Statistical Yearbook.

Similar rural-urban disparities are shown in Table 11.3 with regard to the possession of color television sets and the amount of one's personal income spent on health care. For instance, urban households have 1.5 times more color TVs than rural households. We turn in the next section to an examination of rural-urban differences in demographic structure.

## Age and Sex Structure

Of all the characteristics of human populations, age and sex are the most important and relevant for demographers. Their importance lies in the fact that the interaction of the demographic processes produces a population's age and sex structure (Horiuchi & Preston, 1988), and the demographic processes are themselves affected by the age and sex structure (Poston, 2005).

But the importance of age and sex extends beyond demography. The division of labor in traditional societies is based almost entirely on age and sex. Moreover, changes in the age distribution of a population have consequences for educational, political, and economic life (Keyfitz & Flieger, 1971). A society's age and sex distribution has important implications for socioeconomic and demographic development (Keyfitz, 1965), as well as for labor force participation and gender relations (South & Trent, 1988). Indeed "almost any measurement that can be taken of human beings, or of groups of human beings, will show substantial variation by sex and age" (Bogue, 1969, p. 147).

We now present age and sex pyramids of China's population for the two census years of 1982 and 2000 and compare the rural and urban populations. Figures 11.2 and 11.3 are population pyramids which are graphic representations of the age and sex distributions of populations. A pyramid is a graph of age data (males on the left, females on the right) vertically arranged in 5-year age groups from the bottom (age zero) to the top (age 80 and over). The horizontal line (the base) of the pyramid represents size, and is calibrated in terms of the percentage of the total population represented by each age-sex group.

Figure 11.2 is a population pyramid of the rural and urban populations of China for 1982, and Fig. 11.3 is a pyramid for 2000; the urban population in both pyramids is shaded. Keep in mind that the rural and urban population data in the two figures have been calibrated on the basis of percentages, not absolute numbers. Both pyramids clearly show that the working-age population is more highly concentrated in urban areas. There are about the same percentages of aged persons in the rural as in the urban areas. The pyramids also show that rural China has higher percentages at the younger ages than urban China, a manifestation of the higher fertility rates in the rural areas.

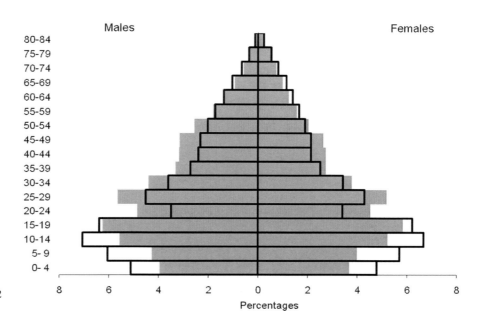

**Fig. 11.2** Urban China 1982 (*shaded*) and rural China 1982

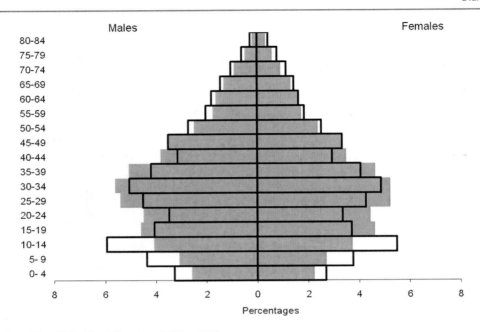

**Fig. 11.3** Urban China 2000 (*shaded*) and rural China 2000

We turn next to specific analyses first of the sex structure of urban and rural China, and then to age structure, specifically age dependency.

The sex ratio is a basic measure of a population's sex structure; it is the number of males per 100 females. Imbalanced sex ratios may arise as a consequence of various factors ranging from war casualties to intentional gender control. In China, the age-old phenomenon of son preference, combined with the one-child policy, has produced the largest, highest, and longest degree of gender imbalance in the world. Moreover, son preference is stronger in rural China than in urban China.

Table 11.4 shows sex ratios for the urban and rural populations for the provinces of China in 2000. Generally speaking, China has a relatively high sex ratio compared to other countries. There were, on average, 106.3 males for every 100 females in 2000. In the same year, the sex ratio for the world was 102, and the sex ratio for the United States was 97. In China the sex ratio varies between urban and rural populations. The sex ratio for rural China of 107 is higher than that for urban China of 105.

For urban populations, Hainan Province has the most unbalanced sex ratio (111.52), while Liaoning Province has the lowest sex ratio (102.13). For rural populations, the sex ratio varies from 114 (in Hainan province) to 100 (in Shanghai). Chongqing has the highest difference in sex ratios between the urban and rural populations. We now turn to an analysis of age structure, specifically age dependency.

Higher numbers of elderly persons in a population are not problematic if there are, at the same time, a large number of producers. It is only when the ratio of elderly to producers increases significantly that economic, social and related problems occur. Aged dependency ratios (ADRs) show empirically the degree of burden that the elderly place on the producers.

The aged dependency ratio is the ratio of persons aged 65 and over to persons aged 15–64. The numerator consists of persons who typically are not employed, hence not serving actively as producers of goods, material resources and sustenance. The denominator, persons aged 15–64, contains the productive members of the population. Most of these people are in the labor force, all of whom, in varying ways, are producing foodstuffs and related goods and services for the population. This ratio is multiplied by 100 and refers to the number of elder dependents in the population per 100 producers.

**Table 11.4** Population by sex and the sex ratio for urban and rural areas: Provinces of China, 2000

| | Urban population[a] | | | | Rural population[a] | | | |
|---|---|---|---|---|---|---|---|---|
| | Total | Male | Female | Sex ratio | Total | Male | Female | Sex ratio |
| Total | 45,877 | 23,526 | 22,351 | 105.3 | 78,384 | 40,501 | 37,883 | 106.9 |
| Beijing | 1,052 | 550 | 502 | 109.7 | 305 | 157 | 148 | 106.3 |
| Tianjin | 709 | 362 | 347 | 104.1 | 276 | 140 | 136 | 103.1 |
| Hebei | 1,756 | 892 | 864 | 103.2 | 4,912 | 2,502 | 2,411 | 103.8 |
| Shanxi | 1,143 | 589 | 555 | 106.1 | 2,104 | 1,091 | 1,012 | 107.8 |
| Mongolia | 996 | 509 | 487 | 104.4 | 1,336 | 697 | 639 | 109.1 |
| Liaoning | 2,297 | 1,160 | 1,136 | 102.1 | 1,886 | 972 | 914 | 106.3 |
| Jilin | 1,331 | 675 | 656 | 102.8 | 1,349 | 697 | 652 | 106.9 |
| Heilongjiang | 1,867 | 947 | 920 | 102.9 | 1,757 | 905 | 851 | 106.4 |
| Shanghai | 1,449 | 747 | 702 | 106.5 | 192 | 96 | 96 | 100.0 |
| Jiangsu | 3,086 | 1,575 | 1,511 | 104.2 | 4,218 | 2,123 | 2,095 | 101.4 |
| Zhejiang | 2,236 | 1,151 | 1,084 | 106.2 | 2,357 | 1,207 | 1,151 | 104.9 |
| Anhui | 1,577 | 814 | 763 | 106.7 | 4,323 | 2,230 | 2,093 | 106.5 |
| Fujian | 1,431 | 738 | 693 | 106.6 | 1,979 | 1,019 | 960 | 106.1 |
| Jiangxi | 1,119 | 578 | 541 | 106.8 | 2,921 | 1,521 | 1,400 | 108.7 |
| Shandong | 3,433 | 1,739 | 1,693 | 102.7 | 5,565 | 2,815 | 2,750 | 102.4 |
| Henan | 2,139 | 1,096 | 1,042 | 105.2 | 6,985 | 3,608 | 3,377 | 106.8 |
| Hubei | 2,409 | 1,246 | 1,163 | 107.2 | 3,542 | 1,852 | 1,690 | 109.6 |
| Hunan | 1,740 | 895 | 845 | 106.0 | 4,588 | 2,404 | 2,183 | 110.1 |
| Guangdong | 4,743 | 2,411 | 2,333 | 103.3 | 3,779 | 1,928 | 1,852 | 104.1 |
| Guangxi | 1,235 | 646 | 589 | 109.5 | 3,150 | 1,678 | 1,472 | 114.0 |
| Hainan | 307 | 162 | 145 | 111.5 | 448 | 238 | 210 | 113.2 |
| Chongqing | 1,010 | 517 | 493 | 104.8 | 2,042 | 1,068 | 974 | 109.6 |
| Sichuan | 2,231 | 1,143 | 1,088 | 105.1 | 6,004 | 3,113 | 2,891 | 107.7 |
| Guizhou | 845 | 439 | 405 | 108.5 | 2,680 | 1,407 | 1,273 | 110.5 |
| Yunnan | 990 | 518 | 473 | 109.5 | 3,246 | 1,702 | 1,544 | 110.2 |
| Tibet | 51 | 27 | 24 | 110.2 | 211 | 106 | 105 | 100.9 |
| Shanxi | 1,137 | 591 | 545 | 108.4 | 2,400 | 1,246 | 1,153 | 108.1 |
| Gansu | 602 | 316 | 286 | 110.4 | 1,911 | 986 | 924 | 106.7 |
| Qinghai | 156 | 81 | 75 | 108.3 | 326 | 168 | 158 | 105.9 |
| Ningxia | 178 | 91 | 87 | 105.6 | 371 | 190 | 181 | 105.1 |
| Xinjiang | 625 | 322 | 303 | 106.3 | 1,221 | 633 | 588 | 107.7 |

[a] Population per 10,000.
*Source*: 2000 China Statistics Press, 2005.

Although when calculating the ADR, demographers almost always use the ages for the producing population of 15 to 64 and the ages of 65 and over for the dependent population (Poston & Bouvier, 2010), Trinh (2006) has suggested that the true ADRs may be even higher in China since the actual retirement ages, which vary by occupation, are much lower, around 50 for females and around 60 for males. This would mean that the true ADR in China would need to be calculated

**Table 11.5** Aged dependency ratios (ADRs) and parental support ratios (PSRs): rural and urban China, by sex, 1982 and 2000

|  | Urban 1982 | | Rural 1982 | | Urban 2000 | | Rural 2000 | |
| --- | --- | --- | --- | --- | --- | --- | --- | --- |
|  | Males | Females | Males | Females | Males | Females | Males | Females |
| ADR | 5.55 | 7.80 | 7.24 | 9.61 | 7.99 | 9.13 | 10.20 | 12.27 |
| PSR | 2.63 | 5.76 | 2.86 | 5.35 | 4.37 | 7.31 | 4.92 | 8.80 |
| Percentage 80+ | 0.33 | 0.70 | 0.35 | 0.66 | 0.62 | 1.06 | 0.76 | 1.34 |
| Percentage 65 + | 3.87 | 5.28 | 4.34 | 5.69 | 5.99 | 6.88 | 6.82 | 8.23 |

*Source*: United Nations and U.S. Census International Database.

with a producing population of from age 15 to around 49 for females, and to around 59 for males.

Another method of calculating the relative degree of aged dependency in a population is the parental-support ratio (PSR), which takes the number of persons 80 years old and over per 100 persons aged 50–64 (Wu & Wang, 2004). The PSR is an indication of the relative burden that the oldest old population, i.e., the elderly parents, have on the population aged 50–64, i.e., the children of the elderly parents.

Table 11.5 shows sex-specific ADRs and PSRs for China in 1982 and 2000, along with percentages of age 65 and older, and of age 80 and older. Clearly, China's rural population is older than its urban population. In 2000, 0.8% of rural males and 1.3% of rural females were over age 80, compared to 0.6% of urban males and 1.1% of urban females.

The dependency ratios show a higher dependency burden in rural China than in urban China for both 1982 and 2000 and for both males and females. We have reported male- and female-specific ratios because these more clearly depict both the age dependency and gender issues which affect the workforce. For example note that females have a wider rural-urban disparity in dependency than do males.

Wealso show in the table that the growth between 1982 and 2000 in the old (age 65+) and the oldest old (age 85+) has been much higher in rural China than in urban China. The oldest old in China are much more rural than they are urban, and, moreover, they have increased more rapidly in the rural compared to the urban areas of the country. We look next at marital status.

## Marital Status

Unfortunately, current data on marital status do not provide the urban and rural status. However, the *China Statistical Yearbook* (2005) provides marital status data by province. In Table 11.6 we present percentage data for 2005 for categories of marital status for persons aged 15 and over, by sex, for each of the provinces, along with data on percent rural. In the country as a whole, most are in the "first marriage" category, 71% of males and 73% of females, but this varies across the provinces. The rural difference is most evident in Tibet, which is 80% rural; 60% of males and 59% of females are in their first marriage. In China, 22.5% of males are never married, this ranges from a high of 35% of males in (largely rural) Tibet to a low of 20.9% of males in (largely urban) Shanghai. The remarriage and divorce percentages are low throughout China, only 1.5% of males and 1.7% of females are remarried. The highest percentage of remarried males and females is in (the very rural) Xinjiang (66.2% rural), namely, 8.1% males and 7.5% females. Nationally, 1.3% of males and 0.9% of females are divorced. There is little variation among the provinces; the standard deviations are only 0.5 for males and 0.7 for females. About 4% of males and 8% of females in China are widowed. The widowed category also has very small standard deviations, but this is slightly higher for females (0.7 versus 1.4). Tibet, the most rural of all the provinces of China, has by far the highest percentages of widows, 11.7%. We turn next to a consideration of the demographic processes of fertility, mortality, and migration.

## The Demographic Processes

We discuss in this section rural-urban differences in fertility, mortality, and migration. First, regarding fertility and mortality, China is now completing its demographic transition from high to low birth and death rates, i.e., the third phase of the transition. As we show in Figs. 11.4 and 11.5, both rural and urban China are now in the third phase of the transition, although rural China is lagging behind urban China. Since the

**Table 11.6** Percentages of marital status by region in China in 2005

| | Aged 15 + | % Male | % Female | Never married % Male | Never married % Female | First marriage % Male | First marriage % Female | Remarried % Male | Remarried % Female | Divorced % Male | Divorced % Female | Widowed % Male | Widowed % Female | % Rural |
|---|---|---|---|---|---|---|---|---|---|---|---|---|---|---|
| Total | 1,011,199 | 50.11 | 49.89 | 22.53 | 16.53 | 71.18 | 72.89 | 1.53 | 1.74 | 1.26 | 0.87 | 3.49 | 7.93 | 63.1 |
| Beijing | 12,798 | 51.12 | 48.88 | 26.38 | 21.60 | 67.78 | 67.79 | 1.85 | 1.84 | 1.35 | 1.61 | 2.64 | 6.85 | 22.5 |
| Tianjin | 8,575 | 48.96 | 51.04 | 19.53 | 16.27 | 74.94 | 73.57 | 1.36 | 1.28 | 0.93 | 1.28 | 3.22 | 7.91 | 28.0 |
| Hebei | 54,547 | 50.52 | 49.48 | 23.57 | 18.15 | 70.66 | 72.78 | 1.32 | 1.66 | 0.98 | 0.55 | 3.47 | 6.72 | 73.7 |
| Shanxi | 25,501 | 51.17 | 48.83 | 24.42 | 17.15 | 70.01 | 73.83 | 1.40 | 1.97 | 1.13 | 0.37 | 3.03 | 6.38 | 64.8 |
| Mongolia | 19,256 | 51.32 | 48.68 | 21.49 | 15.47 | 72.77 | 75.27 | 1.47 | 1.92 | 1.24 | 0.84 | 3.03 | 6.16 | 57.3 |
| Liaoning | 35,385 | 49.88 | 50.12 | 20.04 | 15.63 | 72.82 | 72.79 | 1.69 | 2.00 | 2.32 | 1.95 | 3.12 | 7.67 | 45.1 |
| Jilin | 22,730 | 49.67 | 50.33 | 21.68 | 20.01 | 71.51 | 70.62 | 1.44 | 1.51 | 2.19 | 1.69 | 3.18 | 6.24 | 50.3 |
| Heilongjiang | 31,828 | 50.45 | 49.55 | 20.80 | 16.23 | 72.03 | 73.72 | 2.04 | 2.04 | 1.99 | 1.40 | 3.14 | 6.50 | 48.5 |
| Shanghai | 15,233 | 49.03 | 50.97 | 20.94 | 15.52 | 72.74 | 71.35 | 1.87 | 1.91 | 1.79 | 1.97 | 2.65 | 9.61 | 11.7 |
| Jiangsu | 60,493 | 48.52 | 51.48 | 17.82 | 12.33 | 75.56 | 75.74 | 1.49 | 1.83 | 0.97 | 0.64 | 4.16 | 10.04 | 57.7 |
| Zhejiang | 38,551 | 50.29 | 49.71 | 20.18 | 14.09 | 73.90 | 75.16 | 1.50 | 2.10 | 1.44 | 0.89 | 2.97 | 7.68 | 51.3 |
| Anhui | 49,000 | 50.34 | 49.66 | 21.03 | 14.61 | 72.81 | 74.99 | 1.20 | 1.41 | 1.27 | 0.51 | 3.67 | 8.36 | 73.3 |
| Fujian | 27,488 | 49.31 | 50.69 | 25.29 | 20.10 | 68.83 | 68.88 | 1.34 | 1.58 | 1.18 | 0.64 | 3.36 | 9.05 | 58.0 |
| Jiangxi | 32,561 | 50.27 | 49.74 | 21.58 | 15.09 | 72.86 | 74.44 | 1.23 | 1.25 | 1.07 | 0.56 | 3.26 | 8.56 | 72.3 |
| Shandong | 73,816 | 49.42 | 50.58 | 19.75 | 15.62 | 74.97 | 74.39 | 1.48 | 1.98 | 0.65 | 0.41 | 3.16 | 7.79 | 61.8 |
| Henan | 74,339 | 50.13 | 49.87 | 22.69 | 17.42 | 71.11 | 72.99 | 1.38 | 1.63 | 1.09 | 0.59 | 3.73 | 7.32 | 76.6 |
| Hubei | 47,234 | 49.87 | 50.13 | 24.50 | 17.60 | 69.70 | 72.61 | 1.11 | 1.27 | 1.01 | 0.69 | 3.68 | 7.87 | 59.5 |
| Hunan | 52,986 | 50.67 | 49.33 | 23.51 | 16.55 | 70.27 | 73.14 | 1.12 | 1.29 | 1.21 | 0.61 | 3.88 | 8.18 | 72.5 |
| Guangdong | 58,117 | 50.13 | 49.87 | 28.69 | 22.42 | 66.94 | 67.78 | 0.72 | 0.74 | 0.84 | 0.46 | 2.81 | 8.56 | 44.3 |
| Guangxi | 37,473 | 51.16 | 48.84 | 29.90 | 21.17 | 63.91 | 68.06 | 1.37 | 1.32 | 1.20 | 0.74 | 3.63 | 8.33 | 71.8 |
| Hainan | 6,024 | 51.03 | 48.99 | 31.72 | 23.28 | 64.12 | 67.64 | 0.98 | 0.91 | 0.65 | 0.44 | 2.54 | 7.42 | 59.3 |
| Chongqing | 24,176 | 49.16 | 50.84 | 16.48 | 9.84 | 74.32 | 75.67 | 2.23 | 2.86 | 1.72 | 1.49 | 5.24 | 10.48 | 66.9 |
| Sichuan | 68,253 | 49.81 | 50.19 | 17.89 | 12.37 | 74.94 | 76.32 | 1.86 | 2.13 | 1.44 | 1.17 | 3.87 | 8.07 | 72.9 |
| Guizhou | 28,140 | 51.03 | 48.97 | 25.38 | 17.31 | 67.26 | 71.53 | 1.73 | 1.60 | 1.59 | 1.10 | 4.05 | 8.12 | 76.0 |
| Yunnan | 33,119 | 50.10 | 49.90 | 24.05 | 15.94 | 68.52 | 71.78 | 2.02 | 1.97 | 1.45 | 1.12 | 3.96 | 9.15 | 76.6 |
| Tibet | 1,982 | 48.59 | 51.41 | 34.79 | 28.46 | 59.81 | 58.29 | 0.31 | 0.20 | 0.52 | 2.06 | 4.57 | 11.73 | 80.6 |
| Shaanxi | 28,886 | 50.79 | 49.21 | 23.65 | 17.00 | 70.30 | 73.95 | 1.25 | 1.51 | 1.04 | 0.58 | 3.76 | 6.75 | 67.9 |
| Gansu | 19,797 | 50.95 | 49.05 | 24.11 | 17.11 | 70.67 | 74.20 | 0.72 | 0.81 | 1.03 | 0.58 | 3.47 | 7.01 | 76.0 |
| Qinghai | 3,997 | 50.71 | 49.31 | 22.84 | 15.32 | 69.86 | 72.25 | 1.92 | 2.03 | 2.02 | 2.33 | 3.35 | 7.84 | 67.7 |
| Ningxia | 4,200 | 50.14 | 49.86 | 21.94 | 17.29 | 73.50 | 74.59 | 1.57 | 1.19 | 1.00 | 1.10 | 1.99 | 5.75 | 67.6 |
| Xinjiang | 14,714 | 50.90 | 49.10 | 26.43 | 18.75 | 60.26 | 63.93 | 8.11 | 7.50 | 2.96 | 3.29 | 2.24 | 6.30 | 66.2 |
| Mean | | 50.18 | 49.83 | 23.33 | 17.28 | 70.31 | 71.94 | 1.65 | 1.78 | 1.33 | 1.09 | 3.38 | 7.88 | 60.6 |
| Standard deviation | | 0.79 | 0.79 | 4.03 | 3.59 | 4.05 | 3.88 | 1.27 | 1.18 | 0.54 | 0.69 | 0.67 | 1.36 | 16.6 |

*Source*: China Statistical Yearbook 2005

early 1960s, China experienced a pronounced and rapid decline in fertility (Fig. 11.4), from a crude birth rate of 37 per 1,000 population to a low in the year 2000 of 15 per 1,000. The major decline occurred between 1965 and 1975. The crude birth rates for rural and urban China were very similar in 1962, at 37 per 1,000 and 35 per 1,000, respectively. But by 1975, the birth rate for urban China had fallen to 14, while that for rural China had dropped to 24. Since 1975, however, the birth rate in rural China has decreased more rapidly than in urban China. By the year 2000 the birth rates for rural and urban China were almost as similar as in 1962, albeit considerably lower. So at the start of the demographic transition, birth rates for rural and urban China were similar, with the rural rates slightly higher. During the transition, urban rates

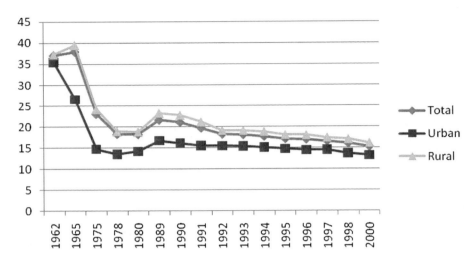

**Fig. 11.4** Crude birth rates, China by rural and urban, 1962–2000

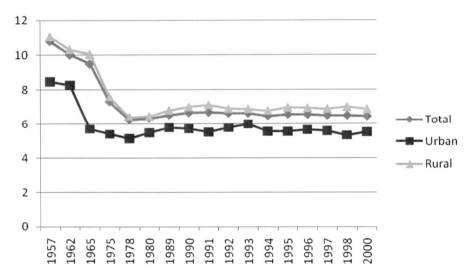

**Fig. 11.5** Crude death rates, China by rural and urban, 1957–2000

dropped much more quickly than the rural rates, and for several years during the transition, the urban crude birth rate was as much as 10 births per 1,000 population less than the rural crude birth rate. By the year 2000 the rural and urban rates were once again close in magnitude, although the urban rate is still slightly less than the rural rate.

The crude death rates for rural and urban China are shown in Fig. 11.5. We have available crude death rate data starting in 1957. The rates then were already somewhat low, but the rural death rates were higher than the urban rates. In 1957 rural China had a crude death rate of 11 per 1,000 and urban China a rate of 8 per 1,000. By the year 2000, the rural rate had dropped to 7, and the urban rate to 6. The crude death rates for rural and urban China were then much closer than they had been more than four decades earlier.

Let us now review some of the dynamics of China's demographic transition, paying special attention to rural and urban differences, so to provide some sociological context for the birth and death rate data shown in Figs. 11.4 and 11.5.

When Mao Zedong and the Chinese Communists took over China in 1949, relatively little attention was paid to the size and growth of the population. As we noted earlier, the population was mostly rural and fertility and mortality were high. Aird (1972) has described the early years of the People's Republic as a period of doctrinaire Marxism. When the initial results of the 1953 census became available in 1954, anxiety was expressed about the size and growth trends of the population, especially in rural China. By the summer of 1956 a birth control campaign was underway. Zhou Enlai, in a report to the People's Congress in August 1956, demanded that "health departments disseminate propaganda and take effective measures for birth control" (Aird, 1972, p. 237). But with the introduction in rural China in 1958 of communes and the Great Leap Forward, China began to reverse its new birth control policy: "A large population was once more regarded as advantageous, and the vicious attacks on Malthusians, 'rightists' and 'bourgeois economists' who championed birth control again shifted into high gear" (Orleans, 1972, p. 40).

The Great Leap Forward, initiated in 1958, was designed to "involve a revolutionary struggle against nature to realize the great potential of agriculture by maximizing the advantages of the collective economy" (Aird, 1972, p. 278). It had a short life because in 1959 China suffered an economic crisis and famine (Ashton et al., 1984), resulting in the premature death of between 30 and 45 million people. The famine was experienced in rural and urban areas, but was particularly disastrous in rural China. Fertility declined from the mid-1950s through the early-1960s, due to the famine. However, Coale has noted that in addition to "famine-induced subfecundity," the fertility decline was also due to the "disruption of normal married life" (1984, p. 57).

During the early years of the 1960s, fertility increased considerably, to birth rates between 37 and 40 in rural and urban China (Fig. 11.4). According to Chen, this occurred in conjunction with an economic recovery in China (1984, p. 45). Coale added that the upsurge also "resulted from the restoration of normal married life, from an abnormally large number of marriages, and from the unusually small fraction of married women who were infertile because of nursing a recently born infant" (1984, p. 57). These years from the early to mid-1960s were the time of China's "baby boom," a demographic event similar to that experienced in the U.S. after World War II. China's "baby boom" was of a shorter duration but of a significantly higher magnitude than in the U.S. Also, rural China had a higher baby boom than urban China.

In early 1962 China resumed its second family planning program, mainly encouraging smaller families. The campaign lasted until 1966. The introduction of the Great Proletarian Cultural Revolution interrupted, the birth control campaign and little focus was given to family planning programs in general.

The third family planning campaign, begun in 1971, was the *wan xi shao* program (meaning *later* marriages, *longer* birth intervals, and *fewer* children). The birth rate declined precipitously through the late 1970s (Fig. 11.4). The *wan xi shao* program was very successful, particularly in urban areas. However, the large numbers of children born during the "baby boom" years caused concern among Chinese leaders in the mid-to-late 1970s due to the demographic momentum and the concomitant growth potential of this extraordinarily large cohort. Banister has written that at this time the Chinese government was "discovering the existence and usefulness of the field of demography" (1987, p. 183), so the leaders were cognizant of the demographic momentum of the population's current age structure, especially in the rural areas. Hence the "one child is best" norm was established and the One-Child Campaign was launched in 1979. This fourth program (which was actually an extension of the third) was undertaken so that, in the words of then Vice-Premier Chen Muhua, "the total population of China will be controlled at about 1.2 billion by the end of the century" (Tien, 1983, p. 32).

The principal goal of the fourth campaign was to restrict births to two per family, and to encourage most families to have only one child, especially in urban areas. The policy was not enforced stringently among the country's minority populations (Poston & Shu, 1987; Poston, 1992), and a number of exceptions were permitted among the majority Han. The program involved a varied series of inducements, touching virtually every aspect of a person's economic and social life, including salary, sustenance, health facilities, employment, and education (Sardon, 1985). The fertility policies were relaxed somewhat in rural China, so that if the first child was a girl families could generally have a second child. This relaxed policy only applied in rural China; the one-child policy was much more strictly enforced in urban China.

Between 1980 and 1982 fertility increased slightly, and then fell back to earlier levels. The increases were due in part to the implementation of China's new Marriage Law of 1981 which raised the legal age at first marriage to age 22 for men and 20 for women. Previously, according to the Marriage Law of 1950, the legal age was 20 and 18 years, respectively (Banister, 1984). Ironically, the new marriage law led to an unanticipated increase in the number of first marriages, with a corresponding increase in the birth rate. This occurred because previously most provincial-level marriage policies required men and women to be quite a few years older, at least 25 for men and 23 for women, although these policies were applied more in urban China than in rural China. With the passing of the new law, many couples found a justification for earlier marriages, and thus the slight marriage-boom (Coale, 1984; Poston, 1986).

By the late 1980s the birth rate increased slightly in rural China, partly due to even greater relaxation of China's "one child per couple" policy. More and more couples in rural areas were allowed to have a second child. Let us now turn our attention to a discussion of migration.

Of the three demographic processes, the one that most distinguishes rural from urban China is internal migration. Unlike most of the countries of the world, China differentiates internal migrants into permanent migrants and floating migrants. A permanent migrant in China is the same as a permanent migrant elsewhere; the person's migration involves a permanent change in residence and the crossing of a county boundary. The difference in China is that the permanent migration must first be approved by the government. A temporary migrant in China, and in a few other countries where internal migration is heavily controlled, is a migrant whose residential move does not have governmental approval. Temporary migrants are referred to in China as floating migrants (*liudong renkou*). The floating migrant moves without government permission. However, in many if not most cases, the migration is not really temporary, but is permanent or relatively permanent. But it is a migration that is not officially sanctioned.

Most internal migration in China is from rural areas to urban areas, and this is especially the case with regard to floating migration. Moreover, much more internal migration is floating than permanent (Poston & Zhang, 2008). Indeed one reason why temporary migration in China is so important is because its volume is so great. The 2000 Census of China counted more than 140 million temporary internal migrants in the country, and more than 100 million of them were from rural areas (Liang & Ma, 2004). The proportions of rural floating migrants in the resident populations of China's large cities these days typically range from one-third to one-fourth of the total city population. Thus, the floating migrants from rural China comprise nearly 40% of the country's total urban population (Solinger, 1999, p. 18). The internal migration of "floaters" from rural China to its cities constitutes the largest stream of peacetime residential mobility in recorded human history (Roberts, 1997).

Who are the rural to urban floating migrants? They are mainly young and unmarried males and females seeking employment in blue-collar, service and household jobs in China's cities. The "average [floating] migrant is less educated than the general population but more educated than the rural population. Few [floating] migrants come from the ranks of the absolute poor, who lack even the few years of schooling and basic Mandarin required for most migrant jobs" (World Bank, 1997, p. 55). Also, they are young, and males predominate over females (also see Yang, 1994, 1996).

There is yet another reason why China's rural to urban floating migrant population is so important. Some could likely become international immigrants and leave China, mainly illegally (Liang, 2001; Massey, 1995). How might this happen? The rural floating migrants in China's big cities earn wages that are much less than those of the permanent residents of the cities, as much as 20 to 40% less. However, the wages of the floaters are several times greater than the wages earned by countrymen in their rural home villages. They send as much as half of their salaries back to their home villages. In the rural counties of some provinces (e.g., Sichuan and Anhui Provinces), remittances from the floaters account for almost one-half of household cash income (World Bank, 1997, pp. 56–57).

If the floaters in the cities of China are unable to find or maintain jobs some could look elsewhere, likely outside China where there are jobs and possibly established Chinese networks. One such location would be the United States. In future years in China there will be more rural surplus workers, as well as more floaters. Indications point to increases in unemployment in China's cities in future years. Liang (2001) has written that the "likelihood of competition for jobs between internal migrants [i.e., the floaters] and unemployed workers [among the permanent residents of the cities] is clear.... Some members of the floating population and unemployed workers [may be pushed] onto the market for illegal transnational migration" (2001, p. 693).

Floaters have been sending remittances back to their home villages. If they were to stop and return home to the villages, this would result in a tremendous embarrassment and loss of "face." Many would look elsewhere, most likely outside China, where there are jobs and where there are already established Chinese networks, in countries such as the United States and many in Europe (Poston, Mao, & Yu, 1994). It is not inconceivable that there could well be many million such migrants to the U.S. from China in the next decade or so (Poston & Bouvier, 2010). Indeed, Massey, has written that "China's movement towards markets and rapid economic growth may contain the seeds of an enormous migration ... that would produce a flow of immigrants [to the U.S.] that would dwarf levels of migration now observed from Mexico" (Massey, 1995, p. 649). In the next and last section of this chapter we consider the situation of ethnic minorities in rural and urban China.

## The Minority Populations

The Chinese government identifies 56 ethnic nationalities, namely, the Han majority and 55 different minority groups. The Han are the most numerous, comprising in the year 2000 over 92% of China's total population. Thus, nearly 8% of the total population consists of the 55 minority nationalities. Although this is a relatively small proportion of China's total population, these 106 million Chinese minorities greatly exceed the actual number of minority group members in the United States. Indeed, if the minorities of China were a single country, it would be the twelfth largest country in the world, outnumbered only by India, the United States, Indonesia, Brazil, Pakistan, Bangladesh, Nigeria, Russia, Japan, Mexico, and the Han population of China.

All 31 provinces of China, and most of the more than 2,800 counties of China, contain some minority residents. Most of the minorities reside in the border areas rather than in the interior regions of the country, and many more minority peoples live in rural areas than in urban areas. In China, the geographic locations of the minority populations have to a significant degree been invariant for centuries.

The Chinese do not think of their minority populations as races. They are seldom distinguished solely by physical and anthropometric criteria. Instead, minority identification is distinguished largely on the basis of persistent cultural, linguistic, and in some cases religious characteristics (Poston, Chang, Deng, & Venegas, forthcoming).

Almost three-quarters (73.8%) of China's minority peoples live in rural China, a much higher figure than the 61.8% of Han people living in rural China. It thus makes good sense here to focus attention on minority peoples in rural China.

Among the 55 minority groups, their representations in rural China vary considerably. In the year 2000, slightly more than 18% of the Russian people were rural residents, whereas over 96% of the Dongxiang people lived in rural areas. Among the 55 minority groups, eight have very high percentages living in rural areas; the top three are the Dongxiang (96%), the Lisu (95%), and the Blang (94%). Most of the Dongxiang people live in the Ningxia Hui Autonomous Region and in the surrounding areas of Gansu Province in Northwestern China. They are Chinese Muslims of Mongol descent. The Lisu and the Blang minority peoples live mainly in Yunnan province in Southwestern China in remote mountainous areas.

The minority peoples as a whole are highly segregated residentially from the Han majority at levels of segregation above those common in the United States between whites and African Americans. Also, in rural China the levels of residential segregation between the minorities and the Han are higher than in urban China. For the 55 minority nationalities, the average dissimilarity index score measuring the degree of residential segregation of a minority from the Han across the rural parts of the more than 2,800 counties of China is 90.1%; the scores vary from a low dissimilarity score of 46.8% for the Gaoshan to a high of 99.3% for the Kazak. This means that over 99% of the Kazak peoples living in rural areas of China would have to move to certain other rural areas of China for their rural percentage residential distribution to be equal to that of the Han. Most of the minority groups have rural segregation scores from the Han of more than 90%. Segregation scores between majority and minority peoples in Western countries do not approach the rural segregation scores of most of China's minority groups from the Han.

Chinese minorities have higher fertility than the majority Han. The total fertility rate (TFR) for all minority populations on average was 1.7 in 2000, which is higher than the TFR of 1.2 for the majority Han. And there is extensive diversity in fertility among the 55 minorities groups. For instance, the Korean nationality has the lowest TFR of all the minority groups: a TFR of 0.7. The Lhoba minority group has the highest TFR, at a value of 2.7. In rural China the fertility differences between the minorities and the Han are even larger. For the whole country, there are eight minority groups with lower TFRs than the Han, but only five minority groups in rural China have TFRs lower than the Han's. That means most rural minority groups (50 groups) have higher fertility rates than the rural majority Han. Among all the rural minorities in the year 2000, the Koreans have the lowest TFR.

The extremely high ethnic segregation has placed Chinese rural minorities at a disadvantage. Since they are segregated in remote regions of China, most of them have very limited access to clinics and hospitals. Moreover, high medical fees often prevent the low-income minorities from accessing public care. Conversely a large proportion of the Han population resides in the interior regions of the country, associated with more resources and better medical care. As a result, the mortality levels for rural minorities are much higher than the mortality for rural Han. Also, in 2000 in China, 36% of all HIV-infected individuals were from rural minority groups.

## Conclusion

In this chapter, we have discussed the demographic structure and dynamics of rural China. We have seen major differences between rural and urban China in age and sex structure, particularly age dependency. Fertility and mortality are higher in rural than in urban China. Migration is a major factor distinguishing the rural and urban areas of China. There is so much preference for urban compared to rural living that more than 100 million rural residents have moved to China's cities in recent decades without the permission of government officials. Why are there such major rural-urban differences in China? Why do millions of rural residents want to live in the cities, and virtually no urban peoples ever move to the rural countryside? The answer lies in the rural-urban divide, the major factor of inequality in China (Farris et al., forthcoming).

Despite the socioeconomic successes that China as a country has achieved since 1949, serious inequalities and differences remain throughout the country. The major reason is the rural-urban divide. Rural-urban demographic and socioeconomic disparities are largely a result of China's household registration system used by the government since 1958, known as the hukou system. At birth, individuals are broadly divided into two categories, agricultural or nonagricultural, which essentially represent a distinction between "rural" and "urban." This basically ascriptive designation plays an important role in determining the person's future. Changing from a rural hukou to an urban hukou has been very difficult in past years (Chan & Buckingham, 2008).

Since China has always had a large rural population comprised mainly of poor farm workers, the hukou system served to limit the mass migration of poor peasants from rural to urban areas, ensuring a certain degree of structural stability, and preventing potential disruptions of China's economic and social order. The household registration system also impacted people's lives in profound ways; it regulated access to benefits provided and funded by the state. It created different life chances for rural and urban peoples. Those in rural areas predominately depended on their own agricultural production, while those in urban areas were able to access government-provided goods and social services.

Because of the advantages associated with nonagricultural living, we saw earlier in this chapter that in past decades over 100 million rural temporary internal migrants have moved to the cities to work, mainly in the manufacturing and service industries (Farris et al., forthcoming).

Socioeconomic and related welfare policies in China distinguish the residents of rural and urban areas. Urban residents benefit much more from those policies than do rural residents, resulting in a highly segregated and disadvantaged population in rural areas. China's household registration system is actually used for not recognizing the peasantry as full and equal citizens of the country (Farris et al., forthcoming). This has important impacts on overall life chances in rural

China, and is at the foundation of the demographic disparities between rural and urban China that we have presented in this chapter.

## References

Aird, J. S. (1972). Population policy and demographic prospects in the People's Republic of China. In *People's Republic of China: An Economic Assessment, A Compendium of Papers Submitted to the Joint Economic Committee, Congress of the United States, 18 May (92nd Congress, 2nd Session)*. Washington, DC: U.S. Government Printing Office.

Ashton, B., Hill, K., Piazza, A., & Zeitz, R. (1984). Famine in China, 1958–61. *Population and Development Review, 10*(4), 613–645.

Banister, J. (1984). An analysis of recent data on the population of China. *Population and Development Review, 10*(2), 241–271.

Banister, J. (1987). *China's changing population*. Stanford, CA: Stanford University Press.

Banister, J., & Hill, K. (2004). Mortality in China 1964–2000. *Population Studies, 58*, 55–75.

Becker, J. (1998). *Hungry ghosts: Mao's secret famine*. New York: Henry Holt and Company.

Bogue, D. J. (1969). *Principles of demography*. New York: Wiley.

Central Intelligence Agency. (2007). *The CIA World Factbook*. New York: Skyhorse Publishing.

Chan, K. W., & Buckingham, W. (2008). Is China abolishing the Hukou system? *The China Quarterly, 195*, 582–606.

Chandler, T. (1987). *Four thousand years of urban growth: An historical census*. Lewiston, NY: Edwin Mellen Press.

Chandler, T., & Fox, G. (1974). *Three thousand years of urban growth*. New York: Academic.

Chen, S. (1984). Fertility of women during the 42-year period from 1940 to 1981. In China Population Information Center, *Analysis on China's National One-per-Thousand Sampling Survey* (pp. 32–58). Beijing: China Population Information Center.

China Statistics Press. (2005). *The China statistical yearbook 2005*. Beijing, China: China Statistics Press. Retrieved November 1, 2010, from http://www.stats.gov.cn/tjsj/ndsj/2005/indexee.htm

China Statistical Yearbooks Database. (1998). *The China statistical yearbook 1997*. Retrieved November 1, 2010, from http://tongji.cnki.net/overseas/engnavi/YearBook.aspx?id=N2006042082&floor=1###

China Statistical Yearbooks Database. (2007). *The China statistical yearbook 2007*. Retrieved November 1, 2010, from http://www.stats.gov.cn/tjsj/ndsj/2007/indexeh.htm

Coale, A. J. (1984). *Rapid population change in China, 1952–1982*. Washington, DC: National Academy Press.

Dikotter, F. (2010). *Mao's great famine: The history of China's most devastating catastrophe, 1958–1962*. New Yor: Walker and Company.

Fairbank, J. K., & Goldman, M. (2006). *China: A new history* (2nd enlarged ed.). Cambridge, MA: Belknap Press.

Fan, S., Chan-Kang, C., & Mukherjee, A. (2005). *Rural and urban dynamics and poverty: Evidence from China and India*. Washington, DC: International Food Policy Research Institute, Discussion Paper 196. Retrieved January 19, 2010, from http://www.ifpri.org/sites/default/files/publications/fcndp196.pdf

Farris, D. N., He, L., Iwinska-Nowak, A., & Poston, D. L., Jr. (forthcoming). Poverty in China. In J. Singelmann & M. Lee (Eds.), *International handbook of poverty populations*. New York: Springer.

Goldstein, S. (1990). Urbanization in China, 1982–1987: Effect of migration and reclassification. *Population and Development Review, 16*, 673–701.

Heilig, G. K. (1999). *China Food: Can China Feed Itself?* Laxenburg, Austria: International Institute for Applied Systems Analysis.

Heilig, G. K. (2003). *Rural development or sustainable development in China: Is China's rural development sustainable?* Paper presented at "ECOLINK Workshop: Ecosites, EcoCenters and the Implementation of European Union Environment and Sustainable Development Policies." Montpellier, France, 18–19 September.

Horiuchi, S., & Preston, S. H. (1988). Age-specific growth rates: The legacy of past population dynamics. *Demography, 25*, 429–441.

Hsu, M. L. (1985). Growth and control of population in China: The urban-rural contrast. *Annals of the Association of American Geographers, 75*, 241–257.

Keyfitz, N. (1965). Age distribution as a challenge to development. *American Journal of Sociology, 70*, 659–668.

Keyfitz, N., & Flieger, W. (1971). *Population: Facts and methods of demography*. San Francisco: W.H. Freeman and Company.

Liang, Z. (2001). Demography of illicit emigration from China: A sending country's perspective. *Sociological Forum, 16*, 677–701.

Liang, Z., & Ma, Z. (2004). China's floating population: New evidence from the 2000 census. *Population and Development Review, 30*, 467–488.

Massey, D. S. (1995). The new immigration and ethnicity in the United States. *Population and Development Review, 21*, 631–652.

Orleans, L. A. 1972. *Every fifth child: The population of China*. Stanford, CA: Stanford University Press.

Poston, D. L., Jr. (1986). Patterns of contraceptive use in China. *Studies in Family Planning, 17*, 217–227.

Poston, D. L., Jr. (1992). China in 1990. In D. L. Poston, Jr. & D. Yaukey (Eds.), *The population of modern China* (pp. 699–718). New York: Plenum Press.

Poston, D. L., Jr. (2005). Age and sex. In D. L. Poston, Jr. & M. Micklin (Eds.), *Handbook of population* (pp. 19–58). New York: Springer Publishers.

Poston, D. L., Jr., & Bouvier, L. F. (2010). *Population and society: An introduction to demography*. New York: Oxford University Press.

Poston, D. L., Jr., Chang, Y., Deng, X., & Venegas, M. (forthcoming). The demography of China's minority nationalities. In R. Saenz, N. Rodriguez, & D. G. Embrick (Eds.), *The international handbook of the demography of race and ethnicity*. New York: Springer.

Poston, D. L., Jr., & Duan, C. C. (2000). The current and projected distribution of the elderly and eldercare in the people's Republic of China. *Journal of Family Issues, 21*, 714–732.

Poston, D. L., Jr., Gu, B., & Luo, H. (2004). The effects of the fertility and mortality transitions on the elderly and eldercare in China, and Shanghai, Beijing, and Tianjin. *The Journal of Gerontology, 8,* 126–166.

Poston, D. L., Jr., Mao, M. X., & Yu, M.-Y. (1994). The global distribution of the overseas Chinese around 1990. *Population and Development Review, 20,* 631–645.

Poston, D. L., Jr., & Shu, J. (1987). The demographic and socioeconomic composition of the major minority groups in China. *Population and Development Review, 13,* 703–722.

Poston, D. L., Jr., Tian, Y., & Jia, Z. (1990). The urban hierarchy of China. In B. D. H. Doan (Ed.), *Urbanization and geographical distribution of population* (pp. 100–130). Pusan, Korea: Social Survey Research Center, Pusan National University.

Poston, D. L., Jr., & Zhang, L. (2008). Ecological analyses of permanent and temporary migration streams in China in the 1990s. *Population Research and Policy Review, 27,* 689–712.

Roberts, K. D. (1997). China's 'tidal wave' of migrant labor: What can we learn from Mexican undocumented migration to the United States? *International Migration Review, 31,* 249–293.

Sardon, J.-P. (1985). Planification Familiale et Pratiques Contraceptives en Chine. *Population, 40,* 774–779.

Solinger, D. J. (1999). *Contesting citizenship in urban China: Peasant migrants, the state, and the logic of the market.* Berkeley, CA: University of California Press.

South, S. J., & Trent, K. (1988). Sex ratios and women's roles: A cross-national analysis. *American Journal of Sociology, 93,* 1096–1115.

Tien, H. Y. (1983). China: Demographic billionaire. *Population Bulletin, 38*(2), 1–42.

Tien, H. Y. (1991). *China's strategic demographic initiative.* New York: Praeger Publications.

Trinh, T. (2006). China's pension system caught between mounting legacies and unfavourable demographics. *Deutsche Bank Research: Special China Issue,* 1–24. Retrieved January 20, 2010, from http://www.dbresearch.de/PROD/DBR_INTERNET_DEPROD/PROD0000000000196025.pdf

United Nations. (1980). *Patterns of urban and rural population growth.* New York: United Nations.

United Nations. (2007). *World urbanization prospects: The 2007 revision population database.* Retrieved May 5, 2010, from http://esa.un.org/unup/

World Bank. (1997). *China 2020: Sharing rising incomes: Disparities in China.* Washington, DC: The World Bank.

Wu, C., & Wang, L. (2004). *Contribution of population control in creating opportunities for China arising from fertility decline should not be neglected.* Paper Presented at the International Symposium on the 2000 Population Census of China, Beijing, April.

Yang, X. (1994). Urban temporary out-migration under economic reforms: Who moves and for what reasons? *Population Research and Policy Review, 13,* 83–100.

Yang, X. (1996). Labor force characteristics and labor force migration in China. In The U.S. Department of Labor, *Changes in China's labor market: Implications for the future* (pp. 13–44). Washington, DC: U.S. Department of Labor.

You, H. X., & Poston, D. L., Jr. (2004). Are floating migrants in China "Child bearing guerillas?": An analysis of floating migration and fertility. *Asian and Pacific Migration Journal, 13*(4), 405–422.

# Rural Population Trends in Mexico: Demographic and Labor Changes

## 12

Landy Sanchez and Edith Pacheco

## Abbreviations

| | |
|---|---|
| CEED | Center for Economic and Demographic Studies (Spanish Acronym) |
| CONAPO | National Population Council (Spanish Acronym) |
| CONEVAL | National Council for the Evaluation of Social Policies (Spanish Acronym) |
| EMIF | National Migration Survey in the Northern Border (Spanish Acronym) |
| ENADID | National Survey of Demographic Dynamic |
| ENE | National Survey of Employment (Spanish Acronym) |
| ENEU | National Survey of Urban Employment (Spanish Acronym) |
| ENOE | National Survey of Occupation and Employment (Spanish Acronym) |
| GDP | Gross Domestic Product |
| IMR | Infant Mortality Rate |
| INAH | National Institute of Anthropology and History (Spanish Acronym) |
| INEGI | National institute of Statistics and Geography (Spanish Acronym) |
| STPS | Secretary of Labor and Social Provision (Spanish Acronym) |

L. Sanchez (✉)
El Colegio de México, A.C. Center for Demographic, Urban, and Environmental Studies, C.P.10740, México, D.F., México
e-mail: lsanchez@colmex.mx

## Demographic Changes

Although there is a long-standing debate on the definition of rural population, the Mexican statistics office designates as rural any individual who lives in a locality with a population under 2,500, regardless of population density or proximity to urban areas, while the urban population lives in localities with 2,500 and more inhabitants (INEGI, 2009b).

This standardized definition makes it possible to analyze some central demographic changes in rural areas in recent decades. Table 12.1 shows that the proportion of rural population has decreased markedly in Mexico since the beginning of the 20th century. In the early 1960s, the rural population still accounted for almost half of the population, but through rapid urbanization, this proportion declined rapidly over the following decades, to the extent that in 2005 it was only 23.5% and estimated at 22.1% in 2009. It is important to note that despite this proportional decline, the rural population maintained an upward trend in absolute numbers until 2000 due to previous high fertility rates, meaning that by 2000 there were 24.7 million living in rural areas and it was only in 2005 that the rural population decreased in absolute as well as proportional terms.

Historical data also allows a rapid look at the main changes in the composition of the rural population. First, as trends in population size have already suggested, fertility rates began to decline significantly in Mexico from the mid-1970s, a shift that was more pronounced in urban areas but also occurred in rural areas albeit at a slower pace. Table 12.2 shows that in rural areas the fertility rate declined from 7.4 in 1974 to

**Table 12.1** Rural population trends in Mexico 1921–2009

|  | Total population | Rural | % Rural population | Growth rate Rural | Urban |
|---|---|---|---|---|---|
| 1921 | 14,334,780 | 10,034,346 | 70.00 | – | – |
| 1930 | 16,560,889 | 11,012,991 | 66.50 | 1.04 | 2.87 |
| 1940 | 19,652,552 | 12,754,506 | 64.90 | 1.64 | 2.45 |
| 1950 | 25,791,016 | 14,804,043 | 57.40 | 1.67 | 5.31 |
| 1960 | 34,923,128 | 17,217,102 | 49.30 | 1.69 | 5.45 |
| 1970 | 48,225,237 | 19,917,023 | 41.30 | 1.63 | 5.35 |
| 1980 | 66,846,831 | 19,786,662 | 29.60 | –0.07 | 5.81 |
| 1990 | 81,249,645 | 23,318,648 | 28.70 | 1.84 | 2.34 |
| 2000 | 97,483,409 | 24,760,786 | 25.40 | 0.67 | 2.56 |
| 2005 | 103,300,617 | 24,275,645 | 23.50 | –0.22 | 0.93 |
| 2010 | 112,322,757 | 26,00,1607 | 23.15 | 0.77 | 0.99 |

*Source*: INEGI, population census, 1921–2010 and population enumeration 1995 and 2005 (INEGI, 2007).

**Table 12.2** Fertility rates by residence, Mexico 1974–2008

|  | Rural | Urban |
|---|---|---|
| 1974 | 7.4 | 5.0 |
| 1980 | 6.8 | 4.0 |
| 1985 | 6.0 | 3.3 |
| 1990 | 4.8 | 2.9 |
| 1996 | 3.5 | 2.3 |
| 1995 | 3.8 | 2.4 |
| 2000 | 3.7 | 2.5 |
| 2005 | 2.8 | 2.1 |
| 2008 | 2.7 | 2.0 |

*Source*: CONAPO estimated based on demographic surveys.

2.7 in 2008. For urban areas, this rate declined from 5 to 2.0 in the same period, since fertility began to decline earlier and rapidly (Romo & Sánchez, 2010). Although there are still noticeable differences across regions in Mexico, there is a general tendency towards a decline in fertility and a narrowing gap between urban and rural contexts. Differences in mothers' ages at birth are also declining between rural and urban women, although young cohorts (20–25, 25–29) still display noticeable differences in their fertility rates which basically account for disparities in global fertility levels (Romo & Sánchez, 2010; ENADID, 2009). Yet, the infant mortality rate (IMR) is noticeable higher in rural than in urban areas: in the period 2006–2008, IMR was 15.7 in rural while it was 13.0 in urban areas (ENADID, 2009).

Trends in rural population volumes can not only be explained by fertility and mortality rates but also by migration patterns. Historically, it is possible to differentiate between a period where rural-urban migration was a central driver of rural demographics, and a second period in which international migration became dominant. The first interlude began in the 1950s as a consequence of industrialization and modernization processes, as well as a drop in traditional agricultural products that expelled population from rural areas. Until the 1980s, metropolitan areas attracted rural population due to the employment opportunities and housing possibilities they offered. It is estimated that during the 1950s, the urban population grew by 4.9 million, with 38% coming from rural areas; whereas in the 1960s, rural-urban migration accounted for 32.2% of the population increase in urban areas (Alba, 1977). Initially, rural migrants tended to be young, single, and more female than male, but as time went by, family migration increased and a balance between the sexes began to be struck (CEED, 1970). During those years, rural-urban migration released the population pressure over land and local labor markets (Appendini, 2008), but demographic growth continued because a sizable proportion was circular migration. In addition, agricultural production and land access still offered some opportunities to those who benefit from the agrarian reform in the 1940s. Circular movements were particularly likely in areas where regional population centers existed and offered employment opportunities (Appendini, 2008).

Rural-urban migration declined from the early 1980s, so that during the 1990s it only accounted for 18.4% of internal movements in Mexico (Partida, 2004). However, the probability of migrate is actually higher among the rural than the population: 3.7 rate versus a 3.3 rate respectively (Partida, 2004). Whereas internal migration diminished, international migration, primarily to the USA, rapidly expanded. Estimates of international migration are still under debate, but all accounts support its rapid growth since 1970, with just some signs of decline in recent years (Passel & Suro, 2005; Corona & Tuiran, 2006; Galindo & Ramos, 2009). In the 1980s, it was estimated that 235,000 people migrated out of Mexico every year, while during the period from 2000 to 2006 it reached an average volume of 460,000 annually, overwhelmingly to the USA (Galindo & Ramos, 2009). The traditional migrant profile included rural, male population of reproductive age, with low educational achievement, often engaged in seasonal agricultural activities (Leite, Ramos, & Gaspar, 2004). Although this sociodemographic profile is changing, rural areas are still experiencing the greatest population losses. Table 12.3 presents estimates of migration to the USA by residence based on EMIF. Although the proportion from urban areas grew between 1995 and 2000, rural areas still contribute an average of 55.6% of migrants, a sizable overrepresentation considering rural population volumes and trends. On the basis of the same source, most of these rural migrants were still males of reproductive and working age, although the data also shows increases in family migration.

The international migration stream and its changes over time have a clear impact on rural population composition. In contrast to early periods of international migration – for example during the bracero program — and also in contrast to circular internal migration, in recent times international migration implies a long-term or permanent move. As we will show below, such a shift responds, at least partially, to deteriorating employment opportunities in rural communities as well as limited access to land, particularly for younger cohorts. Figure 12.1 compares the age structure of the rural and urban population in 2005, using the Population Enumeration data. The first remarkable fact is the larger proportion of population under 20 years old in rural areas as a consequence of their higher fertility rates. However, since fertility differences between urban and rural women are narrowing, the disparities at the bottom of the pyramid (population younger than 10 years old) are not as pronounced as a few decades back. Second, the working-age population losses in rural areas due to migration become apparent by looking at age groups at the peak of their productive participation (20's). This is particularly pronounced among males and in the 25–29 group, where Mexico has a "shortage" in the pyramid, and especially noticeable in rural areas. Third, the pyramid also points towards an older population in rural areas, mostly as a consequence of losses of working-age population (CONAPO, 2008). As we discuss next, this aging population supposes productive challenges:

**Table 12.3** Migrants to the USA by place of birth

|      | Total migrants | Urban   | Nonurban | % Nonurban |
|------|----------------|---------|----------|------------|
| 1995 | 433,452        | 162,076 | 271,376  | 62.61      |
| 1999 | 382,505        | 179,802 | 202,703  | 52.99      |
| 2000 | 327,535        | 144,732 | 182,803  | 55.81      |
| 2001 | 680,875        | 380,445 | 300,430  | 44.12      |
| 2002 | 558,664        | 190,555 | 368,109  | 65.89      |
| 2003 | 324,854        | 141,369 | 183,485  | 56.48      |
| 2004 | 325,911        | 137,851 | 188,060  | 57.70      |
| 2005 | 255,227        | 95,364  | 159,863  | 62.64      |
| 2006 | 363,764        | 179,591 | 184,174  | 50.63      |
| 2007 | 404,494        | 214,749 | 189,745  | 46.91      |

*Source*: EMIF several years.

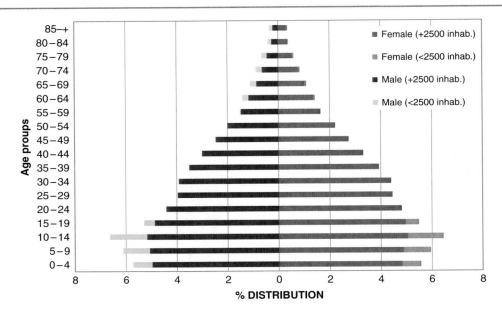

**Fig. 12.1** 2005 Mexico population structure

on the one hand, most individuals need to remain economically active until advanced age but on the other hand, property is also concentrated in older groups, which deepens economic uncertainties in rural communities.

## Land, Poverty, and Spatial Dispersion

The evolution of rural population is closely linked to the development of agricultural production and land property rights in Mexico. The 1917 Constitution, resulting from the Mexican Revolution, gave rise to land redistribution, which peaked during the government of President Lazaro Cardenas (1934–1940). A focal product of such redistribution was the ejido holders, individuals who could operate on a smaller scale in communal land (ejido) but they did not actually own the land. They were allowed to use their allotted parcels indefinitely and they could even pass their rights down to their children, but land sales were banned. This system continued until 1993 when President Carlos Salinas de Gortari promoted major changes in Article 27 of the Constitution. Since then, ejido land can be converted into private property and sold to third parties, including foreigners (Huerta, 2001).

Among the reasons put forward in favor of the reform were the vast and disperse number of existing small properties, their low level of technology and productivity, and the chronic poverty of rural communities (Merino, 2004). However, some of those arguments still hold currently. In 2007, the average property size was 16.8 hectares, but almost 60% of ejido holders had less than 5 hectares (SRA, 2010).[1] Only a third of productive units have access to modern machinery and credits, although the larger proportion of land falls under the private property regime (INEGI, 2009a).

Studies also suggest that even though social policies targeted rural households since the early 1990s, they still experience higher levels of poverty and lagged behind urban households in all relevant socioeconomic indicators (educational attainment, health access, and income) (Scott, 2009). Government poverty estimates show that the rural population remained largely poor (Table 12.4). Between 1992 and 2008, the rural population experienced noticeably higher poverty levels than the urban population: at any single point in time, poverty percentages in rural areas are at least twice as high as in urban areas. Furthermore, poverty estimates also suggest that the rural population is particularly vulnerable to periods of economic downturn, such as 1995 or 2008 after which poverty increased despite antipoverty programs. As Scott claims (2009), rural

---

[1] 5 hectares equivalent to 12.3 acres.

**Table 12.4** Population in poverty (%)

| | Food-subsistence poverty line | Food-subsistence poverty line | Capabilities poverty line | Capabilities poverty line |
|---|---|---|---|---|
| | Rural | Urban | Rural | Urban |
| 1992 | 34.0 | 13.0 | 44.1 | 20.1 |
| 1994 | 37.0 | 10.7 | 47.5 | 18.3 |
| 1996 | 53.5 | 27.0 | 62.6 | 36.8 |
| 1998 | 51.7 | 21.4 | 59 | 30.6 |
| 2000 | 42.4 | 12.5 | 49.9 | 20.2 |
| 2002 | 34.0 | 11.3 | 42.6 | 17.2 |
| 2004 | 28.0 | 11.0 | 36.2 | 17.8 |
| 2005 | 32.3 | 9.9 | 39.8 | 15.8 |
| 2006 | 24.5 | 7.5 | 32.7 | 13.6 |
| 2008 | 31.8 | 10.6 | 39.1 | 17.2 |

*Source*: Coneval (2009).

poverty cannot be understood without paying attention to the structure of agricultural production: to the extent that social programs are dissociated from agricultural subsidies, most rural households only benefit from the former but are unable to maintain agricultural income or to generate alternative employment options. Thus, for these households agriculture becomes either a subsistence or complementary activity, and they are more likely to depend on other income sources, government transfers or remittances (Appendini, 2008; Scott, 2009).[2]

The rural population is not only diminishing in numbers but is also divided among thousands of localities across Mexico. Whereas in 1970, there were almost 20 million rural inhabitants distributed across 95,400 localities, in 2005 the rural population was scattered among a total of 196,400 localities decreasing the average number of inhabitants in rural localities from 208.7 to 125.9 in 2000. Moreover, most of these rural places continue to have poor access to educational and health infrastructure, and almost 32.5% of these localities – with 4.9 million inhabitants in 2000 – are considered to be isolated from roads and transport to larger population centers (Hernández, 2004). Geographical dispersion contributed to high poverty rates in rural areas, although at the core of such impoverishment are agrarian labor-market conditions.

## Labor Changes and Rural Households' Strategies

The previous sections already suggested the interconnections between population structure, migration trends, and poverty. In this section, we attempt to show in detail the transformations in farm work and the way in which they are crucial to understanding the demographic trends described earlier.

Table 12.5 shows the declining weight of farm labor. During the first 30 years of the 20th century, farming accounted for nearly 70%. This figure began to decline in the 1930s, during the period known as the Mexican miracle,[3] activities were diversified and the proportion of the population engaged in agriculture declined. By the early 1970s, just four out of every ten persons were engaged in the agricultural sector and from that year onwards, numbers steadily declined, so that by 2009, the proportion had dropped to 13.4%. In absolute terms, however, the population engaged in

---

[2] Agricultural subsidies are concentrated by middle and large producers, which are relevant in terms of production but not in relation to population (Scott, 2009).

[3] The term "Mexican Economic Miracle" points to a long period of sustained economic growth, from the mid-1940s to the late 1960s. Although a trend of Gross Domestic Product (GDP) was not uniform over the years, a couple of years are illustrative: 8.2% in 1944 or 10% in 1954.

**Table 12.5** Population and labor force, 1900–2006

| | 1900 | 1930 | 1950 | 1970 | 1979 | 1991 | 1995 | 2000 | 2006 |
|---|---|---|---|---|---|---|---|---|---|
| Labor Force | | | | | | | | | |
| (thousands) | 4,195 | 5,352 | 8,272 | 13,873 | 18,784 | 31,088 | 35,951 | 40,162 | 43,575 |
| (growth) | | (0.81) | (2.18) | (2.59) | (3.37) | (4.20) | (3.63) | (2.22) | (1.36) |
| Male LFPR | – | – | 88.0 | 70.1 | 71.3 | 77.7 | 78.2 | 76.8 | 78.7 |
| Female LFPR | – | – | 13.1 | 17.6 | 21.5 | 31.5 | 34.5 | 36.4 | 40.7 |
| LF by sector (%) | | | | | | | | | |
| Primary | 62.5 | 67.8 | 58.3 | 39.4 | 28.9 | 26.8 | 24.7 | 18.6 | 14.3 |
| Secondary | 14.6 | 16.7 | 20.0 | 28.6 | 27.5 | 23.0 | 21.3 | 26.7 | 25.6 |
| Tertiary | 16.2 | 15.6 | 21.7 | 32.0 | 43.1 | 49.5 | 53.1 | 54.8 | 60.1 |
| LF in less urbanized contexts (%) | | | | | | | | | |
| Primary | – | – | – | – | – | 48.9 | 44.0 | 34.9 | 29.3 |
| Secondary | | | | | | | 18.3 | 17.4 | 24.5 | 24.0 |
| Tertiary | | | | | | | 32.8 | 38.6 | 40.6 | 46.7 |

*LFPR* Labor Force Participation Rate.
*Sources*: From 1895 to 1950: Census 1930 to 1950, Direccion General de Estadistica and INEGI-INAH, Estadisticas Historicas de Mexico, INEGI-INAH, Mexico, 1990. From 1970 to 1991: STPS, El mercado de Trabajo en Mexico (1970–1992), STPS, Mexico, 1994; Rendon and Salas, DEMOS 1989 and García, Brígida, DEMOS, 1992, 1995 y 1996. Data for 1995 and 2000, STPS-INEGI, ENE, 1995 and 2000. 2006 Data STPS-INEGI, ENOE.

the agricultural sector totaled 3.6 million in 1910, and by 2009 it reached 5.9 million. There are significant differences in the weight of agricultural labor force across Mexican regions, reaching in the southern state between 40 and 30% of the total labor force, while the central state of Mexico only employs 9% of it (Scott, 2009).

The decline in farming labor occurred in a context where female economic activity rose from nearly 10% to approximately 40% at the beginning of the 21st century. At the same time, the growth of the economically active population rose gradually throughout the 20th century as opposed to the total population growth rate, which had steadily declined since the 1980s. It is only between 1991 and 2000 that a decline was observed in the labor force growth rate. However, until 2009, the labor growth rate continued to be higher than that of population growth (Table 12.5).

Yet, the agricultural sector still employed a significant proportion of the labor force in rural localities, in 2009 it occupied around half of it (48.5%). However, labor occupations have diversified towards other activities such as industry (11.1%), retail trade (12%), construction (8.6%), and services (18.5%). To a certain extent, this diversification is one of the elements giving rise to the analytical perspective called the new rurality.[4] In addition, other studies pointed also to emerging employment opportunities in rural areas, from textile maquiladoras to tourism and new niche trades (Arias & Wilson, 1997; Marsch & Runsten, 2000). Although there are localized new employment sources, as the previous numbers suggest, most of the rural population still works in farming and the new occupations are mainly in personal services and construction, two traditional occupations for rural residents (Appendini, 2008; Pacheco & Florez, 2009).

In fact, as several authors point out, understanding rural as a sphere related to agricultural production in contrast to an urban arena related to industry and services no longer has an explanatory value in the current Mexican context (Garay, 2008; Pérez, 2001; Teubal, 2001; Carton de Grammont, 2004;

---

[4] The concept of new rurality often refers to any change occurring in the rural contexts under the influence of globalization, trade liberalization and structural adjustment policies. This concept includes the changes in agricultural markets, the peri-urban phenomena, the emergence of new social actors, as well as government policies. A group of Latin American researchers use this concept referring exclusively to economy and material structures that change not only by external forces but also by social movements (Pérez, Farah, & Grammont, 2008: 14).

Appendini & Torres, 2008). Although the diversification of economic activities in rural contexts has been shown previously, the common precarious employment conditions faced by agricultural workers and their relationship to population trends in rural Mexico are not often highlighted.

Data from the agrarian module of the National Employment Survey (1991–2003) enables one to estimate the size of farm work, it defines as "agrarian subjects" any individual who declared, at some time during the six months prior to the interview, that he had been engaged in obtaining products from the earth or in livestock production, either directly as a worker or as an organizer and supervisor of the production process as a whole.

A comparison of the age and sex structure of agrarian and nonagrarian subjects yields sharp differences. An initial dissimilarity has to do with gender inequalities, since women's economic participation in agricultural activities is extremely limited compared with their participation in other activities. Partly this is because of the difficulties of making women's work visible, since they often perceive their activity as a form of family help rather than work, and this blending may be particularly strong in farming where family labor is widespread. The difficulty of separating domestic and extra-domestic spheres reinforces the process of women's invisibility in labor statistics (Wainerman & Rechinni, 1981; García, Blanco, & Pacheco, 1999).

The ageing process is also evident. Figure 12.2 shows that agrarian subjects have an older age structure than the rest of the population. There is a higher percentage of people 65 and older among agricultural subjects, suggesting a context where population may work until late in life, given the lack of pension coverage for these workers. In fact, only about 4% of farm subjects have access to social security.

A third difference is seen between the group ages 15 to 19 and 20 to 24. In agrarian subjects' structure, the gap between the two age groups is broad, which could be explained by workers' mobility towards other activities as well as spatial mobility. Conversely, the proportion of younger nonagricultural workers is very small in relation to that group among agrarian subjects. Moreover, the group aged 20 to 24 is larger than the group aged 15 to 19 for nonfarm workers. Conversely, the former age group accounts for a smaller proportion in the farm group, due to occupational shifts and migration.

During the period for which the agricultural module is available (1991–2003), workers comprise the

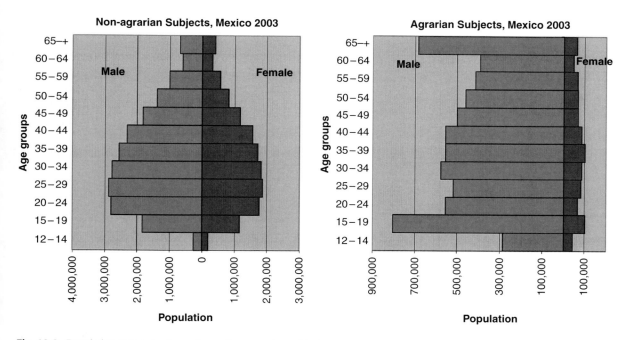

**Fig. 12.2** Population structure of agrarian and nonagrarian subjects

**Table 12.6** Agrarian subjects by type. Less urbanized localities

|  | Male | Female | Male | Female |
|---|---|---|---|---|
|  | 1991 | 2003 | 1991 | 2003 |
| *Producers* | 49.3 | 45.2 | 11.7 | 10.8 |
| Land owners | 13.8 | 14.2 | 6.7 | 4.5 |
| Communal-land owners "Ejidatarios" | 24.8 | 24.3 | 3.2 | 5.1 |
| Tenants | 5.7 | 2.7 | 1.4 | 0.9 |
| Sharecroppers and leaseholders | 4.9 | 4.0 | 0.5 | 0.3 |
| *Landless producers* | 0.7 | 2.0 | 1.9 | 8.5 |
| *Workers* | 50.0 | 52.8 | 86.3 | 80.7 |
| Day workers | 20.5 | 30.1 | 21.1 | 21.3 |
| Employees | 3.8 | 2.1 | 0.5 | 1.0 |
| Unpaid workers | 25.7 | 20.5 | 64.7 | 58.3 |
| *Total* | 8,173,458 | 6,502,376 | 1,671,562 | 1,216,712 |

*Source*: Agrarian module National Employment Survey, INEGI.

largest group.[5] In the case of men, they account for just over 50% of agrarian subjects, whereas in the case of women, the percentage is approximately 80% (Table 12.6). Male producers also occupy a significant proportion of the group of agrarian subjects and it is worth noting that only a slight decline has been observed during the period of study.[6] A close look at the type of producers shows that this group is dominated by ejido holders[7] in the case of men (accounting for nearly a quarter of agrarian subjects) while the group of workers is dominated by unpaid female workers (approximately 60%) as well as day workers of either sex (30 and 20% of men and women respectively in 2003).

As for the question of age and sex structures for the various agrarian subjects, it is important to note that there is a sharp difference between producers and workers, since the former have a relatively old structure, whereas the structure of the latter is quite young (Fig. 12.3). Tenants, sharecroppers, and leaseholders[8] also have a lower average age than other producers. The older age of producers can be explained by the fact that being a producer requires some form of land ownership, which is unusual among the younger population. This does not reflect only the lack of monetary resources of the youth, but mainly the demographic pressures over land: there is not enough land to inherit, as for most young people this is the only way to obtain access to land (Quesnel & del Rey, 2004; Dirven, 2003). Moreover, owners tend to transfer land property rights at late age and, in the past, it was rarely

---

[5] For INEGI (2002), "Agricultural workers are all those individuals who sell their labor for engaging in farm work plus those who, within families or territorial groups are mobilized by producers without the existence of a monetary agreement between them. It also includes direct workers (day workers, farm hands and peons) and employees and operators, but also ancillary personnel." In short, the group of agricultural workers includes workers and peons, employees and unpaid workers. Conversely, the group of producers includes a broad subgroup of agricultural subjects: owners, *ejidatarios* or *comuneros*, tenants, sharecroppers, and leaseholders (footnote no. 8 describes each of these terms in detail).

[6] To a certain extent, this result takes us back to the bibliography that holds that agricultural activity is linked to subjective processes of identity construction (Zendejas & Vries, 1998). In other words, although these workers may not be actively producing in the countryside, landownership makes them define themselves as agrarian subjects.

[7] Ejido holders or owners: previously communal-land owners. Currently, they own land and can sell it after the approval of the community assembly. See section "Land, Poverty, Spatial Dispersion", first paragraph.

[8] These agricultural subjects are defined as follows: (1) tenants: subjects that work land that has been lent or informally ceded without any reciprocal agreement; (2) Sharecroppers: Individuals that ask to work a plot of land belonging to someone else, and promise to share the result of their work on this plot with the landowner, which is usually half of what they have obtained (*medieros*); and (3) Leaseholders: those that declare they have access to arable land they do not own, by paying a monetary sum for the temporary usufruct of this land, without directly having to define what they will do with the result of their agricultural activity (INEGI, 2002, Glossary).

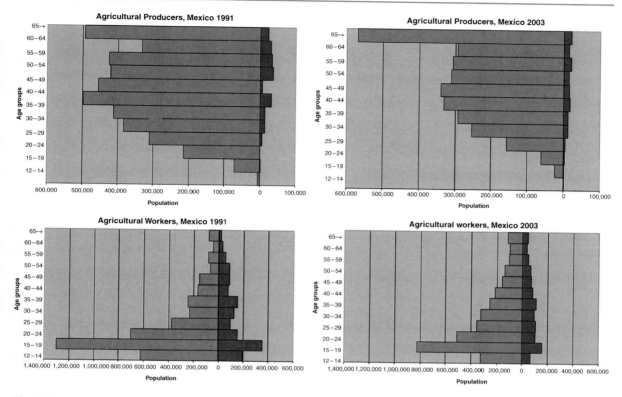

**Fig. 12.3** Agrarian population structure. Producers vs. workers

passed onto daughters. As agriculture loses relevance in household budgets, however, land property became assets as housing and more siblings acquire access to it, but not as agricultural producers.

As for male workers, unpaid work is related with being young (an average age of 20) whereas in the case of women, this situation occurs even later – their average age is nearly 15 years higher than men. This result suggests that for women, the condition of unpaid worker is likely to occur throughout their lifetime. In addition, day workers are the group with the second lowest average age, but this is above 30 and it is likely to comprise a sizable proportion of seasonal, landless labor.

As for the trends by age over time, a process of ageing among the main agrarian subjects is confirmed. The average age of both workers and producers has increased. Among agricultural producers, the average age rose from 46.3 to 50.2 years while the age of male workers rose from 25.2 to 30. In the case of women, it is interesting to note that the age of female producers – 50 – hardly varies, while the average age of female workers rose from 29.7 to 34.4. Once again, this basic data provides some indication as to the effects of migration in rural contexts, since among the general population, the age increase was just 2 years, from 33 to 35 years, whereas among agrarian subjects this change was twice as large, which might be associated with the departure of the youth.

## Working and Family Conditions

The characteristics of agricultural workers are different from those of nonagricultural workers and reflect a situation of social inequality, in which agricultural activities display extremely precarious working conditions. First of all, most nonfarm workers are salaried workers, while the group of farm workers consists mainly of self-employed or unpaid family workers (Table 12.7). Between 1995 and 2009, however, there was an increase in the number of

**Table 12.7** Working conditions. Farm and nonfarm workers

|  | Nonagricultural workers | | | | Agricultural workers | | | |
|---|---|---|---|---|---|---|---|---|
|  | 1995 | 1995 | 2009 | 2009 | 1995 | 1995 | 2009 | 2009 |
|  | Male | Female | Male | Female | Male | Female | Male | Female |
| Labor Force Participation (Millions) | 15.9 | 9.6 | 22.1 | 15.8 | 7.2 | 1.2 | 5.2 | 0.6 |
| Status in Employment (%) | 100 | 100 | 100 | 100 | 100 | 100 | 100 | 100 |
| Wage and salaried workers | 69.1 | 63.5 | 72.7 | 66.5 | 26.8 | 11.8 | 38.5 | 30.2 |
| Self-employed workers | 20.4 | 23.5 | 18.0 | 23.2 | 40.8 | 12.9 | 41.6 | 18.0 |
| Employers | 6.3 | 1.4 | 6.1 | 2.2 | 4.3 | 1.3 | 4.2 | 2.2 |
| Contributing family workers (unpaid workers) | 4.1 | 11.5 | 2.8 | 8.1 | 24.4 | 71.6 | 15.6 | 48.9 |
| Mean hourly earnings (dollars) | 2.63 | 2.09 | 2.42 | 2.21 | 1.06 | 0.91 | 1.18 | 1.39 |
| Median hourly earnings (dollars) | 1.46 | 1.31 | 1.67 | 1.52 | 0.70 | 0.70 | 0.94 | 1.09 |
| Working week (%) | 43.9 | 35.7 | 46.0 | 37.6 | 40.2 | 25.7 | 39.2 | 29.8 |
| Social security (%) | 41.4 | 39.5 | 41.5 | 37.5 | 6.7 | 2.1 | 5.3 | 7.8 |
| Employed in small enterprises (%) | 48.3 | 55.2 | 47.2 | 55.3 | 82.0 | 84.8 | 85.5 | 72.4 |

*Source*: ENE, 1995, ENOE, 2009, INEGI.

salaried farm workers, especially in the case of women.[9]

Although in Mexico being a salaried worker does not guarantee better working conditions (Pacheco, 2004; Valdivia & Pedrero, 2008),[10] a comparison of nonfarm and farm workers shows that being a nonfarm worker implies a lower degree of vulnerability in terms of income and social security. Hourly payment for farm workers is noticeably lower than among nonagricultural workers (Table 12.7). In the case of women, being engaged in farm work means earning one quarter less than female nonfarm workers do. This difference is probably one of the factors that drove women in rural contexts towards growing insertion in agricultural activities, as documented by recent research (see Garay, 2008). The situation is even worse in the case of men. Whereas the median wage for nonfarm workers was nearly 2 dollars an hour in 2009, men engaged in agricultural activities had a median under one dollar per hour. Although this comparison does not account for differences in qualifications between activities, the gap is wide enough to show poorly paid jobs in rural areas, and it is one of the reasons for the migration and the abandonment of agricultural activities.

In addition, a farm workers' working day is shorter than that of nonfarm workers (Table 12.7), which translates into lower total income. One could assume that there is under-declaration of the working week; but it could also be the case of an increase of labor exploitation since productivity in farm work has increased (David, Morales, & Rodríguez, 2001). Lastly, the vulnerability of agricultural workers is particularly acute since only 5.6% of these workers had access to social security in 2009. This situation may be partly related to the context in which farm workers are inserted, since over 80% produce or work in units with fewer than six employees.

In order to finish this section, it is essential to analyze differences in terms of labor income and family strategies for participating in the labor market. Using information from the agricultural module, it is important to note that most households in less urbanized contexts – less than 100,000 inhabitants – rely on nonagricultural income, and that this situation did not change substantially between 1995 and 2003,

---

[9] This section of the study analyzes the changes between 1995 and 2009 since the questionnaires for 1991 and 1993 are slightly different from the questionnaires from 1995 onwards. One of the differences is that agricultural producers' pay is not known for the first two years, which is why it was decided to analyze working conditions from 1995. It is worth noting that the questions designed to record the number of agricultural workers are not different, which is why information from 1991 is used in the previous sections of this study.

[10] It has been found that the incomes of some self-employed occupations are significantly better than salaried jobs.

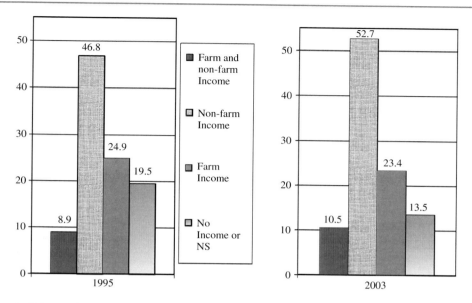

**Fig. 12.4** Household income by source

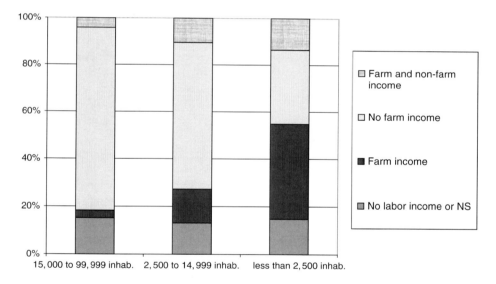

**Fig. 12.5** Farm income by size of place

while the number of households with exclusively non-farm incomes rose (Fig. 12.4).[11] This result supports previous findings on the status of the countryside, namely that conditions are so precarious that people have to earn their livelihood from other income sources (see for example, Carton de Grammont, 2007).

In rural contexts, over 40% of households had exclusively agricultural labor incomes, which is linked to widespread situations of subsistence. Another 30% lived off exclusively nonagricultural income while 14.4% organize themselves by combining agricultural with nonagricultural incomes (Fig. 12.5). However, a large proportion of households (13.5%) fail to declare work income. Although this could result from an under-estimation of their income, another explanation relates to households dependence on government

---

[11] Once again, it should be noted that in 1991 and 1993, producers were not asked about their income, therefore we only used information from 1995 onwards.

transfers, family gifts and remittances, which are not well captured in these questions.

The results of this paper support the findings reported in an extensive specialized bibliography regarding the need to diversify income (see for example, Carton de Grammont, 2007; Lara, 1998; Puyana & Romero, 2008; Yúnez-Naude, 2005) although it has the advantage of providing a national snapshot.

Appendini and Luca (2004) argue that the diversification of employment work and activities including agriculture has always been part of strategies of rural households: even taking land into account, most rural households had not the sufficient resources to live exclusively on agriculture. However, in recent years, the importance of nonagricultural activities has increased and has been displacing agriculture as the axis around which articulates the households' economy. They are also changing traditional strategies earning nonfarm and that international migration and remittances have gained more weight as a source of income, compared with past decades.

## Conclusions

This paper addresses the transformations of the rural population in recent decades. One of the main reasons to focus on this period is the implementation of a new development model since the 1980s; to the extent that the following decades represent the consolidation of a growth model based on an open-market economy. In particular, the rural population faced contrasting alternatives: either to adapt to new forms of farm production or to insert themselves into changing labor markets in nonfarm activities or as migrants in new contexts.

This paper shows population changes in terms of classic demographic variables, while also looking at the labor characteristics of the rural population, in order to suggest that both trends are closely intertwined. In relation to classic demographic variables, the paper shows the decrease of rural population through the past century, explained largely by the rapid process of urbanization that took place in Mexico since the mid-1950s. In fact, Mexico already has urbanization levels similar to most developed countries.

The analysis secondly suggests a more pronounced ageing process in the rural population than in the urban one. While ageing is becoming a salient feature of the population pyramid in Mexico due to fertility and mortality rate decrements, this trend is reinforced by a stream of young out-migrants. There is a feeding process occurring between productive and demographic tendencies: population pressure over land, combined with limited agricultural production and poor prospect of inheritance contributed to the migration of the youth. Once that migration stream is consolidated and transformed from rural-urban to international out-migration, its character will have important consequences for rural populations since it impacts the intensity of migration, the migrant profile, community resources, and probabilities of return (Massey, Alarcon, Duran, & González, 1990).

A third element highlighted in this work is the high levels of poverty and spatial dispersion of the rural population. A larger proportion of rural households have had experience of poverty and this is more severe than in urban areas. For the most part, this poverty is explained by limited employment and productive opportunities for the small landholder, but rural population spreading also contributes to their lack of health, educational and infrastructure services.

Even after agricultural production was modernized in many areas of Mexico, precarious labor conditions prevailed. Given this, we wonder about the survival strategies that rural populations developed. The data suggest that one of these family strategies is to combine agricultural and nonagricultural work. However, there are a significant number of households in rural localities that still depend on self-consumption or subsistence production. Finally, this paper agrees with previous studies in Mexico and other countries arguing that to account for rural population it is not enough to only consider agricultural work. Rural localities have changed greatly in the last decades, and other economic activities are generating jobs in these areas. In Mexico, however, these options are quite limited, basically to petit-trade and construction work for men, while women are getting jobs as domestic workers and also in petit-trade. Even while manufacturing is growing in some rural areas the proportion of the labor force occupied in this activity is still small compared to other activities.

Thus, to better understand changes in the rural population it is necessary to look at the processes shaping labor opportunities and living conditions in these contexts. Families' survival strategies – including labor, fertility, and migration decisions – are influenced by their resources, expectations, family size and structure; an accumulative process shaping demographic changes in rural contexts.

## References

Alba, F. (1977). *La población en México, evolución y dilemas*. México: El Colegio de México.
Appendini, K. (2008). La transformación de la vida rural en tres ejidos del centro de México. In K. Appendini & G. Torres (Eds.), *¿Ruralidad sin agricultura? Perspectivas multidisciplinaria de una realidad fragmentada* (pp. 27–58). México: El Colegio de México.
Appendini, K., & De Luca, M. (2004). *Género y trabajo. Estrategias rurales en el nuevo contexto mexicano*. Roma: Organización de las Naciones Unidas para la Agricultura y la Alimentación (FAO).
Appendini, K., & Torres, G. (Eds.). (2008). *¿Ruralidad sin agricultura? Perspectivas multidisciplinaria de una realidad fragmentada*. México: El Colegio de México.
Arias, P., & Wilson, F. (1997). *La aguja y el surco. Cambio regional, consumo y relaciones de género en la industria de la ropa en México*. Guadalajara: Universidad de Guadalajara-Centre for Development Research.
Carton de Grammont, H. C. (2004). La nueva ruralidad en América Latina. *Revista Mexicana de Sociología*, Año LXVI, Núm. especial.
Carton de Grammont, H. C. (2007). *La desagrarización del campo mexicano*. Paper presented at Congress: Encrucijadas del México Rural: contrastes regionales en un mundo desigual. Asociación Mexicana de Estudios Rurales (AMER). Veracruz, Veracruz, October 22–26, 2007.
CEED. (1970). *Dinámica de la Población en México*. México: El Colegio de Mexico.
CONAPO. (2008). Informe de México: El cambio demográfico, el envejecimiento y la migración internacional en México. Resource document. Special Report to the 32nd Session of the Economic Commission for Latin America (ECLA). Retrieved February 15, 2010, from http://www.conapo.gob.mx/prensa/2008/02cepal.pdf
Coneval. (2009). *Evolución de la pobreza 1992–2008. Poverty Report by CONEVAL (Consejo Nacional de Evaluación)*. México: CONEVAL. Retrieved November 11, 2010, from http://www.coneval.gob.mx/
Corona, R., & Tuiran, R. (2006, July). *Magnitud aproximada de la emigración de mexicanos a Estados Unidos. Congreso Internacional de Migración, Alcances y límites de las políticas migratorias*. Unpublished.
David, M. B. de A., Morales, C., & Rodríguez, M. (2001). Modernidad y heterogeneidad: estilo de desarrollo agrícola y rural en América latina y el Caribe. In David, M. B. de A. (Ed.), *Desarrollo rural en América Latina y el Caribe ¿La construcción de un nuevo modelo?* Bogotá: Alfaomega.

Dirven, M. (2003). La herencia de tierras y la necesidad de rejuvenecimiento del campo. In P. Tejo (Comp.), *Mercados de tierras agrícolas en América Latina y el Caribe: una realidad incompleta* (pp. 127–163). Santiago de Chile: ECLA.
ENADID. (2009). *Encuesta Nacional de la dinámica demográfica. Resultados Preliminares*. México: CONAPO-INEGI.
ENE. (1995). *Encuesta Nacional de Empleo*. Microdata. Mexico: INEGI.
ENOE. (1999). *Encuesta Nacional de Ocupación y Empleo*. Microdata. México: INEGI.
Galindo, C., & Ramos, L. (2009). Un nuevo enfoque para estimarla migración internacional de México. In CONAPO, *La situación demográfica de México 2008* (pp. 45–71). México: CONAPO.
Garay, S. (2008). *Trabajo rural femenino en México: tendencias recientes*. Dissertation to Obtain Doctorate Degree in Demographic Studies, Centro de Estudios Demográficos, Urbanos y Ambientales, El Colegio de México.
García, B., Blanco, M., & Pacheco, E. (1999). Género y trabajo extradoméstico en México. In B. García (Ed.), *Mujer, género y población en México*. México: Sociedad Mexicana de Demografía & El Colegio de México.
Hernández, J. (2004). La distribución territorial de la población rural urbanización. In CONAPO, *La situación demográfica de México 2003* (pp. 63–75). México: CONAPO
Huerta, M. M. C. (2001). *El sector agropecuario mexicano. Antecedentes recientes y perspectivas*. México: Instituto Politécnico Nacional.
INEGI. (2002). *Encuesta Nacional de Empleo*. México: INEGI.
INEGI. (2007). *Resultados Definitivos del Conteo de Población y Vivienda 2005*. México: INEGI.
INEGI. (2009a). *Censo Agrícola, Ganadero y Forestal 2007. Tabulados Estatales*. México: INEGI.
INEGI. (2009b). *México. Compendio censal del siglo XX*. CD. México: INEGI.
Lara, S. (1998). *Nuevas experiencias productivas y nuevas formas de organización flexible del trabajo en la agricultura mexicana*. México: Juan Pablos.
Leite, P., Ramos, L., & Gaspar, S. (2004). Tendencias recientes de la migración México-Estados Unidos. In CONAPO, *La situación demográfica de México 2003* (pp. 97–115) México: CONAPO
Marsch, R., & Runsten, D. (2000). The Organic Produce Niche Market: Can Mexican Smallholders be Stakeholders? In G. Rodriguez & R. Snyder (Eds.), *Strategies for Resource Management, Production, and Marketing in Rural Mexico* (pp. 71–104). La Jolla, CA: University of California-San Diego.
Massey, D., Alarcon, R., Duran, J., & González, H. (1990). *Return to Aztlan: The social process of international migration from Western Mexico*. Berkeley, CA: University of California Press.
Merino, L. (2004). *Conservación o deterioro: el impacto de las políticas públicas en las instituciones comunitarias y en los usos de los bosques en México*. México, DF: Instituto Nacional de Ecología –SEMARNAT.
Pacheco, E., & Florez, N. (2009). *Having More Than One Job as a Family Strategy in Mexican Rural*. Paper presented at XXVI IUSSP International Population Conference, Marrakeck, Marruecos, Sep 27–Oct 2, 2009.

Pacheco Gómez, E. (2004). *Ciudad de México, heterogénea y desigual*. Un estudio sobre el mercado de trabajo, México: El Colegio de México.

Partida, V. (2004). Aspectos demográficos de la urbanización. In CONAPO, *La situación demográfica de México 2003* (pp. 17–26). México: CONAPO.

Passel, J. & Suro, R. (2005). *Rise, peak and decline: Trends in US immigration 1992–2004*. Report, Pew Hispanic Center.

Pérez, E. (2001). *Hacia una visión de lo rural*. In ¿*Una nueva ruralidad en América Latina?* Buenos Aires: CLACSO.

Pérez, E., Farah, M. A., & Grammont, C. de (2008). *La nueva ruralidad en América Latina. Avances teóricos y evidencias empíricas*. Bogotá: Editorial Pontificia Universidad Javariana/ Consejo Latinoamericano de Ciencias Sociales.

Puyana, A., & Romero, J. (2008). *El sector agropecuario mexicano: un decenio con el Tratado de Libre Comercio de América del Norte, Efectos económicos y sociales*. México: El Colegio de México.

Quesnel, A., & del Rey, A. (2004). La construcción de una economía familiar del archipiélago. Movilidad y recomposición de las relaciones intergeneracionales en el medio rural Mexicano. *Estudios Demográficos y Urbanos, 20(2)(59)*, 197–228.

Romo, R., & Sánchez, M. (2010). El descenso de la fecundidad en México, 1974–2009: a 35 años de la puesta en marcha de la nueva política de población. In CONAPO, *La situación demográfica de México 2009* (pp. 23–38). México: CONAPO.

Scott, J. (2009). *The incidence of agricultural subsidies in Mexico*. Agricultural Trade Adjustment and Rural Poverty. Transparency, Accountability, and Compensatory Programs in Mexico. Woodrow Wilson International Center, Mexican Rural Development Research Reports, Report 2. November 11, 2009

SRA. (2010). *Reglas de Operación de los Programas Sociales de la Secretaria de la Reforma Agraria*. México: SRA. Retrieved September 3, 2010, from http://www.sra.gob.mx/sraweb/programas/

Teubal, M. (2001). Globalización y nueva ruralidad en América Latina. In N. Giarraca (Ed.), ¿*Una nueva ruralidad en América Latina?* Buenos Aires: CLACSO.o

Valdivia, M., & Pedrero, M. (2008). *Mercados laborales segmentados y el nivel de educación de la fuerza de trabajo en México: un estudio de la desigualdad salarial a partir de las encuestas urbanas de empleo*. Paper presented at IX reunión Nacional de Investigación demográfica en México, Mérida, Oct. 8–11.

Wainerman, C., & Rechinni, Z. (1981). *El trabajo femenino en el banquillo de los acusados. La medición censal en América Latina*. México: Terra Nova.

Yúnez-Naude, A. (2005). *Sectores de América del Norte: la agricultura*. Paper presented at Seminar: América del Norte los siguientes diez años. El Colegio de México, January 13–14, 2005.

Zendejas, S., & Vries, P. de (Eds.). (1998). *Las disputas por el México rural: transformaciones de práticas, identidades y proyectos*. México: El Colegio de Michoacán.

# Rural Demography of India

T.V. Sekher

## Introduction

In the span of a century, there was a fivefold rise in the population of India – at the start of the 20th century the population was about 238 million, which grew to more than one billion in 2001. With an annual increase of nearly 19 million, India accounts for approximately 18% of the world's population. India has one of the densest rural populations in the world, living in the 600,000 villages scattered throughout the country. The huge density of rural population exerts human pressure on the natural resources and adversely affects the quality of life.

This paper presents the rural demographic scenario in India in the light of its physical, cultural and religious diversity and changing socio-economic trends. According to the 2001 Census, 74% of India's population lives in villages (Fig. 13.1). The size of the Indian villages varies considerably – an overwhelming majority of villages have a population less than 1000. Indian society is deeply influenced by religion, caste, language and tradition. The caste and kinship systems regulate economic and social life, especially at the village level to a great extent. More than 80% of the rural population in India is Hindu and the other religious communities are Muslims, Christians, Buddhists, Sikhs and Jains. The rural population comprises of several castes and tribal (*Adivasi*) communities.

Though India is considered an emerging economic power, in reality life remains largely rooted in villages. A majority of the rural[1] population in India lives on agriculture and related activities. Throughout India the rural population has lower education levels, higher poverty, higher mortality and higher fertility. Rural residents have relatively fewer modern amenities compared to their urban counterparts. It is also a common trend among villagers to migrate to urban areas in search of employment and education opportunities. The literacy rate among India's rural population is about 60%, which is considerable progress since independence. Disparity with regard to education, employment, land ownership and assets are more pronounced in rural areas with considerable variation

---

[1] The unit of classification in Census is "town" for urban areas and "village" for rural areas. In the Census of India 2001, the definition of urban area adopted is as follows:
a) All places with a municipality, corporation, cantonment board or notified town area committee, etc.
b) A place satisfying the following three criteria simultaneously:
  1) A minimum population of 5,000
  2) At least 75% of male working population engaged in non-agricultural pursuits; and
  3) A density of population of at least 400 per sq. km. (1,000 per sq. mile)

Settlements that are not urban are considered as rural. However, the local self-Government Departments in each state have their own rules and regulations based on certain Acts to determine the status of a place as urban or rural. Because of the duality of classification of agencies defining urban, there have been occasions when a place has been regarded as rural by the local Self-Government but as urban by the Census organization. For a detailed discussion on India's demographic scenario, refer to United Nations (1982), Dyson et al. (2004), Haub and Sharma (2006), and Chaurasia and Gulati (2008).

---

T.V. Sekher (✉)
Department of Population Policies and Programmes,
International Institute for Population Sciences (IIPS), Deonar,
Mumbai 400 088, India
e-mail: tvsekher@gmail.com

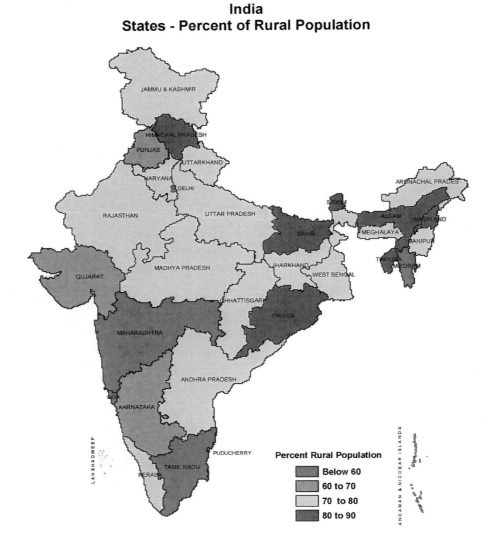

**Fig. 13.1** Percent rural population, 2001

across social groups. Gender differentials prevail in most parts of the rural population. The centuries' old tradition of patriarchal families resulting in a low status for women still remains a characteristic feature of India's rural society.

Three-fourths of Indians still live in rural areas. The persistently high rural fertility in the large Northern states continue to be the major demographic challenge facing India today, despite an overall reduction in the birth rate at the national level. Early marriages and strong preference for sons critically influence India's demographic profile. The social, cultural and regional diversity and heterogeneity of population is mainly responsible for the diverse demographic outcomes across the states. Added to this, the increasing gender discrimination as manifested in female feticide resulting in alarmingly skewed sex ratio is another population challenge the country is facing today.

This study provides an overview of the rural demographic scenario in India. The "Introduction" presents the basic features of the social, economic and demographic situation. The various dimensions of marriage, fertility and family planning are discussed in the Section "Demographic Scenario". The Section "Marriage and Fertility" focuses on the imbalance in sex ratio and dimensions of gender discrimination in

# 13 Rural Demography of India

**Table 13.1** Population size and growth in India, 1901–2001

| Census year | Population | Growth over decade | | Multiple of 1901 population |
|---|---|---|---|---|
| | | Number | Percent | |
| 1901 | 238,396,327 | – | – | 1 |
| 1911 | 252,093,390 | 13,697,063 | 5.7 | 1.1 |
| 1921 | 251,321,213 | −772,177 | −0.3 | 1.1 |
| 1931 | 278,977,238 | 27,656,025 | 11 | 1.2 |
| 1941 | 318,660,580 | 39,683,342 | 14.2 | 1.3 |
| 1951 | 361,088,090 | 42,427,510 | 13.3 | 1.5 |
| 1961 | 439,234,771 | 78,146,681 | 21.6 | 1.8 |
| 1971 | 548,159,652 | 108,924,881 | 24.8 | 2.3 |
| 1981 | 683,329,097 | 135,169,445 | 24.7 | 2.9 |
| 1991 | 846,421,039 | 163,091,942 | 23.9 | 3.6 |
| 2001 | 1,028,737,436 | 182,316,397 | 21.5 | 4.3 |

*Source*: Registrar General and Census Commissioner, India, *Census of India, 2001*.

recent times. Available data and information from various sources – census, governmental statistics, sample surveys, micro-level studies – are utilized to portray the existing rural scenario and its implications for the future.

## Demographic Scenario

### Population Growth

The population of India increased drastically from 361 million in 1951 to 1,028 million in 2001, almost tripling within half a century (Tables 13.1 and 13.2). The percentage of people living in urban areas increased to 28% in 2001. The annual growth rate of the rural population during the decade 1991–2001, was 1.7. Nearly 16% of India's population belongs to Scheduled Castes (SCs) and 8% to Scheduled Tribes (STs).[2]

The growth of India's population since independence hovered around 2% per year for nearly two decades. Population growth has shown a slow down since the 1970s as a result of the gradual decline in birth rate. The decline was slow during 1981–1991, but accelerated later. Despite slowing population growth, the net addition to the population continued to increase. During the 1990s, more than 180 million people were added to the population of the country which is almost 18 million per year (Table 13.1). For the period 2010–11, the net addition would be about 217 million.[3] Though the proportion of rural population in India declined from 89% in 1901 to 72% in 2001 (Table 13.3), India will continue to add huge numbers to its population in the immediate future, more so in its rural areas.

---

[2] The Constitution of India contains a schedule of castes (SCs) and tribes (STs) eligible to receive special benefits, including welfare services, scholarships, and guaranteed places in educational institutions, the civil service and Parliament. These provisions were made for the educational and economic upliftment of weaker sections and to protect them from social injustice and all forms of exploitation.

[3] The 2011 Census count of India's population, one of the largest administrative exercises in the world, is currently in progress (from 9th to 28th February 2011). India's Census enumeration involves more than 2 million enumerators and supervisors. In the year before the Census, the enumerators canvass the entire country listing each and every dwelling. This house listing serves as a basis for actual census count. The motto of Indian Census 2011 is "Our Census, Our Future". Alongside the Census operation, the Government is also preparing the country's first ever National Population Register (NPR) which is designed to be a comprehensive identity data base of all usual residents of India. Census 2011 is the 15th National Census in the country and the seventh since independence, having been conducted uninterruptedly every 10 years since 1872 (www.censusindia.net).

**Table 13.2** Population size and growth of states and union territories of India, 1991–2001

| State/union territory | Total population | | Percentage change | Percent of national population | Percent of rural population |
|---|---|---|---|---|---|
| | 1991 | 2001 | 1991–2001 | 2001 | 2001 |
| **India** | 846,421,039 | 1,028,737,436 | 21.5 | 100 | 72.19 |
| Uttar Pradesh | 132,061,653 | 166,197,921 | 25.9 | 16.2 | 79.14 |
| Maharashtra | 78,937,187 | 96,878,627 | 22.7 | 9.4 | 57.52 |
| Bihar | 64,530,554 | 82,998,509 | 28.6 | 8.1 | 89.39 |
| West Bengal | 68,077,965 | 80,176,197 | 17.8 | 7.8 | 72.00 |
| Andhra Pradesh | 66,508,008 | 76,210,007 | 14.6 | 7.4 | 72.46 |
| Tamil Nadu | 55,858,008 | 62,405,679 | 11.7 | 6.1 | 55.87 |
| Madhya Pradesh | 48,566,242 | 60,348,023 | 24.3 | 5.9 | 73.37 |
| Rajasthan | 44,005,990 | 56,507,188 | 28.4 | 5.5 | 76.57 |
| Karnataka | 44,977,201 | 52,850,562 | 17.5 | 5.1 | 65.87 |
| Gujarat | 41,309,582 | 50,671,017 | 22.7 | 4.9 | 62.55 |
| Orissa | 31,659,736 | 36,804,660 | 16.3 | 3.6 | 84.80 |
| Kerala | 29,098,518 | 31,841,374 | 9.4 | 3.1 | 74.02 |
| Jharkhand | 21,843,911 | 26,945,829 | 23.4 | 2.6 | 77.64 |
| Assam | 22,414,322 | 26,655,528 | 18.9 | 2.6 | 87.22 |
| Punjab | 20,281,969 | 24,358,999 | 20.1 | 2.4 | 65.86 |
| Haryana | 16,463,648 | 21,144,564 | 28.4 | 2.1 | 70.79 |
| Chhattisgarh | 17,614,928 | 20,833,803 | 18.3 | 2 | 79.77 |
| Delhi | 9,420,644 | 13,850,507 | 47 | 1.4 | 6.95 |
| Jammu and Kashmir | 7,837,051 | 10,143,700 | 29.4 | 1 | 74.57 |
| Uttarakhand | 7,050,634 | 8,489,349 | 20.4 | 0.8 | 74.32 |
| Himachal Pradesh | 5,170,877 | 6,077,900 | 17.5 | 0.6 | 90.20 |
| Tripura | 2,757,205 | 3,199,203 | 16 | 0.3 | 82.77 |
| Meghalaya | 1,774,778 | 2,318,822 | 30.7 | 0.2 | 79.93 |
| Manipur | 1,837,149 | 2,293,896 | 24.9 | 0.2 | 79.26 |
| Nagaland | 1,209,546 | 1,990,036 | 64.5 | 0.2 | 82.20 |
| Goa | 1,169,793 | 1,347,668 | 15.2 | 0.1 | 50.09 |
| Arunachal Pradesh | 864,558 | 1,097,968 | 27 | 0.1 | 79.09 |
| Mizoram | 689,015 | 888,573 | 28.8 | 0.1 | 50.64 |
| Sikkim | 689,756 | 540,851 | 33.1 | 0.1 | 88.83 |
| Puducherry[a] | 807,785 | 974,345 | 20.6 | 0.1 | 33.41 |
| Chandigarh[a] | 642,015 | 900,635 | 40.3 | 0.1 | 10.22 |
| Andaman and Nicobar Islands[a] | 280,661 | 356,152 | 26.9 | – | 67.34 |
| Dadra and Nagar Haveli[a] | 138,477 | 220,490 | 59.2 | – | 77.09 |
| Daman and Diu [a] | 101,586 | 158,204 | 55.7 | – | 63.67 |
| Lakshadweep[a] | 51,707 | 60,650 | 17.3 | – | 55.47 |

[a] Union Territories, less than 0.1% of national population.
*Source*: Registrar General and Census Commissioner, India, *Census of India, 1991 and 2001*.

**Table 13.3** Urban and rural population in India, 1901–2001

| Census Year | Population in (000's) | | Change over decade (000's) | | Percent |
|---|---|---|---|---|---|
| | Urban | Rural | Urban | Rural | Rural |
| 1901 | 25,855 | 212,541 | – | – | 89.15 |
| 1911 | 25,948 | 226,145 | 93 | 13,604 | 89.71 |
| 1921 | 28,091 | 223,230 | 2,143 | −2,915 | 88.82 |
| 1931 | 33,463 | 245,515 | 5,371 | 22,285 | 88.01 |
| 1941 | 44,162 | 274,515 | 10,700 | 28,984 | 86.14 |
| 1951 | 62,444 | 274,498 | 18,282 | 24,146 | 81.47 |
| 1961 | 78,937 | 360,298 | 16,493 | 61,654 | 82.03 |
| 1971 | 109,114 | 439,046 | 30,177 | 78,748 | 80.09 |
| 1981 | 159,463 | 523,867 | 50,349 | 84,821 | 76.66 |
| 1991 | 217,611 | 628,810 | 58,148 | 104,943 | 74.29 |
| 2001 | 286,120 | 742,618 | 68,509 | 113,808 | 72.19 |

*Source*: Registrar General and Census Commissioner, India, *Census of India, 2001*.

## Household Type and Size

Change in household type is a significant indicator of social change involving social structure, familial relationships, bond of kinship, etc. There has been a drastic change in the family structure in India during its transformation from a closed agrarian economy to globalization and open markets. The term "household" has been defined in the Indian Census as "usually a group of persons who normally live together and take their meals from a common kitchen unless the exigencies of work prevent any of them from doing so. Persons in a household may be related or unrelated or a mix of both. However, if a group of unrelated persons live in a census house but do not take their meals from the common kitchen, then they are not constituent of a common household. Each such person should be treated as a separate household. The important link to find out whether it is a household or not is a common kitchen. There may be one-member households, two-member households or multi-member households" (p. 1) (Office of the Registrar General, 2009). Contrary to the popular notion that the joint family type in India is on the decline, approximately one in five households in India is a joint household, according to the 2001 Census. The concept of a female heading a household is theoretically non-existent in a patriarchal or a patrilineal society. Even if the female is the main bread earner in a household, the decision-making authority of the households rests generally upon its male members.

According to the 2001 Census, female-headed households account for only 10.3%. However, the National Family Health Survey[4] (IIPS and Macro International, 2007) observed that 14% of the households in India are headed by women.

## Religious Composition

India has the rare distinction of being the land from where many religions, Hinduism, Buddhism, Sikhism and Jainism originated. Islam and Christianity also have a considerable presence in the country. Religion has a major influence on the social life of most Indians. As Nyrop and Shinn (1975) rightly described, "Daily life in India, more than in western societies, is charged with religious meaning. Religion permeates family and personal life as well as most major social and political movements. It underlies and justifies the caste system and consequently regulates interpersonal

---

[4] The National Family Health Survey (NFHS) is the Indian equivalent of Demographic and Health Surveys (DHS). Three rounds of NFHS were undertaken in 1992–93, 1998–99 and 2005–06. NFHS provides wealth of information on fertility, contraception, infant and child mortality, immunization, reproductive health, nutrition of women and children, domestic violence and status of women. In NFHS-3 (2005–06), face-to-face interviews were conducted with nearly 200,000 people covering all 29 states of India (www.nfhsindia.org). However for district level estimates, the only source is the District Level Household and Facility Survey – DLHS (IIPS, 2010) (www.rchiips.org).

and intergroup relations" (p. 157). According to the 2001 Census, Hindus constitute 81.4% of India's population. Muslims, the second largest religious group, account for 12.4%, Christians (2.3), Sikhs (1.9), Buddhists (0.8) and Jains (0.4). Religion is an important factor in fertility differential in India. The differential growth rates of Hindus and Muslims, as well as differences in accepting family planning practices, have always been the subject of controversial debate not only among academicians, but more so among political and religious leaders. The release of the results of the 2001 census data on religion generated a major controversy. Muslims in India have higher fertility than the Hindus. They have similar levels of poverty and female education in rural areas, but in urban areas, the Hindus are much better off than the Muslims. Since all religious communities have experienced a substantial fertility decline in recent decades and contraceptive practice has been well accepted, it is expected that the fertility levels among the communities would converge over time (Bhat & Zavier, 2005; Kulkarni & Alagrajan, 2005).

## Literacy and Education

Literacy[5] is the most generally used indicator of educational development in any country. The first post-independence Census in 1951 illustrated that only 9% of the females and 27% of the males were literate. This pathetic legacy of illiteracy and educational neglect made the government set an ambitious goal of providing free and compulsory education to all children up to the age of 14. A large proportion of India's rural population continues to have little or no education, and this proportion is much higher for females than for males. Among the population aged six and above, 42% of females and 22% of males never attended school and 18% of females and 21% of males have less than 5 years of completed school education. Despite the expansion of educational facilities, the progress achieved has not been satisfactory in rural India both in terms of quality and quantity. Though the government aims at reaching complete literacy, the 2001 census indicated that the effective literacy rate (in the age group 7 years and above) is only 65%. In rural areas, it is only 59% and among females it is only 46%. Considerable regional disparities still exist with regard to literacy levels in India. In many states, female literacy is less than 30%. Only 81% of the children in the primary school age group (6–10 years) attend school in rural areas. The gender disparity in school attendance in rural areas is very significant. In brief, the situation with regard to education at the beginning of the twenty-first century is not very encouraging and rural India has a long way to travel to achieve the set goal of universal elementary education.

## Indian Youth

Young people (10–24 years) constituted about 31% of India's population (315 million) in 2001 and the projected increase is 358 million in 2011. In 2001, children in the age group 0–14 years constitute about 35% of India's population and those in the age group 15–29 years, account for another 27% (Table 13.4). According to a recent survey, a large proportion of Indian youth is exposed to media, mainly television. Among the youth (with 5 or more years of education) nearly 92% of young men and 78% of young women are exposed to newspapers, magazines or books. However, their exposure to the internet is considerably low (15% among boys and 9% among girls). Only 15% of the youth had attended family life or sex education programs either in/outside the school setting. Nearly 15% of young men and 4% of young women reported experiences of pre-marital sex. Almost one-third of the young men reported tobacco consumption and one-sixth reported alcohol consumption. Among those who are eligible to vote, only 71% of the young men and 60% of the young women participated in the last election process. The four leading problems facing the youth in India as expressed by them are unemployment, poverty, lack of amenities and lack of educational opportunities (IIPS and Population Council, 2010).

## Rural Infrastructure and Amenities

With regard to basic amenities and consumer durables, significant differences still persist between rural and urban households. Although 93% of the urban

---

[5] In the Indian Census, the test of literacy is satisfied if a person can both read and write with understanding in any one language.

**Table 13.4** Levels and trends in selected indicators of the age structure of the population of India: 1951–2001

| Indicator | 1951 | 1961 | 1971 | 1981 | 1991 | 2001 |
|---|---|---|---|---|---|---|
| **Age structure** | | | | | | |
| 0–14 years (percent) | 38.42 | 41.04 | 42.03 | 39.57 | 37.46 | 35.44 |
| 15–29 years (percent) | 25.78 | 25.02 | 23.97 | 25.90 | 26.71 | 26.65 |
| 30–59 years (percent) | 30.30 | 28.30 | 28.03 | 28.04 | 29.03 | 30.44 |
| 60 years and above (percent) | 5.50 | 5.63 | 5.97 | 6.49 | 6.80 | 7.47 |
| **Dependency ratio** | | | | | | |
| Young (per 1000) | 685 | 770 | 808 | 734 | 672 | 621 |
| Old (per 1000) | 98 | 106 | 115 | 120 | 122 | 131 |
| Combined (per 1000) | 783 | 875 | 923 | 854 | 794 | 752 |
| Ageing index (percent) | 14.31 | 13.72 | 14.20 | 16.41 | 18.15 | 21.07 |

*Source*: Chaurasia and Gulati (2008).

households have electricity connections, it is only 56% in rural areas. The rural-urban difference is more glaring with regard to toilet facilities. In 2005–06, 83% of the urban households had toilet facilities, whereas it was only 26% in rural areas. The access to television, telephone and computer are much lower in rural areas. Though 73% of urban households have a television at home, it is only 30% in rural areas. In 2005–06, nearly 36% of the households had mobile phones in urban areas, while it was only 7% in rural areas. It needs to be mentioned that considerable improvement has taken place even in rural areas during the last 5 years with regard to possession of mobile telephones, computers, televisions, etc. The bicycle is the most commonly used means of transport in rural areas, with nearly 50% of households owning a bicycle; nearly 11% of rural households have either a motorcycle or a scooter. Nearly one-third of rural households have an account either in a bank or a post office. The coverage of health insurance is relatively low in India, only 2% of rural households have health insurance. The vast majority of the rural households, (93%), own a house and this proportion is higher in rural areas than in urban areas (Fig. 13.2).

## Rural to Urban Migration

According to the Census of India, there were about 309 million internal migrants in India in 2001, which accounted for nearly 31% of the total population of the country. This proportion has remained more or less the same throughout the latter half of the twentieth century except in 1991 when the share of migrants decreased to 27%. Among internal migrants, females dominate. It is a common practice in India that after marriage women move to their husband's place of residence. About 42 million out of 65 million female migrants cited marriage as the reason for their migration. Among males, the most important reason for migration is employment. As per the 2001 Census, rural to urban migration accounted for 18 and 38% of intra-state and inter-state migrants, respectively (Table 13.5). Rural to urban migration is one of the most important factors contributing to the growth of urban population. The total urban population in India increased from 218 million in 1991 to 286 million in 2001, registering a growth rate of 32%. About 21 million people enumerated in urban areas are migrants from rural areas who moved in within the last 10 years. There are six million migrants who have migrated from urban areas to rural areas. So the net addition to the urban population on account of migration is 14 million. The bulk of the rural migrants come from two states, Uttar Pradesh and Bihar. The major states receiving migrants include Maharashtra, Delhi, West Bengal and Haryana. Maharashtra witnessed the largest in-migration during the last 10 years (about 3.2 million), followed by Delhi (2.2 million).

## Emerging Demographic Scenario

One of the most remarkable changes in the 20th century has been the shift from high fertility to low fertility, and this has been described as the greatest

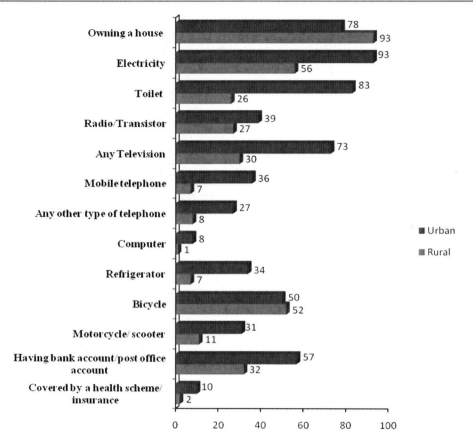

**Fig. 13.2** Household amenities in rural and urban India: 2005–06
*Source*: IIPS and Macro International, 2007.

**Table 13.5** Migrants classified by streams of migration based on place of last residence, and their growth rates, India (0–9 duration)-2001

| Migration Steams | Million | Percentage distribution | Sex- ratio (Males per 100 females) | Growth Rate (percent) | | |
|---|---|---|---|---|---|---|
| | | | | 1971–81 | 1981–91 | 1991–2001 |
| **Intra-state** | | | | | | |
| Rural to Rural | 48.8 | 60.6 | 257 | 14.8 | 0.2 | 12.2 |
| Rural to Urban | 14.2 | 17.6 | 842 | 47.8 | 6.7 | 7.3 |
| Urban to Rural | 5.2 | 6.5 | 651 | 29.4 | −4.8 | 1 |
| Urban to Urban | 9.8 | 12.1 | 796 | 50.0 | −11.2 | 23.6 |
| **Inter-state** | | | | | | |
| Rural to Rural | 4.4 | 26.6 | 648 | 12.1 | 3.4 | 54.0 |
| Rural to Urban | 6.3 | 38.2 | 1480 | 22.8 | 20.1 | 76.5 |
| Urban to Rural | 1.0 | 6.0 | 984 | 14.1 | 9.6 | 11.2 |
| Urban to Urban | 4.4 | 26.7 | 970 | 18.0 | 6.0 | 24.3 |

*Note*: Migrants unclassified by rural-urban streams are not excluded.
*Source*: Census of India 1971, 1981, 1991, 2001.

single demographic change in the second half of that century (Caldwell, 1993). The timing, onset, pace, and magnitude of this decline varies between countries. The 2001 Census indicated that after a large spell of unprecedented population growth, India experienced a gradual decline in fertility levels. However, there is also evidence of a growing disparity between the north and the south, with the southern states having been more successful in controlling population growth. In a vast country like India with considerable demographic diversity and heterogeneity and varying levels of socio-economic development, the levels and phases of fertility decline vary significantly from one state to another (Bhat, 1994; Srinivasan, 1995; Sekher, Raju, & Sivakumar, 2001; Guilmoto & Rajan, 2002). Several studies suggest that cultural factors have played an important role in determining fertility trends (Das Gupta, 1987; Basu, 1992; Jeffery & Jeffery, 1997).

According to the current trends and projections, there could be 190 million poor people in India by 2026 and three-fourths of them live in the five poor states of Bihar, Madhya Pradesh, Orissa, Rajasthan and Uttar Pradesh (Dyson, Cassen, & Visaria, 2004). These are the states with most poverty, slow economic growth and high population growth. Better health and nutrition, better education and clean drinking water are the priority issues for elimination of poverty in rural areas. Along with this, better reproductive health services including family planning will be required. Because the majority of the poor remain in rural areas, the measures to address poverty must concentrate on increasing agricultural growth and non-farm employment. The development of villages in India is seriously constrained by inadequate infrastructure – transport, irrigation, road, telecommunication, sanitation and energy. The continuing decline in fertility, particularly in rural areas, in a way will contribute to the amelioration of poverty among rural households.

## Marriage and Fertility

### Mate Selection, Marriage and Dowry

Marriage is considered a familial and social duty rather than a romantic liaison. Mate selection and marriage ceremonies are important social events. For Hindus, marriage is a sacred duty, an irrevocable union that is not dissoluble during the lifetime. Hindu marriage customs and values have had an influence on other religious communities, because most of them were converts from Hinduism. Though modern values and social changes have slowly started influencing the traditional marriage system in rural areas, even now most marriages are arranged by parents and preformed as per the customs and traditions of each community. Marriages are mutually decided by two families and not by the consent of the partners concerned. Marrying off a daughter is regarded as one of the most important duties of a father in India. Traditional societal norms suggest that the husband should be older than the wife. Marriages between certain categories of relatives are prohibited in northern India and this varies across geographical regions and between communities. Among Hindus, marriages are usually arranged between people belonging to the same caste, but the practice of hypergamy was also seen in different parts of the country. Marriage in Indian social and cultural settings signals the beginning of a socially recognized sexually active reproductive life. Children produced within the institution of marriage are legitimate children with property rights.

An early age at marriage is an indicator of the low status of women in society. It curtails women's access to education, cuts short the time needed to develop and mature; it also has many negative health consequences. In India, the legally prescribed minimum age at marriage is 18 years for girls and 21 years for boys. However, according to the National Family Health Survey (NFHS), more than half of the women get married before attaining 18 years. The median age at first marriage among women was 17.2 years in 2005–06. Men get married more than 6 years later at a median age of 23.4 years. More than one-fourth of the men (27%) in the age group, 21–29 years got married before the legal minimum age of 21. The age at marriage is relatively low among the rural population and among the less educated. Nearly 16% of the women aged 15–49 years are married to men who are 10 or more years older than they are. Not only did marriage occur at young ages, but it was also often arranged without the participation of the young people themselves, particularly young women. According to a youth survey in 2006–07, one in ten young men and one in four young women reported that their parents did not seek their approval while deciding on their marriage partner. About two in three married youth reported that they had met their spouse for the first time on their wedding day (IIPS and Population Council, 2010). Arranged marriages and extensive dowries continue to characterize the marriage patterns in most parts of India.

Dowry is an important part of Indian marriages. Dowry is defined as any property or valuable security which passes directly or indirectly between the parties to their parents etc. at, before, or after the marriage, as consideration for such marriage. The dowry practice has a long history in India. The modern dowry system is a modified version of traditional practices such as *Kanyadan* (gift of the virgin bride) and *Stridhan* (voluntary gifts given to the bride). In 1961, the Indian Parliament passed the Dowry Prohibition Act, which makes the giving, taking and demanding of dowry punishable. Despite the existence of laws against the payment of dowry, nearly three-fourths of the marriages had dowry transactions. In the era of globalization and increase in consumerism, dowry payment is more a rule than an exception. Many rural communities in India where the practice of dowry was totally absent have started making huge dowry payments in recent times. Earlier, the dowry system was restricted to Hindu middle-class families. Today, all castes follow the practice. Even Muslims and Christians among whom dowry was unheard of have started indulging in dowry transactions. In the northern parts of India characterized by hypergamous traditions, dowry is an integral component of marriage. According to the laws of hypergamy, a daughter is married to a man from a superior clan within the same *jati*. Hence, a price has to be paid for such upward mobility. In the traditional Indian system, daughters were denied inheritance rights over parental wealth and "dowry" was their share of parental wealth. It is also a way of "compensating" the groom and his family for the economic support they would provide to the new wife since women had a very limited role in the market economy and were dependent on their husbands and in-laws. Srinivas (1989) argues that there are two types of dowry – traditional and modern. The modern dowry is a comparatively new phenomenon and has become ingrained in recent years in order to attract better qualified and more desirable grooms in the marriage market. Dowry is represented as a "return" on an "investment" made in the son's upbringing and education. Grooms with higher education demand a bigger dowry and recent evidence indicates that dowry prices are increasing and poor families feel the crunch the most. Most families with daughters are forced to spend beyond their means, leading to rural indebtedness. Daughters are clearly perceived by both the educated and the uneducated as a drain on family resources. Women sometimes prefer to use the term, "gifts" for the substantial jewellery, money and consumer goods that are given to the husband's family at the time of marriage. Even among women who labelled the wealth that accompanied their marriages as gifts, the majority indicated that the content and amount of these gifts were negotiated between the families prior to marriage. Hence the distinction between "dowry" and "gifts" becomes blurred (Jejeebhoy & Halli, 2006). The value of dowry has been inflating rapidly and conducting a daughter's marriage may turn out to be a financially devastating experience for many parents. At the same time, dowry symbolizes the social and economic standing of the bride-giving family. An ostentatious dowry display increases the status of the girl's family. In other words, the parents of a girl are willing to provide a huge dowry to get a suitable husband for their daughter. It is also felt that a generous dowry is essential to ensure that the daughter is treated well in her family of procreation. In spite of modernization and the woman's increasing role in the market economy, the practice of dowry in India is becoming more widespread (Srinivasan & Lee, 2004). In many families even after the payment of dowry, there is a continuing uni-directional flow of resources from the woman's parental household to her husband's household (Srinivasan, 2005). Dowry has emerged as a strategy to acquire higher standards of material life with adverse consequences on women's status, including their survival. A large number of incidences are reported every year related to harassment and violence against women for not bringing enough dowry as desired by husbands and in-laws. In other words, insufficient dowry can threaten the physical security of women in many Indian households.

## Fertility Patterns

Though India is generally considered a "demographic laggard" with high fertility and rapid population growth, there has been a considerable decline in fertility in recent decades, including in rural areas (Table 13.6). Contemporary contextual forces like technological development and explosion of media outreach, new consumption aspirations of people,

**Table 13.6** Determinants of population growth in India: 1951–2001

| Year | Population (million) | Absolute increase (million) | CBR (per 1000) | TFR | CDR (per 1000) | Life expectancy at birth | |
|---|---|---|---|---|---|---|---|
| | | | | | | Male | Female |
| 1951 | 361.088 | – | – | – | – | – | – |
| 1961 | 439.235 | 78.147 | 45.5 | 6.11 | 25.9 | 36.8 | 36.6 |
| 1971 | 548.160 | 108.925 | 43.5 | 6.50 | 21.3 | 44.0 | 43.0 |
| 1981 | 683.329 | 135.169 | 38.0 | 5.40 | 16.0 | 50.0 | 49.0 |
| 1991 | 846.421 | 163.092 | 35.0 | 4.60 | 13.6 | 55.5 | 56.0 |
| 2001 | 1028.737 | 182.316 | 28.2 | 3.50 | 9.3 | 60.8 | 62.3 |

*Source*: Census of India (various years), Dyson, Cassen and Visaria (2004).

social and economic benefits of having fewer children, easy availability of contraceptives with choices, and overall improvement in the socio-economic status of women, all contribute to the accelerated pace of fertility decline. Das Gupta, Martine, and Chen (1998) while reviewing the scenario concluded that "Looking at India alone, it is difficult to avoid the conclusion that the pressure of population resources, combined with development efforts, have been responsible for generating a powerful demand for reducing fertility. This has happened regardless of whether the focus was essentially on social or on economic development" (p. 23). Having smaller families not only became advantageous for parents, but also became socially acceptable. The demand for smaller families came as a byproduct of socio-economic changes resulting in a shift from agrarian to non-agrarian occupations, improved mortality conditions, the spread of education, and enhanced participation of women in income-earning occupations.

In a vast country like India with high demographic diversity and heterogeneity, the levels and stages of fertility decline vary significantly from state to state. Even within a state, we observe large-scale regional disparities with regard to health and demographic indicators. At current fertility levels, a woman in India will have an average of 2.7 children in her lifetime. Fertility in rural areas is three children per woman, much higher than in urban areas where the replacement level of fertility of 2.1 children per woman has been already achieved. The greatest differentials in fertility can be seen with regard to the education of women and economic status of the households (IIPS and Macro International, 2007). At current fertility rates, women in the lowest wealth quintile households have two children more than the women from the highest wealth quintile households. The same is true of education. On average, a woman with no education has 3.6 children in her lifetime, whereas women with 12 or more years of education have only half of that, 1.8 children. The fertility rates are below the replacement level in the four south Indian states (Andhra Pradesh, Karnataka, Kerala and Tamil Nadu), Punjab, Maharashtra, Delhi and Himachal Pradesh. In contrast, the fertility rates are highest in Bihar and Uttar Pradesh, where at current fertility levels a woman would have about four children. Most of the other states are close to the replacement level fertility (Table 13.7). The total fertility rate for Muslims (3.1) is slightly higher than that for Hindus (2.7). But this difference has been narrowing significantly in recent times.

Another dimension is the marriage of girls at young ages leading to teenage pregnancy and early motherhood. Young women, who become pregnant and give birth, experience much health, social, economic and emotional problems. In addition, relatively high levels of pregnancy complications are reported among young mothers because of physiological immaturity and inexperience in child-care practices. It also influences maternal and infant health. Moreover, an early start to childbearing greatly reduces the educational and employment opportunity of women, which in turn influences higher level of fertility. Among young women aged 15–19 years, nearly 16% have already begun childbearing. Young women in rural areas are more than twice as likely to be mothers as young women in urban areas. This also reflects the fact that the majority of rural women marry during their teens. In rural India, motherhood is associated with power and prestige in every community. Childless women face abuse, neglect and stigmatization.

**Table 13.7** Projected year of achievement of replacement fertility in India and states

| Sr. No | Country/state | Year by which replacement fertility (TFR = 2.1) will be achieved | Current total fertility rate | |
|---|---|---|---|---|
| | | | NFHS (2005–06) | SRS (2005) |
| | **India** | 2021 | 2.68 | 2.9 |
| 1 | Andhra Pradesh | 2002 | 1.79 | 2.0 |
| 2 | Assam | 2019 | 2.42 | 2.9 |
| 3 | Bihar | 2021 | 4.00 | 4.3 |
| 4 | Chhattisgarh | 2022 | 2.62 | 3.4 |
| 5 | Delhi | Achieved in 2001 | 2.13 | 2.1 |
| 6 | Gujarat | 2012 | 2.42 | 2.8 |
| 7 | Haryana | 2012 | 2.69 | 2.8 |
| 8 | Himachal Pradesh | Achieved in 2002 | 1.94 | 2.2 |
| 9 | Jammu and Kashmir | NA | 2.38 | 2.4 |
| 10 | Jharkhand | 2018 | 3.31 | 3.5 |
| 11 | Karnataka | 2005 | 2.08 | 2.2 |
| 12 | Kerala | Achieved in 1988 | 1.93 | 1.7 |
| 13 | Madhya Pradesh | 2025 | 3.12 | 3.6 |
| 14 | Maharashtra | 2009 | 2.11 | 2.2 |
| 15 | Orissa | 2010 | 2.37 | 2.6 |
| 16 | Punjab | 2006 | 1.99 | 2.1 |
| 17 | Rajasthan | 2021 | 3.21 | 3.7 |
| 18 | Tamil Nadu | Achieved in 2000 | 1.80 | 1.7 |
| 19 | Uttar Pradesh | 2027 | 3.82 | 4.2 |
| 20 | Uttarakhand | 2022 | 2.55 | NA |
| 21 | West Bengal | 2003 | 2.27 | 2.1 |
| 22 | NE states | 2005 | NA | NA |

*Note*: *NE* North-eastern; *NFHS* National Family Health Survey; *SRS* Sample Registration System. *NA* Not Available.
*Source*: Government of India (2006).

## Family Planning

India was the first country in the world to introduce an official family planning program in 1952. The saga of family planning efforts in India has essentially been the story of an official family planning program fully depending upon government initiatives, resources and policies. There are essentially three dimensions to India's family planning efforts – the conceptual foundation of family planning in the context of fertility reduction, the administrative and management structure of providing services and supplies to meet the needs of the population, and the inputs provided for establishing the family planning services delivery system (Chaurasia & Gulati, 2008). However, the strong family planning program has met with differing success in different states of the country. The program has been successful in those states where social and economic development has been significant. In other words, the fertility decline is more "demand-led" rather than "supply-driven", despite the fact that the family planning program in India is fully financed and directed by the national government. Family planning efforts have been closely linked with the healthcare delivery system from the beginning. Because of this, even after 60 years of persistent governmental efforts, the family planning program never became a people's movement. The administration of family planning is essentially bureaucratic and follows a top-down approach. Though in recent years some efforts have been made to assess the needs of the community, yet people are not involved in the program. The target-based approach of the official family planning program dominated the family planning efforts for more than three decades. According to population projections, India will be overtaking China as the most overpopulated country somewhere around the middle of the current century. This means a rapid increase in the country's population in the years to come is almost inevitable, notwithstanding the efforts of the government. The two child norm is yet to emerge as a social norm in rural India. The public health delivery system in rural areas consists of Community Health Centres, Primary Health Centres and Sub-Centres. There is a considerable gap in the number of public health-care institutions and personnel required and the actual number of institutions in place. The main provider of family planning services in the rural areas is the female health worker (ANM) located at the Sub-Centre.

The knowledge of contraception is almost universal in India. Female sterilization is the most widely known method in the rural areas. The government family planning program also promotes three temporary methods – the pill, the IUD and condoms. The contraceptive prevalence rate among currently married women is 53% in rural areas. Female sterilization accounts for two-thirds of contraceptive use. Traditional methods such as rhythm and withdrawal methods are practiced by a small percentage of couples even now (Fig. 13.3). Surveys indicate that women belonging to Muslim

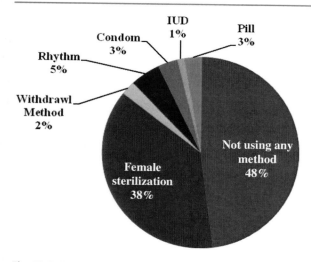

**Fig. 13.3** What contraceptive methods do rural couples use? *Source*: IIPS and Macro International (2007).

so in rural areas. Even today about 300 mothers die because of complications of pregnancy and delivery for every 100,000 live births. It is estimated that more than 92,000 maternal deaths occurred in India in 2001 and 93% of these deaths happened in rural areas. About 70% of the maternal deaths are concentrated in Bihar, Uttar Pradesh, Madhya Pradesh, Rajasthan and Orissa. Socio-economic development – education, health care, household income and infrastructure – will contribute significantly in the reduction of mortality from certain types of infectious diseases like diarrhoea and acute respiratory infections.

## Gender Discrimination

### Imbalance in Sex Ratio

Why are female children still at risk in India despite progress in education, increasing participation of women in economic and political activities, and an overall improvement in the status of women? Is there any significant shift from "son preference" to "daughter discrimination"?

One of the characteristic features of India's population is imbalance in the sex ratio. Globally, the average sex ratio at birth is 105 boys to 100 girls. However in India, it is 113 boys to 100 girls. During the last two decades, it has assumed alarming proportions in some states – in Punjab it is 129 and in Haryana, it is 124. Many Indians show a strong preference for sons, often resulting in the deliberate elimination of female foetuses through sex determination via ultrasound/sonography. This combined with the low status of women in India has resulted in an unusually high ratio of men to women. In the past, the imbalance in sex ratio was attributed to better nutrition and health care for males than for females resulting in high female death rates. However, abortion of female foetuses seems to be the main cause for the "missing girls". The low value of girls in a conservative patriarchal society led to a precarious situation for female children before birth, at birth and during childhood. Girls have been aborted on a massive scale in recent decades simply because they are girls.

religion, those who are less educated and belong to the lowest economic strata are less likely to use family planning methods. It is interesting to note that women are more likely to use contraception if they already have a son. Most men in India consider that contraception is women's business and that a man should not have to worry about it. It is also believed that, in recent years the promotion of the integrated package of reproductive and child health services has resulted in lesser attention on family planning. In short, the family planning program appears to have lost its importance and identity in the last decade.

## Reproductive and Child Health Services

According to the National Family Health Survey (2005–06), about 53% of women (22–24 age group) were married before attaining 18 years of age. The rural-urban differences are clearly visible with regard to institutional deliveries – only 31% of rural women gave birth in health facilities, whereas it was 69% in urban areas. Childhood immunization is another area where the rural-urban dichotomy is significant. Although 68% of the urban children were fully immunized (protection against six vaccine preventable diseases), the coverage was only 38% in rural areas. Recent surveys (IIPS and Macro International 2007) have indicated that nearly four-fifths of the children are anaemic in rural areas (Table 13.8). Infant, child and maternal mortality is unacceptably high in India, more

Considerable attention has been paid by researchers to different aspects of the female deficit in India (Visaria, 1971; Miller, 1981; Sen, 1990; Agnihotri, 2000; Croll, 2000; Bhat, 2002; Kaur, 2004; Patel,

**Table 13.8** Rural-urban differentials in the coverage of reproductive and child health services in India: 2005–2006

| | Indicator | Rural | Urban |
|---|---|---|---|
| | **Reproductive health** | | |
| 1 | Women (20–24) married by age 18 (percent) | 52.5 | 28.1 |
| 2 | Total fertility rate (Births per woman) | 3.0 | 2.1 |
| 3 | Women (15–19) pregnant or mother at survey (percent) | 19.1 | 8.7 |
| 4 | Median age at first birth for women (25–49 years of age) | 19.3 | 20.9 |
| 5 | Mothers with 3 ANC in the last birth (percent) | 42.8 | 73.8 |
| 6 | Mothers consuming IFA tbs for 90 days in the last pregnancy (percent) | 18.1 | 34.5 |
| 7 | Births attended by professionally trained persons | 39.1 | 75.2 |
| 8 | Institutional deliveries (percent) | 31.1 | 69.4 |
| 9 | Mother receiving PNC from professionally trained person (percent) | 28.1 | 60.7 |
| 10 | Current use of any family planning method (percent) | 53.0 | 64.0 |
| 11 | Current use of any modern family planning method (percent) | 45.3 | 55.8 |
| 12 | Total unmet need (percent) | 14.6 | 10.0 |
| 13 | Total unmet need for spacing (percent) | 7.1 | 4.6 |
| 14 | Total unmet need for limiting (percent) | 7.5 | 5.3 |
| | **Child health** | | |
| 1 | Children (12–23) fully immunized (percent) | 38.2 | 57.5 |
| 2 | Children (12–35) received Vitamin A (percent) | 20.4 | 22.7 |
| 3 | Children with diarrhoea received ORS (percent) | 24.0 | 32.7 |
| 4 | Children (<3 years) breastfed within 1 hour (percent) | 21.5 | 28.9 |
| 5 | Children 0–5 months exclusively breastfed (percent) | 48.3 | 40.3 |
| 6 | Children 6–9 months receiving solid or semi-solid food and breast milk (percent) | 53.8 | 62.1 |
| 7 | Children under 3 years who are stunted (percent) | 40.7 | 31.1 |
| 8 | Children under 3 years who are wasted (percent) | 19.8 | 16.9 |
| 9 | Children under 3 years who are underweight (percent) | 49.0 | 36.4 |
| 10 | Children 6–35 months anaemic (percent) | 81.2 | 72.7 |

*Note*: ORS Oral rehydration salt, ANC Antenatal Care, IFA Iron and Folic Acid, PNC Post-natal Care.
*Source*: International Institute for Population Sciences and Macro International (2007).

2007; Guilmoto, 2009; Sekher & Hatti, 2010b). The 2001 Census has generated a debate on the issue focusing on the changes in the juvenile or child sex ratio. Change in the sex ratio of children in the age group 0–6 is a better indicator of the status of the girl child in India. It also reflects the sum-total of intra-household gender relations. Why do millions of girls not survive in contemporary India, despite the overall improvement in welfare and state measures to enhance the status of women?

Although the 2001 Census shows that the overall sex ratio has marginally improved from 927 women per 1,000 men to 933 per 1,000[6] during the last decade, the number of girls to boys in the youngest age group fell from 945 to 927. Regional disparities also appear to have increased – the northern states generally exhibit a worsening trend in sex ratio as compared to the southern states (Table 13.9). The census

---

[6] The Census of India measures the sex ratio as number of females per 1,000 males as opposed to the standard international norm of number of males per 100 females. Defining the sex ratio by covering children in the age group 0–6 may seem arbitrary, but the Census uses it for the purpose of finding literacy status, categorizing the entire population into two groups – those aged 0–6 years and those 7 years and above.

**Table 13.9** The gender balance in the population – India and States: 2001

| Country/state | Number of males per 100 females | | |
|---|---|---|---|
| | All ages | 0–4 years | 0–14 years |
| India | 107 | 107 | 109 |
| Andhra Pradesh | 102 | 104 | 105 |
| Arunachal Pradesh | 112 | 103 | 104 |
| Assam | 107 | 103 | 104 |
| Bihar | 109 | 104 | 110 |
| Chhattisgarh | 101 | 102 | 103 |
| Goa | 104 | 107 | 105 |
| Gujarat | 109 | 113 | 113 |
| Haryana | 116 | 122 | 119 |
| Himachal Pradesh | 103 | 112 | 109 |
| Jammu and Kashmir | 112 | 107 | 106 |
| Jharkhand | 106 | 102 | 106 |
| Karnataka | 104 | 105 | 105 |
| Kerala | 95 | 104 | 104 |
| Madhya Pradesh | 109 | 107 | 109 |
| Maharashtra | 108 | 110 | 109 |
| Manipur | 102 | 104 | 104 |
| Meghalaya | 103 | 103 | 103 |
| Mizoram | 107 | 103 | 103 |
| Nagaland | 111 | 102 | 107 |
| Orissa | 103 | 104 | 104 |
| Punjab | 114 | 126 | 121 |
| Rajasthan | 109 | 110 | 111 |
| Sikkim | 114 | 105 | 103 |
| Tamil Nadu | 101 | 106 | 106 |
| Tripura | 105 | 104 | 104 |
| Uttar Pradesh | 111 | 108 | 112 |
| Uttarakhand | 104 | 110 | 109 |
| West Bengal | 107 | 104 | 105 |
| Delhi | 122 | 115 | 115 |

*Source*: Census of India, 2001.

evidence suggests a clear cultural preference for male children, particularly among some North Indian states (Fig. 13.4). The census lists "sex-selective female abortions", "female infanticide", and "female neglect" – typically through giving girls less food and medical care than boys – as "important reasons commonly put forward" for this shocking anomaly. The accelerated fall in the child sex ratio after 1981 is largely due to the diffusion of prenatal sex-selection techniques in regions with a well-entrenched gender bias (Bhat, 2002; Hatti, Sekher, & Larsen, 2004). Furthermore, as social norms are changing toward smaller families, the availability of and access to new reproductive technology provide an easy way for parents to achieve their goals. While attention has been drawn to the importance of cultural factors in studying demographic behaviour, few studies have examined in detail the relations between the cultural and economic aspects. One important cultural (and economic) feature is the value attached to sons. It is important to analyze the nexus of economic, social and cultural factors that underlie daughter discrimination, thus shifting the focus from son preference to daughter discrimination.

## Fertility Decline and Adverse Sex Ratio

In a significant article titled, "More than 100 Million Women are Missing", Amartya Sen (1990) brought to focus the increasing gender discrimination by analyzing the male-female ratio. He argues that the problem of missing women is "clearly one of the more momentous and neglected problems facing the world today" (p. 9). Miller (1981) in her anthropological study on the neglect of female children in North India has illustrated the strong relationship between culture and mortality. It is the cultural bias against females in North India that brings into play neglect and mistreatment of unknown numbers of children. Many studies have illustrated how the decline in fertility will affect gender bias and greater imbalance in juvenile sex ratios (Das Gupta & Bhat, 1997; Clark, 2000; Bhat & Zavier, 2003). A substantial decline in fertility presupposes a desire for fewer children as well as access to the means to limit the family size. Both these conditions can be achieved with increase in social and economic development. It is generally accepted that the pace of demographic transition is closely associated with the levels of socio-economic development. However, there is evidence to show that, even in the poorer regions, substantial decline in fertility has occurred through political intervention, in the form of family planning programs.

Social and economic development and governmental interventions, however, do not ensure any substantial change in the cultural ethos of society. In South Asian societies, it is believed that a major

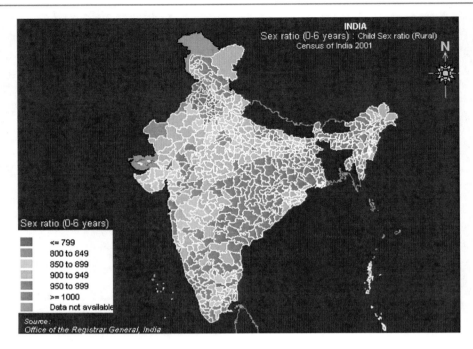

**Fig. 13.4** Sex ratio in India (0–6 years)

barrier for decline in fertility was the prevalence of a strong son-preference, irrespective of social and economic development. It is also argued that with the increase in welfare and economic development, the influence of son preference would decline gradually. These assumptions are being questioned by some studies indicating that there has been an increase in son preference during the years of fertility decline. This occurs not only in poorer communities, but also in populations where women have taken to education and employment and have achieved considerable social status. Das Gupta (1987) has found that excess female mortality for second and subsequent parity daughters was 32% higher than their siblings for uneducated mothers and 136% higher if the mothers were educated. Basu makes a similar observation, "Although her capacity to increase the chances of survival of her children seems to increase with education, the typical Uttar Pradesh woman's ability to treat her male and female offspring equally actually decreases" (1992, p. 196). The existence of strong son-preference has resulted in the desire to prevent the birth of daughters by carefully balancing the desired family size and desired sex composition of the children. In other words, the decline in fertility partly explains the rising masculinity of many populations (Das Gupta & Bhat, 1997; Croll, 2002). It is hypothesized that as fertility declines, two opposing forces could affect the child sex ratio, what is called "parity effect", which leads to a reduction of sex bias, and an "intensification effect", which increases it. Considering this dimension, there is a need to examine the influence of the mirror image of son preference, namely, daughter discrimination in the Indian context.

Does a strong son preference ultimately result in deliberate discrimination against daughters? Miller asserts that, "The problem is that son preference is so strong in some areas of India and amongst some classes that daughters must logically suffer in order that family's personal and culturally mandated needs are fulfilled" (1981, p. 25). Logically, this would mean that the stronger the son preference, the more intense the daughter discrimination. Rather than going through repeated pregnancies bearing daughters in an attempt to produce male progeny, the norm of a small family and reduced fertility seem to imply that unborn daughters are the first to be "sacrificed". Generally, both infanticide and fatal neglect of female children seem to be supplemented by sex identification and sex-selective abortion to achieve the desired family size and desired gender composition. Better opportunities for women's education, increasing labour force participation, and greater exposure to urban life do not necessarily guarantee equal status for daughters. In many Indian communities, daughters are associated with a double loss. Firstly, a daughter leaves the natal family after her marriage and the benefits from investment in her upbringing accrue to the new family, constituting a loss to her natal family. This is further compounded by the expenses of her marriage, particularly dowry, which are a heavy burden for the bride's family. Sons, on the other hand, are considered assets, deserving short and long-term investment. In rural India, the birth of a boy is thus a time for celebration, while the birth of a girl, especially a second or subsequent one, is often viewed as a time of crisis (Bumiller, 1990). Besides economic considerations, there are cultural factors that support son preference. All these factors put together contribute to the firm belief that daughters cannot substitute sons.

A general explanation for son preference is that sons can provide old age support. In India, a majority of the old parents live with married sons. In the Indian context, characterized by high levels of uncertainty, where no institutional alternative to the family as a source of social insurance has emerged, parental decisions are likely to be powerfully motivated by their concerns about their own security in old age. The existence of such an understanding and commitment between parents and sons, known as inter-generational contract, is one factor that appears to have remained unchanged through overall socio-economic changes. Sons are also important because they alone can perform the funeral rituals of their parents. Added to this, most women have very limited opportunities to contribute towards their parents' welfare. This creates an apparent dichotomy between the value of a girl to her parents and that of a woman to her parents-in-law. A South Indian proverb says, "Having a daughter is like watering a flower in the neighbour's garden". There is a growing "realization" among parents, particularly in rural areas, that daughters can rarely substitute sons. It has also become more expensive to raise children, as education has become more important and a necessity in a transforming society. The increasing cost of education and marriage of girls is a major drain on household resources, which acts as a strong disincentive to have daughters. Unless there is a change in the socio-economic attitudes of Indian society towards girl children, the increasing incidences of female feticide will continue to spread as a social epidemic throughout India.

The underlying workings of female discrimination are undoubtedly highly complex. However, many broad factors have been identified which together create a situation where sons are preferred and daughters are neglected. The patterns of inheritance are typically patrilineal in India with property passing from father to son (Miller, 1981; Agarwal, 1994; Kabeer, 1996). Upon marriage, the bride leaves her natal home to live with the family of her husband. In this exogamous lineage system, women are left out. They become dispensable essentially because they count for very little as individuals. In recent years, a major factor directly influencing the imbalance in child sex ratio is the widespread use of sex-determination technology and sex-selective abortion. Misuse of sex-determination tests has been a subject of media attention for many years. Health activists and women's organizations have voiced their concern forcing the government to act. In 1994, the Government of India banned the tests at the national level, with the Pre-natal Diagnostic Techniques (PNDT) (Regulation and Prevention of Misuse) Act. This Act specifies that no prenatal diagnostic procedures may be used unless there is a heightened possibility that the foetus suffers from a harmful condition or genetic disease. It also states that no person conducting prenatal diagnostic procedures shall communicate to the pregnant woman concerned or her relatives the sex of the foetus by words, signs or in any other manner. This Act was again amended in the light of the new techniques of pre-conception tests and the amended law came into effect in 2003. The Act has been renamed Pre-conception and Pre-natal Diagnostic Techniques (Prohibition of Sex-selection) Act, 1994. This legislation has been a miserable failure in preventing couples from seeking sex-determination tests and abortions, and medical practitioners from performing them for material gain.[7]

Female foetuses are liable to victimization on the basis of their sex alone even before they are born. Only far-reaching social changes that aim at increasing female autonomy, female economic power and the

---

[7] The first court case and conviction under this Act did not happen until recently when a doctor and his assistant in the state of Haryana were sentenced to 2 years in jail (*The Hindu* Newspaper, March 30, 2006).

value of the girl child are likely to make a significant impact on the demand for sex-selective abortion. Interestingly, there are no reliable statistics available on sex-selective abortion at the state or national level in India. An indirect estimate using the data from two rounds of National Family Health Survey (NFHS) indicates more than 100,000 sex-selective abortions in India every year (Arnold, Kishor, & Roy, 2002). The evidence of substantial sex-selective abortion in states such as Punjab, Haryana, Delhi and Maharashtra is consistent with the high rates of use of ultrasound and amniocentesis (Retherford & Roy, 2003).

How does fertility decline and son preference manifest at the village level, particularly in the context of widespread availability of sex-selection techniques at low cost? By studying two villages in the low fertility regions of South India, Sekher and Hatti (2007, 2010a) found that with the substantial decline in fertility in these regions, the son preference appears to have resulted in an increased as well as intensified manifestation of deliberate discrimination towards daughters. The widespread use of sex-selection techniques has provided an opportunity for couples to choose a son rather than a daughter. With increasing pressure on limited land on the one hand, and the spiralling cost of bringing up children (particularly girls, due to dowry) on the other, parents prefer not to have daughters. Medical technology has come in handy for many for achieving the desired sex-composition and the desired family-size. Rapid fertility decline, unaccompanied by changes in cultural values and gender inequality, is in a way responsible for the intensification of gender bias and the deliberate attempt to deny the girls from being "born at all". In other words, female foetuses are increasingly being "victimized" on the basis of their sex alone, even among affluent communities.

In Indian families known for persisting gender discrimination, one main reason for the pathetic condition of the girl child is the diversion of limited funds and facilities towards the boy child. One can see different levels of discrimination against girl children at every stage of their lives – feticide, infanticide, little or no access to education, lack of health care and nutrition, child labour, child marriage, early motherhood, frequent pregnancy, etc. In order to reverse the distorted sex ratio at birth (SRB) and to improve the survival and welfare of the girl children, both national and state governments have launched special financial incentive schemes to girl children at different stages of their life cycle. By providing Conditional Cash Transfers (CCTs), the families were encouraged to ensure certain minimum requirements such as registration of births, childhood immunization, enrolment in school, retention in school and delaying age at marriage beyond 18 years. Some of the well-known schemes are Dhan Lakshmi Scheme of the Government of India, Ladli Scheme of Delhi, Ladli Lakshmi Yojana of Madhya Pradesh, Bhagyalakshmi Scheme of Karnataka, Ladli Scheme of Haryana, Kanyadan scheme of Madhya Pradesh, Kanya Vivah Yojana of Bihar and Girl Child Protection Scheme in Andhra Pradesh. These incentive schemes have been aimed at improving the value of the girl child with the premise that financial benefits would trigger behavioural changes among parents and community and that this will go a long way towards ensuring the survival and a decent life for the girls. The CCTs are a marked departure from the traditional approaches in social service measures. By providing money to poor families under certain conditions, CCTs seek to address short-term income support objectives and also promote long-term accumulation of human capital through supply of health and educational services. CCTs can be an effective way of targeting limited resources to the poor and socially disadvantaged sections which will result in better education and health care for their children. Though CCTs offer governments the scope for positive discrimination in favour of girls, it is not clear how far they have influenced parental preferences and attitudes towards girls. Though most of these schemes are steps in the right direction, little is known about their implementation and effectiveness.

## Status of Women

Women's autonomy in the family and in society, consisting of their control of physical and financial resources, has implications for fertility behaviour. Therefore, improving the status of women is essential for lowering fertility and mortality rates. Though the principal of gender equality is entrenched in the Constitution, there is a considerable gap between the written word and reality at the ground level. Strong patriarchal traditions continue to persist in India with women's rights being influenced by centuries-old customs and traditions. This is reflected not only in the imbalance in the male-female ratio, but also in many other aspects of social and economic development including education, employment and health conditions (Table 13.10). Education is one of the most important indicators of the status of women which enhances their capabilities and decision-making power. Despite improvement in the educational level of girls, the gender gap continues to persist.

The same is true with regard to women's participation in economic activity. In rural India, most women work at home and also in agriculture. However, their work is not considered economically productive activity. According to the 2001 Census, the proportion of the working-age population (15–59 years) was around 61% with a gender gap of 41 percentage points. In

**Table 13.10** Status of women in India: selected indicators

| Country/states | Female literacy rate | Proportion of 15+ women at least matriculate | Female work participation rate | Female married by 18 years of age | Women 15–19 years pregnant or mothers | Median age at first birth |
| --- | --- | --- | --- | --- | --- | --- |
| India | 53.7 | 8.3 | 25.6 | 44.5 | 16.0 | 19.8 |
| Jammu and Kashmir | 43.0 | 8.1 | 22.5 | 14.0 | 4.2 | 21.4 |
| Himachal Pradesh | 67.4 | 14.2 | 43.7 | 12.3 | 3.1 | 21.2 |
| Punjab | 63.4 | 15.4 | 19.1 | 19.4 | 5.5 | 21.4 |
| Uttarakhand | 59.6 | 9.5 | 27.3 | 22.6 | 6.2 | 20.5 |
| Haryana | 55.7 | 9.9 | 27.2 | 39.8 | 12.1 | 20.3 |
| Delhi | 74.7 | 16.4 | 9.4 | 21.2 | 5.0 | 21.7 |
| Rajasthan | 43.9 | 3.7 | 33.5 | 57.1 | 16.0 | 19.6 |
| Uttar Pradesh | 42.2 | 5.5 | 16.5 | 53.0 | 14.3 | 19.4 |
| Bihar | 33.1 | 4.4 | 18.8 | 60.3 | 25.0 | 18.7 |
| Sikkim | 45.0 | 8.1 | 27.3 | 30.1 | 12.0 | 21.9 |
| Arunachal Pradesh | 43.5 | 5.8 | 36.5 | 40.6 | 15.4 | 19.9 |
| Nagaland | 61.5 | 11.4 | 38.1 | 21.1 | 7.5 | 21.8 |
| Manipur[a] | 60.53 | 13.2 | 39.0 | 12.7 | 7.3 | 23.7 |
| Mizoram | 86.8 | 8.3 | 47.5 | 20.6 | 10.1 | 22.3 |
| Tripura | 64.9 | 4.8 | 21.1 | 41.0 | 18.5 | 20.3 |
| Meghalaya | 59.6 | 6.8 | 35.2 | 24.5 | 8.3 | 21.7 |
| Assam | 54.6 | 9.5 | 20.7 | 38.0 | 16.4 | 20.7 |
| West Bengal | 59.6 | 6.6 | 18.3 | 53.3 | 25.3 | 19.0 |
| Jharkhand | 38.9 | 5.6 | 26.4 | 61.2 | 27.5 | 18.9 |
| Orissa | 50.5 | 7.2 | 24.7 | 36.3 | 14.4 | 20.0 |
| Chhattisgarh | 51.9 | 4.6 | 40.0 | 51.8 | 14.6 | 18.8 |
| Madhya Pradesh | 50.3 | 5.0 | 33.2 | 53.0 | 13.6 | 19.4 |
| Gujarat | 57.8 | 10.1 | 27.9 | 33.5 | 12.7 | 20.6 |
| Maharashtra | 67.0 | 11.9 | 30.8 | 38.8 | 13.8 | 19.9 |
| Andhra Pradesh | 50.4 | 8.5 | 35.1 | 54.7 | 18.1 | 18.8 |
| Karnataka | 56.9 | 11.0 | 32.0 | 41.2 | 17.0 | 19.9 |
| Goa | 75.4 | 20.9 | 22.4 | 11.7 | 3.6 | 25.0 |
| Kerala | 87.7 | 19.6 | 15.4 | 15.4 | 5.8 | 22.7 |
| Tamil Nadu | 64.4 | 11.4 | 31.5 | 21.5 | 7.7 | 21.0 |

[a] Excluding 3 Sub-Divisions of Senapati District viz., Mao-Maram, Paomata and Purul in 2001 Census.
*Source*: Census of India 2001, IIPS and Macro International (2007).

other words, four out of five working-age males are engaged in productive activity, while among females it is only two out of five. However, a recent study of women employed in the booming information technology (IT) sector suggests that a partial reversal of daughter devaluation is currently emerging in the families of young women (Clark & Sekher, 2007). When young women find opportunities to improve their financial autonomy, mobility and social acceptance in a male-dominated society, there are far-reaching implications for social demographic change and also for gender equality. These young women in the IT sector, with their assertive attitudes, large incomes and renegotiated family relationships may begin to be imitated by others in a movement toward greater gender equity, and become role models for young women from less-privileged backgrounds.

## References

Agarwal, B. (1994). *A field of one's own: Gender and land rights in South Asia*. Cambridge: Cambridge University Press.

Agnihotri, S. B. (2000). *Sex ratio patterns in the Indian population: A fresh exploration*. New Delhi: Sage.

Arnold, F., Kishor, S., & Roy, T. K. (2002). Sex-selective abortions in India. *Population and Development Review, 28*(4), 759–785.

Basu, A. (1992). *Culture, the status of women and demographic behaviour*. Oxford: Clarendon Press.

Bhat, M. P. N. (1994). Levels and trends in Indian fertility. *Economic and Political Weekly, 29*(51–52), 273–280.

Bhat, M. P. N. (2002). On the trail of "Missing" Indian females (I and II). *Economic and Political Weekly, 37*(51 and 52), 5105–5118 and 5244–5263.

Bhat, M. P. N., & Zavier, F. (2003). Fertility decline and gender bias in northern India. *Demography, 40*(4), 637–657.

Bhat, M. P. N., & Zavier, F. (2005). Role of religion in fertility decline: The case of Indian Muslims. *Economic and Political Weekly, 40*(5), 385–402.

Bumiller, E. (1990). *May you be the mother of a thousand sons: A journey among women in India*. New York: Penguin Books.

Caldwell, J. (1993). The Asian fertility revolution: Its implications for transition theories. In R. Leete & I. Alam (Eds.), *The revolution in Asian fertility: Dimensions, causes and implications* (pp. 299–316). Oxford: Clarendon Press.

Chaurasia, A. R., & Gulati, S. C. (Eds.). (2008). *India: The state of population 2007*. New Delhi: Oxford University Press.

Clark, A., & Sekher, T. V. (2007). Can career-minded young women reverse gender discrimination? A view from Bangalore's High-Tech sector. *Gender, Technology and Development, 11*(3), 285–319.

Clark, S. (2000). Son preference and sex composition of children: Evidence from India. *Demography, 37*(1), 95–108.

Croll, E. J. (2000). *Endangered daughters: Discrimination and development in Asia*. New York: Routledge.

Croll, E. J. (2002). Fertility decline, family size and female discrimination: A study of reproductive management in East and South Asia. *Asia-Pacific Population Journal, 17*(2), 11–38.

Das Gupta, M. (1987). Selective discrimination against female children in rural Punjab, India. *Population and Development Review, 13*(1), 77–100.

Das Gupta, M., & Bhat, P. N. M. (1997). Fertility decline and increased manifestation of sex bias in India. *Population Studies, 51*(3), 307–315.

Das Gupta, M., Martine, G., & Chen, L. C. (1998). Reproductive change in India and Brazil: Implications for understanding fertility decline. In G. Martine, M. Das Gupta, & L. C. Chen (Eds.), *Reproductive change in India and Brazil* (pp. 1–34). Delhi: Oxford University Press.

Dyson, T., Cassen, R., & Visaria, L. (Eds.). (2004). *Twenty-first century India: Population, economy, human development and the environment*. New Delhi: Oxford University Press.

Government of India. (2006). *Report of the working group on empowerment of women for the XI plan*. Ministry of Women and Child Development, New Delhi.

Guilmoto, C. Z. (2009). The sex ratio transition in Asia. *Population and Development Review, 35*(3), 519–549.

Guilmoto, C. Z., & Rajan, S. I. (2002). Spatial patterns of fertility transition in Indian districts. *Population and Development Review, 27*(4), 713–738.

Hatti, N., Sekher, T. V., & Larsen, M. (2004). *Lives at risk: Declining child sex ratios in India*. Lund Papers in Economic History, No. 93. Lund, Sweden: Lund University.

Haub, C., & Sharma, O. P. (2006). India's population reality: Reconciling change and tradition. *Population Bulletin, 61*(3), 1–20.

International Institute for Population Sciences. (2010). *District Level Household and Facility Survey-2007–08*. India, Mumbai: IIPS.

International Institute for Population Sciences (IIPS) and Macro International. (2007). *National Family Health Survey (NFHS-3) – India 2005–06*. Mumbai: IIPS.

International Institute for Population Sciences (IIPS) and Population Council. (2010). *Youth in India: Situations and Needs 2006–07*. Mumbai: IIPS.

Jeffery, P., & Jeffery, R. (1997). *Population, gender and politics: Demographic change in rural north India*. Cambridge: Cambridge University Press.

Jejeebhoy, S., & Halli S. S. (2006). Marriage Patterns in rural India: Influence of sociocultural context. In C. R. Lloyd, J. R. Behrman, N. P. Stromquist, & B. Cohen (Eds.), *The changing transitions to adulthood in developing countries: Selected studies* (pp. 172–199). Washington, DC: The National Academies Press.

Kabeer, N. (1996). *Gender, demographic transition and the economics of family size: Population policy for a human-centred development*. Occasional paper 7. Geneva: UNRISD.

Kaur, R. (2004). Across-region marriages: Poverty, female migration and the sex ratio. *Economic and Political Weekly, 39*(25), 2595–2616.

Kulkarni, P. M., & Alagrajan, M. (2005). Population growth, fertility and religion in India. *Economic and Political Weekly, 40*(5), 403–410.

Miller, B. D. (1981). *The endangered sex: The neglect of female child in rural North India*. Ithaca, NY: Cornell University Press.

Nyrop, R., & Shinn, R. (1975). *Area handbook for India*. Washington, DC: The American University.

Office of the Registrar General, India. (2009). *Households Composition and Size, Census of India, 2001*. New Delhi.

Patel, T. (2007). Informal social networks, sonography and female foeticide in India. *Sociological Bulletin, 56*(2), 243–262.

Retherford, R. D., & Roy, T. K. (2003). *Factors affecting sex-selective abortion in India and 17 major states. NFHS Series – No.21*. Mumbai: IIPS and Hawaii: East-West Centre.

Sekher, T. V., & Hatti, N. (2007). Vulnerable daughters in a modernising society: From son preference to daughter discrimination in rural South India. In I. Attane, & C. Z. Guilmoto (Eds.), *Watering the neighbour's garden: The growing demographic female deficit in Asia* (pp. 295–323). Paris: CICRED.

Sekher, T. V., & Hatti, N. (2010a). Disappearing daughters and intensification of gender bias: Evidences from two village studies in South India. *Sociological Bulletin, 59*(1), 111–133.

Sekher, T. V., & Hatti, N. (Eds.). (2010b). *Unwanted daughters: Gender discrimination in modern India*. Jaipur: Rawat Publications.

Sekher, T. V., Raju, K. N. M., & Sivakumar, M. N. (2001). Fertility transition in Karnataka: Levels, trends and implications. *Economic and Political Weekly, 36*(51), 4742–4752.

Sen, A. (1990). More than 100 million women are missing. *New York Review of Books, 37*(20), 61–66.

Srinivas, M. N. (1989). *The cohesive role of Sanskritisation and other essays*. Oxford: Oxford University Press.

Srinivasan, K. (1995). *Regulating reproduction in India's population: Efforts, results and recommendations*. New Delhi: Sage.

Srinivasan, P., & Lee, G. (2004). The dowry system in Northern India: Women's attitudes and social change. *Journal of Marriage and Family, 66*(6), 1108–1117.

Srinivasan, S. (2005). Daughters or dowries? The changing nature of dowry practices in South India. *World Development, 33*(4), 593–615.

United Nations. (1982). *Population of India, Country Monograph series No. 10*. Economic and Social Commission for Asia and the Pacific, Bangkok.

Visaria, P. (1971). *The sex ratio of the population of India, Monograph 10 – Census of India*. New Delhi: Office of the Registrar General of India.

# The Aboriginal People of Canada: A Rural Perspective

Gustave Goldmann

## Introduction

Canada's population is a rich mosaic of people representing many cultures, speaking different languages and with a varied history with respect to settlement in this country. Although numerous theories exist about the origins of human habitation in North America, it is a commonly accepted anthropological view that the land mass that is Canada today was first inhabited by indigenous people who migrated from Asia via a land bridge that spanned the Bering Strait (Dickason, 2002). This migration is considered to be the first settlement of Aboriginal people in North America. This chapter presents a socio-demographic profile of the first inhabitants of this territory, the Aboriginal people living in Canada, with emphasis on the rural population.

Who are the Aboriginal people of Canada? Very often, expressions such as "Aboriginal", "Native", "Indian", "Registered Indian", "Treaty Indian" and "First Nations" are used interchangeably, irrespective of the specific history and meanings of these words. In Canada, the word "Aboriginal" includes many groups with unique heritages, languages, cultural practices, and spiritual beliefs, as well as distinct needs and aspirations. Section 35 of the 1982 Constitution Act of Canada recognizes three distinct groups of Aboriginal people: Indians (First Nations), Métis, and Inuit. Many definitions of the concept of "Aboriginality" have been proposed over the years, and more so since the early 1980s, mirroring the growing awareness of Canadian society towards Aboriginal issues. The socio-demographic profiles presented in this chapter will be organized by the three groups recognized in the 1982 Constitution Act of Canada.

The primary concepts and the data that will be used in this analysis are defined in the next section of the chapter. It is inevitable in a presentation of this type that comparisons are made with the non-Aboriginal population living in Canada. Comparisons and contrasts will also be made between the Aboriginal people living in rural and urban areas and between the three major aboriginal groups listed above. It is important to understand where the Aboriginal people live in Canada, including the distribution of the population in rural and urban areas. All subsequent sections dealing with the socio-demographic characteristics of the Aboriginal population will consider where they live in the analysis.

## Data and Concepts

The Census of Canada, the primary source of demographic and socio-economic data covering all Aboriginal groups in Canada, gathers information on four concepts of Aboriginality: ethnic origin, self-identification as an Aboriginal person, Registered Indian and membership to a First Nation. Such data serve to estimate the size and characteristics of Aboriginal populations in Canada, in whole or in part. The first three concepts, i.e. those appearing most often in definitions, are described in detail below.

G. Goldmann (✉)
University of Ottawa, Ottawa, ON, K1N 6N5, Canada

Carleton University, Ottawa, ON, K1S 5B6, Canada
e-mail: ggoldman@uottawa.ca

For the longest time, ethnic origin was the ethnocultural characteristic most widely used in Canada to establish Aboriginal affiliation. Since 1871, all Canadian censuses have enumerated Aboriginal populations by means of a question on ethnic origin. The concept of origin refers to the ethnic or cultural group to which a person's ancestors belonged. In theory, this concept could serve to identify the descendents of populations who lived in America when Europeans arrived in the 16th and 17th centuries (Robitaille & Choinière, 1987). In reality, however, since very few people have thorough knowledge of their ethnocultural genealogy, only a fraction of true descendents from pre-colonial Aboriginal people report an Aboriginal origin during a census. In addition to genealogy, census data on ethnic origin varies according to societal concerns in general and the nature of the socio-political relations the Canadian society maintains (or not) with Aboriginal populations (Goldmann, 1993). The Census of Canada shows that 1.678 million persons reported at least one Aboriginal origin in 2006.

Currently, the concept of Aboriginal self-identity is increasingly used to define affiliation to an Aboriginal group. Ethnic identity is a subjective indicator of a person's affiliation to an ethnic group. Considering the growing ineffectiveness of objective indicators of ethnic affiliation (such as "real" ethnic origins and mother tongue) for reasons of acculturation and exogamy (intermarriage), ethnic identity is one of the best ethnicity indicators available. The concept of Aboriginal identity emerged in 1986 with the goal of improving the enumeration of Aboriginal populations (Statistics Canada, 1989). According to the Census of Canada, about 1.146 million persons self-identified as Aboriginal in 2006.

In Canada, like in many other countries with an Aboriginal population, there are legal definitions of Aboriginality (Lee, 1990). The Indian Act is the main Canadian legislative document explicitly defining a specific subset of Aboriginal populations: Registered Indians (or Status Indians). The concept of Registered Indian was established to determine the right of residency on Indian reserves. The first version of the Indian Act in the confederative era dates backs to 1876. Since then, the federal government has made several amendments to it. The latest amendments to the Indian Act were made in 1985. According to the 2006 Census of Canada, 623,780 persons self-reported as Registered Indian, as defined by the Indian Act.

Intuitively, one would be led to believe that there is a "hierarchical structure" to these three concepts of Aboriginality: the Registered Indian population could be a subset of the population with Aboriginal identity, which in turn could be a subset of the population with Aboriginal origin. However practical or logical this worldview may appear, the actual data show a much more complex reality. Indeed, the populations as defined by these three concepts overlap in part (Fig. 14.1). Together, the concepts of Aboriginal origin, Aboriginal identity and Registered Indian define seven subsets of different sizes, the total of which comes to 1.8 million persons. The two largest subsets are composed of people self-reporting Aboriginal origin, Aboriginal identity and Indian legal status (572,140) and people reporting Aboriginal origin only (632,760). The other two "one-dimensional" subsets – Aboriginal identity and Indian legal status only – respectively include 80,735 and 9,810 persons.

Another interesting observation resulting from the analysis of Census data is that, independently of the concept used to define Aboriginality, Aboriginal populations experienced a demographic explosion since the 1980s. From 1981 to 2006, the size of the population with Aboriginal origin (Table 14.1) went from about 491,000 to 1.678 million people, an overall relative increase of 242%, which is more than eight times the relative increase observed for the entire Canadian population (30%). The observed growth of Aboriginal populations is not limited to fertility, mortality and migration, and is not simply the result of coverage errors (Guimond, 1999, 2009).

From this brief analysis of definitions, concepts and population statistics, it is clear that there is no simple and single answer to this question: "Who is an Aboriginal person in Canada?" Evidently, the concept of Aboriginality in Canada is multidimensional, with each dimension showing a different population count and its own level of complexity. In other words, "Aboriginal group boundaries" are fuzzy in Canada. But it was not always the case. At the time of first contact between Aboriginal populations and European explorers, these group boundaries were clearly defined. Why is it harder to define and enumerate Aboriginal populations today? The answer to this question is to be found in the concept of ethnic mobility, which we will develop in the next section.

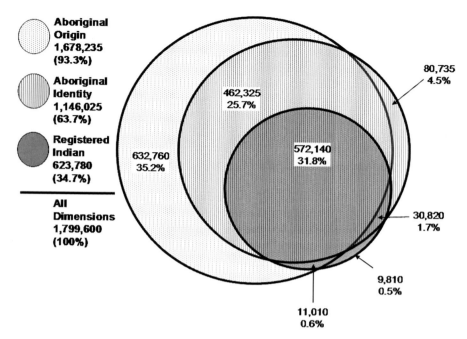

**Fig. 14.1** Three dimensions of Aboriginality in Canada, 2006
*Source*: Statistics Canada, 2006 Census of Canada, custom tabulations.

**Table 14.1** Aboriginal population counts based on concepts of origin, identity, Indian registration and first nation/band membership, Canada, 1981–2006

| | Population | | | | | | % Increase | |
|---|---|---|---|---|---|---|---|---|
| | 1981 | 1986 | 1991 | 1996 | 2001 | 2006 | 1986–2006 | 1996–2006 |
| Aboriginal origin population | 491,465 | 711,720 | 1,002,675 | 1,101,960 | 1,319,890 | 1,678,235 | 241.5% | 52.3% |
| Aboriginal identity population[a] | | | | 779,790 | 952,895 | 1,034,470 | | 32.7% |
| Registered Indian population | 320,140 | 263,245 | 385,805 | 488,040 | 558,175 | 623,780 | 94.8% | 27.8% |
| First Nation/Indian band population | | | | 461,760 | 554,860 | 620,345 | | 34.3% |
| Canada – Total (in millions) | 24,083.5 | 25,022.0 | 26,994.0 | 28,528.1 | 29,639.0 | 31,241.0 | 29.7% | 9.5% |

[a] Includes only persons who have self-reported an Aboriginal identity (First Nations, Métis or Inuit). Data on the Aboriginal identity of the Aboriginal origin population is available for 1986 and 1991 (Guimond, 2009).
*Source*: Statistics Canada, 1981–2006 censuses of population, custom tabulations prepared by Indian and Northern Affairs Canada.

## Ethnic Mobility

Ethnic mobility is the phenomenon by which changes in ethnic affiliation happen among individuals and families. In relation to a group, ethnic mobility is a multi-directional phenomenon, composed of entries and exits that supply or tap the group. Such changes in ethnic affiliation, or ethnic transfers, affect the size and characteristics of ethnic groups. Different terms have been used in the demographic literature to designate that phenomenon: ethnic switching, transfer, passing, changing identities and changes in self-reporting of ethnic identity.

Two types of ethnic mobility are to be distinguished. The first, intergenerational ethnic mobility refers to the universe of families and may happen when a child's ethnic affiliation is reported for the first time. Parents and children do not necessarily have the same affiliation, especially when the parents do not belong to the same ethnic group. Intergenerational ethnic mobility has long been a component of the demographic growth of Aboriginal populations in Canada. The Métis, the second largest Aboriginal population, are a "product" of this type of ethnic mobility. Historical, geopolitical, commercial and cultural circumstances related to colonization of Western Canada led to the emergence of this third Aboriginal cultural entity, originally uniting descendents of First Nations women and European men, very often fur traders. By fostering the emergence of "new types of Aboriginal people", intergenerational ethnic mobility contributes to the imprecision of "Aboriginal group boundaries" previously noted (Fig. 14.1).

The second type, intragenerational ethnic mobility, results from a change in the ethnic affiliation of a person over time. This type of ethnic mobility is responsible for the exceptional growth of Aboriginal populations since the 1980s. According to estimates based on the residual method, nearly 42,000 Indians living off-reserve in 2001 did not self-identify as Indian in 1986, which amounts to one in eight Indians living off-reserve (13%). Over 101,000 Métis in 2001 did not self-identify as Métis in 1986, or four Métis in ten (39%). Among the Inuit, the contribution of intragenerational ethnic mobility appears to be negligible (Guimond, 2009).

The phenomenon of intragenerational ethnic mobility was also recognized among Aboriginal populations in the United States and Australia. In the United States, several researchers became interested in the exceptional demographic growth of the American Indian population observed between 1960 and 1990 (Passel, 1996; Eschbach, 1993; Eschbach, Supple, & Snipp, 1998). They found that changes in self-reporting of ethnic and racial affiliations are a significant component, sometimes the most significant, of the demographic growth observed in the American Indian population of the United States during this period. In Australia, it was observed that over half of the total Aboriginal population growth during the 1991–1996 period is explained by variations in data quality combined with changes in ethnic affiliation reporting (Ross, 1996).

Though there is no definitive explanation for ethnic mobility among First Nations, Métis, Inuit and non-Aboriginal populations in Canada, three types of factors may be considered (Guimond, 1999, 2009). First, there are predisposing demographic factors. In Canada's main urban centres, people of various ethnocultural affiliations meet, form couples and have children. Given their mixed ethnocultural origins, once they are adults those children may "choose" their ethnic affiliation, and such a choice may vary depending on the circumstances. In a nutshell, mixed origins could favour intragenerational ethnic mobility.

Social factors could also foster intragenerational ethnic mobility toward Aboriginal populations. Different socio-political events – spontaneous like the Oka crisis in the summer of 1990 or organized like the Royal Commission on Aboriginal People from 1991 to 1996 – as well as their media coverage raised public awareness and contributed to restoring Aboriginal people's pride. Increased public attention and an improved overall perception Aboriginal people have of themselves could therefore have induced some people to report to be Aboriginal people.

Finally, political and legal decisions could also further foster ethnic mobility toward Aboriginal populations, especially if such decisions have spin-offs considered to be favourable. For example, the 1985 amendments to the Indian Act had a considerable demographic impact on the size and growth of the Registered Indian population: on December 31, 2000, 114,512 people had acquired (or reacquired) Indian status under the 1985 amendments (INAC, 2001). In addition to those amendments to the Indian Act, territorial claim settlements and employment equity policies are also likely to generate ethnic mobility.

## Where Do the Aboriginal People Live?

Aboriginal people in Canada live in urban and rural areas as well as on Indian reserves.[1] Indian reserves are classified as rural communities for the purposes

---

[1] "The on-reserve population is a derived census variable that is captured by using the census subdivision (CSD) type according to criteria established by Indian and Northern Affairs Canada

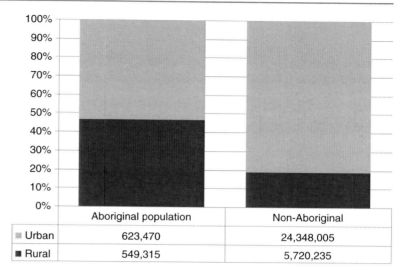

**Fig. 14.2** Urban-rural distribution of the Aboriginal and non-Aboriginal population of Canada (2006) *Source*: Statistics Canada, 2006 Census of Canada, custom tabulations, calculations by the author.

of the analysis presented in this chapter. While the population of Canada lives primarily in urban areas (less than 20% live in rural areas), the overall distribution of the Aboriginal people is closer to 50% rural and 50% urban (see Fig. 14.2).

It is important to note that the demography of rural Canada is not defined by the demography of the Aboriginal people since they do not necessarily represent the majority. If we accept the 60th parallel as the dividing line between the North and the South, the data show that the Aboriginal people represent a majority of the population in the North. Approximately 85% of the population living in Nunavut, one of the three northern territories, is Aboriginal. The corresponding proportions for the Northwest Territories and the Yukon are 50% and 25%, respectively. It is reasonable to conclude that their influence on the demographic structure of the population is much stronger in these regions than in the south where they represent between 1.3% (in Prince Edward Island) and 15% (in Manitoba) of the population.

The proportions vary substantially between the three Aboriginal groups. Over 60% of the Inuit, 55% of the First Nations people and 30% of the Métis people live in rural areas (see Fig. 14.3). The Inuit live primarily in the Northern parts of the country, concentrated in the three territories (Yukon, Northwest Territories and Nunavut) and in the Northern parts of the provinces. The Indian reserves are distributed across the country with concentrations in British Columbia. The Métis live primarily in the Prairie Provinces (Manitoba, Saskatchewan and Alberta).

As indicated earlier in this chapter, the influence that a population group has on the overall territory is a function of its proportion in the overall population. Focusing specifically on the Inuit in the northern territories (the dark bars in Fig. 14.3), one quarter of the population of the Yukon, half the population of the Northwest Territories and 85% of the population of Nunavut is Aboriginal. These proportions indicate a very strong Aboriginal influence in these territories. For example, the Territorial Government of Nunavut conducts its business in Inuktitut and the Inuit culture and values permeate the policies and programs developed and implemented in the Territory. The Government of the Northwest Territories also represents the values and cultures of the Aboriginal people living in that region. The Dene People and the Inuvialuit are well represented in Government at the political and bureaucratic level and there are departments that focus on each of these cultures. The

(INAC). On-reserve population includes all people living in any of eight CSD types legally affiliated with First Nations or Indian Bands (...), as well as selected CSDs of various other types that are northern communities in Saskatchewan, the Northwest Territories and the Yukon Territory (...)." (Statistics Canada, 2009, 215).

The census subdivision types are based on the legal definition of communities affiliated with First Nations or Indian Bands. They are : Indian reserve (IRI); Indian settlement (S-É); Indian government district (IGD); Terres réservées aux Cris (TC); Terres réservées aux Naskapis (TK); Nisga'a village (NVL); Nisga'a land (NL); Teslin land (TL). (Statistics Canada, 2009)

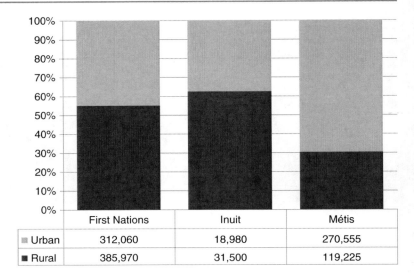

**Fig. 14.3** Distribution of Aboriginal people by group identity in Canada, 2006
*Source*: 2006 Census of Canada, calculations by the author.

Government of the Yukon is also structured to reflect the concentration of Aboriginal people living in the Territory, although to a lesser extent than its northern neighbours.

Furthermore, the data show that slightly more than half of the Aboriginal people living in the Yukon reside in rural areas or on reserves. The comparable proportion for both the Northwest Territories and Nunavut is 2/3.

## A Younger Population

The age structure of the population is an important distinguishing feature of the Aboriginal people in Canada. A series of age-sex pyramids are presented in this section to illustrate the differences between the Aboriginal and non-Aboriginal populations as well as the differences between the Aboriginal people living in rural and urban areas in Canada.

Overall, the Aboriginal people are substantially younger than the non-Aboriginal population in Canada. The median age of the Aboriginal population is 27 compared to 40 for the non-Aboriginal population. The median ages for the individual groups are 25 for First Nations, 30 for the Métis and 22 for the Inuit (Statistics Canada, 2008). Focussing on the rural populations, we see from the age-sex structures presented in Fig. 14.4 that there are relatively a greater number of Aboriginal people under the age of 25 living in rural areas when compared to the non-Aboriginal population. We also see that there are relatively fewer Aboriginal people over the age of 45 living in rural areas. Given that the growth of the population for the Aboriginal people is due to net natural increase and to ethnic mobility[2] (described earlier) the shape of the pyramid shows a good potential for population growth, assuming that the life expectancy is the same for Aboriginal and non-Aboriginal people. While the gap between Aboriginal and non-Aboriginal people is narrowing, the latest projections of life expectancy in 2017 show that a significant difference still exists. These latest projections indicate that life expectancy for the non-Aboriginal population is 79 years for men and 83 years for women. The comparable projections for the Aboriginal people show that Inuit men can expect to live to the age of 64 and Inuit women can expect to live to the age of 73. Métis and First Nations men can expect to live to 74 years and women can expect to live to 80 years (Statistics Canada, 2010). Although these data apply to the total population, they can be taken as reasonable proxy indicators for the rural population.

Figure 14.5 shows the age-sex comparison between the urban and rural Aboriginal people. We can see from the comparative distributions that there are relatively

---

[2] The Aboriginal people can be considered to be a "closed population" for the purposes of estimating population growth and decline since immigration and emigration are not significant factors of population flow.

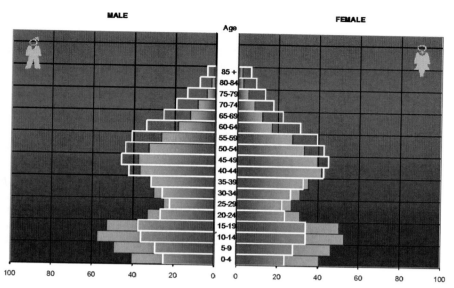

**Fig. 14.4** Aboriginal (*solid bars*) and non-Aboriginal (*hollow bars*) people living rural areas, 2006
*Source*: 2006 Census of Canada, calculations by the author.

fewer Aboriginal women between the ages of 20 and 39 living in rural areas (hollow bars in Fig. 14.5). Given that this is the prime age cohort for family formation, this pattern has an important impact on family structures. The data show that between 2 and 3% of Aboriginal children under the age of 15 were living solely with their grandparents in 2006 while less than 0.5% of non-Aboriginal children live only with their grandparents (Statistics Canada, 2010).

It should be noted that these types of family arrangements may be temporary for some of the Aboriginal people. Young Aboriginal women migrate to urban centres for a variety of reasons, ranging from family-related issues to acquiring education to seeking employment opportunities. Some move alone while others bring their children with them. A recent study

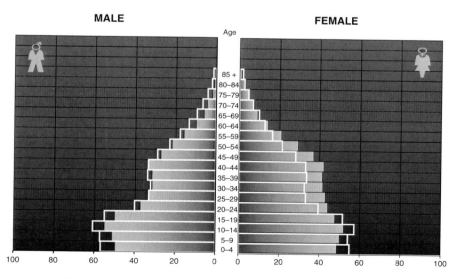

**Fig. 14.5** Aboriginal people living in urban (*solid bars*) and in rural (*hollow bars*) areas in Canada, 2006
*Source*: 2006 Census of Canada, calculations by the author.

published by Indian and Northern Affairs Canada observed that

> Women have tended to leave the reserves for family-related and housing reasons. Many are single parents moving with their children. Nearly one in four families are lone-parent families. (INAC, 2009).

The data also show that well over half (58%) of the Inuit and Indian women in that age cohort living in rural areas and on reserves respectively are single.

When we disaggregate the Aboriginal population into the three major groups (First Nations, Métis and Inuit), we see very little difference from the overall pattern described above. We see that in all cases the rural population appears to be somewhat younger, with a larger proportion of people under the age of 19. We also notice substantial differences in the proportions of Indian women (when compared to men) between the ages of 20 and 59 on reserves and Inuit women in rural areas.

## Language Characteristics of the Aboriginal People Living in Canada

Language was an important aspect of the cultural identity of the Aboriginal people of Canada. Aboriginal nations in Canada were defined as much by language as they were defined by territory. As with most other Aboriginal people in the world, oral tradition played (and continues to play) a central role in the transmission of culture and history from one generation to the next.

The Census captures five fundamental language characteristics of the population:
- mother tongue – defined as the language first learned in childhood and still understood;
- home language – defined as the language spoken either most often or on a regular basis in the home;
- knowledge of one or both of the official languages in Canada;
- knowledge of a heritage language; and
- the language used either most often or on a regular basis at work.

This section focuses on mother tongue, home language and the retention ratio (which is defined below) for the Aboriginal people living in rural and urban areas. Given the historical importance of language to Aboriginal culture, this section explores the degree to which Aboriginal languages are preserved and/or revitalized in Canada.

While more than 30 Aboriginal languages are separately tabulated in the Census data, the analysis in this section is conducted at the aggregate level for those declaring an Aboriginal identity. Table 14.2 shows the distribution of the declared mother tongue by broad age cohorts for the rural and urban Aboriginal people. Previous work on this topic highlights some of the factors that may contribute to language retention. For instance, Norris (1998) and Beaujot and Kerr (2004) comment on the importance of age in maintaining a language. It is often the elderly who are most proficient. The middle-aged generation is often less proficient since they were the group that experienced the Residential School system – a system that emphasized non-Aboriginal languages in its programs.

**Table 14.2** Distribution of Aboriginal population in Canada by mother tongue and identity showing retention ratio, 2006

| Identity | 0–14 years | | | 15–64 years | | | 65 years and older | | |
| --- | --- | --- | --- | --- | --- | --- | --- | --- | --- |
| | n | % | Retention ratio | n | % | Retention ratio | n | % | Retention ratio |
| | *Rural (including the on-reserve population)* | | | | | | | | |
| First Nations | 37,465 | 29.1 | 0.96 | 98,225 | 41.4 | 0.89 | 12,665 | 64.6 | 0.82 |
| Inuit | 8,365 | 73.0 | 1.04 | 14,160 | 75.1 | 0.97 | 915 | 78.5 | 0.91 |
| Métis | 1,040 | 3.5 | 0.78 | 4,325 | 5.3 | 0.85 | 905 | 12.2 | 0.83 |
| | *Urban* | | | | | | | | |
| First Nations | 2,555 | 2.7 | 1.31 | 21,055 | 10.4 | 0.62 | 2,740 | 22.4 | 0.49 |
| Inuit | 2,830 | 45.5 | 1.04 | 5,955 | 49.5 | 0.91 | 435 | 63.0 | 0.78 |
| Métis | 365 | 0.5 | 1.18 | 2,840 | 1.5 | 0.59 | 730 | 6.0 | 0.45 |

*Source*: Statistics Canada, 2006 Census of Canada, custom tabulations, calculations by the author.

Geography is also important. Aboriginal people who live in communities in which there is a larger concentration of indigenous speakers "appear to find it easier to retain their language" (Beaujot & Kerr, 2004).

The selection of the age cohorts was based on the nature of the exposure to Aboriginal languages that the individuals are likely to experience. For example, those under the age of 15 are generally exposed to the language in their homes and in school. The second cohort covers the transition from school to the labour market. The final cohort represents the elders of the communities.

Language retention is calculated by dividing the number of people who use the language in the home by the number who declares it as their mother tongue. A ratio that is close to 1 indicates that the likelihood of language retention exists. A ratio substantially below 1 (<0.8) suggests that some degree of language loss will occur. The ratios in these tables are calculated at the aggregate level. Therefore, they may mask conditions that apply for specific language groups. Nevertheless, one can assume that if a language is spoken in the home it is likely that all members of the household are exposed to it, thereby improving the likelihood of retention.

It is difficult to discuss the use or knowledge of Aboriginal languages for the Métis people since they are essentially the product of intermarriage between an Aboriginal person and someone from one of the two majority groups (French and English). They tend to speak either English or French – the result of their heritage. Therefore, they are not included in the analysis presented in this section.

Focusing on the people belonging to the First Nations (North American Indian), the data show that fewer than 1 in 3 children under the age of 15 living on reserves or in rural areas declared an Aboriginal mother tongue. That proportion increases for the older cohorts. Other studies have shown that the situation varies by language group (see Lachapelle & Goldmann, 2011). This is in sharp contrast to the pattern that is observed for those living in urban areas, where the proportions are substantially lower. This finding suggests that the conditions necessary to retain an Aboriginal mother tongue are stronger in rural areas, or conversely one may conclude that language assimilation occurs in urban areas.

Conditions for the Inuit differ substantially from those of the First Nations. As was shown earlier in this chapter, the Inuit tend to live in more homogenous communities in Canada's northern territories. Their language characteristics reflect these differences. Higher proportions of Inuit declare an Aboriginal language (Inuktitut) as their mother tongue in rural areas, regardless of the age cohort. The retention ratios are also close to 1 for all age groups, indicating that the language is often used in the home. Again, we see differences between the Inuit living in rural areas and those living in urban centres. Although the differences are not as dramatic as for the First Nations people, proportionally fewer Inuit living in urban areas declare an Aboriginal mother tongue.[3] For those who do, however, the retention ratio remains high, indicating that they use an Aboriginal language in the home.

## Educational Characteristics of the Aboriginal People

It has been shown in prior research on education for Aboriginal people that their returns to post-secondary education are equal to, or superior to, the other members of the population (White, Maxim, & Gymah, 2003). Furthermore, education is often cited as an important contributor to social and economic change for a society (Côté & Allahar, 2007; Ghosh & Ray, 1991). Therefore, the educational outcome of Aboriginal people will be examined in this section. It should be noted that no attempt is made in this section of the chapter to draw a comparison of the educational attainments between the Aboriginal and non-Aboriginal people since it would serve no productive purpose. It is more meaningful to compare the outcomes for Aboriginal people living in rural and urban areas since isolation from main metropolitan centres appears to result in lower educational attainment (Spence, White, & Maxim, 2007).

The Canadian Census of population includes a number of questions dealing with the educational attainment of respondents. Given that we are concerned with the education that an individual has acquired, the analysis in this section focuses on the highest

---

[3] It should be noted that very few urban areas exist in the Northern territories in Canada.

**Fig. 14.6** Highest level of education achieved by First Nations living in rural (including on-reserve) and urban areas in Canada, 2006 *Source*: 2006 Census of Population of Canada, calculations by the author.

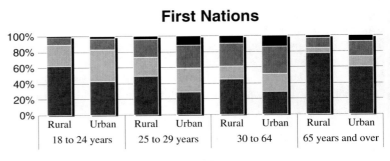

■ No degree, certificate or diploma
■ High school diploma or equivalent only
■ Trades/apprenticeship or other non university
■ University certificate or degree

**Fig. 14.7** Highest level of education achieved by the Inuit living in rural and urban areas in Canada, 2006 *Source*: 2006 Census of Population of Canada, calculations by the author.

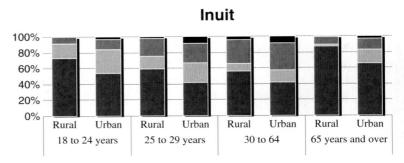

■ No degree, certificate or diploma
■ High school diploma or equivalent only
■ Trades/apprenticeship or other non university
■ University certificate or degree

level achieved.[4] It is generally the case in Canada that most students graduate from high school by the age of 18. Therefore, this analysis will concentrate on the Aboriginal people who are 18 years of age and older. Furthermore, the population is divided into the following four broad age groups that correspond to some of the life-course stages of early and advanced adulthood: post-secondary education (ages 18–24), entry into the full-time labour market (ages 25–29), family formation and progression in the labour market (ages 30–64) and retirement (ages 65 and older). Educational achievement in Figs. 14.6, 14.7, and 14.8 has been summarized into the following four categories: no degree, certificate or diploma (which is the equivalent of less than secondary school); high school completion (with a certificate); non-university post-secondary certificate or qualification; and a university certificate or degree (undergraduate, graduate and postgraduate).

The data show that a substantial proportion of the Aboriginal population has not completed high school. The proportion is more pronounced for those living in rural areas and there are variations between the groups. For instance, over 50% of the First Nations (Fig. 14.6) and Inuit (Fig. 14.7) and about 1/3 of the Métis (Fig. 14.8) living in rural areas do not have a secondary school diploma. This outcome confirms the conclusions drawn by Spence et al. (2007) concerning the impact on educational outcomes for Aboriginal

---

[4] The highest level of education is a derived variable that summarizes the educational qualifications of the respondent (Statistics Canada, 2009).

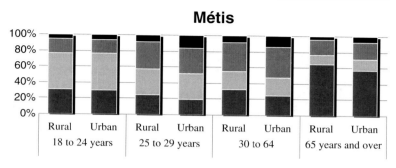

**Fig. 14.8** Highest level of education achieved by the Métis living in rural and urban areas in Canada, 2006 *Source*: Statistics Canada, 2006 Census of Canada, custom tabulations, calculations by the author.

people living in rural communities. Although the opportunities for secondary schooling exist, the fact that so many young Aboriginal people (ages 18–24) do not complete their studies may be a reflection of the employment prospects within their communities. It is interesting and encouraging to note that the secondary school completion rates improve substantially for the 25–29-year old and the 20–64-year old cohorts. This pattern is true across all Aboriginal groups living in rural and urban settings and it may reflect a trend to return to school to obtain a high school diploma.

It was noted earlier that the returns to post-secondary education are strong for the Aboriginal people (White et al., 2003). While the proportion of Aboriginal people obtaining post-secondary qualifications is generally lower in rural areas when compared to those living in urban areas, they are nevertheless substantial. We see that approximately ¼ of the 25–29-year old First Nations and Inuit living in rural areas have either a trades certificate or a university degree. That proportion increases to approximately 1/3 for the 30–64-year old cohort.

Although the people live in rural areas, the post-secondary qualifications were not necessarily obtained in the areas where they live. There are very few post-secondary institutions located in rural areas in Canada. This situation is slowly changing with the institution of branches of universities and colleges in the North and in some of the more remote areas of Canada, and with the development of distance learning programs. It is also important to note that many universities in Canada have Aboriginal studies programs and that an Aboriginal University exists in Saskatchewan.[5]

The results presented in this section of the chapter are a cross-section snap shot based on 2006 Census data. They show an improvement in completion rates over the results cited in other studies conducted with older data (Spence et al., 2007; Walters, White, & Maxim, 2004; White et al., 2003). It is important to continue this analysis with more current data when they become available in order to establish whether or not a fundamental change has occurred in the educational pattern for Aboriginal people in Canada.

## Aboriginal People and the Labour Market

We have seen in the previous section that a rural-urban divide exists in the educational outcomes for Aboriginal people in Canada. We also know from previous research that there is a direct relationship between educational outcomes and labour market success. We will now examine the labour outcomes for the Aboriginal people.

Employment and the labour market encompass a number of dimensions for the Aboriginal people. Some are engaged in traditional activities such as hunting, fishing and the harvesting of natural resources. Others are employed in enterprises that are owned and

---

[5] The First Nations University of Canada has campuses in Regina, Saskatoon and Prince Albert, Saskatchewan. (http://www.firstnationsuniversity.ca/).

**Table 14.3** Labour force activity of the Canadian Aboriginal population by identity and by area of residence, 2006

| | Total | Participation rate (%) | Unemployment[a] rate (%) | Employment rate (%) |
|---|---|---|---|---|
| | | On-reserve | | |
| First Nations | 198,330 | 52 | 24.9 | 39 |
| Inuit | 290 | 64.9 | 24.3 | 47.4 |
| Métis | 3,295 | 62.5 | 19.2 | 50.5 |
| | | Rural | | |
| First Nations | 58,675 | 62.5 | 14.6 | 53.4 |
| Inuit | 19,740 | 59.4 | 23.9 | 45.2 |
| Métis | 85,685 | 66.6 | 12 | 58.7 |
| | | Urban | | |
| First Nations | 216,235 | 64.1 | 13.8 | 55.3 |
| Inuit | 12,745 | 64.2 | 15 | 54.6 |
| Métis | 202,350 | 71.7 | 9.1 | 65.2 |
| Canada | | 66.8 | 6.6 | 62.4 |

[a] The employment and unemployment rates do not sum to 100 since they are calculated with different denominators (see footnote 6).
*Source*: Statistics Canada, 2006 Census of Canada, custom tabulations.

operated by Aboriginal communities (both on and off reserves). Yet others are part of the larger Canadian labour market. The analysis in this section will focus primarily on the latter category – the conventional Canadian labour market.

The integration and assimilation of Aboriginal people in the Canadian labour market has not been studied extensively by social scientists in Canada (Kuhn & Sweetman, 2002; Mueller, 2004). This is due in part to insufficient data and to the different labour market conditions faced by Aboriginal people. What is clear in the limited research conducted so far is that education and contact with the dominant culture are "... predictors of Aboriginal labour market success in Canada". (Kuhn & Sweetman, 2002, 332) There is very little contact with the non-Aboriginal Canadian culture on reserves or in rural areas. Therefore, these areas are "... isolated from the mainstream economy and culture". (Kuhn & Sweetman, 2002, 340).

Table 14.3 shows the labour force participation rate and the employment and unemployment rates[6] for the Aboriginal people and for the total Canadian population in 2006. The rates are shown separately for the on-reserve and rural populations in this table since the data were not available to calculate aggregate rates for the combination of these areas.

The data show that employment rates are at least 10 percentage points lower for the Aboriginal people when compared with the total population of Canada and their unemployment rates are more than double. In fact, the unemployment rate for the First Nations living on reserves is approximately 4 times the national average.

Care must be taken when analyzing these statistics since they likely reflect the fact that employment in rural areas and reserves is largely limited to either traditional activities (that may not be captured in the official statistics on employment) or local industries whereas the Aboriginal people living in urban areas are generally part of the "mainstream" labour market.

Environmental and contextual factors are not the only explanation for this disparity. Education is a direct determinant of success in the labour market. There

---

[6] The participation rate is defined as the ratio of the labour force and the population 15 years of age and older (excluding institutional residents). The employment rate is the number employed expressed as a percentage of the non-institutional population 15 years of age and over. The unemployment rate is the number of unemployed divided by the available labour force, expressed as a percentage (Statistics Canada, 2009).

is a strong positive correlation between labour force participation and levels of educational achievement. Research has shown that the employment prospects for Aboriginal people suffer substantially for those with less than a grade 9 education (Sloane-Seale, Wallace, & Levin, 2000) and, as we saw in the previous section, a substantial proportion of the Aboriginal people living in rural areas have less than a high school education.

## A Global Perspective

Does national context make a difference in the socio-economic and demographic characteristics of the Aboriginal people? Aboriginal populations exist in essentially all regions in the World. The geopolitical boundaries by which we tend to analyze national data are considered by some to be artificial when conducting an analysis of Aboriginal people since they are the result of a colonial process. Nevertheless, most of the socio-economic characteristics of the regions in which Aboriginal people live are shaped and defined along the commonly accepted geopolitical boundaries that we all recognize. The socio-economic and political conditions for the Aboriginal people living in Canada, the United States, Australia, Russia, New Zealand, Mexico, Peru, among others, are a function of the state in which they live. Therefore, it is helpful to complete the analysis by making a brief comparison between the characteristics of the Aboriginal population living in Canada with those of other countries with similar socio-political histories and comparable economies.

The data shown in Table 14.4 are at the National level and no distinction is made between different Aboriginal groups. For instance, the values for the United States are aggregates for all American Indians and Alaska Natives. Similarly, the characteristics for the indigenous population of Australia include the people who declared Aboriginal origins as well those who declared Torres Strait Islander origins.

It is important when presenting comparisons of this nature to inform the reader of the limitations of the analysis since some variations may exist in the specific concepts and definitions used by the respective national statistical offices. For instance, the classifications for the highest level of education are not always comparable. In this particular instance the author used the absence of a non-university or post-secondary certificate as evidence that the individuals did not complete secondary school.

The four nations described in this section share one important historical feature – they are all the product of a British colonial history. The impact of this history is particularly noticeable in the proportions of people who use an Aboriginal language in the home. In general, fewer than one in four Aboriginal people currently speak an Aboriginal language in the home. This demographic fact points to an area of concern for the preservation of Aboriginal languages in the future. It also shows the impact of linguistic assimilation.

The distributions in Table 14.4 also show that the Aboriginal people living in these four countries face similar challenges in the labour market. The unemployment rate for Aboriginal people tends to be higher than for the non-Aboriginal population. The differences are more pronounced in rural areas, reflecting the differences in job opportunities between the rural and urban labour markets – especially for the lower skilled occupations. This outcome reinforces the impact of the lower levels of education for the Aboriginal people. The proportion of Aboriginal people with less than secondary school qualifications ranges from 29% in Australia and the United States to over 40% in Canada.

**Table 14.4** Selected characteristics of the Aboriginal populations living in Canada, Australia, New Zealand and the United States

| Characteristic | Canada | Australia | New Zealand | United States |
|---|---|---|---|---|
| Proportion of the population (%) | 3.3 | 2.3 | 14.6 | 0.9 |
| Proportion of the population living in rural areas (%) | 46.8 | 23.9 | 16.6 | 35.9 |
| Median age of the population (years) | 27.0 | 21.0 | 22.7 | 28.5 |
| Aboriginal language spoken in the home (%) | 16.4 | 12.0 | 23.7 | 28.1 |
| Proportion completing less than high school (%) | 43.9 | 29.0 | 39.9 | 29.1 |
| Unemployment rate (%) | 15 | 16 | 11 | 12 |

*Sources*: Australian Bureau of Statistics, 2010, Statistics New Zealand, 2007, U.S. Census Bureau, 2003 and calculations by the author.

While the characteristics of the Aboriginal populations in Canada, Australia, New Zealand and the United States tend to be similar, we see a very interesting continental pattern in their respective age structures. In all cases, we see that the Aboriginal population is younger than the non-Aboriginal population. However, the data show that the Aboriginal people living in North America are younger than their homologues living in Australia and New Zealand (median age in the low 20s compared to median age in the high 20s). No attempt is made in this chapter to explain the difference, although it would be interesting to explore this phenomenon further to determine whether the pattern observed in Oceania is an indication of demographic assimilation.

## Conclusion

The analysis presented in this chapter has shown that the characteristics of the Aboriginal population living in rural areas in Canada vary substantially by group. These differences appear to be more acute when comparing the rural population with those living in urban areas. Classical theorists would likely interpret these urban-rural variations as important gaps in the welfare of the Aboriginal people. In fact, many of the works cited in this chapter extend this comparison to include an Aboriginal/non-Aboriginal component which serves to accentuate the perceived gap.

Students of rural demography of Aboriginal people in Canada must consider a number of important factors. First, the Aboriginal population of Canada is not homogenous. There are three distinct groups – the First Nations, the Métis and the Inuit – and they tend to inhabit different regions of the country. The Inuit are concentrated in the North, far from urban population centres in the south and major land transportation networks. This shapes their socio-economic and political realities. The majority of First Nations (North American Indians) who are not in urban centres live on Indian reserves. They are largely self-governing (through the local tribal councils) and can be located near major transportation routes or urban population centres. The Métis live in rural communities that are generally located in the southern parts of the Prairie Provinces and in which there is a mixed population. Their economic activity is often integrated with that of the non-Aboriginal population.

The second point to consider is the impact that geography and remoteness have on the population. The provision of social services such as health care and education is more difficult and costly in rural areas. Those communities located in relative proximity to population centres (mostly First Nations communities and Indian Reserves) benefit from the infrastructure that exists to serve the non-Aboriginal population. However, those in more remote areas (the Inuit and some First Nations communities) must migrate to urban centres for health services and to obtain post-secondary qualifications.

Similar arguments may be made for economic opportunities, which leads to the third consideration. The rural economy in Canada is largely resource-based. The major sectors in which employment can be found in rural areas are agriculture, forestry, mining and energy. Large-scale economic activity for the Aboriginal people living in the rural areas, whether through self-employment or through the wage labour market, depends on the non-Aboriginal economy. While some economic opportunities exist in Indian Reserves and in northern communities, there is generally a structural economic dependence on non-traditional employment.

To summarize, classical demographic analyses of Aboriginal people must incorporate the three considerations mentioned above. Furthermore, population flows cannot be measured in traditional ways. The impact of ethnic mobility must be incorporated in all analyses. Finally, the Aboriginal population is experiencing a series of transitions that are accelerating over time. Conditions for the Aboriginal people have improved over the past 25 years. We have observed significant changes in both the size and composition of the population of the Aboriginal groups (Goldmann & Delic, 2010; Guimond, 2009). Research has shown that the socio-economic conditions of the Aboriginal people have improved substantively over this period of time (O'Sullivan & McHardy, 2007). While this research was conducted using data from the 1981 to 2006 Censuses of population, it is reasonable to assume that the trend that was established over 25 years is likely to continue for the foreseeable future.

**Acknowledgements** The author acknowledges the significant contributions to this chapter made by Dr. Eric Guimond of Indian and Northern Affairs Canada and the University of Western Ontario.

# References

Australian Bureau of Statistics. (2010). Population Characteristics, Aboriginal and Torres Strait Islander Australians. 4713.0.

Beaujot, R., & Kerr, D. (2004). *Population change in Canada*. Toronto, ON: Oxford University Press.

Côté, J., & Allahar, A. L. (2007). *Ivory tower blues: A university system in crisis*. Toronto, ON: University of Toronto Press.

Dickason, O. P. (2002). *Canada's first nations: A history of founding peoples from earliest times*. Don Mills: Oxford University Press.

Eschbach, K. (1993). Changing identification among American Indians and Alaska Natives. *Demography, 30*(4), 635–652.

Eschbach, K., Supple, K., & Snipp, C. M. (1998). Changes in racial identification and the educational attainment of American Indians, 1970–1990. *Demography, 35*(1), 35–43.

Ghosh, R., & Ray, D. (1991). *Social change and education in Canada*. Toronto, ON: Harcourt Brace Jovanovich, Canada.

Goldmann, G. (1993). *The aboriginal population and the census*. 120 Years of Information—1871 to 1991, presented at the Conference of the International Union for the Scientific Study of Population (IUSSP), Montreal.

Goldmann, G., & Delic, S. (2010). Ethnic mobility – An historical and contemporary outcome for Aboriginal peoples in Canada: Evidence drawn from past trends and current census data. In F. Trovato & A. Romaniuk (Eds.), *Aboriginal population in transition*. Toronto, ON: University of Toronto Press.

Guimond, E. (1999). *Ethnic mobility and the demographic growth of Canada's Aboriginal populations from 1986 to 1996*. Report on the Demographic Situation in Canada, 1998–1999, directed by A. Bélanger, Statistics Canada, Ottawa: Industry Canada, Catalogue No. 91-209-XPE, 187–200.

Guimond, E. (2009). *L'explosion démographique des populations autochtones du Canada de 1986 à 2001*. Ph.D. thesis, Département de démographie, Université de Montréal.

Indian and Northern Affairs Canada (INAC). (2001). Basic Departmental Data 2000, Ottawa, Information Management Branch, Corporate Information Management Directorate, First Nations and Northern Statistics Section, 76p.

Indian and Northern Affairs Canada (INAC). (2009). *Fact Sheet – Urban Aboriginal population in Canada*. http://www.ainc-inac.gc.ca/ai/ofi/uas/fs/index-eng.asp. Accessed April 2010.

Kuhn, P., & Sweetman, A. (2002). Aboriginals as unwilling immigrants: Contact, assimilation and labour market outcomes. *Journal of Population Economics, 15*(2), 331–355.

Lachapelle, R., & Goldmann, G. (2011). Language and demography. In E. Fong & B. Edmonston (Eds.), *The changing Canadian population*. Montreal: McGill-Queens University Press.

Lee, T. (1990). *Definitions of indigenous peoples in selected countries*. Working Paper Series; 90-4, 29p. Indian and Northern Affairs Canada, Finance and Professional Services, Quantitative Analysis and Socio-Demographic Research.

Mueller, R. E. (2004). The relative earnings position of Canadian Aboriginals in the 1990s. *Canadian Journal of Native Studies, XXIV*(1), 37–63.

Norris, M. J. (1998). Canada's Aboriginal languages. *Canadian Social Trends, 51*(36), 19–27.

O'Sullivan, E., & McHardy, M. (2007). The community well-being index (CWB): Well-being in first nations communities, present, past, and future. In J. P. White, D. Beavon, & N. Spence (Eds.), *Aboriginal well-being: Canada's continuing challenge* (pp. 111–148). Toronto, ON: Thompson Educational Publishing.

Passel, J. S. (1996). The growing American Indian population, 1960–1990: Beyond demography. In G. D. Sandefur, R. R. Rindfuss, & B. Cohen (Eds.), *Changing numbers, changing needs: American Indian demography and public health* (pp. 79–102). Washington, DC: National Academy Press.

Robitaille, N., & Choinière, R. (1987). L'accroissement démographique des groupes autochtones du Canada au XX$^e$ siècle. *Cahiers québécois de démographie, 16*(1), 3–35.

Ross, K. (1996). *Population issues, indigenous Australians, Australian Bureau of Statistics*. 4708.0 – Occasional Paper.

Sloane-Seale, A., Wallace, L., & Levin, B. (2000). Labour market outcomes of students in the University of Manitoba access program. *The Canadian Journal of Native Studies, XX*(2), 347–370.

Spence, N., White, J., & Maxim, P. (2007). Modeling success of first nations students in Canada: Community level perspectives. *Canadian Ethnic Studies, 39*(1–2), 145–167.

Statistics Canada. (1989). *General review of the 1986 census*. Catalogue No. 99-137E. Canada, Ottawa: Department of Supply and Services.

Statistics Canada. (2008). *Aboriginal Peoples in Canada in 2006: Inuit, Métis and First Nations, 2006 Census*. Catalogue No. 97-558-XIE, 53p.

Statistics Canada. (2009). *2006 Census Dictionary*. Catalogue no. 92-566x.

Statistics Canada. (2010). *Aboriginal statistics at a glance*. http://www.statcan.gc.ca/pub/89-645-x/89-645-x2010001-eng.htm. Accessed March 2010.

Statistics New Zealand. (2007). *QuickStats About Maori, Census 2006*.

U.S. Census Bureau. (2003). *2000 Census of Population and Housing, Characteristics of American Indians and Alaska Natives by Tribe and Language: 2000 PHC-5*. Washington, DC: U.S. Census Bureau.

Walters, D., White, J., & Maxim, P. (2004). Does postsecondary education benefit Aboriginal Canadians? An examination of earnings and employment outcomes for recent Aboriginal graduates. *Canadian Public Policy, 30*(3), 283–301.

White, J. P., Maxim, P., & Gymah, S. O. (2003). Labour force activity of women in Canada: A comparative analysis of Aboriginal and non-Aboriginal women. *Canadian Review of Sociology and Anthropology, 40*(4), 391–416.

# Rural Race and Ethnicity

Rogelio Sáenz

## Rural Race and Ethnicity

Throughout much of the last century, rural areas of the United States have been characterized by out-migration, aging populations, and population decline. Furthermore, these places have traditionally had little racial and ethnic heterogeneity. Indeed, persons of color experienced the greatest level of racism, discrimination, and inequality in rural settings in the southern and western portions of the United States. Thus, over the course of several decades in the early to mid 20th century, blacks fled the Jim-Crow South, Mexican Americans ventured out of the southwest away from the segregation and racism rampant in places such as Texas, and Native Americans left reservations in search of better social and economic opportunities in urban areas. Nonetheless, populations of racial and ethnic minorities have continued to inhabit rural areas of the country where they have been clustered in enclaves primarily located in the South, West, and Midwest regions.

Furthermore, over the last several decades global forces involving the restructuring of the meat processing industry have stimulated the movement of Latinos into rural areas of the country that have traditionally not had large Latino populations. As such, many rural communities have been reinvigorated demographically through the movement of Latinos originating from Mexico and Central America. These newcomers have been attracted to rural communities in the South and Midwest by jobs in meatpacking, agriculture, and construction (Kandel and Parrado, 2005; Lichter & Johnson, 2006; see also Chapter 3 in this volume). While these areas are commonly referred to as Latino new destinations, Latinos are increasingly setting roots in these locations (Saenz, 2006). Finally, due to the significant aging of the white population, the Latino population is playing a major role in the changing demography of many rural areas in new destinations as well as in the traditional southwestern region (Johnson & Lichter, 2008).

Despite such changes, there continues to be relatively little information about persons of color in rural areas. The existing literature for the most part has been limited to periodic interest among rural sociologists in rural minorities and more recently in Latino new destination areas. There is a lack of current knowledge about the social and economic characteristics of the major groups of color that inhabit rural areas of the country. This chapter seeks to address this research need. The chapter has two major aims. First, we present a general descriptive overview of the social and economic characteristics of four racial and ethnic groups (blacks, Latinos, Native Americans, and whites) in rural areas. Second, we examine the extent to which the three minority groups face disparities in rural job markets through the multivariate analysis of employment and earnings. The analysis conducted in this chapter is based on data from the 2009 1% American Community Survey (ACS). Before presenting the analysis, we turn to a discussion of the historical context of the existence of persons of color living in rural areas of the country.

R. Sáenz (✉)
College of Public Policy, University of Texas at San Antonio, San Antonio, TX 78207, USA
e-mail: Rogelio.Saenz@utsa.edu

## Historical Overview of Rural-Urban Migration of Rural Racial and Ethnic Groups

Rural areas of the country have historically lagged significantly behind urban areas in socioeconomic status. As the U.S. economy increasingly shifted from an agricultural to a manufacturing economy early in the 20th century, many people migrated out of rural areas to urban ones where manufacturing plants were concentrated. The movement of whites was stimulated greatly by the disproportionate benefits that they received from the G.I. Bill following World War II (Katznelson, 2005). These benefits allowed them to attend and graduate from college and become homeowners in suburban areas of the country. Whites benefitted tremendously from their whiteness as they gained valuable societal resources that permitted them to take advantage of enriched economic opportunities in the post-WWII period. Indeed, it is whites—rather than persons of color—who are the subject of the "lucky few" generation that experienced significant upward mobility and became the parents of the baby boomers (Carlson, 2008).

Blocked from higher education for upward mobility, people of color undertook other routes to escape the major oppression that they faced in rural areas. African Americans exemplify the primary movement out of rural areas. This movement was so significant that it became known as the Great Migration, a social movement spanning from 1915 to 1970 (Fligstein, 1981; Gregory, 2005; Henri, 1975; Johnson & Campbell, 1981; Marks, 1989; Wilkerson, 2010). Blacks making this move sought to escape the horrendous Jim Crow and sharecropping system of the South where their social and economic fate was sealed in the region especially in rural areas. Wilkerson (2010) documents the movement of individuals from Van Vleet, Mississippi to Chicago; Eustis, Florida to New York City; and Monroe, Louisiana to Los Angeles. Langston Hughes memorializes the conditions that forced blacks to leave the South in search of better opportunities elsewhere in his poem titled "The South" which includes the following lines:

> ....That is the South.
> And I, who am black, would love her
> But she spits in my face.
> And I, who am black,
> Would give her many rare gifts
> But she turns her back upon me.
>> So now I seek the North—
>> The cold-faced North,
>> For she, they say,
>> Is a kinder mistress....(Rampersad & Roessel, 1994, p. 27).

By the time that the Great Migration ended, the percentage of blacks outside of the South had risen from 10% in 1910, at the outset of the movement, to 47% by 1970 (Wilkerson, 2010).

Mexican Americans, too, set their sights out of the rural areas of the Southwest, especially from Texas where segregation and Jim Crow-like laws and customs kept them cemented to the bottom of the stratification system (Montejano, 1987). It was in Three Rivers, a rural community in Texas, in 1949 where the body of Felix Longoria, a soldier who died in battle in the Philippines, was denied service in the local mortuary because "whites would not like it" (Carroll, 2003). The movement of Mexican Americans out of Texas began in the early 20th century when they were recruited to work in agriculture, meatpacking plants, railroads, and steel plants in states such as Illinois, Indiana, Kansas, Michigan, Minnesota, Nebraska, Pennsylvania, and Washington (Saenz, 1991). Furthermore, Mexican Americans increasingly moved to urban areas of the Southwest including Dallas, Houston, Los Angeles, and San Antonio in search of better opportunities especially in the manufacturing sector. Nonetheless, there has been a revival of Latinos in rural areas outside of the traditional Southwest region over the last several decades (see below). Thus, the share of Mexican Americans living outside of the Southwest (Arizona, California, Colorado, New Mexico, and Texas) rose from 17% in 1980 to 28% in 2009 (Saenz, 1991; U.S. Census Bureau, 2010).

Native Americans also experienced a significant movement to urban areas beginning in the mid 20th century. At this time, the U.S. government established policies to terminate its special relationship with Native American tribes in an effort to assimilate the population into the mainstream society. The Urban Indian Relocation Program, established in 1952, represented an effort to assist Native Americans in moving from reservations to selected cities with the major processing centers located in Chicago, Denver, Los Angeles, Oakland, Oklahoma City, St. Louis,

San Francisco, San Jose, Seattle, and Tulsa (Snipp, 1989). Upwards of 100,000 Native Americans participated in the program although many others also moved to urban areas during this period without assistance from the program (Margon, 1992; Snipp, 1989). In a short period of time, the number of Native Americans in Chicago rose sharply from 274 in 1940 to 6,575 in 1970 (LaGrand, 2002). Between 1950 and 1970, the percentage of Native Americans in urban areas increased significantly from 13.4% in 1950 to 44.5% in 1970 (Thornton, 1987).

## The New Migration of Latinos to Rural America

Despite the significant urbanization of minority groups, global forces have stimulated the movement of Latinos, originating from Mexico and Central America, into rural regions of the country that have traditionally had few Latinos (Gouveia & Saenz, 2000; Kandel & Parrado, 2005; Stull, Broadway, & Griffith, 1995). Beginning in the late 1970s and early 1980s, the U.S. meatpacking industry experienced major competition on a global scale. In efforts to reduce costs, jobs moved from urban centers, many of these in the Midwest, to rural areas of the Midwest as well as the South. The move cut transportation costs as cattle and poultry did not have to be moved from rural to urban areas and labor costs as unions were relatively scarce in these rural communities (Stull et al., 1995).

The reduced wages for meat processing jobs did not attract locals and many of these communities, especially those in the Midwest, had aging populations since young people moved to urban areas in search of higher education or better economic opportunities. Thus, Latino workers were recruited directly from Mexico or from California and Texas (Cohen, 1998; Stull et al., 1995). In a relatively short period of time, Latino workers made their way into rural communities in the South and Midwest. This movement has transformed rural communities tremendously demographically, economically, and linguistically. Put simply, global forces have linked rural communities in sending communities in Mexico and Central America and receiving communities in rural parts of the South and Midwest (see Zúñiga & Hernández-León, 2006).

Moreover, international policies have also affected the flow of people from rural areas in Mexico to rural areas in the United States. In particular, the North American Free Trade Agreement (NAFTA) has profoundly affected the lives of many rural peasants in Mexico. As U.S. corn entered the Mexican consumer market, small-scale rural Mexican corn growers, the country's major crop, could not compete with U.S. growers. Consequently, the rising migration from Mexico to the United States is partly due to this new segment of migrants from rural areas (Bacon, 2008). In addition, given that the impact of NAFTA has been particularly felt in indigenous areas of the country, such as Chiapas and Yucatan, we have also seen the development of Mexican new-origin areas, places that have traditionally not participated significantly in migration to the United States (Batalova & Terrazas, 2009). Thus, global forces have resulted in the emergence of new-origin and new-destination rural communities in Mexico and the United States, respectively.

## Spatial Inequality and Minority Groups in Rural America

Despite the significant urbanization of African Americans, Native Americans, and Latinos, significant portions of these populations continue to inhabit rural areas. In studying issues of racial inequality and more generally poverty, rural sociologists have recognized the importance of spatial dimensions which create such inequality (Henderson & Tickamyer, 2008; Lichter & Johnson, 2007; Lobao, 2004; Lobao, Hooks, & Tickamyer, 2007; Lobao & Saenz, 2002; Poston et al., 2010; Schafft, Jensen, & Hinrichs, 2009; Slack, 2010). Put simply, space matters when it comes to understanding inequality. Indeed, the geographic settings in which people live set contextual parameters that can enhance or inhibit opportunities for social and economic enhancement.

As the United States became more industrial, rural residence has been associated with more limited opportunities for socioeconomic success. Thus, rural areas lag significantly behind urban areas on a wide variety of social and economic characteristics. Furthermore, research has also demonstrated that location within rural America is important in two respects. In particular, rural areas that are located closer to metropolitan areas and those with scenic amenities tend to have more favorable population growth (Albrecht, 2010).

However, rural residence has historically been particularly punishing for persons of color. Indeed, as we illustrated above, African Americans, Native Americans, and Latinos were long shackled to rural environments where they faced severe levels of racism, segregation, and inequality. Although many persons of color eventually migrated out of rural areas into urban settings in search of better social and economic opportunities, pockets of minority groups persist in much of rural America. The nation's persistently poor counties are predominantly located in rural areas and feature high and immutable rates of impoverishment (Jolliffe, 2004; Saenz, 1997). Thus, we find enduring pockets of poverty among blacks throughout the South, Mexican Americans along the Texas-Mexico border, Native Americans in reservations, as well as whites in Appalachia. These places have been poor for a long period of time. Jolliffe (2004) in his overview of rural poverty highlights the profound impoverishment of minorities in rural settings:

> More than one out of every four nonmetro Hispanics, Blacks, and Native Americans live in poverty. The nonmetro poverty rates in 2002 for non-Hispanic Blacks (33 percent) and Native Americans (35 percent) were more than three times the nonmetro poverty rate for non-Hispanic Whites (11 percent). The rate for Hispanics (27 percent) was more than twice as high. Sixty-eight percent of nonmetro Hispanics who are poor have less than a high school education, compared with 40 percent of nonmetro non-Hispanic Whites who are poor. Fifty-two percent of nonmetro Native Americans who are poor have incomes that are less than half of the poverty line. Poverty rates for non-Hispanic Blacks and Native Americans are more than 10 percentage points higher in nonmetro areas than in metro areas, the largest gap among minority population groups (2).

Jolliffe's (2004) report shows a dismal socioeconomic profile of persons of color in rural areas.

## Rural Inequality and New Latino Immigrants

U.S. employers in many industries have shown a major preference for Latino immigrant labor (Waldinger, 1997; Hyde & Leiter, 2000; Powers, 2005; Saucedo, 2006). They tend to view native-born minority workers, particularly blacks, as undesirable workers because they ascribe to them attributes of laziness and lack of motivation (Wilson, 1996). In contrast, they view Latino immigrant workers as motivated hard workers who do not complain. While, indeed, Latino immigrant workers are hard workers and often do not complain about their work situations, employers exploit them in many ways including paying them very low wages. In particular, employers exploit the vulnerability of Latino immigrant workers, especially in the case of those who lack proper documentation. Because of the lack of U.S. citizenship among many Latino workers, Massey (2007) has referred to Mexicans as the "new blacks." Put simply, U.S. employers in many industries prefer Latino immigrant workers but they do not pay them adequate wages.

Transformations in the U.S. economy and in particular industries have resulted in the conversion of well-paying stable jobs to low-wage jobs with high turnover. Such transformations, for example, have taken place in the meat processing industry. Kandel and Parrado (2005) illustrate the transformation of the meat processing industry as "a formerly urban, unionized, and semi-skilled workforce employed in production plants, supermarkets, and butcher shops in the 1950s was transformed into one with rural, mostly nonunion, and unskilled workers concentrated at the industrial processing end of the meat production chain by the end of the 1980s" (p. 458). The workforce in the meat processing industry changed dramatically between 1980 and 2000, with the share of white workers declining from 74% to 49% and the percentage of Latino workers rising from 9% to 29% (Kandel, 2006). Furthermore, among Latino meat processing workers the share of foreign-born Latinos employed in this industry increased from 50% in 1980 to 82% in 2000 (Kandel, 2006). The presence of Latino immigrant labor has increased substantially in a variety of other industries including forestry (Casanova & McDaniel, 2005; McDaniel & Casanova, 2003), blue crab processing, tobacco, apple harvesting (Griffith, 2006), agriculture (Schlosser, 2004), and janitorial services (Cranford, 2005).

Thus, U.S. employers who rely heavily on Latino immigrant workers pit them against native-born workers (Griffith, 2006; Taylor, 2006; Jordan, 2007). For instance, Casanova and McDaniel (2005) illustrate the lack of rural development in Alabama communities in which the timber service industry went through a significant transformation in its labor force:

> "Timber dependency" has helped maintain racially based social inequities and segmented labor markets, inadequately funded public schools, and inequitable land concentrations that can be traced back to slave-based

agriculture in the pre-Civil war era. The shift to guest workers to fill jobs previously performed by local workers represents a continued marginalization of local labor, and evidence that the linchpin of local economic activity is effectively divorced from the lives of people in rural Alabama (51).

Many Latino workers perform dangerous jobs that place them at risk of injury or, worse, death. Over the period between 1992 and 2001, the fatality rate of Latino workers (the majority Mexican immigrants) rose by 15%, while the fatality rate of non-Latino workers fell by 15% (Hopkins, 2003). The lack of English fluency as well as their desperation for taking any job contribute to the high level of worksite mortality among Latino immigrants (Hopkins, 2003). Hopkins (2003) points out that Latino immigrants:

> ...died, in part, because they took some of the nation's most dangerous, thus hard-to-fill, jobs in construction and factories, government data show. They were often too scared of losing jobs to press for safer working conditions, advocates say. There weren't enough government inspectors to help ensure their safety, and lax penalties failed to discourage safety-law violations. Although lawmakers, regulators and prosecutors are stepping up efforts to reverse the trend, labor advocates worry it may take a major disaster—such as the 1911 Triange Shirtwaist Factory fire that killed 146 immigrants, later spurring workplace reform—before real change is made.

The vulnerability of Latino immigrant workers makes them an ideal labor force for many U.S. employers who prefer them to native-born workers. These workers face exploitation on the job and often toil in dangerous conditions.

In the analysis presented below, we will examine various social and economic dimensions of the three major minority groups in rural areas (blacks, Latinos, and Native Americans) along with whites. We will also assess differences between native- and foreign-born Latinos. Moreover, we will examine variations in employment and earnings across rural racial and ethnic groups in order to assess how Latino immigrants fare relative to other groups.

## Methods

The data analysis consists of descriptive and multivariate analysis. Both of these analyses are based on data derived from the 2009 1% American Community Survey (ACS). In particular, the data for the descriptive analysis were obtained from the Census Bureau's American Community Survey 1-Year Estimates (herein referred to as the 2009 1% aggregate ACS) accessed through the American Factfinder website (U.S. Census Bureau, 2010). Data were obtained for whites, blacks, Native Americans (American Indians and Alaskan Natives), and Latinos living in nonmetropolitan (nonmetro) areas. Unfortunately, the available data do not allow us to disaggregate blacks and Native Americans on the basis of Hispanic and non-Hispanic membership. Thus, the data for blacks and Native Americans include Latinos who identified themselves as belonging to each of these racial groups. Latinos who classified themselves racially as black accounted for 1.1% of all blacks in nonmetro areas while those who identified themselves racially as American Indian or Alaskan Native comprised 7.4% of all Native Americans in nonmetro areas. Data for nonmetropolitan areas were obtained using the Geo Component option in the American Factfinder website.

The descriptive analysis involves the comparison of the four racial and ethnic groups in nonmetro areas on a variety of social and economic dimensions. The four racial and ethnic nonmetro groups are also compared to their respective metropolitan (metro) counterparts on these four dimensions. Furthermore, given the great diversity found in the Latino population on the basis of nativity, the analysis will also highlight differences between native- and foreign-born Latinos on the various dimensions.

The multivariate part of the analysis focuses on the employment and earnings of nonmetro workers across the four racial and ethnic groups. In particular, this analysis will allow us to assess racial and ethnic disparities on the basis of employment and earnings in a multivariate context. Data for this part of the analysis come from the 2009 1% American Community Survey (herein referred to as the 2009 1% individual-level ACS) downloaded from the Integrated Public Use Microdata Series (IPUMS) website (Ruggles et al., 2010).

The first part of the multivariate analysis, based on persons 16 and older in the civilian labor force, uses employment as the dependent variable with the independent variable of interest being racial and ethnic membership. Employment is a dichotomous variable indicating whether the person was employed (value of 1) or unemployed (value of 0) at the time of the survey.

Racial and ethnic membership is measured on the basis of four dummy variables (blacks, Native Americans, native-born Latinos, and foreign-born Latinos), with whites representing the reference category. A series of control variables is included in the analysis: age, education, marital status, and region. The analysis will be conducted with logistic regression given the dichotomous categorization of the dependent variable, employment. The analysis will be conducted separately for males and females.

The second part of the analysis, based on persons who worked and had earnings in 2008, uses the logged form of the wage and salary income with the major independent variable of interest being, again, racial and ethnic membership. The control variables for this part of the analysis include those presented above in addition to usual hours worked per week and weeks worked in 2008. This part of the analysis is conducted with ordinary least squares regression. Again, the analysis is executed separately for males and females.

Note that a portion of the sample in the ACS public-use file does not have information to be able to identify persons as residents of nonmetro or metro areas. Thus, the analysis includes only persons who are uniquely identified as living in nonmetro areas.

## Results

### Descriptive Results

We begin with a discussion of the descriptive results comparing the four racial and ethnic groups on the basis of four sets of dimensions—demographic, language, socioeconomic status, and health.

### Demographic Dimension

The 2009 American Community Survey estimates that there were approximately 39.8 million whites, 4.1 million blacks, 3.5 million Latinos, and 879,000 Native Americans living in nonmetro areas in 2009. Whites comprise the large majority of the nonmetro population accounting for four-fifths of the nation's nonmetro inhabitants, with African Americans constituting about 8%, Latinos 7%, and Native Americans 3% (Fig. 15.1). The nonmetro population is more racially and ethnically homogeneous compared to the metro population, with nonwhites comprising 38% of the metro population compared to 20% of the nonmetro population.

There are major differences in the extent to which the different racial and ethnic groups are located in nonmetro settings. For example, Native Americans are by far the most likely to be living in nonmetro areas with about 45% of the nation's Native American population living in nonmetro places, as do one-fifth of whites. In contrast, blacks (11%) and Latinos (7%) are much less likely to be located in nonmetro areas.

The four groups also vary with respect to the geographic concentration of their nonmetro populations. Figure 15.2 highlights the ten most populous (in absolute numbers) states for the nonmetro populations of each racial and ethnic group. The black nonmetro population is particularly clustered in the South extending from Virginia in the northeastern portion down to Texas in the southwestern portion of the region.

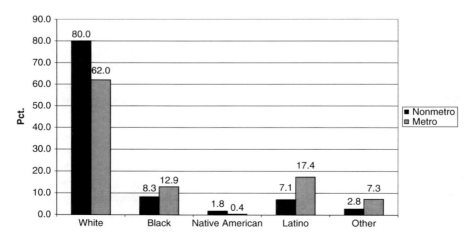

**Fig. 15.1** Racial and ethnic distribution of the nonmetro and metro population, 2009
*Source*: 2009 American community survey 1-year estimates.

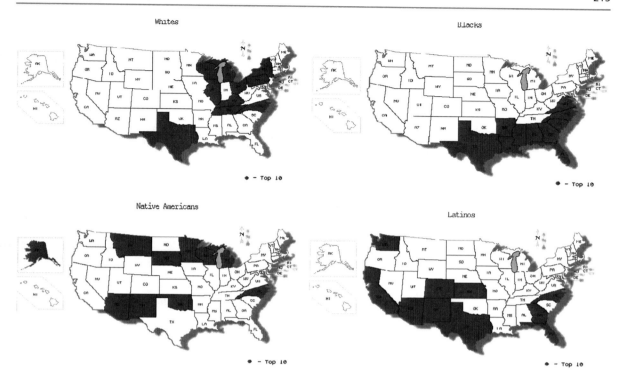

**Fig. 15.2** Top-ten states in terms of nonmetro whites, blacks, Native Americans, and Latinos, 2009
*Source*: U.S. Census Bureau, 2010.

Approximately 83% of the black nonmetro population is located in the top-ten states. The nonmetro populations of the other three racial and ethnic groups are a bit more widely distributed encompassing states in various regions. Nonmetro whites are the least concentrated in the ten most populous states with 42% of all nonmetro whites living in these ten states. In contrast, 71% of Native Americans and 62% of Latinos in nonmetro areas are located in each respective set of top-ten states.

The four nonmetro racial and ethnic groups vary significantly in other demographic characteristics as well. For example, whites are the oldest population with a median age of 42.6, reflecting an aging population with relatively low fertility (Table 15.1). In contrast, Latinos are the youngest nonmetro population with a median age of 25.6, revealing a relatively high level of fertility. Blacks and Native Americans are somewhat older than Latinos, but much younger than whites. Figure 15.3 shows the age distributions across the four racial and ethnic groups. Note that an equal share of whites are less than 15 years of age and 65 years of age or older, suggesting that the nonmetro population is not likely to increase much in the coming decades. The youthfulness of the Latino population is aptly demonstrated as almost one-third are less than 15 years of age. These age patterns suggest that the future labor force of nonmetro areas is likely to be comprised increasingly of Latinos.

There are also variations in the sex distribution of nonmetro residents across the racial and ethnic groups. In particular, if we examine an important component of the labor force—persons 25–44 years of age—there are more males than females across the four groups ranging from about 104 males per 100 females among whites and Native Americans to a sex ratio of 128 among Latinos (Table 15.1). At first glance, it appears that this is the case even among blacks, as there are 115 males per 100 females. However, black males tend to have elevated rates of incarceration and correctional facilities are much more likely to be situated in nonmetro areas than in metro areas. Thus, using data from the 2009 1% individual-level ACS (Ruggles et al., 2010), we find that the sex ratio among nonmetro blacks 25–44 years of age who are not living in group quarters is 82 males per 100 females; among

**Table 15.1** Selected characteristics for nonmetro population by race/ethnicity

| Dimensions and indicators | White | Black | Native American | Latino |
|---|---|---|---|---|
| *Demographic dimension:* | | | | |
| Median age | 42.6 | 33.2 | 29.6 | 25.6 |
| Sex ratio: | | | | |
| Total | 97.3 | 101.6 | 98.8 | 114.8 |
| Age 25–44 | 103.7 | 114.5 | 103.4 | 128.4 |
| Place of birth: | | | | |
| Born in state of residence | 70.0 | 80.7 | 77.5 | 49.3 |
| Native-born other | 29.0 | 17.8 | 20.4 | 19.9 |
| Foreign-born | 1.0 | 1.5 | 2.1 | 30.8 |
| Pct. women 15–50 having birth in past year | 5.5 | 6.6 | 7.7 | 8.8 |
| Pct. unmarried | 33.3 | 73.4 | 64.5 | 38.0 |
| *Language dimension:* | | | | |
| Language patterns of persons 5 and older: | | | | |
| Native-born: | | | | |
| English | 97.8 | 98.3 | 74.0 | 44.4 |
| Bilingual | 1.7 | 1.4 | 20.3 | 44.0 |
| Native language | 0.5 | 0.3 | 5.7 | 11.6 |
| Foreign-born: | | | | |
| English | 55.0 | 44.7 | 15.8 | 5.4 |
| Bilingual | 29.9 | 32.5 | 17.4 | 25.1 |
| Native language | 15.1 | 22.8 | 66.8 | 69.5 |
| *Socioeconomic dimension:* | | | | |
| Pct. of persons 25 and older high school graduates | 85.8 | 71.1 | 75.4 | 56.0 |
| Pct. of persons 25 and older college graduates | 18.8 | 8.8 | 9.5 | 7.6 |
| Percent unemployed: | | | | |
| Total | 8.8 | 17.7 | 17.2 | 12.3 |
| Male | 10.0 | 20.9 | 20.6 | 11.8 |
| Female | 7.5 | 14.9 | 13.8 | 13.0 |
| Occupational distribution: | | | | |
| Males: | | | | |
| Professional, management, and related occups. | 26.5 | 12.4 | 19.3 | 11.0 |
| Service occupations | 12.5 | 21.4 | 22.1 | 18.1 |
| Sales and office occupations | 14.6 | 12.0 | 11.0 | 9.5 |
| Farming, fishing, and forestry occupations | 2.2 | 2.4 | 3.3 | 11.1 |
| Construction, extraction, maintenance, and repair occups. | 20.8 | 14.3 | 24.3 | 23.1 |
| Production, transportation, and material moving occups. | 23.4 | 37.5 | 20.0 | 27.2 |

**Table 15.1** (continued)

| Dimensions and indicators | White | Black | Native American | Latino |
|---|---|---|---|---|
| Occupational distribution: | | | | |
| Females: | | | | |
| Professional, management, and related occups. | 35.5 | 25.0 | 31.2 | 21.3 |
| Service occupations | 22.3 | 34.1 | 31.0 | 34.6 |
| Sales and office occupations | 34.0 | 25.5 | 28.4 | 27.2 |
| Farming, fishing, and forestry occupations | 0.4 | 0.4 | 0.7 | 2.9 |
| Construction, extraction, maintenance, and repair occups. | 0.7 | 0.7 | 1.1 | 0.6 |
| Production, transportation, and material moving occups. | 7.1 | 14.3 | 7.6 | 13.4 |
| Median family income | 52,350 | 28,005 | 33,672 | 34,792 |
| Percent families in poverty: | | | | |
| All families | 9.9 | 31.5 | 28.0 | 26.1 |
| *Health dimension:* | | | | |
| Percent with a disability: | | | | |
| 0–17 | 4.8 | 5.2 | 5.9 | 4.2 |
| 18–64 | 13.7 | 18.3 | 18.4 | 10.5 |
| 65 and Older | 39.6 | 51.1 | 54.9 | 47.0 |
| Pct. lacking health insurance: | | | | |
| Total | 13.4 | 20.6 | 32.7 | 32.2 |
| 0–17 | 7.9 | 8.8 | 23.5 | 17.9 |
| 18–64 | 19.0 | 29.5 | 41.7 | 45.1 |
| 65 and older | 0.3 | 0.7 | 2.7 | 3.0 |

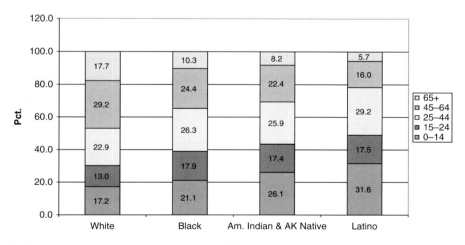

**Fig. 15.3** Age distribution of nonmetro population by race/ethnicity
*Source*: 2009 American community survey 1-year estimates.

the nonmetro black population of the same age group living in group quarters the sex ratio is 655 males per 100 females. The higher presence of males compared to females among whites, Native Americans, and Latinos reflects the greater relative presence of jobs that tend to be filled by males (e.g., agriculture, manufacturing, mining, etc.) in nonmetro areas compared to metro areas. Indeed, overall across racial and ethnic groups, sex ratios are lower in metro areas. In the case of blacks, the disproportionate presence of females in nonmetro areas might reflect the relatively high mortality and incarceration rates among black males.

The four groups differ noticeably also on the basis of their place of birth. African Americans (80.7%) and Native Americans (77.5%) in nonmetro areas are the most likely to have been born in the same state where they are residing at the time of the survey (Table 15.1). Whites are the most likely to have migrated to their state of residence from another U.S. state (29.0%), while Latinos are the most likely to be foreign-born (30.8%). Overall, metro residents across the four racial and ethnic groups are less likely to have been born in their current state of residence compared to nonmetro residents.

There are also differences across the four racial and ethnic groups on the basis of the percentage of women 15–50 years of age who gave birth in the past year. Latina women (8.8%) were the most likely to have given birth in the previous year, while white women (5.5%) were the least likely to have had a baby at that time (Table 15.1). However, there are significant differences across groups with respect to the percentage of such women who gave birth within the past year who are currently not married. Nearly three-fourths of black women and close to two-thirds of Native American women who had a baby in the past year are not currently married; a significant portion of Latina (38.0%) and white (33.3%) women who gave birth in the past year are not married as well. In general, nonmetro women who gave birth in the last year are more likely than their metro counterparts to be currently unmarried.

## Language Dimension

The ACS asked persons 5 years of age and older to indicate the language that they spoke at home and, for those who did not speak English at home, their ability to speak English. The responses were used to construct three categories: English speakers (those persons who speak English at home); bilingual speakers (those who speak a language other than English at home and who speak English "very well"); and non-English language speakers (those who speak a language besides English at home and who do not speak English "very well"). Note that while the language patterns are broken down by nativity, the data for the foreign-born are most appropriate for Latinos due to the very small number of non-Latinos who are foreign-born. White and African Americans in nonmetro areas are almost exclusively English speakers (Table 15.1). While Native Americans are largely English speakers, one fifth of the native-born are bilingual speakers. Finally, while an equal share of native-born Latinos are English speakers (44.4%) or bilingual speakers (44.0%), the large majority of foreign-born Latinos are non-English speakers (69.5%) with an additional one-fourth being bilingual speakers. These language patterns reflect the significant presence of foreign-born persons among Latinos. Overall, there are relatively minor differences in the language patterns of nonmetro and metro Latinos, although among the native-born those in nonmetro areas are more likely to be English speakers (44.4% versus 37.5% among those in metro areas).

## Socioeconomic Status Dimension

There are fairly consistent patterns related to the percentage of persons 25 and older who have completed a high school degree or a bachelor's degree. Whites have the highest levels of educational attainment followed by Native Americans and blacks (Table 15.1). Latinos have the lowest levels of educational attainment. Whites are twice as likely to have completed a bachelor's degree compared to the three minority groups. In general, females have higher rates of educational attainment compared to males across racial and ethnic groups in nonmetro areas. However, nonmetro persons, regardless of race and ethnicity, lag significantly behind their metro counterparts with respect to educational attainment. For instance, whites 25 and older in metro areas are almost twice as likely to have a bachelor's degree compared to their white counterparts in nonmetro areas, with similar gap magnitudes also apparent among blacks.

The current economic crisis has had a major impact on the economic standing of wide swaths of the country. Among the nonmetro civilian labor force, all racial and ethnic groups across both sexes had double-digit unemployment rates in 2009, the exception being white females with an unemployment rate of 7.5% (Table 15.1). In fact, across each racial and ethnic group except among Latinos, females have lower unemployment rates than males. Furthermore, while Latino males (11.8%) have an unemployment rate that is somewhat higher than that of white males (10.0%), the unemployment rates of black and Native American males are twice as high as those of white males. Similarly, nonwhite females are approximately twice as likely as white females to be without a job. Overall, nonmetro residents have higher unemployment rates compared to their metro counterparts.

There are significant differences in the occupations of whites and minorities across gender groups. For example, regardless of sex group, whites are more likely than minorities to be employed in professional, management, and related occupations and in sales and office occupations (Table 15.1). In contrast, minorities are more likely to be working in service occupations and in farming, fishing, and forestry occupations. Among males, Latinos exhibit high levels of work in farming, fishing, and forestry occupations; Native Americans in construction, extraction, maintenance, and repair occupations; and African Americans in production, transportation, and material moving occupations. In general, metro male and female workers are more likely to be employed in professional, management, and related occupations compared to their nonmetro counterparts, while metro males are also more likely to be working in sales and office occupations in comparison to nonmetro males.

There are significant gaps in the median incomes of white and minority families. Compared to the median income of white families, the median income of black families is only 53% as high, while the income of Native American and Latino families is only about 65% as high (Table 15.1). Across all racial and ethnic groups, median family incomes are higher in metro areas than in nonmetro areas, with the gap being the widest among white families (the median income of white families in nonmetro areas is 20% lower than that of white families in metro areas) and the smallest among Latino families (where the median income of nonmetro families is only 3% lower than that of metro families).

Similarly, minority families are much more likely to be in poverty compared to white families in nonmetro areas. While 10% of white families are impoverished, 32% of black families are poor as are 28% of Native American families and 26% of Latino families (Table 15.1). The highest levels of poverty are found among families with a female householder without a husband present and with children: blacks (58%), Latinos (56%), Native Americans (53%), and whites (43%). Across all racial and ethnic groups, nonmetro families are more likely to be in poverty compared to their metro counterparts.

## Health Dimension

The ACS has limited information to assess the health conditions of the population. The only measures involve whether or not a person has a variety of disabilities. The prevalence of disability increases with age as can be seen in Table 15.1. Across the three age categories, Native Americans and blacks consistently have the highest rates of disability. However, Latinos actually have lower rates of disability compared to whites in the 0–17 and 18–64 age categories. Nevertheless, there is a disability crossover at the oldest age group in which Latinos are much more likely to be disabled compared to whites. These findings to a certain extent reflect the epidemiological paradox in which Latinos—especially Mexican immigrants—despite having low socioeconomic standing have low levels of mortality and high life expectancy (Palloni & Arias, 2004). In the case of the disability patterns observed here, it is likely that foreign-born Latinos are selected on the basis of health well-being from their countries of origin with the result being that the overall Latino population has relatively low levels of disability. It is likely that among Latinos, especially the foreign-born, disabilities arise in older ages due to the wear-and-tear on the body associated with the physically demanding jobs that Latinos perform. Across racial and ethnic groups, nonmetro residents have a higher prevalence of disabilities compared to their metro counterparts.

There are significant differences across whites and minority groups on the basis of the lack of health insurance. Overall, approximately one-third of Native Americans and Latinos lack any health insurance, as do about one-fifth of African Americans. In contrast, about one-seventh of whites do not have insurance. These patterns hold across the 0–17 and 18–64 age groups. The high prevalence of the lack of insurance reflects the kinds of jobs that the poor especially the foreign-born (particularly, unauthorized workers) perform, jobs that offer few employment benefits. Across all racial and ethnic groups, persons living in nonmetro areas are more likely to lack health insurance compared to their counterparts living in metro areas.

The descriptive analysis examining the four dimensions of interest revealed important differences across the four racial and ethnic groups. Among the three minority groups, there tends to be greater variability across some of the indicators, particularly in the socioeconomic dimension. Thus, compared to blacks and Native Americans, Latinos tend to do better in the areas of unemployment, income, and poverty, but relatively worse in the areas of education and occupational attainment. It is likely that these fluctuations reflect the diversity that exists within the group with nonmetro Latinos being almost evenly split between U.S.- and foreign-born individuals. We next examine the nonmetro Latino population in more depth paying particular attention to nativity differences.

## The Special Case of Latinos: Nativity-Status Differences

We use microdata from the 2009 1% individual-level ACS (Ruggles et al., 2010) to examine the extent to which native- and foreign-born Latinos in nonmetro areas differ on the various dimensions of interest. Compared to the native-born Latinos, foreign-born Latinos are somewhat more likely to be Mexican or Central American. The foreign-born are also less likely to live in the five southwestern states (Arizona, California, Colorado, New Mexico, and Texas) where Mexicans have been clustered, but are more likely to live in the South, consistent with the observation that foreign-born Latinos are more likely to move to new destination areas compared to their native-born counterparts. Furthermore, in accordance with patterns among immigrants, foreign-born Latinos are much more likely to have a greater presence of males (sex ratio of 145 among the population 25–44 years of age) compared to the native-born (sex ratio of 116). In addition, foreign-born Latinas were somewhat more likely (11%) to have given birth in the past year compared to native-born Latinas (8%).

There are also significant differences between native- and foreign-born Latinos in terms of socioeconomic status. Indeed, in many ways, native-born Latinos are more similar socioeconomically to African Americans and Native Americans than they are to foreign-born Latinos. For example, native-born Latinos are almost twice as likely as foreign-born Latinos to have completed high school or a four-year college degree. In addition, native-born individuals tend to work in certain occupations that tend to have higher status (e.g., managerial, professional, and related occupations; service occupations; and sales and office occupations) compared to foreign-born persons. The native-born also tend to have higher income levels, lower levels of poverty, and lower rates of noninsurance compared to their foreign-born counterparts.

However, foreign-born Latinos tend to fare better than native-born Latinos in two areas. First, the foreign-born as a whole—and males in particular—are less likely to be unemployed compared to native-born Latinos. Second, foreign-born Latinos are less likely than native-born Latinos to have a disability, consistent with the notion that there is health selectivity among immigrants in the country of origin.

Having provided a detailed descriptive overview of the four major racial and ethnic groups in nonmetro areas across the four dimensions of interest, we now turn to the multivariate analysis to assess the degree to which racial and ethnic disparities persist in the areas of employment and earnings after taking into account appropriate demographic and socioeconomic differences.

## Multivariate Analysis of Employment

We first use logistic regression to examine the relationship between racial and ethnic group membership and employment in nonmetro areas taking into account relevant control variables. The results for nonmetro males and females are shown in the first two columns in Table 15.2. For the most part, minority groups are less likely to be employed compared to whites even after taking into account age, educational attainment, marital status, and region. Among males and females, blacks and Native Americans are especially less likely than whites to have a job. However, the one difference concerns foreign-born Latino males, who are actually 33% more likely than white males to be employed.

**Table 15.2** Odds ratios based on logistic regressional analysis examining the relationship between selected variables and employment among persons in the civilian labor force

| Selected variables | Nonmetro | | Metro | |
|---|---|---|---|---|
| | Males | Females | Males | Females |
| Black | 0.542** | 0.639** | 0.569** | 0.593** |
| Native American | 0.436** | 0.585** | 0.624** | 0.742** |
| Native-born Latino | 0.802** | 0.765** | 0.805** | 0.804** |
| Foreign-born Latino | 1.330** | 0.784** | 1.219** | 0.766** |
| [Reference category = White] | | | | |
| Age 25–34 | 1.345** | 1.342** | 1.576** | 1.512** |
| Age 35–44 | 1.551** | 1.790** | 1.726** | 1.765** |
| Age 45–54 | 1.638** | 2.163** | 1.584** | 2.001** |
| Age 55–64 | 1.607** | 2.371** | 1.447** | 2.214** |
| Age 65 and Older | 2.160** | 3.890** | 1.632** | 2.443** |
| [Reference category = 16–24] | | | | |
| Some High School | 0.789** | 1.079 | 0.824** | 0.869** |
| High School Graduate | 1.244** | 1.832** | 1.356** | 1.507** |
| Some College | 1.855** | 2.775** | 1.971** | 2.159** |
| College Graduate | 3.372** | 4.771** | 3.055** | 3.363** |
| [Reference category = 0–8 years] | | | | |
| Married | 2.342** | 1.490** | 2.083** | 1.353** |
| [Reference category = not married] | | | | |
| Southwest (AZ, CA, CO, NM, TX) | 1.067 | 1.152** | 0.943** | 0.958** |
| Northeast | 1.008 | 1.320** | 0.966* | 1.018 |
| Midwest | 0.975 | 1.143** | 0.848** | 0.956** |
| West | 0.869** | 1.134** | 0.872** | 0.955 |
| [Reference category = South] | | | | |
| Chi-square likelihood ratio | 7,383.7** | 4,722.0** | 26,614.0** | 17,240.90** |
| df | 18 | 18 | 18 | 18 |
| N | 139,346 | 125,925 | 546,324 | 505,391 |

\* Statistically significant at the 0.05 level.
\*\* Statistically significant at the 0.01 level.
*Source*: Ruggles et al. (2010).

Foreign-born (female) Latinas do not have such an employment advantage. These findings echo the patterns observed earlier in the descriptive analysis.

The control variables are related to employment in the expected directions. For example, the probability of employment increases with age, level of education, and being married. Regional differences are stronger in the case of females compared to males, with women being more likely to be employed if they are living outside of the South.

The results for metro areas are consistent with the patterns observed for nonmetro areas. In particular, while all nonwhite groups are significantly less likely to be employed compared to whites, foreign-born Latino males represent the exception. In this case, foreign-born Latino males are 22% more likely than white males to hold a job.

**Table 15.3** Results from the ordinary least squares multiple regression examining the relationship between selected variables and the log earnings among workers

| Selected variables | Nonmetro | | Metro | |
|---|---|---|---|---|
| | Males | Females | Males | Females |
| Intercept | 6.273** | 5.814** | 6.177** | 5.707** |
| Black | −0.184** | −0.090** | −0.179** | −0.045** |
| Native American | −0.054** | −0.009 | −0.126** | −0.097** |
| Native-born Latino | −0.087** | −0.030** | −0.070** | −0.033** |
| Foreign-born Latino | −0.127** | −0.059** | −0.189** | −0.173** |
| [Reference category = White] | | | | |
| Age 25–34 | 0.435** | 0.316** | 0.428** | 0.378** |
| Age 35–44 | 0.593** | 0.437** | 0.661** | 0.541** |
| Age 45–54 | 0.650** | 0.493** | 0.738** | 0.589** |
| Age 55–64 | 0.622** | 0.493** | 0.698** | 0.602** |
| Age 65 and Older | 0.302** | 0.341** | 0.477** | 0.467** |
| [Reference category = 16–24] | | | | |
| Some high school | 0.029* | 0.015 | 0.031** | 0.057** |
| High school graduate | 0.234** | 0.185** | 0.228** | 0.265** |
| Some college | 0.333** | 0.359** | 0.360** | 0.428** |
| College graduate | 0.595** | 0.666** | 0.753** | 0.776** |
| [Reference category = 0–8 years] | | | | |
| Worked 14–26 weeks | 0.947** | 0.938** | 0.928** | 0.967** |
| Worked 27–39 weeks | 1.420** | 1.431** | 1.403** | 1.427** |
| Worked 40–47 weeks | 1.768** | 1.744** | 1.745** | 1.778** |
| Worked 48–49 weeks | 1.922** | 1.850** | 1.919** | 1.900** |
| Worked 50–52 weeks | 2.039** | 2.023** | 2.062** | 2.072** |
| [Reference category = worked 1–13 weeks] | | | | |
| Usual hours worked per week | 0.027** | 0.038** | 0.031** | 0.040** |
| Married | 0.224** | 0.077** | 0.223** | 0.058** |
| [Reference category = not married] | | | | |
| Southwest (AZ, CA, CO, NM, TX) | 0.017* | −0.007 | 0.077** | 0.079** |
| Northeast | 0.028** | 0.064** | 0.099** | 0.117** |
| Midwest | −0.033** | −0.014** | −0.012** | −0.010** |
| West | 0.040** | 0.040** | 0.046** | 0.045** |
| [Reference category = south] | | | | |
| Adjusted $R$-square | 0.660 | 0.707 | 0.686 | 0.712 |
| N | 132,577 | 125,943 | 525,124 | 498,859 |

* Statistically significant at the 0.05 level.
** Statistically significant at the 0.01 level.
*Source*: Ruggles et al. (2010).

These results provide support for the notion that inequality continues to be a fact of life in obtaining employment among minority groups, although this pattern is equally true for nonmetro and metro areas. However, the advantageous position of foreign-born Latinos presents an interesting aberration to the general pattern. We now turn to the examination of earnings.

## Multivariate Analysis of Earnings

For this part of the analysis, we use OLS multiple regression to examine the association between racial and ethnic group membership and logged earnings in 2009. We first examine the results for nonmetro workers (Table 15.3, first two columns). The results indicate that for the most part minority workers have significantly lower earnings compared to white workers even after controlling for age, education, weeks worked, usual hours worked per week, marital status, and region. Black men and women are especially disadvantaged in their earnings, as is the case with foreign-born Latino men. The one exception to the general pattern concerns Native American women whose earnings do not differ significantly from those of white women.

The control variables are related to the logged earnings in the expected directions. For example, earnings tend to increase with age, education, weeks worked, usual hours worked per week, being married, and generally living outside of the South, although Midwest residence is associated with lower wages.

As was the case with earnings, the results for metro workers generally mirror the results based on nonmetro workers. All minority groups have significantly lower wages than white workers regardless of sex. The earnings of black men, Native American men, and foreign-born Latino men and women are especially low in metro areas.

The findings examining the relationship between racial and ethnic group membership and earnings provide additional support for the persistence of racial and ethnic disparities in nonmetro areas. However, as is the case in the analysis of employment, such inequality is not limited to nonmetro areas but appears to be even stronger in the case of metro areas at least with respect to earnings.

## Conclusion

This chapter has sought to provide a wide overview of rural (nonmetro) racial and ethnic groups in relation to demographic, language, socioeconomic status, and health dimensions. The results show major differences across groups with whites faring much better socially and economically compared to minority groups. It was also shown that there is a significant amount of diversity within the Latino population revolving around nativity status. Multivariate analysis examining the relationship between racial and ethnic group membership and employment and earnings demonstrated the persistence of racial and ethnic disparities in nonmetro as well as metro settings. The case of foreign-born Latino men is particularly interesting when looking at employment, for this group exhibits high levels of employment, even surpassing those of white men in both nonmetro and metro areas.

The findings call attention to the attractiveness of Latino immigrants to U.S. employers. Latino immigrants tend to be preferred to native-born minorities because they are perceived to be hard workers who do not complain. Moreover, the wages that are paid to Latino immigrants, particularly those that are unauthorized workers, are very low. Employers, then, pit Latino immigrants against native-born minorities which tends to create animosities between workers with limited human capital. In order to avoid the exploitation of Latino immigrants, to allow them to be rewarded fairly, and to participate fully as members of our society, it is essential that immigration reform policies be established that create paths for citizenship for undocumented workers who are already here in the United States.

Our results demonstrate that nonmetro minorities fare worse than metro minorities on a wide variety of socioeconomic measures. Indeed, rural minorities—and rural whites as well for that matter—have lower levels of education, lower levels of income, higher unemployment rates, higher levels of the lack of health insurance, and higher rates of disability. Rural development policies need to be established to decrease the disparities between rural and urban communities and their residents. Given the youthfulness of rural minority populations, especially in the case of Latinos, rural community leaders also need to establish programs and policies to better integrate persons of color in their communities and to make sure that minorities succeed in the educational institution. Indeed, the future of rural communities will increasingly depend on the fortunes of today's minority youth.

## References

Albrecht, D. E. (2010). Nonmetropolitan population trends: Twenty-first century updates. *Journal of Rural Social Sciences, 25*(1), 1–21.

Bacon, D. (2008). *Illegal people: How globalization creates migration and criminalizes immigrants*. Boston: Beacon Press.

Batalova, J., & Terrazas, A. (2009). *Frequently requested statistics on immigrants and immigration in the United States*. Washington, DC: Migration Policy Institute. Retrieved February 21, 2011, http://www.migrationinformation.org/feature/display.cfm?ID=747

Carlson, E. (2008). *The lucky few: Between the greatest generation and the Baby Boom*. New York: Springer.

Carroll, P. J. (2003). *Felix Longoria's wake: Bereavement, racism, and the rise of Mexican American activism*. Austin, TX: University of Texas Press.

Casanova, V., & McDaniel, J. (2005). "No sobra y no falta": Recruitment networks and guest workers in southeastern U.S. forest industries. *Urban Anthropology and Studies of Cultural Systems and World Economic Development, 34*(1), 45–84.

Cohen, L. (1998, October 15). Free ride: With help from INS, U.S. meatpacker taps Mexican work force. *Wall Street Journal*, A1.

Cranford, C. (2005). Networks of exploitation: Immigrant labor and the restructuring of the Los Angeles janitorial industry. *Social Problems, 52*(3), 379–397.

Fligstein, N. (1981). *Going North: Migration of blacks and whites from the South, 1900–1950*. New York: Academic.

Gouveia, L., & Saenz, R. (2000). Global forces and Latino population growth in the Midwest: A regional and subregional analysis. *Great Plains Research, 10*(Fall), 305–328.

Gregory, J. N. (2005). *The southern Diaspora: How the great migration of African American and White Southerners transformed America*. Chapel Hill, NC: University of North Carolina Press.

Griffith, D. (2006). *American guestworkers: Jamaicans and Mexicans in the U.S. labor market*. University Park, PA: Pennsylvania State University Press.

Henderson, D. A., & Tickamyer, A. R. (2008). Lost in Appalachia: The unexpected impact of welfare reform on older women in rural communities. *Journal of Sociology and Social Welfare, 35*(3), 153–171.

Henri, F. (1975). *African American migration: Movement North, 1900–1920* (1st ed.). Garden City, NJ: Anchor Press.

Hopkins, J. (2003). Fatality rates increase for Hispanic workers. *USA Today*, March 13. www.usatoday.com/money/workplace/2003-03-12-hispanic-workers_x.htm. Accessed 21 February 2011.

Hyde, K., & Leiter, J. (2000). Overcoming ethnic intolerance. *The Journal of Common Sense, 5*(4), 14–19.

Johnson, D., & Campbell, R. R. (1981). *Black migration in America: A social demographic history*. Durham, NC: Duke University Press.

Johnson, K. M., & Lichter, D. T. (2008). Natural increase: A new source of population growth in emerging Hispanic destinations in the United States. *Population and Development Review, 34*(2), 327–346.

Jolliffe, D. (2004). *Rural poverty at a glance*. Rural Development Research Report No. 100. Washington, DC: United States Department of Agriculture, Economic Research Service.

Jordan, M. (2007). Blacks vs. Latinos at work. In P. S. Rothenberg (Ed.), *Race, class, and gender in the United States* (7th ed., pp. 277–279). New York: Worth Publishers.

Kandel, W. (2006). Meat-processing firms attract Hispanic workers to rural America: Hispanics increasingly meet labor demand arising from industry restructuring. Amber Waves. Washington, DC: U.S. Department of Agriculture. www.ers.usda.gov/AmberWaves/June06/Features/MeatProcessing.htm. Accessed 21 February 2011.

Kandel, W., & Parrado, E. (2005). Restructuring of the U.S. meat processing industry and new Hispanic migrant destinations. *Population and Development Review, 31*(3), 447–471.

Katznelson, I. (2005). *When affirmative action was white: An untold history of racial inequality in twentieth-century America*. New York: W.W. Norton & Company.

LaGrand, J. B. (2002). *Indian metropolis: Native Americans in Chicago, 1945–75*. Urbana, IL: University of Illinois Press.

Lichter, D. T., & Johnson, K. M. (2006). Emerging rural settlement patterns and the geographic redistribution of America's new immigrants. *Rural Sociology, 71*(1), 109–131.

Lichter, D. T., & Johnson, K. M. (2007). The changing spatial concentration of America's rural poor population. *Rural Sociology, 72*(3), 331–358.

Lobao, L. (2004). Continuity and change in place stratification: Spatial inequality and middle-range territorial units. *Rural Sociology, 69*(1), 1–30.

Lobao, L., Hooks, G., & Tickamyer, A. R. (Eds.). (2007). *The sociology of spatial inequality*. Albany, NY: State University of New York Press.

Lobao, L., & Saenz, R. (2002). Spatial inequality and diversity as an emerging research tradition. *Rural Sociology, 67*(4), 497–511.

Margon, A. (1992). Indians and immigrants: A comparison of groups new to the city. In R. L. Nichols (Ed.), *The American Indian: Past and present* (4th ed., pp. 259–267). New York: McGraw-Hill.

Marks, C. (1989). *Farewell—we're good and gone: The Great Black migration*. Bloomington, IN: Indiana University Press.

Massey, D. S. (2007). *Categorically unequal: The American stratification system*. New York: Russell Sage.

McDaniel, J., & Casanova, V. (2003). Pines in lines: Tree planting, H2-B guest workers, and rural poverty in Alabama. *Southern Rural Sociology, 19*(1), 73–96.

Montejano, D. (1987). *Anglos and Mexicans in the making of Texas, 1836–1986*. Austin, TX: University of Texas Press.

Palloni, A., & Arias, E. (2004). Paradox lost: Explaining the Hispanic adult mortality advantage. *Demography, 41*(3), 385–415.

Poston, D. L., Jr., Singelmann, J., Siordia, C., Slack, T., Robertson, B. A., Saenz, R., et al. (2010). Spatial context and poverty: Area-level effects and micro-level effects of household poverty in the Texas borderland and lower Mississippi Delta: United States, 2006. *Applied Spatial Analysis and Policy, 3*, 139–162.

Powers, R. S. (2005). Working it out in North Carolina: Employers and Hispanic/Latino immigrants. *Sociation Today, 3*(2). Available online at http://www.ncsociology.org/sociationtoday/v32/powers.htm. Accessed 21 February 2011.

Rampersad, A., & Roessel, D. (Eds.). (1994). *The collected poems of Langston Hughes*. New York: Vintage Classics.

Ruggles, S., Alexander, J. T., Genadek, K., Goeken, R., Schroeder, M. B., & Sobek, M. (2010). *Integrated public use microdata series: Version 5.0 [Machine-readable database]*. Minneapolis, MN: University of Minnesota, 2010. Retrieved December 20, 2010, from http://usa.ipums.org/usa/index.shtml

Saenz, R. (1991). Interregional migration patterns of Chicanos: The core, periphery, and frontier. *Social Science Quarterly, 72*(1), 135–148.

Saenz, R. (1997). Ethnic concentration and Chicano poverty: A comparative approach. *Social Science Research, 26*, 205–228.

Saenz, R. (2006). Latino births increase in nontraditional destination states. *Population Reference Bureau*. http://www.prb.org/Articles/2006/LatinoBirthsIncreaseinNontraditionalDestinationStates.aspx. Accessed 23 December 2010.

Saucedo, L. M. (2006). The employer preference for the subservient worker and the making of the brown collar workplace. *Ohio State Law Journal, 67*(5), 961–1022.

Schafft, K. A., Jensen, E. B., & Hinrichs, C. C. (2009). Food deserts and overweight schoolchildren: Evidence from Pennsylvania. *Rural Sociology, 74*(2), 153–177.

Schlosser, E. (2004). *Reefer madness: Sex, drugs, and cheap labor in the American black market*. New York: Houghton Mifflin.

Slack, T. (2010). Working poverty across the metro-nonmetro divide: A quarter century in perspective, 1979–2003. *Rural Sociology, 75*(3), 363–387.

Snipp, C. M. (1989). *American Indians: The first of this land*. New York: Russell Sage.

Stull, D. D., Broadway, M. J., & Griffith, D. (Eds.). (1995). *Any way you cut it: Meat processing and small-town America*. Lawrence: University Press of Kansas.

Taylor, K.-Y. (2006). "Life ain't been no crystal stair": Blacks, Latinos and immigrant civil rights. *International Socialist Review, 48*(July–August). Available online at http://www.isreview.org/issues/48/blackslatinos.shtml. Accessed 22 February 2011.

Thornton, R. (1987). *American Indian holocaust and survival: A population history since 1942*. Norman: University of Oklahoma Press.

U.S. Census Bureau. (2010). *2009 American Community Survey 1-Year estimates*. Retrieved December 20, 2010, from http://factfinder.census.gov/servlet/DatasetMainPageServlet?_program=ACS&_submenuId=&_lang=en&_ts

Waldinger, R. (1997). Black/immigrant competition re-assessed: New evidence from Los Angeles. *Sociological Perspectives, 40*(3), 365–386.

Wilkerson, I. (2010). *The warmth of other suns: The epic story of America's Great Migration*. New York: Random House.

Wilson, W. J. (1996). *When work disappears: The world of the new urban poor*. New York: Alfred A. Knopf.

Zúñiga, V., & Hernández-León, R. (Eds.). (2006). *New destinations: Mexican immigration in the United States*. New York: Russell Sage.

# Family Matters: Gender, Work Arrangements, and the Rural Myth

Leann M. Tigges and Hae Yeon Choo

## Introduction

As is the case throughout the Western World, the *myth of rural life* has long held sway within American culture. It involves idyllic images of a peaceful countryside and morally upright, hard-working, self-sufficient peoples. It is characterized by agrarian ideologies about family structure, values, and community – ideologies predicated upon traditional gender roles. In this paper, we respond to the challenge raised by Tickamyer (1996) to demythologize rural life and the gender roles that undergird it. We do so by examining the ways in which rural men and women structure their work lives, considering which individual, family and labor market factors explain the character and extent of their engagement in paid employment. We build our study upon Naples's (1994) assertion that "despite continuity in traditional gender role ideology, its hegemony is challenged by the material reality of men's and women's economic lives" (p. 123). The "material reality" of their economic lives involves the decisions and opportunities for paid work, and the ways in which couples arrange their schedules to provide income and care for their families (see Chapters 19 and 21 in this volume).

In rural America, the bifurcation of social classes is coming to the fore (Struthers & Bokemeier, 2000; Tickamyer & Duncan, 1990). This bifurcation often stems from family members' work arrangements, in particular, the extent they can rely on their jobs as a stable source of income. Nelson and Smith's (1998, 1999) study of survival strategies in rural Vermont shows that families with different work arrangements, what they call "good-job" and "bad-job" households, respond to economic restructuring in different ways. Good-job households have at least one earner with a full-time, year-round job that is stable and offers benefits and paid vacations, whereas bad-job households are those whose members hold either a seasonal or temporary job, or a full-time job that lacks benefits (1998, p. 111). Nelson and Smith argue that good-job households depend more on a dual-earner strategy and use their considerable resources to strengthen their financial base through moonlighting. Bad-job households, in contrast, tend to rely on a single male breadwinner model, not because of gender ideology but because of the difficulties of costly childcare and inflexibility of their jobs.

Although Nelson and Smith's study offers insight into the bifurcation of work arrangements and its gendered implications, their conceptualization of good-job and bad-job households neglects the fact that having a full-time, year-round job, what we will call simply "standard work," is itself a gendered phenomenon with very different causes and ramifications for men and women in the same household. The division between standard and nonstandard work has long been constructed around traditional gender roles, with nonstandard work being "women's work" that is supplementary to men's main income and flexible to meet family needs (Gringeri, 1993). It is the connection between the family household and standard work that we explore in this chapter.

L.M. Tigges (✉)
Department of Community and Environmental Sociology,
University of Wisconsin-Madison, Madison, WI 53706, USA
e-mail: lmtigges@wisc.edu

Our data from nonmetropolitan Wisconsin allow us to examine the work arrangements of the household and to explore the gendered underpinnings of the division between standard and nonstandard work. We note that the single male breadwinner model is losing its power, as the realities of rural lifestyle require a second earner to make ends meet. Yet, when it comes to the types of work arrangements, our data show disparate patterns between men and women. Half of married women have standard work, while nearly three quarters of their husbands do. Even more telling is the patterning of work arrangements within the household. We use multivariate models to predict wives' labor force participation, wives' and husbands' standard work, and finally, which couples work the same shift as opposed to sequential scheduling. Our models take into account individual and family characteristics, the characteristics of jobs held by the husbands and wives, and the characteristics of the labor market. Before discussing our data and findings, we delve into what the sociological literature tells us about the gendered underpinnings of the rural myth, and then link it to standard employment relations.

## The Rural Myth and Realities of Gendered Work Lives

In the rural myth, the image of rural families is of two parents with a small-scale, independent male producer living on the land with his wife and children (Fink, 1992; Naples, 1994). Women in this picture are portrayed as traditional stay-at-home mothers (Coontz, 1992; Rosenblatt, 1997). This image is consistent with the facts that nonmetropolitan women were historically less likely to be in the labor force, more likely to be married, and to have more children than their metro counterparts (Jones & Tertilt, 2006; Rogers, 1997). However, Jones and Tertilt's (2006) analysis of US historical trends shows that the strong negative relationship between income and fertility accounts for much of rural-urban difference in fertility. Further, they show near convergence of rural and urban fertility rates for the 1956–1960 birth cohort.

Women's paid employment has long provided an important source of income for many rural families, especially farm families (Bokemeier & Tickamyer, 1985). For the past several decades, rural married women have been more likely to be in the labor force than their urban counterparts, and this is even more the case for those with children under age 6 (Cotter, DeFiore, Mermsen, Kowaleski, & Vanneman, 1996; Smith, 2008). Further, despite their substantial earnings disadvantage and limited professional opportunities, college-educated rural mothers are even more likely to be employed than their urban counterparts (85 vs. 71%) (Smith, 2008, 14). Ironically given this high level of labor force participation, rural women work in jobs that provide lower returns to their human capital (McLaughlin & Perman, 1991), are more sex segregated (Cotter et al., 1996), and are less likely to provide adequate hours (Findeis & Hsu, 1997) and adequate wages (Jensen, Findeis, Hsu, & Schachter, 1999).

The contradictory characteristics of community in the rural myth – individualism and gemeinschaft – also play out differently for men and women. Individualism emphasizes the self-sufficiency of rural living, whereas gemeinschaft emphasizes community spirit and mutual help (Naples, 1994). Prior research has demonstrated the gendered nature of these contradictory tendencies with rural men emphasizing the importance of self-sufficiency and women emphasizing the benefits of small town life (Tigges, 1998). However, the ideology of self-sufficiency persists for women as well, and is closely linked to their desires to be the ones who raise their children (Struthers & Bokemeier, 2000, 25). In order to be self-sufficient in child rearing, dual-earner couples often choose to arrange their work schedules sequentially (Hanson & Pratt, 1995; Presser, 1994; Preston, Rose, Norcliffe, & Holmes, 2000). In a study of women's work in a small Massachusetts city, Hanson and Pratt (1995) found that in almost a third of dual-earner families with children younger than 13, the husband and wife worked sequential shifts. The most common sequential arrangement in Hanson and Pratt's study, occurring for two out of ten working couples, is for the wife to work the day shift and the husband to work at some other time. National data demonstrate that paid work is scheduled to meet household and family demands, with the timing of men's work less restricted than women's (Presser, 2003). Regardless of parents' desires to be the primary caregivers for young children, greater difficulties finding adequate childcare and the lack of after-school care in rural areas may make sequential scheduling one of a few viable options for dual-worker families.

Another contradiction can be found between the gemeinschaft notions of rural community life and the lack of family friendly workplace policies among rural employers. Analyzing data from the National Longitudinal Survey of Youth (NLSY), Glauber (2009) finds that rural mothers, whether single or married, are less likely than urban mothers to have paid sick days, paid vacation days, health insurance, parental leave, and flextime. Of course, there are variations by education, occupation, industry, and establishment size, but in each case, rural mothers fare worse than their urban counterparts. For example, among all comparison groups, lack of sick or vacation days is highest for rural mothers who had not completed high school, those in service and sales occupations, those in retail trade and personal service industries, and those who work in small establishments. Rural jobs are less "family friendly" despite the family-oriented culture of small town America and the high levels of labor force involvement by rural mothers (see Chapter 17 in this volume).

The gendered rural myth is not limited to the United States, nor is rural women's disadvantage in the labor market solely an American phenomenon. Research from the UK shows that the cultural construction of the rural idyll, particularly its emphasis on the community, helps maintain traditional gender relations in rural areas (Little & Austin, 1996). Gender ideology that puts childcare mainly under women's domain within a gendered household division of labor (Little, 1994), combined with lower levels of formal childcare available in rural areas (Halliday, 1997), relegates rural women in the UK to a more disadvantaged employment market with temporary and part-time, low-paid jobs (Halliday & Little, 2001; Little, 1997; Mauthner, McKee, & Strell, 2001). Rural employment conditions in Europe, although improved since the early 1990s, show persisting gender inequality (Bock, 2004). We now turn to a brief review of some of the factors other studies have identified as salient for standard employment within the US, especially for women and rural workers.

## Nonstandard Employment and Women's Work

Contrary to the construction of standard work as male breadwinner's work, nonstandard work has since its inception been predicated on women's secondary earner role (Vosko, 2000). Vosko notes that the norm of standard employment in the Fordist era was only possible because of the segmented labor market structure where women and immigrants were located at the bottom strata doing nonstandard work. In this postwar era, temporary work utilized the labor of married women whose right to work was denied by both Canadian national policy and an ideology of domesticity. In other words, nonstandard work was accepted because it was "women's work" that did not threaten men's standard work. This changed in the 1970s when nonstandard work began replacing standard work, "feminizing" employment relations in terms of both norm and practice. Today, throughout developed societies, nonstandard work is no longer just women's work, but is increasingly shared by men.

The divide between standard work and nonstandard work is an important domain for gender ideologies, not just gender roles. Williams (2000) argues that the construction of "the ideal worker" norm in standard work was modeled on a male breadwinner with a full-time homemaker spouse. This norm renders women, and mothers in particular, as deficient workers since they generally lack the support of a homemaker spouse. Not able to fit the ideal worker norm, women are more likely than men to be employed in the marginalized nonstandard jobs with lower earning and limited benefits and are excluded from men's informal networks (Reskin, McBrier, & Kmec, 1999). Among women, Hanson and Pratt (1995) argue, those who work in female-dominated occupations and those working part-time schedules are further marginalized with limited work options.

Metropolitan and nonmetropolitan areas differ substantially in the levels of nonstandard work. McLaughlin and Coleman-Jensen (2008) report that 25% of the nonmetropolitan labor force is employed in nonstandard work compared with 21% of central city and of suburban workers. They note that the rural disadvantage cannot be completely explained by differences in industry or occupational structure, nor by the sociodemographic characteristics of workers. In addition, they find "less variation in the odds of nonstandard work across industries and occupations in nonmetro than metro areas. This suggests more similarity in the nature of employment in nonmetro areas, perhaps as a result of the size of labor markets and employer knowledge of the availability of standard jobs and alternative employment opportunities" (p. 653).

These studies suggest that nonstandard employment is not simply a response to the desires of workers for more flexibility or time at home. It is both a gendered phenomenon and one affected by the structure of local economies. Certainly, workers' human capital (education and work experience) and family circumstances (age and number of children) affect their desires for full-time employment and their ability to get the jobs that are worth the cost of being there. But the evaluation of whether work is worthwhile is clearly influenced by gender ideology. Tigges (1998) finds that men and women alike think of women's, but not men's, wages in relation to the cost of childcare. Mothers, but not fathers, need to earn enough to offset the cost of childcare, or bring in valuable health insurance for the family. Other studies show that married women's labor force participation is normative during certain stages of life. Budig (2003) demonstrates that fertility and women's employment are interdependent, but the relationships are influenced by the age of the children – preschool age children reduce women's employment participation but older children appear to increase full-time employment.

Social factors also influence women's labor market experiences. Hanson and Pratt (1995) identify one especially relevant factor for the women in their study of Worchester, Massachusetts. Many families in that city lived in homes that had been or were still owned by a relative of one of the couple. For example, the couple may have purchased their home from one of their parents, or they may be paying some rent to the parent, or working out an informal exchange. Hanson and Pratt refer to the family being *rooted* in the location by this arrangement. They find that rootedness affects the way women engage the labor market, restraining them to working in certain geographical areas and narrowing their employment options. The consequences of rootedness in nonmetropolitan areas might be different from metropolitan areas in Hanson and Pratt's study, but it is seldom studied because data are lacking. Our Wisconsin data show that for 18% of nonmetropolitan couples, either their house or their land was currently or had been previously owned by a relative. We investigate here the significance of this strong tie to location for women's and men's standard employment.

McLaughlin and Coleman-Jensen (2008, 655) note that men and women alike are affected by the prevalence of nonstandard work in rural areas, which suggests that rural households, in particular, may be likely to experience some combination of standard and nonstandard jobs. Thus the household, not just the workers, must respond to the changing work arrangements available within their local labor markets. Our data, to which we now turn, allow us to look inside the household, to see how the employment situation of one partner affects the chances of standard employment for the other.

## Data

In order to examine the pattern of standard employment within families, we need data that provide similarly useful data on the human capital and jobs of both working spouses, as well as information about childcare, family structure, and labor market structure. We also need the data to be representative of a rural population and to be of adequate sample size to allow multivariate statistical analysis. The ideal data for our analysis come from a random telephone survey of nonmetropolitan Wisconsin family households. Although rural Wisconsin is not typical of the whole of nonmetropolitan America – no rural sample from any state would be, the data represent well the rural Midwest of the 1990s, with its vast majority white population largely nonfarm in residence, and employed in manufacturing and service occupations. It is also important to note that Wisconsin's economy was particularly vibrant in the mid-1990s, making the study of nonstandard work all the more interesting, since it is likely to reflect workers' "choice" and employment opportunities. In the next section of this chapter, we describe the economic conditions in the state at the time of the survey.

The survey was conducted from November 1995 through April 1996 (Leann Tigges, Principle Investigator). A modified random-digit-dialing method was used to select both listed and unlisted numbers in the 52 nonmetropolitan counties of the state. The response rate was 58%.[1] The interviews lasted an

---

[1] O'Neil (1979) notes that those who resist telephone surveys are likely to be either younger than 19 or older than 65 (outside the age boundaries for eligible respondents to our survey). Thus, it seems likely that the refusal rate is lower than 42% (the rate based on the assumption that households refusing before eligibility could be determined are as likely to be eligible as households that did not refuse).

average of 30 min. Households in the study sample included those headed by couples (married or in a marriage-like relationship) and by single mothers with children age 18 or under living in the home. Households were excluded if one of the heads was 65 or older. Within couple households, the woman or the man of the couple was randomly selected for interviewing.[2] A total of 1610 interviews were completed.[3]

The focus of our analysis is on the work arrangements of couples, therefore we do not include single mothers in this analysis. Although not all couples in the sample are legally married, all are in "marriage-like" arrangements. For convenience we will refer to the women as wives and the men as husbands. Respondents to the survey were asked detailed questions about their own employment situation and about that of their spouses or partners. We have coded information from these questions to allow us to analyze the employment and earnings of husbands and wives in the sample.

We define a "standard work arrangement" as working at one's main job at least 35 h a week for at least 50 weeks (that is, a full-time, year-round job). Those working either part-time or part-year are considered to have nonstandard work arrangements. The exception to this rule is that teachers who reported working at least 36 weeks (reflecting the standard nine month school year in Wisconsin) are considered to hold standard employment. Table 16.1 provides descriptive data for the variables used in this study.

## The Setting: Rural Wisconsin

In the mid-1990s, at the time of our study, Wisconsin's economy was frequently portrayed as vibrant. In 1995, standard business measures indicated that Wisconsin was in a strong economic situation. The state experienced growth in total income and employment and its unemployment rates were among the lowest in the nation (Dresser, Rogers, & Whittaker, 1996). Yet the benefits of this economy fell unevenly between working families and an elite group of business owners and professionals. The income gap between metropolitan and nonmetropolitan areas widened. Wisconsin nonmetropolitan areas' earnings per job and per-capita income were well below metropolitan levels (by about 25% in 1997) and their unemployment rates higher (4.1 vs. 3.0% for metropolitan areas) (USDA, 2000). Not surprisingly, rural residents were disproportionately represented among Wisconsin's working poor families with children, due in part to the concentration of seasonal and part-time jobs in nonmetropolitan industries, jobs which are disproportionately filled by women (Center on Wisconsin Strategy, 2000).

Under such economic circumstances, the families in nonmetropolitan Wisconsin responded to their economic difficulties by using multiple strategies to "get by." One common way households increase their income is to maximize the employment of family labor (Ziebarth & Tigges, 2000). Rather than relying on a single breadwinner, multiple family members join the labor force. This reality of working wives does not fit the rural myth that emphasizes women's domestic roles as stay-at-home mothers. In rural Wisconsin, the norm

---

[2] Nonmetropolitan counties are those without a central city of at least 50,000 residents, or commuting connections to an area with 50,000 or more residents and a metropolitan area of 100,000 people total.

[3] Although the sample is intended to represent working-age family households, there are two ways in which this sample could be biased. First, the survey excluded homes without telephones. Only 2.8% of Wisconsin households did not have a telephone in 1990 (U.S. Census Bureau, 2004). Research in the U.S. indicates that households without phones are significantly poorer, are more likely to be either in a central city or outside a metropolitan statistical area, and are more likely to have a young householder (Keeter, 1995). Second, the survey could suffer from nonresponse bias due to refusals. To check whether the survey was representative of the desired population we compared it with data from the March 1995 Current Population Survey (CPS) conducted by the Census Bureau. We approximated our sample specifications by age, residence, and household headship. There are no significant differences in labor force status of respondents, household income, and personal earnings. There are some differences in occupation and industry, however. Our sample has more people in technical and related occupations (4% of our sample versus 1% in the CPS) and administrative and clerical occupations (13 vs. 5%), and fewer people in precision production and craft occupations (12 vs. 24%). It has more people in "other services" industries – defined as hospital, medical, education, social and other professional services, than the CPS sample does (26 vs. 18% in the CPS). Finally, our sample contains more self-employed than the CPS sample (14 vs. 8% in the CPS). Thus, our sample may over-represent higher status occupational groups.

**Table 16.1** Family, personal and demographic characteristics of husbands and wives

| | N | Mean | Std. deviation |
|---|---|---|---|
| Presence of child age 18 or younger | 1490 | 0.6362 | 0.48124 |
| # Children in household | 1472 | 1.3628 | 1.31153 |
| Youngest child age < 6 | 1479 | 0.2650 | 0.44151 |
| Child aged 6–17 present | 1472 | 0.5088 | 0.50009 |
| Uses paid childcare | 1479 | 0.1197 | 0.32469 |
| Rooted (home/land owned by relative) | 1468 | 0.1839 | 0.38755 |
| Farm household | 1437 | 0.0835 | 0.27674 |
| # Jobs both spouses, past year | 1477 | 2.4279 | 1.12123 |
| Both spouses employed | 1485 | 0.7414 | 0.43801 |
| Husband has standard work | 1347 | 0.7632 | 0.42529 |
| Wife has standard work | 1245 | 0.5068 | 0.50015 |
| Husband works day shift | 1409 | 0.7175 | 0.45036 |
| Wife works day shift | 1288 | 0.7725 | 0.41937 |
| Husband's age | 1481 | 42.3720 | 10.54585 |
| Husband's education beyond high school, but not college graduate | 1477 | 0.2864 | 0.45223 |
| Husband college graduate | 1477 | 0.1821 | 0.38608 |
| Husband in female-dominated occupation | 1407 | 0.0426 | 0.20212 |
| Husband self-employed | 1484 | 0.2156 | 0.41140 |
| Husband's hourly wage | 1048 | 19.3030 | 32.30945 |
| Husband's income (main job) | 1057 | 33642.0096 | 28865.41838 |
| Wife's age | 1477 | 40.1009 | 10.39921 |
| Wife's education beyond high school, but not college graduate | 1490 | 0.2685 | 0.78716 |
| Wife college graduate | 1490 | 0.1383 | 0.73643 |
| Wife self-employed | 1485 | 0.1333 | 0.34005 |
| Wife returned to school to improve job | 1481 | 0.3410 | 0.47420 |
| Share female in wife's occupation | 1284 | 0.6451 | 0.26979 |
| Wife's hourly wage | 1026 | 12.0769 | 15.80153 |
| Wife's income (main job) | 1009 | 17749.0975 | 16286.75044 |

of rural lifestyle is the dual-earner model in which husbands and wives both work for pay, mostly outside the home. Our survey shows that 74% of rural couples had both partners in the labor force. As the dual-earner model becomes a norm among rural families, childcare becomes an increasingly important factor when deciding the kind of work arrangement for the families. Among the families who have a child younger than 13 years, 70% of our respondents did not use any outside care. Only 21% of them use formal care, whereas 9% depend on paid or unpaid informal care, such as extended family members and neighbors.

## Results: Gender, Family and Standard Work

Our data reveal a gender hierarchy in women and men's earnings and work arrangements. While wives' average annual income from her main job was $17,749 in 1995, husbands made $33,642, nearly twice as much. This is partly because men worked more hours per week (48 compared to women's 37) and more weeks per year (47 vs. 43). But women's hourly wages, which averaged $12.08, are also significantly lower than men's average of $19.30. (See Table 16.1 for more detail on work and family characteristics.) When we take a close look at the family level, in 41% of the households where both partners are employed, wives and husbands both have standard work. In 35% of households, only husbands have standard work and complement it with wives' nonstandard work; for 14% of couples, neither partner has standard work. The least common situation, occurring for one in ten dual-working households, is one in which the wife has standard employment and the husband has nonstandard work. The overall pattern shows the predominance of standard work for men and suggests that couples make decisions about who should work, when, and for how long.

In households where men have standard work, we find a family model that fits relatively well with the rural myth (Table 16.2). Compared to the households where men have nonstandard work, these couples are more likely to have children at home. These families have more children overall and more school-aged children in particular. These households experience more employment stability because of less frequent job changes for men and women combined. Employed wives of men with standard work are also more likely to have standard work than are the employed wives of men in nonstandard work arrangements (54 vs. 42%). The portrait that emerges here is of concentrated advantage, linked to husband's standard work. On average, these families, similar to the "good-job households" in Vermont (Nelson & Smith, 1998), are in better economic conditions. They have higher household income due to the higher annual wage of male standard workers ($37,345 compared to $21,647 in families where men have nonstandard work).

Different from the case of men, the households of women with standard work display characteristics that are often contradictory to the rural myth (see Table 16.2). As noted above, about half of the wives in our study have standard work. Because of their full-time work arrangements, these women have higher annual incomes than their nonstandard counterparts ($24,272 vs. $10,910), but husbands' wages do not differ significantly between the two groups. The hourly wages for women with standard work are about the same as wives in nonstandard work; the same was true of their husbands. Whereas male standard work households had about the same number of children as their nonstandard work counterparts, women with standard work have significantly fewer children at home than women in nonstandard employment.

Overall, households with wives in standard work have higher total income and higher job stability. The husbands of these women with standard work are more likely to also have standard work than the husbands of women in nonstandard work (80 vs. 72%). Women with standard employment are more likely to work the day-shift (81 vs. 73%) and in slightly less "feminine" occupations (62 vs. 67% female in the occupation in Wisconsin). These characteristics might put these women's households in Nelson and Smith's "good-job households" category (1999). On the basis of our data, we argue that the category of good-job households, where one earner regardless of gender has good employment, is problematic. As demonstrated in the comparisons above, depending on whether this earner is male or female, the family composition and the gendered implications of their family strategy vary significantly.

This becomes more evident regarding child-care decisions in the households. Childcare is an important terrain where families maintain and challenge the rural myth. Whether men have standard work or not

**Table 16.2** Average sample characteristics by standard work of husband and wife

| Work arrangement | Has children under 18 | Use paid childcare | Spouse has standard work | # of children in hhld | Husband's income | Wife's income | # of jobs in hhld in past year |
|---|---|---|---|---|---|---|---|
| Husband nonstandard | 61% | 12% | 42% | 1.32 | $21,647 | $16,855 | 2.83 |
| Husband standard | 67% | 13% | 54%*** | 1.44 | $37,345*** | $18,532 | 2.43*** |
| Wife nonstandard | 70% | 12% | 69% | 1.54 | $33,914 | $10,910 | 2.80 |
| Wife standard | 60%*** | 16%* | 80%*** | 1.23*** | $31,960 | $24,272*** | 2.47*** |

T-test for difference in means between nonstandard and standard work among husbands and among wives, significant at 0.05 level*, at 0.01 level**, at 0.001 level*** does not affect the households' decision about childcare. Conversely, women's work arrangement makes a significant difference in such decisions. For example, among those households with children younger than 13 where women have nonstandard work, 72% do not use any type of care. This proportion drops to 57% among the households where women have standard work. Families with wives in standard work rely much more on formal childcare than do female nonstandard work households (31 vs. 19%). Using paid child-care services, particularly formal childcare, appears necessary for wives to have standard work. The gendered implications regarding rural myth are further explored in the following regression analysis.

Next, we examine women and men's employment and family in relation to the ways in which the rural myth is maintained and challenged by the realities of rural living. First, we look at the wife's employment and various characteristics that might influence her decision to hold a job (Table 16.3). Our model controls for various labor market characteristics, including the industrial structure of the local labor market within the commuting zone and county population.

The results show the strong influence of family and social characteristics on wives' decision to work. Family constraints such as having more children at home or having a preschool-age child reduce the odds of wives' employment. Yet, women seem to have an opportunity to find work outside the home when children become school age, or they are compelled to do so by the costs of raising children at this age (Budig, 2003). Human capital characteristics, especially education, increase the probability of women's employment. Having a college degree and having returned to school in order to improve employment prospects increase the odds of employment by about 45% compared to lacking these education achievements. As husbands' income increases, women are less likely to be in the labor force. This is consistent with the gender ideology that women's employment is secondary to

**Table 16.3** Logistic regression of wife's labor force participation

|  | B | S.E. | Exp(B) |
|---|---|---|---|
| # Children | −0.178 | 0.098 | 0.837 |
| Preschooler*** | −1.181 | 0.223 | 0.307 |
| School age child*** | 0.917 | 0.237 | 2.501 |
| Rooted | 0.243 | 0.217 | 1.276 |
| Wife's age*** | −0.036 | 0.009 | 0.965 |
| Wife's educ. beyond HS | −0.191 | 0.121 | 0.826 |
| Wife college grad** | 0.364 | 0.133 | 1.438 |
| Wife returned to school for job* | 0.391 | 0.167 | 1.478 |
| Husband standard empl. | 0.156 | 0.181 | 1.169 |
| Husband self-employed | 0.086 | 0.201 | 1.089 |
| Farm household | 0.516 | 0.344 | 1.675 |
| Husband's income (ln)*** | −0.435 | 0.122 | 0.647 |
| Husband's income not reported* | 0.386 | 0.189 | 1.471 |
| % l.f. in extractive indus. | 0.590 | 3.505 | 1.804 |
| % l.f. in manufacturing | −1.256 | 3.772 | 0.285 |
| % l.f. in professional services | −1.478 | 5.066 | 0.228 |
| % l.f. in consumer services | −9.374 | 5.180 | 0.000 |
| County population (ln.) | 0.198 | 0.140 | 1.219 |
| Constant | 7.665 | 4.044 | 2131.681 |

*$p<0.05$, **$p<0.01$, ***$p<0.001$
Log likelihood = 1126.369; Pseudo $R^2 = 0.153$
l.f. = area labor force. HS = high school

men's, and thus is only required when men are "deficient workers" and do not earn enough money. When we take a close look at men and women's standard employment in the next models, we gain a better understanding of how gender ideology affects the work arrangements of those in the labor force.

Comparing the models of standard work for women and men (Tables 16.4 and 16.5), we see that wives' standard work is more contingent on household constraints than is the case for husbands. As in the women's employment model above, having more children and having a preschool age child impede women's standard employment. This again reflects the findings of Budig (2003), who shows that preschool children reduce women's employment participation. However, unlike Budig, we do not find school age children increase the odds of their mothers' full-time year-round employment. Those wives who use paid child-care services are nearly three times as likely to be in standard employment situations. They are also more likely to work the day-shift, a likely accommodation to children's school hours.

Conversely, for men, family characteristics matter much less (see Table 16.5). Their standard employment is not affected by the number of children at home, having a preschooler, the type of child-care arrangements, or which shift they work. Interestingly, men with standard employment are more likely to have a school-age child, which can be interpreted as the burden of the financial support required by the school-age children that falls onto men's backs.

In addition to family demographic characteristics, our models include "rootedness" as a measure of the social embeddedness of the households in their communities. Following Hanson and Pratt (1995), we define rootedness as the household obtaining the land

**Table 16.4** Logistic regression of wife's standard employment

|  | B | S.E. | Exp(B) |
|---|---|---|---|
| # Children** | −0.228 | 0.086 | 0.796 |
| Preschool child** | −0.596 | 0.217 | 0.551 |
| School age child | 0.226 | 0.204 | 1.254 |
| Use paid childcare*** | 1.069 | 0.233 | 2.913 |
| Rooted* | 0.413 | 0.174 | 1.511 |
| Husband standard work* | 0.320 | 0.155 | 1.378 |
| # Jobs in hhld past year*** | −0.329 | 0.072 | 0.720 |
| Husband day shift | −0.154 | 0.145 | 0.858 |
| Wife day shift* | 0.327 | 0.165 | 1.387 |
| % Female wife's occupation*** | −0.849 | 0.249 | 0.428 |
| Wife's age | 0.013 | 0.008 | 1.013 |
| Wife's educ. beyond HS | −0.033 | 0.105 | 0.968 |
| Wife college grad. | 0.019 | 0.113 | 1.019 |
| Farm household | 0.356 | 0.260 | 1.428 |
| Wife self-employed | −0.059 | 0.191 | 0.943 |
| % l.f. in extractive indus. | 0.632 | 2.972 | 1.881 |
| % l.f. in manufacturing | 1.461 | 3.196 | 4.310 |
| % l.f. in professional services | 1.019 | 4.355 | 2.772 |
| % l.f. in consumer services | 1.361 | 4.793 | 3.900 |
| County population (ln.) | −0.215 | 0.125 | 0.807 |
| Constant | 2.023 | 3.344 | 7.561 |

*$p<0.05$, **$p<0.01$, ***$p<0.001$
Log likelihood = 1409.709; Pseudo $R^2 = 0.137$
l.f. = area labor force. HS = high school

**Table 16.5** Logistic regression of husband's standard employment

|  | B | S.E. | Exp(B) |
|---|---|---|---|
| # Children | −0.141 | 0.093 | 0.868 |
| Preschooler | 0.154 | 0.238 | 1.167 |
| School age child | 0.526 | 0.232 | 1.691* |
| Use paid childcare | −0.085 | 0.257 | 0.918 |
| Rooted | 0.331 | 0.210 | 1.393 |
| Wife standard work | 0.284 | 0.154 | 1.328 |
| # Jobs in household past year | −0.352 | 0.074 | 0.703** |
| Husband day shift | 0.118 | 0.165 | 1.126 |
| Wife day shift | 0.386 | 0.175 | 1.471* |
| Husband's occupation female-dominated | 0.654 | 0.432 | 1.924 |
| Husband's age | −0.002 | 0.009 | .998 |
| Husband's educ. beyond HS | 0.346 | 0.174 | 1.414* |
| Husband college grad. | 0.339 | 0.213 | 1.403 |
| Farm household | 1.010 | 0.347 | 2.746*** |
| Husband self-employed | −0.056 | 0.194 | 0.945 |
| % l.f. in extractive indus. | −2.144 | 3.443 | 0.117 |
| % l.f. in manufacturing | 0.671 | 3.764 | 1.955 |
| % l.f. in professional services | 4.282 | 5.101 | 72.415 |
| % l.f. in consumer services | −1.809 | 5.503 | 0.164 |
| County population (ln.) | 0.246 | 0.139 | 1.280 |
| Constant | −2.008 | 3.850 | 0.134 |

*$p<0.05$, **$p<0.01$, ***$p<0.001$. l.f. = area labor force. HS = high school
Log Likelihood = 1134.067; Pseudo $R^2 = 0.096$

or house through a family member. Almost one fifth of the survey respondents (18%) reported that their home or land is or was owned by a family member. Over half of farm households were rooted in this way. Our analysis shows that rootedness is significantly and positively related to women's standard work arrangements. Women who are socially embedded through generational links in the locality seem to benefit from having these "roots." Rootedness works for them as employment-relevant social capital. This result contrasts with Hanson and Pratt's (1995) Massachusetts study where rootedness works to constrain rather than empower women by "grounding" them within the areas with limited work options. The fact that men's standard work is not significantly influenced by household rootedness demonstrates again the gendered character of the household.

Another interesting factor in the standard work for men and women is the percent female in the occupation, which measures the degree of sex segregation. Consistent with previous literature that shows female-dominated occupations tend to be part-time and seasonal, as the percent of female in the occupation increases, women are less likely to have standard employment (Reskin et al., 1999). However, working in a female-dominated occupation (at least 75% female) does not hurt men's chances of having standard employment. This may be evidence of the "glass escalator" that men in female-dominated occupations ride to the top, giving them access to authority and stability denied the women they supervise (Williams, 1992).

Demonstrating the ways in which standard work is a household arrangement (McLaughlin & Coleman-

Jensen, 2008) and also a situation that compounds advantage (Nelson & Smith, 1999), our data show that women whose husbands have standard work are about 38% more likely to also have standard work than women whose husbands are in nonstandard employment. (The association in the men's model is significant only at the .1 level.) Age and education, common indicators of human capital do not significantly increase wives' chances of having standard work in our model, and technical college education (beyond high school but not college graduation) is the only human capital characteristic increasing the odds of men's standard employment. Women in standard work are more likely to work the day shift, a likely accommodation to family responsibilities and possibly an indication of the work schedules available to women who seek year-round, full-time jobs. Although we expected the industrial structure of the local labor market to affect access to standard work, these variables are not significant for women or men.

Finally, we examine one way that working couples may provide for the care of their children – through the practice of sequential scheduling. Our model tests which work and family characteristics affect the partners working the same shift, rather than choosing sequential scheduling (Table 16.6). Working the same shift, in most cases, means that wives and husbands are both working during the day (77% of wives and 72% of husbands worked the dayshift).

The regression analysis shows that couples in which husbands have standard work are more likely to work the same shift (i.e., less likely to have sequential scheduling). These households approximate Nelson and Smith's "good-job households" – one aspect of which is not having to juggle schedules in order to meet child-care responsibilities. Interestingly, against common perceptions, "same-shift households" are more likely than those with staggered work schedules to have children younger than 6 and children between 6 and 12, who require extensive care. The key to parents' ability to manage their family lives with children and avoid the "tag-team" approach of sequential scheduling is formal and paid childcare (i.e., not relying on informal child-care arrangements). Wages also matter, but again it is only women's hourly wages that influence the decision to have both partners working the same shift. This suggests that couples make decisions about their work schedules by considering whether women's wages are sufficient to pay for childcare during work hours. Women's employment becomes an opportunity cost in these decisions, whereas men's employment is not subject to such consideration. The gender ideology that childcare is women's work persists, but in a changed form for these Wisconsin rural families, even while their dual-earner strategy and paid child-care services seem to be challenging to the gender ideology underlying the rural myth.

**Table 16.6** Logistic regression of couple working the same shift

|  | B | S.E. | Exp(B) |
|---|---|---|---|
| Wife standard employment | 0.003 | 0.162 | 1.003 |
| Husband standard employment | 0.467 | 0.177 | 1.595* |
| Wife's hourly wage (ln) | 0.366 | 0.150 | 1.442** |
| Husband's hourly wage (ln) | 0.038 | 0.149 | 1.039 |
| # Jobs in household per year | −0.105 | 0.074 | 0.900 |
| # Children | −0.006 | 0.079 | 0.994 |
| Preschool child | 1.014 | 0.307 | 2.756*** |
| Youngest child age 6–12 | 1.159 | 0.346 | 3.188*** |
| Use informal childcare | −1.102 | 0.276 | 0.332*** |
| Rooted | 0.151 | 0.202 | 1.162 |
| Wife's age | 0.031 | 0.010 | 1.032* |
| Farm household | −0.454 | 0.282 | 0.635 |
| Constant | −1.794 | 0.686 | 0.166 |

*$p<0.05$, **$p<0.01$, ***$p<0.001$
Log Likelihood = 1010.180; Pseudo $R^2 = 0.090$

## Conclusions and Discussion

In this chapter, we demythologize rural ideology by examining the reality of employment strategies among rural couples. We take issue with the gender indifference of the category of good-job households, where one earner regardless of gender has good employment (Nelson & Smith, 1999). We use unique data from nonmetropolitan Wisconsin to identify the gendered implications of good jobs, particularly year-round, full-time (standard) employment. In particular, we explore the workings of and changes in gender ideology by focusing on men and women's work arrangements.

When considering which individual, family and labor market factors explain the extent of men's and women's paid employment, we find women's standard work is more contingent on household constraints and social characteristics than is men's. Family constraints, such as the number and age of children, as well as being socially embedded in a place affect women's involvement in standard work, but matter much less for men. Furthermore, social characteristics such as being rooted in one's home through family linkages increase probabilities of women's standard work. That rootedness operates for rural women as employment-relevant social capital while constraining urban women in Hanson and Pratt's study poses interesting questions about how social factors may play very different roles in rural and urban labor markets. This is certainly an issue which would benefit from increased research.

Our analysis demonstrates the multiple ways gender ideology is reinforced and challenged within rural families. Virtually gone are the kinds of families portrayed by the rural myth, that is, the male farmer living independently with his dependent wife and children. The gendered character of the rural myth has not died out, but has changed its face, adapting to the changes in rural economies. Thus, it is important to discover the new domains where myth finds its place, in order to deconstruct the myth. Nonmetropolitan wives and mothers actively participate in the labor market. Yet, the values in the rural myth, such as self-sufficiency and gender hierarchy, persist in rural residents' lives. Some rural families struggle through sequential scheduling of the couple's jobs in order to remain self-sufficient in child rearing. When they make decisions to spend the money on childcare, women's earnings become the deciding factor, based on the ideology of women's domestic role as caregivers. Although this finding fits well with the gendered ideology of rural life, we suspect that it is neither uniquely rural, nor uniquely Midwestern American. But we need more employment research that includes all kinds of socially relevant characteristics, not only demographic and human capital characteristics but locational and family characteristics as well. Rather than assuming that individuals make decisions in a social vacuum, we need to consider the ways in which individuals make employment and child-care decisions as members of households.

Of course, not everyone who desires standard work can obtain it. McLaughlin and Coleman-Jensen (2008, 655) note that men and women alike are affected by the prevalence of nonstandard work in rural areas, which suggests that rural households, in particular, may be likely to experience some combination of standard and nonstandard jobs. Thus the household, not just the workers, must respond to the changing work arrangements available within their local labor markets. Our data allowed us to look inside the household, to see how the employment situation of one partner affects the chances of standard employment for the other. Other studies of household employment dynamics in urban or non-U.S. settings are needed.

## References

Bock, B. (2004). It still matters where you live: Rural women's employment throughout Europe. In H. Buller & K. Hoggart (Eds.), *Women in the European countryside* (pp. 14–41). Aldershot: Ashgate.

Bokemeier, J. L., & Tickamyer, A. R. (1985). Labor force experiences of nonmetropolitan women. *Rural Sociology, 50*(1), 51–73.

Budig, M. J. (2003). Are women's employment and fertility histories interdependent? An examination of causal order using event history analysis. *Social Science Research, 32*(3), 376–401.

Center on Wisconsin Strategy. (2000). *Barely getting by: Wisconsin's working poor families*. Retrieved August 10, 2010, from http://www.cows.org/pdf/rp-wrkgpoor-00.pdf

Coontz, S. (1992). *The way we never were: American families and the nostalgia trap*. New York: Basic Books.

Cotter, D., DeFiore, J., Mermsen, J. M., Kowaleski, B. M., & Vanneman, R. (1996). Gender inequality in nonmetropolitan and metropolitan areas. *Rural Sociology, 61*(2), 272–288.

Dresser, L., Rogers, J., & Whittaker, J. (1996). *The state of working Wisconsin*. Center on Wisconsin Strategy, University of Wisconsin-Madison. Retrieved August 10, 2010, from http://www.cows.org/pdf/rp-soww-96.pdf

Findeis, J., & Hsu, W. L. (1997). Employment. In G. Goreham (Ed.), *Encyclopedia of rural America: The land and people* (Vol. 1, pp. 623–626). Santa Barbara, CA: ABC-CLIO.

Fink, D. (1992). *Agrarian women: Wives and mothers in rural Nebraska 1880–1940*. Chapel Hill, NC: University of North Carolina Press.

Glauber, R. (2009). *Family-friendly policies for rural working mothers*. Carsey Institute Policy Brief No.15. Retrieved August 10, 2010, from http://www.nera.umd.edu/landGrant/papers/CarseyInstituteFamilyPolicies.pdf

Gringeri, C. (1993). Inscribing gender in rural development. *Rural Sociology, 58*(1), 30–52.

Halliday, J. (1997). Children's services and care: A rural view. *Geoforum, 28*, 103–119.

Halliday, J., & Little, J. (2001). Amongst women: Exploring the reality of rural childcare. *Sociologia Ruralis, 41*(4), 423–437.

Hanson, S., & Pratt, G. (1995). *Gender, work, and space*. New York: Routledge.

Jensen, L., Findeis, J. L., Hsu, W., & Schachter, J. P. (1999). Slipping into and out of underemployment: Another disadvantage for nonmetropolitan workers? *Rural Sociology, 64*(3), 417–438.

Jones, L. E., & Tertilt, M. (2006). *An economic history of fertility in the U.S.: 1826–1960*. NBER working paper No.W12796. Retrieved August 10, 2010, from http://ssrn.com/abstract=953361

Keeter, S. (1995). Estimating telephone noncoverage bias with a telephone survey. *Public Opinion Quarterly, 59*(2), 196–217.

Little, J. (1994). Gender relations and the rural labour process. In S. Whatmore, T. Marsden, & P. Lowe (Eds.), *Gender and rurality* (pp. 11–30). London: David Fulton.

Little, J. (1997). Employment marginality and women's self-identity. In P. J. Cloke & J. Little (Eds.), *Contested countryside cultures* (pp. 138–157). London: Routledge.

Little, J., & Austin, P. (1996). Women and the rural idyll. *Journal of Rural Studies, 12*(2), 101–111.

Mauthner, N., McKee, L., & Strell, M. (2001). *Work and family life in rural communities*. York: York Publishing Services.

McLaughlin, D. K., & Coleman-Jensen, A. J. (2008). Nonstandard employment in the nonmetropolitan United States. *Rural Sociology, 73*(4), 631–659.

McLaughlin, D. K., & Perman, L. (1991). Returns vs. endowments in earnings attainment process for metropolitan and nonmetropolitan men and women. *Rural Sociology, 56*(3), 339–365.

Naples, N. (1994). Contradictions in agrarian ideology: Restructuring gender, race-ethnicity, and class. *Rural Sociology, 59*(1), 110–135.

Nelson, M. K., & Smith, J. (1998). Economic restructuring, household strategies and gender: A case study of a rural community. *Feminist Studies, 24*(1), 79–114.

Nelson, M. K., & Smith, J. (1999). *Working hard and making do: Surviving in small town America*. Berkeley, CA: University of California Press.

O'Neil, M. J. (1979). Estimating the nonresponse bias due to refusals in telephone surveys. *Public Opinion Quarterly, 43*(2), 218–232.

Presser, H. B. (1994). Employment schedules among dual-earner families and the division of household labor by gender. *American Sociological Review, 59*(3), 348–364.

Presser, H. B. (2003). Race-ethnic and gender differences in nonstandard work shifts. *Work and Occupations, 30*(4), 412–439.

Preston, V., Rose, D., Norcliffe, G., & Holmes, J. (2000). Shift work, childcare and domestic work: Divisions of labor in Canadian paper mill communities. *Gender, Place and Culture, 7*(1), 5–29.

Reskin, B., McBrier, D. B., & Kmec, J. A. (1999). The determinants and consequences of workplace sex and race composition. *Annual Review of Sociology, 25*, 335–361.

Rogers, C. C. (1997). *Changes in the social and economic status of women by metro-nonmetro residence*. Agriculture Information Bulletin No. (AIB732) Economic Research Service/USDA.

Rosenblatt, P. C. (1997). Marriage. In G. Goreham (Ed.), *Encyclopedia of rural America: The land and people* (Vol. 2, pp. 451–454). Santa Barbara, CA: ABC-CLIO.

Smith, K. (2008). Working hard for the money: Trends in women's employment, 1970–2007. *Carsey Institute Reports on Rural America, 1*(5). Retrieved August 10, 2010, from http://www.carseyinstitute.unh.edu/publications/Report-Smith-WorkingHard.pdf

Struthers, C. B., & Bokemeier, J. L. (2000). Myths and realities of raising children and creating family life in a rural county. *Journal of Family Issues, 21*(1), 17–46.

Tickamyer, A. R. (1996). *Rural myth, rural reality: Diversity and change in rural America for the 21st century*. Santa Fe, NM: Keynote address at the NEC*TAS Rural Conference.

Tickamyer, A. R., & Duncan, C. M. (1990). Poverty and opportunity structure in rural America. *Annual Review of Sociology, 16*, 67–86.

Tigges, L. M. (1998). Constructing gender and rural lifestyles in the American heartland. In G. M. Franberg (Ed.), *The social construction of gender in different cultural contexts* (pp. 143–155). Stockholm: Fritzes.

U.S. Census Bureau. (2004). *Historical census of housing tables: Telephones*. Retrieved August 10, 2010, from http://www.census.gov/hhes/www/housing/census/historic/phone.html

USDA Economic Research Service. (2000). *Wisconsin fact sheet*. Retrieved August 10, 2010, from http://www.ers.usda.gov/epubs/other/usfact/WI.HTM

Vosko, L. (2000). *Temporary work*. Toronto, ON: University of Toronto Press.

Williams, C. (1992). The glass escalator: Hidden advantages for men in the "female" professions. *Social Problems, 39*(3), 253–267.

Williams, J. (2000). *Unbending gender: Why family and work conflict and what to do about it*. New York: Oxford University Press.

Ziebarth, A., & Tigges, L. M. (2000). Earning a living and building a life: Income-generating and income-saving strategies of rural Wisconsin families. In W. W. Falk, M. Schulman, & A. Tickamyer (Eds.), *Communities of work* (pp. 316–338). Athens, OH: Ohio University Press.

# Rural Families in Transition

Kristin E. Smith and Marybeth J. Mattingly

## Introduction

America has witnessed a transformation of the family and family life since the postwar baby boom years of the 1950s (see, for example: Glick, 1977; Stevenson & Wolfers, 2007; Casper & Bianchi, 2002). In the past, the typical life course for women was to complete high school, marry and move out of the parental home, and bear children within marriage (Glick, 1977). Some women worked for pay, but often only prior to marriage (Sørensen, 1983).[1] Conversely for men, the usual sequence of family life events was to complete schooling, enter the labor force, marry and leave the parental home. Couples generally stayed together as divorce and remarriage were uncommon (Cherlin, 1981, 2009) and few women had children outside of marriage (Wu, 2008).

The timing and sequencing of life events is dramatically different today. Many young adults stay in their parents' homes even after completing high school (Furstenberg, 2010) or return after college (Schnaiberg & Goldenberg, 2003) as they accrue more years of schooling or wait for higher paying jobs. Young adults increasingly live alone, or with other young adults, and in cohabiting relationships (Smock, 2000; Seltzer, 2000). Marriage is delayed and it is increasingly common for women to bear children outside of marriage, and these women are often well beyond their teenage years (Hamilton, Martin, & Ventura, 2009). Marriages that do form often occur later in life (Arnett, 2000; Lichter & Qian, 2004) and have a high likelihood of dissolution (Cherlin, 2009). This translates into an increasing percentage of children raised by single parents, most frequently the mother (Snyder, McLaughlin, & Findeis, 2006). Additionally, couples are living together prior to, or instead of, marriage and are more often comprised of people of the same sex.

Economic change has occurred alongside changing demographics and family life. Education levels have increased (Crissey, 2009) and in turn earnings and family income have risen (DeNavas-Walt, Proctor, & Smith, 2009). With the rise in women's employment, many families now rely on two breadwinners instead of one, again contributing to a rise in family income (Smith, 2008). Although overall earnings and family income have risen, the increase has been uneven and income inequality has increased substantially (Ellwood & Jencks, 2004).

In addition, dramatic attitudinal changes accompany these shifts in behavior. For example, there have been notable changes in Americans' perceptions of gender roles. In 1977, an estimated 74% of men and 52% of women agreed with the statement, "it is better for all involved if the man earns the money and the woman takes care of the home and children" (Galinsky, Aumann, & Bond, 2009). By 2008 that percentage had dropped to only 42% of men and 39% of women—a

---

K.E. Smith (✉)
The Carsey Institute and Department of Sociology, University of New Hampshire, Durham, NH 03824, USA
e-mail: kristin.smith@unh.edu

[1] This was particularly true for white, middle-class women but there have been historical variations in these patterns. For example, black women have historically had high labor force participation rates, even after the birth of a child (see, for example, Jones, 2010).

decrease of 32 and 13 percentage points, respectively. Similarly, in 1977, 71% of women and 49% of men somewhat or strongly agreed that "a mother who works outside the home can have just as good a relationship with her children as a mother who does not work." By 2008 this had shifted to 80% of women and 67% of men (Galinsky et al., 2009).

Although very broad, these general patterns in family life have been observed throughout America, even in rural communities (Lichter & Jensen, 2002, see also Chapter 16 in this volume), though sometimes to a lesser degree, despite the common perception that rural places have not changed. Even though rural people may prefer a "rural way of life"—where children are reared in intact families surrounded by supportive kin and community networks—rural families increasingly resemble those of urban families, due, in part, to increasing nonmarital fertility, rising divorce rates and increased cohabitation (Glasgow, 2003; O'Hare, Manning, Porter, & Lyons, 2009). Rural America has been altered by economic restructuring (Smith & Tickamyer, 2011), as communities and families that were dependent on manufacturing, farming, or resource extraction find those jobs disappearing (Tickamyer & Duncan, 1990; Falk & Lobao, 2003). Without many viable employment alternatives, many rural communities are facing dramatic shifts in age structure and substantial declines in family income. Increased in-migration of minorities and continued out-migration of youth contribute to the changing face of rural communities (Johnson & Lichter, 2010).

Using 1970, 1990, and 2009 Current Population Survey data, this chapter documents the changes in rural and urban families, and sheds light on the nuances that exist and how the patterns vary across place and for different demographic groups. Specifically, we consider how two of the most important changes in American family life—changes in family structure and changes in women's employment and family breadwinning (Bianchi, Robinson, & Milkie, 2006)—play out in rural families compared with urban families. We begin with a discussion of demographic changes in rural America to set the stage for our discussion of changes in family life. Next, we document change in family structure and discuss the contributing factors of this change on families in rural areas. The following section similarly examines the change in family breadwinning patterns. We then discuss the implications of these changes in family structure and family employment patterns for income inequality and poverty. We close with conclusions.[2]

## Changing Population Dynamics

Similar to the United States population at large, rural populations are aging, fueled by lower fertility and increased life expectancy. The post-World War II baby boom generation is now aging and this population bubble has moved upward on the population pyramid (see Fig. 17.1). Further, due to the rising cost of children and women's increased labor force participation, fertility rates have declined substantially. In 1970 nearly 55% of rural adults resided with at least one child under age 18. By 2009, this had dropped to just over 41%. While only 20% of the rural population was age 55 or over in 1970, the percentage rose to 28% by 2009, according to our analyses of CPS data. Glasgow and Brown (2008) reported that 12% of the population was over age 65, (and 15% in rural areas), but noted that when baby boomers reach retirement age, that number will swell by at least 5%. The changing age structure in rural places is visually shown in Fig. 17.1.

Figure 17.1 shows two rural population pyramids overlaid (1970 and 2009), derived from Current Population Survey (CPS) data. Clearly, the 1970 population is characterized by a younger age structure reflected in the wider base and narrower top of the

---

[2] We analyze 1970, 1990, and 2009 Current Population Survey (CPS) data (1970 and 1990 March Supplements and 2009 Annual Social and Economic Supplement data) to document change in families residing in rural, suburban, and central city places. The CPS is a nationally representative sample of American households and collects demographic, economic, and employment information. We analyze both the individual (with analyses including all respondents age 18 and over, and the total population) and family data (with analyses including all families and subfamilies with a household head 18 and over). Dollar values are inflated to 2009 using the Bureau of Labor Statistics inflation calculator. Comparisons presented in the text are statistically significant at the 0.05 level. The term "rural" and nonmetropolitan are both used to refer to persons or families living outside the officially designated metropolitan areas. Central city refers to those residing within metropolitan areas inside the central core, and suburban refers to those residing within metropolitan areas outside the central core. Those living in areas not identified by the US Census Bureau for reasons of confidentiality are not included in the analysis by place. Metropolitan residence is based on Office of Management and Budget delineation at the time of data collection.

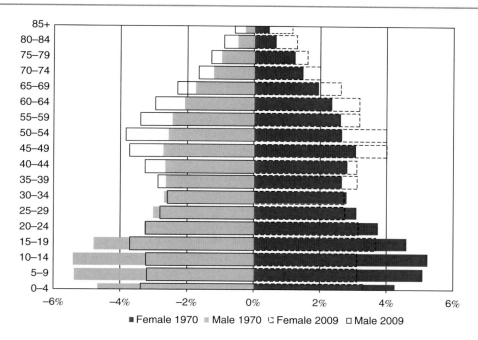

**Fig. 17.1** Population pyramids for rural America, 1970 and 2009

pyramid. In contrast, 2009 has a much narrower base and more similar distribution of ages, reflecting an aging population. We also examined population pyramids for central cities and the suburbs (data not shown).[3] In 2009, these population pyramids had a wider base and narrower top than did the 2009 rural population pyramid, reflecting a younger age distribution. However, for both suburban and, to a lesser extent, central city places, the age pyramid bases were narrower and tops were wider than 1970 (when rural and suburban places had the youngest populations), showing that although aging is more pronounced in rural areas, it is also occurring in metropolitan America.

Migration is also dramatically changing the face of rural America. Many young people are leaving rural places after high school, in search of better or broader opportunities (Demi, McLaughlin, & Snyder, 2007). Some rural places, those with more amenities such as mountains or proximity to rivers and streams, are seeing in-migration of retirees (Glasgow & Brown, 2008).

In addition to the changing age composition and migration patterns, the racial profile of rural America is changing (see Chapter 15 in this volume). Our own analyses of CPS data suggest a smaller percent of rural America is white. In 1990, 88% of adults in rural America were white (see Table 17.1). By 2009, only 84% were white. While we see stability, or modest increases for other racial groups (except Blacks), the bulk of this change is driven by larger Hispanic representation in rural America. Hispanics are increasingly migrating to rural areas, and have higher fertility rates than other groups (see Johnson & Lichter, 2010; Lichter & Johnson, 2009). Despite these changes, it is worth noting that rural areas remain the most racially homogenous type of place in America.

**Table 17.1** Racial distribution of all adults, 1990 and 2009

| Race/ethnicity | Rural | | Central city | | Suburban | |
|---|---|---|---|---|---|---|
| | 1990 | 2009 | 1990 | 2009 | 1990 | 2009 |
| White, non-Hispanic | 87.7 | 83.6 | 59.4 | 50.0 | 83.1 | 71.2 |
| Black, non-Hispanic | 8.1 | 7.0 | 21.9 | 18.9 | 6.3 | 9.6 |
| Other, non-Hispanic | 1.8 | 3.8 | 5.1 | 9.4 | 3.3 | 6.2 |
| Hispanic | 2.4 | 5.6 | 13.7 | 21.7 | 7.2 | 13.1 |

*Note*: Includes people 18 and over.
*Source*: Current Population Survey, 1990 and 2009.

---

[3] Population pyramid data for central cities and suburban areas for 1970 and 2009 are available upon request.

The racial composition of the entire nation is changing, and white Americans may soon be the largest minority rather than the majority group. In 1990, nearly two-thirds of births were white, non-Hispanic children, but by 2008, white, non-Hispanic births represented only about half of all births in America (Johnson & Lichter, 2010). Indeed, we find that across America, black, Hispanic and other races/ethnicities are representing a larger share of the American population. In 1990, America was just under 80% white. By 2009, this had declined by over 9 percentage points, representing a decline of over 20%, according to our analyses of CPS data. This aggregate, however, masks the larger representation of white, non-Hispanics at older ages, who will be replaced by younger generations with greater minority representation (see Johnson & Lichter, 2010). It is with this picture of changing demographics that we turn to changes in the family.

## Changing Rural Families

### Changing Family Structure

Family demographers widely acknowledge dramatic shifts in family formation and composition over the past 60 years. Cohabitation, delayed marriage and childlessness have become more common. However, we have also seen increases in births outside marriage and divorce, both of which lead to increased single motherhood. Economic and cultural shifts accompanying these changes have made it both more enticing for women to invest in their own human capital and enter the labor force *and* more difficult for families to survive on one income.

Scholars recognize historical differences between metropolitan and nonmetropolitan places that have implications for family formation. Snyder (2011) cites the trend for more traditional marital and fertility behaviors in rural America but also acknowledges research showing increases in single motherhood that may be an indicator of change toward some of the patterns more typically observed in nonmetro places. Brown and Snyder (2006) recognize that rural places tend to have tighter knit communities that lend themselves to "shared morals and values that encourage conformity to local norms" (p. 313). Further, rural places can often be characterized as more traditional and conservative than their urban counterparts (see also Larson, 1978; Willits, Bealer, & Crider, 1982, as cited in Brown & Snyder, 2006).

These characteristics of rural America might lead us to expect higher rates of marriage, younger ages at marriage and first birth, fewer births to unmarried mothers, and lower cohabitation rates than in urban places. Indeed, the research largely supports this. Snyder, Brown, and Condo (2004) found rural women marry more often and at younger ages than their urban counterparts. Rural women are more likely than urban women to both have sex and marry younger (Heaton, Lichter, & Amoateng, 1989), and are more likely to have their first birth within marriage (Snyder et al., 2004). Heaton et al. therefore conclude that "rural residents are more inclined to legitimize sexual activity and parenthood through marriage" (1989, p. 9). Rural women are also more likely than urban women to marry following a nonmarital birth (Albrecht & Albrecht, 2004).

Despite cultural differences between rural and urban places, many of the trends observed across America are also evident in rural places. Indeed the economic restructuring of rural America provides ample reason for us to expect family patterns have undergone dramatic shifts. These may even occur faster in some rural places than in urban areas, where rates of nontraditional family formation may already be high.

Our own analyses of Current Population Survey data from March 1970, 1990, and 2009 suggest that marriage rates have declined over time for rural places, as shown in Fig. 17.2. Slight increases are evident over time in the percent of respondents never married and divorced or separated and declines in widowhood are evident.

The proportion of adults currently married was highest for rural and suburban residents and lowest for those residing in central cities in 1970, and remained higher for them in 1990 and 2009. However, the percent of rural and suburban residents who were married dropped precipitously during these forty years from over 70% to well below 60%. Declines were also evident in central cities where the percent of adults currently married declined from 63% to 46%. Part of this decline can be explained by rising rates of cohabitation, as discussed below. However, research suggests that relative to their urban counterparts, rural women may have a higher preference for marriage

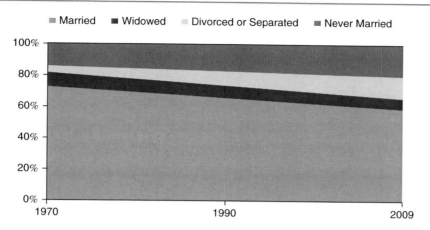

**Fig. 17.2** Marital status of people ages 18 and over in rural places over time

(Snyder, 2011). Snyder (p. 135) finds that "compared to suburban metro and central city metro women, nonmetropolitan women spend a significantly larger percentage of their lives in the married state, have lower odds of divorce from a first marriage, remarry quicker following the end of a first marriage, and have higher odds of remarriage." Thus, despite the similar trend away from marriage observed across place, rural families may still reflect more traditional patterns than do urban and suburban families.

Recent research by O'Hare et al. (2009) describes children residing with cohabiting partners in rural America. Although they acknowledge that cohabitation rates are similar across place for unmarried single women without children, they are higher for rural single mothers (see Snyder et al., 2006). O'Hare et al. (2009) find that, as a result of more rapid increases in rates of cohabitation in rural places, the percent of children living in cohabitating families is higher in rural America than it is in urban places. Specifically, in 1995, 3% of rural and urban children lived with cohabiting adults. By 2005–2006, this number had only increased to 4% among urban children, but had risen to 7% of rural children. O'Hare et al. (2009) suggest this trend may be attributable, at least in part, to greater perceived financial pressure among rural single parents. O'Hare et al.'s (2009) findings suggest that these families are more often in poverty than are children in married couple families (more than one in five rural children in cohabiting households is poor compared to only one in ten children in married couple households), yet they fare better than children in families headed by single mothers without cohabiting partners.

Cohabitation appears to be one strategy employed by poor rural mothers to offset financial stress (O'Hare et al., 2009). Rural cohabiting parents are less likely to have any college education than their urban counterparts and face higher unemployment rates (O'Hare et al., 2009) and thus may face such stresses more frequently.

Casper and Sayer (2000) identified several types of cohabiting relationships: those acting as substitutes for marriage, precursors to marriage, trial marriages, and coresidential dating. They find the highest rates of separation 5–7 years later in couples whose partnerships resembled trial marriages or coresidential dating. Cohabiting women in rural America are somewhat more likely to marry their cohabiting partners than are their urban counterparts (see Brown and Snyder 2006 who find slightly higher entry into marriage among nonmetro cohabitors within 2 years of cohabiting), suggesting cohabitation more often acts as a precursor to marriage in rural America and that cohabiting relationships in rural America may be different in nature than cohabiting relationships in other places. This is also supported by Sherman (2009) who studied a very poor rural place in California. Her findings suggest that many cohabiting couples would like to marry, but are waiting until they can afford a wedding.

According to our analyses of the CPS, being divorced or separated was a less common marital status in rural America than in central cities in 1970 and 1990. In 1970, 4% of rural adults were divorced or separated (and not remarried), while by 2009 this had risen to more than 13%, on par with central

**Table 17.2** Number of children by marital status, 1970–2009

|  | Total | | | Rural | | | Central city | | | Suburban | | |
| --- | --- | --- | --- | --- | --- | --- | --- | --- | --- | --- | --- | --- |
|  | 1970 | 1990 | 2009 | 1970 | 1990 | 2009 | 1970 | 1990 | 2009 | 1970 | 1990 | 2009 |
| Married |  |  |  |  |  |  |  |  |  |  |  |  |
| No children | 42.6 | 53.0 | 57.2 | 43.4 | 54.2 | 63.4 | 47.9 | 53.6 | 54.3 | 38.1 | 51.7 | 56.0 |
| 1 Child | 18.4 | 18.4 | 16.6 | 17.5 | 17.8 | 14.5 | 18.5 | 18.9 | 18.2 | 19.1 | 18.6 | 16.8 |
| 2 Children | 18.0 | 18.7 | 16.7 | 17.5 | 17.9 | 13.8 | 16.0 | 17.3 | 17.1 | 20.0 | 20.0 | 18.0 |
| 3 or More children | 21.0 | 9.9 | 9.4 | 21.6 | 10.0 | 8.4 | 17.6 | 10.2 | 10.4 | 22.9 | 9.7 | 9.3 |
| Never married |  |  |  |  |  |  |  |  |  |  |  |  |
| No children | 76.3 | 37.6 | 39.2 | 79.5 | 34.6 | 31.6 | 71.2 | 32.9 | 39.0 | 83.1 | 46.6 | 42.9 |
| 1 Child | 10.8 | 34.5 | 32.4 | 8.0 | 38.6 | 35.3 | 13.7 | 33.5 | 32.2 | 7.7 | 32.9 | 31.4 |
| 2 Children | 5.4 | 16.4 | 17.9 | 3.0 | 16.9 | 21.8 | 7.1 | 18.6 | 16.9 | 4.8 | 13.1 | 16.7 |
| 3 or More children | 7.6 | 11.6 | 10.5 | 9.5 | 9.9 | 11.4 | 8.0 | 15.0 | 12.0 | 4.4 | 7.3 | 9.1 |

*Source*: Current Population Survey, 1970, 1990, and 2009.

cities[4] and *higher* than in the suburbs (data not shown). Overall, 12% of the rural population aged 15 and older is divorced, compared to 10% in suburban areas and 11% in urban areas. As noted above, recent research suggests that rural residents remarry quicker than their urban peers (Snyder, 2011), suggesting these observed differences in presently being divorced are somewhat smaller than the place differences in divorce rates.

Not only is marriage changing across America, including in rural places, but family size is changing as well. Rural households, historically larger than urban households, are now smaller, reflecting the aging population and lower birth rates (MacTavish & Salamon, 2003). This is echoed and detailed by O'Hare and Johnson (2004, p. 1):

> Just as the rural economy has changed, so too has the rural family. Urban families are now larger than their rural counterparts. Data from the 2000 Census show the average family size inside metropolitan areas was 3.2 persons compared with 3.0 outside metropolitan areas. Two important demographic forces account for this transformation. First, fertility rates in rural areas have declined, and rural women now have about the same number of children as urban women. Second, the rural population is now considerably older on average than the urban population. The median age in 2000 was 37.2 in nonmetropolitan America, compared with 34.9 in the nation's metropolitan areas. Rural areas also have a higher proportion of people ages 65 and older (15%), compared with urban areas (12%). Family size in rural areas has decreased because a growing share of rural households are headed by older Americans, who are less likely to have children in the household.

Our own analyses of CPS data reveal that both the average family size, and the number of children among families with children have declined over time. In 1970, the average family size in rural America was 3.6, slightly larger than in central cities (3.5) and marginally lower than in the suburbs (3.7). By 2009, that number declined to 3.0 in rural America, not substantively different than urban places (3.1 in both central cities and the suburbs). Similar declines are evident in the number of children present in families with children under age 18. In 1970, the mean number of children was 2.4 in rural America, 2.3 in the suburbs and central cities. By 2009 that number fell to 1.9 in each place type (data not shown).

As shown in Table 17.2, there has also been an increasing trend towards living without children (under age 18) in both rural and urban (suburbs and central cities) places among married couples, yet a declining trend among the never married in rural and suburban America. In rural America, the rate of living without children among these adults fell from nearly 80% in 1970 to just over 30% in 2009. In 2009, rural never married adults had the lowest rate, followed by those residing in central cities and the suburbs. The picture is rather different when we look at previously married adults. Small declines in childlessness (from about 54

---

[4] Although substantively similar, the difference between rural (13.3%) and central city (13.2%) places is statistically significant given large sample size.

to 47%) exist in rural America, but small increases are evident in suburban places and central cities (data not shown).

An increasing number of children are growing up with single mothers. We illustrated the declines in marriage and rise in nonmarital childbearing in rural America. McLaughlin and Coleman-Jensen (2011) document an increase in the prevalence of single mother families between 1980 and 2000, and show that the rural-urban gap in single motherhood is narrowing. A vast array of literature has documented the challenges faced by such families, as discussed below.

Before concluding our discussion of changes in family formation and family structure across rural America, it is worth noting the increased presence of same sex couples across the country. Although many such couples are heavily concentrated in progressive urban locales, estimates suggest gay and lesbian families are more geographically dispersed than one might think. Smith and Gates (2001) examined unmarried same sex couples using 2000 census data and estimated that roughly 15%, or over 88,000 gay and lesbian families, reside in rural places. Romero, Baumle, Badgett, and Gates (2007) echo this, noting that same sex couples are located in all county types, rural and urban alike. They further explain that these couples are, in many ways, like their heterosexual counterparts: racially and ethnically diverse, participating in the economy (as consumers and workers), and about one in five same sex couples are raising children.

## Changing Family Work Patterns and Breadwinning

A second notable change in American families over the past 60 years is the large influx of women, and notably wives and mothers, into the labor force (Bianchi et al., 2006). Women's employment grew sharply in the 1970s and 1980s, before slowing in the 1990s and decreasing slightly in the early 2000s (Smith, 2008), raising the question of whether the plateauing of women's employment, along with other indicators, is indicative of a larger phenomenon: the stalling of women's equality (Cotter, DeFiore, Hermsen, Kowalewski, & Vanneman, 1996). Trends in employment rates among rural and urban women were parallel from 1970 to 2000. However, after decades of slightly higher employment rates among urban women (Rogers, 1997), employment rates of rural and urban women converged in 2003, owing to a larger decline in employment among urban women over the 2001 recession (Smith, 2008). Since 1990, our analyses show that rural women have had higher employment rates than women in central cities, but lower employment rates than women in the suburbs (data not shown).

Variations in employment patterns exist among single mothers and married mothers by place. Historically single mothers had higher employment rates than married mothers in both rural and urban areas. Large increases in married mothers' employment and a leveling of employment rates among single mothers over the 1980s reversed that pattern (Smith, 2011). However, single mothers' employment rose substantially over the 1990s, particularly in urban areas. By the turn of the century, rural married and single mothers had similar employment rates, and urban single mothers were more likely to be employed than urban married mothers.

Today, married rural women and rural mothers are more likely to work and work more hours per week than their urban counterparts. In 2006, 70% of married women with children under age 6 in rural areas worked for pay compared with 64% in urban areas (Smith, 2008). Furthermore, since 2000, more married than single women have been in the workforce in rural areas. This is the first time America has witnessed this pattern.

Concurrent with increased employment among rural women has been an increase in rural women's work hours and earnings. Research illustrates that rural women earn less than urban women (Cotter et al., 1996; McLaughlin & Perman, 1991; Vera-Toscano, Phimister, & Weersink, 2004) and they are disproportionately concentrated in low paying occupations and industries (Bokemeier & Tickamyer, 1985). Smith (2008) finds that rural women's real earnings rose from $23,538 in 1969 to $27,000 in 2006—an increase of 15%. However, urban women's earnings grew by 25% during the same time period, from $28,015 to $35,000, thus widening the spatial earnings gap among women. This disparity remains even after accounting for differences in marital status, motherhood, race, education, and age. Smith and Glauber (2009) find that urban women earn 19% more per hour than rural women. Further, they find that the spatial earnings gap increases as women's education increases. Their results suggest the gap can be explained by variations in the labor markets available to women residing in different place types. Rural women with college degrees are concentrated in lower-paying education and health industries, while their urban counterparts are concentrated in higher-paying industries, such as professional services and finance.[5]

Wives employment and increased earnings have also contributed to a shift in breadwinning patterns among married couples in both rural and urban America. Decades ago, more than half of all married couples relied on husbands as the sole breadwinner (Raley, Mattingly, & Bianchi, 2006). Yet, today a large majority of couples are dual providers, relying on both husbands' and wives' earnings to make ends meet, and wives are increasingly acting as equal or primary providers. Indeed, the fastest growing category is equal provider couples, where both husbands and wives contribute about half of total family earnings.

Trends in breadwinning patterns among rural, central city and suburban married couple families are remarkably similar,[6] with a shift away from husbands as sole providers and toward equal providers and wives as sole providers (see Figs. 17.3A, 17.3B, and 17.3C). Yet some differences remain. By 2009, rural married couples were less reliant on husbands as sole providers than married couples in central cities or suburban areas.

Many rural families today are turning to women as economic providers as they need a second income to alleviate the family's strained budget. Traditionally male-dominated fields like farming, mining, logging, and paper mills continue to disappear due to economic restructuring and accelerated during the "Great Recession" of 2008–2009 (Smith & Tickamyer, 2011), with few replacement jobs and some growth in the service economy. Since 1980, rural men are less likely to be working and earn less than their urban peers; their wages have been declining as well (Smith, 2011). Unemployment and chronic underemployment are higher in the rural U.S. for both men and women (Jensen & Jensen, 2011). Inadequate employment is especially problematic for rural women (Lichter, 1989). Even in more traditionally minded rural areas, wives have become primary earners when their husbands have lost their jobs (Tickamyer & Henderson, 2003).

Further evidence of families' increasing dependence on women's earnings is the growing share of employed wives' contribution to total family earnings. In both rural and urban families, wives' economic contribution to family economic stability increased. During the second year of the "Great Recession" (roughly in 2009), employed wives' contribution to family earnings rose from 45 to 47%—the largest single-year increase in the past ten years (Smith, 2010). Additionally, almost half of the total increase in employed wives' share of family earnings over the past 15 years occurred during the "Great Recession" from 2007 to 2009.

Recent research by Mattingly and Smith (2010) further documents the toll the "Great Recession" has had on families' economic well-being in light of men's massive job loss, and the role that wives' earnings play in bolstering families during an economic downturn. They found that rural wives were less likely to enter the labor force during the recession than their urban counterparts, driven by their lower propensity to look for work. These findings may be indicative of a tighter job market in rural areas during the recession, or to more traditional gender norms among rural families.

## Factors Contributing to the Shift in Breadwinning Patterns Among American Families

Large shifts in how women allocate their time and negotiate their work and family responsibilities are due to several contributing factors. First, as discussed above, social change and shifting family structure exemplified in delays in marriage, declines in fertility, and the rise in cohabitation and divorce result in women spending less time married and raising children, leaving more time for paid market work (Casper & Bianchi, 2002).

---

[5] Some of the differences in wages may be attributable to differences in the cost of living in rural and other areas (Debertin & Goetz, 1994; Kurre, 2003).

[6] Our analyses differ from the Raley et al. (2006) analyses in several ways: our estimates (a) are place-based, (b) report estimates using earnings rather than income, (c) include both primary and secondary families, and (d) include couples with neither spouse employed. Our estimates for 1990 and 2009 are not substantially different from the Raley et al. (1990) and (2001) estimates. However, we report lower levels of husbands as sole providers and higher levels of husbands as primary providers in 1970 compared with the Raley et al. (1970) estimates, but the general trends are the same.

**Fig. 17.3A** Married couple earner status in rural places over time

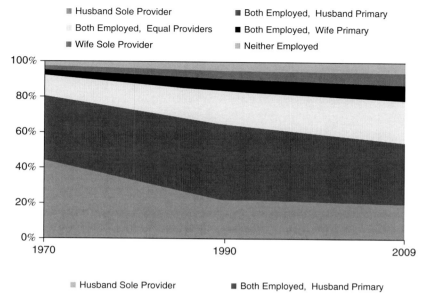

**Fig. 17.3B** Married couple earner status in central cities over time

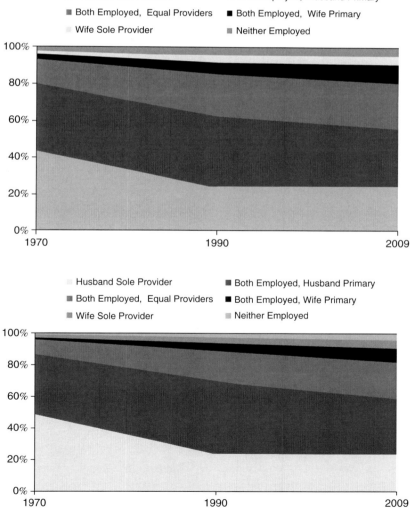

**Fig. 17.3C** Married couple earner status in suburban places over time

Second, the rise in single mother families, stagnant and in some cases declining men's wages, and job loss in industries that traditionally employ men (such as manufacturing and agriculture) have increased the need for women to work for pay (Levy, 1998). Concurrent with the increased need for women's earnings, opportunities for women in the labor market have increased. Both the rise in educational attainment among women and an increased demand in typically female jobs in the service sector due to economic restructuring have increased opportunities for women to secure employment in the paid labor market (Blau, Ferber, & Winkler, 2002; Falk & Lobao, 2003; Sayer, Cohen, & Casper, 2004).

Furthermore, attitudes have become more accepting of women working outside the home for pay, even women with young children, making it more acceptable for women to engage in market work (Goldin, 2006).

Finally, parallel with the rise in women's employment, policymakers have introduced legislation to ease work and family conflict (such as the Family Medical Leave Act of 1993), and also legislation that mandates paid work for single mothers who otherwise might seek welfare (such as Temporary Assistance for Needy Families). In addition, flexible workplace policies are more prevalent today; all of which translates into a climate that is more supportive of workers with family responsibilities encouraging women to work and remain working (Glauber, 2009).

## Implications of Changes in Family Structure and Women's Employment

The rise in single parenthood and mothers' employment has some worrying that today's parents have less time for children, as mothers now juggle the dual roles of worker and family caretaker in ways not seen before (Bianchi et al., 2006). Social observers and researchers alike voice concern about the well-being of children and the quality of family life. For example, two decades ago, James Coleman (1988) pointed to the rise in maternal employment and the rise in single parenting as two factors within the family that were reducing time and attention children were receiving from parents, thus diminishing the parent-child relationship and therefore reducing children's social capital. Bianchi et al. (2006) in their careful analysis of changing trends in parents' time use refute these claims and show that despite increased employment and single parenting, mothers have managed to guard their time with children and fathers have increased their time with children, such that parents are spending as much, and in some cases more, time with children than in 1965.

Nevertheless, changes in marriage patterns have had implications for children (McLanahan & Sandefur, 1994). As marriage and fertility sequencing are often reversed, people marry later or forego marriage, and divorce is fairly normative, it is not surprising that an increasing number of children are growing up with single parents, most commonly mothers. A vast array of literature has documented the challenges facing such families including higher poverty rates (e.g., Cancian & Reed, 2009), underemployment or unemployment (see English, Hartmann, & Hegewisch, 2009; Grall, 2009), severe depression (Pascoe et al., 2010), and experiencing intimate partner violence (Huang, Son, & Wang, 2010). While rural America trails urban America on many dimensions of family change, McLaughlin and Coleman-Jensen (2011) show that the rural-urban gap in single motherhood is narrowing. Children growing up in female-headed households in rural places are increasing and are more likely to face these same challenges, including living in poverty.

Research consistently shows that poverty in rural America rivals that in urban (suburb and central city combined) places (Joliffe, 2004; Lichter & Eggebeen, 1992; see also Chapter 20 in this volume), despite public opinion to the contrary. However, when comparisons are made between rural, suburban, and central city places since the 1990s, rural poverty is higher than poverty rates in the suburbs, but lower than the rates seen in central cities (data not shown). In addition, one in five rural children is growing up poor, and half of these children live in "deep poverty," in families with income less than half the poverty line (O'Hare, 2009). The rural poor tend to live in poverty longer than their urban counterparts, and more rural than urban places are characterized as persistently poor for decades (Miller & Weber, 2003).

Place-based differences in poverty may, in part, be explained by differences in family structure and human capital. It is widely known that poverty rates are especially high for those raised by single mothers and among families where parents have limited educational attainment (see Snyder et al., 2004). In fact, we find that poverty rates among rural married couples are lower than those seen among rural single-headed families. While families with two earners have made economic gains over the past decades, single-earner families and single-parent families have been left behind (Casper & Bianchi, 2002). Evidence of increasing inequality among American families is visible when looking at median family income over time and the rise in the gap between the highest earning families and the lowest earning families by marital status and employment status.

Past research suggests income inequality is greatest within central cities, followed by nonmetropolitan places and lowest in the suburbs (Levernier, Partridge, & Rickman, 1998). Rising income inequality within rural places results largely from the economic restructuring these places have undergone over the past four decades. Indeed, Parrado and Kandel (2010) suggest it is population growth and economic expansion that underlie this trend, and while they explicitly examined the role of an increasing Hispanic presence in rural America, they did not find evidence that this contributed to economic inequality.

Our own analysis shows that median family income has been rising since the 1970s, such that rural families experienced income growth over the past five decades (data not shown). Patterns of growth in family income among those living in central cities are similar to those seen in rural areas, with two differences. First, family income levels in central cities are higher than those in rural areas, and second, the overall gains in family income from 1970 to 2009 were larger in rural areas. Median family income levels are consistently higher in the suburbs than in other areas, and suburban families have seen a flattening of family income since 1990.[7]

One measure of income inequality is the gap, or the ratio of the median family income among the lowest earning quintile and the highest earning quintile. We find that this gap has been rising over the past five decades (see Table 17.3). In 1970, families at the highest quintile earned 6 times more than families at the bottom quintile. By 2009, this gap had risen to 9 times more, a rise of 53% (data not shown). The gap in median family income has grown in rural and urban places, but to a lesser extent in rural areas. Income inequality is highest among families living in central cities, with those at the top earning nearly 12 times more than those at the bottom. Historically income inequality was higher among rural than suburban families, but our analysis shows that by 2009 rural family income inequality was slightly lower than that seen in the suburbs.

Rural areas experienced smaller increases in income inequality compared to urban places due to different patterns in wage growth among the lower quintiles. Wage growth occurred for all the quintiles in rural areas, but at a slightly faster rate among the highest earning families. In contrast, families in the two lowest quintiles living in central cities and suburbs experienced declines in family income while their counterparts in the highest two quintiles saw large increases in family income. Thus, income inequality grew at a faster pace in central cities and suburbs.

Income inequality is higher among single-headed families than married couple families (see Table 17.3). In 2009, rural married couples at the top earned 5.9 times those at the bottom, while rural single-headed families at the top earned 10.3 times more. Yet, income inequality did not rise dramatically among either group in rural areas over the past 50 years. This was not the case in urban areas, where income inequality grew among married couple and single-headed families. Increased inequality was the greatest among families living in central cities.

Not only do families with two earners have the highest median family income and lowest poverty rates, but they also experienced the lowest income inequality compared with married, one earner couples and single-headed families. Income inequality grew by a minimal amount (just by 3%) among married dual-earner families in rural areas. In contrast, income inequality among married dual-earner families rose by 52% in central cities and by 37% in the suburbs.

Rural places have lower levels of income inequality than urban places and since 1970 income inequality has grown at a slower pace in rural areas. For some rural families, income inequality has actually declined—among married couples with one earner.

The growth in income inequality may be slower in rural areas due to differing labor markets by place. Rural residents typically face more limited employment options, have lower income growth, and earn less than their metropolitan peers (Jensen & Jensen, 2011).

---

[7] Dollar values are inflated to 2009 using the Bureau of Labor Statistics inflation calculator; substantive earnings differences are discussed.

**Table 17.3** Income inequality by place, 1970–2009

| | Rural | | | Percent change | Central city | | | Percent change | Suburban | | | Percent change |
|---|---|---|---|---|---|---|---|---|---|---|---|---|
| | 1970 | 1990 | 2009 | 1970–2009 | 1970 | 1990 | 2009 | 1970–2009 | 1970 | 1990 | 2009 | 1970–2009 |
| All families | 6.6 | 7.3 | 7.9 | 20.0 | 5.9 | 10.2 | 11.9 | 100.0 | 4.7 | 6.6 | 8.1 | 74.0 |
| Single | 9.4 | 10.0 | 10.3 | 10.0 | 7.3 | 12.2 | 12.2 | 66.0 | 1.3 | 10.0 | 10.9 | 23.0 |
| Married | 5.9 | 5.7 | 5.9 | 1.0 | 4.9 | 6.6 | 8.7 | 77.0 | 4.2 | 5.5 | 6.6 | 56.0 |
| Dual–earner | 3.7 | 4.1 | 3.8 | 3.0 | 3.4 | 4.3 | 5.2 | 52.0 | 3.0 | 3.8 | 4.1 | 37.0 |
| One earner | 5.4 | 5.9 | 5.2 | −4.0 | 4.5 | 6.3 | 8.3 | 86.0 | 3.9 | 6.2 | 7.2 | 81.0 |

*Note*: Income inequality measure is the ratio of the median family income among the lowest earning quintile and the median family income among the highest earning quintile.
*Source*: Current Population Survey, 1970, 1990, and 2009.

Some research suggests that rural Americans may suffer from higher rates of underemployment, working at jobs for fewer hours than they would ideally like. Slack and Jensen (2002) suggest that residing in a nonmetropolitan place is an obstacle to full employment, as is being a member of a minority group. As a result, rural minorities are doubly challenged in the labor market. However, there are little differences in the employment of Hispanics and white adults in nonmetropolitan places and black-white differences in nonmetropolitan America are declining, minorities residing in nonmetropolitan America are more likely than their metro counterparts to experience underemployment. Additionally, research suggests that relative to their metropolitan counterparts, nonmetropolitan adults are more likely to be employed in contingent work or to work varied hours (McLaughlin & Coleman-Jensen, 2008). Such nonstandard work schedules are associated with lower wages and fewer benefits. McCrate (2011) finds that rural workers are more likely to work nonstandard work schedules with less control over their work schedule; and Nelson (2011) demonstrates that low-income rural families with less job flexibility fare much worse than those with more.

## Conclusions

Rural families are in transition. Population dynamics such as a growing minority population, lower fertility, and aging populations contribute to the changing face of rural families. On many measures rural families resemble urban families; though nuanced differences still exist. All places have seen a general decline in marriage; yet, rural families still reflect more traditional marriage patterns than urban families as rural women spend more time married, have lower levels of divorce, remarry quicker, and have higher odds of remarriage.

Similarly, employment patterns of women in rural and urban places have converged. However, rural women (and men) have lower earnings and married couples in rural areas exhibit more equitable breadwinning patterns, with a lower reliance on husbands as sole breadwinners in rural areas compared with suburban and central city places. This may be due to a greater need in rural areas for a second earner to help families make ends meet. Wives are making important contributions to family economic well-being and rural families are increasingly relying on wives' employment and earnings. Over the past decades this reflects a growing need for two earners, and more recently may reflect declines in men's employment concurrent with the recession. With more mothers working outside of the home, access to child care becomes crucial as does paid sick leave and workplace flexibility, both of which allow working parents the tools necessary to balance their family and work demands, such as time off to care for sick children or supervise children when school is closed.

Finally, income inequality is growing in all places, yet rural family income inequality has grown at a slower pace than that seen in central cities or suburban areas, and some rural families have actually seen a decline in income inequality. While it may seem optimistic that the pace of inequality is slower in rural America, we must remember that incomes are also typically lower in rural America and income growth has been lower in rural areas as well. Thus, those at the bottom may be earning salaries somewhat closer to those at the top, but those at the top of the income distribution in rural America are typically earning less than those at the top of the income distribution in urban places. Further, rural places, like urban places, are also confronting increasing poverty, and child poverty rates continue to be higher in rural America (Mattingly & Stransky, 2010). Thus, policies and programs aimed at alleviating financial stress must consider rural populations and pay attention to the specific needs faced by various rural communities.

While rural populations may be starting to resemble urban populations in terms of family structure and employment patterns, important distinctions remain in these and other domains. The nature of rural life is very different from that in urban places: population density is lower, amenities and services are more widely distributed, there is often a sense that "everyone knows everyone" and thus people are cautious to avoid stigma and to keep private matters close. The emerging similarities between rural and urban places suggest many similar needs: needs for affordable, quality child care, access to jobs that offer benefits, flexibility, and growth opportunities, opportunities for youth, services for older Americans, and so forth. However, the implementation of delivery of programs and services may look very different across place. Transportation continues to be a challenge for rural residents. Providing services is incredibly challenging when there is not a population center and outreach efforts take longer. Finally, rural America is not homogenous. The places that have experienced high rates of poverty for decades will need a different array of policies and services than those places rich in natural beauty and tourist opportunities: places that attract "the best and the brightest" and are destinations for both vacation and retirement.

Future research that further describes differences within rural places and situates those differences within the context of rural-urban differences will be valuable as we enter the coming decades and consider how to develop policies and practices that are most advantageous given shrinking resources.

**Acknowledgements** The authors would like to thank Jessica Bean and Michelle Stransky for research assistance. This work was supported by the Annie E. Casey Foundation, the W. K. Kellogg Foundation, and anonymous donation.

# References

Albrecht, D. E., & Albrecht, C. M. (2004). Metro/nonmetro residence, nonmarital conception, and conception outcomes. *Rural Sociology, 69*(3), 430–452.

Arnett, J. J. (2000). Emerging adulthood: A theory of development from the late teens through the twenties. *American Psychologist, 55*(5), 469–480.

Bianchi, S. M., Robinson, J. P., & Milkie, M. A. (2006). *Changing rhythms of American family life*. New York: Russell Sage Foundation Publications.

Blau, F. D., Ferber, M. A., & Winkler, A. E. (2002). *The economics of women, men, and work* (4th ed.). Upper Saddle River, NJ: Prentice Hall.

Bokemeier, J., & Tickamyer, A. (1985). Labor force experiences of nonmetropolitan women. *Rural Sociology, 50*, 51–73.

Brown, S. L., & Snyder, A. R. (2006). Residential differences in cohabitors' union transition. *Rural Sociology, 71*(2), 311–334.

Cancian, M., & Reed, D. (2009). Family structure, childbearing, and parental employment: Implications for the level and trend in poverty. *Focus, 26*(2), 21–26.

Casper, L. M., & Bianchi, S. M. (2002). *Continuity and change in the American family*. Thousand Oaks, CA: Sage.

Casper, L. M., & Sayer, L. C. (2000). *Cohabitation transitions: Different attitudes and purposes, different paths*. Presented at the annual meeting of the Population Association of America, March, Los Angeles.

Cherlin, A. J. (1981). *Marriage, divorce, and remarriage*. Cambridge, MA: Harvard University Press.

Cherlin, A. J. (2009). *The marriage-go-round: The state of marriage and the family in America today*. New York: Alfred A. Knopf, Random House, Inc.

Coleman, J. (1988). Social capital in the creation of human capital. *American Journal of Sociology, Supplement 94*, S95–S120.

Cotter, D. A., DeFiore, J., Hermsen, J. M., Kowalewski, B. M., & Vanneman, R. (1996). Gender inequality in nonmetropolitan and metropolitan areas. *Rural Sociology, 61*, 272–288.

Crissey, S. R. (2009). Educational Attainment in the United States: 2007. *Current Population Reports*, U.S. Census Bureau.

Debertin, D. L., & Goetz, S. J. (1994). *Differences in rural and urban schools: Issues for policymakers*. Lexington, KY: Department of Agricultural Economics, University of Kentucky.

Demi, M. A., McLaughlin, D., & Snyder, A. R. (2007). *Rural youth—Stayers and leavers*. Paper presented at the Annual Meeting of the Rural Sociological Society, Santa Clara, CA, August 2, 2007.

DeNavas-Walt, C., Proctor, B. D., & Smith, J. C. (2009). Income, poverty, and health insurance coverage in the United States: 2009. *Current Population Reports*, P60-238. U.S. Census Bureau.

Ellwood, D. T., & Jencks, C. (2004). The uneven spread of single-parent families: What do we know? In K. M. Neckerman (Ed.), *Social inequality* (pp. 3–78). New York: Russell Sage Foundation.

English, A., Hartmann, H., & Hegewisch, A. (2009). *Unemployment among single mother families*. Fact Sheet

#C369. Washington, DC: Institute for Women's Policy Research.

Falk, W., & Lobao, L. (2003). Who benefits from economic restructuring? Lessons from the past, challenges for the future? In D. Brown & L. Swanson (Eds.), *Challenges for rural America in the twenty-first century* (pp. 152–165). University Park, PA: Pennsylvania State University Press.

Furstenberg, F. F. (2010). On a new schedule: Transitions to adulthood and family change. *Transition to Adulthood, 20*(1), 67–87.

Galinsky, E., Aumann, K., & Bond, J. T. (2009). *Times are changing: Gender and generation at work and at home.* New York: Families and Work Institute.

Glasgow, N. (2003). Older rural families. In D. Brown & L. E. Swanson (Eds.), *Challenges for rural America in the twenty-first century* (pp. 86–96). University Park, PA: Penn State University Press.

Glasgow, N., & Brown, D. L. (2008). *Grey gold: Do older in-migrants benefit rural communities?* Policy Brief No. 10. Durham, NH: Carsey Institute.

Glauber, R. (2009). *Family-friendly policies for rural working mothers.* Policy Brief No. 15. Durham, NH: Carsey Institute.

Glick, P. C. (1977). Updating the life cycle of the family. *Journal of Marriage and Family, 39*(1), 5–13.

Goldin, C. (2006). The quiet revolution that transformed women's employment, education, and family. *The American Economic Review, 96*(2), 1–21.

Grall, T. S. (2009). *Custodial mothers and fathers and their child support: 2007.* Current Population Reports. Washington, DC: U.S. Census Bureau.

Hamilton, B. E., Martin, J. A., & Ventura, S. J. (2009). Births: Preliminary data for 2007. *National Vital Statistics Reports, 57*(12). National Center for Health Statistics, Center for Disease Control and Prevention, U.S. Department of Health and Human Services.

Heaton, T. B., Lichter, D. T., & Amoateng, A. (1989). The timing of family formation: Rural-urban differentials in first intercourse, childbirth, and marriage. *Rural Sociology, 54*(1), 1–16.

Huang, C., Son, E., & Wang, L. (2010). Prevalence and factors of domestic violence among unmarried mothers with a young child. *Families in Society, 91*(2), 171–177.

Jensen, L., & Jensen, E. B. (2011). Employment hardship among rural men. In K. Smith & A. Tickamyer (Eds.), *Economic restructuring and family well being in rural America* (pp. 40–59). University Park, PA: Pennsylvania State University Press.

Johnson, K. M., & Lichter, D. T. (2010). *The changing faces of America's children and youth.* Issue Brief No. 15. Durham, NH: The Carsey Institute.

Joliffe, D. (2004). Rural poverty at a glance. *Rural Development Research Report No. 100.* Economic Research Service, U.S. Dept. of Agriculture.

Jones, J. (2010). *Labor of love, labor of sorrow: Black women, work, and the family, from slavery to the present.* New York: Basic Books.

Kurre, J. A. (2003). Is the cost of living less in rural areas? *International Regional Science Review, 26*, 86–116.

Larson, O. (1978). Values and beliefs of rural people. In T. R. Ford (Ed.), *Rural U.S.A.: Persistence and change* (pp. 91–112). Ames, IA: Iowa State University Press.

Levernier, W., Partridge, M. D., & Rickman, D. S. (1998). Differences in metropolitan and nonmetropolitan U.S. family income inequality: A cross-county comparison. *Journal of Urban Economics, 44*, 272–290.

Levy, F. (1998). *The new dollars and dreams: American incomes and economic change.* New York: Russell Sage Foundation.

Lichter, D. T. (1989). The underemployment of American rural women: Prevalence, trends and spatial inequality. *Journal of Rural Studies, 5*, 199–208.

Lichter, D., & Eggebeen, D. (1992). Child poverty and the changing rural family. *Rural Sociology, 57*(2), 151–172.

Lichter, D. T., & Jensen, L. (2002). Rural America in transition: Poverty and welfare at the turn of the 21st century. In B. Weber, G. Duncan, L. & Whitener (Eds.), *Rural dimensions of welfare reform* (pp. 77–110). Kalamazoo, MI: W.E. Upjohn Institute.

Lichter, D. T., & Johnson, K. M. (2009). Immigrant gateways and Hispanic migration to new destinations. *International Migration Review, 43*(3), 496–518.

Lichter, D. T., & Qian, Z. (2004). *Marriage and family in a multiracial society.* New York: Russell Sage Foundation and Washington, DC: Population Reference Bureau.

MacTavish, K., & Salamon, S. (2003). Mobile home park on the prairie: A new rural community form. *Rural Sociology, 66*(4), 487–506.

Mattingly, M. J., & Smith, K. (2010). Changes in wives' employment when husbands stop working: A recession-prosperity comparison. *Family Relations, 59*, 343–357.

Mattingly, M. J., & Stransky, M. L. (2010). *Young child poverty in 2009: Rural poverty rate jumps to nearly 29 percent.* Issue Brief No. 17. Durham, NH: Carsey Institute.

McCrate, E. (2011). Parents' work time in rural America: The growth of irregular schedules. In K. Smith & A. Tickamyer (Eds.), *Economic restructuring and family well being in rural America* (pp. 177–193). University Park, PA: Pennsylvania State University Press.

McLanahan, S., & Sandefur, G. D. (1994). *Growing up with a single parent: What hurts, what helps.* Cambridge, MA: Harvard University Press.

McLaughlin, D. K., & Coleman-Jensen, A. J. (2008). Nonstandard employment in the metropolitan United States. *Rural Sociology, 73*(4), 631–659.

McLaughlin, D. K., & Coleman-Jensen, A. J. (2011). Economic restructuring and family structure, 1980–2000: A focus on female-headed families with children. In K. Smith & A. Tickamyer (Eds.), *Economic restructuring and family well being in rural America* (pp. 105–123). University Park, PA: Pennsylvania State University Press.

McLaughlin, D. K., & Perman, L. (1991). Returns vs. endowments in the earnings attainment process for metropolitan and nonmetropolitan men and women. *Rural Sociology, 56*, 339–365.

Miller, K. K., & Weber, B. A. (2003). *Persistent poverty across the rural-urban continuum.* Working Paper 03-01. Columbia, MO: Rural Poverty Research Center.

Nelson, M. (2011). Job characteristics and economic survival strategies: The effect of economic restructuring and marital status in a rural county. In K. Smith & A. Tickamyer (Eds.), *Economic restructuring and family well being in rural America* (pp. 136–157). University Park, PA: Pennsylvania State University Press.

O'Hare, W. (2009). *The forgotten fifth: Child poverty in rural America*. Report No. 10. Durham, NH: Carsey Institute.

O'Hare, W. P., & Johnson, K. M. (2004). Child poverty in rural America. *PRB Reports to America, 3*(1). Washington, DC: Population Reference Bureau.

O'Hare, W., Manning, W., Porter, M., & Lyons, H. (2009). *Rural children are more likely to live in cohabiting-couple households*. Policy Brief No. 14. Durham, NH: Carsey Institute.

Parrado, E. A., & Kandel, W. A. (2010). Hispanic population growth and rural income inequality. *Social Forces, 88*(3), 1121–1450.

Pascoe, J. M., Miryoung, L., Specht, S., McNicholas, C., Spears, W., Gans, A., et al. (2010). Mothers with positive or negative depression screens evaluate a maternal resource guide. *Journal of Pediatric Health Care, 24*(6), 378–384.

Raley, S., Mattingly, M. J., & Bianchi, S. M. (2006). How dual are dual income couples? Documenting change from 1970 to 2001. *Journal of Marriage and the Family, 68*, 11–28.

Rogers, C. (1997). *Changes in the social and economic status of women by metro-nonmetro residence*. Agriculture Information Bulletin No. 732. Washington, DC: Rural Economy Division, Economic Research Service, U.S. Department of Agriculture.

Romero, A., Baumle, A., Badgett, M., & Gates, G. (2007). *Census snapshot: Illinois*. Los Angeles, CA: The Williams Institute.

Sayer, L., Cohen, P. N., & Casper, L. (2004). Women, men, and work. In *The American People: Census 2000*. New York: Russell Sage Foundation & Washington, DC: Population Reference Bureau.

Schnaiberg, A., & Goldenberg, S. (2003). From empty nest to crowded nest: The dynamics of incompletely launched adults. In H. Z. Lopata & J. A. Levy (Eds.), *Social problems across the life course* (pp. 97–118). Lanham, MD: Rowman & Littlefield Publishers.

Seltzer, J. A. (2000). Families formed outside of marriage. *Journal of Marriage and the Family, 62*, 1247–1268.

Sherman, J. (2009). *Those who work, those who don't: Poverty, morality, and family in rural America*. Minneapolis, MN: University of Minnesota Press.

Slack, T., & Jensen, L. (2002). Race, ethnicity, and underemployment in nonmetropolitan America: A 30-year profile. *Rural Sociology, 67*, 208–233.

Smith, D. M., & Gates, G. J. (2001). Gay and lesbian families in the United States: Same-sex unmarried partner households. *A Human Rights Campaign Report*. Washington, DC: Human Rights Campaign.

Smith, K. (2008). Working hard for the money: Trends in women's employment 1970–2007. *National Reports, 1*(5). Durham, NH: The Carsey Institute.

Smith, K. (2010). Wives as Breadwinners: Wives Share of Family Earnings Hits Historic High during the Second Year of the Great Recession. Factsheet No. 20. Durham, NH: Carsey Institute.

Smith, K. (2011). Changing roles: Women and work in rural America. In K. Smith & A. Tickamyer (Eds.), *Economic restructuring and family well being in rural America* (pp. 60–81). University Park, PA: Pennsylvania State University Press.

Smith, K., & Glauber, R. (2009). *Exploring the spatial wage penalty for women: Does it matter where you live?* Paper presented at the American Sociological Association meetings in San Francisco, CA.

Smith, K., & Tickamyer, A. (2011). *Economic restructuring and family well being in rural America*. University Park, PA: Pennsylvania State University Press.

Smock, P. J. (2000). Cohabitation in the United States: An appraisal of research themes, findings, and implications. *Annual Review of Sociology, 26*, 1–20.

Snyder, A. (2011). Patterns of family formation and dissolution in rural American and implications for well-being. In K. Smith & A. Tickamyer (Eds.), *Economic restructuring and family well being in rural America* (pp. 124–135). University Park, PA: Pennsylvania State University Press.

Snyder, A. R., Brown, S. L., & Condo, E. P. (2004). Residential differences in family formation: The significance of cohabitation. *Rural Sociology, 69*(2), 235–260.

Snyder, A. R., McLaughlin, D. K., & Findeis, J. (2006). Household composition and poverty among female-headed households with children: Differences by race and residence. *Rural Sociology, 71*(4), 597–624.

Sørensen, A. (1983). Women's employment patterns after marriage. *Journal of Marriage and Family, 45*(2), 311–321.

Stevenson, B., & Wolfers, J. (2007). Marriage and divorce: Changes and their driving forces. *Journal of Economic Perspectives, 21*(2), 27–52.

Tickamyer, A. R., & Duncan, C. M. (1990). Poverty and opportunity structure in rural America. *Annual Review of Sociology, 16*, 67–86.

Tickamyer, A., & Henderson, D. (2003). Rural women: New roles for the new century? In D. Brown & L. Swanson (Eds.), *Challenges for rural America in the twenty-first century* (pp. 109–117). University Park, PA: Pennsylvania State University Press.

Vera-Toscano, E., Phimister, E., & Weersink, A. (2004). Panel estimates of the Canadian rural/urban women's wage gap. *American Journal of Agricultural Economics, 86*, 1136–1151.

Willits, F. K., Bealer, R. C., & Crider, D. M. (1982). Persistence of rural/urban differences. In D. A. Dillman & D. J. Hobbs (Eds.), *Rural society in the U.S.: Issues for the 1980s* (pp. 58–68). Boulder, CO: Westview Press.

Wu, L. (2008). Cohort estimates of nonmarital fertility for U.S. women. *Demography, 45*(1), 193–207.

# Rural Health Disparities

P. Johnelle Sparks

## Introduction

Two common arguments are offered to elucidate potential geographical variations in health outcomes, and these arguments largely focus on compositional or contextual explanations of health disparities (Macintyre & Ellaway, 2003). Compositional explanations of health disparities focus on individual attributes of people in certain places leading to differences in health outcomes over space, while contextual explanations highlight the importance of differences between places as they influence differences in health outcomes. Compositional and contextual explanations of health disparities may serve as an overarching perspective to address potential rural-urban health disparities in the United States and internationally. However, it is important to note that most disparities observed for health outcomes are not the result of composition or context operating in isolation. Instead both compositional and contextual factors likely contribute to variations in health and health-care outcomes across rural and urban areas throughout the world.

Contextual explanations have gained more attention in recent literature with the use of multilevel theoretical and statistical methods. However, most research finds that contextual-based associations with individual health or mortality outcomes tend to be much weaker than individual level, or more traditional compositional, characteristics in offering explanations for differences in health outcomes across place (Pickett & Pearl, 2001). From a rural demography perspective, it is necessary to consider both compositional and contextual factors, since social and physical environments, as well as characteristics of individuals within places, have been shown to be important determinants of population health (Macintyre & Ellaway, 2003; Pearce & Boyle, 2005; Reijneveld, 2002). From a policy perspective it is also important to consider how contextually based programs may impact the health and well-being of a large number of people, knowing that compositional factors may be the driving force behind rural health disparities. Diversity in and between rural areas presents some challenges to a single policy that deals with health disparities noted for rural residents, and both composition and context for different rural areas must be examined.

Research examining rural-urban health disparities documents varied associations across residential locations depending on the health outcome studied. Heterogeneity across rural places, in both composition and context, presents additional layers of complexity when considering rural-urban health disparities in the United States, as well as across diverse settings internationally. Studies of mortality rates in the U.S. find somewhat of a paradox in that age-, sex-, and race-adjusted mortality rates tend to favor a rural mortality advantage (Geronimus, Bound, Waidmann, Colen, & Steffick, 2001; Hayward, Pienta, & McLaughlin, 1997; Kitagawa & Hauser, 1973; McLaughlin, Stokes, & Nonoyama, 2001; Miller, Stokes, & Clifford, 1987). This is considered a paradox, because the compositional characteristics in rural places, including lower levels of education, lower incomes, higher rates of

P.J. Sparks (✉)
Department of Demography, University of Texas at San Antonio, San Antonio,
TX 78207, USA
e-mail: johnelle.sparks@utsa.edu

poverty, should indicate higher mortality level for rural residents. However, wide variation in general and infant mortality rates have been observed in studies that examine these mortality patterns across varied rural-urban categorization schemes that consider issues of adjacency to an urban area or differences in population size (Cossman, Cossman, Cosby, & Reavis, 2008; McLaughlin, Stokes, Smith, & Nonoyama, 2007; Morton, 2004; Sparks, McLaughlin, & Stokes, 2009). These studies find that the most rural and isolated areas have increased mortality rates compared to rural areas that are located next to a small urban area with a somewhat larger population.

International studies of rural-urban mortality patterns find mixed area-based associations, in that some research finds a rural mortality advantage (Fukuda, Nakamura, & Takano, 2004; Kravdal, 2009; Luo, Kierans, Wilkins, Liston, Uh et al., 2004; Pollan et al., 2007; van Hooijdonk, Droomers, Deerenberg, Mackenbach, & Kunst, 2008), while other studies evidence a rural mortality disadvantage (Hu, Baker, & Baker, 2010; Kim, Subramanian, Kawachi, & Kim, 2007; Van de Poel, O'Donnell, & Van Doorslaer, 2007, 2009; Zimmer, Kaneda, & Spess, 2007). Again, differences in the compositional characteristics of rural residents in these settings compared to their urban counterparts should lead to a rural health disadvantage in international settings. Further, international rural health disparities are not consistent among developed and developing country settings. Disparities in rural-urban morbidity and health-care access and usage patterns present even more varied and complex associations based on the outcomes examined and the definitions used to classify a place as rural or urban.

The study of health disparities between rural and urban locations is important; rural populations face unique environmental exposures (contextual factors), and people in rural areas often have different sociodemographic profiles compared to their urban counterparts (compositional factors). These environmental and sociodemographic characteristics may increase a rural individual's chances of experiencing poor health outcomes or limit their access to health-care resources. Several contextually based factors have been argued to impact the health of residents, and rural residents may be at a particular disadvantage. Pearce, Witten, Hiscock, and Blakely (2008) summarize several of the potential contextual characteristics that may independently impact the health outcomes of individuals living in rural areas, including poor investment in infrastructure and overall area deprivation, segregation, social and economic inequality, differential access to natural and build resources, and harmful environments due to air pollutions, landfills, etc.

The U.S. Department of Health and Human Services and the United Nations have identified rural residence as one potential barrier to better health outcomes for rural populations in the U.S. and globally. Healthy People 2010 aims to promote health and prevent morbidities and premature death for the U.S. population with the goal of eliminating health disparities by a variety of demographic characteristics, including gender, race/ethnicity, and socioeconomic status (SES), while also focusing on geographic location, or rural residence (U.S. Department of Health and Human Services, 2000). Primary attention is given to the study and elimination of health disparities based on geographic location, because rural residents are at increased risk of experiencing injury-related mortality, have higher rates of heart disease, cancer, diabetes, and obesity, and rural residents have higher rates of uninsurance compared to urban residents (U.S. Department of Health and Human Services, 2000). These increased health and health-care risk factors for rural residents, combined with the unique composition of rural areas in the United States, discussed more thoroughly below, warrant the attention of federal agencies to offer programmatic goals and policies targeted at the elimination of health disparities for rural populations.

From an international perspective, the United Nations set eight millennium development goals to be reached by 2015 that advocate ending poverty and hunger, providing universal education, promoting gender equality, improving child and maternal health, preventing and reversing the spread of HIV/AIDS, offering environmental sustainability, and promoting global partnerships in an effort to enhance equity and sustainability of the world population, with particular attention given to people in developing countries (UN Millennium Project, 2005). Rural residence is a specific focus of these goals, because uneven development and limited access to resources such as fresh water and food, education, safe housing, and health-care services in rural areas throughout the developing world place rural populations at high risk for premature mortality, morbidity, and poor health status. Although the goals identified here largely focus on contextual-based approaches, these factors, combined with extreme poverty and ethnic minority status among rural individuals, increase poor health outcomes for many rural populations throughout diverse regions of the world (United Nations, 2009).

Both domestic and international trends in rural health disparities are discussed below as they relate to compositional and contextual factors to offer a broad overview of current rural and urban health and health-care usage patterns for rural and urban populations. Two key points emerge from this review. First, heterogeneity is present among rural areas in both composition and context, and more variability is often noted between health outcomes across different designations of rural areas than between comparisons of rural and urban areas or populations. Second, diverse socioeconomic (composition) and environmental circumstances (context) influence health disparities for rural or urban residents alike for most health and health-care outcomes.

## Trends in US Rural Health Disparities

Demographic, or compositional, characteristics of the rural population in the United States would indicate that rural residents should be at a health disadvantage compared to their urban counterparts. Rural residence is associated with lower household incomes, higher rates of poverty, lower rates of health insurance, lower rates of employment in stable and higher-paying professional jobs, older housing structures, lower levels of education, and population aging (Brown & Swanson, 2003; McLaughlin et al., 2001; Morton, 2004). Differences in racial/ethnic minority concentration in various parts of the rural U.S. also contribute to the unique sociodemographic and health profiles of rural residents (Johnson, 2003, see also Chapter 15 in this volume). Contextual factors, such as insufficient and aging health infrastructures and physician shortages, including both general practitioners and specialists, and lower access to preventative and specialized health-care services in rural areas, present additional problems when examining rural health disparities (Casey, Call, & Klingner, 2001; Gazewood, Rollins, & Galazka, 2006; Gong et al., 2009; Morton, 2003; O'Connor & Hooker, 2007; Rabinowitz, Diamond, Markham, & Hazelwood, 1999).

And while a rural mortality paradox has been observed, as noted above, several rural health disadvantages are noted for specific morbidities and other health-related outcomes. For example, higher infant mortality rates have been observed in rural compared to urban areas (Clarke, Farmer, & Miller, 1994; Miller, Clarke, Albrecht, & Farmer, 1996; Nesbitt, Connell, Hart, & Rosenblatt, 1990; Sparks et al., 2009). Among other maternal and infant health outcomes, low birthweight and premature births are higher among rural residents compared to urban residents (Alexy, Nichols, Heverly, & Garzon, 1997; Baffour, Jones, & Contreras, 2006; Bailey & Cole, 2009; Hillemeier, Weisman, Chase, & Dyer, 2007; Laditka, Laditka, & Probst, 2006), adequate levels of prenatal care are lower for rural mothers (Epstein, Grant, Schiff, & Kasehagen, 2009; Laditka, Laditka, Bennett, & Probst, 2005), and breastfeeding initiation and continuation are lower among rural mothers compared to urban mothers (Flower et al., 2008; Grummer-Strawn, Scanlon, Darling, & Conrey, 2006; Sparks, 2010). These outcomes are often worse for rural minority women, particularly American Indians and Alaska Natives (Baldwin et al., 2002, 2009), and African Americans (Baffour & Chonody, 2009; Laditka et al., 2006). Potential explanations for these rural maternal and infant health disparities include higher rates of smoking during pregnancy among rural women (Bailey & Cole, 2009) and inadequate prenatal care use, lower rates of health insurance, long travel times to seek health care, and limited public transportation options to seek appropriate and timely obstetric or gynecological care for women in rural areas (Armstrong Schellenberg et al., 2008; Braveman, Marchi, Egerter, Pearl, & Neuhaus, 2000; Epstein et al., 2009; Nesbitt, Larson, Rosenblatt, & Hart, 1997; Sontheimer, Halverson, Bell, Ellis, & Bunting, 2008). Both individual compositional and structural contextual barriers for rural residents likely contribute to these infant and maternal health disadvantages for rural residents.

Rural health disparities have been noted across all age ranges, another compositional characteristic of rural areas. For example, higher prevalence of asthma, obesity, and high cholesterol have been noted for rural children and adolescents compared to urban children and adolescents (Chrischilles et al., 2004; Wickrama, Elder, & Abraham, 2007). Obesity and health problems associated with overweight and obesity, such as metabolic syndrome or diabetes, have been documented to be much higher among rural children and adolescents compared to their urban counterparts, largely due to limited physical activity of rural youth (Davy, Harrell, Stewart, & King, 2004; Joens-Matre et al., 2008; Lewis et al., 2006; Moore, Davis, Baxter, Lewis, & Yin, 2008; O'Hara Tompkins, Rye, Zizzi, & Vitullo, 2005); these associations are often magnified among rural minority children and adolescents (Drummond et al., 2009; Felton et al., 2002). Vaccination rates among children are also lower in rural areas compared to urban areas (Luman, Ching, Jumaan, & Seward, 2006); although other researchers find no significant differences in vaccination rates for rural, urban, and suburban children (Steyer, Mainous, & Geesey, 2005; Stokley, Smith, Klevens, & Battaglia, 2001; Zhao & Luman, 2010). Young children in rural areas also experience contextual barriers that limit their access to health-care infrastructure; lower rates of health insurance and limited access to preventative health care and dental care among children are observed in rural areas compared to urban areas (DeVoe, Krois, & Stenger, 2009; Probst, Moore, & Baxley, 2005).

Mixed associations are noted for morbidity patterns based on rural or urban residential location among adults in the U.S., but most explanations for these patterns focus on compositional differences in rural areas by race/ethnicity, age, or socioeconomic status. Although rural adults may have longer life expectancy and lower mortality risks compared to urban adults, this may come with the burden of having higher rates of disability and fewer years of active life expectancy (Geronimus et al., 2001; Laditka, Laditka, Olatosi, & Elder, 2007). Clear rural-urban health differences do not emerge in research considering multiple risk factors for specific morbidities. For example, early research on cardiovascular disease found higher mortality rates from coronary heart disease in urban areas compared to rural areas, but more current data indicate that the prevalence of heart disease is higher among white middle-aged men in nonmetro areas, while there are elevated risks for heart disease among black men and women in both nonmetro areas and central cities (Barnett & Halverson, 2000). Conversely, Feresu, Zhang, Puumala, Ullrich, and Anderson (2008) found that older, minority, and less-educated rural women were at increased risk for experiencing cardiovascular diseases. Incomplete evidence exists to make claims regarding a rural health advantage or disadvantage relative to asthma (Chrischilles et al., 2004; Grineski, 2009; Ownby, 2005), and current research finds variation in asthma prevalence relative to the measure of rural residence that is used (Morrison, Callahan, Moorman, & Bailey, 2009). Self-rated health has become a common measure of overall health status in studies of population health, and research evidence from the U.S. indicates a rural health disadvantage exists for poor self-rated health among adults (Auchincloss & Hadden, 2002; Wickrama et al., 2007; Coburn & Bolda, 1999). Studies indicate that self-rated health is strongly correlated with later survival chances, even with the inclusion of appropriate health status, behavioral, and other sociodemographic covariates (Idler & Benyamini, 1997; Rogers, Hummer, & Nam, 2000).

Diabetes prevalence has been reported higher in rural areas compared to urban areas, and diabetes is more heavily concentrated among rural minority residents compared to white rural residents (Koopman, Mainous, & Geesey, 2006; Krishna, Gillespie, & McBride, 2010). A rural diabetes disadvantage raises particular concerns for older, low-income, minority residents of rural areas, because poor access to resources to self-manage diabetes and specialty medical care are often compounded with other health problems for these vulnerable rural residents (Bell et al., 2005, 2007; Quandt et al., 2005). Overweight and obesity, a risk factor for diabetes, has consistently been shown to be higher in rural compared to urban areas, and this rural obesity/overweight disparity may in part be the result of limited access to healthy foods in rural areas (Hosler, 2009; Larson, Story, & Nelson, 2009). Literature has noted higher rates of overweight and obesity for both men and women in nonmetropolitan areas compared to metropolitan areas, even with controls for appropriate sociodemographic and behavioral characteristics (Borders, Rohrer, & Cardarelli, 2006). Further, a national study of women from rural and urban areas finds that rural women have increased odds of being obese and reporting poor overall health, leading to an increased health burden for overweight and obese rural women (Ramsey & Glenn, 2002). And while compositional differences between rural and urban areas may partly explain higher rates of diabetes and obesity for rural residents, most research emphasizes contextual factors, such as access to timely health care and healthy food environments, as important to eliminating these disparities.

Results are mixed regarding cancer incidence and prevalence between rural and urban areas, particularly with the type of cancer, indicating a rural cancer disadvantage is not always observed (Friedell et al., 2001; Higginbotham, Moulder, & Currier, 2001; Howe, Keller, & Lehnherr, 1993; Lengerich et al., 2005; Pozet et al., 2008; Prehn & West, 1998; Schootman & Fuortes, 1999; Sung, Blumenthal, AlemaMensah, & McGrady, 1997). However, rural residents have increased odds of having late-stage diagnoses of cancer compared to their urban counterparts which may lead to high cancer mortality rates in rural areas (Amey, Miller, & Albrecht, 1997; Baldwin et al., 2008; Huang, Dignan, Han, & Johnson, 2009; Liff, Chow, & Greenberg, 1991; Paquette & Finlayson, 2007; Sankaranarayanan et al., 2009). Rural health disadvantages in the United States have also been noted for mental health (Burris & Andrykowski, 2010; Hauenstein et al., 2006, 2007; Petterson, Williams, Hauenstein, Rovnyak, & Merwin, 2009; Roberts, Johnson, Brems, & Warner, 2007; Tudiver, Edwards, & Pfortmiller, 2010), oral health (Allison & Manski, 2007; Quandt et al., 2009; Vargas, Dye, & Hayes, 2002), and general health-care access and utilization (Beachler, Holloman, & Herman, 2003; Diaz-Perez, Farley, & Cabanis, 2004; Glover, Moore, Probst, & Samuels, 2004). However, there are no clear patterns to indicate a distinct rural health disadvantage once controls for sociodemographic and behavioral factors are controlled for in these studies. These findings highlight the importance of considering both compositional and contextual differences between rural and urban areas to understand how populations are at risk of poor health outcomes.

## Trends in International Rural Health Disparities

Literature addressing international rural health disparities notes mixed associations between health outcomes for rural and urban residents depending on the outcome and definitions of rural-urban employed. Rural-urban differences or similarities of diverse health outcomes vary across and within developed and developing countries internationally as well. Smith, Humphreys, and Wilson (2008) completed a comprehensive literature review of rural-urban health disparities among several developed countries, including Australia, New Zealand, Canada, the United Kingdom, other western European countries, and the United States. Their review finds that for certain individual health outcomes, including suicide, some cancers, cardiovascular diseases, and obesity, prevalence rates for these health outcomes are higher in rural areas compared to urban areas. The authors then go further to argue that health disparities noted between rural and urban areas in developed countries are the result of a complex interplay between individual characteristics (composition) and local social and physical environments (context), and taken together, these factors put rural residents more at risk for poor health outcomes than urban residents.

Compositional characteristics like race/ethnicity and socioeconomic position of individuals in Canada are addressed in the research literature and lead to more complicated associations for health outcomes among rural and urban residents. More generally, rural Canadians report poorer health status than their urban counterparts; yet when more comparisons are made between rural designations, residents of the most isolated rural areas report poorer health than the least rural areas. A similar pattern holds for Australia (Pong, DesMeules, & Lagacé, 2009). Black Canadian women in rural areas have poorer maternal and infant health outcomes than white rural women in Canada (Etowa, Bernard, Oyinsan, & Clow, 2007). Socioeconomic gradients are noted for birth outcomes across the rural-urban continuum for Canadian women including low birthweight, small for gestational age, and preterm birth (Auger, Authier, Martinez, & Daniel, 2009). Other studies find that a socioeconomic disadvantage is only observed for infant health outcomes in urban areas of Canada, not rural areas (Luo, Kierans, Wilkins, Liston, Mohamed, et al., 2004; Luo, Kierans, Wilkins, Liston, Uh, et al., 2004; Luo, Wilkins, Kramer, & Canadian Fetal Infant Health Study Group, 2006). Therefore compositional explanations for rural health disparities exhibit a mixed pattern across different definitions of rural areas in this setting.

In more developed regions of Asia, mixed rural-urban health disparities focusing on compositional factors have been noted. Stroke mortality is higher for women in rural areas of Japan, even though the health profiles of urban residents, both men and women, indicate that urban adults are at increased risk for experiencing stroke (Nishi, 2008; Nishi et al., 2007). Dong and Simon (2010) found that rural residents were more likely to report poorer overall health, lower quality of life, more changes in recent health status, and more depression symptoms compared to urban residents in a study of an aging Chinese population. Overall this study finds that the physical and mental health status of older, rural Chinese residents is less favorable than their urban counterparts. However, research using data representative of the adult Chinese population finds that urban residents are more likely to report poor self-rated health, activity limitations, and to have been diagnosed with a serious illness/disease compared to rural residents. Additionally, urban residents were less likely to visit a physician for an illness than residents of rural areas in this study (Fang, Chen, & Rizzo, 2009). Uneven economic development in China in recent decades has led to potentially wider rural-urban health disparities in this country from a contextual perspective, in that infant and maternal mortality rates, infectious disease incidence, HIV/AIDS, poor mental health ratings and suicides are higher in rural areas, and less investment is being made in health infrastructures in rural areas of China (Dummer & Cook, 2007). Further, injury-related mortality accounts for a large portion of the rural-urban mortality differential noted in China (Hu et al., 2010).

Rural health disparities in developing countries are generally the result of lack of health-care services and infrastructure, high levels of poverty, and poor maternal and child health, i.e., a combination of compositional and contextual factors. It is often difficult to compare health outcomes between rural and urban areas of many developing countries due to uneven development and socioeconomic resource differentials between residents of these areas. In India, the major cause of mortality in rural areas is attributable to infections and communicable diseases. Malnutrition and illnesses and death associated with pregnancy and childbirth remain primary causes of morbidity and mortality in rural India (Patil, Somasundaram, & Goyal, 2002). In a comprehensive study of 47 developing countries using Demographic and Health Surveys, Van de Poel et al. (2007) find that stunting and mortality under the age of five is consistently higher in rural areas compared to urban areas. However, education and income gradients are important for these child health outcomes and indicate that the urban poor have worse child health outcomes measured by child stunting and mortality compared to poor children in rural areas. When these authors examine rural-urban differences in infant mortality rates in six sub-Saharan African countries (Benin, Central African Republic, Chad, Guinea, Mail, and Niger), they find a rural infant mortality disadvantage that is largely attributable to lower levels of maternal education, lower awareness of contraception, and limited access to safe drinking water in rural areas (Van de Poel et al., 2009). Maternal and child health issues pose serious health problems for rural women in Bangladesh, as well, with health complications during pregnancy and limited access to health-care facilities during pregnancy leading to high maternal morbidity for rural women (Islam, Chowdhury, & Singh, 2006). However, many of these problems are similar for poor urban populations in these developing countries, leading to less clear rural-urban health disparities based on compositional differences alone.

## Summary

Overall research exploring rural-urban health disparities in the United States and internationally largely focuses on the two competing but also complimentary explanations for these disparities: compositional and contextual factors. Although compositional factors, such as race/ethnicity, age, socioeconomic status, gender, and health behaviors, most likely contribute to the differences noted above in diverse mortality and morbidity outcomes, rural places are unique in their context. Contextual characteristics of rural areas offer a more localized assessment of how local place-based factors, such as access to health-care resources, may contribute to or exacerbate health problems for rural residents based on their sociodemographic profiles.

## Empirical Example

An empirical example is presented next to assess potential rural-urban disparities in self-rated health, diabetes, heart attack (myocardial infarction), coronary health disease or angina, stroke, and asthma among U.S. adults using a current and comprehensive data source. This example serves as a way to assess how differences in the composition and context of rural and urban populations may influence health outcomes and possible rural-urban disparities in these various health outcomes. Multilevel modeling techniques permit the analysis of associations between potential contextual factors on individual level outcomes (Macintyre & Ellaway, 2003). As a first step, the analytic strategy used in this example takes a broader view of contextual associations, one that examines the variation in associations across the general rural-urban spectrum.

## Data and Methods

### Data Source and Variables

Data for this analysis come from the 2008 Behavioral Risk Factor Surveillance System survey (BRFSS), which consists of a cross-sectional, nationally representative sample of noninstitutionalized adults 18 years of age or older from all U.S. states conducted using telephone interviews. This data source was selected because it asks respondents to assess their health status and specific morbidities, and also includes information on compositional factors (sociodemographic and behavioral characteristics, and health-care usage) and contextual factors (rural/urban).[1]

Variables included in this analysis can be grouped into three categories: health conditions (dependent variables); compositional characteristics; and contextual characteristics. The dependent variables, or health conditions, were based on several questions that ask each respondent to rate their general health or report a specific morbidity condition. Self-assessed health was measured by a question that asked the responded to rate their health as excellent, very good, good, fair, or poor. A dichotomous variable was created to measure poor self-rated health, and responses of fair or poor were used to construct this measure. Respondents were also asked if they had been diagnosed with any of the following health conditions: (1) diabetes, (2) heart attack (myocardial infarction), (3) coronary health disease or angina, (4) stroke, or (5) asthma, and dichotomous measures were recoded to correspond with each of these morbidities.

Compositional factors were measured using sociodemographic characteristics of respondents, health behaviors, and health-care usage. Sociodemographic characteristics included: race/ethnicity (Non-Hispanic Whites, Non-Hispanic Blacks, Hispanics, and other races/ethnicities); gender; current age (18–24, 25–34, 35–44, 45–54, 55–64, and 65 years of age or older); highest level of education completed (less than high school, high school graduate or its equivalent, some college or more); household income (income at or below $25,000 compared to income above $25,000); current employment status (employed or not); and current marital status (married or member of an unmarried couple compared to respondents that were divorced, widowed, separated, or never married). Health behavior measures included: if the respondent reported activity limitations or not; an index of the total number of chronic health conditions each respondent reported; self-reported body mass index (BMI) [normal weight (BMI $\leq$ 24.9), overweight (BMI $=$ 25–29.9), or obese (BMI $\geq$ 30)]; if the respondent drank alcohol in the 30 days prior to the interview date or not; current smoking status (current smoker, former smoker, never smoker); and whether or not the respondent had exercised in the 30 days prior to the interview. Health-care usage variables were operationalized with dichotomous variables that measured (1) whether or not the respondent reported they had some type of health-care coverage (either private or public); (2) if the respondent had a personal doctor or not; and (3) if the respondent indicated that health-care costs were too high to see a physician or not.

Lastly, contextual factors were measured by the residential status of the respondent. Of the large national survey data sources available to study population health, few provide a measure of rural residential status in public use data. A variable indicating if the respondent lived in a metropolitan statistical area (MSA) (urban) or nonmetropolitan statistical area (rural) was used to assess rural-urban differences in health conditions and compositional factors. The more detailed MSA coding scheme (MSA, city center; MSA outside city center; MSA, suburban county; MSA, no center city; non-MSA) was used to present results from the multiple variable models and to explore the implications of the rural context.

---

[1] While the BRFSS uses metropolitan statistical areas (MSA) as their measure of rural or urban status, MSAs/non-MSAs and rural/urban designations are not interchangeable when discussing rural populations. MSAs refer to county designations based on size of place, while rural/urban designations are based on U.S. Census Bureau defined places. These terms are used interchangeably, although conceptually the two measures mean very different things and refer to different geographic units.

## Statistical Methods

Survey procedures in SAS 9.2 were used to estimate all statistical procedures due to the complex survey design of the BRFSS. First, the SURVEYFREQ procedure was used to estimate chi-square tests for equal distributions of compositional variables detailed above among rural and urban residents. Second, logistic regression models with each of the health conditions were estimated using the SURVEYLOGISTIC procedure in SAS 9.2, and results from these models are presented in a graphical format based on differences in MSA status, or contextual factors, first. Then the second graph for each outcome shows the change in odds in each outcome with controls for all compositional factors. The survey design procedure was used to adjust the calculation of standard errors using the Taylor series approximation method (An, 2002), and these adjustments allow the results to be generalized to the adult, noninstitutionalized population in the United States in 2008.

## Results

Statistically significant differences were found among all health condition variables between rural and urban residents, except for an asthma diagnosis, based on bivariate tests (see Table 18.1). Rural residents were more likely to report their general health as fair or poor (19.17%) compared to urban residents (15.40%). Among the specific morbidity diagnoses, rural residents were more likely to be diagnosed with any of the conditions, except for asthma, than urban residents. Rural residents were also more likely to have more chronic health conditions than urban residents. Activity limitations were more common among rural compared to urban adults, and rural adults were more likely to be overweight or obese while urban adults were more likely to be normal weight.

Table 18.1 highlights the difference in compositional characteristics between rural and urban residents. There is less racial/ethnic diversity among adult respondents living in rural areas as compared to respondents in urban areas. The age distribution of adults in rural areas was significantly older than urban areas. Adults in urban areas were more likely to have some college education or more compared to rural adults, 62% compared to 50%, respectively. Adults in rural areas were more likely to live in households with incomes below $25,000 compared to adults in urban areas. Urban adults were more likely to be currently employed (60.41%) compared to rural adults (57.11%). Additionally rural adults were more likely to be married than their urban counterparts.

Health behaviors, additional compositional characteristics, also varied significantly between adults in rural and urban areas. Urban adults were more likely to have consumed alcohol and exercised in the past 30 days compared to rural adults, while rural adults were more likely to be current or former smokers, and urban adults are more likely to have been never smokers. Health-care usage varied by rural or urban residence. Rural residents were less likely to report having some type of health-care coverage than their urban counterparts, while rural residents reported that medical care costs were too high to see a physician at higher rates than urban residents.

On the basis of the significant differences in compositional differences between rural and urban residents and somewhat less favorable profiles noted among rural adults, it is assumed that adults in rural areas will have higher odds of reporting poor health and more morbidity diagnoses compared to urban adults with only contextual factors of residential location considered in the multiple variable models. However, it is not clear if compositional variables may explain away these contextual-based health differences once the compositional characteristics are controlled for in the models.

Figure 18.1 presents the change in odds of poor self-rated health, diabetes, heart attack, coronary heart disease, stroke, and asthma with only MSA status included (contextual factors) and with all variables included from Table 18.1 (compositional and contextual factors). With only MSA status in the model, a strong, significant change in odds was noted between adults living in MSAs with a center city compared to adults living in a non-MSA for poor self-rated health. Adults in non-MSAs had 20% higher odds of reporting poor self-rated health compared to adults in center cities of MSAs. However, adults living in MSAs outside of the center city have much lower odds of reporting poor self-rated health compared to adults in core central cities in MSAs. Significant associations between different MSA types with only contextual factors in the model become insignificant when all compositional variables are included in the logistic

# 18 Rural Health Disparities

**Table 18.1** Weighted percentages of health conditions, compositional, and contextual characteristics among adults by MSA/non-MSA residential status with adjustments for survey design, Behavioral Risk Factor Surveillance System data, $n = 406{,}747$

| Variables | MSA | Non-MSA | Rao-Scott Chi-Square | $p$-value |
|---|---|---|---|---|
| **Health Conditions** | | | | |
| Poor or Fair Self-Rated Health | | | | |
|   Yes | 15.40 | 19.17 | 235.81 | <0.0001 |
|   No | 84.60 | 80.83 | | |
| Ever Told by A Doctor you Have: | | | | |
|   Diabetes | 9.50 | 10.91 | 63.90 | <0.0001 |
|   Heart Attack (Myocardial Infarction) | 3.98 | 5.59 | 194.71 | <0.0001 |
|   Coronary Heart Disease or Angina | 4.13 | 5.38 | 121.16 | <0.0001 |
|   Stroke | 2.52 | 3.40 | 102.42 | <0.0001 |
|   Asthma | 86.57 | 86.39 | 0.53 | 0.4647 |
| **Compositional Characteristics** | | | | |
| *Sociodemographic Characteristics* | | | | |
| Race/Ethnicity | | | | |
|   Non-Hispanic White | 66.17 | 82.47 | 2,028.63 | <0.0001 |
|   Non-Hispanic Black | 10.66 | 6.50 | | |
|   Hispanic | 7.30 | 4.80 | | |
|   Non-Hispanic Other Races | 15.87 | 6.23 | | |
| Gender | | | | |
|   Male | 48.78 | 48.10 | 3.80 | 0.0511 |
|   Female | 51.22 | 51.90 | | |
| Current Age | | | | |
|   18–24 | 12.51 | 11.53 | 253.56 | <0.0001 |
|   25–34 | 18.52 | 16.79 | | |
|   35–44 | 19.33 | 17.12 | | |
|   45–54 | 19.17 | 19.05 | | |
|   55–64 | 14.23 | 16.12 | | |
|   65 Years of Age or Older | 16.24 | 19.39 | | |
| Educational Level | | | | |
|   Less than High School | 10.95 | 13.15 | 1,031.79 | <0.0001 |
|   High School Diploma | 27.41 | 37.02 | | |
|   Some College or More | 61.64 | 49.83 | | |
| Household Income | | | | |
|   Income at or below $25,000 | 21.24 | 26.58 | 315.94 | <0.0001 |
|   Income more than $25,000 | 78.76 | 73.42 | | |
| Current Employment Status | | | | |
|   Employed | 60.41 | 57.11 | 95.74 | <0.0001 |
|   Not Employed | 39.59 | 42.89 | | |
| Current Marital Status | | | | |
|   Married | 63.57 | 65.47 | 30.09 | <0.0001 |
|   Not Married | 36.43 | 34.53 | | |

**Table 18.1** (continued)

| Variables | MSA | Non-MSA | Rao-Scott Chi-Square | p-value |
|---|---|---|---|---|
| *Health Behavior Characteristics* | | | | |
| Number of Chronic Health Conditions | | | | |
| 0 | 10.88 | 10.32 | 204.04 | <0.0001 |
| 1 | 76.01 | 73.81 | | |
| 2 | 9.67 | 11.30 | | |
| 3 | 2.54 | 3.24 | | |
| 4 | 0.77 | 1.11 | | |
| 5 | 0.13 | 0.22 | | |
| Respondent Has Activity Limitations | | | | |
| Yes | 19.54 | 23.55 | 241.04 | <0.0001 |
| No | 80.46 | 76.45 | | |
| Weight Status | | | | |
| Normal Weight | 40.53 | 36.30 | 245.61 | <0.0001 |
| Overweight | 34.72 | 34.63 | | |
| Obese | 24.75 | 29.07 | | |
| Drank Alcohol in Past 30 Days | | | | |
| Yes | 53.03 | 44.44 | 609.22 | <0.0001 |
| No | 46.97 | 55.56 | | |
| Current Smoking Status | | | | |
| Current Smoker | 17.93 | 22.40 | 361.38 | <0.0001 |
| Former Smoker | 24.14 | 25.50 | | |
| Never Smoked | 57.93 | 52.10 | | |
| Exercised During Past 30 Days | | | | |
| Yes | 75.47 | 70.96 | 224.83 | <0.0001 |
| No | 24.53 | 29.04 | | |
| *Health-Care Usage* | | | | |
| Respondent Has Some Type of Health-Care Coverage | | | | |
| Yes | 84.84 | 82.40 | 63.54 | <0.0001 |
| No | 15.16 | 17.60 | | |
| Respondent Has a Personal Doctor | | | | |
| Yes | 80.15 | 81.29 | 12.67 | 0.0004 |
| No | 19.85 | 18.71 | | |
| Medical Care Costs Too High to See Physician | | | | |
| Yes | 13.73 | 15.46 | 42.38 | <0.0001 |
| No | 86.27 | 84.54 | | |

Analysis weighted by _finalwt

regression model. Additionally, the magnitude and strength of the MSA central city and non-MSA difference in poor self-rated health is weakened substantially with the addition of compositional variables; stated differently, no substantive differences are noted in adults reporting poor health among MSA designations with the inclusion of compositional factors.

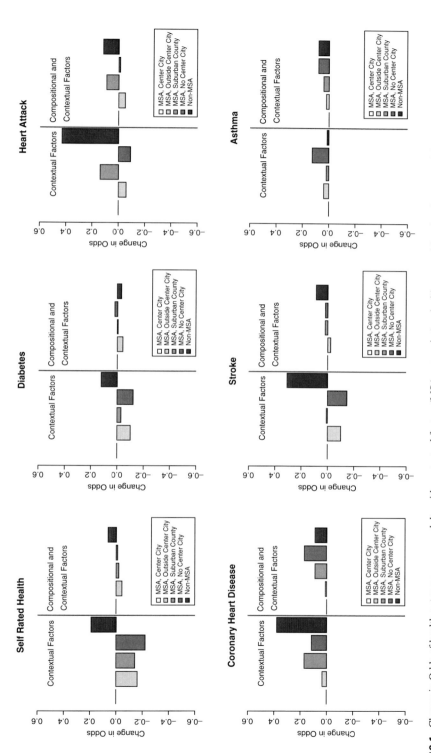

**Fig. 18.1** Change in Odds of health outcomes among adults with contextual factors (MSA categories) and with compositional and contextual factors controlled, BRFSS 2008
*Note*: Referent is MSA, Center City.

Similar patterns are noted for specific morbidity diagnoses of diabetes, heart attack, coronary heart disease, and stroke in Fig. 18.1. When only considering contextual factors, adults in non-MSAs have 12% higher odds of having a diabetes diagnosis compared to adults in center city MSAs. A rural health disadvantage seems even larger for heart attack, coronary heart disease, and stroke diagnoses compared to the other health outcomes. Rural adults have 43% higher odds of a heart attack diagnosis, 38% higher odds of a coronary heart disease diagnosis, and 31% higher odds of a stroke diagnosis compared to adults in central city MSAs. However, the addition of compositional characteristics to each of the models indicates marginal differences in health risks for the most rural residents compared to the most urban residents. Compositional differences between residential locations largely accounts for these initial contextual differences in health status. Conversely asthma witnesses a somewhat different pattern. When only accounting for contextual factors, no differences are noted in asthma diagnoses between the five MSA categories. With the inclusion of compositional factors, a marginally significant health disadvantage is noted for adults in non-MSAs compared with adults in MSAs with a center city.

## Conclusions and Future Directions

Rural health disparities are present when examining many outcomes, including mortality, morbidity, and access to care, both in the U.S. and internationally. However, there is not always a rural health disadvantage when comparing outcomes between rural and urban populations. Two themes guided the literature reviewed and empirical analysis presented: the roles of compositional and contextual factors in determining health disparities for rural populations.

The composition of rural areas appeared very different to the composition of urban areas and would indicate a disadvantage on many characteristics, including sociodemographic composition, health behaviors, and health-care usage. Results from the empirical example above highlight the diverse health, sociodemographic, and behavioral characteristics between adults in MSAs and non-MSAs in the United States. On the basis of a bivariate assessment of these characteristics between adults in these two residential locations, it would appear that non-MSA, or rural adults, would have a health disadvantage relative to their MSA counterparts. Other research literature documented at the beginning of this chapter provides a similar portrait of lower sociodemographic profiles of rural populations in the U.S. compared to urban populations (Brown & Swanson, 2003). It is interesting to note that the compositional factors give meaning to the observed difference in health outcomes between rural and urban populations in this analysis. However, the compositional factors do not explain away these differences. In addition, a stronger SES gradient is noted for poor self-rated health among MSA residents, indicating that these differences may contribute more to self-rated health differences among urban residents than between rural and urban residents. To a large extent this comparison provides a generalization of these differences between rural and urban areas.

After reviewing a broad and comprehensive set of literature, two patterns emerged as important for future empirical research when considering health disparities based on residential location. First, variations and disparities in health outcomes across rural classification schemes may be stronger than comparisons between rural and urban areas. Second, strong socioeconomic gradients between the highest and lowest SES groups in urban areas often contribute to more of a disparity between health outcomes for populations of urban areas than between populations of rural and urban areas. These two findings when assessing area-based health disparities highlight the importance of considering both the composition and context of placed-based associations when examining health outcomes for rural and urban populations due to the diversity of characteristics and local political, social, and economic dynamics found among populations in diverse residential settings.

Future research on rural health disparities must acknowledge and give thoughtful consideration to the unique composition of rural populations while also recognizing the infrastructures and social systems that may elevate risks for rural residents to experience poor health outcomes. For example, numerous research studies highlight issues of limited availability and accessibility to health-care facilities and medical professionals in rural areas, particularly for the most remote and isolated rural areas (Beachler et al., 2003; Dansky & Dirani, 1998; Krishna et al., 2010). Costs associated with travel distances, time missed from paid employment, and opportunity costs to seek medical care, which to some degree are compositional measures, also present rural residents with increased risks for seeking health care requiring treatment instead of prevention, receiving late-stage diagnoses, and not managing existing health problems based on physician recommendations (DeVoe et al., 2009; Glover et al., 2004). Changing demographic compositions of rural populations throughout the world, but specifically in the U.S., mean that researchers must consider the additional health risks that rural minority, low-income, and poorly educated populations may face in addition to access barriers to seeking appropriate and timely health care (Baffour & Chonody, 2009). Overall the diverse composition of rural places warrants the use of more localized policies and research agendas that can identify the unique contextual constraints that may exacerbate unique compositional characteristics of rural places. Additionally, recommendations about potential pathways by which compositional or contextual factors influence health disparities can be difficult to make based on the diversity of rural places and populations. The empirical analysis presented here serves as a guide to think about these issues.

While Healthy People 2010 explicitly focused on elimination of health disparities by geographic locations, Healthy People 2020 remains committed to eliminating health disparities across a variety of demographic characteristics and geographic locations for the U.S. population. Healthy People 2020 sets ambitious goals to increase the proportion of persons receiving timely and appropriate health care, ongoing care, and the number of practicing primary care providers and reduce the proportion of persons with delays in seeking medical care (U.S. Department of Health and Human Services, 2009). It will be essential for local health and education policies in rural areas to address these specific health care and health-care workforce-related concerns if these goals are to be met and lead to reductions in health disparities for rural populations. Likewise international rural health disparities will continue to persist as long as uneven development creates differential access to health-promoting resources for rural and low-income urban residents, making it difficult to achieve the millennium development goals to reduce health disparities by residential location. Population aging in many parts of the world also presents an additional layer of complexity for many rural populations and their health status as they age. However, more work is needed that assesses why rural populations see a health advantage for some health outcomes and a disadvantage for others and if these differentials are indeed place-based or due to compositional differences between rural and urban populations.

## References

Alexy, B., Nichols, B., Heverly, M. A., & Garzon, L. (1997). Prenatal factors and birth outcomes in the public health service: A rural/urban comparison. *Research in Nursing & Health, 20*(1), 61–70.

Allison, R. A., & Manski, R. J. (2007). The supply of dentists and access to care in rural Kansas. *Journal of Rural Health, 23*(3), 198–206.

Amey, C. H., Miller, M. K., & Albrecht, S. L. (1997). The role of race and residence in determining stage at diagnosis of breast cancer. *Journal of Rural Health, 13*(2), 99–108.

An, A. B. (2002). *Performing Logistic Regression on Survey Data with the New SURVEYLOGISTIC Procedure*. Paper read at Proceedings of the Twenty-Seventh Annual SAS® Users Group International Conference, at Orlando, Florida.

Armstrong Schellenberg, J. R., Mrisho, M., Manzi, F., Shirima, K., Mbuya, C., Mushi, A. K., et al. (2008). Health and survival of young children in southern Tanzania. *BMC Public Health, 8*, 194.

Auchincloss, A. H., & Hadden, W. (2002). The health effects of rural-urban residence and concentrated poverty. *Journal of Rural Health, 18*(2), 319–336.

Auger, N., Authier, M. A., Martinez, J., & Daniel, M. (2009). The association between rural-urban continuum, maternal education and adverse birth outcomes in Quebec, Canada. *Journal of Rural Health, 25*(4), 342–351.

Baffour, T. D., & Chonody, J. M. (2009). African-American women's conceptualizations of health disparities: A community-based participatory research approach. *American Journal of Community Psychology, 44*(3–4), 374–381.

Baffour, T. D., Jones, M. A., & Contreras, L. K. (2006). Family health advocacy – An empowerment model for pregnant and parenting African American women in rural communities. *Family & Community Health, 29*(3), 221–228.

Bailey, B. A., & Cole, L. K. J. (2009). Rurality and birth outcomes: Findings from Southern Appalachia and the potential role of pregnancy smoking. *Journal of Rural Health, 25*(2), 141–149.

Baldwin, L. M., Cai, Y., Larson, E. H., Dobie, S. A., Wright, G. E., Goodman, D. C., et al. (2008). Access to cancer services for rural colorectal cancer patients. *Journal of Rural Health, 24*(4), 390–399.

Baldwin, L. M., Grossman, D. C., Casey, S., Hollow, W., Sugarman, J. R., Freeman, W.L., et al. (2002). Perinatal and infant health among rural and urban American Indians/Alaska natives. *American Journal of Public Health, 92*(9), 1491–1497.

Baldwin, L. M., Grossman, D. C., Murowchick, E., Larson, E. H., Hollow, W. B., Sugarman, J. R., et al. (2009).

Trends in perinatal and infant health disparities between rural American Indians and Alaska natives and rural whites. *American Journal of Public Health, 99*(4), 638–646.

Barnett, E., & Halverson, J. (2000). Disparities in premature coronary heart disease mortality by region and urbanicity among black and white adults ages 35–64, 1985–1995. *Public Health Reports, 115*(1), 52–64.

Beachler, M., Holloman, C., & Herman, J. (2003). Southern rural access program: An overview. *Journal of Rural Health, 19*(S5), 301–307.

Bell, R. A., Arcury, T. A., Stafford, J. M., Golden, S. L., Snively, B. M., & Quandt, S. A. (2007). Ethnic and sex differences in ownership of preventive health equipment among rural older adults with diabetes. *Journal of Rural Health, 23*(4), 332–338.

Bell, R. A., Quandt, S. A., Arcury, T. A., Snively, B. M., Stafford, J. M., Smith, S. L., et al. (2005). Primary and Specialty medical care among ethnically diverse, older rural adults with type 2 diabetes: The ELDER diabetes study. *Journal of Rural Health, 21*(3), 198–205.

Borders, T. F., Rohrer, J. E., & Cardarelli, K. M. (2006). Gender-specific disparities in obesity. *Journal of Community Health, 31*(1), 57–68.

Braveman, P., Marchi, K., Egerter, S., Pearl, M., & Neuhaus, J. (2000). Barriers to timely prenatal care among women with insurance: The importance of prepregnancy factors. *Obstetrics and Gynecology, 95*(6), 874–880.

Brown, D. L., & Swanson, L. E. (Eds.). (2003). *Challenges for rural America in the twenty-first century*. University Park, PA: Penn State Press.

Burris, J. L., & Andrykowski, M. (2010). Disparities in mental health between rural and nonrural cancer survivors: A preliminary study. *Psycho-Oncology, 19*(6), 637–645.

Casey, M. M., Call, K. T., & Klingner, J. M. (2001). Are rural residents less likely to obtain recommended preventive healthcare services? *American Journal of Preventive Medicine, 21*(3), 182–188.

Chrischilles, E., Ahrens, R., Kuehl, A., Kelly, K., Thorne, P., Burmeister, L., et al. (2004). Asthma prevalence and morbidity among rural Iowa schoolchildren. *Journal of Allergy and Clinical Immunology, 113*(1), 66–71.

Clarke, L. L., Farmer, F. L., & Miller, M. K. (1994). Structural determinants of infant mortality in metropolitan and nonmetropolitan America. *Rural Sociology, 59*(1), 84–99.

Coburn, A. F., & Bolda, E. J. (1999). The rural elderly and long-term care. In T. A. Ricketts (Ed.), *Rural health in the United States* (pp. 179–189). New York: Oxford University Press.

Cossman, R. E., Cossman, J. S., Cosby, A. G., & Reavis, R. M. (2008). Reconsidering the rural-urban continuum in rural health research: A test of stable relationships using mortality as a health measure. *Population Research and Policy Review, 27*(4), 459–476.

Dansky, K. H., & Dirani, R. (1998). The use of health care services by people with diabetes in rural areas. *Journal of Rural Health, 14*(2), 129–137.

Davy, B. M., Harrell, K., Stewart, J., & King, D. S. (2004). Body weight status, dietary habits, and physical activity levels of middle school-aged children in rural Mississippi. *Southern Medical Journal, 97*(6), 571–577.

DeVoe, J. E., Krois, L., & Stenger, R. (2009). Do children in rural areas still have different access to health care? Results from a statewide survey of Oregon's food stamp population. *Journal of Rural Health, 25*(1), 1–7.

Diaz-Perez, M. D., Farley, T., & Cabanis, C. M. (2004). A program to improve access to health care among Mexican immigrants in rural Colorado. *Journal of Rural Health, 20*(3), 258–264.

Dong, X., & Simon, M. A. (2010). Health and aging in a Chinese population: Urban and rural disparities. *Geriatrics & Gerontology International, 10*(1), 85–93.

Drummond, R. L., Staten, L. K., Sanford, M. R., Davidson, C. L., Ciocazan, M. M., Khor, K.-N., et al. (2009). A pebble in the pond: The ripple effect of an obesity prevention intervention targeting the child care environment. *Health Promotion Practice, 10*(2 Suppl), 156S–167S.

Dummer, T. J. B., & Cook, I. G. (2007). Exploring China's rural health crisis: Processes and policy implications. *Health Policy, 83*(1), 1–16.

Epstein, B., Grant, T., Schiff, M., & Kasehagen, L. (2009). Does rural residence affect access to prenatal care in Oregon? *Journal of Rural Health, 25*(2), 150–157.

Etowa, J. B., Bernard, W. T., Oyinsan, B., & Clow, B. (2007). Participatory action research (PAR): An approach for improving black women's health in rural and remote communities. *Journal of Transcultural Nursing, 18*, 349–357.

Fang, H., Chen, J., & Rizzo, J. A. (2009). Explaining urban-rural health disparities in China. *Medical Care, 47*(12), 1209–1216.

Felton, G. M., Dowda, M., Ward, D. S., Dishman, R. K., Trost, S. G., Saunders, R., et al. (2002). Differences in physical activity between black and white girls living in rural and urban areas. *Journal of School Health, 72*(6), 250–255.

Feresu, S. A., Zhang, W. Q., Puumala, S. E., Ullrich, F., & Anderson. J. R. (2008). The frequency and distribution of cardiovascular disease risk factors among Nebraska women enrolled in the WISEWOMAN screening program. *Journal of Womens Health, 17*(4), 607–617.

Flower, K. B., Willoughby, M., Cadigan, R. J., Perrin, E. M., Randolph, G., & Investigative Family Life Project. (2008). Understanding breastfeeding initiation and continuation in rural communities: A combined qualitative/quantitative approach. *Maternal and Child Health Journal, 12*(3), 402–414.

Friedell, G. H., Rubio, A., Maretzki, A., Garland, B., Brown, P., Crane, M., et al. (2001). Community cancer control in a rural, underserved population: The Appalachian leadership initiative on cancer project. *Journal of Health Care for the Poor and Underserved, 12*(1), 5–19.

Fukuda, Y., Nakamura, K., & Takano, T. (2004). Increased excess deaths in urban areas: Quantification of geographical variation in mortality in Japan, 1973–1998. *Health Policy, 68*(2), 233–244.

Gazewood, J. D., Rollins, L. K., & Galazka, S. S. (2006). Beyond the horizon: The role of academic health centers in improving the health of rural communities. *Academic Medicine, 81*(9), 793–797.

Geronimus, A. T., Bound, J., Waidmann, T. A., Colen, C. G., & Steffick, D. (2001). Inequality in life expectancy, functional status, and active life expectancy across selected black and white populations in the United States. *Demography, 38*(2), 227–251.

Glover, S., Moore, C. G., Probst, J. C., & Samuels, M. E. (2004). Disparities in access to care among rural working-age adults. *Journal of Rural Health, 20*(3), 193–205.

Gong, G., Braddock, E., Zhang, Y., Hudson, C., Lefforge, D., & O'Bryant, S. (2009). Trend and racial disparities in infant mortality rate in Texas From 1990 to 2004. *Journal of the National Medical Association, 101*(11), 1149–1153.

Grineski, S. E. (2009). Predicting children's asthma hospitalizations: Rural and urban differences in Texas. *Rural Sociology, 74*(2), 201–219.

Grummer-Strawn, L., Scanlon, K. S., Darling, N., & Conrey, E. J. (2006). Racial and socioeconomic disparities in breastfeeding – United States, 2004. *Morbidity and Mortality Weekly Report, 55*(12), 335–339.

Hauenstein, E. J., Petterson, S., Merwin, E., Rovnyak, V., Heise, B., & Wagner, D. (2006). Rurality, gender, and mental health treatment. *Family & Community Health, 29*(3), 169–185.

Hauenstein, E. J., Petterson, S., Rovnyak, V., Merwin, E., Heise, B., & Wagner, D. (2007). Rurality and mental health treatment. *Administration and Policy in Mental Health and Mental Health Services Research, 34*(3), 255–267.

Hayward, M. D., Pienta, A. M., & McLaughlin, D. K. (1997). Inequality in men's mortality: The socioeconomic status gradient and geographic context. *Journal of Health and Social Behavior, 38*(4), 313–330.

Higginbotham, J. C., Moulder, J., & Currier, M. (2001). Rural v. urban aspects of cancer: First-year data from the Mississippi central cancer registry. *Family & Community Health, 24*(2), 1–9.

Hillemeier, M. M., Weisman, C. S., Chase, G. A., & Dyer, A. M. (2007). Individual and community predictors of preterm birth and low birthweight along the rural-urban continuum in central Pennsylvania. *Journal of Rural Health, 23*(1), 42–48.

Hosler, A. S. (2009). Retail food availability, obesity, and cigarette smoking in rural communities. *Journal of Rural Health, 25*(2), 203–210.

Howe, H. L., Keller, J. E., & Lehnherr, M. (1993). Relation between population-density and cancer incidence, Illinois, 1986–1990. *American Journal of Epidemiology, 138*(1), 29–36.

Hu, G., Baker, S. P., & Baker, T. D. (2010). Urban-rural disparities in injury mortality in China, 2006. *Journal of Rural Health, 26*(1), 73–77.

Huang, B., Dignan, M., Han, D., & Johnson, O. (2009). Does distance matter? Distance to mammography facilities and stage at diagnosis of breast cancer in Kentucky. *Journal of Rural Health, 25*(4), 366–371.

Idler, E., & Benyamini, Y. (1997). Self-rated health and mortality: A review of twenty-seven community studies. *Journal of Health and Social Behavior, 38*(1), 21–37.

Islam, M. A., Chowdhury, R. I., & Singh, K. P. (2006). Statistical methods for analysis of repeated measures on maternal morbidity. *Australian Journal of Rural Health, 14*(4), 154–159.

Joens-Matre, R. R., Welk, G. J., Calabro, M. A., Russell, D. W., Nicklay, E., & Hensley, L. D. (2008). Rural-urban differences in physical activity, physical fitness, and overweight prevalence of children. *Journal of Rural Health, 24*(1), 49–54.

Johnson, K. M. (2003). Unpredictable directions of rural population growth and migration. In D. L. Brown & L. E. Swanson (Eds.), *Challenges for rural America in the twenty-first century* (pp. 19–31). University Park, PA: The Pennsylvania State University Press.

Kim, M. H., Subramanian, S. V., Kawachi, I., & Kim, C. Y. (2007). Association between childhood fatal injuries and socioeconomic position at individual and area levels: A multilevel study. *Journal of Epidemiology and Community Health, 61*(2), 135–140.

Kitagawa, E. M., & Hauser, P. M. (1973). *Differential mortality in the U.S.: A study in socioeconomic epidemiology*. Cambridge, MA: Harvard University Press.

Koopman, R. J., Mainous, A. G., & Geesey, M. E. (2006). Rural residence and Hispanic ethnicity: Doubly disadvantaged for diabetes? *Journal of Rural Health, 22*(1), 63–68.

Kravdal, O. (2009). Mortality effects of average education: A multilevel study of small neighbourhoods in rural and urban areas in Norway. *International Journal for Equity in Health, 8*(41), 1–9.

Krishna, S., Gillespie, K. N., & McBride, T. M. (2010). Diabetes burden and access to preventive care in the rural United States. *Journal of Rural Health, 26*(1), 3–11.

Laditka, J. N., Laditka, S. B., Olatosi, B., & Elder, K. T. (2007). The health trade-off of rural residence for impaired older adults: Longer life, more impairment. *Journal of Rural Health, 23*(2), 124–132.

Laditka, S. B., Laditka, J. N., Bennett, K. J., & Probst, J. C. (2005). Delivery complications associated with prenatal care access for Medicaid-insured mothers in rural and urban hospitals. *Journal of Rural Health, 21*(2), 158–166.

Laditka, S. B., Laditka, J. N., & Probst, J. C. (2006). Racial and ethnic disparities in potentially avoidable delivery complications among pregnant Medicaid beneficiaries in South Carolina. *Maternal and Child Health Journal, 10*(4), 339–350.

Larson, N. I., Story, M. T., & Nelson, M. C. (2009). Neighborhood environments: disparities in access to healthy foods in the US. *American Journal of Preventive Medicine, 36*(1), 74–81.

Lengerich, E. J., Tucker, T. C., Powell, R. K., Colsher, P., Lehman, E., Ward, A. J., et al. (2005). Cancer incidence in Kentucky, Pennsylvania, and West Virginia: Disparities in Appalachia. *Journal of Rural Health, 21*(1), 39–47.

Lewis, R. D., Meyer, M. C., Lehman, S. C., Trowbridge, F. L., Bason, J. J., Yurman, K. H., et al. (2006). Prevalence and degree of childhood and adolescent overweight in rural, urban, and suburban Georgia. *Journal of School Health, 76*(4), 126–132.

Liff, J. M., Chow, W. H., & Greenberg, R. S. (1991). Rural-urban differences in stage at diagnosis – possible relationship to cancer screening. *Cancer, 67*(5), 1454–1459.

Luman, E. T., Ching, P., Jumaan, A. O., & Seward, J. F. (2006). Uptake of varicella vaccination among young children in the United States: A success story in eliminating racial and ethnic disparities. *Pediatrics, 117*(4), 999–1008.

Luo, Z. C., Kierans, W. J., Wilkins, R., Liston, R. M., Mohamed, J., & Kramer, M. S. (2004). Disparities in birth outcomes by neighborhood income: Temporal trends in rural and urban areas, British Columbia. *Epidemiology, 15*(6), 679–686.

Luo, Z. C., Kierans, W. J., Wilkins, R., Liston, R. M., Uh, S. H., & Kramer, M. S. (2004). Infant mortality among First Nations versus non-First Nations in British Columbia:

Temporal trends in rural versus urban areas, 1981–2000. *International Journal of Epidemiology, 33*(6), 1252–1259.

Luo, Z. C., Wilkins, R., Kramer, M. S., & Canadian Fetal Infant Health Study Group. (2006). Effect of neighbourhood income and maternal education on birth outcomes: A population-based study. *Canadian Medical Association Journal, 174*(10), 1415–1421.

Macintyre, S., & Ellaway, A. (2003). Neighborhoods and health: An overview. In I. Kawachi & L. F. Berkman (Eds.), *Neighborhoods and health* (pp. 20–44). New York: Oxford University Press.

McLaughlin, D. K., Stokes, C. S., & Nonoyama, A. (2001). Residence and income inequality: Effects on mortality among US counties. *Rural Sociology, 66*(4), 579–598.

McLaughlin, D. K., Stokes, C. S., Smith, P. J., & Nonoyama, A. (2007). Differential mortality across the United States: The influence of place-based inequality. In L.M. Lobao, G. Hooks, & A. R. Tickamyer (Eds.), *The sociology of spatial inequality* (pp. 141–152). Albany, NY: State University of New York Press.

Miller, M. K., Clarke, L. L., Albrecht, S. L., & Farmer, F. L. (1996). The interactive effects of race and ethnicity and mother's residence on adequacy of prenatal care. *Journal of Rural Health, 12*(1), 6–18.

Miller, M. K., Stokes, C. S., & Clifford, W. B. (1987). A comparison of the rural-urban mortality differential for deaths from all causes, cardiovascular disease and cancer. *Journal of Rural Health, 3*(2), 23–33.

Moore, J. B., Davis, C. L., Baxter, S. D., Lewis, R. D., & Yin, Z. N. (2008). Physical activity, metabolic syndrome, and overweight in rural youth. *Journal of Rural Health, 24*(2), 136–142.

Morrison, T., Callahan, D., Moorman, J., & Bailey, C. (2009). A national survey of adult asthma prevalence by urban-rural residence US 2005. *Journal of Asthma, 46*(8), 751–758.

Morton, L. W. (2003). Rural health policy. In D. L. Brown & L. E. Swanson (Eds.), *Challenges for rural America in the twenty-first century* (pp. 290–304). University Park: The Pennsylvania State University Press.

Morton, L. W. (2004). Spatial patterns of rural mortality. In N. Glasgow, N. E. Johnson, & L. W. Morton (Eds.), *Critical issues in rural health* (pp. 37–48). Ames: Blackwell.

Nesbitt, T. S., Connell, F. A., Hart, L. G., & Rosenblatt, R. A. (1990). Access to obstetric care in rural areas: Effect on birth outcomes. *American Journal of Public Health, 80*(7), 814–818.

Nesbitt, T. S., Larson, E. H., Rosenblatt, R. A., & Hart, L. G. (1997). Access to maternity care in rural Washington: Its effect on neonatal outcomes and resource use. *American Journal of Public Health, 87*(1), 85–90.

Nishi, N. (2008). Baseline cardiovascular risk factors and stroke mortality by municipality population size in a 19-year follow-up study-NIPPON DATA80. *Journal of Epidemiology, 18*(4), 135–143.

Nishi, N., Sugiyama, H., Kasagi, F., Kodama, K., Hayakawa, T., Ueda, K., et al. (2007). Urban-rural difference in stroke mortality from a 19-year cohort study of the Japanese general population: NIPPON DATA80. *Social Science & Medicine, 65*(4), 822–832.

O'Connor, T. M., & Hooker, R. S. (2007). Extending rural and remote medicine with a new type of health worker: Physician assistants. *Australian Journal of Rural Health, 15*(6), 346–351.

O'Hara Tompkins, N., Rye, J. A., Zizzi, S., & Vitullo, E. (2005). Engaging rural youth in physical activity promotion research in an after-school setting. *Preventing Chronic Disease, 2*(Special Issue), 1–7.

Ownby, D. R. (2005). Asthma in rural America. *Annals of Allergy Asthma & Immunology, 95*(5), S17–S22.

Paquette, L., & Finlayson, S. R. G. (2007). Rural versus urban colorectal and lung cancer patients: Differences in stage at presentation. *Journal of the American College of Surgeons, 205*(5), 636–641.

Patil, A. V., Somasundaram, K. V., & Goyal, R. C. (2002). Current health scenario in rural India. *Australian Journal of Rural Health, 10*(2), 129–135.

Pearce, J., & Boyle, P. (2005). Is the urban excess in lung cancer in Scotland explained by patterns of smoking? *Social Science & Medicine, 60*(12), 2833–2843.

Pearce, J., Witten, K., Hiscock, R., & Blakely, T. (2008). Regional and urban-rural variations in the association of neighbourhood deprivation with community resource access: A national study. *Environment and Planning A, 40*(10), 2469–2489.

Petterson, S., Williams, I. C., Hauenstein, E. J., Rovnyak, V., & Merwin, E. (2009). Race and ethnicity and rural mental health treatment. *Journal of Health Care for the Poor and Underserved, 20*(3), 662–677.

Pickett, K. E., & Pearl, M. (2001). Multilevel analyses of neighbourhood socioeconomic context and health outcomes: A critical review. *Journal of Epidemiology and Community Health, 55*(2), 111–122.

Pollan, M., Ramis, R., Aragones, N., Perez-Gomez, B., Gomez, D., Lope, V., et al. (2007). Municipal distribution of breast cancer mortality among women in Spain. *BMC Cancer, 7*(78), 1–14.

Pong, R. W., DesMeules, M., & Lagacé, C. (2009). Rural & urban disparities in health: How does Canada fare and how does Canada compare with Australia? *Australian Journal of Rural Health, 17*(1), 58–64.

Pozet, A., Westeel, V., Berion, P., Danzon, A., Debieuvre, D., & Breton, J. L. (2008). Rurality and survival differences in lung cancer: A large population-based multivariate analysis. *Lung Cancer, 59*(3), 291–300.

Prehn, A. W., & West, D. W. (1998). Evaluating local differences in breast cancer incidence rates: A census-based methodology (United States). *Cancer Causes & Control, 9*(5), 511–517.

Probst, J. C., Moore, C. G., & Baxley, E. G. (2005). Update: Health insurance and utilization of care among rural adolescents. *Journal of Rural Health, 21*(4), 279–287.

Quandt, S. A., Bell, R. A., Snively, B. M., Smith, S. L., Stafford, J. M., Wetmore, L. K., et al. (2005). Ethnic disparities in glycemic control among rural older adults with type 2 diabetes. *Ethnicity & Disease, 15*(4), 656–663.

Quandt, S. A., Chen, H., Bell, R. A., Anderson, A. M., Savoca, M. R., Kohrman, T., et al. (2009). Disparities in oral health status between older adults in a multiethnic rural community: The rural nutrition and oral health study. *Journal of the American Geriatrics Society, 57*(8), 1369–1375.

Rabinowitz, H. K., Diamond, J. J., Markham, F. W., & Hazelwood, C. E. (1999). A program to increase the number of family physicians in rural and underserved areas – Impact after 22 years. *Journal of the American Medical Association, 281*(3), 255–260.

Ramsey, P. W., & Glenn, L. L. (2002). Obesity and health status in rural, urban, and suburban Southern women. *Southern Medical Journal, 95*(7), 666–671.

Reijneveld, S. A. (2002). Neighbourhood socioeconomic context and self reported health and smoking: A secondary analysis of data on seven cities. *Journal of Epidemiology and Community Health, 56*(12), 935–942.

Roberts, L. W., Johnson, M. E., Brems, C., & Warner, T. D. (2007). Ethical disparities: Challenges encountered by multidisciplinary providers in fulfilling ethical standards in the care of rural and minority people. *Journal of Rural Health, 23*(s1), 89–97.

Rogers, R. G., Hummer, R. A., & Nam, C. B. (2000). *Living and dying in the USA: Behavioral, health, and social differentials of adult mortality*. San Diego: Academic Press.

Sankaranarayanan, J., Watanabe-Galloway, S., Sun, J. F., Qiu, F., Boilesen, E., & Thorson, A. G. (2009). Rurality and other determinants of early colorectal cancer diagnosis in Nebraska: A 6-year cancer registry study, 1998–2003. *Journal of Rural Health, 25*(4), 358–365.

Schootman, M., & Fuortes, L. J. (1999). Breast and cervical carcinoma – The correlation of activity limitations and rurality with screening, disease incidence, and mortality. *Cancer, 86*(6), 1087–1094.

Smith, K. B., Humphreys, J. S., & Wilson, M. G. A. (2008). Addressing the health disadvantage of rural populations: How does epidemiological evidence inform rural health policies and research? *Australian Journal of Rural Health, 16*(2), 56–66.

Sontheimer, D., Halverson, L. W., Bell, L., Ellis, M., & Bunting, P. W. (2008). Impact of discontinued obstetrical services in rural Missouri: 1990–2002. *Journal of Rural Health, 24*(1), 96–98.

Sparks, P. J. (2010). Rural-Urban Differences in Breastfeeding Initiation in the United States. *Journal of Human Lactation, 26*(2), 118–129.

Sparks, P. J., McLaughlin, D. K., & Stokes, C. S. (2009). Differential neonatal and postneonatal infant mortality rates across US counties: The role of socioeconomic conditions and rurality. *Journal of Rural Health, 25*(4), 332–341.

Steyer, T. E., Mainous, A. G., & Geesey, M. E. (2005). The effect of race and residence on the receipt of childhood immunizations: 1993–2001. *Vaccine, 23*(12), 1464–1470.

Stokley, S., Smith, P. J., Klevens, R. M., & Battaglia, M. P. (2001). Vaccination status of children living in rural areas in the United States – Are they protected? *American Journal of Preventive Medicine, 20*(4), 55–60.

Sung, J. F. C., Blumenthal, D. S., AlemaMensah, E., & McGrady, G. A. (1997). Racial and urban/rural differences in cervical carcinoma in Georgia Medicaid recipients. *Cancer, 80*(2), 231–236.

Tudiver, F., Edwards, J. B., & Pfortmiller, D. T. (2010). Depression screening patterns for women in rural health clinics. *Journal of Rural Health, 26*(1), 44–50.

UN Millennium Project. (2005). *Investing in development: A practical plan to achieve millennium development goals*. New York: United Nations Development Programme.

United Nations. (2009). *The millennium development goals report 2009*. New York: United Nations.

U.S. Department of Health and Human Services. (2000). *Healthy people 2010: Understanding and improving health* (2nd ed.). Washington, DC: U.S. Government Printing Office.

U.S. Department of Health and Human Services. (2009). Healthy People 2020 Public Meetings: 2009 Draft Objectives.

Van de Poel, E., O'Donnell, O., & Van Doorslaer, E. (2007). Are urban children really healthier? Evidence from 47 developing countries. *Social Science & Medicine, 65*(10), 1986–2003.

Van de Poel, E., O'Donnell, O., & Van Doorslaer, E. (2009). What explains the rural-urban gap in infant mortality: Household or community characteristics? *Demography, 46*(4), 827–850.

van Hooijdonk, C., Droomers, M., Deerenberg, I. M., Mackenbach, J. P., & Kunst, A. E. (2008). Higher mortality in urban neighbourhoods in The Netherlands: Who is at risk? *Journal of Epidemiology and Community Health, 62*(6), 499–505.

Vargas, C. M., Dye, B. A., & Hayes, K. L. (2002). Oral health status of rural adults in the United States. *Journal of the American Dental Association, 133*(12), 1672–1681.

Wickrama, K. A. S., Elder, G. H., Jr., & Abraham, W. T. (2007). Rurality and ethnicity in adolescent physical illness: Are children of the growing rural latino population at excess health risk? *Journal of Rural Health, 23*(3), 228–237.

Zhao, Z., & Luman, E. T. (2010). Progress toward eliminating disparities in vaccination coverage among US children, 2000–2008. *American Journal of Preventive Medicine, 38*(2), 127–137.

Zimmer, Z., Kaneda, T., & Spess, L. (2007). An examination of urban versus rural mortality in china using community and individual data. *Journals of Gerontology Series B-Psychological Sciences and Social Sciences, 62*(5), S349–S357.

# Perspectives on U.S. Rural Labor Markets in the First Decade of the Twenty-First Century

## 19

Alexander C. Vias[†]

## Introduction

In recent years scholars have developed very robust notions of what makes a rural community prosperous, especially the idea that there is more to a community's long term sustainability than employment or income growth alone (Isserman, Feser, & Warren, 2009). Nevertheless, it is also apparent that a fundamental characteristic of any rural community's success is a healthy labor market that offers good, decent paying job opportunities for the local population that match the skill set of the labor force (see Chapter 21 in this volume). The recent recession that started in late 2007 makes understanding the nature of rural labor markets even more important because as national indicators begin to show improvement in the economy, there has been a remarkable lag in an employment rebound. More unsettling is that throughout this recession, unemployment rates in rural areas have remained persistently higher than those in urban areas, a trend that stretches back over a century (Bishop & Gallardo, 2009). So for many people in rural areas, the recession and unemployment remains an ongoing event, perhaps even more so than for urban areas in general.

In this chapter I examine the nature of rural labor markets as we enter the second decade of the twenty-first century, including a review of the better known theoretical approaches developed by social scientists. Since labor markets in general represent a set of exchange relationships between employers and workers, we need to understand contemporary theory on: how the demand for labor works in rural areas; availability and constraints on the supply of labor; and the variety of factors that can interfere with efficient labor markets. To examine these issues empirically, the demand for labor is shown through a range of data from the past decade on broad changes in the structure of labor markets, especially in terms of the industrial and occupational structure of employment, with comparisons between rural (nonmetropolitan) and urban (metropolitan) areas. Additionally, supply-side information is provided to show some of the demographic and socioeconomic changes in the human capital of the rural population and workforce in recent years, and how broad structural issues in the rural labor supply may continue to constrain some aspects of economic growth and rural prosperity. Finally, data are presented on some of the outcomes of the rural labor market in action, especially in terms of wages and unemployment across the U.S., along with a brief discussion on how rural labor markets are coping with the economic problems associated with the recent recession.

---

[†]This handbook represents the collective efforts of many contributors, but sadly, this chapter's author will not see the final product. Alex Vias passed away suddenly on April 25, 2011 at far too young an age. Throughout his productive, albeit too short, academic career, Alex's work focused on the changing economic and demographic landscapes in the rural United States. We are grateful for Alex's contributions to our understanding of rural migration patterns, the changing retail geography in rural areas, and complex health disparities emerging between urban and rural regions. Most of all, however, we will miss Alex as a colleague and friend who brought us a wonderfully dry sense of humor and an unending curiosity about places.

Peter B. Nelson, Department of Geography, Middlebury College, Middlebury College, VT 05753, USA
e-mail: pbnelson@middlebury.edu

Overall, one of the most profound changes in rural labor markets—changes that are taking place in other developed nations—is the increasing integration of rural economies into the global marketplace and the continued restructuring of national economies. Today, globalization processes represent more than a geographic expansion of markets for agricultural and natural resource commodities. In fact, labor markets themselves have become more globalized as (im)migration changes the human capital of rural areas. Perhaps more importantly, globalization is affecting rural areas much in the way it has reordered urban and suburban economies that rely on service-oriented labor markets. This is especially relevant as economic restructuring continues to increase the percentage of people employed in service and trade jobs, that is, sectors of the economy increasingly linked directly to global partners and the postindustrial economy. In many ways, it could be argued that these broad level changes driving the demand side of the economy are more important than inadequate human capital or poorly functioning labor markets in rural areas today. These overlying trends are extremely important and are worth keeping in mind as this review of the rural labor market proceeds.

## Demand Driven Theory of Labor Markets

Over the decades, social scientists have developed a set of theories and conceptual models that try to explain how labor markets work, including the role of space and location, important factors that differentiate urban versus rural labor markets (Summers, Horton, & Gringeri, 1990; Shaffer, Deller, & Marcouiller, 2004). Although offering insights on certain (dis)advantages associated with rural labor markets, the theories are often inadequate in an age of global trade and instantaneous economic interactions over long distances. As a result, over the past few decades scholars have published thousands of papers and books describing the effects of economic restructuring and globalization at multiple spatial scales, and a sizeable portion of that literature focuses on rural labor markets in developed countries. The paragraphs below briefly summarize some of the more important theories that inform our knowledge of rural labor markets and the demand for workers.

## Spatial Location Models and Export Base Theory

A number of spatial location theories developed over the past century (and earlier) have attempted to explain the location of economic activities, and hence the labor required to support those activities (e.g., von Thunen, Christaller, Weber, to name a few). As a result, these are demand-oriented labor market theories that explain the needs of firms and industries located in particular types of places (such as rural versus urban areas). Besides this geographic emphasis, the theories often have specific foci in terms of the sectors or occupations of the jobs and employment analyzed.

At the broadest level, one can consider fundamental differences in the nature of urban versus rural locations, and the types of economic activities possible in each location. Clearly, agriculture and natural resource extraction have been and will remain primarily rural activities due to land requirements and the location of natural resources in remote areas. However, a number of changes have led this particular strand of thought to diminish in importance over time, including mechanization in these sectors that has drastically reduced labor demand, with simultaneous increases in labor demand in urban areas as the industrial revolution progressed. As a result, this is a small part of the rural economy today, even in such regions as the Great Plains or Midwest, where farming-related jobs represent less than 20% of all employment (see below). Of course, in many parts of rural America, these sectors remain very important, and can provide a sound economic base even in this era of globalization and economic restructuring, but farmers face another set of global-scale challenges (discussed in more detail below). That said, much of the economy in rural areas today is related to manufacturing and services (broadly defined), and any examination of labor demand needs to move away from any traditional notion that rural areas are simply about farms, other extractive activities, and a limited set of service activities for the local population.

Moving on, a well-known set of theories is related to the location of manufacturing activities (Smith, 1971). For example, Weberian theory posits a "least cost" rationale for locating certain types of manufacturing operations close to markets or to resource inputs, depending on the nature of the manufacturing process and associated transportation costs. Although this approach still makes some sense for a specific subset of manufacturing where rural areas still dominate—like resource extraction and processing—it is a decidedly small fraction of the rural economy. Other manufacturing location theories, related to a "demand maximization" or "profit maximization" rationale for industrial location, along with a host of other spatial theoretical traditions (especially in regional science), also still offer some interesting insights on firm behavior and the location decision for producing goods, especially why it might be more profitable to locate in urban over rural areas due to market size (Isard, 1975). However, all these models rely on strict neoclassical assumptions of behavior that often do not work as well in today's increasingly complicated global markets. Clearly, manufacturing can and does locate almost anywhere today, however the problem today is not so much rural versus urban, but is more often related to the following question: whether or not to locate in the U.S. at all. A final theory for manufacturing location is the product cycle (Vernon, 1966). In this theory, manufacturing goes through several stages such as development, growth, routine production, and decline as the product and its markets mature over time, with the latter stages of production more likely to locate in rural areas. Still, the same drive for low costs that moved factories to rural areas is now pushing them offshore as well, and Vernon's theory really works best at explaining the location of factories for a small segment of the manufacturing sector, like consumer electronics.

Though widely ignored today, where older spatial location theories still offer some valuable insights on the demand for labor is related to services (Berry, Parr, Epstein, Gosh, & Smith, 1988). For example, "Central Place Theory" still explains some fundamental differences in terms of low versus higher order goods and services in small towns versus bigger cities, and the types of jobs available in those places with respect to certain sectors. For a long time this explained why low-skilled and low-paying service jobs dominated labor markets in rural areas, while both lower and higher paying jobs would be found in cities, where those services could be supported with a sizeable threshold population. This is still true to some extent in personal or consumer services and parts of the retail sector that really need to be close to the consumer (convenience goods/services). But in many other parts of the larger service or tertiary sector, changes in technology (Internet) and the nature of many transnational corporations (in retail and financial services) operating in this part of the economy have made the location decision for firms much more complex, or even irrelevant as far as consumers are concerned (Vias, 2004). Further complicating the ideas behind central place theory is the degree to which rural residents are willing to travel to obtain their required goods and services, leading to significant declines in many once-thriving rural CBDs (Central Business Districts) (Tigges & Fuguitt, 2003; Vias, 2007).

Export base theory—although dated and simplistic in many ways—also offers important conceptual ideas on rural labor markets to this day because it can account for changing sectoral structures within a local economy (Krikelas, 1992). The notion here is simple: increasing exports (from the basic sectors like manufacturing) lead to increasing demand for local services (from the nonbasic sectors like retail). The theory has been adapted to take into account broad restructuring in the overall economy, and the potential for many services (like tourism) to act as part of the export base, as well as the increasingly important role of nonemployment income in rural areas (Hirschl & Summers, 1982), which can induce local demand for services without any changes in exports (think high-amenity locations). The problem with this model is that it really only works well for isolated areas because of cross-hauling and overlapping markets.

## Globalization and Economic Restructuring

In many ways, the spatial theories that have traditionally been used to understand rural labor market demand have become outmoded in light of broad structural changes that have taken place in the U.S. economy, and globalization processes leading to an increasingly interconnected world economy (Bluestone & Harrison, 1982; Held & McGrew, 2007). Both of these interlinked processes have had profound impacts on rural areas in the U.S. (Glasmeier & Leichenko, 2000; Falk, Schulman, & Tickamyer, 2003). Clearly, as the fortunes of different types of firms rise and fall based on the vagaries of local and global markets, so does the nature of rural labor markets. When analyzing the impact of globalization and economic restructuring on labor markets, it makes sense to start with the agricultural sector, once the primary employer in rural areas. This sector has been buffeted by a range of global forces, perhaps more so than any part of the rural economy (Blank, 2008; Lobao & Meyer, 2001). Since the end of World War II, and especially since the 1970s, agriculture has become increasingly important as an export commodity sold around the world. In fact, this is one of the few parts of the U.S. economy where a trade surplus exists (Stutz & Warf, 2007). For sure, American farms remain very competitive in many parts of the agricultural sector, especially in the trade of grains like corn, wheat, and soybeans, but also in more specialized agricultural commodities as well (U.S. Department of Agriculture, 2009).

Growth in exports represents a positive outcome for rural areas in terms of jobs (especially considering the export base model), but the export orientation of large parts of this sector has linked rural areas directly with the global economy and all its inherent volatility (Buttel, 2003; McMichael, 2003). So, while globalization means an increase in potential markets for farmers, it will also entail more competition from abroad, especially should the protective tariffs eventually disappear (as advocated by free-trade enthusiasts). For example, the very profitable soybean sector in the U.S. faces strong competition from countries like Brazil, which continues to add new production capabilities in once forested areas (Schnepf, Dohlman, & Bolling, 2001). At home, the agricultural sector continues to experience changes such as increasing corporate ownership, and new technology that increases productivity (Lobao, 1990; Lobao & Meyer, 2001). This had led to lower demand for workers and fewer family farmers, which might endanger some of the favorable treatment the sector has traditionally received in Washington DC (Hansen, 1991).

Despite the trade surplus enjoyed by the agricultural sector, and emerging opportunities in such areas as energy-related production (ethanol), the demand for all these commodities can be fickle at times, and will change as other nations enter the market, or as government policies evolve (Carolan, 2009; Gehlhar, 2009). In all likelihood, a stable farm sector and consistent demand for labor is probably the best prospect for jobs in this sector. However, there are some other opportunities for helping this sector and the rural labor market. Potential areas for agricultural development are emerging due to increasing demand in niche markets like organically grown foods, and the "buy-local" movement in and around urban areas (Lyson, Gillespie, & Hilcheya, 1995; Greene & Kremen, 2003). Nontraditional activities on farms related to tourism also provide employment opportunities in some parts of the U.S. (Bender & Davis, 2000), but overall, prospects for significant new demand for farm labor seem limited.

For several decades in the second half of the last century, it looked like manufacturing would provide a core of long-term employment opportunities in rural areas as factories continued to decentralize out of large metropolitan areas in the Manufacturing Belt (Barkley & Hinschberger, 1992; Mack & Schaeffer, 1993). In fact, by the end of the past century, manufacturing was a larger source of employment in rural areas than urban areas (17 to 13% based on Census 2000 data). This has been a fortunate outcome in many ways because the jobs in this sector have been among the highest found in rural areas (Vias & Nelson, 2006). However, manufacturing has not been the broad job generator once envisioned. One of the reasons is that the economic restructuring process will continue to shift jobs out of manufacturing and into services (Collins & Quark, 2006; Miller, 2007). A more important reason for the dim prospects in manufacturing is related to the forces of globalization that have opened new regions abroad for factories that utilize low skill labor that was the core of rural manufacturing in the U.S. This has been especially true, for example, in industries such as textiles in the South, which have been decimated by the movement of factories to Asia (Bascom, 2000). Furthermore, much of the manufacturing that remains in the U.S. relies on highly skilled workers more commonly found in urban areas (more on this below) (Gibbs, 2002).

The largest portion of the rural economy is based on tertiary or service sector activities, and as the broader economy shifts to a higher proportion of all employment in this very broad sector, this would seem to be an area of interest for rural areas (Glasmeier & Howland, 1995; Beyers & Nelson, 2000). This sector has become increasingly differentiated, with some types of services still based close to sources of demand (low level goods/services), hence they can still be found in rural communities. But, many of these are among the lowest paying jobs found in rural areas (especially consumer/personal and social services), and even these jobs are increasingly concentrated in regional centers, leaving the most remote towns with virtually no jobs and dead CBDs (Vias, 2007). This will continue to be a major problem for many of the most isolated rural towns, and changes in the retail sector that favor big-box stores will further enhance this regional center phenomena, much to the detriment of the traditional "mom and pop" store owners in many small towns across rural America (Vias, 2004; Bonanno, 2007).

Other issues for rural areas arise because the most sought-after service-related jobs like information technologies, financial services and other producer services, along with management and professional jobs, are likely to be most highly concentrated in and around metropolitan areas (Garnick, 1984; Glasmeier & Howland, 1995). Still, changes in technology have allowed the shift of some types of services to more rural locales (Beyers & Lindahl, 1996), especially routine back-office operations for many types of financial services, telemarketing, or customer service operations (Glasmeier & Howland, 1995), but growth in this area seems limited, and could be threatened by international competition (e.g., Indian customer service operations).

Areas where rural America still has opportunities include jobs related to public administration, although this is hardly what might be considered a sound economic base, especially in rough economic/fiscal times (Vias & Nelson, 2006). Even so, increasing numbers of rural residents are employed by local and state and national government agencies, especially in health care and education (Bull, 1998). A better prospect in many rural areas, especially in some of the most remote parts of the U.S., is tourism and economic development for regions that enjoy high-quality environmental amenities (Green, Deller, & Marcouiller, 2005; Moss, 2006). One problem that remains with respect to these jobs, especially if they are in the service-related sectors is that many are seasonal in nature, and low paying. So, while some may benefit from growth in these types of jobs, especially the owners of the operations, they often form an unstable/volatile economic base for long-term economic success. The same characteristics that make rural areas appealing for recreation and tourism can also attract retirees with mobile sources of income, which in turn can generate significant consumer spending in the local economy (Brown & Glasgow, 2008). But once again, the vagaries of the national and global economy can have significant impacts on these activities, as seen in many parts of the U.S. that were once booming as a result of in-migration and housing construction, and have now crashed in the most recent economic downturn (think Arizona and Nevada).

## Supply-Oriented Approaches, and Other Theoretical Issues in Rural Labor Markets

If one is to follow the assumptions of the neoclassical approach to labor markets, then the opposite side of the demand-driven approaches is a focus on the supply side. In that respect, much of the theory here revolves around human capital theory and the quality and structure of the labor force (Becker, 1964; Mincer, 1974). For rural areas this has indeed been a long-term area of concern because of marked socioeconomic disparities between urban and rural areas (Singelmann & Deseran, 1993). Additionally, scholars have proposed a whole host of additional theories that explore the role of institutions and social constraints, and how these are mediating the supply and demand of labor, thereby disrupting many of the assumptions underlying the neoclassical approaches to labor markets (Doeringer & Piore, 1971; Gordon, Edwards, & Reich, 1982). Probably most well known of these approaches centers on dual or segmented labor markets, and the role of informal work.

## Supply-Oriented Approaches: Human Capital Theory

From the perspective of the supply side, workers enter the job market to sell their labor, subject to their skills and training, and labor demand (Summers et al., 1990; Shaffer et al., 2004). What determines the level of human capital in rural areas? This is related to the level/amount of schooling, specialized training and health care for workers, along with a host of policies aimed at improving the productive capacity of the workforce. Furthermore, a demand for labor creates incentives for workers to increase their skill sets in anticipation of a rise in wages in the future. Of course all this assumes markets work perfectly in competitive markets, and all information is available to all.

The theory of human capital does offer an important way of understanding labor markets, especially because it helps highlight some of the impediments that rural areas may face in creating and keeping high-quality jobs (Lyson & Falk, 1992; Wojan, 2000). For example, simple disparities in education levels between rural and urban places can often put rural areas at a severe disadvantage (Gibbs, 2000; Kusmin, Gibbs, & Parker, 2008). If a rural area is already suffering economic losses because of declines in the economic base in such sectors as agriculture or even manufacturing, this process can be self-reinforcing, as job losses create even fewer incentives for workers to stay and increase skill sets. It is easier to simply leave and move to nearby cities. Making the impact associated with disparities in human capital and labor skills even worse are the types of jobs often found in rural areas that emphasize lower labor skills, thus making the jobs more susceptible to international competition and the movement of jobs offshore, as described above with respect to globalization processes (Mazie & Killian, 1991). It is hard to overstate how this declining market for relatively cheap and relatively unskilled labor—a huge advantage when manufacturing first started to decentralize from urban areas—is what now puts rural areas at a disadvantage when it comes to the demands of the postindustrial economy.

Unfortunately, new programs that train and educate the local workforce may not help develop the human capital needed if the characteristics of the local population make these efforts too difficult or costly. This could happen if local populations are dominated by certain demographic groups, such as the very young or old, or recent immigrants who might require special efforts to train because of language/cultural barriers (Jensen & Tienda, 1989; Saenz, 2000). Additionally, there are uneven outcomes for women versus men who face different constraints in terms of their ability to enter/leave/stay in the labor market (Bokemeier & Tickamyer, 1985; Jensen, Findeis, & Wang, 2000). Besides differences in training, education and skill sets related to these groups that disadvantage them in the labor market, there are long-term historical issues that have led to discrimination and marginalization in the work force, which are discussed in more detail below.

Despite the importance of human capital theory in explaining some fundamental shortcomings of the rural labor supply, some argue that the theory places too much emphasis on rational thinking with respect to returns in the labor market—that is, workers do not have perfect information, and there are simply too many social and personal issues that interfere with these types of decisions (Shaffer et al., 2004). Perhaps more fundamentally, human capital theory does not take into account a number of broad structural problems with how workers and employers interact in labor markets, as discussed next.

## Institutional Theories: Dual/Segmented and Informal Labor Markets

In response to problems with neoclassical approaches to labor markets, social scientists have developed several high-profile institutional theories that try to explain the reasons why rural labor markets do not provide consistently high quality, long-term employment (Summers et al., 1990; Shaffer et al., 2004). The institutional approaches generally argue that a narrow analysis of supply and demand as the sole forces working in the labor market is too simplistic. For example, historical precedents have set up some long-term relations and inequalities in the labor market that often may favor people in urban areas. Though there are many variants of what may fall into the institutional approach, here I focus on two important ideas, dual/segmented labor markets, and informal labor markets. The reader is referred elsewhere for a more in-depth discussion of alternative institutional approaches to labor markets (such as the role of implicit contracts and transaction costs for rural areas) (see Summers et al., 1990; Shaffer et al., 2004).

In the dual/segmented labor markets, it is posited that the economy is divided into two primary components, core and periphery economies (Doeringer and Piore, 1971; Snipp & Bloomquist, 1989). The variant of this model of most interest here is the division that exists between urban areas at the core and rural areas at the periphery within developed countries like the U.S. (Wojan, 2000). The thinking here is that differences between urban and rural areas are not simply about dissimilar sectoral emphases, but also exist in terms of the ability of firms in core versus periphery economies to manipulate the labor market and workers, and control the jobs in each of these areas.

For example, it is argued that jobs in the core (or urban areas) are more secure and higher paying, and with highly skilled workers that exert greater control over their own destiny (Summers et al., 1990; Shaffer et al., 2004). Moreover, firms in urban areas are also larger and more sophisticated, and better equipped to operate in today's increasingly competitive global markets. Conversely, labor in the periphery (or rural areas) work in jobs that are extremely low skilled and volatile in nature—constantly appearing and disappearing according to market demand. Also, firms operating in rural areas are smaller and less likely to be flexible and/or competitive in the face of market forces beyond their control. Even within the limited confines of rural labor markets, many workers are disadvantaged, especially marginalized groups like immigrants, minorities, and women who encounter discriminatory practices that keep wages low and work conditions poor (Tickamyer & Bokemeier, 1988; Davila & Mora, 2000; Saenz, 2000). Thus, rural labor markets have faced long-term structural disadvantages in terms of the types of jobs that might be available compared to urban areas. Workers in rural areas face additional hurdles because of historical and social factors that often have limited their ability to successfully engage in labor markets. This scenario describes the prevailing disparities between rural and urban labor markets, and especially why these disparities are so persistent and difficult to eliminate.

Another topic related to inadequately working labor markets focuses on economic activities related to informal work. While a lot of research on informal work has focused on developing nations and urban enclaves, this part of the economy is important in rural areas of developed countries as well (Edgcomb & Armington, 2003; Slack, 2007). Overall, these types of jobs often thrive because of efforts to circumvent taxes, and because firms and workers may be trying to reduce oversight from various regulatory agencies. Of course, this type of work is also generally unstable in nature, lower paying, and subject to abuse by employers. Many scholars note that growth in the informal economy, including in rural areas, is a result of the continued globalization process and the eternal search for lower costs and practices by firms (Portes, Castells, & Benton, 1989; McLaughlin & Coleman-Jensen, 2008).

On the plus side, these informal activities offer income opportunities often not found in the formal economy of rural areas, both for those living on the margin as well as those gainfully employed. This also applies to younger cohorts of the rural population capable of working, as well as women, minorities, and immigrants who may face various types of discrimination in the formal labor market (Deseran & Keithly, 1994; Jensen, Cornwell, & Findeis, 1995). Another similar category of labor, sometimes termed "nonstandard employment" (part-time, seasonal, contingent jobs) offers legal opportunities where a permanent labor market is weak (McLaughlin & Coleman-Jensen, 2008). However, it is very possible that a growing informal sector will further entrench inequalities and segmentation in the labor market, thus perpetuating rural/urban differences in the number and quality of jobs, and will not form the basis for long-term stable economic growth and development in rural areas.

## Trends in the Rural Labor Market of the U.S.

Data to comprehensively analyze current labor market trends, especially in the context of the theories described above, are often not available at the proper geographic scale or time frame. For example, labor markets may vary in size from a town/city to a multistate area depending on the definition used (see Killian & Tolbert, 1993 for a review of these issues). Unfortunately, the various databases available do not consistently match up with any single spatial scale, a problem that worsens if a temporal analysis is required. However, data are available that do point out some of the major employment trends such as industrial and occupational structure at the national and regional levels, but this analysis requires using county-level data for metropolitan and nonmetropolitan (which include micropolitan) areas to serve as proxies for urban or rural. This is always problematic, and care is required in any interpretation of the data. Still, this methodological approach reveals many of the broad trends in urban versus rural labor markets, including information on the demand and supply of labor, as well as outcomes of labor market interactions.

## Employment Trends in Metropolitan and Nonmetropolitan Counties in the U.S.

The data used to analyze population and employment change in this section come from the U.S. Bureau of Economic Analysis (BEA) (2010) Regional Economic Information System (REIS) data set (note that data are based on 2008 OMB Metropolitan Classification). The real advantage of this data set is its time series characteristics. Unfortunately, the change between SIC (Standard Industrial Classification) and NAICS (North American Industrial Classification System) categories for employment that was completed at the start of the century means that for the more detailed sectoral breakdowns, the data only go from 2001 to 2007. It is also important to note that these data are based on "place of work" rather than "place of residence" (as done with Census data), and that the employment data include part-time positions. Still, important trends emerge that are quite relevant to the various theoretical perspectives on rural labor markets just outlined.

For decades, population change in nonmetropolitan areas trailed that of metropolitan areas as the U.S. continued the urbanization process. However, as Fig. 19.1 shows, this trend was reversed for a brief period in the 1970s during the rural renaissance, when for a brief time, nonmetropolitan areas did grow faster, but by the 1980s this trend had reversed, and has generally continued to this day (there was a brief reprieve in the early 1990s) (Fuguitt, 1995). The inability of these areas to grow as fast as metropolitan areas has been a persistent problem in areas where population densities are exceptionally low to begin with. This is especially hard on service sectors that cater to the local population, and which employ a sizeable percentage of the workforce (see below). When local populations decline, these service sector businesses often do not have the population thresholds needed to survive, leading to the loss of these businesses entirely, or they may cluster in regional centers where they can take advantage of economies of scale.

In terms of employment growth, the impact of business cycles on long-term trends is quite obvious, especially when compared to population change, which is generally smoother and subject to a different set of forces. Virtually throughout this time period annual employment growth rates in nonmetropolitan areas have been slower than metropolitan growth rates (Vias & Nelson, 2006). Clearly, metropolitan areas are favored when it comes to growing jobs, a problem that continues to this day, often resulting in higher unemployment rates in nonmetropolitan areas, or additional commuting to metropolitan areas located near nonmetropolitan areas. While this out-commuting has allowed many to persevere and cope in the face of local job shortages in rural areas, the fact that so many need to commute long distances to find decent employment says much about the weak labor markets in rural areas (Fuguitt, 1991; Tigges & Fuguitt, 2003).

Although an analysis of the broad national trends on population/employment is useful, it is also important to note that the fortunes of nonmetropolitan areas around the U.S. differ significantly by region. This regional differentiation in population/employment change is apparent utilizing the eight regions developed by the Bureau of Economic Analysis. (Note again that employment data include part-time jobs, hence much larger growth rates). Although not shown here, the data indicate that between 1969 and 2007, employment growth was greatest in the Rocky Mountain (152%) and Far West (138%) regions, where high-amenity areas have fared well, despite the loss of many natural resource-related jobs (Shumway & Davis, 1996). Lagging far behind in growth are the Mideast (52%), Plains (45%), and Great Lakes (51%) regions of the

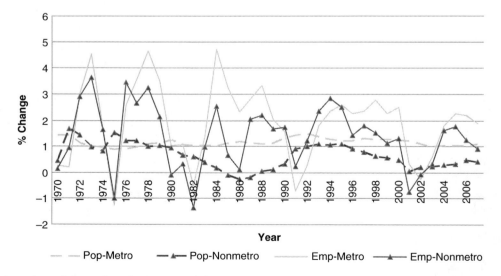

**Fig. 19.1** Annual population and employment growth for metropolitan and nonmetropolitan areas, 1969–2007
*Source*: REIS 1969–2007. On the basis of 2000 and 2008 OMB metro classifications.
*Note*: Micro and nonmetro areas are aggregated.

U.S., all with sizeable nonmetropolitan populations, and often viewed as the traditional agricultural heartland of the U.S. In terms of population growth, nonmetropolitan areas have again fared better in the Far West (89%) and Rocky Mountain (62%) regions, while the Great Lakes (17%), Plains (0.5%), and Mideast (17%) regions lagged. As stated above, these differences in population change are problematic for the workforce in the service sectors (especially in the Great Plains), and may actually have a greater impact on local labor markets if the composition of the population is changing at the same time (see Section "Human Capital Differences in Metropolitan and Nonmetropolitan Counties in the U.S." below).

Digging deeper into the structure of employment in nonmetropolitan areas, the long-term reliance on sectors of the economy not favored in today's globalized economy—especially compared to metropolitan areas—is quite clear. The data in Table 19.1 provide a glimpse of these deficiencies by showing regional trends in the U.S. in terms of the percentage of the workforce employed in farming and manufacturing. Although this obscures the degree of complexity really found in such sectors as manufacturing (high-skill versus low-skill manufacturing jobs), the data still show some regions are much more dependent on these primary and secondary sectors than other parts of the U.S. In terms of farming, the Southwest and Plains still have close to 10% of their employment based on farming. Except for New England and the Midwest, the other regions all still have about 5% of their workforce in farming as well. Between 2001 and 2007, there have been across the board declines in farming employment in every region of the U.S., although the regions of the U.S. most dependent on farming are not losing these jobs as fast as other less-dependent regions. As the economy continues to restructure, the declining trend in farm employment is likely to continue, thereby providing fewer job opportunities in rural areas.

In some ways the picture in manufacturing is a bit more optimistic as the filtering-down process has made rural America more dependent on manufacturing jobs. As of 2007, nonmetropolitan areas had 11.4% of their jobs in manufacturing compared to metropolitan

**Table 19.1** Regional patterns of employment in manufacturing and farming, 2001 and 2007

| BEA region | County type | % Employment in farming | | % Employment in manufacturing | |
|---|---|---|---|---|---|
| | | 2001 | 2007 | 2001 | 2007 |
| USA | Metro | 1.0 | 0.8 | 9.2 | 7.2 |
| | Nonmetro | 6.6 | 5.9 | 13.5 | 11.2 |
| New England | Metro | 0.4 | 0.3 | 10.4 | 8.0 |
| | Nonmetro | 1.9 | 1.6 | 10.9 | 8.8 |
| Midwest | Metro | 0.5 | 0.4 | 7.8 | 5.8 |
| | Nonmetro | 3.6 | 3.0 | 13.7 | 11.5 |
| Great Lakes | Metro | 0.9 | 0.8 | 13.6 | 11.0 |
| | Nonmetro | 5.6 | 5.3 | 18.6 | 15.9 |
| Plains | Metro | 1.6 | 1.4 | 9.9 | 8.5 |
| | Nonmetro | 10.3 | 9.5 | 12.6 | 11.5 |
| Southeast | Metro | 1.1 | 0.9 | 8.7 | 6.7 |
| | Nonmetro | 5.5 | 4.8 | 16.5 | 12.7 |
| Southwest | Metro | 1.1 | 0.9 | 8.3 | 6.6 |
| | Nonmetro | 10.5 | 9.1 | 7.3 | 6.4 |
| Rocky Mountain | Metro | 1.1 | 0.9 | 7.7 | 6.3 |
| | Nonmetro | 7.2 | 5.9 | 4.9 | 4.3 |
| Far West | Metro | 1.4 | 1.1 | 9.2 | 7.2 |
| | Nonmetro | 5.4 | 4.6 | 6.8 | 6.1 |

*Source*: REIS 2009. On the basis of 2000 and 2008 OMB metro classification.
*Note*: Micro and nonmetro areas are aggregated for 2008.

areas, which had 7.4%. Some regions of the U.S. (Midwest, Great Lakes, Plains, and Southeast) show much higher percentages of the nonmetropolitan workforce employed in manufacturing than the national average. Although manufacturing jobs generally pay well compared to jobs in other sectors, the literature shows that nonmetropolitan areas have traditionally been less oriented to the parts of the manufacturing sector that pay higher wages (McGranahan, 2003). Additionally, trends between 2001 and 2007 show that the proportion of manufacturing jobs of all types is declining in every region of the U.S.

While the data in Table 19.1 do show some broad perspectives on manufacturing and farming in nonmetropolitan areas, to assess today's rural/urban economy, it is important to understand the nature of service or tertiary sector employment, now the largest part of the economy in the U.S. Table 19.2 breaks down employment using the new NAICS categories of the economy. Furthermore, the sectors are aggregated a bit from the 2-digit level to form more meaningful groups, in a classification commonly used by the Bureau of Labor Statistics (BLS). This breakdown highlights quite well many of the deficiencies in the types of jobs available in rural labor markets. The heavy reliance on the goods-producing sectors related to farming/natural resources, and manufacturing generally reflects data already shown above, including declines in these jobs since 2001 (slight differences exist because of different sectoral aggregations). One bright spot in the economy was construction, (both metropolitan and nonmetropolitan areas had over 6% of their jobs in this sector in 2007), which experienced significant growth over the time period, clearly a reflection of the housing industry, which has since crashed in the recent recession.

Of more interest are metropolitan versus nonmetropolitan employment disparities in tertiary sectors like financial services (9.7% metropolitan versus 6.2% nonmetropolitan—percentage of total employment), professional/business services (14.9 versus 7.6%), and education/health services (12.5 versus 10.6%), which also happen to be the fastest growing sectors of employment. Interestingly, highly touted information services form a very small part of the service sector in both metropolitan and nonmetropolitan areas (2.1 versus 1.0%), and the sector actually shows declines in terms of the number of jobs in both metropolitan and nonmetropolitan areas in recent years. However, this may be more a reflection of the dot.com crash after 2001. One other aspect worth noting is the strength of public administration jobs which form over 15% of

**Table 19.2** Distribution of employment in metropolitan and nonmetropolitan areas in 2007, and employment growth, 2001 and 2007

| Code # | Industry sector name | % of Total employment 2007 | | % Growth in employment 2001–2007 | |
|---|---|---|---|---|---|
| | | Metro | Nonmetro | Metro | Nonmetro |
| NAICS | Goods producing | | | | |
| 11, 21 | Farms, resources and mining | 1.6 | 8.7 | −0.6 | −1.5 |
| 21 | Construction | 6.4 | 6.9 | 18.1 | 19.1 |
| 31–33 | Manufacturing | 7.4 | 11.4 | −15.1 | −12.6 |
| | Service providing | | | | |
| 42, 44–45, 48–49, 22 | Trade, transp. and utilities | 17.9 | 17.8 | 4.8 | 5.3 |
| 51 | Information | 2.1 | 1.0 | −13.2 | −7.5 |
| 52–53 | Financial services | 9.7 | 6.2 | 23.7 | 23.8 |
| 54–56 | Prof. and business services | 14.9 | 7.6 | 13.2 | 21.6 |
| 61–62 | Education & health services | 12.5 | 10.6 | 18.7 | 13.9 |
| 71–72 | Leisure and hospitality | 8.9 | 8.2 | 14.4 | 9.1 |
| 81 | Other | 5.6 | 5.9 | 12.2 | 11.0 |
| 92 | Public administration | 13.0 | 15.7 | 5.1 | 2.6 |

*Source*: REIS 2009. On the basis of 2000 and 2008 OMB metro classification.
*Note*: Micro and nonmetro areas are aggregated for 2008. Using BLS Sectoral Aggregation and 2007 Dollars.

the jobs in nonmetropolitan areas (2.7% points higher than metropolitan areas), and which continues to grow, although slowly compared to other service sectors (less than 3% growth between 2001 and 2007).

Many of these differences in sectoral employment are also apparent when the focus is on occupation. For example, readily accessible data (not shown here) from the American Community Survey for 2008 and Census 2000 show that the higher paying management and professional occupations are more strongly represented in metropolitan areas (35.2%) than nonmetropolitan areas (28%). The data also reflect the higher proportion of people in nonmetropolitan areas in occupations related to the primary and secondary sectors like farming (1.8% nonmetropolitan versus 0.5% metropolitan), construction/extractive (11.8% nonmetropolitan versus 8.9% metropolitan), and production (17.6% nonmetropolitan versus 11.5% metropolitan). These occupational differences are significant because in many ways they also reflect differences in human capital between metropolitan and nonmetropolitan areas, with the more highly skilled occupations found in higher percentages in metropolitan areas, an issue we return to later in this chapter.

## Wage and Salary Differences in Metropolitan and Nonmetropolitan Areas

Besides employment and occupational disparities between metropolitan and nonmetropolitan areas, perhaps more disturbing are the wages and salaries associated with particular types of jobs, and how uneven this compensation is for the same sectors just discussed. Table 19.3 highlights the distribution of average wages/salaries in 2007. Looking simply within the nonmetropolitan areas, we see the significance of manufacturing since it is the highest paying job on average at over $48,000 a year as of 2007 (all figures are in 2007 dollars). Also important are the low wages in the natural resource sectors like agriculture that have always been so important in rural areas, at an average of less than $20,000 a year. Finally, high employment nonmetropolitan sectors like trade/transportation (around $27,000) and education health services (around $30,000) have much lower average wages than manufacturing.

The real stark divisions and issues arise when these wages/salaries are compared to those in metropolitan areas (Kusmin et al., 2008). To be sure, some of these wage/salary disparities reflect cost of living

**Table 19.3** Distribution of average wages/salaries in metropolitan and nonmetropolitan areas in 2007, and wage/salary growth, 2001–2007

| Code # | Industry sector name | Average wage/salary 2007 | | % Growth in wage/salaries 2001–2007 | |
|---|---|---|---|---|---|
| | | Metro | Nonmetro | Metro | Nonmetro |
| NAICS | Goods producing | | | | |
| 11, 21 | Farms, resources and mining | 28,264 | 15,878 | 41.8 | 41.5 |
| 21 | Construction | 40,750 | 23,764 | 14.2 | 17.8 |
| 31–33 | Manufacturing | 71,477 | 48,874 | 30.0 | 27.2 |
| | Service providing | | | | |
| 42, 44–45, 48–49, 22 | Trade, transp. and utilities | 40,301 | 26,932 | 18.6 | 23.1 |
| 51 | Information | 76,097 | 35,849 | 20.9 | 19.7 |
| 52–53 | Financial Services | 47,381 | 18,055 | 14.6 | 12.6 |
| 54–56 | Prof. and business services | 49,533 | 24,041 | 22.4 | 24.1 |
| 61–62 | Education and health services | 40,829 | 30,277 | 23.6 | 25.4 |
| 71–72 | Leisure and hospitality | 20,477 | 14,513 | 21.2 | 23.0 |
| 81 | Other | 22,820 | 15,431 | 18.0 | 21.5 |
| 92 | Public administration | 62,651 | 46,919 | 32.6 | 30.9 |

*Source*: REIS 2009. On the basis of 2000 and 2008 OMB metro classification.
*Note*: Micro and nonmetro areas are aggregated for 2008. Using BLS Sectoral Aggregation and 2007 Dollars.

differences between metropolitan and nonmetropolitan areas, but even these differences do not negate the huge inequalities in the compensation data. For example, even in the relatively high-paying (for nonmetropolitan areas) economic mainstay of manufacturing, wages/salaries in metropolitan areas are almost 50% higher than nonmetropolitan areas. The same situation, with metropolitan areas exhibiting average wages/salaries significantly higher than nonmetropolitan areas, is apparent in other key "new economy" sectors such as information services (112% higher than nonmetropolitan areas), financial services (162% higher), professional/business services (106% higher), and education/health services (35% higher). Many of the discrepancies are related to the quality of the jobs in metropolitan versus nonmetropolitan areas, or segmentation within these NAICS sectors (that is, they are too aggregated), with the lower paying jobs more important (percentage wise) in nonmetropolitan areas (Freshwater, 1996; McGranahan, 2003). This is especially easy to see in manufacturing, where rural areas have relied on lower skilled manufacturing in such areas as textiles, food processing, or routine manufacturing, versus high-tech manufacturing jobs in metropolitan areas (Mazie & Killian, 1991; Freshwater, 1996). Unfortunately, the manufacturing jobs—often among the best paying jobs in nonmetropolitan counties—are often among the most susceptible to be exported overseas in the coming years.

## Human Capital Differences in Metropolitan and Nonmetropolitan Counties in the U.S.

Besides issues related to the job opportunities in rural areas that are inadequate compared to cities, rural America has long had a problem in terms of human capital (Gibbs, 2002; Pickering, Harvey, Summers, & Mushinski, 2006). This is a fundamental problem for a part of the country that is trying to move beyond its agricultural and natural resource heritage, and is starting to come to grips with a decline in manufacturing as well. In a globalizing world, education and training are increasingly important, especially in higher-end services. Besides deficiencies in terms of the number of these types of jobs, rural areas are at a real disadvantage because many of the people who do have these skills choose to live and work in urban areas with all their amenities, and because this is where these types of jobs are more likely to be located. The end result of this is that many of the people who do get the education needed for highly skilled jobs end up leaving the rural areas in a "brain drain" effect (Artz, 2003).

Table 19.4 below provides a glimpse at some of these differences using metropolitan and nonmetropolitan data for 2000 (Census) and 2008 (ACS). In terms of demography, nonmetropolitan areas have experienced long-term change related to an aging population base, reflected in the percentage of the population over 65 (14.7% in 2000 and 15.7% in 2008), which is much higher than found in metropolitan

**Table 19.4**
Sociodemographic characteristics of metropolitan and nonmetropolitan populations, 2000 and 2008

| Census/ACS variable | Census 2000 | | ACS 2008 | |
|---|---|---|---|---|
| | Metro | Nonmetro | Metro | Nonmetro |
| Total population | 80.6 | 19.4 | 83.5 | 16.5 |
| % of pop. over 65 | 11.9 | 14.7 | 12.2 | 15.7 |
| % of pop. 25–44 | 31.0 | 27.3 | 27.7 | 25.3 |
| % pop. under 18 | 25.8 | 25.3 | 24.6 | 22.9 |
| % White | 72.8 | 84.8 | 73.1 | 85.0 |
| % Black | 13.2 | 8.6 | 13.1 | 8.4 |
| % Hispanic | 14.2 | 5.6 | 17.1 | 6.8 |
| % over 25 w/HS graduate | 81.3 | 76.7 | 85.5 | 82.6 |
| % over 25 w/BA graduate | 26.6 | 15.4 | 29.8 | 17.2 |
| % foreign-born | 13.0 | 3.1 | 14.2 | 3.6 |
| % families below poverty level | 8.7 | 10.9 | 9.2 | 11.9 |

*Source*: Census 2000 and ACS 2008. On the basis of 2000 and 2008 OMB metro classification.
*Note*: Micro and nonmetro areas are aggregated for 2008.

areas (11.9% in 2000 and 12.2% in 2008). The flip side of this aging scenario for nonmetropolitan areas is reflected in the percentage of the population less than 18 years of age, which is lower than found in metropolitan areas, and declining over time. This trend means added stress on local public services as many people continue to age-in-place, with associated decreases in the core working age population of 25–45 year olds required for a robust economy (Rogers, 2002). An alternative and positive view of an aging population emerges from areas that experienced significant in-migration of retirees due to attractive local amenities, especially scenic natural environments. This in-migration can actually lead to growth in local employment as migrants consume services using income generated from elsewhere (Brown & Glasgow, 2008), but this phenomena is isolated to those rural areas that are attractive to retirees.

Another interesting trend in rural demography is related to race and ethnicity changes in recent years (see Kirschner, Berry, & Glasgow, 2006 for a review). A large literature has emerged on the rising Hispanic presence in many remote counties far from big cities, a trend that is also reflected in the data presented here, where Hispanics have gone from 5.6% of the population in 2000 to 6.8% in nonmetropolitan areas in 2008 (Saenz & Torres, 2003; Kandel, 2005). Although this percentage is not high compared to metropolitan areas (17.1% in 2008), it is often highly concentrated in a few areas, so the relative impact can be very large in small rural communities. This influx of people different to the local population is also apparent in the data for nonmetropolitan areas that shows increases in the percentage of foreign-born (3.1% in 2000 and 3.6% in 2008).

In recent years scholars have published a large number of studies on the significant impact of recent immigrants in nonmetropolitan counties, however, the outcomes have been uneven (Saenz & Torres, 2003; Kandel, 2005; Broadway & Stull, 2006; see also Chapters 3 and 15 in this volume). For example, immigrants represent the only in-migration taking place in many areas that would otherwise be losing population, and provide a reliable and cheap source of labor in agriculture and many food-processing businesses (Donato, Tolbert, Nucci, & Kawano, 2007). Also, immigrants can often boost business at local service and trade establishments that may exist on the margin due to population losses (Broadway & Stull, 2006). Conversely, for cultural reasons many smaller communities may be poorly equipped and/or unaccustomed to such sudden changes in the composition of the local population, often creating a contentious political environment (Broadway, 2007). Additionally, on average many of the migrants do not have the same level of education as rural Americans (or those immigrants going to metropolitan areas), thus they do not enhance the base of human capital that is often needed to participate in many of the high-end sectors that provide higher incomes in today's global economy (Saenz & Torres, 2003; Kandel, 2005; Farmer & Moon, 2009).

Besides changes in the racial/ethnic makeup of rural America, probably the most important human capital consideration for employment in the new postindustrial economy is the education level of the local workforce (Gallardo & Bishop, 2010). According to the data in Table 19.4, differences in education based on the percentage of students with a high school diploma between metropolitan areas (85.5%) and nonmetropolitan areas (82.6%) are now quite small, and the gap has decreased over time. However, the same is not true with respect to the percentage of the population with a BA degree, where metropolitan areas (29.8%) clearly surpass nonmetropolitan areas (17.2%) in terms of higher education levels. Furthermore, the gap with respect to this key human capital variable is not declining over time, as it has with respect to the percentage of high school graduates. Overall, it seems apparent that rural areas continue to face a number of difficult issues related to the quality of the local labor workforce, virtually all of which put rural areas at a severe disadvantage in today's global economy, especially compared to urban and suburban locations.

## Rural Labor Market Outcomes: Unemployment and Poverty

The last part of this empirical discussion focuses on rural labor market outcomes. The primary question is the following: are there differences between urban and rural areas in the prevalence of unemployment? Figure 19.2 shows aggregate trends in unemployment for metropolitan and nonmetropolitan counties (including micropolitan areas) in the U.S. between 2000 and 2008, which are based on BLS annual averages for county-level employment that

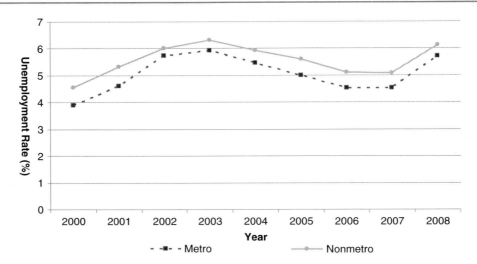

**Fig. 19.2** Annual unemployment rates for metropolitan and nonmetropolitan areas, 2000–2008
*Source*: Local Unemployment Statistic, BLS, 2000–2008. On the basis of 2000 and 2008 OMB metro classification.
*Note*: Micro and Nonmetro areas are aggregated.

were aggregated up based on the 2008 OMB classification. (Note that because the data are aggregated in this manner, they can sometimes vary with other estimates published for metro/nonmetro areas [e.g., Bishop & Gallardo, 2009]). Although both areas have experienced the ups and downs of the business cycle in a remarkably consistent fashion, there has been a persistent gap, with nonmetropolitan areas always experiencing a rate of unemployment about one percentage point higher than metropolitan areas over this time period, a gap found by others (Kusmin, 2006). This gap exists even with the large amount of commuting that takes place as people in nonmetropolitan areas drive to nearby metropolitan areas that offer better job opportunities and higher wages (Fuguitt, 1991; see also Chapter 22 in this volume). Unhappily, this trend in increased commuting, combined with the fact that unemployment rates are based on place of residence, probably means job opportunities in nonmetropolitan labor markets are worse than portrayed by the actual unemployment rates.

As might be expected, unemployment rates are spatially uneven across the U.S. As shown in Table 19.5, some parts of the U.S. experience much higher/lower unemployment rates, with differences in these rates between metropolitan and nonmetropolitan areas also varying by region (Bishop & Gallardo, 2009). The highest rates of nonmetropolitan unemployment are in the Great Lakes and Far West regions, with rates over 7% in 2008, with the lowest amounts of unemployment in the Southwest and Rocky Mountain regions, with a rate less than 5%. Interestingly, where the rates are highest is also where the gaps between metropolitan and nonmetropolitan areas are generally the greatest. For example, in the Southeast the unemployment rate is 5.6% in metropolitan areas but 6.8% in nonmetropolitan areas. Large gaps also exist in the Great Lakes and Far West. Interestingly, a region often associated with rural economic distress, the Great Plains, shows little difference in the unemployment rates between metropolitan and nonmetropolitan areas, and in fact, has among the lowest unemployment rates in 2000 and 2008. However, statistics for such regions as the Great Plains need to be viewed with care, since outmigration of the past few decades may have cleared some of the potential labor pool that would otherwise lead to higher unemployment numbers.

Although the picture with respect to unemployment makes it seem as if problems in many rural areas may not be dire, many studies highlight other labor market outcomes that are more difficult to analyze than unemployment, but which still significantly affect the ability to earn a living. Probably the most notable problem is related to underemployment. This term may apply to several related situations where workers: may not have a full-time job; may be employed in nonstandard type jobs; or may need several jobs to survive because of low wages (Tigges & Tottle, 1990; Jensen

**Table 19.5** Unemployment rates for metropolitan and nonmetropolitan areas by region, 2000 and 2008

| BEA region | % Unemployment 2000 | | % Unemployment 2008 | |
| --- | --- | --- | --- | --- |
| | Metro | Nonmetro | Metro | Nonmetro |
| USA | 3.9 | 4.5 | 5.7 | 6.1 |
| New England | 2.7 | 3.0 | 5.4 | 5.1 |
| Midwest | 4.1 | 4.6 | 5.2 | 6.0 |
| Great Lakes | 3.8 | 4.2 | 6.5 | 7.1 |
| Plains | 3.0 | 3.5 | 4.9 | 4.8 |
| Southeast | 3.5 | 5.0 | 5.6 | 6.8 |
| Southwest | 4.1 | 4.9 | 4.9 | 4.7 |
| Rocky Mountain | 3.1 | 4.3 | 4.5 | 4.3 |
| Far West | 4.8 | 6.2 | 6.8 | 7.2 |

*Source*: Local Area Unemployment. Statistics, BLS, 2000 and 2008. On the basis of 2000 and 2008 OMB metro classification.
*Note*: Micro and nonmetro areas are aggregated for 2008.

et al., 2000; McLaughlin & Coleman-Jensen, 2008). An abundance of data has been developed through case studies, but good aggregate statistics of the U.S. as a whole, or regional data good enough for comparative purposes, are woefully inadequate because the U.S. Bureau of Labor Statistics (2010) has had problems developing consistent objective criteria on what constitutes "underemployed." Thus, questions related to underemployment are not part of the monthly Current Population Survey from which the BLS draws its employment numbers.

Besides high unemployment rates, another undesirable outcome of a poorly functioning labor market is a population mired in poverty. The causes of rural poverty, and differences in poverty rates based on demographic, social, and geographic differences, have been a very fertile area of research for rural scholars (Cotter, 2002; Jensen, Goetz, & Swaminathan, 2006; see also Chapter 20 in this volume). As shown in other parts of Table 19.4, the outcomes are worse with respect to the percentage of families below the poverty level for those in nonmetropolitan areas versus metropolitan areas in 2008 (11.9 versus 9.2%, respectively) (U.S. Department of Agriculture, 2003). Furthermore, this disparity has remained pretty stable over the decade, although the rates did go up slightly for both types of areas over the eight years. Besides poverty rate differences visible at the aggregate level, social scientists continue to study poverty because it has remained incredibly persistent over time, and is often concentrated in certain regions of the U.S., and among specific segments of the population (Summers, 1995; U.S. Department of Agriculture, 2003). Part of this concentration of poverty may be due to the mobility of the poor, and their desire to seek out cheaper places to live, thereby leading to significant clusters of poor people, which may in turn make the problem all the more intractable (Nord, 1998; Foulkes & Schafft, 2010).

## Summary: Rural Labor Markets in Turbulent Economic Times

In a time of increasing economic unease across the United States due to the recent recession, along with a sluggish recovery, the long-term prospects for the national economy remain a fundamental concern for most Americans. The nature and severity of the recession has meant its impact has been felt across all sectors of the economy, and in all regions of the U.S. That said, the theoretical perspectives and empirical analysis presented above highlight a number of concerns that are particular to rural America, a part of the country that tends to emerge from recession even slower than urban areas (Parker, Kusmin, & Marre, 2010).

The theoretical perspectives surveyed point to a number of long-term problems that social scientists have long recognized with respect to rural areas. Neoclassical approaches to labor market analysis outline many of the persistent disadvantages rural areas face when compared to urban areas, especially in terms of geography (low density and remoteness of many areas), and the needs of many firms to be in or near urban markets in terms of labor supply and consumers. Perhaps of more concern are broad structural changes in the economy that do not favor the sectors that have traditionally formed the rural economic base for decades—farming and natural resources. Furthermore, continued globalization is creating a competitive environment that favors the internationalization of manufacturing in a way that hurts this sector across the U.S., but even more so in rural areas that rely on low skill types of routine production, and where manufacturing employs a larger percentage of workers than urban areas.

The literature also points to other problems in rural labor markets, like disparities in terms of human capital, especially in the area of education, that continue to make it less likely that rural areas will be able to attract high-quality jobs in numbers sufficient to ensure a stable economic base and a properly functioning labor market. To some extent the deficiencies in human capital are a result of the structural shift in the economy toward tertiary activities, and the tendency for the best of these jobs to locate in or near major metropolitan areas. This creates a downward spiral of jobs losses of the most highly educated in rural areas, which in turn makes the areas even less desirable to the firms that form the postindustrial economy. The major demographic shifts taking place in rural areas, the aging of the population and increased immigration raises a number of other potential problems. Overall, rural areas face persistent structural differences in the quality of urban versus rural jobs, and the types of jobs and work conditions available for marginalized segments of the population.

Despite some data shortcomings associated with the broadly constructed empirical analysis of urban/rural (metro/nonmetro areas to be precise) labor markets, many of the problems cited in the literature are readily apparent in data for the last decade. Especially apparent are disparities in terms of the types of jobs available in rural and urban areas and associated compensation, problems that seem likely to remain in the foreseeable future. Besides these economic and labor market issues, a host of demographic changes show the very face of rural America is changing. Although this change is problematic and contentious in some areas, the infusion of population in many areas represents a positive force for communities subject to long-term out-migration and depopulation pressures.

It is interesting to note that this pessimistic outlook contrasts with some data and stories now emerging on the nature of the 2008 recession's impact in terms of unemployment. For example, not all rural areas have been broadly impacted by this recession—unemployment rates have generally remained lowest in the states of the American agricultural heartland, though the rural South has suffered (Bishop & Gallardo, 2009; Parker et al., 2010). Additionally, once the economy starts to revive, and the housing market rebounds even a bit, a reinvigorated exurbanization process could mean that many rural areas within commuting distance of major cities and their suburbs might continue to grow, even if few decent jobs are produced locally by this growth. In fact, it is difficult to overestimate how important commuting to jobs in metro areas and their fringes is to rural labor markets. Much of the same potential for labor market expansion applies to rural areas experiencing amenity-driven migration, despite some issues related to job quality. Finally, the American farmer still is the dominant player worldwide in many parts of the agricultural sector, and a good source of income for many rural areas. That said, it would seem that many of the global processes driving economic growth today do not portend good things for rural labor markets in general, and policymakers have a robust set of issues and problems that require innovative solutions.

## References

Artz, G. (2003). Rural brain drain: Is it a reality? *Choices, 18*(4), 11–16.

Barkley, D., & Hinschberger, S. (1992). Industrial restructuring: Implications for the decentralization of manufacturing to nonmetropolitan areas. *Economic Development Quarterly, 6*, 64–79.

Bascom, J. (2000). Revisiting the rural revolution in East Carolina. *Geographical Review, 90*(3), 432–445.

Becker, G. (1964). *Human capital: A theoretical and empirical analysis, with special reference to education.* Chicago: University of Chicago Press.

Bender, N., & Davis, N. (2000). Developing agricultural and nature-based tourism in Eastern Connecticut. In P. Schaeffer & S. Loveridge (Eds.), *Small town and rural economic development* (pp. 99–106). Westport, CT: Praeger.

Berry, B., Parr, J., Epstein, B., Gosh, A., & Smith, R. (1988). *Market centers and retail location: Theory and application.* Englewood Cliffs, NJ: Prentice Hall.

Beyers, W., & Lindahl, D. (1996). Lone eagles and high fliers in rural producer services. *Rural Development Perspectives, 11*, 2–10.

Beyers, W. B., & Nelson, P.B. (2000). Service industries and employment growth in the nonmetro South: A geographical perspective. *Southern Rural Sociology, 15*, 139–169.

Bishop, B., & Gallardo, R. (2009). *Rural unemployment lower than city rates*. Main Street Economics. Retrieved March 1, 2010, from http://www.dailyyonder.com/rural-unemployment-lower-city-rates/2009/12/07/2485.

Blank, S. C. (2008). *The economics of American agriculture: Evolution and global development*. Armonk, NY: M.E. Sharpe Inc.

Bluestone, B., & Harrison, B. (1982). *The deindustrialization of America*. New York: Basic Books.

Bokemeier, J., & Tickamyer, A. (1985). Labor force experiences of nonmetropolitan women. *Rural Sociology, 50*(1), 51–73.

Bonanno, A. (2007). *Economics of emerging retail formats: Wal-Mart, wages and service competition*. PhD dissertation. Storrs, CT: Agricultural and Resource Economics Department, University of Connecticut.

Broadway, M. J. (2007). Meatpacking and the transformation of rural communities: A comparison of Brooks Alberta and Garden City Kansas. *Rural Sociology, 72*(4), 560–582.

Broadway, M. J., & Stull, D. D. (2006). Meat processing and Garden City, KS: Boom and bust. *Journal of Rural Studies, 22*(1), 55–66.

Brown, D. L., & Glasgow, N. (Eds.). (2008). *Rural retirement migration*. Dordrecht: Springer.

Bull, C. N. (1998). Aging in rural communities. *National Forum, 78*(2), 38–42.

Buttel, F. H. (2003). Continuities and disjunctures in the transformation of the U.S. Agro-food complex. In D. L. Brown & L. E. Swanson (Eds.), *Challenges for rural America in the twenty-first century* (pp. 177–189). University Park, PA: Penn State Press.

Carolan, M. S. (2009). A sociological look at biofuels: Ethanol in the early decades of the twentieth century and lessons for today. *Rural Sociology, 74*(1), 86–112.

Collins, J. L., & Quark, A. (2006). Globalizing firms and small communities: The apparel Industry's changing connection to rural labor markets. *Rural Sociology, 71*(2), 281–310.

Cotter, D. A. (2002). Poor people in poor places: Local opportunity structures and household poverty. *Rural Sociology, 67*(4), 534–555.

Davila, A., & Mora, M. T. (2000). English skills, earnings, and the occupational sorting of Mexican Americans along the U.S.-Mexico border. *International Migration Review, 34*(1), 133–157.

Deseran, F. A., & Keithly, D. (1994). Teenagers in the US labor force: Local labor markets. *Race and Family, 59*(4), 668–692.

Doeringer, P. B., & Piore, M. J. (1971). *Internal labor markets and manpower analysis*. Boston, MA: D.C. Heath and Company.

Donato, K. M., Tolbert, C. M., Nucci, A., & Kawano, Y. (2007). Recent immigrant settlement in the nonmetropolitan United States: Evidence from internal census data. *Rural Sociology, 72*(4), 537–559.

Edgcomb, E. L., & Armington, M. M. (2003). *The informal economy: Latino enterprises at the margins*. Microenterprise Fund for Innovation, Effectiveness, Learning and Dissemination (FIELD), The Aspen Institute: Washington, DC. Retrieved March 1, 2010, from http://www.fieldus.org/publications/IE_Latino.pdf

Falk, W., Schulman, M., & Tickamyer, A. (2003). *Communities of work: Rural restructuring in local and global contexts*. Columbus, OH: Ohio State University Press.

Farmer, F. L., & Moon, Z. K. (2009). An empirical examination of characteristics of Mexican migrants to metropolitan and nonmetropolitan areas of the United States. *Rural Sociology, 74*(2), 220–240.

Foulkes, M., & Schafft, K. A. (2010). The impact of migration on poverty concentrations in the United States, 1995–2000. *Rural Sociology, 75*(1), 90–110.

Freshwater, D. (1996). The future role of low-wage, low-skill jobs in rural areas. *International Advances in Economic Research, 2*(4), 498–499.

Fuguitt. G. V. (1991). Commuting and the rural-urban hierarchy. *Journal of Rural Studies, 7*(4), 459–466.

Fuguitt, G. V. (1995). Population change in nonmetropolitan America. In E. M. Castle (Ed.), *The changing American countryside: Rural people and places* (pp. 77–100). Lawrence, KS: University of Kansas Press.

Gallardo, R., & Bishop, B. (2010). *A reason for higher rural unemployment: Education*. Main Street Economics. Retrieved March 3 2010, from http://www.dailyyonder.com/reason-higher-rural-unemployment-education/2010/02/26/2613

Garnick, D. (1984). Shifting balances in U.S. metropolitan and nonmetropolitan area growth. *International Regional Science Review, 9*(3), 257–273.

Gehlhar, M. (2009). A weakening global economy interrupts agricultural trade. *Amber Waves, 7*(2), 23–29.

Gibbs, R. M. (2000). College graduates in the nonmetropolitan South: Origins and prospects. *Southern Rural Sociology, 16*, 36–59.

Gibbs, R. M. (2002). Rural labor markets in an era of welfare reform. In B.A Weber, G. Duncan, & L. A. Whitener (Eds.), *Rural dimensions of welfare reform* (pp. 51–76). Detroit, MI: WE Upjohn Institute for Employment Research.

Glasmeier, A., & Howland, M. (1995). *From combines to computers: Rural services and development in the age of information technology*. Albany, NY: State University of New York Press.

Glasmeier, A. K., & Leichenko, R. M. (2000). What does the future hold? What globalization might mean for the rural south. *Southern Rural Sociology, 15*, 59–83.

Gordon, D. M., Edwards, R., & Reich, M. (1982). *Segmented work, divided workers: The historical transformation of work in the United States*. Cambridge, MA: Cambridge UP.

Green, G., Deller, S. C., & Marcouiller, D. (Eds.). (2005). *Amenities and rural development: Theory, methods and public policy*. Northampton, MA: Edward Elgar Publishing.

Greene, C., & Kremen, A. (2003). *U.S. organic farming in 2000–2001: Adoption of certified systems*. Agriculture Information Bulletin No. 780. Washington, DC: U.S. Department of Agriculture, Economic Research Service, Resource Economics Division.

Hansen, J. (1991). *Gaining access: Congress and the farm lobby, 1919–1981*. Chicago: University of Chicago Press.

Held, D., & McGrew, A. (Eds.). (2007). *Globalization theory: Approaches and controversies*. Cambridge: Polity.

Hirschl, T., & Summers, G. F. (1982). Cash transfers and the export base of small communities. *Rural Sociology, 47*, 295–316.

Isard, W. (1975). *Introduction to regional science*. Englewood Cliffs, NJ: Prentice-Hall.

Isserman, A. M., Feser, E., & Warren, D. E. (2009). Why some rural places prosper and others do not. *International Regional Science Review, 32*(3), 300–342.

Jensen, L., Cornwell, G. T., & Findeis, J. L. (1995). Informal work in nonmetropolitan Pennsylvania. *Rural Sociology, 60*(1), 91–107.

Jensen, L., Findeis, J. F., & Wang, Q. (2000). Labor supply and underemployment in the Southern United States. *Southern Rural Sociology, 16*, 96–124.

Jensen, L., Goetz, S. J., & Swaminathan, H. (2006). Changing fortunes: Poverty in rural America. In D. L. Brown & W. Kandel (Eds.), *Population change and rural society* (pp. 131–152). Dordrecht: Springer.

Jensen, L., & Tienda, M. (1989). Nonmetropolitan minority families in the United States: Trends in racial and ethnic economic stratification, 1959–1986. *Rural Sociology, 54*, 509–532.

Kandel, W. (2005). *Rural Hispanics at a glance*. Economic Information Bulletin No. 8. Washington, DC: Economic Research Service, U.S. Department of Agriculture.

Killian, M. S., & Tolbert, C. M. (1993). Mapping social and economic space: The delineation of local labor markets. In J. Singelmann & F. Deseran (Eds.), *Inequalities in labor market areas* (pp. 69–81). Boulder, CO: Westview Press.

Kirschner, A., Berry, E. H., & Glasgow, N. (2006). The changing faces of rural America. In W. Kandell & D. Brown (Eds.), *Population change and rural society* (pp. 53–74). Dordrecht: Springer.

Krikelas, A. C. (1992). Why regions grow: A review of research on the economic base model. *Economic Review from the Federal Reserve Bank of Atlanta, July Issue*, 16–29.

Kusmin, L. (2006). *Rural employment at a glance*. Economic Information Bulletin Number 21. Washington, DC: Economic Research Service, United States Department of Agriculture.

Kusmin, L., Gibbs, R., & Parker, T. (2008). Education's role in the metro-nonmetro earnings divide. *Amber Waves, 6*(1), 30–35.

Lobao, L. (1990). *Locality and inequality: Farm structure, industry structure, and socioeconomic conditions*. Albany, NY: The State University of New York Press.

Lobao, L., & Meyer, K. (2001). The great agricultural transition: Crisis, change, and social consequences of twentieth century US farming. *Annual Review of Sociology, 27*, 103–124.

Lyson, T., & Falk, W. (1992). *Forgotten places: Uneven development and the loss of opportunity in rural America*. Lawrence, KS: University of Kansas Press.

Lyson, T. A., Gillespie, G. W., & Hilcheya, D. (1995). Farmers' markets and the local community: Bridging the formal and informal economy. *American Journal of Alternative Agriculture, 10*, 108–113.

Mack, R. S., & Schaeffer, P. V. (1993). Nonmetropolitan manufacturing in the United States and product cycle theory: A review of the literature. *Journal of Planning Literature, 8*(2), 124–139.

Mazie, S. M., & Killian, M. S. (1991). Growth and change in rural America: The experience of the 1980s and prospects for the 1990s. In N. Walzer (Ed.), *Rural community economic development* (pp. 1–20). New York: Praeger.

McGranahan, D. (2003). How people make a living in rural America. In D. L. Brown & L. E. Swanson (Eds.), *Challenges for rural America in the twenty-first century* (pp. 135–151). University Park, PA: Penn State Press.

McLaughlin, D. M., & Coleman-Jensen, A. J. (2008). Nonstandard employment in the nonmetropolitan United States. *Rural Sociology, 73*(4), 631–659.

McMichael, P. (2003). The impact of global economic practices of American farming. In D. L. Brown & L. E. Swanson (Eds.), *Challenges for rural America in the twenty-first century* (pp. 375–384). University Park, PA: Penn State Press.

Miller, C. D. (2007). *Niagara falling: Globalization in a small town*. Lanham, MD: Lexington Books.

Mincer, J. (1974). *Schooling, experience, and earnings*. New York: Columbia University Press.

Moss, L. (Ed.). (2006). *The amenity migrants: Seeking and sustaining mountains and their cultures*. Wallingford: CABI Publishers.

Nord, M. (1998). Poor people on the move: County-to-county migration and the spatial concentration of poverty. *Journal of Regional Science, 38*(2), 329–351.

Parker, T. S., Kusmin, L. D., & Marre, A. W. (2010). Economic recovery: Lessons learned from previous recessions. *Amber Waves, 8*(1), 42–47.

Pickering, K., Harvey, M., Summers, G., & Mushinski, D. (2006). *Welfare reform in persistent rural poverty*. University Park, PA: Penn State University Press.

Portes, A., Castells, M., & Benton, L. A. (Eds.). (1989). *The informal economy: Studies in advanced and less developed countries*. Baltimore, MD: The Johns Hopkins University Press.

REIS. (2008). *Regional economic information system*. Bureau of Economic Analysis. Department of Commerce. Washington, DC. Retrieved January 12, 2009, from http://www.bea.gov/regional/reis/

Rogers, C. (2002). The older population in 21st century rural America. *Rural America, 17*(3), 2–10.

Saenz, R. (2000). Earnings patterns of Mexican workers in the Southern Region: A focus on nonmetro/metro distinctions. *Southern Rural Sociology, 16*, 60–95.

Saenz, R., & Torres, C. C. (2003). Latinos in rural America. In D. L. Brown & L. E. Swanson (Eds.), *Challenges for rural America in the twenty-first century* (pp. 57–71). University Park, PA: Penn State Press.

Schnepf, R. D., Dohlman, E., & Bolling, C. (2001). *Agriculture in Brazil and Argentina: Developments and prospects for major field crops*. Agriculture and Trade Report No. (WRS013). Washington, DC: U.S. Department of Agriculture.

Shaffer, R., Deller, S., & Marcouiller, D. (2004). *Community economics: Linking theory and practice* (2nd ed.). London: Blackwell.

Shumway, J. M., & Davis, J. A. (1996). Nonmetropolitan population change in the mountain west. *Rural Sociology, 61*(3), 512–528.

Singelmann, J., & Deseran, F. (Eds.). (1993). *Inequalities in labor market areas*. Boulder, CO: Westview Press.

Slack, T. (2007). The contours and correlates of informal work in rural Pennsylvania. *Rural Sociology, 72*(1), 69–89.

Smith, D. M. (1971). *Industrial location: An economical geographical analysis*. New York: Wiley.

Snipp, C. M., & Bloomquist, L. (1989). Sociology and labor markets. In W. Falk & T. Lyson (Eds.), *Research in rural sociology and development* (pp. 1–27). New York: JAI Press.

Summers, G. F. (1995). Persistent rural poverty. In E. M. Castle (Ed.), *The changing American countryside: Rural people and places* (pp. 213–228). Lawrence, KS: University of Kansas Press.

Summers, G. F., Horton, F., & Gringeri, C. (1990). Rural labour-market changes in the United States. In T. Marsden, P. Lowe, & S. Whatmore (Eds.), *Rural restructuring: Global processes and their responses* (pp. 129–164). London: David Fulton.

Stutz, F. B., & Warf, B. (2007). *The world economy: Resources, location trade and development.* New York: Pearson.

Tickamyer, A., & Bokemeier, J. L. (1988). Sex differences in labor market experiences. *Rural Sociology, 53*(2), 166–190.

Tigges, L. M., & Fuguitt, G. (2003). Commuting: A good job nearby. In D. L. Brown & L. E. Swanson (Eds.), *Challenges for rural America in the twenty-first century* (pp. 166–176). University Park, PA: Penn State Press.

Tigges, L. M., & Tottle, D. M. (1990). Labor supply, labor demand and men's underemployment in rural and urban labor markets. *Rural Sociology, 55*(3), 328–356.

U.S. Bureau of Economic Analysis. (2010). *Local area personal income.* Regional Economic Information System (REIS). Retrieved March 1, 2010, from http://www.bea.gov/regional/reis/

U.S. Bureau of Labor Statistics. (2010). *Labor force statistics from the current population survey.* Retrieved June 1, 2010, from http://www.bls.gov/cps/faq.htm

U.S. Department of Agriculture. (2003). *Rural income, poverty, and welfare: Rural poverty.* ERS Briefing Room. Retrieved March 1, 2010, from http://www.ers.usda.gov/Briefing/incomepovertywelfare/RuralPoverty

U.S. Department of Agriculture. (2009). *World agricultural report.* Foreign Agricultural Service Circular Series WAP 12-09. Retrieved March 1, 2010, from http://www.fas.usda.gov/wap/circular/2009/09-12/WAPfull12-09.pdf

Vernon, R. (1966). International investment and international trade in the product cycle. *Quarterly Journal of Economics, 80*, 190–207.

Vias, A. C. (2004). Bigger stores, more stores or no stores: Paths of retail restructuring in rural America, 1988–1999. *Journal of Rural Studies, 20*(3), 303–318.

Vias, A. C. (2007). Population change, economic restructuring, and the evolving landscape of retail activities. *Southern Rural Sociology, 21*, 1–22.

Vias, A. C., & Nelson, P. (2006). Restructuring, globalization, and altered livelihoods. In W. Kandell & sD. Brown (Eds.), *Population change and rural society* (pp. 75–102). Dordrecht: Springer.

Wojan, T. R. (2000). Functional skill requirements of manufacturing employment in the rural South. *Southern Rural Sociology, 15*, 104–138.

# 20. Race and Place: Determinants of Poverty in the Texas Borderland and the Lower Mississippi Delta

Joachim Singelmann, Tim Slack, and Kayla Fontenot

## Introduction

Forty years after the War on Poverty, the United States poverty rate remains one of the highest among industrial countries. Today, 17% of the U.S. population live in households with less than 50% of median income,[1] compared to an average of about 10.5% for all OECD countries (OECD, 2008); only Mexico and Turkey have a higher poverty rate than the United States. The above-average poverty rate in the United States mirrors the much greater U.S. income inequality (gini coefficient = 0.38) than is the case for the average OECD country (gini coefficient = 0.32). The poorest 10% of U.S. citizens have an income of US$5,800 per year during the mid-2000s, which is about 20% lower than the average for OECD countries.

While the War on Poverty initially halved the poverty rate of U.S. families (from 20.8% in 1959 to 9.7% in 1973, using the domestic poverty threshold definition), the deep recession of the 1970s brought a halt to poverty reduction. After the end of this major recession, a new welfare regime set in, questioning the expansion of the welfare state and the function of government as an agent of social change. As a result, the poverty rate that increased during the mid-1970s recession did not decrease much and fluctuated between 11 and 14% during the period 1975–1993. Only the economic expansion of the 1990s brought it close to the 1973 level, with the family poverty rate of 9.9% in 2000. For most of the current decade, family poverty ranged between 11 and 12%. Much of the increase in poverty is related to the distribution of earnings that widened by 20% since the mid-1980s. Other factors contributing to the lack of progress in bringing down poverty include a steadily rising proportion of single-parent families and a relatively weak safety net that lifted fewer families out of poverty.

In spite of the amount of social change that took place during the past four decades, the two key findings of the President's National Advisory Committee on Rural Poverty (1967) continue to hold true: rural poverty rates remain substantially higher than those in urban areas, and those places characterized by the greatest economic distress are in the rural South and Southwest, and home to high proportions of racial and ethnic minorities.

First, Table 20.1 shows that for the past 60 years, poverty in nonmetro areas has been substantially higher than in metro areas. While the metro-nonmetro gap has narrowed over the decades, nonmetro poverty by 2009 still exceeded that of metro areas by almost 20%. Table 20.1 further demonstrates that both metro and nonmetro areas experienced growing poverty after 2000, but that increase affected metro areas to a greater extent than nonmetro areas. By 2009, the poverty rate in nonmetro areas approximately matched their 1970 rate, whereas 2009 poverty in metro areas was more similar to their rates during the 1960s.

---

J. Singelmann (✉)
Department of Demography, The University of Texas at San Antonio, 501 W. Durango Blvd., San Antonio, TX 78207, USA

Wissenschaftszentrum Berlin (WZB), Berlin, Germany
e-mail: Joachim.Singelmann@utsa.edu

---

[1] European countries and the OECD use a relative measure of poverty rather than an absolute threshold level as in the United States.

**Table 20.1** Poverty rates by metro status, 1959–2009

| Year | Total | Metro | Nonmetro | Nonmet as percent of Met |
|------|-------|-------|----------|--------------------------|
| 1959 | 22.4  | 15.3  | 33.2     | 217.0                    |
| 1970 | 12.6  | 10.2  | 16.9     | 165.7                    |
| 1980 | 13.0  | 11.9  | 15.4     | 129.4                    |
| 1990 | 13.5  | 12.7  | 16.3     | 128.3                    |
| 2000 | 11.3  | 10.8  | 13.4     | 124.1                    |
| 2005 | 12.6  | 12.2  | 14.5     | 118.8                    |
| 2009 | 14.3  | 13.9  | 16.6     | 119.4                    |

*Source*: U.S. Bureau of the Census (2011), Current Population Survey, Annual Social and Economic Supplements.

Second, nearly 40 years after the rural poverty report, the two poorest regions in the United States continue to be the Texas Borderland, characterized by a higher proportion of the population that is Latino (primarily of Mexican descent), and the Lower Mississippi Delta with its historically high proportion of African Americans.[2]

This chapter examines the patterns and dynamics of poverty among the counties in the two aforementioned high-poverty regions using data from the 2000 U.S. Census. We develop and test a comparative model to determine whether and, if so, how the patterns and dynamics of poverty differ between the Borderland and the Delta, and between the sociological majorities and minorities in those two regions. Aside from an overall analysis, we estimate separate models for four populations: (1) the non-Hispanic white population of the Borderland counties, (2) the Latino population of the Borderland counties, (3) the non-Hispanic white population of the Delta counties, and (4) the black population of the Delta counties. Our research aims to broaden our understanding of the relationships between race, ethnicity, and poverty in a largely nonmetro setting. As we note below, the Delta's economy historically was based on a plantation economy that relied on slave labor. Much of the Borderland is as rural and economically based on agriculture as is the Delta. Although rural Latino laborers have not been slaves, the employment conditions in agriculture have not been unlike those in the Delta once slavery was abolished. In both regions, many workers, especially in rural areas, were disenfranchised and exploited. By comparing the two regions and differentiating by race/ethnicity, we can assess if the poverty of blacks and Latinos is correlated with similar factors.

## Past Research

Since the War on Poverty, much research has been conducted trying to understand the mechanisms that produce poverty. More recently, a promising new approach to examining poverty has highlighted the importance of place in this mechanism (Friedman & Lichter, 1998; Glasmeier, 2002; Lobao, 1990; Lobao & Saenz, 2002; Lyson & Falk, 1993; Massey & Denton, 1993; Massey & Eggers, 1990; Rosenbaum, Reynolds, & Deluca, 2002; Rural Sociological Society Task Force on Persistent Rural Poverty, 1993; Saenz & Thomas, 1991; Tickamyer & Duncan, 1990; Weinberg, 1987). For example, research has identified pockets of persistent poverty in the United States, including central Appalachia, the Mississippi Delta, the Ozarks, the Texas Borderland, and Native American reservations. With the exception of Appalachia and the Ozarks, these places are the homes of concentrated populations of rural racial/ethnic minorities who face escalated racial/ethnic inequality and socioeconomic hardships due to the historical legacies of these locations (Saenz, 1997a; Snipp, 1996; Swanson, Harris, Skees, & Williamson, 1994).

But the existing literature lacks a comparative perspective regarding the conditions of racial and ethnic minority groups in such places, including Latinos and blacks. Some studies examined poverty of the Latino population along the Texas border (Davila & Mattila, 1985; Fong, 1998; Maril, 1989; Saenz & Ballejos, 1993; Tan & Ryan, 2001), while others focused on the black population in the Delta (Allen-Smith, Wimberley, & Morris, 2000; Duncan, 1997, 2001; Kodras, 1997; Lee & Singelmann, 2006) and the Black Belt (Allen-Smith et al., 2000; Falk & Rankin, 1992; Hattery & Smith, 2007; Rankin & Falk, 1991; Wimberley & Morris, 2002). Yet hardly any research compares the mechanism of poverty for Latinos and blacks living in persistently poor areas, especially in the Delta and the Borderland (for an exception based on a brief descriptive piece, see Shaw, 1997).

---

[2] For the remainder of this chapter the Texas Borderland will be referred to as the "Borderland" and the Lower Mississippi Delta will be referred to as the "Delta."

This chapter assesses the extent to which there are commonalities in the relationships between selected predictors and poverty rates. We first provide a brief overview of the two study regions, the Borderland and the Delta. We then review past research on factors found to be associated with aggregate-level poverty. We group those factors into the following four dimensions (cf. Hirschl & Brown, 1995): economic structure, demographic structure, human capital, and metropolitan (metro)/nonmetropolitan (nonmetro) location.

## The Two Regions

Both the Borderland and the Delta have a long history of poverty. Their traditional economy was based on agriculture, with few efforts made towards industrialization until late in the 20th century. The economies of both regions were based on economic systems that did not rely on labor markets, for such markets assume that workers have choices of where to work. The legacy of oppression in these two regions resulted in disenfranchisement of the social minority populations that remains to be fully overcome. Given those conditions, the concentration of minorities in the two regions resulted in especially high rates of aggregate poverty.

The proximity of the Borderland to Mexico continued to fuel a steady supply of Mexican labor and, more recently, of immigrants from other Central American countries such as Guatemala, El Salvador, and Honduras (Betts & Slottje, 1994; Snipp, 1996). Immigration laws such as the *Bracero* program that started during World War II and lasted until 1964 provided U.S. agribusiness with cheap and steady labor. Those workers had little to no labor mobility once in the United States. Subsequently, and especially after the implementation of the North American Free Trade Act (NAFTA), labor-intensive manufacturing plants known as *maquiladoras* were set up on both sides of the border and served as magnets for low-skilled labor (see Slack et al., 2009). The indirect effect of Mexican *maquiladoras* on the labor market in the Borderland has been to lower U.S. wages because of the lower wage level in Mexico. Despite low wages, the Borderland has experienced substantial population growth over the past decades. Although in-migrants tend to seek out higher-wage areas, they also consider their chances of obtaining a job. Thus, the labor-intensive manufacturing plants with their demands for low-skilled labor attract migrants with lower human capital who reason that they would be less competitive in higher-wage labor markets. The special form of industrialization does not include much value added and thus has benefited the region relatively little. As Yoskowitz, Giermanski, and Pena-Sanchez (2002, p. 30) said, the economy remains "one dimensional with regard to trade, mainly transportation and warehousing, leaving little possibilities for growth in other areas."

A consequence of low wages that often do not raise families out of poverty has been the expansion of *colonias*, unincorporated subdivisions with small plots and little infrastructure, where houses often lack such basic amenities as electricity and plumbing. Residents in the *colonias* are both socially and geographically isolated. According to one estimate, about 400,000 people in the Borderland live in such subdivisions (Texas Secretary of State, 2009). Such residential concentration of poverty has been shown to have many socially undesirable outcomes (Massey & Denton, 1993), including lack of job opportunities and the absence of social networks with resources.

The Delta's legacy is the plantation system that relied on slavery for economic survival. To control labor and keep it cheap after the end of slavery, land owners and power brokers systematically kept industries out of the region that would compete with agriculture for labor, thus likely raising its wages. Although slavery was abolished after the Civil War, slave-like conditions (e.g., Jim Crow laws; voting conditions; tenant farming) continued after the end of Reconstruction in 1877 and lasted through the middle of the 20th century (Hyland & Timberlake, 1993). The rejection of industrialization went hand in hand with ready access to the U.S. rail system and, especially, the road system, keeping the Delta economically isolated. Although the Delta includes some of the most fertile agricultural soil in the nation—found in the Mississippi River floodplain that benefited from the rich sediments of the river—the concentration of land ownership among a few families per county has meant a high level of income inequality, with a few families very well off and many in poverty. That inequality largely persists through today. Those conditions gave rise to the Great Migration toward the North, mostly during the period 1916–1930, and the second Great Migration of the period 1930–1970 (Lemann, 1991). As a lingering consequence of those adverse conditions, population growth in the Delta remains largely stagnant or negative.

The brief description of conditions in the Borderland and the Delta show some similarities but also differences. In terms of race and ethnicity, the minority in the Borderland is Latinos, whereas it is blacks in the Delta. Both regions are characterized by high poverty, but the Borderland has embarked on industrialization, albeit without substantial structural regional improvements, that has drawn large numbers of in-migrants. The Delta, in contrast, has been struggling with the decline of agriculture without many industrial alternatives so far. Thus, many counties lose more migrants than they bring in, and much of the region remains underdeveloped.

## Dimensions of Poverty Correlates

### Economic Structure

*FIRE, manufacturing, and agriculture.* A large body of research exists that has shown that the economic structure (or industrial structure) of a place has an impact on poverty rates. For example, we know that poverty at the aggregate level is negatively associated with the percentage of the working-age population employed in finance, insurance, and real estate (FIRE) (Singelmann, 1978; Parisi, McLaughlin, Grice, Taquino, & Gill, 2003; Rupasingha & Goetz, 2007) and the prevalence of manufacturing (Brady & Wallace, 2001; Cotter, 2002; Rupasingha & Goetz, 2007). When examined separately by race, the percent employed in manufacturing has a similar dampening effect on both black and white poverty rates (Adelman & Jaret, 1999). Although most studies conclude that the percent employed in agriculture has a positive relationship with poverty (Levernier, Patridge, & Rickman, 2000; Albrecht, Albrecht, & Albrecht, 2000), some research has found that agriculture has a negative effect on poverty in the rural South (Rupasingha & Goetz, 2007).

*Employment.* Previous research has also shown a negative association between the percent of the working-age population employed and poverty (Cotter, 2002; Gundersen, 2006; Rupasingha & Goetz, 2007; see also Chapter 19 in this volume). Although this has been found for both metro and nonmetro locations, the employment rate is more influential in metro areas (Gundersen, 2006; Jensen, Findeis, Hsu, & Schachter, 1999). It may be the case that structural impediments such as longer commutes and limited childcare options hinder nonmetro residents' ability to capitalize on some of the benefits of employment (Gundersen, 2006). On the level of counties, it could also be that the employment rate fluctuates less among nonmetro counties than it does among metro counties.

### Demographic Structure

*Female-headed households.* It has been well established that household structure has an impact on poverty rates. Previous research has consistently found that poverty is positively associated with the prevalence of households with unmarried/unpartnered females (Albrecht et al., 2000; Goe & Rhea, 2000; Lichter, Graefe, & Brown, 2003; Lichter & McLaughlin, 1995; Parisi, Grice, Taquino, & Gill, 2005; see also Chapter 17 in this volume). It is estimated that about 60% of all poor children today live in female-headed households (Ellwood & Jencks, 2004). Among female-headed households, poverty rates are highest for blacks, Hispanics, and Native Americans (Snyder, McLaughlin, & Findeis, 2006).

*Net migration.* Positive net migration can be viewed as a proxy for economic growth. Migrants flock to areas that have significant employment growth (Frey & Liaw, 2005). Net migration of the nonpoor is more strongly associated with a county's industrial and occupational structures than is net migration of the poor (Nord, 1998), suggesting that an area's economic opportunities provide a strong draw for individuals with greater human capital. Nationally, counties with less in-migrants tend to have higher rates of poverty (Rupasingha & Goetz, 2007).

*Population youthfulness.* Having a young age structure has also been shown in previous research to be positively associated with poverty (Cotter, 2002; Rupasingha & Goetz, 2007). This may be particularly salient for minority populations who typically have younger age structures. Adelman and Jaret (1999) found that metro areas with large percentages of young blacks have higher poverty than metropolitan areas where the black population is older.

*Foreign-born.* The percent of an area's foreign-born population also has an effect on poverty. Poverty among Mexican immigrants is substantially higher than among those that are native-born (Crowley, Lichter, & Qian, 2006). The higher poverty rates among immigrants have significantly increased the overall size of the total American population living in poverty (Camarota, 2001). The percent of the population foreign-born tends to reduce poverty for metro areas, but it was not found to be significant for nonmetro areas, including the nonmetro South (Rupasingha & Goetz, 2007). Again, until very recently, the nonmetro South attracted very few recent immigrants and, historically, the nonmetro South has not had a large diversity of white ethnicity. According to Adelman and Jaret (1999), the percent of an area's foreign-born population in metro areas decreased black poverty but not white poverty. Moreover, the percentage of foreign-born immigrants depresses earnings for natives in low-skill occupations but not in high-skill occupations (Camarota, 1997).

## Human Capital

*Education.* A strong consensus exists that educational attainment is an important factor in reducing poverty rates (Saenz, 1997a; Adelman & Jaret, 1999; Rupasingha & Goetz, 2007; Crowley et al., 2006).

*Ability to speak English.* Speaking English well results in better economic outcomes for immigrants (Davila, Bohara, & Saenz, 1993). Immigrants who speak poor English are economically penalized in both border and nonborder metro areas (Davila & Mora, 2000). In their study of Mexican immigrants, Crowley et al. (2006) found that speaking English "very well" reduced the odds of poverty by 16%.

Counties with a less educated population and one that is limited in its ability to speak English are less likely to attract investment and higher paying jobs than counties with a population commanding higher human capital.

## Nonmetro Status

*Nonmetro.* Poverty has consistently been found to be positively associated with *nonmetro location* (Jensen, McLaughlin, & Slack, 2003; Jensen & Tienda, 1989; O'Hare, 1988; Parisi et al., 2003; Rank & Hirschl, 1988; Rural Sociological Society Task Force on Persistent Rural Poverty, 1993; Saenz & Thomas, 1991; Singelmann, Davidson, & Reynolds, 2002). The economic disadvantage of rural places is related to geographic isolation and substantial underrepresentation of higher-wage industries such as manufacturing and FIRE and social services and is especially pronounced among rural racial/ethnic minorities (Slack & Jensen, 2002). In 1999, the rural South had the highest shares of families living under the poverty line (Rupasingha & Goetz, 2007). The positive association between nonmetro status and poverty in models that include other factors such as industry structure and human capital suggests that nonmetro captures unmeasured positive correlates of poverty. For example, other research in the Delta has shown that persons in nonmetro areas tend to "have networks that have fewer resources, are smaller regarding help and reciprocal help, and are less diverse than the networks of respondents in [metro areas]" (Singelmann, 2001, p. 39). Network size and resources are positively related to the likelihood of finding a job; persons with small networks that command few resources therefore are at a greater risk of being in poverty. The full legacy of the plantation system in the Delta, and the plantation-like working conditions in the Borderland, is also unlikely to be fully captured by the models used in past research as well as by the ones estimated by us. That legacy is mostly relevant to nonmetro areas which, in part because of that legacy, are more prone to remain poor places.

## Data and Measurements

### Data

The analysis presented in this paper is based on data from the 2000 U.S. Census. Our units of analysis are counties. Our choice of counties is governed by the fact that these are the smallest units for which socioeconomic data are available at the level of detail required for our analyses. We estimate models separately for the Borderland and the Delta and, within each region, separately for non-Hispanic whites and minorities (Latinos in the Borderland and blacks in the Delta). The independent variables in the race/ethnic-specific models are also race/ethnic specific. For example, the percent FIRE in the models for non-Hispanic whites refers to the percent of non-Hispanic employed in FIRE services, and so on.

The two study regions are defined as follows. The Borderland stretches from El Paso in the West along the Rio Grande River to Brownsville in the East (see Fig. 20.1). Following Saenz (1997b), we

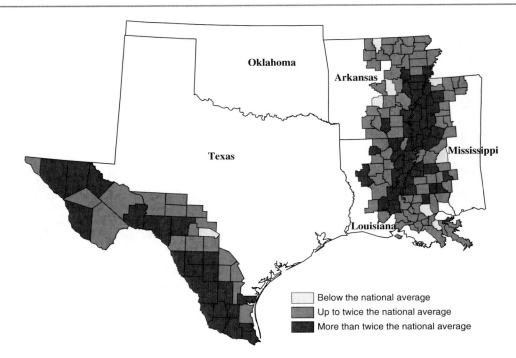

**Fig. 20.1** Poverty in the Borderland and Delta relative to the national average, 2000
*Source*: U.S. Bureau of the Census, 2000 U.S. Census Summary Files.

include all counties in this region whose largest city is within 100 miles of the U.S.-Mexican border. Latinos represent the largest racial/ethnic minority group in the Borderland, making up 80.2% of the total population. In fact, Latinos are the numerical majority in 30 of the 41 counties in the Borderland, reaching as high as 98%.

The Delta is defined according to the geography delineated by the Lower Mississippi Delta Development Commission, as established by the U.S. Congress in the 1980s (now the Delta Regional Authority). In our paper, we restrict the analysis to the core Delta area made up of counties in the states of Arkansas, Louisiana, and Mississippi (see Fig. 20.1). We use the term core Delta here because in many ways these counties include the cultural, social, and economic geography that is called the Delta. Even in this core, political pressures lead to the inclusion of counties whose connection to the Delta is debatable (e.g., a number of Ozark counties in Arkansas). In these three states, 133 counties belong to the Delta area. Blacks are the largest racial/ethnic minority group in the Delta, making up 35% of the total population. In 30 of the 133 counties in the Delta, blacks represent a majority of the population, reaching as high as 86%.

In our paper, to be included in the analysis, we require every county to have at least 1,000 non-Hispanic whites; and we require at least 1,000 Hispanics in each of the Borderland counties, and at least 1,000 non-Hispanic blacks in each of the Delta counties. All 41 Borderland counties meet these requirements. However, 14 of the 133 Delta counties (largely in the Ozarks) do not have the minimum number of 1,000 blacks and were dropped. Thus, our analyses of poverty in the Delta are based on 119 counties in Arkansas, Louisiana, and Mississippi.

The Delta and Borderland areas have been among the poorest regions in the United States (see Table 20.2). In fact, most of the counties in the two regions are designated as "persistent poverty" counties

**Table 20.2** Percent poor for the United States, Delta, and Borderland by race/ethnicity, 2000

| | Total families | White | Black | Latino |
|---|---|---|---|---|
| United States | 9.2 | 5.5 | 21.6 | 20.0 |
| Delta | 16.1 | 7.9 | 32.4 | – |
| Borderland | 25.2 | 6.8 | – | 3.4 |

U.S. Bureau of the Census (2002).

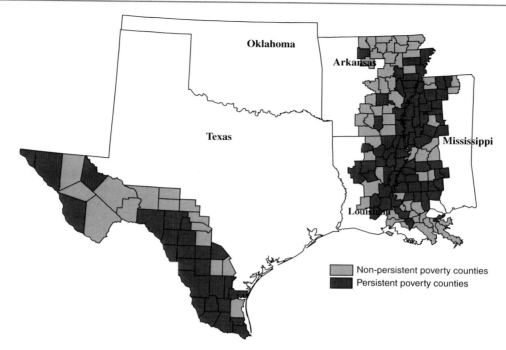

**Fig. 20.2** Persistent poverty in the Borderland and Delta, 2000
*Source*: U.S. Bureau of the Census, 2000 U.S. Census Summary Files.

(i.e., 20% or more of residents were poor as measured in each of the last four censuses, 1970, 1980, 1990, and 2000) (see Fig. 20.2). In 2000, all but 7 of the 119 Delta counties had poverty rates exceeding the national average; the same was true of 40 of the 41 Borderland counties. Indeed, of the nation's 100 poorest counties, 48 are located in one of these two regions (16 in the Borderland and 32 in the Delta). Table 20.2 also shows the even greater relative poverty of blacks, compared to non-Hispanic whites, in the two regions.[3] In the Borderland, poverty of Latinos is 45% higher than is poverty for all Latinos in the United States. That compares with a 24% difference between non-Hispanic white poverty in the Borderland vis-à-vis the nation. Similarly, black poverty in the Delta exceeds U.S. poverty of blacks by 50%, whereas it is 44% for non-Hispanic whites.

## Measurement of Independent and Dependent Variables

The *dependent* variable in this analysis is county-level (and race-/ethnic-specific) poverty, based on 2000 Census data. It is measured in three ways in the Delta counties, namely, the percentage of all families below the poverty line, the percentage of non-Hispanic white families below the poverty threshold, and the percentage of black families below the poverty threshold. In the Borderland counties, poverty is also measured in three ways, namely, the percentage of total families below the poverty line, the percentage of non-Hispanic white families below the poverty threshold, and the percentage of Hispanic families below the poverty threshold. The official poverty thresholds are calculated based on family size, the number of related children, and the age of the householder.

We test an assortment of substantive hypotheses examining the effects on racial/ethnic minority and majority poverty of four groups of *independent* variables: economic structure, demographic structure, human capital, and metro/nonmetro location.

Regarding the economic structure of a county, we estimate the effects of four factors: the percentages

---

[3] The percent poor in Tables 20.1 and 20.2 (means) for the Delta and the Borderland are not fully comparable. The data in Table 20.1 are based on a weighted average of all Delta counties in order to match the procedure used for the national reporting of poverty rates, whereas the mean poverty in Table 20.2 is the unweighted average of all Delta county poverty rates.

of the working-age population employed in finance, insurance, and real estate (FIRE); the percentage of the working-age population employed in manufacturing; the percentage of the working-age population employed in agriculture; and the percentage of the working-age population employed. The FIRE, manufacturing, and employed variables are expected to be negatively associated with poverty, while we expect the agriculture variable to be positively related with poverty.

We estimate the effects of the population structure of a county on poverty via the following four factors: percentage of families headed by females without a spouse; the county's net migration rate; percentage of the population age 15 and under; and the percentage of the population foreign-born (for the Borderland). We anticipate percent female-headed families, percent under 15 years of age, and percent foreign-born to be negatively associated with the poverty rate of a county but expect a positive effect for net migration.

Two variables are used to assess the influence of human capital variables on poverty: the percentage of the population 25 years of age and older without a high-school degree (or its equivalent), and the percentage of the population that does not speak English "well" or "very well" for the Borderland models. Both less than high-school diploma and low English-language ability are expected to be positively associated with poverty.

Finally, our estimated models include nonmetro status of a county, and we expect nonmetro counties to have higher poverty than metro counties.

As part of our analysis, we carried out diagnostics for possible spatial autocorrelation which would violate the assumptions of ordinary least squares (OLS) regressions (Rupasingha & Goetz, 2007; Voss, Long, Hammer, & Friedman, 2006; Cressie, 1993).[4] The results of our tests for spatial autocorrelation showed no need for models accounting for spatial effects.

## Findings

Table 20.3 presents the means and standard deviations for the variables of our Borderland and Delta models. They show similarities and differences between the two regions as well as between the race/ethnic groups. In terms of Borderland-Delta differences, the manufacturing sector is substantially larger in the Delta than it is in the Borderland, with the reverse being the case for agriculture; and Delta counties have a much higher percent female-headed families, on average, than do counties in the Borderland. In terms of white-black difference in the Delta, the county-average for blacks working in FIRE service is substantially below that for whites, whereas the percentage of blacks in manufacturing exceeds that of whites. Overall, the employment rate of blacks is about one-fifth below that of whites, and the average percent less than high school for blacks is almost twice that for whites. On average, the black population in Delta counties is younger than is the white population, and the percent of black families headed by a single female is over five times the corresponding percent for whites. On balance, the white-Latino differences in the Borderland are somewhat smaller that the white-black differences in the Delta. The one exception is education: the ethnic differential for the percent less than high school is much greater in the Borderland than it is in the Delta. As in the case of blacks in the Delta, Latinos have a higher percent of the population under age 15, a lower percent employed, and a higher percent of families headed by single females than does the white population in the Borderland.

We turn now to an examination of the results of OLS regression models of white and minority poverty among the counties of the Delta and the counties of the Borderland presented in Table 20.4 (Delta) and Table 20.5 (Borderland). We tested the three Delta models for multicollinearity and found no problems. The Delta model for the total population shows that all variables but two (percent FIRE and percent agriculture) are statistically significant predictors of a county's percent poverty, and all effects are in the direction as hypothesized. Percent FIRE approaches statistical significance, and

---

[4] When using geographically defined units of analysis, one must examine whether variables are independently distributed through space or if the value of a variable in one location is influenced by the value in a neighboring area (i.e., spatially autocorrelated). Our method for assessing possible autocorrelation involved the examination of Moran's I statistic (queen 1st order contiguity). This statistic quantifies the degree to which the characteristics and spatial units are correlated with those of its neighbors. Our diagnostics showed that Moran's I did not exceed ±0.2 (for conceptual and measurement issues regarding spatial autocorrelation, see Voss, White, & Hammer, 2006).

**Table 20.3** Delta and Borderland characteristics by race/ethnicity, 2000

| Variables | Delta | | | | | | Borderland | | | | | |
|---|---|---|---|---|---|---|---|---|---|---|---|---|
| | Total | | White | | Black | | Total | | White | | Latino | |
| | Mean | S.D. | Mean | S.D. | Mean | S.D. | Mean | S.D. | Mean | S.D. | Mean | S.D. |
| Percent poor | 19.1 | 6.3 | 9.2 | 3.0 | 35.9 | 7.1 | 22.3 | 8.6 | 9.9 | 4.9 | 29.0 | 6.9 |
| Percent FIRE | 4.2 | 1.4 | 5.4 | 1.7 | 2.0 | 1.3 | 3.9 | 1.4 | 5.0 | 2.6 | 3.1 | 1.4 |
| Percent manufacturing | 16.9 | 7.2 | 14.2 | 6.5 | 22.5 | 10.6 | 5.6 | 3.4 | 4.5 | 2.6 | 6.5 | 4.7 |
| Percent agriculture | 5.3 | 4.2 | 6.0 | 5.1 | 4.0 | 3.4 | 9.3 | 8.2 | 11.3 | 8.1 | 8.4 | 8.6 |
| Net migration | −1.7 | 8.9 | – | – | – | – | 1.0 | 17.2 | – | – | – | – |
| Percent less than h.s. | 32.1 | 7.0 | 24.9 | 6.5 | 44.0 | 8.3 | 39.6 | 11.4 | 16.9 | 5.2 | 54.7 | 8.0 |
| Nonmetro | 0.7 | – | – | – | – | – | 0.8 | 0.4 | – | – | – | – |
| Percent under age 15 | 24.1 | 2.2 | 20.0 | 2.5 | 29.1 | 3.2 | 24.3 | 3.7 | 17.4 | 3.5 | 30.1 | 2.3 |
| Percent employed | 60.4 | 7.3 | 68.7 | 5.0 | 48.8 | 8.6 | 60.6 | 9.2 | 68.2 | 8.5 | 57.0 | 7.4 |
| Percent female-headed | 17.6 | 6.0 | 6.8 | 1.7 | 36.1 | 5.0 | 11.4 | 3.4 | 5.8 | 2.7 | 14.2 | 3.0 |
| Percent foreign-born | | | | | | | 13.7 | 10.5 | – | – | – | – |
| Percent no English | | | | | | | 11.6 | 7.5 | – | – | – | – |

*Notes*: S.D. standard deviation. Net migration is the domestic net migration rate between 1990 and 2000. h.s. High school. $N = 119$.
U.S. Bureau of the Census (2002).

**Table 20.4** OLS regression models of Delta total, white, and black family poverty, 2000

| Variables | Total | White | Black |
|---|---|---|---|
| Percent FIRE | −0.081† | −0.201** | −0.124* |
| Percent manufacturing | −0.117** | −0.301*** | −0.150* |
| Percent agriculture | 0.044 | −0.079 | 0.035 |
| Net migration | −0.075* | −0.046 | −0.077 |
| Percent less than high school | 0.206*** | 0.579*** | 0.159* |
| Nonmetro | 0.143*** | 0.227*** | 0.115* |
| Percent under age 15 | 0.143** | 0.080 | 0.389*** |
| Percent employed | −0.184** | −0.098 | −0.519*** |
| Percent female-headed | 0.471*** | 0.194** | 0.187** |
| Intercept | 5.783 | 5.376† | 18.721*** |
| Adjusted $R$-square | 0.902 | 0.737 | 0.757 |

†$p < 0.1$; *$p < 0.05$; **$p < 0.01$; ***$p < 0.001$.
*Note*: Cell entries are standardized OLS coefficients. Race-specific variables are used for the race-specific models with the exception of net migration and nonmetro ($N = 119$).

**Table 20.5** OLS regression models of Borderland total, white, and Latino family poverty, 2000

| Variables | Total | White | Latino |
|---|---|---|---|
| Percent FIRE | – | – | −0.354** |
| Percent agriculture | – | 0.253* | – |
| Percent employed | −0.482*** | – | −0.661*** |
| Nonmetro | 0.161* | – | – |
| Percent female-headed | – | 0.401** | – |
| Education/age/language/nativity | 0.512*** | – | – |
| Percent less than high school | – | 0.471*** | – |
| Nativity | – | – | – |
| Language/nativity | – | – | 0.279* |
| Constant | 46.480*** | −3.567 | 69.337*** |
| Adjusted $R$-square | 0.794 | 0.459 | 0.650 |

*$p < 0.05$; **$p < 0.01$; ***$p < 0.001$.
*Note*: Cell entries are standardized OLS coefficients. Race-specific variables are used for the race-specific models with the exception of nonmetro. Education/age/language/nativity is a factor score comprised of percent less than high school, percent under the age of 15, percent that do not speak English, and percent foreign-born. Language/nativity is a factor score comprised of percent that do not speak English and percent foreign-born. We present a reduced model because of the small number of countries in the Borderland ($N = 41$).

it affects poverty as expected. A comparison of the two race-specific models shows that the correlates of poverty differ somewhat for blacks and whites.[5] Again, all statistically significant effects are as previously hypothesized. Among counties, higher percent FIRE and percent manufacturing tend to lower the percent of both black and white poverty, whereas high percent with less than high school, percent female-headed families, and nonmetro status tend to increase the poverty rate for both blacks and whites. Two additional variables influence black poverty: percent employed lowers and percent under age 15 increases the black poverty rate. It appears that there is greater variation in the employment rate for blacks among counties than there is for whites, thus making this a more important correlate of black poverty. No factor has a significant effect on white poverty and not on black poverty.

Our models for the Borderland differ substantially from those for the Delta because the small number of counties ($N = 41$) in the Borderland made it impossible to estimate the full Delta model. For that reason, we employed factor analysis to reduce the number of variables; and through various model reiterations, we omitted those variables that were not statistically significant. The resulting models for the Borderland are presented in Table 20.4 and include no more variables than can be defended given the number of counties in the analysis. Unfortunately, the necessity for data reduction makes it impossible to directly compare the Delta and Borderland models.

For the overall model, the statistically significant correlates of poverty in Borderland counties are percent employed, nonmetro status, and the human-capital factor education/age/language ability/nativity. The direction of their effects is as expected: among counties, the greater the employment rate, the lower the poverty rate. The four variables making up the human capital factor were all hypothesized to increase poverty, and the effect of this factor on poverty is positive. Finally, metro counties have a higher poverty rate than nonmetro counties, net of their socioeconomic and demographic structure.

In contrast to the Delta where the mechanisms of black and white poverty were quite similar, the model results show no commonality of factors for Latino and white poverty in the Borderland. Poverty of whites is a function of percent agriculture, percent female-headed families, and percent less than high school, with all three variables increasing poverty as we hypothesized. For Latino poverty in the Borderland, percent FIRE, percent employed, and the factor language ability/nativity are the significant correlates, and they are in the expected direction as well. Particularly noteworthy is the insignificance of Latino percent female-headed households for Latino poverty. This finding suggests that Latinos are rewarded less for having two-parent families (or less penalized when having single female-headed families) compared to their white counterparts in the Borderland, and whites and blacks in the Delta. Further examination of the data show that part of the reason is the lower employment rate among married Latinas, but more significant is the fact that income for Latinos and Latinas is sufficiently depressed so that family type does not affect the likelihood of Latinos to be in poverty, net of the other correlates. Furthermore, Latinos in the Borderland are the only demographic group whose poverty rate is not influenced by their percent with less than high school; for whites in the Borderland and whites and blacks in the Delta, a higher percent with less than high school is positively correlated with higher poverty. Although we cannot rule out that these differences, in part, are the result of the small number of Borderland counties for our analysis, they do raise the important issue that poverty-reduction strategies must be targeted to specific demographic groups to be most successful.

## Discussion

This paper presented a comparative analysis of poverty in the Texas Borderland and the Lower Mississippi Delta, which for a long time have been the two poorest regions in the United States. With the use of data from 2000 U.S. Census Summary Files, we estimate race/ethnic-specific models of county-level poverty in each of the two regions. Our goal was to examine the correlates of aggregate-level poverty by focusing on indicators of several dimensions of poverty that have been identified in past research: employment structure, population structure, human capital, and nonmetro residence; previous research guided our expectations for the effects of the model factors on poverty. We further

---

[5] As a reminder, the independent variables for the race/ethnic-specific models are the respective values for each demographic group, as indicated in Table 20.3.

aimed to uncover similarities and differences in those effects for race/ethnic differentials in the Borderland and the Delta. Finally, we wanted to ascertain if the correlates of county-level poverty are the same in the two regions. As we noted above, while the Borderland and the Delta share some common characteristics, they do have distinct histories that have shaped race and ethnic relations and the opportunities for social and economic development.

Our analyses yielded a number of findings. First, compared to national poverty rates, poverty in the Borderland and the Delta is relatively more severe for Latinos and blacks than it is for whites. This finding reflects the legacy of past exploitation and underdevelopment that remains to be fully overcome. Second, the model results showed a similar structure of correlates of county-level poverty for whites and blacks in the Delta.[6] Key factors to reduce both white and black poverty are the percentage of total (white or black) employment in FIRE services and in manufacturing industries. Conversely, common factors to favor poverty are the percent less than high school, the percent female-headed families, and a county's nonmetro status. All statistically significant effects were in the direction as hypothesized. Third, while the small number of counties in the Borderland makes it impossible to estimate the same full model that we employed in the Delta, and thus precludes a precise Borderland-Delta comparison, it appears that similar factors condition poverty in the Borderland and the Delta. Finally, while acknowledging the same small-N caveat for the white-Latino comparison in the Borderland, we interpret the results to show that different factors affect white poverty than do Latino poverty. In particular, we note the absent effect on Latino poverty of the percent female-headed households. Further, as in the white-black comparison in the Delta, the percent employed was the most important factor reducing poverty of Latinos, yet the employment rate of whites had no effect on their poverty rate.

These findings demonstrate the importance of targeting poverty-reduction strategies at specific demographic groups to assure the success of those programs. For both Latinos in the Borderland and blacks in the Delta, for example, a higher employment rate would greatly reduce their poverty rates; no such effect is obtained for whites in either of the two regions. Moreover, in finalizing our models, we also examined the effects of nonrace/ethnic-specific independent variables on the poverty rates of whites, blacks, and Latinos. Those results (not reported here but available upon request from the authors) showed, for example, that the overall percent FIRE tends to reduce white poverty in the Delta but not black poverty. Yet the race/ethnic-specific models show that percent FIRE lowers both white and black poverty. The reason for those divergent findings is the fact that blacks are much less likely to be employed in the higher-wage FIRE services than are whites (see Table 20.2). Thus, a development strategy to reduce poverty that only focuses on increasing the amount of FIRE service employment in high-poverty counties would have little effect on reducing the poverty rate of blacks *unless* that program assured that banks, insurance companies, and realtors actually do employ black workers.

In sum, the results of the analysis presented in this paper reveal a continued disadvantage of blacks in the Delta and Latinos in the Borderland that, we believe, reflect the legacy of the plantation system and coercive employment conditions. The results, however, also point to socioeconomic conditions that can be changed through policy intervention. Finally, the analysis shows the importance of policies that are targeted at specific demographic groups and regions in order for them to be successful in alleviating poverty for all population groups.

To return to the international context of the introduction to this chapter: a key component of poverty in the United States is the proportion of the working poor. According to Slack (2010), who relied on a conservative definition of "working poverty," the percentage of working poor as a share of all poor families has fluctuated between about one third and two fifths during the period 1979–2003; further weakening of the U.S. labor regime during the first decade of the new millennium makes it unlikely that this percentage has fallen since. A family of four with one wage earner working full-time/year-round (about 2,000 h) will remain in poverty if the work is minimum wage; a second wage earner working at minimum wage would have to work at least half-time/year-round (about 1,000 h) for the family to leave poverty. With small children and the

---

[6] The importance of the correlates examined here is further demonstrated by an analysis of change in these factors that we carried out elsewhere (Fontenot et al., 2010).

fragility of many jobs, such an amount of labor supply is unrealistic for many families. No other industrial nation has such a high proportion of the working poor among all poor families.

The significance of the working poor for overall poverty is especially pronounced in nonmetro areas where between 1979 and 2003 the prevalence of working poverty was 9% higher on average compared to metro areas, with differences approaching twice that size in some years (Slack, 2010). While the metro-nonmetro gap has decreased during this period, well over two fifths of all poor nonmetro families have family members with significant labor market attachment.

While not eliminating overall poverty, a minimum wage pegged to the poverty threshold level, in conjunction with the earned income tax credit system (EITC) would substantially reduce poverty by making work pay, i.e., provide a wage sufficiently high to lift working families out of poverty. A more challenging implementation of the concept of a living wage would further reduce the risk that families fall back into poverty at the slightest distress affecting their labor supply.

**Acknowledgements** This is a revised version of a paper presented at the XXVI IUSSP International Population Conference in Marrakech, Morocco, September–October 2009. This project was supported by the National Research Initiative (NRI) of the Cooperative State Research, Education and Extension Service (CSREES), U.S. Department of Agriculture (USDA), Rural Development Program, Grant #2006-35401-17432. Dudley L. Poston, Jr., and Rogelio Saenz from Texas A&M University were part of the grant and provided very helpful comments. We thank Huizhen Niu of the Agricultural Economics Geographic Information Systems (AEGIS) Lab. in the Department of Agricultural Economics and Agribusiness, LSU AgCenter, for her assistance in developing the maps presented in this paper and used to diagnose spatial effects.

## References

Adelman, R. M., & Jaret, C. (1999). Poverty, race, and US metropolitan social and economic structure. *Journal of Urban Affairs, 21*(1), 35–56.

Albrecht, D. E., Albrecht, C. M., & Albrecht, S. L. (2000). Poverty in nonmetropolitan America: Impacts of industrial, employment, and family structure variables. *Rural Sociology, 65*, 87–103.

Allen-Smith, J. E., Wimberley, R. C., & Morris, L. V. (2000). America's forgotten people and places: Ending the legacy of poverty in the rural south. *Journal of Agricultural and Applied Economics, 32*, 319–329.

Betts, D. C., & Slottje, D. J. (1994). *Crisis on the Rio Grande: Poverty, unemployment, and economic development on the Texas-Mexico border*. Boulder, CO: Westview Press.

Brady, D., & Wallace, M. (2001). Deindustrialization and poverty: Manufacturing decline and AFDC recipiency in lake country, Indiana 1964–93. *Sociological Forum, 16*, 321–358.

Camarota, S. A. (1997). The effect of immigrants on the earnings of low-skilled native workers: Evidence from the June 1991 current population survey. *Social Science Quarterly, 78*(2), 417–431.

Camarota, S. A. (2001). Immigrants in the United States – 2000. *Spectrum: Journal of State Government, 74*(2), 1–5.

Cotter, D. A. (2002). Poor people in poor places: Local opportunity structures and household poverty. *Rural Sociology, 67*, 534–555.

Cressie, N. A. (1993). *Statistics for spatial data*. New York: Wiley.

Crowley, M., Lichter, D. T., & Qian, Z. (2006). Beyond gateway cities: Economic restructuring and poverty among Mexican immigrant families and children. *Family Relations, 55*, 345–360.

Davila, A., Bohara, A. K., & Saenz, R. (1993). Accent penalties and the earnings of Mexican Americans. *Social Science Quarterly, 74*(4), 902–916.

Davila, A., & Mattila, J. P. (1985). Do workers earn less along the U.S.-Mexico border? *Social Science Quarterly, 66*, 310–318.

Davila, A., & Mora, M. T. (2000). English skills, earnings, and the occupational sorting of Mexican Americans along the U.S.-Mexico border. *International Migration Review, 34*(1), 133–157.

Duncan, C. M. (1997). *Worlds apart: Why poverty persists in Rural America*. New Haven, CT: Yale University Press.

Duncan, C. M. (2001). Social capital in America's poor rural communities. In S. Saegert, J. Thompson, & M. R. Warren (Eds.), *Social capital and poor communities* (pp. 60–86). New York: Russell Sage Foundation.

Ellwood, D., & Jencks, C. (2004). The spread of single-parent families in the United States since 1960. In D. Moynihan, T. Smeeding, & L. Rainwater (Eds.), *The future of the family* (pp. 25–65). New York: Russell Sage Foundation.

Falk, W. W., & Rankin, B. H. (1992). The cost of being black in the black belt. *Social Problems, 39*, 299–313.

Fong, L. Y.-S. (1998). Borderland poverty: The case of the Rio Grande valley at the United States-Mexican border. *Social Development Issues, 20*, 107–115.

Fontenot, K., Singelmann, J., Slack, T., Siordia, C., Poston, D. L., Jr., & Saenz, R. (2010). Understanding falling poverty in the poorest places: An examination of the experience of the Texas Borderland and Lower Mississippi Delta, 1990–2000. *Journal of Poverty, 14*, 216–236.

Frey, W. H., & Liaw, K.-L. (2005). Migration within the United States: Role of race-ethnicity. *Brookings-Wharton Papers on Urban Affairs, 6*, 207–262.

Friedman, S., & Lichter, D. T. (1998). Spatial inequality and poverty among American children. *Population Research and Policy Review, 17*, 91–109.

Glasmeier, A. K. (2002). One nation, pulling apart: The basis of persistent poverty in the USA. *Progress in Human Geography, 26*, 155–173.

Goe, W. R., & Rhea, A. (2000). The spatial shift in the growth of poverty among families headed by employed females, 1979–89. *Journal of Sociology and Social Welfare, 27*, 79–95.

Gundersen, C. (2006). Are the effects of the macroeconomy and social policies on poverty different in nonmetro areas in the United States? *Rural Sociology, 71*(4), 545–572.

Hattery, A., & Smith, E. (2007). Social stratification in the new/old South: The influence of racial segregation on social class in the Deep South. *Journal of Poverty, 11*, 81.

Hirschl, T., & Brown, D. L. (1995). The determinants of rural and urban poverty. In E. Castle (Ed.), *The changing American countryside* (pp. 229–246). Lawrence, KS: University Press of Kansas.

Hyland, S., & Timberlake, M. (1993). The Mississippi Delta: Change or continued trouble. In T. A. Lyson, & W. W. Falk (Eds.), *Forgotten places: Uneven development in rural America* (pp. 78–101). Lawrence, KS: University Press of Kansas.

Jensen, L., Findeis, J., Hsu, W.-L., & Schachter, J. P. (1999). Slipping into and out of underemployment: Another disadvantage for nonmetropolitan workers? *Rural Sociology, 64*, 417–438.

Jensen, L., McLaughlin, D. K., & Slack, T. (2003). Rural poverty: The persisting challenge. In D. L. Brown, & L. E. Swanson (Eds.), *Challenges for rural America in the twenty-first century* (pp. 118–131). University Park, PA: The Pennsylvania State University Press.

Jensen, L., & Tienda, M. (1989). Nonmetropolitan minority families in the United States: Trends in racial and ethnic economic stratification, 1959–1986. *Rural Sociology, 54*, 509–532.

Kodras, J. E. (1997). The changing map of American poverty in an era of economic restructuring and political realignment. *Economic Geography, 73*, 67–93.

Lee, M. A., & Singelmann, J. (2006). Welfare reform amidst chronic poverty in the Mississippi Delta. In W. A. Kandel, & D. L. Brown (Eds.), *Rural population change and rural society* (pp. 381–403). Dordrecht, The Netherlands: Springer Press.

Lemann, N. (1991). *Promised land: The great migration and how it changed America.* New York: Alfred A. Knopf.

Levernier, W., Patridge, M. D., & Rickman, D. S. (2000). The causes of regional variations in US poverty: A cross-county analysis. *Journal of Regional Science, 40*(3), 473–497.

Lichter, D. T., Graefe, D. R., & Brown, J. B. (2003). Is marriage a Panacea? Union formation among economically disadvantaged unwed mothers. *Social Problems, 50*, 60–86.

Lichter, D. T., & McLaughlin, D. K. (1995). Changing economic opportunities, family structure, and poverty in rural areas. *Rural Sociology, 60*, 688–706.

Lobao, L. M. (1990). *Locality and inequality: Farm and industry structure and socioeconomic conditions.* Albany, NY: State University of New York Press.

Lobao, L. M., & Saenz, R. (2002). Spatial inequality and diversity as an emerging research area. *Rural Sociology, 67*, 497–511.

Lyson, T. A., & Falk, W. W. (Eds.). (1993). *Forgotten places: Uneven development in rural America.* Lawrence, KS: University Press of Kansas.

Maril, R. L. (1989). *Poorest of Americans: The Mexican-Americans of the lower Rio Grande Valley of Texas.* Notre Dame, IN: University of Notre Dame Press.

Massey, D. S., & Denton, N. A. (1993). *American Apartheid: Segregation and the making of the underclass.* Cambridge, MA: Harvard University Press.

Massey, D. S., & Eggers, M. L. (1990). The ecology of inequality: Minorities and the concentration of poverty, 1970–1980. *American Journal of Sociology, 95*, 1153–1188.

National Advisory Committee on Rural Poverty. (1967). *The people left behind: A report.* Washington, DC: U.S. Government Printing Office.

Nord, M. (1998). Poor people on the move: County-to-county migration and the spatial concentration of poverty. *Journal of Regional Science, 38*(2), 329–351.

OECD. (2008). *Growing unequal? Income distribution and poverty in OECD countries.* Paris: OECD.

O'Hare, W. P. (1988). *The rise of poverty in rural America.* Washington, DC: Population Reference Bureau.

Parisi, D., Grice, S. M., Taquino, M., & Gill, D. A. (2005). Community concentration of poverty and its consequences on nonmetro county persistence of poverty in Mississippi. *Sociological Spectrum, 25*, 469–483.

Parisi, D., McLaughlin, D. K., Grice, S. M., Taquino, M., & Gill, D. A. (2003). TANF participation rates: Do community conditions matter? *Rural Sociology, 68*, 491–512.

Rank, M. R., & Hirschl, T. A. (1988). A rural-urban comparison of welfare exits: The importance of population density. *Rural Sociology, 53*, 28–35.

Rankin, B. H., & Falk, W. W. (1991). Race, region, and earnings: Blacks and whites in the South. *Rural Sociology, 56*, 224–237.

Rosenbaum, J. E., Reynolds, L., & Deluca, S. (2002). How do places matter? The geography of opportunity, self-efficacy and a look inside the black box of residential mobility. *Housing Studies, 17*, 71–82.

Rupasingha, A., & Goetz, S. A. (2007). Social and political forces as determinants of poverty: A spatial analysis. *The Journal of Socio-Economics, 36*, 650–671.

Rural Sociological Society Task Force on Persistent Rural Poverty. (1993). *Persistent poverty in rural America.* Boulder, CO: Westview Press.

Saenz, R. (1997a). Ethnic concentration and Chicano poverty: A comparative approach. *Social Science Research, 26*, 205–228.

Saenz, R. (1997b). *Mexican American poverty in Texas border communities: A multivariate approach.* Unpublished manuscript presented at the Borderlands Landscapes Conference, Texas A&M International University.

Saenz, R., & Ballejos, M. (1993). Industrial development and persistent poverty in the lower Rio Grande Valley. In T. A. Lyson, & W. W. Falk (Eds.), *Forgotten places: Uneven development in rural America* (pp. 102–123). Lawrence, KS: University Press of Kansas.

Saenz, R., & Thomas, J. K. (1991). Minority poverty in nonmetro Texas. *Rural Sociology, 56*, 204–223.

Shaw, W. (1997). Regionally specific strategies to alleviate rural poverty. *Economic Development Review, 15*, 52–58.

Singelmann, J. (1978). *From agriculture to services: The transformation of industrial employment.* Beverly Hills, CA: Sage.

Singelmann, J. (2001). *Louisiana welfare survey wave III: Selected results*. Baton Rouge: Louisiana State University, Department of Sociology.

Singelmann, J., Davidson, T., & Reynolds, R. (2002). Welfare, work, and well-being in metro and nonmetro Louisiana. *Southern Rural Sociology, 18*, 21–47.

Slack, T. (2010). Working poverty across the metro-nonmetro divide: A quarter century in perspective, 1979–2003. *Rural Sociology, 75*, 363–387.

Slack, T., & Jensen, L. (2002). Race, ethnicity, and underemployment in nonmetropolitan America: A 30-year profile. *Rural Sociology, 67*, 208–233.

Slack, T., Singelmann, J., Fontenot, K., Poston, D. L., Jr., Saenz, R., & Siordia, C. (2009). Poverty in the Texas Borderland and Lower Mississippi Delta: A comparative analysis of differences by family type. *Demographic Research, 20*, 353–376.

Snipp, C. M. (1996). Understanding race and ethnicity in rural America. *Rural Sociology, 61*, 125–142.

Snyder, A. R., McLaughlin, D. K., & Findeis, J. (2006). Household composition and poverty among female-headed households with children: Differences by race and residence. *Rural Sociology, 71*(4), 597–624.

Swanson, L. E., Harris, R. P., Skees, J. R., & Williamson, L. (1994). African Americans in southern rural regions: The importance of legacy. *The Review of Black Political Economy, 22*, 109–124.

Tan, P. P., & Ryan, E. (2001). Homeless Hispanic and Non-Hispanic adults on the Texas-Mexico border. *Hispanic Journal of Behavioral Science, 23*, 239–249.

Texas Secretary of State. (2009). Colonias FAQ's. Retrieved September 12, 2009, from http://www.sos.state.tx.us/border/colonias/faqs.shtml.

Tickamyer, A. R., & Duncan, C. M. (1990). Poverty and opportunity structure in rural America. *Annual Review of Sociology, 16*, 67–86.

U.S. Bureau of the Census. (2002). Census 2000 Summary file 3. Washington, D.C

U.S. Bureau of the Census. (2011). *Historical poverty tables – People*. Tables 2 and 8. Retrieved March 6, 2011, from http://www.census.gov/hhes/www/poverty/data/historical/people.html

Voss, P. R., Long, D. D., Hammer, R. B., & Friedman, S. (2006). County-child poverty rates in the U.S.: A spatial regression approach. *Population Research and Policy Review, 25*, 369–391.

Voss, P. R., White, K. C., & Hammer, R. B. (2006). Explorations in spatial demography. In W. Kandel & D. L. Brown (Eds.), *Population change and rural society: Demographic research for a new century* (pp. 407–429). Dordrecht, The Netherlands: Springer.

Weinberg, D. H. (1987). Rural pockets of poverty. *Rural Sociology, 52*, 398–408.

Wimberley, R. C., & Morris, L. V. (2002). The regionalization of poverty: Assistance for the Black Belt South? *Southern Rural Sociology, 18*, 294–306.

Yoskowitz, D. W., Giermanski, J. R., & Pena-Sanchez, R. (2002). The influence of NAFTA on socio-economic variables for the US-Mexico border region. *Regional Studies, 36*, 25–31.

# Rural Jobs: Making a Living in the Countryside

Gary Paul Green

## Introduction

Farming is no longer the primary rural occupation in most developed countries. Even in agricultural-dependent regions, farming does not provide the majority of jobs or income for rural households. In rural regions dependent on mining, fishing, or forestry, the demand for labor in these industries has declined dramatically. Much of the decline in demand for jobs in extractive industries can be attributed to technological change, global competition, and economies of scale. While the extractive sector's share of employment has declined significantly over the past few decades, the service sector has grown rapidly. In many respects, rural labor markets appear on the surface to look more like urban labor markets.

In this chapter, I explore the changing nature of rural employment. I pay special attention to the restructuring of rural labor markets and the challenges of building the "high road" in rural areas. There are some unique obstacles to providing good jobs for rural workers. Education and training are lagging in many regions. Workers in rural areas tend to be older because many young workers migrate to urban areas where they can find jobs with better wages and more benefits. Employers invest very little in upgrading the skills of the workforce and rural areas lack many of the institutional mechanisms that could address labor market weaknesses. The emerging green economy may offer some unique opportunities to rural communities. I discuss the potential of green-collar jobs in rural areas and the need for workforce development efforts in this area.

## Rural Jobs in a Global Context

Developing countries remain largely dependent on extractive industries. As one might expect, the rural population is proportionately large in Africa and Asia and small in Europe, Latin America, and North America (Table 21.1). Latin American countries have the smallest percentage of rural residents—about one-fifth. The rate of urbanization throughout Latin America has accelerated during the 1990s. The U.S. nonmetropolitan population is about 30% of the total. For much of the past century, rural areas have experienced a net out-migration of residents. The 1970s and early 1990s were two exceptions. During these decades, many rural areas had a net in-migration. In recent years, the demographic patterns have returned to the long-term pattern of a net out-migration in rural areas.

The vast majority of rural workers in Africa and Asia continue to work in the agricultural sector (broadly defined as agriculture, hunting, fishing, and forestry). Most African countries have relatively few rural residents in the nonfarm sector. Several countries (e.g., Mali, Malawi, and Rwanda) have less than 10% of their rural population in nonfarm activities (Lanjouw & Lanjouw, 2001). Although it has a relatively small rural population, Latin America has a relatively high proportion of rural residents working in the agricultural sector as well.

G.P. Green (✉)
Department of Community and Environmental Sociology,
University of Wisconsin-Madison, Madison, WI 53706, USA
e-mail: gpgreen@wisc.edu

**Table 21.1** Percentage of rural and agricultural population by geographic region, 2008

| Region | Percent rural | Percent agricultural |
|---|---|---|
| Africa | 61 | 51 |
| Latin America | 21 | 17 |
| Asia | 59 | 48 |
| Europe | 28 | 6 |

*Note*: Rural population refers to the population not residing in urban areas. Usually the urban areas and hence the urban population are defined according to national census definitions which can be roughly divided into three major groups: classification of localities of a certain size as urban; classification of administrative centers of minor civil divisions as urban; and classification of centers of minor civil divisions on a chosen criterion which may include type of local government, number of inhabitants or proportion of population engaged in agriculture, as urban. Agricultural population is defined as all persons depending for their livelihood on agriculture, hunting, fishing, and forestry. It comprises all persons economically active in agriculture as well as their nonworking dependents.
*Source*: United Nations (2009).

International development agencies, such as the World Bank, have focused many of their programs on supporting the rural nonfarm sector as a means of alleviating rural poverty. Investments in this sector, especially financial support for entrepreneurs, can be an effective strategy for providing economic opportunities for the poor who may not have access to land in rural areas. Although there are concerns with the low productivity of the rural nonfarm sector, the experience in many developing countries is that promoting the nonfarm reduces income inequality and promotes growth in the rural areas. Given the relative size of the rural population in most developing countries, this strategy may help reduce out-migration to urban areas.

One-fourth of the rural population of Europe works in the agricultural sector. The percentage of rural residents in agriculture is even lower (less than 10%, depending on definitions) in the U.S. In this context, promotion of nonfarm activities in rural areas has several goals. Nonfarm employment provides support for the farming population. More than 90% of farm families in the U.S. have a family member who earns wages in the nonfarm sector. For small farm operators, nonfarm earnings are critical to the survival of the farm operation.

Generating nonfarm economic development activities is also considered a mechanism for adding value to farm production. Rather than producing commodities that are processed somewhere else, value is added closer to the production site. Value-added economic developing activities that are tightly linked to the farming sector are likely to have a stronger impact on the regional economy. It also may reduce some of the vulnerability that farm operators face in their markets.

Finally, promotion of nonfarm economic activities in rural areas may slow down rural-to-urban migration in many developing countries. High concentrations of poverty in urban areas may generate more political instability and additional obstacles to economic development.

The difference in the relative size of the agricultural workforce in developing and developed countries can be attributed to several interrelated factors: agricultural productivity, technology, and capital availability (Lanjouw & Lanjouw, 2001). In developing countries, farmers are much less productive and cannot adopt new technology. In addition, the lack of financial capital makes it difficult to purchase inputs, land and machinery. The gap also reflects the obstacles to nonagricultural investments in many developing countries. Inadequate roads, communication, and educational systems make it more difficult to invest in nonfarm economic activities in rural areas. In developing countries, improvements in transportation and infrastructure have facilitated investments in rural areas.

## Occupations and Industries in the Rural U.S.

Because of the lack of data on rural employment in most countries, I focus most of the discussion in the following section on rural jobs in the U.S. I examine the nature of employment, structural changes occurring in rural areas, and factors influencing income (see Chapter 19 in this volume).

There are more than 25 million workers in nonmetropolitan areas of the U.S., with almost 80% of them in wage and salary employment (Table 21.2). Fewer than 6% of the workers are in farming. Many of the jobs classified as either manufacturing or service sector employment are related to agriculture, such as food processing and farm machinery production and sales, or other resource-based industries.

Manufacturing employment in rural areas continues to receive a great deal of attention by policy makers. Manufacturing jobs have traditionally paid relatively high wages, offered good benefits, and provided

**Table 21.2** Employment by industry in nonmetropolitan areas of the U.S. (2007)

| | |
|---|---:|
| Total employment | 26,539,913 |
| Wage and salary employment | 19,774,277 |
| Proprietors employment | 6,765,636 |
|   Farm proprietors employment | 1,254,300 |
|   Nonfarm proprietors employment | 5,511,336 |
| Farm employment | 1,557,490 |
| Nonfarm employment | 24,982,423 |
| Private employment | 20,806,462 |
|   Forestry, fishing, related activities, and other | 375,922 |
|   Mining | 372,516 |
|   Utilities | 120,877 |
|   Construction | 1,833,971 |
|   Manufacturing | 3,027,708 |
|   Wholesale trade | 686,474 |
|   Retail trade | 3,055,718 |
|   Transportation and warehousing | 858,988 |
|   Information | 271,067 |
|   Finance and insurance | 748,865 |
|   Real estate and rental and leasing | 891,503 |
|   Professional, scientific, and technical services | 858,180 |
|   Management of companies and enterprises | 122,259 |
|   Administrative and waste services | 1,037,752 |
|   Educational services | 326,290 |
|   Health care and social assistance | 2,477,692 |
|   Arts, entertainment, and recreation | 414,540 |
|   Accommodation and food services | 1,756,719 |
|   Other services, except public administration | 1,569,421 |
| Government and government enterprises | 4,175,961 |
|   Federal, civilian | 320,394 |
|   Military | 286,052 |
|   State and local | 3,569,515 |
|     State government | 859,605 |
|     Local government | 2,709,910 |

*Source*: Bureau of Economic Analysis (2009).

opportunities for income mobility within the firm (Cohen & Zysman, 1987). Rural communities continue to concentrate much of their economic development effort on providing incentives, such as tax breaks and subsidies, to manufacturing firms. There is growing evidence, however, that manufacturing jobs in rural areas may not confer as many advantages for workers as they once did (Green & Sanchez, 2007). Competitive pressures from other low-wage regions have led to stagnant wages, reduced benefits, and fewer opportunities to advance oneself within the firm. Although manufacturing wages are probably still higher than many other industrial sectors, these jobs are not as advantageous as they once were.

Looking at employment by occupation in nonmetropolitan areas, we find that the occupations with the largest number of workers are office and administrative support, production, and sales (Table 21.3). Food preparation and related occupations also are overrepresented in rural areas. These occupations correspond closely to the dominant industries in nonmetropolitan areas, such as food processing.

Wages in rural areas generally lag behind those in urban areas, and the gap has increased over the past few decades. On average, earnings by rural workers are about 65% of earnings in urban areas. There are several factors that explain the earnings gap between urban and rural areas. First, the industrial and occupational structure is different in rural and urban areas. Although the service sector has grown rapidly in both urban and rural areas, professionals and other high skilled workers are more likely to reside in urban centers. Low-wage service sector employment is proportionally much higher in rural areas.

Second, rural residents are on average older than urban residents. Older workers generally earn less because many of them are semi-retired. There also is a tendency for older workers to invest less in training, which lowers their earnings. In addition, out-migration of younger and more educated workers to urban areas contributes to the wage gap.

Third, rural residents generally have less education and training than urban residents. Some of the disparity in education can be attributed to the age difference; older workers tend to have less education. Not only do rural workers invest less in job training, employers in these areas tend not to invest in their workforce. Employers in urban areas are more likely to find other firms with similar training needs. This provides more opportunities to collaborate and to reduce the costs of training. Collaboration with other employers is especially important for small firms because they have fewer resources to train their workforce.

Fourth, many rural areas do not have access to two-year or technical colleges. Teixeira and McGranahan (1998) report that employers in counties with these

**Table 21.3** Employment and wages by occupation in non-metropolitan areas of the U.S. (2008)

| Occupation | Number | Mean wage (dollars) |
|---|---|---|
| Management occupations | 668,250 | 74,826 |
| Business and financial operations occupations | 449,580 | 51,119 |
| Computer and mathematical science occupations | 138,460 | 55,202 |
| Architecture and engineering occupations | 215,490 | 58,081 |
| Life, physical, and social science occupations | 124,530 | 50,236 |
| Community and social services occupations | 281,160 | 36,291 |
| Legal occupations | 62,400 | 59,851 |
| Education, training, and library occupations | 1,325,140 | 40,572 |
| Arts, design, entertainment, sports, and media occupations | 144,740 | 34,152 |
| Health-care practitioners and technical occupations | 945,460 | 57,597 |
| Health-care support occupations | 604,530 | 23,063 |
| Protective service occupations | 445,310 | 35,776 |
| Food preparation and serving related occupations | 1,650,220 | 18,630 |
| Building and grounds cleaning and maintenance occupations | 636,230 | 22,436 |
| Personal care and service occupations | 409,840 | 20,853 |
| Sales and related occupations | 1,790,780 | 27,222 |
| Office and administrative support occupations | 2,725,530 | 27,649 |
| Farming, fishing, and forestry occupations | 105,370 | 26,545 |
| Construction and extraction occupations | 991,820 | 36,022 |
| Installation, maintenance, and repair occupations | 846,900 | 36,979 |
| Production occupations | 2,086,970 | 30,020 |
| Transportation and material moving occupations | 1,493,100 | 28,746 |

*Source*: Bureau of Labor Statistics, http://www.bls.gov/oes/2008/may/oesdl.htm#2008. Accessed 3 December 2009.

training institutions were more likely to indicate that labor quality was less of a problem. Without these key institutions, employers are less likely to provide workplace training.

Fifth, firms locating in rural areas tend to be in mature industries. Mature industries are usually characterized by lower rates of innovation and less demand for a skilled workforce. In addition, the industry structure is typically very competitive, and in many cases the firms are competing in international markets. These factors combined usually lead to lower profit rates and ultimately lower wages.

Finally, rural areas have fewer unions. Collective bargaining arrangements have historically improved wages and benefits for workers in these industries (Freeman, 1985).

There may be several reasons for this. The culture of individualism is much stronger in rural than in urban areas. Workers are less inclined to see the benefits of collectively negotiating with employers. Employers also tend to be smaller and may have less capacity to bargain with unions.

Jobs in manufacturing and government sectors tend to provide higher wages than other industries in rural areas (Table 21.4). As I mentioned above, manufacturing jobs continue to offer advantages, but the gap between these jobs and others may be narrowing. Wages are relatively low in recreation and food services industries, which are often associated with tourism. Similarly, wages in real estate and retail trade are especially low as well. Both of these sectors have a large percentage of part-time and seasonal workers which contributes to their low wages.

As can be seen from Table 21.3, service-related, forestry, and fishing occupations tend to be among the lowest paid occupations in rural America. Workers in entertainment, recreation and food service, on average, have comparatively low wages. The number of jobs in these occupations has grown significantly in the past few decades with the expansion of the recreation and tourism industries (McGranahan, 1999). Low wages in these occupations are often due to part-time or seasonal work.

## Structural Changes in Rural Labor Markets

In many respects, rural and urban labor markets have become more similar as extractive industries have constituted a smaller share of jobs. This may be especially true for workers on the rural-urban fringe. Workers in rural areas close to metropolitan areas are likely to commute to urban regions for higher paying jobs

**Table 21.4** Mean annual wage for nonmetropolitan U.S. employment by industry (2007)

| Industry | Mean wage (dollars) |
|---|---|
| Farm employment | 6,053 |
| Nonfarm employment | 30,835 |
| Private employment | 27,607 |
| Forestry, fishing, related activities, and other | 16,658 |
| Mining | 56,171 |
| Utilities | 83,087 |
| Construction | 23,764 |
| Manufacturing | 48,874 |
| Wholesale trade | 41,926 |
| Retail trade | 19,632 |
| Transportation and warehousing | 33,017 |
| Information | 35,849 |
| Finance and insurance | 31,467 |
| Real estate and rental and leasing | 6,789 |
| Professional, scientific, and technical services | 27,300 |
| Management of companies and enterprises | 62,485 |
| Administrative and waste services | 16,816 |
| Educational services | 21,856 |
| Health care and social assistance | 31,386 |
| Arts, entertainment, and recreation | 12,943 |
| Accommodation and food services | 14,884 |
| Other services, except public administration | 15,431 |
| Government and government enterprises | 46,919 |

*Source*: Bureau of Economic Analysis (2009).

(Tigges & Fuguitt, 2003). As a result, rural and urban residents in these regions have very similar jobs. Similarly, manufacturing and service firms have located in these areas because of lower costs of land and labor.

In more isolated rural areas, however, labor markets function differently (Marsden, Lowe, & Whatmore, 1992). First, labor markets in rural regions tend to be "thin," which means that there are few opportunities for most jobs. This quality has several consequences for labor markets. First, this characteristic may result in less competition for workers, especially for unskilled or semiskilled workers. Less competition typically results in lower wages and fewer benefits for workers. The balance of power in these situations is clearly in the hands of employers who have more options.

A second related consequence of thin labor markets is that they lead to lower returns to human capital in rural than in urban areas. Investments in education and training generally do not have the same payoff for rural workers as they do for urban workers. Obtaining training in computer repair, for example, will have a larger return on the investment for urban than rural workers.

Third, thin labor markets are more vulnerable to fluctuations in the economy. The loss of a major employer in a rural community can have devastating effects on the local economy. As a result, major employers may have a significant influence on local political decisions and obtain large subsidies to remain in the community.

Finally, thin labor markets may also increase the likelihood of underemployment because of fewer job opportunities. Almost all indicators of economic well-being (underemployment, poverty, and earnings) are lower in rural than in urban areas (Lichter, 1989). One of the primary reasons for the high level of underemployment is that part-time and seasonal jobs are more likely to be located in rural areas (Lichter, 1989). Many of the part-time and seasonal jobs are in the recreation and tourism industries.

In the 1960s and 1970s, rural America experienced an industrial invasion (Summers, Evans, Clemente, Beck, & Minkoff, 1976). The primary factor driving this transition was the push to lower production costs. Firms moving to rural areas tend to be later in the profit/product cycle than those firms in metropolitan areas (Markusen, 1987). Innovative and high profit firms are more likely to be located in metropolitan areas where they have better access to producer services and financial capital, and are in closer proximity to markets and other firms with whom they can collaborate. Rural areas generally have lower rates of unionization, which also made them an attractive location for manufacturers.

There are other differences in the types of manufacturing jobs that locate in rural areas. Metropolitan areas are much more likely to have durable manufacturing jobs that typically pay good wages and provide benefits. Manufacturing activities in rural areas tend to be resource-based, such as food, timber products, or energy-related.

There are some important regional differences in manufacturing employment throughout rural areas of the U.S. The South has historically had a high concentration of manufacturing jobs in textiles and apparel. The Midwest has a much larger share of high-wage manufacturing jobs, especially in machinery production and printing (Fuguitt, Brown, & Beale, 1989).

In the 1980s and 1990s, however, many manufacturers moved to even lower cost areas, such as Mexico, and eventually China (Bluestone & Harrison, 1982). With the loss of these jobs, rural America became much more dependent on service sector employment. Growth in the service sector was fueled by rapid expansion of recreation and tourism industries, as well as migration of retirees to rural areas. These industries grew especially fast in the Western and upper Midwest states during this period. Many of these jobs, however, were part-time and/or seasonal.

There is considerable debate in the literature whether the skill demands of rural employers have decreased or increased in recent years (see Gibbs, Swaim, & Teixeira, 1998 for a good summary of the issues). On the one hand, research suggests that there has been a de-skilling of the workforce as the workplace has been mechanized. De-skilling breaks down the work process so that specific tasks become more repetitive. In essence, there are fewer skills required to perform these tasks. These types of jobs are more likely to be located in rural than in urban areas.

On the other hand, competition for low-skilled workers has left more skilled workers in rural areas (Gibbs, Kusmin, & Cromartie, 2004). Jobs not requiring skilled workers are most likely to be shifted to other low-cost areas. These regions have a supply of workers willing to work at low wages. Technological change also reduces the demand for many of the low-skilled jobs, especially in the manufacturing sector.

Overall, the evidence suggests that both processes may be occurring, but the net outcome is a higher percentage of skilled jobs that remain in rural areas. Technology upgrades the skills of some jobs, while de-skilling others. As some jobs are de-skilled, they are more likely to be lost to low-cost areas with more unskilled workers. The composition of jobs in rural areas, then, shifts to relatively more skilled positions.

## Workforce Development Strategies

Policies intended to improve rural jobs have generally emphasized either the supply- or demand-side of the labor market. By far, supply-side programs have been the favored approaches in the U.S. (Bartik, 2001). Supply-side approaches point to increased labor productivity as the key to increasing profits and wages. Labor market policies usually consider education and training programs as the primary mechanisms for increasing productivity. The federal government has established a plethora of programs intended to support increased worker training. Many of these programs are not strongly tied to the local demand for skills. As a result, workers may not be trained for the types of jobs that are available in the area. These training programs also tend to be fragmented, spread out across various agencies and departments. Finally, because most of these programs are directed at specific populations (such as displaced workers), there is very little flexibility in how these funds can be used.

It is difficult to provide job training programs in rural areas. Educational and training institutions in rural areas offer a much more limited curriculum than do urban institutions. In rural areas, training can be more costly because of the small scale of most programs and the relatively weak demand for specific positions. For example, to set up an apprenticeship program in a rural community college for electricians is more costly because there are fixed costs associated with these programs regardless of the number of students. Finally, rural workers may receive training, but move to urban areas where there are more job opportunities. Thus, rural areas may bear the costs of training many workers for urban jobs. This situation creates disincentives for rural communities to invest a great deal in job training and post-high-school educational programs unless it is subsidized by state or federal governments.

Demand-side approaches focus on job creation as the primary means of improving opportunities in labor markets. These policies include wage subsides to employers for hiring new workers or economic development incentives to firms to locate in rural areas. Research suggests that demand-size policies can generally be more effective than supply-side approaches (Bartik, 2001). There are, however, some serious concerns with these policies. Subsidies to employers may have little impact on their actual hiring decisions. The employers may be planning to hire additional workers even without the subsidy, so there is a net loss of government funds for these programs. Increased competition for capital investment has led to an "arms race" for economic development that has raised the level of subsidies to businesses to the point that there are questions about the extent to which these policies make good economic sense (Fleischmann, Green, & Kwong, 1992). The evidence that these policies have a direct impact on job creation remains mixed (Green, Fleischmann, & Kwong, 1996).

In rural areas, demand-side policies are often not matched well with the supply of workers, so employers may face difficulty in finding skilled workers to fill positions. Employers are often forced to recruit skilled workers outside the region, which does not have the intended impact for local workers or the economy.

A growing body of literature points to the importance of workforce development networks in the functioning of rural labor markets and as an alternative to demand- and supply-side policies (Green, 2007). Workforce development is more than training. It involves the set of activities from orientation to the work world, recruiting, placement, and mentoring to follow-up counseling and crisis intervention (Harrison & Weiss, 1998, 5). The primary objective is to provide stronger linkages between the supply- and demand-sides of the labor market. Workforce development networks also help prepare workers for entry into the labor market by emphasizing "soft skills" that many employers report are lacking in their workforce (Holzer, 1996).

Workforce development networks influence the functioning of the labor market in several ways. First, networks increase the information available to both employers and workers. Employers generally lack good information about the productivity of job applicants. As a result, employers often rely on credentials or other signals about the potential productivity of workers. Networks improve the information about the work ethic of potential hires and provide the specific types of skills required by employers (Holzer, 1996). Workers obtain information on the availability of jobs in the area through networks. Most workers find jobs through their informal networks, so improving the flow of information will make job searches more effective, especially for minority workers (Granovetter, 1974).

Second, workforce development networks address a critical problem in many rural labor markets—floundering. Floundering refers to the tendency for young workers entering the labor market to go through multiple jobs in a short time span. One of the explanations for this phenomenon is that these workers lack adequate information about existing jobs. Workforce development networks often create school-to-work and apprenticeship programs that are designed to provide young workers with more information and to reduce the high turnover rates during this period (Green, Galetto, & Haines, 2003).

Third, many rural employers fail to invest in their workforce through additional training. The primary reason for this lack of investment is the fear of losing workers to another employer after they are trained. It is essentially a collective action problem. All employers have an interest in raising the skills of workers, but individual employers are reluctant to take on that expense. Workforce development networks address these concerns by establishing collaborative training efforts. These collaborative networks provide training for similar skill needs, and thereby minimize the collective action problem faced by employers (Green et al., 2003). Although this sounds promising, these collaborations are often more difficult to create and maintain (Green & Galetto, 2005). This is because there are fewer employers in the region with similar training needs, and there are few opportunities for employer associations or other collaborative efforts in rural areas as well.

Traditional supply- and demand-side policies are challenged in rural areas. It is more difficult to link labor supply and demand in rural areas. The low population density and thin labor market create some unique obstacles. Institutional changes are needed to more adequately address these obstacles in rural areas.

## Green Jobs

The concept of a green economy suggests that it is possible to create good jobs and protect the environment at the same time (Green & Dane, 2010). In recent years, businesses have begun to recognize the shift in consumer preferences toward products that are less harmful to the environment. Likewise, entrepreneurs are developing new green products and services. Millions of new green jobs will be created, so the argument goes, ranging from renewable energy installers to mass transit employees, from sustainability analysts to water resource technicians. Many of the jobs are blue-collar in nature, and they may provide pathways out of poverty for low-skilled, low-income earners (Jones, 2008).

The green economy may offer unique opportunities for rural communities. Most renewable natural resources are located in rural areas and there are economic benefits to locating firms near these resources. Green jobs that are most likely to grow in rural areas will be in the following sectors:

1. *Renewable Energy.* Renewable energy is growing rapidly as an alternative to fossil fuel usage. Renewable energy includes wind, solar, biofuels, geothermal, and hydropower. It is seen as a significant generator of green-collar jobs both in terms of manufacturing and in design, installation, and servicing of the systems themselves. Most of the investments in this area are in wind (43%) and photovoltaic cells (30%). Most of the interest in biofuels has been in sustainable approaches that focus on fast-growing switch grasses and tree species that are harvested quickly. Communities can promote renewable energy development through conventional means such as offering tax incentives, credits, and other mechanisms to encourage renewable energy manufacturing in their own backyards. They can also develop creative financing mechanisms that provide incentives to homeowners and businesses to deploy renewable energy on site.

2. *Energy Efficiency and Green Buildings.* The jobs related to energy efficiency are often concentrated in traditional building trades and construction industries. The jobs related to green buildings include green construction jobs, sustainability analysts, planners specializing in brownfield redevelopment, and other development professionals with green design experience. Estimates suggest that about ten jobs are created per $1 million investment in high-performance buildings (Center on Wisconsin Strategy, 2007). Energy efficiency jobs may offer the potential for creating the largest number of green-collar jobs.

3. *Smart Grid.* The current electrical grid is widely seen as a barrier to achieving significant improvements in both energy efficiency and renewable energy growth. The system prevents the full deployment of wind, for example, because the transmission lines simply do not exist to connect our nation's largely rural high plains wind resource to our urban population centers. The grid is also highly localized and disjointed which prevents the effective movement of power throughout the country when demand exceeds supply in a given region. A Smart Grid would provide a system for relaying information on the demand, supply, and price of electrical power as well. Jobs associated with a Smart Grid would likely encompass a broad range of occupations including system designers, project developers, marketers, public relations, supply chain managers, and several types of field technicians.

4. *Environmental Management.* Included in this sector would be many technologies that directly benefit the natural environment, including water, solid and hazardous waste, and air quality technologies among others.

The transition to a green economy in rural areas, however, faces numerous obstacles. First, green-collar jobs will require additional training programs. In some cases, training programs are already in place, and will simply need to be revised for these new jobs. For example, training programs for heating systems and mechanics will need to provide additional training on new equipment. In other places, it may be possible to develop new regional collaborations to provide training for green-collar jobs. This may be difficult for rural areas because of the expense of training a relatively small number of workers.

Second, training programs for the trades have had a difficult time recruiting young workers into these fields. Green-collar training programs may face some of the same problems. School-to-work and apprenticeship programs have had some success in recruiting young workers into these types of positions.

Third, green jobs programs have been advanced primarily through federal and state programs. Tax incentives for businesses and consumers have been the primary means of encouraging energy-savings efforts. There is considerable concern that green jobs would not be created without these government programs. David Goldstein (2007), however, presents evidence indicating that investments in energy savings have between a 10 and 50% return for businesses and consumers (without government incentives). Thus, it would appear that it makes good economic sense for businesses and consumers to make these investments.

Additional educational programs are needed to overcome some of the initial opposition and concerns with these investments.

Overall, the shift to a green economy will provide new opportunities for job growth in rural areas. The basic questions that need to be answered concern how many jobs will be created and what is the appropriate role for the government in the green economy. Most estimates suggest that green-collar jobs are relatively small in number at this time (Pinderhughes, 2007). It will be difficult to generate enough green-collar jobs to replace many of the extractive and manufacturing jobs in rural areas that have been lost over the past few decades. Second, there will continue to be debate over how the government should promote green job creation. Tax policies will be critical in encouraging businesses and households to become more energy efficient. Goldstein (2007) argues that regulations promoting greater efficiency may have the greatest impact. These regulations not only save energy, but they often create innovation that is so critical to the green economy.

The potential for green jobs exists not only for developed countries, but many developing countries may benefit from this transition as well. Promotion of renewable energy sources may have an especially important impact on creation of nonfarm jobs in these regions.

## Prospects for Rural Jobs

Rural areas face numerous obstacles in promoting economic and workforce development. Population size and density are critical problems that are difficult to overcome. On the supply-side, it is increasingly expensive to train and educate the workforce in rural settings for 21st century jobs. Improved technology and communication have not yet resolved these issues in most areas. Rural areas also tend to have an older workforce and tend to lose many young, educated workers who migrate to urban areas. An older workforce may reduce the likelihood that individuals will invest in additional training. Rural areas with high levels of out-migration may be concerned about investing in education and training because the workers do not stay in the region. The aging workforce in rural areas makes it less attractive to employers that require a skilled and productive workforce. On the demand-side, innovative firms continue to prefer to locate in urban areas where they have better access to skilled workers, markets, and services they will require. Many nonfarm industries need a better infrastructure than is available in most rural areas.

The growth of green jobs, combined with innovative workforce development strategies, offers new hope for rural areas. The success of workforce development efforts in rural areas will depend on several key factors. Employer participation is critical. Many state and federal training programs have failed to sufficiently link employer demand to programs. Manufacturing employers often consider their training needs are unique. Small firms typically are concerned that the programs only benefit the larger firms that are able to pay higher wages to attract the skilled workforce. These obstacles can be overcome by developing institutional arrangements, such as career ladders, which create a "win-win" solution for most actors involved in the workforce development networks. Career ladders create paths of mobility within the local labor market. If low-wage workers obtain training and job experience, they have access to better paying jobs that require more training and skills. These systems help the smaller firms hold on to workers and reduces their costly turnover rates. Larger firms have improved access to a skilled and trained workforce. The most successful workforce development efforts in rural areas tend to work through existing organizations and institutions (Green, 2007). These organizations and institutions have access to other local resources, as well as good information on job opportunities and workers. Successful workforce development networks recognize the need to address a broader set of issues than just job training. Workers face numerous obstacles related to child care, transportation, and housing. Many younger workers need additional support with time management, financial counseling, and basic "soft" skills.

A key to promoting the green economy in rural areas is to link economic and workforce development programs more effectively to the demand-side of labor markets. Additional incentives and programs at the state and federal level need to target the special needs of rural areas in developing the renewable energy and energy efficiency sectors, as well as building a smart grid that will enable new sources of energy to be transmitted to urban areas. Finally, green-collar programs need to be more tightly integrated with workforce development networks to provide stronger linkages between the demand and supply of labor in local areas.

The prospects for rural labor markets in developing countries are markedly different to those in developed countries, but they share some of the same obstacles and opportunities. Nonfarm development is critical to provide job opportunities and to stem the flow of migrants into the cities. The experience of China of indirectly encouraging rural-to-urban migration as part of the development process illustrates the concerns with this growth model. Rural areas have been gutted of young workers, while cities have experienced many of the social problems associated with rapid growth. Expansion of nonfarm development activities will depend largely on renewable energy sources and a more skilled workforce.

**Acknowledgements** This research was supported by the College of Agriculture and Life Sciences, University of Wisconsin Agricultural Experiment Station, Hatch Project #WIS01510.

## References

Bartik, T. J. (2001). *Jobs for the poor: Can labor demand policies help?* New York: Russell Sage Foundation.

Bluestone, B., & Harrison, B. (1982). *The deindustrialization of America: Plant closings, community abandonment, and the dismantling of basic industry*. New York: Basic Books, Inc.

Bureau of Economic Analysis. (2009). *Regional footnotes. Regional economic information system*. US Department of Commerce. Retrieved December 3, 2009, from http://www.bea.gov/regional/docs/footnotes.cfm?tablename=CA25N.

Center on Wisconsin Strategy. (2007). *Milwaukee retrofit: Capturing home energy savings in Milwaukee*. Retrieved January 20, 2010, from http://www.cows.org/pdf/bp-milwaukeeretrofit_050807.pdf.

Cohen, S. S., & Zysman, J. (1987). *Manufacturing matters: The myth of the post-industrial economy*. New York: Basic Books, Inc.

Fleischmann, A., Green, G. P., & Kwong, T. M. (1992). What's a city to do? Explaining differences in local economic development policies. *Western Political Quarterly, 45*, 677–699.

Freeman, R. (1985). *What do unions do?* New York: Basic Books.

Fuguitt, G. V., Brown, D. L., & Beale, C. L. (1989). *Rural and small town America*. New York: Russell Sage Foundation.

Gibbs, R., Kusmin, L., & Cromartie, J. (2004). Low-skill jobs: A shrinking share of the rural economy. Amber Waves (November). Retrieved December 17, 2009 from http://www.ers.usda.gov/AmberWaves/November04/Features/lowskilljobs.htm.

Gibbs, R. M., Swaim, P. L., & Teixeira, R. (Eds.). (1998). *Rural education and training in the new economy: The myth of the rural skills gap*. Ames, IA: Iowa State University Press.

Goldstein, D. B. (2007). *Saving energy, growing jobs: How environmental protection promotes economic growth, profitability, innovation and competition*. Richmond, CA: Bay Tree Publishing.

Granovetter, M. (1974). *Getting a job: A study of contacts and careers*. Cambridge, MA: Harvard University Press.

Green, G. P. (2007). *Workforce development networks in rural areas: Building the high road*. Northampton, MA: Edward Elgar Publishing.

Green, G. P., & Dane, A. (2010). Green-collar jobs. In C. Laszio, D. S. Fogel, P. Whitehouse, K. Christensen, & G. Wagner (Eds.), *The business of sustainability* (pp. 251–255). Great Barrington, MA: Berkshire.

Green, G. P., Fleischmann, A., & Kwong, T. M. (1996). The effectiveness of local economic development policies in the 1980s. *Social Science Quarterly, 77*, 609–625.

Green, G. P., & Galetto, V. (2005). Employer participation in workforce development networks. *Economic Development Quarterly, 19*, 225–231.

Green, G. P., Galetto, V., & Haines, A. (2003). Collaborative job training in rural America. *Journal of Research in Rural Education, 18*, 78–85.

Green, G. P., & Sanchez, L. (2007). Does manufacturing still matter? *Population Research and Policy Review, 26*, 529–551.

Harrison, B., & Weiss, M. (1998). *Workforce development networks: Community-based organizations and regional alliances*. Thousand Oaks, CA: Sage.

Holzer, H. J. (1996). *What employers want: Job prospects for less-educated workers*. New York: Russell Sage Foundation.

Jones, V. (2008). *The green collar economy*. New York: HarperCollins Publishers.

Lanjouw, J. O., & Lanjouw, P. (2001). The rural non-farm sector: Issues and evidence from developing countries. *Agricultural Economics, 26*, 1–23.

Lichter, D. T. (1989). Race, employment hardship, and inequality in the American nonmetropolitan South. *American Sociological Review, 54*, 436–446.

Markusen, A. (1987). *Regions: The economics and politics of territory*. Totowa, NJ: Rowman and Littlefield.

Marsden, T., Lowe, P., & Whatmore, S. (1992). *Labour and locality: Uneven development and the rural labour process*. London: David Fulton Press.

McGranahan, D. (1999). *Natural amenities drive rural population change*. Washington, DC: Economic Research Service, U.S. Department of Agriculture.

Pinderhughes, R. (2007). Green collar jobs: An analysis of the capacity of green businesses to provide high quality jobs for men and women with barriers to employment. Retrieved January 20, 2009, from http://www.greenforall.org/resources/An-Analysis-of-the-Capacity-of-Green-Businesses-to.

Summers, G. F., Evans, S. D., Clemente, F., Beck, E. M., & Minkoff, J. (1976). *Industrial invasion of nonmetropolitan America: A quarter century of experience*. New York: Praeger Publishers.

Teixeira, R., & McGranahan, D. A. (1998). Rural employer demand and worker skills. In R. M. Gibbs, P. L. Swaim, & R. Teixeira (Eds.), *Rural education and training in the new economy: The myth of the rural skills gap* (pp. 115–129). Ames, IA: Iowa State University Press.

Tigges, L. M., & Fuguitt, G. (2003). Commuting: A good job close by? In D. L. Brown & L. E. Swanson (Eds.), *Challenges for rural America in the twenty-first century* (pp. 166–176). University Park, PA: Penn State University Press.

United Nations. (2009). *National accounts main aggregated database.* Retrieved December 3, 2009, from http://unstats.un.org/unsd/

# The Spatial Heterogeneity and Geographic Extent of Population Deconcentration: Measurement and Policy Implications

Joanna P. Ganning and Benjamin D. McCall

## Introduction

At least since von Thunen published *Isolated State* in 1826 (1966), researchers have studied mechanisms of population growth at the urban-rural fringe. The body of modern theory began to develop in earnest in the 1970s (e.g., Berry, 1970). The 1980s saw the theoretical development of spread-backwash theory (i.e., Gaile, 1980) and deconcentration/restructuring theories (e.g., Frey, 1993), with which this chapter is concerned. By the early 1990s, more descriptive, data-driven work elucidated the mechanisms of household and firm relocation to the urban fringe (e.g., Clark & Kuijpers-Linde, 1994). Soon thereafter, more predictive models of deconcentration and restructuring were developed (e.g., Renkow & Hoover, 2000), adding to the growing theory that urban fringe locations develop first by household relocation, with firm location following.

Scholars have continued to expand and refine this research by studying variation in growth patterns found internationally and within different demographic segments of the population. For example, research finds that while urban land conversion associated with population deconcentration is significantly higher in the United States than elsewhere, population growth at the urban-rural fringe is occurring in both "more developed" and "less developed" countries worldwide (e.g., Schneider & Woodcock, 2007). Additionally, life course stage affects migration patterns along the urban hierarchy (e.g., Plane, Henrie, & Perry, 2005). The continued improvement of deconcentration models expands demographic research by more precisely explaining the intricacies of population change in transitioning urban, rural, and suburban places.

Since 2000, scholars have re-popularized place-based economic development policies, primarily for isolated rural locations (e.g., Partridge & Rickman, 2006). Simultaneously, econometric modeling and policy research have focused on transportation, technology, infrastructure, and commuting-based development strategies for urban fringe locations with substantial linkages to the urban core (e.g., Renkow, 2003). The conclusions of this research favor policies managing or encouraging growth regionally (Partridge, Bollman, Olfert, & Alasia, 2007). Between these studies lie places neither geographically isolated nor significantly tied to central cities. As shown in this chapter, these counties sometimes neighbor metropolitan areas and experience suburbanization with the metropolitan counties at the same or at varying degrees of intensity or magnitude; sometimes these counties truly fall outside the geographic range of suburbanization.

This chapter focuses on these places by creating a model of deconcentration and restructuring reflecting spatial heterogeneity in regional growth around Chicago, IL, USA. This is accomplished by constructing a traditional Ordinary Least Squares (OLS) model of deconcentration, then using the coefficients from a Geographically Weighted Regression (GWR) to derive subregions within the study area. These subregions are incorporated into the OLS model, allowing measurement of the variation in and the spatial extent of deconcentration across the region. The results of

J.P. Ganning (✉)
Department of Public Policy Studies, Saint Louis University, Saint Louis, MO 63103, USA
e-mail: jganning@slu.edu

this model are used to inform a discussion of rural and regional development policy for the United States, Canada, and Europe, the predominant sites of related studies. Since any temporal difference in movement to the periphery between firms and households must be accommodated through commuting, commuting is the lens through which deconcentration and restructuring are analyzed.

The remainder of this chapter follows in five sections. The following section provides background literature on the hypotheses of deconcentration and restructuring. The section entitled "Chicago, IL MSA Study Region" gives an overview of the study region and the components of its growth between 1990 and 2000. The form of the econometric analysis and background on the data and methods are provided in the section "Econometric Analysis". The results section follows. Overall, the model shows spatial heterogeneity in the mechanism of deconcentration and a spatial extent that reaches beyond MSA boundaries. The final section discusses the policy implications.

## Background

This section provides an overview of the literature on the theories of deconcentration and restructuring and popular metrics for their measurement. This literature supports the hypothesis that deconcentration and restructuring vary in magnitude across a region.

## Deconcentration and Restructuring

Though they focus primarily on the role of information technology, Audirac and Fitzgerald (2003) provide an excellent overview of the concepts of deconcentration and restructuring. This review draws heavily on the sources identified there, including direct quotations to introduce each term.

As Audirac and Fitzgerald introduce it, "In the deconcentration group...we find works in the human ecology tradition of urban sociology and microeconomic neoclassical approaches in location decision theories" (2003, p. 482). This theory is straightforward: technology and infrastructure reduce the cost of travel and communication, allowing households to move to the periphery of a region. Peripheral areas afford larger lots and homes with the full range of bucolic amenities (Rouwendal & Meijer, 2001). Brian Berry (1970) was among the earliest scholars to discuss deconcentration. He posited its development on the compression of time (see also Fishman, 1990) and space, as permitted by technology, and the mobility of social classes, which would lead to increased education attainment and mobility. At its root, deconcentration stems from atomistic decision making about commuting, lifestyle amenities, and access to employment.

Conversely, the restructuring school "has its intellectual roots in Marxist political economy and regulation theories....Since theories in this school are vastly heterogeneous, it can simply be said that they emphasize economic and spatial restructuring resulting from (1) technological change, which is the result of, and the transformational force affecting, the (capitalist) mode of production, and (2) the role of the state in shaping the conditions for economic growth (capital accumulation)" (Audirac & Fitzgerald, 2003, p. 483). One of the more consistent themes in the restructuring literature is the transformation of the urban hierarchy from one based on global ports to one based on global centers of command and control with the spatial dispersion of standardized or "less intellectual" (Storper, 1997) activities and back-office functions (Audirac & Fitzgerald, 2003; Coffey & Bailly, 1992; Sassen, 1994, 2002; Scott, 1988). Unlike the deconcentration literature, restructuring studies "reflect the regulation regimes and the interests of corporate and public-sector actors" (Audirac & Fitzgerald, 2003, p. 484).

A popular conceptual measurement for deconcentration and restructuring is the relationship between in-migration and out-commuting within a jurisdiction (usually the county). A positive relationship between in-migration and out-commuting is called "complementarity"; the inverse is "substitution" (Evers, 1989; Renkow & Hoover, 2000). Conceptually, if households are moving into counties and continuing to work elsewhere (complementarity), deconcentration is occurring. Periphery lifestyle amenities have outweighed commuting costs. Households moving into counties to replace commuting to those counties (substitution), are following corporate spatial movement decisions. Complementarity and substitution are conceptual measurements for the theoretical constructs of deconcentration and restructuring.

In constructing typologies, academics group observations to allow analysis of empirical data. Although productive, categorization of observations obscures within-group variability. In reality, deconcentration and restructuring (and complementarity and substitution) happen simultaneously within regions; as discrete concepts they are the polar ends of a spectrum of more plausible scenarios. Even while population deconcentration may dominate regional expansion, some households move nearer to work and some firms move into unsettled areas. Classifying a region as deconcentrating or restructuring as a whole masks the heterogeneity within the region.

Theoretically, there are many hybrid perspectives. Deconcentration and restructuring can be seen as simultaneous results of the interaction of information technology and development (Amirahmadi & Wallace, 1995). Deconcentration suggests that workers move to the suburbs for lifestyle amenities (e.g., Hirschorn, 2000). Restructuring argues that corporations move for profit gains. A hybrid theory suggests that while the New Economy catalyzes the spatial reorganization of metropolitan companies, some firms move to the periphery for the lifestyle amenities (Beyers, 2000), an atomistic approach to corporate decision making (see also Henton & Walesh, 1998). Spatial variation in lifestyle amenities and infrastructure provision are only two examples of the many potential forces suggesting the theoretical spatial heterogeneity of deconcentration and restructuring.

## Chicago, IL MSA Study Region

This paper focuses on the Chicago-Naperville-Joliet CMSA plus its surrounding nonmetropolitan counties (Fig. 22.1). Only the smallest selection of counties surrounding Chicago excludes counties with obvious linkages to at least one other MSA. The selection shown in Fig. 22.1 extends far enough from Chicago to be bounded by smaller MSAs to which the Chicago fringe counties likely have linkages. Including these counties provides a coherent view of the relationship between commuting and migration for counties at the urban fringe outside Chicago. The sample extends roughly 110 miles outward from Chicago. Of the 65 counties in the region, 12 are in the Chicago CMSA, five are in the Milwaukee-Racine, WI CMSA, and 15 are spread across another 11 MSAs. In addition to Chicago's economic engine, each of these MSAs exerts growth effects, potentially including population deconcentration.

The region's outlying metropolitan counties grew the fastest by a wide margin between 1990 and 2000, at 17.0% (Table 22.1). Through the 1990s, four counties in the study region converted from nonmetropolitan to "outlying metropolitan" status. The fastest-growing county in the region (McHenry, IL), converted from "outlying metropolitan" to "central metropolitan" status over the decade. Of the ten fastest-growing counties in the region, four were central metropolitan, four were outlying metropolitan, and two were nonmetropolitan in 1990. These trends resemble the national experience, where suburban population growth outpaced central city growth between 1990 and 2000 (Pisarski, 2006). Figure 22.2 shows population change by county over this period. The strongest growth occurred to the west of Chicago and north into Wisconsin. Interestingly, while Chicago maintained its rank as the third largest city in the U.S. over the decade, the region as a whole and most counties in it (45 of 65) grew slower than the nation, which grew by 13.2% over the decade.

Across the study region between 1990 and July 1999, the population grew by 1,245,416 net people through natural growth (births minus deaths) and lost 66,206 people on net via migration. The region lost over half a million people (net of −500,824) via domestic migration and gained (on net) 434,618 through international migration. Though these sources of change and their magnitudes seem surprising, they are not unusual; this pattern occurred in the eight largest U.S. cities between 1995 and 2000 (Pisarski, 2006). In megacities, the net migration rate is positive only in the age bracket 25–29 years, indicating the role of household formation and childbearing on regional demographic change (Plane et al., 2005). Evidence of lifecycle-related movement up and down the urban hierarchy appears in the fact that households moving into Chicago in the 1990s were smaller and earned less than households moving out of the Chicago MSA (Yu, 2009). Traditionally, young individuals or couples move to the city, start building careers and families, then out-migrate with higher incomes and larger households than when they arrived. Consequently, the roles of migration and commuting at the urban-rural fringe become increasingly important metrics for mechanisms of regional growth.

Given the empirical support for the theory of deconcentration over regional restructuring (e.g., Renkow & Hoover, 2000), it may seem likely that much of

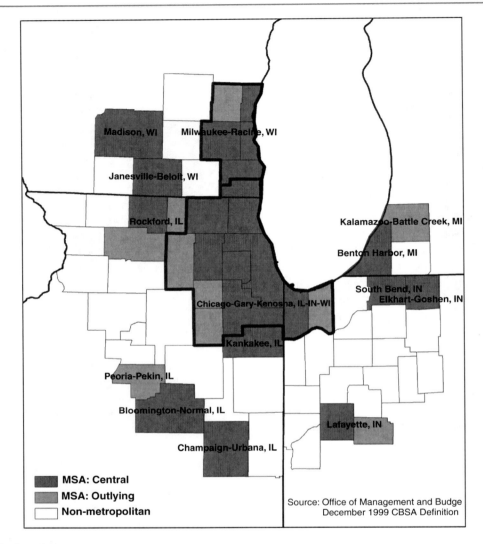

**Fig. 22.1** Study region

**Table 22.1** Population growth in the study region, 1990–2000

| County type | # of counties[a] | 1990 population | 2000 population | Percent change |
|---|---|---|---|---|
| Nonmetropolitan | 33 | 1,287,551 | 1,361,166 | 5.7 |
| Outlying metropolitan | 10 | 584,392 | 683,755 | 17.0 |
| Central metropolitan | 22 | 11,230,000 | 12,348,884 | 10.0 |
| All study counties | 65 | 13,101,943 | 14,393,805 | 9.9 |

[a] Using Office of Management and Budget 1999 definition.

the spatial expansion of economic activity is done through commuting. Yet this is only part of the picture. An analysis of Bureau of Labor Statistics, Quarterly Census of Employment and Wages data from 1990 and 2000 shows strong growth in the number of business establishments across the region, with the strongest growth in the outlying metropolitan counties (Table 22.2; using Office of Management and Budget [OMB] 1999 definitions). Growth in the number of private establishments actually outpaced population

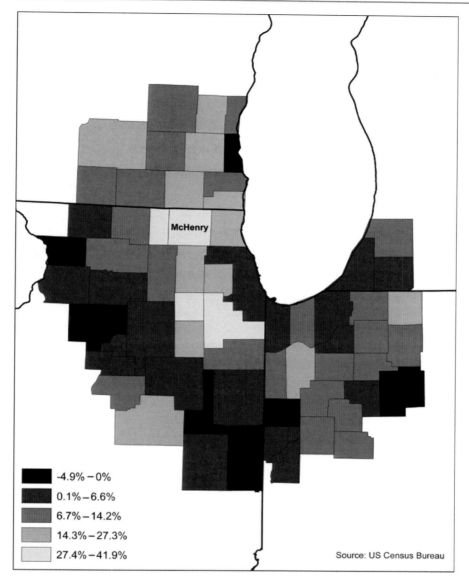

**Fig. 22.2** County population change, 1990–2000

**Table 22.2** Number of establishments by county type, 1990–2000

| County type | Establishments in 1990 | Establishments in 2000 | Percentage change |
| --- | --- | --- | --- |
| Nonmetropolitan | 27,621 | 31,477 | 14.0 |
| Outlying metropolitan | 10,789 | 14,707 | 36.3 |
| Central metropolitan | 244,623 | 305,628 | 24.9 |

growth in each of the three types of counties. Although previous research (and the conclusions of the analysis herein) find deconcentration rather than restructuring, clearly business movement toward the periphery influences regional growth.

Bureau of Economic Analysis data demonstrates the magnitude of the economic consequences of commuting. Residents of the region who commuted outside their home county (to counties within or outside the region) earned nearly $92.9 billion, moving that money into the home county. Workers commuting to a county within the region (though not necessarily living in the region) moved nearly $94 billion across county lines (Bureau of Economic Analysis, REIS, Table CA91). It is critical for municipalities to analyze commuting to capture more of that multibillion dollar practice.

## Econometric Analysis

Deconcentration theory posits that with decreasing transportation costs, people can afford more land, and so choose to commute to work. In restructuring, industry faces changing economic constraints and opportunities that motivate increased distance from the central city; workers follow (Audirac & Fitzgerald, 2003; Clark & Kuijpers-Linde, 1994; Renkow & Hoover, 2000). The deconcentration/restructuring model investigates the relationship between commuting and migration in a county at one point in time. Simultaneous out-commuting and in-migration indicate that deconcentration has occurred.

Using Renkow and Hoover (2000) as a starting point, the ability to out-commute from a county is assumed to face budget constraints where household earnings cannot exceed household expenditures, including commuting costs. Therefore, net commuting is modeled as a function of net migration and the following budget constraints: wage differential, housing cost differential, educational attainment differential, and distance. The econometric model uses county-county pairs as the unit of analysis, with the data lending itself to conclusions at that level of geography. Importantly, this deconcentration/restructuring model varies from a household location model, which would include all varieties of locational and housing amenities.

Equation (22.1) gives the empirical form, with the variable definitions and data sources following in Table 22.3.

The empirical form given is

$$C_{ij} = f(M_i, W_{ij}, D_{ij}, H_{ij}, E_{ij}) \quad (22.1)$$

Where

$C_{ij}$ = net number of workers commuting from county $i$ to county $j$, normalized by the employed population of county $i$

$M_i$ = net migration into county $i$ in the previous period, normalized by the population in county $i$ in the previous period

$W_{ij}$ = wage in county $j$ minus wage in county $i$ (*1000)

$D_{ij}$ = distance between counties $i$ and $j$, using population-weighted centroids

$H_{ij}$ = standardized housing cost in county $j$ minus county $i$

$E_{ij}$ = four-year college degree attainment rate in county $j$ minus county $i$

Net commuting is normalized by the employed population of county $i$ to scale the value of commuting. The wage, distance, and housing variables are included as significant budget constraints in the decision to migrate or commute. The wage data represents wages at the place of employment rather than residence. This figure is the relevant one in modeling commuting since people commute to earn a wage offered somewhere other than the home county. College education attainment includes all county residents 25+ who have

**Table 22.3** Variables for geographically weighted regression

| Variable | Definition | Source |
|---|---|---|
| $C_{ij}$ | Net commuting from county $i$ to county $j$, standardized by the employed population of county $i$ | Census 2000b |
| $M_i$ | Net migration into county $i$ in the previous year, normalized by population in the previous year | IRS county-to-county migration tables, 1998–1999 |
| $W_{ij}$ | Difference in wages between county $i$ and county $j$ (*1000) | Bureau of Economic Analysis, 2000 |
| $D_{ij}$ | Distance between counties $i$ and $j$, with distance measured from the block group population-weighted centroid of each county | Census 2000a, and ArcMap 9.3 |
| $H_{ij}$ | Difference in the Fair Market Rent of a 2-bedroom apartment between county $i$ and county $j$ | HUD Fair Market Rent |
| $E_{ij}$ | Difference in four-year college degree attainment rates between county $i$ and county $j$ | Census 2000a |

earned a four-year degree or higher; those with some college or associates degrees are not counted as having attained a four year degree. The difference in educational attainment provides a crude measure of skill mismatch between counties, since labor demand is often skill-specific.

Finally, rather than using the difference in median housing costs for all units between counties, HUD's Fair Market Rent statistics (Department of Housing and Urban Development, 2000) allow an estimate of the difference in housing costs for similar units. This marks a departure from the literature, where traditionally housing prices have been compared across geographic units at the median, without respect to characteristics (e.g., McMillen, 2004a). Using Fair Market Rents allows a control for the size and general quality of housing units. This is important considering the key demographic that moves into and out of megacities—young people and new households, respectively. Housing units of equal price in a central city and a suburb or smaller city are unequal, with unit size being one of several key distinctions (Pisarski, 2006). Housing size needs present budget constraints in residential location choices.

This paper relies primarily on three databases: the U.S. Census of Population and Housing (2000a), the U.S. Census Transportation Planning Package (Census, 2000b), and migration data from the Internal Revenue Service (IRS, 1990–2000). The county is the unit of analysis for two primary reasons. First, though the Census databases provide information for a finer level of geography, the IRS files are available only at the county level. Additionally, CTPP commuter flow data contains a trade-off between spatial resolution and data disclosure. In densely populated areas, data nondisclosure is minimal; however, in regions inclusive of less densely settled areas, nondisclosure below the county level inhibits analysis.

Additionally, to reduce the error in estimated distance traveled for commuters between counties $i$ and $j$, block group population for 2000 was used to estimate the population-weighted centroid for each county. In some counties, large portions of the population live around a dominant town or city, which may or may not be in the center of the county. Thus, the population-weighted centroids are more likely to be closer to the points of origin and destination for commuters than are the geographic centroids of the counties. The full range of regression variables by data source used is given in Table 22.3.

The econometric analysis is completed in four stages. In the first stage, an OLS regression is carried out to create a baseline for comparison to the literature and against which to interpret the subsequent model. In stage two, the initial model is converted to a GWR. In stage three, a clustering algorithm uses the GWR coefficients to define subregions in the study area. Finally, dummy variables for the subregions are interacted with the variables in the empirical specification and re-tested via OLS to test the hypotheses that deconcentration varies with space and has a spatial limit beyond the MSA border. Although the analysis ultimately relies on a standard spatial regime approach, the definition of subregions incorporates an original application of the GWR method. The use of regimes provides a proxy for spatial heterogeneity.

Observations include the set of $ij$ county pairs that had nonzero net commuting. The set includes only the observations with positive net commuting, as is established in the literature to avoid selection bias (Renkow & Hoover, 2000). Finally, non-neighboring $ij$ pairs were excluded (using a second-order, first-order inclusive, queen weights matrix). Invoking a spatial limit helps to eliminate observations with commute flows so small as to be within a reasonable margin of error. The final sample size is 388 $ij$ pairs. As its dependent variable, the model uses the log of net commuting to ensure linearity.

## Geographically Weighted Regression (GWR)

Within $R$, the function gwr.sel (spgwr) assisted in the selection of the GWR bandwidth, which is 94012.66 m. On average, this bandwidth covers 13.7 counties including county $i$. GWR is a technique used "to examine the spatial variability of regression results across a region and so inform on the presence of spatial nonstationarity" (Fotheringham, Charlton, & Brunsdon, 1998, p. 1907). Its general form, GWR can be expressed as:

$$y_i = a_0 + \sum a_k(u_i, v_i)x_{ik} + \varepsilon_i \qquad (22.2)$$

where $u$ and $v$ are coordinates of the $i$th point, allowing a continuous surface of parameter values. This technique produces localized regression diagnostics (Fotheringham et al., 1998). To allow calibration of the model, points nearer to point $i$ are given more weight in the estimation of the parameter value for point $i$,

$$\hat{a}(u_i, v_i) = \left[X^T W(u_i, v_i) X\right]^{-1} X^T W \cdot (u_i, v_i) y. \quad (22.3)$$

One technical consideration of this approach is that it is meant to model values at $i$. However, the dependent variable used in this paper is the commuting flow between $ij$ pairs of counties, meaning there are multiple data points for each sending county $i$. A hierarchical approach may be more ideal.[1] However, this paper uses GWR to delineate subregions on which to test the spatial heterogeneity of the mechanism of deconcentration, not as a positivistic, conclusion-drawing method. The statistical significance of subregions in the final specification is sufficient evidence that the GWR has functioned satisfactorily for the purpose of this research.

**Table 22.4** OLS results from basic model, 2000

|  | Coefficient | White s.e. | Significance |
|---|---|---|---|
| Constant | 2.0558 | 0.200339 | *** |
| Net migration | 0.2537 | 0.075471 | *** |
| Wage differential | 0.0746 | 0.014016 | *** |
| Distance | −0.1073 | 0.004524 | *** |
| Housing cost differential | 0.0050 | 0.000730 | *** |
| Education differential | 3.6396 | 0.804092 | *** |

Residual standard error: 1.232 on 382 degrees of freedom
Multiple $R$-squared: 0.6707, adjusted $R$-squared: 0.6664
$F$-statistic: 155.6 on 5 and 382 DF, $p$-value: < 2.2e−16
Significance code: ***$p < 0.01$

counties ($i$ of the $ij$ pairs) into six groups. The choice of six groups creates reasonably spatially coherent subregions in comparison to other numbers of clusters. Figure 22.3 shows the subregions created by running a fuzzy clustering algorithm (using $R$) on the GWR coefficients. Only 60 of the original 65 counties are shown here; the other five (including Cook County, IL) are not in the positive half of the net commuting relationship with any neighboring county and are not included here or in the following section (Table 22.5).

## Results

### Geographically Weighted Regression

The existing OLS model of commuting flows is robust and statistically significant. Not only do Renkow and Hoover (2000) report reasonable strength in their OLS models, but the straight OLS model of commuting near Chicago is strong (Table 22.4). These results are shown with White-corrected standard errors (White, 1980; $R$ code for White correction by Gianfranco Piras and provided by Kathy Baylis). The model did not show multicollinearity. The variables common to this and the Renkow and Hoover (2000) approach show the same signs, giving a measure of external validity.

The data was then modeled using GWR, the coefficients of which were used to cluster the sending

### Respecified OLS Model

Using the $ij$ county pairs in subregion one as the comparison group, dummy variables for each region were interacted with each of the independent variables and put into a new OLS regression model. Here again, $ij$ county pairs constitute the unit of analysis ($n = 388$). Results are given in Table 22.5. Table 22.5 elicits several conclusions that warrant interpretation and discussion, most notably: the spatial limits of deconcentration; the spatial heterogeneity of deconcentration; the consistency of signs across subregions; and the varying premium put on wages across space.

First, and perhaps most importantly, the model shows a spatial limit to deconcentration that is constrained yet reaches well beyond the MSA boundaries. The migration term shows statistical significance in two subregions, numbers four and six. Although these subregions most closely frame the Chicago and Milwaukee MSAs, more than half of their constituent counties lie outside MSA boundaries. Deconcentration occurs beyond the MSA, in a selection of outer-ring counties framing the region's major cities. In contrast, the more remote portions of the study area do not demonstrate deconcentration or restructuring;

---

[1] Certainly, other criticisms of GWR exist, most notably that it is appropriate only in cases where explanatory variables are linearly related to the dependent variable at specific locations (McMillen, 2004b). Additionally, the fixed weighting scheme used here to select the bandwidth is insensitive to variation in the density of data; the selection of a bandwidth must balance bias versus variance (Zimmerman, 2003).

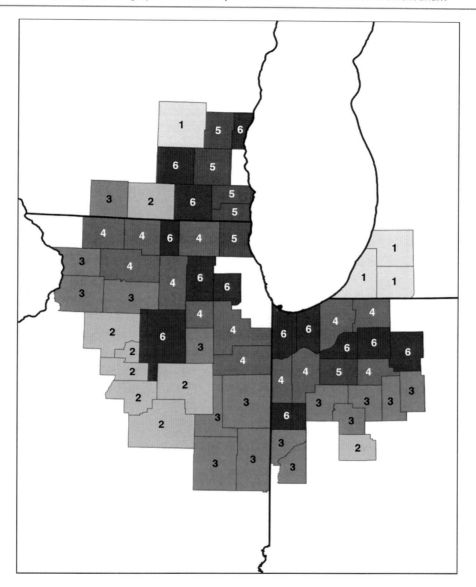

**Fig. 22.3** Subregions created by clustering the GWR coefficients

growth here occurs through alternate mechanisms such as employment growth in the home county rather than through commuting to either Chicago or peripheral, lower-tier cities. As found in Ali, Olfert, and Partridge (2010), there is spatial heterogeneity in growth mechanisms according to geography and placement along the urban hierarchy.

Second, the model shows spatial heterogeneity in the magnitude of deconcentration. Subregion six has a migration coefficient of 0.45, signaling stronger suburbanization when compared to subregion four's coefficient of 0.29. Relative to subregion four, subregion six more closely frames Chicago. Additionally, subregion six includes suburban Milwaukee. The difference in coefficients signals stronger suburbanization in subregion six, but may also signal that in-migrants in subregion four find employment more evenly through both commuting and the local economy; this suggests the possibility of growth in traditionally rural communities through partial suburban use.

Third, all independent variables show consistency of signs across subregions. This provides a measure of

**Table 22.5** OLS output with subregional dummies

| | Subregion | Coefficient | White s.e. | Significance |
|---|---|---|---|---|
| Constant | | 1.1765 | 0.2542 | *** |
| Net in-migration | 2 | 0.1193 | 0.3433 | |
| | 3 | −0.0726 | 0.2639 | |
| | 4 | 0.2860 | 0.1328 | ** |
| | 5 | 0.5995 | 0.3836 | |
| | 6 | 0.4492 | 0.1542 | *** |
| Wage differential | 2 | 0.0146 | 0.0374 | |
| | 3 | 0.0150 | 0.0251 | |
| | 4 | 0.1022 | 0.0291 | *** |
| | 5 | 0.1950 | 0.0523 | *** |
| | 6 | 0.1030 | 0.0274 | *** |
| Distance | 2 | −0.0809 | 0.0077 | *** |
| | 3 | −0.0895 | 0.0058 | *** |
| | 4 | −0.0915 | 0.0062 | *** |
| | 5 | −0.0866 | 0.0074 | *** |
| | 6 | −0.0940 | 0.0068 | *** |
| Housing cost differential | 2 | 0.0013 | 0.0018 | |
| | 3 | 0.0060 | 0.0013 | *** |
| | 4 | 0.0044 | 0.0014 | *** |
| | 5 | 0.0024 | 0.0034 | |
| | 6 | 0.0072 | 0.0019 | *** |
| Education differential | 2 | 5.5182 | 2.0988 | *** |
| | 3 | 4.9199 | 1.3227 | *** |
| | 4 | 4.5608 | 1.7430 | *** |
| | 5 | 0.1030 | 2.8329 | |
| | 6 | 2.7635 | 1.9197 | |

Residual standard error: 1.356 on 362 degrees of freedom
Multiple $R$-squared: 0.6223, Adjusted $R$-squared: 0.5962
$F$-statistic: 23.86 on 25 and 362 DF, $p$-value: $< 2.2e-16$
Significance codes: ***$p < 0.01$; **$p < 0.05$

internal validity for the use of subregions and provides preliminary support for the hypothesis that, while the coefficients do vary, the set and general effect of budgetary constraints on commuting are consistent across the region. Finally, the variation in coefficients across subregions is minimal except in the wage term (and migration, as discussed above). The coefficient for the wage differential for subregion five is approximately double its value in subregions four and six. This suggests that the wage differential between Milwaukee County and its neighbors drives commuting more strongly than in other areas of the study region.

It is important to ask if the results shown in Table 22.5 indicate the significance of spatial heterogeneity in deconcentration because the independent variable values (x-bar) vary, because the coefficients vary, or due to an average effect. Using the county-level output from the GWR, Moran's I values (calculated using a first-order Queen-based weight in GeoDa) for the β, x-bar, and βx terms for each independent variable (Table 22.6) overwhelmingly show that an average effect drives the significance of the model shown in Table 22.5. Both the coefficients and the values of independent variables vary across space. This warrants more investigation into the mechanisms of commuting (McMillen, 2004b). The coefficients may be biased toward having a spatial pattern by virtue of having been created through a GWR.

Tables 22.5 and 22.6, taken together, reveal spatial heterogeneity in the magnitude of deconcentration and a spatial limit to its reach. Perhaps as interesting, Tables 22.5 and 22.6 reveal that regardless of the presence of deconcentration, the aggregated households within counties choose to expend their aggregate household budgets (for housing and commuting costs) similarly across space, with high relative wages in Milwaukee driving commuting more than the wage differential across the Chicago region.

## Conclusion and Policy Recommendations

This work has shown spatial heterogeneity and limits in the geographic scope of population deconcentration in the region surrounding the Chicago CMSA. In its simplest interpretation, this work has three conclusions: the magnitude of deconcentration varies within a region; the geographic scope of deconcentration is much smaller than the universe of counties with proximity to both the megacity (Chicago) and lower-tier cities, like Kankakee, Illinois, and; with the exception of the wage differential between central and suburban Milwaukee, the budgetary constraints to commuting act similarly across the region, regardless of the presence of deconcentration. In particular, estimating the spatial limit of deconcentration signals the need for

Table 22.6 Moran's I values for GWR output

| | β | x-bar | βx-bar |
|---|---|---|---|
| Net in-migration | 0.9028*** | 0.2192*** | 0.2601*** |
| Wage differential | 0.9179*** | 0.023 | 0.0268 |
| Distance | 0.9033*** | 0.3594*** | 0.2519*** |
| Housing cost differential | 0.7719*** | 0.2697*** | 0.2681*** |
| Education differential | 0.8440*** | 0.5148*** | 0.1474** |

***$p < 0.01$; **$p < 0.05$ (pseudo $p$-values)

more in-depth understanding of the mechanisms of growth in counties at the urban fringe. These counties are neither remote nor connected via strong commuting streams to cities. Further research on urban fringe development could replicate the statistical method presented here for estimating the spatial extent of deconcentration.

This research adds a new level of precision to existing models of deconcentration and adds nuance to crude categorizations of metropolitan or nonmetropolitan counties in growth models. Scholars in the United States, Canada, and Europe have argued that place-based rural policies must recognize spatial heterogeneity and properly identify functional regions to be most effective (Partridge, Olfert, & Ali, 2009; Pezzini, 2001). Therefore, the findings of this chapter should prove useful to policymakers seeking more effective planning efforts and growth policies within regions.

This chapter has identified nonmetropolitan counties in subregions with significant ties to urban centers. Based on previous research in the United States, Canada, and Ireland, population retention or growth in rural places with substantial linkages to major urban areas can best be achieved through regional growth policies (Henry, Barkley, & Bao, 1997; Khan, Orazem, & Otto, 2001; Moss, Jack, & Wallace, 2004; Partridge et al., 2007; Partridge & Rickman, 2006). Supporting growth in urban centers that serve as employment hubs for neighboring rural counties positively impacts households in those communities by expanding employment opportunities within established commuting distances (Moss et al., 2004; Partridge & Rickman, 2006; Partridge et al., 2009; Portnov & Schwartz, 2009). These policies will be particularly effective for counties in the initial stages of deconcentration because delays in firms' movements to the periphery result in a period of households' increased reliance on commuting.

Based on the magnitude of the migration coefficient in this work, policymakers can estimate where counties fall in the range of deconcentration and restructuring at a particular point in time. Counties with higher migration coefficients are likely to be in early stages of deconcentration (Clark & Kuijpers-Linde, 1994; Renkow & Hoover, 2000), where households have deconcentrated but employment has not. Policymakers who correctly identify the current stage and predict the near-future stage of their county's growth can better plan for the social service and business needs of their communities. Regional governments and planning agencies can use this information to target planning efforts towards areas likely to experience rapid growth or to encourage business development in areas well suited to becoming future employment hubs. This information is particularly relevant in countries where land use change dramatically outpaces population growth, such as the U.S., in some cases Canada, and in rare cases China (Schneider & Woodcock, 2007).

Regional transportation planning and investment aimed at improving the accessibility of urban clusters to rural workers is also supported by the research (Moss et al., 2004; Renkow & Hoover, 2000; Rephann & Isserman, 1994). Traditionally rural areas, particularly areas that have experienced local structural change and increased reliance on out-commuting, will benefit from such policies (i.e., Moss et al., 2004). Coordinating zoning and environmental policies with regional transportation plans has the potential to benefit residents and businesses in both rural and urban locations (Partridge et al., 2007). Based on this work's findings, regional policies, plans, and investments should pay careful attention to the variation and extent of deconcentration within a region to avoid inefficient outcomes.

This research has also more clearly identified places where spread effects are unlikely to occur. While the counties in the study area are not geographically isolated, the policies recommended for such places are largely applicable. Based on prior research, isolated rural counties are less likely to benefit from regional policies attached to urban centers (Henry et al., 1997; Partridge et al., 2007; Partridge & Rickman, 2006; Renkow & Hoover, 2000). Instead, community-specific programs designed to improve a community's vitality and its residents' quality of life are more appropriate. Critics of rural place-based policies argue that they waste public dollars by artificially suppressing out-migration from areas unlikely to achieve self-sustaining population or employment levels and by creating employment opportunities likely to be awarded to new commuters and in-migrants (Partridge & Rickman, 2006; see also Bolton, 1992). However, community-specific programs should be particularly effective in isolated rural counties because remoteness decreases competition for jobs from commuters in proximate urban areas (Partridge & Rickman, 2006). Additionally, place-based programs in isolated rural places are more likely to identify and address the specific "contextual effects" that most influence a rural community's vitality (Blank, 2005).

Research on successful nonmetropolitan counties suggests that building local capacity in the areas of entrepreneurialism, community leadership, social-capital, and community planning leads to positive prosperity and population outcomes (Cook et al., 2009; Green, 2008; Low, Henderson, & Weiler, 2005; Partridge & Rickman, 2006; Schultz, 2004). Community leadership can stimulate population retention or growth by improving housing, focusing on quality of life issues, and coordinating economic development strategies with neighboring nonmetropolitan communities (Cook et al., 2009; Henry et al., 1997; Khan et al., 2001; Partridge & Rickman, 2006). For the smallest counties, regionally cooperative economic development policies rewarding job creation are likely to be more successful than those targeting high-wage jobs (Khan et al., 2001). From the state and federal level, education investments, technical assistance, and technical infrastructure development are also appropriate aids to these communities (Blank, 2005; Cook et al., 2009; Duncan, 1999; Fuguitt & Beagle, 1996; Garcia-Milà & McGuire, 1992; Low et al., 2005; Oden & Strover, 2002; Partridge & Rickman, 2006; Strover, Oden, & Inagaki, 2002). Such policies will improve the quality of life for existing residents and may attract some new residents; however, they are less likely to attract firms (Henry et al., 1997) and may influence future out-migration of young adults as increased educational attainment drives workers to find higher incomes in urban areas (Berry, 1970; Cushing & Poot, 2004; Plane et al., 2005).

Finally, this chapter highlights counties neither geographically isolated nor significantly tied to cities. The mechanisms of population growth and factors of location key to effective policymaking in other nonmetropolitan counties are less important factors of growth in these places, and their policies should reflect this difference. For these counties, policymakers must act prudently to select a pragmatic, flexible policy mix. Most importantly, strategic planning should serve these areas by facilitating scenario planning and proactive community dialogue about growth goals. Counties wishing to maintain a traditionally rural status may embrace place-based development strategies tied to growth management policies that protect open space and restrict population growth (Nelson & Dawkins, 2004). Counties envisioning a longer-term transition to suburban land use may pursue infrastructure and residential amenity development to facilitate commuting to proximate urban areas. These areas should also strengthen relationships and coordinated planning efforts with neighboring jurisdictions, regional governments, and metropolitan planning agencies (Scott & Storper, 2003).

In conclusion, this chapter has evaluated a mechanism of population growth at the urban-rural fringe. Primarily, this work finds a spatial limit to deconcentration that exceeds and cross-cuts metropolitan boundaries while also finding spatial heterogeneity in subregions experiencing deconcentration. Public policy work elucidates development strategies for areas with strong urban attachments and place-based policies for isolated areas. The study region includes counties neither geographically isolated nor significantly tied to cities. One-size-fits-all approaches based on regional growth dynamics are not sufficient or appropriate for these places; instead, these counties should advance policy portfolios that emphasize community goals and leverage existing community assets.

## References

Ali, K., Olfert, M. R., & Partridge, M. D. (2010). Urban footprints in rural Canada: Employment spillovers by city size. *Regional studies*. doi: 10.1080/00343400903241477.

Amirahmadi, H., & Wallace, C. (1995). Information technology, the organization of production, and regional development. *Environment and Planning A, 27*, 1745–1775.

Audirac, I., & Fitzgerald, J. (2003). Information technology (IT) and urban form: An annotated bibliography of the urban deconcentration and economic restructuring literatures. *Journal of Planning Literature, 17*(4), 480–511.

Berry, B. J. L. (1970). Labor market participation and regional potential. *Growth & Change, 1*(4), 3–10.

Beyers, W. B. (2000). Cyberspace or human space: Wither cities in the age of telecommunications? In J. O. Wheeler, Y. Aoyama, & B. Warf (Eds.), *Cities in the telecommunications age* (pp. 161–180). New York: Routledge.

Blank, R. M. (2005). Poverty, policy, and place: How poverty and policies to alleviate poverty are shaped by local characteristics. *International Regional Science Review, 28*(4), 441–464.

Bolton, R. (1992). 'Place prosperity vs people prosperity' revisited: An old issue with a new angle. *Urban Studies, 29*(2), 185–203.

Bureau of Economic Analysis. (2000). *REIS Table CA34, "Average wage per job."* Washington, DC.

Bureau of Labor Statistics. (2000). *Quarterly census of employment and wages*. Washington, DC.

Clark, W. A. V., & Kuijpers-Linde, M. (1994). Commuting in restructuring urban regions. *Urban Studies, 31*(3), 465–483.

Coffey, W. J., & Bailly, A. S. (1992). Producer services and systems of flexible production. *Urban Studies, 29*(6), 857–868.

Cook, C. C., Crull, S. R., Bruin, M. J., Yust, B. L., Shelley, M. C., Laux, S., et al. (2009). Evidence of a housing decision chain in rural community vitality. *Rural Sociology, 74*, 113–137.

Cushing, B., & Poot, J. (2004). Crossing boundaries and borders: Regional science advances in migration modeling. *Papers in Regional Science, 83*, 317–338.

Department of Housing and Urban Development. (2000). *Fair market rents*. Retrieved August 1, 2009, from http://www.huduser.org/portal/datasets/fmr.html.

Duncan, C. M. (1999). *Worlds apart: Why poverty persists in rural America*. New Haven, CT: Yale University Press.

Evers, G. (1989). Simultaneous models for migration and commuting: Macro and micro economic approaches. In J. van Dijk, H. Folmer, H. W. Herzog, Jr., A. M. Schlottmann (Eds.), *Migration and labour market adjustment* (pp. 177–197). Dordrecht, Netherlands: Kluwer.

Fishman, R. (1990). America's new city: Megalopolis unbound. *Wilson Quarterly, 14*(1), 25–45.

Fotheringham, A. S., Charlton, M. E., & Brunsdon, C. (1998). Geographically weighted regression: A natural evolution of the expansion method for spatial data analysis. *Environment & Planning A, 30*(11), 1905–1927.

Frey, W. H. (1993). The new urban revival in the United States. *Urban Studies, 30*(4–5), 741–774.

Fuguitt, G. V., & Beagle, C. L. (1996). Recent trends in nonmetropolitan migration: Toward a new turnaround? *Growth & Change, 27*(2), 156–174.

Gaile, G. L. (1980). The spread-backwash concept. *Regional Studies, 14*(1), 15–25.

Garcia-Milà, T., & McGuire, T. J. (1992). The contribution of publicly provided inputs to states' economies. *Regional Science and Urban Economics, 22*(2), 229–241.

Green, J. J. (2008). Community development as social movement: A contribution to models of practice. *Community Development, 39*(1), 50–62.

Henry, M. S., Barkley, D. L., & Bao, S. (1997). The hinterland's stake in metropolitan growth: Evidence from selected southern regions. *Journal of Regional Science, 37*(3), 479–501.

Henton, D., & Walesh, K. (1998). *Linking the new economy to the livable community. A report to the James Irvine Foundation*. San Francisco: The James Irvine Foundation.

Hirschorn, J. S. (2000). *Growing pains: Quality of life in the new economy*. Washington, DC: National Governors' Association. Retrieved December 13, 2009, from http://www.nga.org/cda/files/GROWINGPAINS.pdf

Internal Revenue Service. (1999). *County-to-county migration data*. Washington, DC.

Khan, R., Orazem, P. F., & Otto, D. M. (2001). Deriving empirical definitions of spatial labor markets: The roles of competing versus complementary growth. *Journal of Regional Science, 41*(4), 735–756.

Low, S. A., Henderson, J., & Weiler, S. (2005). Gauging a region's entrepreneurial potential. *Economic Review, Third Quarter*, 61–89.

McMillen, D. P. (2004a). Employment subcenters and home price appreciation rates in metropolitan Chicago. In J. P. Lesage & R. K. Pace (Eds.), *Spatial and spatiotemporal econometrics (Advances in Econometrics*, vol.18, pp. 237–257). Emerald Group Publishing Limited.

McMillen, D. P. (2004b). Review: Geographically weighted regression. *American Journal of Agricultural Economics, 86*(2), 554–556.

Moss, J., Jack, C., & Wallace, M. (2004). Employment location and associated commuting patterns for individuals in disadvantaged rural areas in Northern Ireland. *Regional Studies, 38*(2), 121–136.

Nelson, A. C., & Dawkins, C. J. (2004). *Urban containment in the United States: History, models, and techniques for regional and metropolitan growth management*. American Planning Association: Planning Advisory Service Report Number 520.

Oden, M., & Strover, S. (2002). *Links to the future: The role of information and telecommunications technology in Appalachian economic development*. Washington, DC: Appalachian Regional Commission.

Office of Management and Budget. (1999). *Metropolitan areas and components*. Washington, DC.

Partridge, M. D., Bollman, R. D., Olfert, M. R., & Alasia, A. (2007). Riding the wave of urban growth in the countryside: Spread, backwash, or stagnation? *Land Economics, 83*(2), 128–152.

Partridge, M. D., Olfert, M. R., & Ali, K. (2009). Towards a rural development policy: Lessons from the United States and Canada. *Journal of Regional Analysis & Policy, 39*(2), 109–125.

Partridge, M. D., & Rickman, D. S. (2006). *The geography of American poverty*. Kalamazoo, MI: W.E. Upjohn Institute for Employment Research.

Pezzini, M. (2001). Rural policy lessons from OECD countries. *International Regional Science Review, 24*, 134–145.

Pisarski, A. E. (2006). *Commuting in America III*. Washington, DC: Transportation Research Board of the National Academies, NCHRP Report 550/TCRP Report 110.

Plane, D. A., Henrie, C. J., & Perry, M. J. (2005). Migration up and down the urban hierarchy and across the life course. *Proceedings of the National Academy of Sciences of the USA, 102*(43), 15313–15318.

Portnov, B. A., & Schwartz, M. (2009). Urban clusters as growth foci. *Journal of Regional Science, 49*(2), 287–310.

Renkow, M. (2003). Employment growth, worker mobility, and rural economic development. *American Journal of Agricultural Economics, 85*(2), 503–513.

Renkow, M., & Hoover, D. (2000). Commuting, migration, and rural-urban population dynamics. *Journal of Regional Science, 40*(2), 261–287.

Rephann, T., & Isserman, A. (1994). New highways as economic development tools: An evaluation using quasi-experimental matching methods. *Regional Science and Urban Economics, 24*, 723–751.

Rouwendal, J., & Meijer, E. (2001). Preferences for housing, jobs, and commuting: A mixed logit analysis. *Journal of Regional Science, 41*(3), 475–505.

Sassen, S. (1994). *Cities in a world economy*. Thousand Oaks, CA: Pine Forge Press.

Sassen, S. (2002). Cities in a world economy. In S. Fainstein & S. Campbell (Eds.), *Readings in urban theory* (2nd ed., pp. 32–56). Malden, MA: Blackwell.

Schneider, A., & Woodcock, C. E. (2007). Compact, dispersed, fragmented, extensive? A comparison of urban growth in twenty-five global cities using remotely sensed data, pattern metrics and census information. *Urban Studies, 45*(3), 659–692.

Schultz, J. M. (2004). *Boomtown USA: The 7-1/2 keys to big success in small towns*. Herndon, VA: National Association of Industrial and Office Properties.

Scott, A. (1988). *Metropolis: From the division of labor to urban form*. Berkeley, CA: University of California Press.

Scott, A. J. & Storper, M. (2003.) Regions, globalization, development. *Regional Studies, 37*(6/7), 579–593.

Storper, M. (1997). *The regional world*. New York: Guilford.

Strover, S., Oden, M., & Inagaki, N. (2002). Telecommunications and rural economies: Findings from the Appalachian region. In L. F. Craner & S. Greenstein (Eds.), *Communications policy and information technology: Promises, problems, prospects* (pp. 317–346). Cambridge: MIT Press.

U.S. Census Bureau. (2000a). *Census 2000: SF3 tables P84 and P86*. Washington, DC.

U.S. Census Bureau. (2000b). *Census transportation and planning package*. Washington, DC.

von Thunen, J. H. (1966). *Von Thunen's isolated state* (C. M. Wartenberg, Trans.). Oxford: Pergamon Press.

White, H. (1980). A heteroskedasticity-consistent covariance matrix estimator and a direct test for heteroskedasticity. *Econometrica, 48*(4), 817–838.

Yu, C. (2009). *Net migration drains $1.6 billion from Illinois economy each year*. Urbana, IL: Regional Economics Applications Laboratory, University of Illinois Urbana-Champaign.

Zimmerman, D. (2003). Review: Geographically weighted regression. *Journal of the American Statistical Association, 98*(463), 765–766.

# Integrating Ecology and Demography to Understand the Interrelationship Between Environmental Issues and Rural Populations

Christopher A. Lepczyk, Marc Linderman, and Roger B. Hammer

## Introduction

Understanding the linkages between population and the environment has been a rich area of theory and research among both demographers and natural scientists for centuries. Starting at the end of the 18th century with Thomas Malthus's seminal *An Essay on the Principle of Population* (Malthus, 1798), both demographers and natural scientists have sought to integrate their fields into an understanding of how population can shape the environment, and likewise how the environment can shape population. Interest in the interrelationships between population and the environment grew during the nineteenth century with such works as *Walden* (Thoreau, 1854), in which Thoreau noted how the country (rural areas) supports the city, such that "All the Indian huckleberry hills are stripped, all the cranberry meadows are raked into the city" (Thoreau, 1854). In fact, even by Thoreau's time, finding rural locations in New England that were untouched by modern day humans was challenging.

The second half of the twentieth century saw a marked increase in academic research and popular press books related to population and the environment. Perhaps the two most notable were *The Population Bomb* by Paul Ehrlich (Ehrlich, 1968), who wrote of an alarming future of famine, poverty, and resource wars in the same tone as Rachel Carson's *Silent Spring* (Carson, 1962) had done several years earlier, and *The Tragedy of the Commons* (Hardin, 1968). During the era of *The Population Bomb* and *The Tragedy of the Commons*, demographers and ecologists collectively noted the great impact that unrestrained population growth was having on the environment, in such manifest ways as increased pollution, desertification, and famine. The result of this acknowledgement included international conferences sponsored by the United Nations, new government policies, and increased research efforts, all aimed at addressing questions of overpopulation. Such seminal works as the IPAT (Influence = Population × Affluence × Technology; initially developed in Ehrlich & Holdren, 1971) model and *Limits to Growth* (Meadows et al., 1972) were produced during this era.

While interest and research on the linkages between population and the environment continued, the advent of the green revolution reduced problems such as starvation and famine markedly, thus diminishing the attention to issues such as overpopulation, while at the same time demographic transition theory became a dominant view. In fact, it essentially became a taboo topic to discuss overpopulation after the mid-1970s. Green revolutions, in turn, have significantly influenced regional to national populations. For instance, rural migration, household size and incomes have been markedly impacted by changes in agricultural practices, prices, and market interactions (Rhoda, 1983; Estudillo, Sawada, & Otsuka, 2006). Although questions pertaining to population and the environment were less a part of policy discussions and fell out of view of the media and public, research on the linkages continued in many directions. By the 1990s there was a

C.A. Lepczyk (✉)
Department of Natural Resources and Environmental Management, University of Hawai'i at Mānoa, Honolulu, HI 96822, USA
e-mail: lepczyk@hawaii.edu

considerable wealth of new research on their interrelationships, in both demographic and ecological journals and books (e.g., Hardin, 1993; Cohen, 1995; Vitousek, Mooney, Lubchenco, & Melillo, 1997; Hammond, 1998). Moreover, the past decade has witnessed a strong integration between demographers and ecologists as new data sources have become available, new technologies developed or applied, new funding initiatives started (e.g., the urban Long-Term Ecological Research [LTER] sites of Phoenix, AZ and Baltimore, MD; National Science Foundation's Biocomplexity program which has now become the Coupled Human-Nature Systems program, etc.), and new paradigms have been developed (e.g., Liu, Dietz, Carpenter, Alberti, et al., 2007; Liu, Dietz, Carpenter, Folke, et al., 2007).

The increasing integration between demography and ecology comes as more and more people now live in cities or urban areas. Globally more than half of the world's population now lives in urban areas, which are expected to continue growing for the foreseeable future (Cohen, 2005a, 2005b; see also Chapter 5 in this volume). Thus, this trend towards urbanization means reciprocally that rural areas are home to a smaller percentage of the population. With the notable exception of the "rural rebound" in the US during the 1970s and the early 1990s (Vining & Strauss, 1977; Johnson & Beale, 1998, 2002; Johnson & Fuguitt, 2000), the reduction in the rural population has been evident for decades. However, while the proportion of the overall US population has become more urban, this is not to say that all rural areas experienced population declines. In fact, many rural areas have experienced notable increases in their population over the past thirty years as people have migrated and built new homes near locations of high amenity value or on former agricultural land (Johnson & Beale, 2002; Brown, Johnson, Loveland, & Theobald, 2005; Radeloff et al., 2005; Lepczyk, Hammer, Stewart, & Radeloff, 2007). This increase, coupled with decreasing household sizes and settlement densities (Liu, Daily, Ehrlich, & Luck, 2003), results in what we can call "rural sprawl" (Brown et al., 2005). Similarly, in other parts of the globe, particularly Africa, Asia, and several locations in Latin America, rural populations have increased markedly in recent decades, due to migration that is driven by new agricultural opportunities (e.g., Bilsborrow, 2002; Carr, 2009). For instance, over the past thirty years farmers in Burkina Faso, led by high quality soils, have been migrating into rural areas, resulting in a significant increase in the rural population (Ouedraogo et al., 2009). Because rural areas often harbor unique habitats, ecosystems, and species, this rural sprawl can have serious repercussions on the environment (Hansen et al., 2002). Moreover, around the world there are relatively few rural locations in which humans are absent from the environment (Sanderson et al., 2002), highlighting the relevance of coupling demography and ecology.

While the field of rural sociology has addressed issues of rural demography and the environment, it is an area of growing research interest to ecologists. This interest stems in part from the fact that rural areas house much of the world's biodiversity and also provide many of the resources and ecosystems services that humans require. Hence, understanding how rural populations operate and change over time is of great importance given the ecological value of rural areas. Furthermore, it is imperative to understand how populations and the environments are interrelated in order to advance our knowledge and thereby guide decision making, policy, natural resource management, and conservation (see Chapter 24 in this volume). As a first step, then, we need to consider how ecologists view the environment and how that relates to demography, followed by an understanding of how population can influence the environment. We then present a case study of the integration of demographics and landscape ecology to highlight the important relationships between and challenges integrating population and ecology.

## Conceptual View of the Environment

Because an ecologist looking at the environment likely sees a very different world than a demographer, it is essential to provide a conceptual view of how ecologists consider and interpret the environment. While there are congeners in some of the conceptual views between ecologists and demographers, such as how systems can be hierarchically structured (e.g., Grove et al., 2006), there are also many differences. As a result, prior to discussing the linkages between population and the environment, we need to consider an ecological viewpoint of the environment and then how population fits within this viewpoint.

## Scale

One of the first concepts that influences an ecological viewpoint, but has not been commonly considered in demography or other social sciences, is that of scale (Vogt et al., 2002). Ecological phenomena, such as the timing and location of breeding in a species, can operate at very different spatial and temporal scales. Furthermore, different phenomena occur at different levels of ecological organization (Fig. 23.1). For instance, forest fires often occur at meters to kilometers in physical extent and cause changes in the entire forest ecosystem, compared to a wolf preying upon a moose, which is simply two species interacting. Thus, scale is one of the "central problems" in ecology, as ecologists seek to unify different spatial, temporal, and organizational levels together (Levin, 1992). As a result, "there is no single natural scale at which ecological phenomena should be studied... (Levin, 1992)." The question, hypothesis, or goal of the study, coupled with the system of interest often dictates the scale chosen for research. Likewise, data availability can also drive the scale chosen for a study. In ecological studies, such data availability questions often arise when monitoring/citizen science data (e.g., Audubon's Christmas Bird Count, North American Amphibian Monitoring Program) or remotely sensed imagery (e.g., Landsat) are used. The issue of data availability is also extremely relevant in demography as demographic data are often available only at certain scales that may or may not correspond to political boundaries, but certainly differ from ecological boundaries. Hence, population and the environment or coupled human-nature studies may well be dictated in large part by the data availability.

Because scale is linked to concepts of hierarchy, a well-designed ecological investigation considers three hierarchical levels. Specifically, a study contains a focal level, as well as the level above which constrains and/or controls the focal level, and the level below which provides the context and/or details needed to explain the behavior at the focal level (Turner, Gardner, & O'Neill, 2001). One classic way in which this ecological hierarchy is considered is in terms of species, populations, communities, ecosystems, landscapes, ecoregions, biomes, and the globe. Notably, as a means to help integrate demography (and sociology) with ecology, there have been similar hierarchical constructions in demography (Fig. 23.2). Finally, it is important to recognize that many ecological phenomena do not scale in any linear fashion, but are complex and often have thresholds.

In terms of the scale that ecologists often consider demographics or human activities, it is typically at the landscape scale or greater (i.e., ecoregion, continental, or global). Conversely, many demography studies are more site specific or state/region/national level (for a good review of scale in geography and ecology see Wu, 2007). Thus, in many instances where ecologists integrate humans into their analysis, they tend to look at larger scales than demographers (Cincotta, Wisnewski, & Engelman, 2000). This is not to say that one discipline is any more correct than the other in their views, simply that due to issues such as bounding (see next section), questions of interest, and perspective, that they conduct their research differently.

## Boundaries

While both ecologists and demographers delineate areas of interest or phenomena using some type of bounding scheme, it is extremely rare for boundaries delineated by each discipline to coincide. Demographers often use administrative or governmental jurisdictional lines as boundaries, which tend to be straight lines and laid out in geometric fashion. In contrast, ecologists typically use boundaries that are defined by such aspects as dominant vegetation type, ecosystem, watershed, or even home range of an organism. Hence, ecological boundaries tend to have very unusual shapes and jagged edges, with few straight lines. Furthermore, ecological boundaries can be either open or closed. That is, a boundary can be impenetrable (closed) to an ecological process(es) or interaction(s), or open, allowing ecological processes and interactions to cross the boundary. Conversely, demography does not typically have closed boundaries, except in such cases as national borders. While there are understandable reasons why social and ecological bounding systems are different, it makes integrating ecology and demography challenging.

In many instances when integrating existing data from ecological and demographic arenas, a trade-off must be made in terms of bounding. Because the bounds in the two disciplines rarely correspond to one another, this might mean using an ecological boundary that splits a social boundary (e.g., a

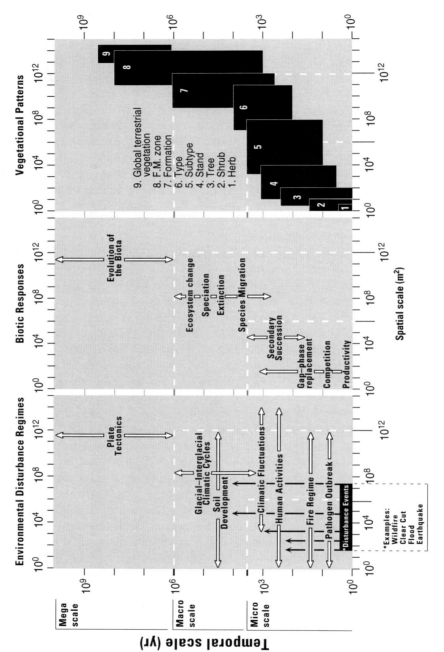

**Fig. 23.1** Example of how different ecological processes occur at different spatial and temporal scales, based upon Delcourt, Delcourt, and Webb (1983)

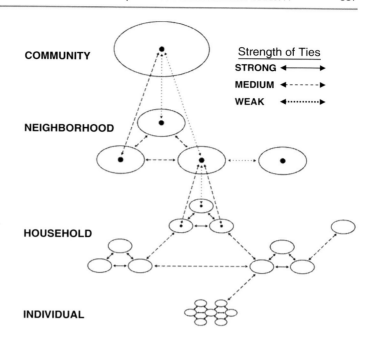

**Fig. 23.2** Example of hypothesized social hierarchy, based upon Grove et al. (2006)

county or school district; Rutledge & Lepczyk, 2002). Depending upon the resolution of the data, such a split may pose relatively few problems or many. For instance, US census blocks are small enough that splitting a county into parts means that the subcounty population estimates will likely be markedly closer to the actual value than if the county were split using only county-level resolution data. As a result, one must recognize the potential for error and bias in any analyses that seek to integrate ecological and demographic boundaries. Similarly, studies across political boundaries are often limited by data availability and consistency, socioeconomic and environmental characteristics, and perceptions of processes and states. Recognizing policy, cultural, infrastructure and other socioeconomic differences and potential influences on ecological and demographic interactions is often difficult, but necessary. Ecological and ecosystem characteristics, structure, function, and perception can vary across international and cultural boundaries (Baudry, Bunce, & Burel, 2000). For example, comparing disturbance and urbanization on ground beetle community structure across three countries, Niemelä et al. (2002) found differences in local factors of urban areas have potential impacts on landscape processes. In addition, difficulties in collecting consistent demographic and socioeconomic data at regional to global scales often limit analyses or comparisons. Rowhani, Degomme, Guha-Sapir, and Lambin (2011), for example, limited by data availability across the Horn of Africa examined the application of remotely sensed data and international indices of child malnutrition to estimate climate variability impacts on food security.

## Ecosystems and Landscapes

Ecologists often study questions at a number of different levels of organization, such as individual species, populations, etc., depending upon the question of interest. But in terms of integrating ecology and demography, the two levels that are of greatest relevance are ecosystems and landscapes. While these two words are often used interchangeably, they are different concepts in practice. Typically an ecosystem is described as a biological community plus all of the abiotic (nonliving) factors influencing that community. Conversely, a landscape can be considered as heterogeneous areas composed of clusters of interacting ecosystems (Forman & Godron, 1986) or as spatially heterogeneous areas that are characterized by structure, function, and change (Turner, 1989). One caveat to note is that while this definition of landscape appears to be at an anthropocentric scale, it is in fact scale independent (see Lepczyk, Lortie, & Anderson, 2008 for discussion), meaning that the term should not be indicative of large physical expanses. Rather, that a landscape encompasses the concept of ecosystem (or structure and function) in a spatial perspective. Ultimately, the ideas of ecosystems and landscapes are the most useful for demography because they can be translated into useful units or ideas for research, planning, and policy.

## Disturbance

Historically, ecologists viewed the natural world from a static perspective in which there was a "balance of nature" and systems were in equilibrium (Wu & Loucks, 1995). However, by the latter decades of the twentieth century, ecologists came to view the natural world from a nonequilibrium paradigm, in part because of the role of disturbance (Pickett & Ostfeld, 1995). Ecologically, "a disturbance is defined as a relatively discrete event that disrupts the structure of an ecosystem, community, or population and changes resource availability or the physical environment" (Turner et al., 2001). Thus, disturbances occur over relatively short periods of time and can be biotic (e.g., spread of an invasive species), abiotic (e.g., tornado, flood, volcanic eruption), or both, and can leave very different patterns on the landscape (e.g., Foster, Knight, & Franklin, 1998). Hence, often times what society calls natural disasters are in fact equivalent to the concept of disturbance in ecology and often inherent to ecological cycles and ecosystem dynamics. Notably, disturbance is not limited to natural phenomena, but can also be the product of mankind. Specifically, anthropogenic disturbances, such as land use change, elicit similar ecological responses to natural disturbances.

While disturbance events are singular occurrences, it is most relevant to consider them in terms of regimes on a landscape. Namely, a disturbance regime describes the spatial and temporal characteristics of disturbance over long periods of time and large geographical areas. When describing a disturbance regime, the most common characteristics are frequency, intensity, predictability, severity, and extent. Because many landscapes have disturbance regimes that impact human society, it is important to note how they may influence populations. Likewise, as people alter the landscape around them, they can alter the natural disturbance regime. For instance, wildland fire suppression can alter the frequency and intensity of wildfires, especially near populated areas.

## How Demographic Change Influences the Environment

Humans are like any other species on Earth in that they both influence and are influenced by the world around them. Specifically, because humans rely on the earth's ecosystems for food, fiber, shelter, water, and other ecosystem services, they are intimately tied to the environment, interacting with it both directly and indirectly. Hence, just as an ecologist understands how the composition, size, and structure of a species' population influences the ecosystem or landscape around it, a demographer understands that the human population likewise influences the ecosystem (including urban ecosystems) they live in or near. Since populations are dynamic, their relationship with, and influence on, both the surrounding ecosystems and global ecology change over time and space. This dynamism occurs as one or more aspect of the population changes, such as composition, size, or structure, or as the population changes in how it uses or interacts with the environment. For instance, a changing composition of ethnicities in the rural Pacific Northwest of the US has led to changes in harvest rates of nontimber forest products (forest vegetation other than industrial lumber that is harvested by people; e.g., craft materials, floral greens, edible and medicinal plants and mushrooms, seeds, saps and resins; Jones & Lynch, 2007). Since harvesting of nontimber forest products can affect ecological processes from individual species through ecosystem levels (Ticktin, 2004), demographic changes likely influence the ecological processes present in the forest (Linderman et al., 2006). Another case in point is how changes in age structure, marriage, sex ratio, and other demographic measures may have differential effects on giant panda (*Ailuropoda melanoleuca*) habitat specifically, and biodiversity conservation generally, in rural China (Liu, Ouyang, Tan, Yang, & Zhang, 1999; An, He, Liang, & Liu, 2006). In particular, because fuelwood remains a major energy source for households in rural China (and around the world), fuelwood collection has resulted in decreased forest area, which in turn has significant impacts on species habitat and ecological communities (Bearer et al., 2008). Essentially, then, rural life and population influence land use and management practices, which themselves affect species distribution and composition (i.e., species population biology), land cover juxtaposition, disturbance regimes, and biogeochemical cycles (for a thorough review of how changes in land use/management result in ecological change see Dale, Archer, Chang, & Ojima, 2005).

Demographic changes can occur in myriad ways, each of which can influence the environment. For instance, a population can increase in size due to an increase in fertility, migration, life expectancy, or the combination of them. However, each of these mechanisms responsible for increasing the population may have a different relationship with the environment. Moreover, while beyond the scope of this paper, we must remain cognizant of the fact that population alone often does not describe impacts on the environment, but rather should be considered within the social, economic, and political arena in which it is a part (Lambin et al., 2001).

One of the most direct ways in which demographic change influences the environment is through changes in the population size, either through growth or decline. Specifically, increasing populations require more resources (or more efficient uses of resources), which invariably means that they will have greater impacts on the environment. For instance, rural population growth typically results in loss and fragmentation of habitat (or ecosystems) due to land conversion for food, housing, roads, and other uses needed to maintain the population (Brown et al., 2005; Lepczyk et al., 2007). Because population growth itself can arise via migration, increased fertility, increased life expectancy, or some combination of these mechanisms, it is important to consider how they each may influence the environment differentially. In terms of the rate of change, increases in migration may have a much more sudden impact on the environment than increases in fertility. Specifically, increased migration may result in rapid changes to the environment as a result of a need for increased infrastructure, services, and use of recreational facilities compared to a rise in fertility which might take many more years to have any noticeable impact. A case in point is the current population explosion in rural North Dakota, where there has been a rapid influx of workers (primarily men) needed to work in oil exploration (Lindholm, 2010). In the case of increased life expectancy, a noticeable trend that is occurring in the rural US is the aging of the population. Specifically, more people over the age of 65 live in rural than urban areas within the US, which is due to both aging and migration (Brown & Glasgow, 2008). As a greater proportion of the rural population moves into retirement age classes, they will require new facilities, infrastructures, and modifications to homes, each of which can alter the ecosystem and landscape. For instance, when new homes replace forests or farmlands, populations of lady slipper (*Paphiopedilum villosum*) flower have been eliminated (Dale et al., 2005).

While ecologists have typically focused on the growth of the human population, it is also important to note that decreases in population can have a marked affect on the environment. For example, in the rural Carpathian Mountains of Eastern Europe (i.e., the triangle region of Poland, Slovakia, Ukraine), depopulation occurred in some regions of Southeast Poland during the time the Soviet Union occupied the country, resulting in forests that were more contiguous and thus supported the highest densities of herbivores and top carnivores (e.g., wolf, brown bear, and European bison; Kuemmerle, Hostert, Radeloff, Perzanowski, & Kruhlov, 2007). Similarly, depopulation in Eastern Europe led to farmland abandonment, resulting in agriculture fields becoming fallow and afforestation (Kuemmerle, Hostert, Radeloff, Perzanowski, & Kruhlov, 2008). Such depopulation is not atypical of rural locations in the US either, where natural resources become depleted (e.g., removal of high-grade iron ore and copper from Michigan's Upper Peninsula), agricultural lands are consolidated, or other economic changes occur.

## Case Study: The Utility of Using Housing to Measure Demographic Influence on the Environment

### Rationale

Historically, ecologists have typically used the human population as the main demographic factor relating people to the environment (e.g., Ehrlich, 1968). However, houses and housing units (hereafter "houses"), offer a different and perhaps more meaningful way to ascertain and investigate how population influences the environment. One of the first and foremost reasons is that over the past century houses have been increasing at a faster rate than the human population in many rural locations in the US and around the world (Liu et al., 2003; Lepczyk et al., 2007). Concurrent with this faster growth, is the fact that the physical dimensions of the average house have increased, while the average number of people occupying them have decreased. The net result of this is that over time there are fewer people per unit area, which translates into a less efficient allocation of land, demonstrating that housing may capture the ecological footprint better than population size (Theobald, 2001; Liu et al., 2003).

A second reason why houses offer value in considering demographic influences on the environment is that they also represent second homes. As such, houses can capture increasing ecological pressure even in the absence of recorded population growth. Furthermore, many second homes are seasonal homes located in amenity-rich areas, which are often of high ecological and conservation value (Hammer, Stewart, Hawbaker, & Radeloff, 2009; Radeloff et al., 2010).

Third, is that houses are not isolated features of the landscape, but rather are representative of a host of other attributes that also influence the environment, such as associated infrastructure like roads (Dwyer & Childs, 2004; Forys & Allen, 2005). For instance, as road density increases, the amount of habitat, such as forest, decreases, resulting in a more fragmented ecological system (Hawbaker & Radeloff, 2004). Likewise, recreational infrastructure (e.g., hiking trails), can change the relationships between predator and prey (e.g., Miller, Knight, & Miller, 1998).

Fourth, rural housing growth has been identified as one of the major threats to ecosystems, due to its effects on land use (Matlack, 1997; Parks, Hardie, Tedder, & Wear, 2000), water quality (Wear, Turner, & Flamm, 1996), forest management (Marcin, 1993), wildlife populations (Soulé, 1991; Cincotta et al., 2000), biodiversity (McKinney, 2002; Hansen et al., 2005; Lepczyk, Flather, et al., 2008), endangered species (Czech, Krausman, & Devers, 2000), habitat loss (Theobald, 2000), and encroachment on protected areas and national parks (Radeloff et al., 2010; Wade & Theobald, 2010). Notably, even an individual home impacts the environment as evidenced by the fact that a number of animal species demonstrate a threshold effect with varying distances from a house, with some showing minimal effects and others showing dramatic effects (Odell & Knight, 2001). Moreover, impacts from ruins of ancient houses have a long ecological legacy, as demonstrated by markedly different patterns of species composition and richness where houses were located compared to adjacent locations in the Aleutian Island (Warren et al., 2006). Thus, whether at the scale of a single home or an entire housing development, houses and housing growth results in marked ecological impact.

Fifth, houses can provide a useful way to measure landscape change (i.e., the shift of one land use or land cover type to another over time). Specifically, all measures of the landscape, and hence landscape change, stem from two main types of data: remotely sensed imagery (aerial photos, satellite imagery) and published data/censuses (Dunn, Sharpe, Guntenspergen, Stearns, & Yang, 1990). Housing units at the partial block group level are a recently developed data set that falls in the latter category and offers a substantial advantage with regard to the limitations identified in traditional landscape change studies (Hammer, Stewart, Winkler, Radeloff, & Voss, 2004). If we assume that the addition of new houses on the landscape results in the conversion of one land use into a residential land use then we can identify three advantages of these data. First, housing growth data at the partial block level are a finer scale representation of landscape change relative to many human influence databases collected over time, allowing for more spatially detailed analyses of houses and housing growth (Lepczyk et al., 2007). Second, housing data has been collected over a longer period of time than remotely sensed information, thus allowing for more extensive temporal analysis. Finally, the spatially consistent nature of the data allows for temporal analyses not previously possible with US Census data, given the problem of shifting census boundaries each decade (Hammer et al., 2004).

Finally, houses can be conceived of in a hierarchical manner (Fig. 23.2), whereby households contain families and/or individuals (i.e., the level below) that may provide the context of the household, and are part of neighborhoods (or such levels as townships in rural areas), which can constrain the household (e.g., through zoning; Grove, Hinson, & Northrop, 2003; Grove et al., 2006). By considering houses within such a hierarchical framework, it allows for easier integration with ecology. Thus, houses, whether measured individually, over time, or within a social framework, offer a very useful approach for integrating demographic and ecological research.

## Example of Housing Growth and Wildlife Habitat

Because landscape change leads to a corresponding change in habitat for plants and animals, the ability to use housing data to measure environmental change offers a great opportunity for broadening the scale at which we examine such questions. Considering the importance of landscape change on ecological systems, we demonstrate how changes in the number of housing units leads to changes in the amount and arrangement of habitat across the landscape for a Neotropical bird of conservation importance, the Ovenbird (*Seiurus aurocapillus*). Ovenbirds are an ideal focal species for investigating the relationship between housing growth and habitat change, because they have a strong association to housing density with abundances decreasing as housing numbers increase (Kluza, Griffin, & Degraaf, 2000; Lepczyk, Flather, et al., 2008), and they are a forest interior species inhabiting rural areas that can be used as an umbrella species for conservation (Hess & King, 2002).

To investigate the utility of measuring changes in housing density as a proxy for changes in Ovenbird habitat availability, we selected the state of Massachusetts, USA. Our selection was based on both the marked increase in the number of housing units from 1970 to 2000 as well as the presence of Ovenbirds, which have declined statewide at an average annual rate of nearly 2.4% since 1990 (Sauer, Hines, & Fallon, 2008). Within Massachusetts, we used a geographic information systems (GIS) dataset of fine-resolution housing unit density in vector format. Specifically, the housing data are US decennial census data at the partial block group level (see Hammer et al., 2004 for details), along with projections of past and future growth trends, that are spatially consistent by decade from 1940 to 2030. Partial block groups fall between blocks and block groups in the hierarchy of US Census Bureau geographies (see http://www.census.gov/geo/www/reference.html), and are roughly equivalent, in social terms, to subdivision-sized neighborhoods. A total of 24,511 partial block groups (excluding water polygons) occur in Massachusetts, with a mean area of 82.8 ha.

Since the abundance of Ovenbirds is strongly correlated to housing density, we investigated a number of general linear models (Lepczyk et al., unpublished data) to create a habitat suitability measure. The simplest model of habitat suitability, based upon adjusted $R^2$ and AIC (Akaike's information criterion), was mean ovenbird abundance = constant +

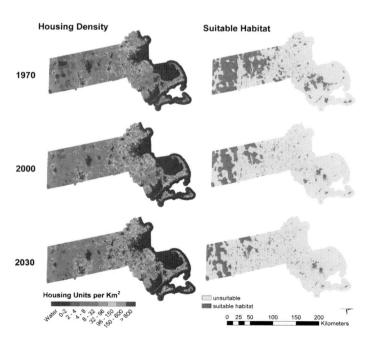

**Fig. 23.3** Temporal dynamics of housing growth and suitable Ovenbird habitat loss from 1970 to 2030 in Massachusetts

$\log_{10}$ housing density ($F_{1,68} = 38.22$; adjusted $R^2 = 0.38$; $p < 0.0001$). Next, to predict habitat suitability for the entire state, we first converted the housing data from vector to grid format with 250 × 250 m cells (6.25 ha cells), and restricted our area of analysis only to forested locations (predominately rural areas in Massachusetts, which were derived from the National Landcover Data; Vogelmann et al., 2001) as that is where Ovenbirds nest. With the software program RAMAS GIS (Akçakaya, 2002), we then used the habitat suitability model to create habitat suitability maps in the rural forested areas of the state from 1970 to 2030, by decade. To determine if significant change occurred over time in the number of houses and amount of habitat we used linear regression, with a $p < 0.05$ considered significant.

From 1970 to 2030, the total number of housing units within the rural forested portion of the state was projected to increase significantly from 360,293 to 974,013 ($F_{1,5} = 455.42$; $R^2 = 0.99$; $p < 0.0005$), representing a 170% increase. This increase in houses resulted in a 56% decline in Ovenbird habitat from ~6,000 km² in 1970 to ~2,600 km² in 2030 (Fig. 23.3). In other words, suitable habitat across the state will have been reduced from ~30% of the landscape in 1970 to ~13% in 2030. Spatially this loss of habitat is predicted to occur through the break-up of several large habitat patches in the western half of the state (Fig. 23.3). In 1970, this western half had one or two large, contiguous, blocks of habitat that are predicted to become greatly reduced and isolated by 2030 as housing numbers increase in this portion of the state.

## Future Directions and Challenges

Although the Ovenbird example is relatively basic in its approach, it offers the potential to link demographic change with ecological change. By integrating an approach such as this with other models and data researchers can investigate much more detailed linkages between demography and ecology. For instance, the next step of the Ovenbird study to incorporate the changes in housing density with changes in the Ovenbird population (Lepczyk et al., unpublished data).

The rising interest in interdisciplinary research offers great promise for further integration of ecology and demography. Already the past decade has seen a marked increase in integrative approaches, especially through the coupled human-nature systems model (Liu, Dietz, Carpenter, Alberti, et al., 2007; Liu, Dietz, Carpenter, Folke, et al., 2007). In addition, there has been a push to move the LTER sites towards including a social and economic component (Haberl et al., 2006). Such integration will be increasingly needed in the coming decades as society faces a number of serious threats to the environment.

Foremost among the current and upcoming challenges is climate change. Because climate change affects all regions of the globe, it is not an urban or rural issue, per se, but rather one that must be investigated at a multitude of scales. Likewise, climate change does not affect all locations to the same degree or in the same manner (IPCC, 2007), meaning that regions will experience differential impacts relative to one another. Within rural locations, climate change will likely influence agricultural production, natural resources, and ecosystem services, as local weather patterns change. In fact, we are already witnessing the migration of ecosystems (Loarie et al., 2009). As a result, we may see changes in net migration of people either to or from rural locations, depending upon how climate change influences urban areas relative to rural areas in terms of such things as the economy, disturbance regimes, etc. Moreover, given the uneven spatial distribution of people around the world coupled with the differential influence of climate change, it is clear that populations will be differentially affected. Thus, one area of research that is urgently needed is to understand how climate change will influence land cover and land use, and in turn how that will influence population.

A second and related area is simply improving our understanding of how land use and population are interrelated. Estimating historical changes and predicting future impacts of human activities requires an improved understanding of the demographic drivers of land use and the potential feedbacks and interactions of ecosystem dynamics on human populations. Increasingly it is recognized that the modification of land cover or intensification of land management activities have significant local to regional environmental, and demographic, implications. For example, the intensification of agricultural management and the continued reliance of households on selective logging for fuelwood have significant and complex effects on ecosystem and land use processes. Increases in farm sizes and decreases in diversity of cropping, as well as increasing uses of synthetic fertilizers and pesticides have significantly modified ecological communities, water quality, and greenhouse gas emissions. These changes in agricultural technology and activities have resulted in marked increases in yield and total productivity likely decreasing the total area required for agriculture. In turn, changes in agricultural technology have had profound impacts on rural labor demands and population structure. Questions remain, however, on how these changes in production influence households, the extent of agriculture land use, and overall environmental impacts (Rudel et al., 2009).

The increased availability of remotely sensed data and information technologies such as GIS now allows researchers to directly couple households, populations, and institutions with the spatial distribution of ecosystem resources and characteristics, land use activities, and environmental impacts and feedbacks. Remotely sensed data have allowed the mapping of land use and land cover change at scales previously not feasible in terms of cost or time. Aerial photographs have been used to map agriculture and land cover characteristics in the US and around the world since the 1930s. Aerial platforms continue to provide high-resolution imagery for a wide range of studies on human-environment interactions. More recently, sensors such as Landsat, SPOT, AVHRR, and others have provided systematic global coverage. While remotely sensed data do not provide direct information on demographics, these data do provide contextual and indirect estimates of the employment of the land. These repeated and extensive measurements permit regular estimates of the extent and spatial patterns of land use activities as well as surface dynamics. Coupling households to these digital measurements, or pixels, of the Earth's surface have resulted in enhanced models of the drivers of human activities and land use (Liverman, Moran, Rindfuss, & Stern, 1998).

While human activities often alter the landscape at relatively fine scales (10s–100s m) and long time periods (annual to decadal changes), it is often unclear how these activities scale to regional processes (Bounoua, DeFries, Collatz, Sellers, & Khan, 2002). Difficulties remain in the ability to gather detailed information on ecosystem dynamics and the basic differences across a range of land use intensities and land cover types to be able to capture the complexity of these systems and the potential impact ecosystem dynamics have on human populations (Waide et al., 1999; McCann, 2000). High frequency (~daily – biweekly) measurements of vegetation characteristics coupled with high-resolution land use delineations may provide a better understanding of demographic impacts on surface characteristics and dynamics and, in turn, how surface dynamics impact social systems (Running, 2008). Coupling land use complexity and regional ecosystem dynamics, however, requires measurements capable of scaling between fine-scale and broad-scale demographic and biophysical process (Lambin & Linderman, 2006). Fine-scale remote sensing data typically lack sufficient temporal resolution or repeat acquisitions to examine intra- and interannual dynamics (Lambin & Ehrlich, 1997). Conversely, coarser resolution data sets such as the MODerate resolution Imaging Spectroradiometer (MODIS) and Advanced Very High Resolution Radiometer (AHRR) provide nearly daily global coverage of earth surface measurements. The growing interest in the application of moderate spatial (250 m–1 km), high temporal (~daily) resolution data is based on the need to examine the mechanisms through which regional demographics influence hydrological responses, biodiversity, and other ecosystem characteristics (Rowhani et al., 2008; Basu et al., 2010). The combination of high spatial and temporal resolution data provides enhanced insight into the interactions and potential feedbacks between demographic patterns and ecosystem processes (Brown et al., 2007; Scott et al., 2008; Linderman, Zeng, & Rowhani, 2010).

## Conclusion

Demography has long been of great interest to ecologists in terms of how humans interact with the environment. While much of the early interest was on how a growing human population was detrimental to the environment, this interest expanded greatly in the past several decades to investigate how demographic characteristics and their dynamics were coupled to nature. Moreover, as the subdisciplines of landscape and urban ecology emerged, there was a growing interest in understanding how ecological patterns and processes influenced the human population as well as being influenced by it. Thus, we are now moving quickly to integrated approaches that can connect both disciplines together.

One demographic measure that allows for strong coupling between the disciplines is houses (or households). Because houses have both a physical presence on the landscape, which affect the ecosystem, and can be integrated into both social and ecological hierarchies, they represent a more robust measure than population numbers. To illustrate the utility of houses, we used their growth to measure how rural forested systems in Massachusetts are impacted in terms of their ability to provide habitat for Ovenbirds. Using a spatiotemporally consistent set of housing data, the growth resulted in a loss of more than half of the habitat for the Ovenbirds over a 60 year period. While relatively simple, the example provides an easy way to see how households can be integrated into both demography and ecology.

In a world facing marked changes due to climate change and a growing human population, the need to integrate demography and ecology will continue to grow. Regional to global losses of environmental services and ecological systems, the interactions between agriculture and climate change, environmental impacts on health, and demographic impacts on land use and ecological systems represent significant pressing problems and research challenges in the near future (Hazell & Wood, 2008). Consistent measures of demographics and ecosystem states across administrative boundaries are essential to examine the interaction of demographic processes and environmental systems at regional to global scales. In addition, demographic insights into the conceptual differences and changes in the drivers and interactions of population and environmental processes that often act to limit broad-scale comparisons are necessary for future international comparisons and collaborations (Geist & Lambin, 2002). Some of the best approaches for this integration are through the current technological advances of remote sensing, GIS, modeling, and the incorporation of field or plot data where appropriate. By using the cutting-edge methods of remote sensing, landscape ecology, and GIS, we can start addressing such pressing questions as how human migration and settlement change over time in relation to land use, and in turn, how these are coupled to ecosystem stability. In answering such questions, we can not only advance the unification of the disciplines, but provide greatly needed information to policymakers and managers.

# References

Akçakaya, H. R. (2002). *RAMAS GIS: Linking landscape data with population viability analysis, version 4.0t*. Setauket, NY: Applied Biomathematics.

An, L., He, G. M., Liang, Z., & Liu, J. (2006). Impacts of demographic and socioeconomic factors on spatio-temporal dynamics of panda habitat. *Biodiversity and Conservation, 15*(8), 2343–2363.

Basu, N. B., Rao, P. S. C., Winzeler, H. E., Kumar, S., Owens, P., & Merwade, V. (2010). Parsimonious modeling of hydrologic responses in engineered watersheds: Structural heterogeneity versus functional homogeneity. *Water Resources Research, 46*, W04501.

Baudry, J., Bunce, R. G. H., & Burel, F. (2000). Hedgerows: An international perspective on their origin, function and management. *Journal of Environmental Management, 60*, 7–22.

Bearer, S., Linderman, M., Huang, J., Ana, L., He, G., & Liu, J. (2008). Effects of fuelwood collection and timber harvesting on giant panda habitat use. *Biological Conservation, 141*, 385–393.

Bilsborrow, R. E. (2002). Migration, population change, and the rural environment. *Environmental Change and Security Project Report, 8*, 69–94.

Bounoua, L., DeFries, R., Collatz, G. J., Sellers, P., & Khan, H. (2002). Effects of land cover conversion on surface climate. *Climatic Change, 52*, 29–64.

Brown, D. G., Johnson, K. M., Loveland, T. R., & Theobald, D. M. (2005). Rural land use trends in the coterminous U.S. 1950–2000. *Ecological Applications, 15*, 1851–1863.

Brown, D. L., & Glasgow, N. (2008). *Rural retirement migration*. New York: Springer.

Brown, J. C., Jepson, W. E., Kastens, J. H., Wardlow, B. D., Lomas, J. M., & Price, K. P. (2007). Multitemporal, moderate-spatial-resolution remote sensing of modern agricultural production and land modification in the Brazilian Amazon. *GIScience & Remote Sensing, 44*, 117–148.

Carr, D. (2009). Rural migration: The driving force behind tropical deforestation on the settlement frontier. *Progress in Human Geography, 33*, 355–378.

Carson, R. (1962). *Silent spring*. Boston: Houghton Mifflin.

Cincotta, R. P., Wisnewski, J., & Engelman, R. (2000). Human population in the biodiversity hotspots. *Nature, 404*, 990–992.

Cohen, J. E. (1995). Population-growth and Earths human carrying-capacity. *Science, 269*, 341–346.

Cohen, J. E. (2005a). Human population grows up. *Scientific American, 293*, 48–55.

Cohen, J. E. (2005b). *How many people can the Earth support?* New York: W.W. Norton and Company.

Czech, B., Krausman, P. R., & Devers, P. K. (2000). Economic associations among causes of species endangerment in the United States. *BioScience, 50*, 593–601.

Dale, V., Archer, S., Chang, M., & Ojima, D. (2005). Ecological impacts and mitigation Strategies for rural land management. *Ecological Applications, 15*, 1879–1892.

Delcourt, H. R., Delcourt, P. A., & Webb, T., III (1983). Dynamic plant ecology: The spectrum of vegetational change in space and time. *Quaternary Science Review, 1*, 153–175.

Dunn, C. P., Sharpe, D. M., Guntenspergen, G. R., Stearns, F., & Yang, Z. (1990). Methods for analyzing temporal changes in landscape pattern. In M. G. Turner & R. H. Gardner (Eds.), *Quantitative methods in landscape ecology* (pp. 173–198). New York: Springer.

Dwyer, J. F., & Childs, G. M. (2004). Movement of people across the landscape: A blurring of distinctions between areas, interests and issues affecting natural resource management. *Landscape and Urban Planning, 69*, 153–164.

Ehrlich, P. R. (1968). *The population bomb*. New York: Ballantine Books.

Ehlrich, P. R., & Holdren, J. P. (1971). Impact of population growth. *Science, 171*, 1212–1217.

Estudillo, J. P., Sawada, Y., & Otsuka, K. (2006). The Green Revolution, development of labor markets, and poverty reduction in the rural Philippines, 1985–2004. *Agricultural Economics, 35*, 399–407.

Forman, R. T. T., & Godron, M. (1986). *Landscape ecology*. New York: Wiley.

Forys, E. A., & Allen, C. R. (2005). The impacts of sprawl on biodiversity: The ant fauna of the lower Florida Keys. *Ecology and Society, 10*(1), 25.

Foster, D. R., Knight, D. H., & Franklin, J. F. (1998). Landscape patterns and legacies resulting from large, infrequent forest disturbances. *Ecosystems, 1*, 497–510.

Geist, H. & Lambin, E. F. (2002). Proximate causes and underlying driving forces of tropical deforestation. *Bioscience, 52*(2), 143–150.

Grove, J. M., Hinson, K. E., & Northrop, R. J. (2003). A social ecology approach to understanding urban ecosystems and landscapes. In A. R. Berkowitz, C. H. Nilon, & K. S. Hollweg (Eds.), *Understanding urban ecosystems* (pp. 167–186). New York: Springer.

Grove, J. M., Troy, A. R., O'Neil-Dunne, J. P. M., Burch, W. R., Cadenasso, M. L., & Pickett, S. T. A. (2006). Characterization of households and its implications for the vegetation of urban ecosystems. *Ecosystems, 9*, 578–597.

Haberl, H., Winiwarter, V., Andersson, K., Ayres, R. U., Boone, C., Castillo, A., et al. (2006). From LTER to LTSER: Conceptualizing the socioeconomic dimension of long-term socioecological research. *Ecology and Society, 11*(2), 13.

Hammer, R. B., Stewart, S. I., Hawbaker, T. J., & Radeloff, V. C. (2009). Housing growth, forests, and public lands in Northern Wisconsin from 1940 to 2000. *Journal of Environmental Management, 90*, 2690–2698.

Hammer, R. B., Stewart, S. I., Winkler, R. L., Radeloff, V. C., & Voss, P. R. (2004). Characterizing dynamic spatial and temporal residential density patterns from 1940–1990 across the North Central United States. *Landscape and Urban Planning, 69*, 183–199.

Hammond, A. (1998). *Which world? Scenarios for the 21st century*. Washington, DC: Island Press.

Hansen, A. J., Knight, R. L., Marzluff, J. M., Powell, S., Brown, K., Gude, P. H., et al. (2005). Effects of exurban development on biodiversity: Patterns, mechanisms, and research needs. *Ecological Applications, 15*, 1893–1905.

Hansen, A. J., Rasker, R., Maxwell, B., Rotella, J. J., Johnson, J. D., Parmenter, A. W., et al. (2002). Ecological causes and consequences of demographic change in the New West. *BioScience, 52*, 151–162.

Hardin, G. (1968). The tragedy of the commons. *Science, 162*, 1243–1248.

Hardin, G. (1993). *Living within limits: Ecology, economics, and population taboos*. New York: Oxford University Press.

Hawbaker, T. J., & Radeloff, V. C. (2004). Road and landscape pattern in northern Wisconsin based on a comparison of four road data sources. *Conservation Biology, 18*, 1233–1244.

Hazell, P., & Wood, S. (2008). Drivers of change in global agriculture. *Philosophical Transactions of the Royal Society B Biological Sciences, 363*, 495–515.

Hess, G. R., & King, T. J. (2002). Planning open spaces for wildlife I. Selecting focal species using a Delphi survey approach. *Landscape and Urban Planning, 58*, 25–40.

IPCC. (2007). *Climate change 2007: The physical science basis. Contribution of working group I to the fourth assessment report of the Intergovernmental Panel on Climate Change*. Cambridge, UK: Cambridge University Press.

Johnson, K. M., & Beale, C. L. (1998). The rural rebound. *The Wilson Quarterly, 22*, 16–27.

Johnson, K. M., & Beale, C. L. (2002). Nonmetro recreation counties: Their identification and rapid growth. *Rural America, 17*(4), 12–19.

Johnson, K. M., & Fuguitt, G. V. (2000). Continuity and change in rural migration patterns, 1950–1995. *Rural Sociology, 65*, 27–49.

Jones, E. T., & Lynch, K. A. (2007). Nontimber forest products and biodiversity management in the Pacific Northwest. *Forest Ecology and Management, 246*, 29–37.

Kluza, D. A., Griffin, C. R., & Degraaf, R. M. (2000). Housing developments in rural New England: Effects on forest birds. *Animal Conservation, 3*, 15–26.

Kuemmerle, T., Hostert, P., Radeloff, V. C., Perzanowski, K., & Kruhlov, I. (2007). Post-socialist forest disturbance in the Carpathian border region of Poland, Slovakia, and Ukraine. *Ecological Applications, 17*, 1279–1295.

Kuemmerle, T., Hostert, P., Radeloff, V. C., Perzanowski, K., & Kruhlov, I. (2008). Post-socialist farmland abandonment in the Carpathians. *Ecosystems, 11*, 614–628.

Lambin, E. F., & Ehrlich, D. (1997). Land-cover changes in Sub-Saharan Africa (1982–1991): Application of a change index based on remotely sensed surface temperature and vegetation indices at a continental scale. *Remote Sensing of the Environment, 61*, 181–200.

Lambin, E. F., & Linderman, M. (2006). Time series of remote sensing data for land change science. *IEEE Transactions on Geoscience and Remote Sensing, 44*, 1926–1928.

Lambin, E. F., Turner, B. L., Geist, H. J., Agbola, S. B., Angelsen, A., Bruce, J. W., et al. (2001). The causes of land-use and land-cover change: Moving beyond the myths. *Global Environmental Change, 11*, 261–269.

Lepczyk, C. A., Flather, C. H., Radeloff, V. C., Pidgeon, A. M., Hammer, R. B., & Liu, J. (2008). Human impacts on regional avian diversity and abundance. *Conservation Biology, 22*, 405–446.

Lepczyk, C. A., Hammer, R. B., Stewart, S. I., & Radeloff, V. C. (2007). Spatiotemporal dynamics of housing growth hotspots in the North Central U.S. from 1940 to 2000. *Landscape Ecology, 22*, 939–952.

Lepczyk, C. A., Lortie, C. J., & Anderson, L. (2008). An ontology of landscapes. *Ecological Complexity, 5*, 272–279.

Levin, S. A. (1992). The problem of pattern and scale in ecology. *Ecology, 73*, 1943–1983.

Linderman M., An, L., Bearer, S., He, G., Ouyang, Z., & Liu, J. (2006). Interactive effects of natural and human disturbances on vegetation dynamics across landscapes. *Ecological Applications, 16*, 452–463.

Linderman, M., Zeng, Y., & Rowhani, P. (2010). Climate and land-use effects on interannual fAPAR variability from MODIS 250 m data. *Photogrammetric Engineering and Remote Sensing, 76*, 807–817

Lindholm, M. (2010) Flock To N.D. Oil Town Leads To Housing Crisis. NPR, All Things Considered. Broadcast 28 May 2010.

Liu, J., Daily, G. C., Ehrlich, P. R., & Luck, G. W. (2003). Effects of household dynamics on resource consumption and biodiversity. *Nature, 421*, 530–533

Liu, J., Dietz, T., Carpenter, S. R., Alberti, M., Folke, C., Moran, E., et al. (2007). Complexity of coupled human and natural systems. *Science, 317*, 1513–1516.

Liu, J., Dietz, T., Carpenter, S. R., Folke, C., Alberti, M., Redman, C. L., et al. (2007). Coupled human and natural systems. *Ambio, 36*, 639–649.

Liu, J., Ouyang, Z., Tan, Y., Yang, J., & Zhang, H. (1999). Changes in human population structure: Implications for biodiversity conservation. *Population and Environment, 21*, 45–58.

Liverman, D., Moran, E. F., Rindfuss, R. R., & Stern, P. C. (1998). *People and pixels: Linking remote sensing and social science*. Washington, DC: National Academy Press.

Loarie, S. R., Duffy, P. B., Hamilton, H., Asner, G. P., Field, C. B. & Ackerly, D. D. (2009). The velocity of climate change. *Nature, 462*, 1052–1055.

Malthus, T. R. (1798). *An essay on the principle of population*. London: J. Johnson. Reprinted 2007, Mineola, MN: Dover.

Marcin, T. C. (1993). Demographic-change – Implications for forest management. *Journal of Forestry, 91*, 39–45.

Matlack, G. R. (1997). Four centuries of forest clearance and regeneration in the hinterland of a large city. *Journal of Biogeography, 24*, 281–295.

McCann, K. S. (2000). The diversity-stability debate. *Nature, 405*, 228–233.

McKinney, M. L. (2002). Urbanization biodiversity and conservation. *BioScience, 52*, 883–890.

Meadows, D. H., Meadows, D. L., Randers, J., & Behrens, W. W., III (1972). *The limits to growth*. New York: Universe Books.

Miller, S. G., Knight, R. L., & Miller, C. K. (1998). Influence of recreational trails on breeding bird communities. *Ecological Applications, 8*, 162–169.

Niemelä, J., Kotze, D. J., Venn, S., Penev, L., Stoyanov, I., Spence, J., et al. (2002). Carabid beetle assemblages (Coleoptera, Carabidae) across urban-rural gradients: An international comparison. *Landscape Ecology, 17*, 387–401.

Odell, E. A., & Knight, R. L. (2001). Songbird and medium-sized mammal communities associated with exurban development in Pitkin County Colorado. *Conservation Biology, 5*, 1143–1150.

Ouedraogo, I., Savadogo, P., Tigabu, M., Cole, R., Odén, P. C., & Ouadba, J.-M. (2009). Is rural migration a threat to environmental sustainability in Southern Burkina Faso? *Land Degradation and Development, 20*, 217–230.

Parks, P. J., Hardie, I. W., Tedder, C. A., & Wear, D. N. (2000). Using resource economics to anticipate forest land use change in the US mid-Atlantic Region. *Environmental Monitoring and Assessment, 63*, 175–185.

Pickett, S. T. A., & Ostfeld, R. S. (1995). The shifting paradigm in ecology. In R. L. Knight & S. F. Bates (Eds.), *A new century for natural resources management* (pp. 261–278). Washington, DC: Island Press.

Radeloff, V. C., Hammer, R. B., Stewart, S. I., Fried, J. S., Holcomb, S. S., & McKeefry, J. F. (2005). The wildland urban interface in the United States. *Ecological Applications, 15*, 799–805.

Radeloff, V. C., Stewart, S. I., Hawbaker, T. J., Gimmi, U., Pidgeon, A. M., Flather, C. H., et al. (2010). Housing growth in and near United States' protected areas limits their conservation value. *Proceedings of the National Academy of Sciences, 107*, 940–945.

Rhoda, R. (1983). Rural development and urban migration: Can we keep them down on the farm? *International Migration Review, 17*, 34–64.

Rowhani, P., Degomme, O., Guha-Sapir, D. & Lambin, E. F. (2011). Climate variability, malnutrition, and armed conflicts in the Horn of Africa. *Climatic change, 105*(1–2), 207–222.

Rowhani, P., Lepczyk, C. A., Linderman, M. A., Pidgeon, A. M., Radeloff, V. C., Culbert, P. D., et al. (2008). Variability in energy influences avian distribution patterns across the USA. *Ecosystems, 11*(6), 854–867.

Rudel, T. K., Schneider, L., Uriarte, M., Turner, B. L., DeFries, R., Lawrence, D., et al. (2009). Agricultural intensification and changes in cultivated areas, 1970–2005. *Proceedings of the National Academy of Sciences of the US A, 106*(49), 20675–20680.

Running, S. W. (2008). Climate change – Ecosystem disturbance, carbon, and climate. *Science, 321*, 652–653.

Rutledge, D. T., & Lepczyk, C. A. (2002). Landscape change: Patterns, effects, and implications for adaptive management of wildlife resources. In J. Liu & W. W. Taylor (Eds.), *Integrating landscape ecology into natural resources management* (pp. 312–333). Cambridge: Cambridge University Press.

Sanderson, E. W., Jaiteh, M., Levy, M. A., Redford, K. H., Wannebo, A. V., & Woolmer, G. (2002). The human footprint and the last of the wild. *BioScience, 52*, 891–904.

Sauer, J. R., Hines, J. E., & Fallon, J. (2008). *The North American breeding bird survey, results and analysis 1966–2007*. Version 5.15, 2008. Laurel, MD: USGS Patuxent Wildlife Research Center

Scott, R. L., Cable, W. L., Huxman, T. E., Nagler, P. L., Hernandez, M., & Goodrich, D. C. (2008). Multiyear Riparian evapotranspiration and groundwater use for a semiarid watershed. *Journal of Arid Environments, 72*, 1232–1246.

Soulé, M. E. (1991). Land-use planning and wildlife maintenance–guidelines for conserving wildlife in an urban landscape. *Journal of the American Planning Association, 57*, 313–323.

Theobald, D. M. (2000). Fragmentation by inholdings and exurban development. In R. L. Knight, F. W. Smith, S. W. Buskirk, W. H. Romme, & W. L. Baker (Eds.), *Forest fragmentation in the Southern Rocky mountains* (pp. 155–174). Boulder, CO: University Press of Colorado.

Theobald, D. M. (2001). Land-use dynamics beyond the American urban fringe. *Geographical Review, 91*, 544–554.

Thoreau, H. D. (1854). *Walden*. Reprinted in 2009 as "Walden and Civil Disobedience" by Ann Arbor Media Group LLC, Ann Arbor, MI.

Ticktin, T. (2004). The ecological implications of harvesting non-timber forest products. *Journal of Applied Ecology, 41*, 11–21.

Turner, M. G. (1989). Landscape ecology: The effect of pattern on process. *Annual Review of Ecology and Systematics, 20*, 171–197.

Turner, M. G., Gardner, R. H., & O'Neill, R. V. (2001). *Landscape ecology in theory and practice*. New York: Springer.

Vining, D. R., Jr., & Strauss, A. (1977). A demonstration that the current deconcentration of population in the United States is a clean break with the past. *Environment and Planning A, 9*, 751–758.

Vitousek, P. M., Mooney, H. A., Lubchenco, J., & Melillo, J. M. (1997). Human domination of Earth's ecosystems. *Science, 277*, 494–499.

Vogelmann, J. E., Howard, S. M., Yang, L., Larson, C. R., Wylie, B. K., & van Driel, N. (2001). Completion of the 1990s National Land Cover Data Set for the conterminous United States from Landsat Thematic Mapper data and ancillary data sources. *Photogrammetric Engineering and Remote Sensing, 67*, 650–662.

Vogt, K. A., Grove, M., Asbjornsen, H., Maxwell, K. B., Vogt, D. J., Sigurđardóttir, R., et al. (2002). Linking ecological and social scales for natural resource management. In J. Liu & W. W. Taylor (Eds.), *Integrating landscape ecology into natural resources management* (pp. 143–175). Cambridge: Cambridge University Press.

Wade, A. A., & Theobald, D. M. (2010). Residential development encroachment on U. S. protected areas. *Conservation Biology, 24*, 151–161.

Waide, R. B., Willig, M. R., Steiner, C. F., Mittelbach, G., Gough, L., Dodson, S. I., et al. (1999). The relationship between productivity and species richness. *Annual Review of Ecology and Systematics, 30*, 257–300.

Warren, P., Tripler, C., Bolger, D., Faeth, S., Huntly, N., Lepczyk, C., et al. (2006). Urban food webs: Predators, prey, and the people who feed them. *Bulletin of the Ecological Society of America, 87*, 387–393.

Wear, D. N., Turner, M. G., & Flamm, R. O. (1996). Ecosystem management with multiple owners: Landscape dynamics in a southern Appalachian watershed. *Ecological Applications, 6*, 1173–1188.

Wu, J. (2007). Scale and scaling: A cross-disciplinary perspective. In J. Wu & R. Hobbs (Eds.), *Key topics in landscape ecology* (pp. 115–142). Cambridge: Cambridge University Press.

Wu, J., & Loucks, O. L. (1995). From balance of nature to hierarchical patch dynamics: A paradigm shift in ecology. *The Quarterly Review of Biology, 70*, 439–466.

# 24. Boom or Bust? Population Dynamics in Natural Resource-Dependent Counties

**Richelle Winkler, Cheng Cheng, and Shaun Golding**

## Introduction

People have long departed natural-resource-dependent rural areas for more urban locales, a trend which has contributed to steady population loss and left rural communities with comparatively low levels of human, social, and financial capitals (Lichter, Heaton, & Fuguitt, 1979; Carr & Kefalas, 2009; Domina, 2006). Contrasting trends, however, have emerged in some rural places. Many people value the natural environment for amenity qualities, including scenic views, recreational opportunities, wildlife habitat, and rural culture (see Chapter 23 in this volume). Numerous rural communities around the world have come to rely on attracting people toward this alternative vision of natural resources presuming that amenity migrants bring skills and resources into the community. Research has clearly established that destination communities experience population growth; but how do characteristics of in-migrants and out-migrants change the resulting population composition? How do migration flows to and from different types of natural resource-dependent communities shape key community assets? Does destination development stem the outflow of rural communities' "best and brightest" young people? This chapter investigates these questions.

R. Winkler (✉)
Department of Social Sciences, Michigan Technological University, Houghton, MI 49931, USA

Applied Population Laboratory, Department of Community and Environmental Sociology, University of Wisconsin-Madison, Madison, WI 53706, USA
e-mail: rwinkler@mtu.edu

Generally speaking, fertility and mortality rates across the more developed countries have been slowly declining over the last several decades. In the absence of migration, the completion of the demographic transition has left more developed countries in a relatively stable, aging, and eventually declining population state. Migration, however, continues to have dramatic impacts on population change especially at more local levels. Today, differences in population change between communities depend almost entirely on migration patterns. Although aging and natural decrease are certainly important issues affecting rural communities, these problems are ultimately driven by migration patterns. For these reasons, this study focuses on migration as the most important component of population change within more developed countries.

Migration influences community vitality not only by contributing to population growth or decline, but also by changing compositional factors such as age, educational attainment, income, and labor force status. Migration *selectivity* alters the socioeconomic structure of communities as people with certain demographic and socioeconomic characteristics are more or less likely to move to and from different types of communities. Different types of natural resource dependence produce distinctive migration patterns that ultimately shape the assets that localities can engage for community development. For example, young adults and more highly educated people are particularly likely to move *out* of farming-dependent counties, while high-income adults at retirement ages are more likely to move *into* amenity destination counties. The resulting population composition influences communities' ability to mobilize resources and weather economic difficulties. In sum, exchanges of human, financial, and social capitals associated with migration produce demographic conditions that contribute to or detract from community well-being.

This chapter evaluates how migration flows changed the population composition of rural counties in the United States in the 1990s and how this process differs in amenity destination counties in comparison to extractive resource-dependent counties. Using data from Census 2000 on migration flows between 1995 and 2000 and age-specific net migration estimates between 1990 and 2000; we test for differences by age, educational attainment, household income, and labor force participation for in-migrants and out-migrants in farming-dependent, mining-dependent, and destination-dependent counties. We analyze the degree to which migration alters population composition in these county types by comparing the observed population structure (by age, education, income, and labor force participation) to the expected population structure had there been no migration over the study period. Finally, we employ Flora and Flora's (2008) community capitals framework (CCF) to analyze how migration selectivity affects community assets, namely human, financial, and social capitals.

The United States in the 1990s offers a particularly interesting context for studying migration's impacts on rural communities. The decade brought sustained economic expansion and increases in personal income in the United States and other high-income countries. Similarly, neoliberalism expanded global capital and labor markets, and the internet and other media sources brought global media and communication streams to new areas. At the same time, the first of the Baby Boom generation reached early retirement age, a time in the life course when people tend to be more mobile than during prime working adulthood. Together these forces produced a more mobile, educated, and wealthy populace with increasing information about previously unheard of rural destinations than at any other point in history. For these reasons, migration to rural destination communities was elevated during the 1990s and had important impacts on the socioeconomic structure of destination communities. Farming- and especially mining-dependent communities, conversely, experienced significant out-migration of young adults in the 1990s as labor markets and agricultural markets globalized and technologies continued to mechanize extractive processes, reducing domestic labor demands in these industries.

Although our research is focused on the United States, a growing catalog of international research illustrates that similar patterns are occurring in other industrialized nations (see Gosnell & Abrams, 2009 for a review). The rural migration trend playing out in the United States has a parallel in most wealthy nations, and destination-oriented development is becoming a development strategy in developing nations as well (Ma & Chow, 2006; Sunil, Rojas, & Bradley, 2007), which may also experience similar effects.

## Community Capitals and Migration Selectivity

Flora and Flora's community capitals framework offers a way to evaluate how rural communities may fare amidst changes in their demographic composition. It is a well-developed strategy for analyzing rural community well-being that has been employed in sites around the world (Emery & Flora, 2006; Fey, Bregendahl, & Flora, 2006; Gasteyer, 2009), but not specifically to study the effects of migration. CCF contends that all communities have assets that can be thought of as different forms of capital (community capitals). When community capitals are well balanced and invested in community development, they foster social inclusion, economic vitality, and healthy ecosystems. The seven community capitals include: natural capital, cultural capital, human capital, social capital, political capital, financial capital, and built capital (Flora & Flora, 2008).

In this study, we posit that the ways in which natural resources (natural capital) are used for economic gain affect migration flows which, in turn, shape communities' accumulation of human, financial, and social capitals. We analyze three different types of natural resource-dependent communities (farming, mining, and amenity destination). While each enjoys abundant natural capital, the ways in which the stocks of natural capital are used and enjoyed vary considerably. We presume that these different uses and associated social and economic conditions influence migrant characteristics and flows.

Migration affects community capitals by changing the population composition of rural communities. Migration is highly selective by age, labor force status, income, and educational attainment. The propensity for migration to be selective heightens the likelihood that it will change the population structure of both sending and receiving communities and consequently impact community capitals. Put simply, inflows bring certain types of new people into communities, outflows take certain types away, and the resulting balance influences a community's demographic assets. While migration patterns may affect each of the seven community capitals and though they are each important components of community sustainability, we specifically examine migration's influence on human, financial, and social capitals because these are the most likely to be transparently manifest in migration data.

**Human capital** is the foundation of labor force and community development. It refers to the skills and productive capacity of the community (including labor force, education, health, and leadership) that may attract employers to an area and provide a generally capable set of residents to engage in and lead community projects (Flora & Flora, 2008; Becker, 2002). One of the most important factors impacting human capital in rural communities is out-migration of young adults (Alston, 2004; Fey et al., 2006; Rye, 2006; Carr & Kefalas, 2009). Alston (2004) explains how out-migration of young adults from rural Australia threatens rural community sustainability by removing future leaders, small business owners, entrepreneurs, and community drivers. Communities where migration generates an increase in education levels, a growing number of people at prime working ages and in the labor force, and/or an increase in the younger and healthier population experience increasing stocks of human capital.

**Financial capital** refers to money within a community that can be used for further investment in the community, like starting new businesses, funding the local government in the form of taxes, and contributing to charitable causes. Financial capital is closely related to the success of local banks who can offer loans to key local businesses that support local economic development, and in turn, to the financial well-being of community residents (Flora & Flora, 2008; Green, 1991). Here, migration flows that increase the income level of the population should correspondingly increase community financial capital.

**Social capital** is the value of connections between individuals and groups based on norms of reciprocity and mutual trust. The more connected residents are to one another, the more likely they are to share a sense of common identity and to work together toward meeting community goals (Flora & Flora, 1996, 2008; Putnam, 2000; Larsen et al., 2004). In this sense, social capital stimulates participation in community action, solidifies community pride, and strengthens productive capacity as individuals and groups within the community take advantage of networks to meet needs.[1] Still, it is important to recognize that social capital can be *inclusionary*, promoting the incorporation of disadvantaged groups into social and community life and strengthening a broad sense of community, or *exclusionary*, promoting the interest of powerful groups and those who "are connected" often at the expense of less advantaged residents. Furthermore, social capital may include close ties between local community members who are closely "bonded" and interact regularly or weaker ties between local residents and people outside the local area or acquaintances by "bridging" physical and social distance between groups. Putnam (2000) distinguishes these types as differences between "bonding" and "bridging" social capital. For the purposes of this study, we focus on bonding social capital, but recognize that newcomers to a community may increase capacity for bridging social capital.

We operationalize the bonding social capital concept by examining population turnover. Turnover refers to the amount of migration into and out-of a community. The development of inclusive community social capital requires time in the community to build trust and networks. High levels of in- and out-migration (population turnover) disrupt trust-building processes and limit development of a shared identity and of a "we're in it together" attitude that is integral for inclusive community action (Salamon, 2003; Flora & Flora, 1996). Newcomers bring the *potential* for social capital and especially for bridging social capital between residents of origin and destination communities; but they may actually increase conflict in the community and contribute to the development of social capital within certain groups that exclude others (Flora & Flora, 1996). In the end, communities that experience

---

[1] Please note that social capital is only one component of community well-being and cannot replace economic opportunities in promoting community and economic development. Furthermore, social capital is inherently neutral in that it can create either positive or negative impacts depending on one's position and perspective (Coleman, 1988; Fukuyama, 2002; Portes, 1998; Dasgupta & Serageldin, 1999).

less migration (in or out) may best develop higher levels of inclusionary bonding social capital.

## Natural Resource Dependence, Migration, and Community Capitals

Decades of net out-migration have plagued rural communities around the world, especially those that depend on resource extraction or agriculture. Industry concentration, global competition, and continual mechanization have reduced the number of workers needed and reduced the number of overall jobs in communities without diversified economies (Galston & Baehler, 1995; Freundenburg, 1992; see also Chapters 19 and 21 in this volume). The subsequent out-migration of educated and financially secure individuals has limited resource-dependent communities' ability to cope with social and economic change (Freundenburg, 1992). In particular, resource dependence has been associated with low levels of human capital (Birdsall, Pinckney, & Sabot, 2001; Johnson & Stallman, 1994) and inclusive social capital (Alao, 2007). Community problems associated with natural resource dependence (particularly mining) are so great that scholars refer to the "resource curse" of places rich in natural resources, but with poor economies, poverty, and social problems (Sachs & Warner, 2001; Humphrey et al., 1993; Auty, 1993, 2001).

Farming-dependent counties in the US have experienced consistent population loss since 1940 (White, 2008; Albrecht, 1993). Out-migration from farming counties has been particularly stark among young adults (Johnson, Voss, Hammer, Fuguitt, & McNiven, 2005). In a case study of an Iowa farming community, Carr and Kefalas (2009) demonstrate how out-migration of young adults and more highly educated people has depleted available human and financial capitals and restricted the ability of the community to reinvigorate itself. They argue that the widespread out-migration of the "best and brightest" young people across farming-dependent communities of the American Heartland is "hollowing out the middle" of the country. The phenomenon has been observed internationally as well, as agricultural production continues to consolidate around global markets. In the United Kingdom and Australia, for example, scholars note that rural places' social landscapes have experienced a similar transition away from agricultural production entailing many of the same population shifts observed in the United States (Halfacree, 1997; Marsden, 1998).

Mining-dependent communities around the world are known to follow a boom and bust pattern of growth and expansion followed by sharp population and economic decline. For instance, the mining industry expanded dramatically in the 1970s with the worldwide energy sector boom following the 1973 Oil Embargo and the parallel expansion of coal-fired electricity. The energy sector then busted in the 1980s and 1990s as oil prices declined and the industry further contracted. Paralleling these economic trends, mining-dependent counties in the US experienced little net migration in the 1950s and 1960s, significant net *in*-migration in the 1970s, and significant net *out*-migration in the 1980s and 1990s.[2] At the same time, mining-dependent communities around the world face some of the most challenging social, economic, and environmental problems. For example, Kuyek and Coumans (2003) explain how Canadian mining communities struggle with poverty, inequality, political corruption, environmental devastation, and health problems that are exacerbated by the cyclical in- and out-migration of young adults, skilled workers, and more highly educated residents.

In sum, industrialized nations have seen major structural changes in their rural economies over the past several decades that have contributed to out-migration and sustained population loss in extractive natural-resource-dependent rural communities. At the same time, some rural communities have increasingly subscribed to a new regime of rural natural resource dependence whereby the scenic and recreational values of natural resources fuel the local economy. These amenity destination-dependent communities depend on attracting residents and visitors in what Boyle and Halfacree (1998) refer to as a postproductivist countryside that is built upon a nostalgic idealization of rural environments and community life (the rural idyll).

The amenity migration phenomenon has been a primary focus for demographers and scholars from several disciplines. Counterurbanization patterns

---

[2] Estimates of net migration for mining-dependent counties are derived from county-specific net migration estimates by age downloaded from ICPSR based on the work of Bowles and Tarver (1965); Bowles, Beale, and Lee (1975); White, Mueser, and Tierney (1987); Fuguitt and Beale (1993); and Voss et al. (2004).

(migration from urban to rural areas) are well documented across more developed countries (Gosnell & Abrams, 2009; Moss, 2006; Champion, 1994; Fuguitt, 1985; Dahms & McComb, 1999; Casado-Diaz, Kaiser, & Warnes, 2004; Hugo, 1988; see also Chapter 5 in this volume),[3] and much of the in-migration to rural areas can be explained by the presence of natural, recreational, and cultural amenities (McGranahan, 1999; Johnson & Beale, 2002; Jobes, 2000). Baby Boomers are particularly likely to move to idyllic rural locales, and as this large cohort reaches retirement years, amenity-related development in rural areas is likely to intensify (Plane, Henrie, & Perry, 2005; Cromatie & Nelson, 2009).

Although amenity migration has been most prominent in industrialized nations, the developing world is also experiencing destination-oriented development in attractive locations from China (Ma & Chow, 2006) to Argentina (Otero et al., 2006) and South Africa (Visser, 2004). Following the rapid growth of eco-tourism, a growing number of expatriates from developed nations are choosing to purchase seasonal property or permanently migrate to popular destinations (Sunil et al., 2007). Expatriate living in amenity destinations has become trendy, as exemplified by television shows such as "House Hunters International" and websites such as www.retire-abroad.org. Amenity migration will likely increase over the next several years in both more and less developed countries as the number of people worldwide with economic means, retirement age, strong quality of life values, and conceptions of a scenic rural idyll grows. As amenity-related development increases in the developing world, it is particularly important to understand how migration patterns impact population composition and the well-being of communities in areas where the original population is materially disadvantaged in comparison to in-migrants.

Finally, reliance on destination development is becoming increasingly formal and institutionalized, making it imperative to examine this new type of resource dependence more closely. Community development agencies promote it as an alternative economic base to grow rural economies and to promote sustainable rural communities (Reeder & Brown, 2005; Chipeniuk, 2004; Galston & Baehler, 1995; Power, 1996). The strategy relies on in-migrants, tourists, and seasonal homeowners bringing money and demand for goods and services into the community, increasing tax rolls, and spurring economic development (Reeder & Brown, 2005). In contrast to more traditional economic base theory (where jobs attract people to place), destination communities bank on the idea that jobs *follow* people to place. This alternative type of resource dependency may reverse the out-migration problem facing many rural communities by attracting in-migrants. But does destination development alleviate problems of low human, financial, and social capitals that extractive resource-dependent communities experience?

It is well documented that amenity destinations experience population growth and net in-migration; yet, little research attempts to link characteristics of both in-migrants and out-migrants to changes in population composition. Shumway and Otterstrom's work (2001) provides an important exception. In an analysis of counties in the US Mountain West, they find that amenity destination counties experience significant net gains in income (financial capital) due to migration flows. Also, Plane et al. (2005) analyze migration up and down the urban hierarchy by age and educational attainment. They find that young, single, and well-educated adults tend to move toward the largest metropolitan areas and away from the most rural areas. Conversely, retirement age people move from urban toward more rural areas. They do not, however, compare counties with different economic bases or evaluate migration's impacts on population composition. Johnson et al. (2005) and Cromatie and Nelson (2009) investigate net migration by age in nonmetropolitan recreation counties and retirement destination counties; but these studies do not examine inflows and outflows, which would be necessary to reveal the total effects of migration.

Our study is unique in that it examines migration *flows* by migrant characteristics and natural resource base. We examine the extent to which communities with different types of natural resource dependence experience unique migration patterns by age, educational attainment, income, and labor force status; and how these patterns shape population composition. Rural demographers should be particularly concerned

---

[3] See proceedings of Understanding and Managing Amenity-led Migration in the Mountain Regions international conference held in Banff, Canada in May 2008.

with migration to and from rural communities and its influence on population composition because migration has an important impact on the local social structures within which rural people meet their daily needs, and thus, affects individuals' and families' life chances and well-being. Ultimately, cumulative migration patterns are intricately related to rural community sustainability, helping to determine which communities flourish and which fizzle.

## Data and Methods

This study analyzes data from US Census 2000, Gross Migration Flows Files which estimate migration flows by county between 1995 and 2000, based on the 1 in 6 household sample census question: "where did you live five years ago?" Data are reported by multiple demographic and socioeconomic characteristics including age, educational attainment, household income, and labor force status. These are the only US data that allow for detailed analysis of migration flows by multiple characteristics for individual counties; yet, they are limited in that short duration moves that occur *within* the five-year time period are not captured and so they likely underestimate the true amount of migration that has occurred. Unlike annual migration data published by the Internal Revenue Service, census flow data include characteristics such as age, educational attainment, and labor force status; and they are not limited to households that file tax returns, allowing for a more robust account of lower income and rural populations, who may be more reliant on informal employment. Secondarily, we draw on county-specific net migration estimates by age 1990–2000 generated by Voss, McNiven, Hammer, Johnson, and Fuguitt (2004) to examine the impact of net migration flows on age structure.[4]

Nonmetropolitan counties are classified according to natural resource dependence. Farming- and mining-dependent counties follow the USDA's Economic Research Service (ERS) 2004 definitions. Amenity destination counties are defined according to a destination development scale developed by Winkler in a related study (see Winkler, 2010 for a detailed description). This measure is based on the proportion of housing units for seasonal or recreational use, the proportion of residents that are recent in-migrants from a metropolitan area, and the proportion of owner-occupied housing units valued at $200,000 or more.[5] Unlike McGranahan's natural amenity index (1999) or Johnson and Beale's nonmetropolitan recreation counties (2002), the destination scale measures the degree to which counties experience amenity development, in contrast to environmental characteristics or recreational infrastructure. In total, 182 counties are classified as destination dependent, 394 are farming dependent, and 106 are mining dependent. The remaining 1,342 nonmetro counties are classified as "other" and are mostly manufacturing, government, or service dependent or have more diverse economies. These types of counties might be expected to have more stable populations than the natural resource-dependent communities. Destination counties are dispersed across the United States, with concentrations in the Intermountain West, southern Appalachia, the Upper Midwest lakes areas, the Ozarks, coastal areas, the Sierra Nevadas, and the Texas hill country. Farming-dependent counties are highly concentrated in the Great Plains. Mining-dependent counties are clustered in Appalachia, the Texas and Oklahoma oil country, Nevada, and dispersed across the Intermountain West.

A move is recorded when a respondent lives in a different county at Census 2000 than where he/she lived five years before (in 1995). Only domestic moves are considered, excluding in-migration from abroad due to the fact that data on corresponding out-migration from the US are not available. For each county, we calculate four migration indicators: an in-migration ratio (IMR), an out-migration rate (OMR), a gross migration rate (GMR), and a migration efficiency index (MEI) by

---

[4] Nonmetropolitan counties (as of 2003 definitions) in the contiguous 48 states are included in this analysis for a total of 2,024 observations. Alaska and Hawaii are excluded because of their great distance from other US counties, their proclivity for generating outliers, and because the amenity destination measure is not available at this time.

[5] A county is coded as "destination" if its score exceeds one standard deviation from the mean for all nonmetropolitan counties and it does not have more than 4% of its population living in group quarters. So that categories are mutually exclusive, destination county status trumps all other types. The destination classification correlates with McGranahan's (1999) natural amenity index at 0.32 and with Johnson and Beale's nonmetropolitan recreation counties at 0.67.

age group, educational attainment, household income level, and labor force status. For the IMR, OMR, and GMR the denominator is the original population who resided in the county in 1995, or the number of nonmigrants plus the number of out-migrants. So, the out-migration measure is truly a rate in that it divides the number of out-migrants from the county by the population at risk of out-migrating. Conversely, the IMR is not a true rate. Rather than dividing in-migrants by the population at risk of in-migrating (those living in all *other* counties in 1995), it divides them by the destination county's original population. Thus, it is a ratio of in-migrants to what the population would have been had there been no migration.

Looking together at the IMR and OMR offers a sense of population turnover. If in-migration and out-migration are both high, there is a high degree of turnover. If, conversely, both are low, there is low population turnover. The GMR more directly measures the degree to which moves into and out-of a county affect the population. It is calculated by summing the number of in-migrants and out-migrants and dividing the total by the starting population in 1995.

Table 24.1 indicates that between 1995 and 2000, nonmetropolitan counties, on average, experienced slight net out-migration, while metro counties experienced net in-migration. It is important to recognize that these values are county medians, rather than sums of migrant flows, by county type. If migration flow counts for nonmetro and metro counties are summed, the opposite finding holds, with nonmetro counties experiencing a net *in*-migration of about 246,000 residents and metro counties experiencing net *out*-migration. Overall, migration flows between urban and rural counties largely balanced one another out in the late 1990s, so that neither group experienced significant net gain or loss. Considerable variation by county type, however, exists. Farming- and mining-dependent counties experienced net out-migration and destination-dependent counties experienced substantial net in-migration. In metro areas, central cities experienced net out-migration at similar rates as farming- and mining-dependent counties, while suburban metro counties experienced considerable net in-migration.

Following Shryock, Siegel, and Larmon (1980), the migration efficiency index is the ratio of net migration to gross migration. It is calculated as follows.

$$\text{MEI} = [(\text{in-migrants} - \text{out-migrants})/ (\text{in-migrants} + \text{out-migrants})]*100$$

The MEI measures the degree to which migration streams are cancelling each other out (low efficiency) as opposed to changing the structure of the population (high efficiency). Values closer to zero suggest little net gain or loss of population, but perhaps substantial turnover. Values farther from zero suggest significant population change due to migration. Rather than taking the absolute value, we retain the directional component of the measure allowing it to capture both net migration and migration efficiency. This means that values above zero indicate positive net migration, whereas values below zero indicate net out-migration. MEIs are less intuitive to interpret than more basic migration rates, but they can be understood in relation to one another as relatively "high" or relatively "low." For all US counties between 1995 and 2000, the mean MEI was 0.7 per 100, with a standard deviation of 15.7. For this reason, we suggest that values of ±10 represent a moderately efficient migration flow and values of ±15 or more represent high efficiency.

**Table 24.1** Summary of migration by county type, 1995–2000

|  | n | Median population | IMR | OMR | NMR |
|---|---|---|---|---|---|
| **Nonmetro total** |  | 15,869 | 17.8 | 18.9 | −0.7 |
| Destination | 182 | 17,275 | 26.0 | 21.0 | 3.7 |
| Farming | 394 | 4,881 | 16.9 | 21.4 | −4.3 |
| Mining | 106 | 12,153 | 15.6 | 20.4 | −4.3 |
| Other Nonmetro | 1,342 | 20,882 | 17.5 | 17.7 | −0.04 |
| **Metro total** |  | 83,217 | 21.8 | 18.8 | 2.20 |
| Central city | 54 | 972,260 | 15.6 | 17.5 | −4.1 |
| Suburban | 346 | 81,911 | 25.1 | 19.6 | 5.1 |
| Other metro | 666 | 77,799 | 20.3 | 18.4 | 1.5 |

IMR = $\bar{x}$ ((inflow/starting population) *100)
OMR = $\bar{x}$ ((outflow/starting population) *100)
NMR = $\bar{x}$ (((inflow − outflow)/(starting population)) *100)
Within metro classes follow a modified version of ERS urban influence codes 2003.
*Source*: US Census Bureau, Gross Migration Summary Files by County.

## Results

As expected, migration flows are highly selective and vary considerably by type of resource dependency. Highly educated and high-income residents moved into destination counties, increasing the socioeconomic status (SES) of the resulting population. Conversely, farming- and mining-dependent counties experienced out-migration of higher SES residents. At the same time, however, destination counties saw similar migration patterns by age as farming and mining counties. Almost 50% of the young adults living in destination counties in 1995 had moved out by 2000. Similarly, migration flows contributed to the aging of the population in destination counties as well as in farming and mining counties. In general, in-migration rates across age, income, education, and labor force groups were higher in destination counties than other rural counties; but out-migration rates in destination counties were also high making population turnover a defining feature of destination counties. Turnover is especially striking among young adults. Overall, migration flows detracted from human, financial, and social capitals in farming and mining counties. Destination counties fared only somewhat better, as migration increased financial capital, but had inconsistent effects on human and social capitals.

Table 24.2 shows in-migration ratios (IMR), out-migration rates (OMR), and migration efficiency indexes (MEI) by age, educational attainment, household income, and labor force status for farming-, mining-, and destination-dependent counties. Scheffe means comparison tests reveal statistically significant differences between destination counties and other rural county types at p <= 0.01, except where italicized. Differences in migration indexes by age, educational attainment, household income level, and labor force status highlight significant migration selectivity. Migration index values statistically significantly different from the most desirable state (in terms of supporting development of human, financial, and social capitals) are noted with an asterisk. These comparison states include: prime working age (age 30–54), college degree, upper middle class income ($50–$74,999), and employed in the labor force.

Table 24.3 evaluates the degree to which migration changed the population structure in the 1990s. Following an approach used by Shin (1978) and Lichter et al. (1979), our study compares the socioeconomic structure of the observed population at Census 2000 to the *expected* population had there been no migration. This counterfactual population is generated by placing movers back into their county of origin (where they lived in 1995) and equals the population of nonmigrants plus out-migrants, whereas the *observed* population equals the population of nonmigrants plus in-migrants.

The compositional changes depicted in Table 24.3 may seem small enough to call into question how consequential migration flows are, but it is important to remember that these effects occur within a short (5–10 year) time frame and that they are compounded over time. Lichter et al. (1979) similarly found that in the short run, migration has little direct impact on the population composition by age, educational attainment, or occupational status, because of a relatively small net volume of migrants in comparison to nonmigrants and because migration streams tend to counterbalance one another (flow and counterflow). Still, because these patterns are found to persist over time, the potential for long-term compositional effects is great (Lichter et al., 1979).

## Migration and Human Capital

Migrants' age, educational attainment, and labor force status each affect a community's accumulation of human capital. Young adults (age 20–29), prime working-age adults (age 30–54), highly educated adults, and employed workers boost stocks of human capital. Older adults and unemployed workers detract from human capital, as they increase dependency ratios and draw on local resources. Young adults are of particular importance for human capital.

Out-migration of young adults is one of the most striking problems facing rural communities, and oftentimes it is the most skilled, intelligent, and well-connected young people who out-migrate (Carr & Kefalas, 2009; Domina, 2006; Rye, 2006; Lichter, McLaughlin, & Cornwell, 1995; Plane et al., 2005). Because many of the young people who move out of rural areas do so to achieve a higher education and few return, young adult out-migration contributes to what has often been called a rural "brain drain." In other words, the human capital effects of young adult

**Table 24.2** Migration flows by county type and migrant characteristics, 1995–2000

|  | Farming dependent | | | Mining dependent | | | Destination dependent | | |
|---|---|---|---|---|---|---|---|---|---|
|  | IMR | OMR | MEI | IMR | OMR | MEI | IMR | OMR | MEI |
| Age |  |  |  |  |  |  |  |  |  |
| 20–29 | *31.1 | *54.2 | *−28.1 | *24.4 | *43.7 | *−29.7 | *39.6 | *49.3 | *−13.7 |
| 30–54** | 19.7 | 19 | 0.7 | 17.8 | 18.5 | −4.4 | 28.5 | 20.8 | 14.9 |
| 55–74 | *10.0 | *9.6 | 0.6 | *10.9 | *10.7 | −1.4 | *23.6 | *13.4 | *26.0 |
| 75 plus | *8.5 | *13.2 | *−19.9 | *10.5 | *11.2 | −2.8 | *12.0 | *15.9 | *−12.0 |
| Education |  |  |  |  |  |  |  |  |  |
| No degree | *14.9 | *15.8 | −4 | *14.2 | *15.0 | −3.6 | *21.3 | *18.9 | *4.9 |
| High school | *14.5 | *14.7 | −2 | *15.1 | *15.7 | −4.4 | *22.4 | *17.5 | 11.9 |
| Some college | *19.1 | *19.0 | −0.8 | 18.6 | *20.4 | −6.6 | *29.1 | *21.5 | 14 |
| 4 year college** | 22.8 | 22.3 | 1.5 | 22.4 | 24.6 | −7.6 | 35.8 | 25.1 | 16 |
| Grad/Prof | *27.4 | *26.0 | 1 | 23 | 22.9 | −3.5 | 39.4 | 22.5 | 24.3 |
| Income |  |  |  |  |  |  |  |  |  |
| <$25,000 | 18.1 | 21.3 | −8.6 | 16.9 | 20.7 | −10.4 | 25.9 | 23.3 | 5 |
| $25–$49,999 | 18.2 | 20.3 | −6.1 | 17.3 | *19.6* | −10.7 | 26.1 | 21.9 | 8.7 |
| $50–$74,999** | 16.3 | 20.6 | −12.1 | 15.1 | *19.3* | −14.7 | 25.2 | 20.8 | 8.9 |
| $75–$99,999 | 15.3 | 19.1 | −10.8 | 14.2 | *19.6* | −17.9 | 25.6 | 21.8 | 7.4 |
| $100–$199,999 | 15.6 | 18.8 | −10 | 15.3 | *21.7* | −15.4 | 31.4 | 21.2 | 17 |
| $200,000 plus | 14.7 | *12.5 | −3.3 | 18.1 | 22.5 | −14.1 | *35.1 | 18.8 | *28.1 |
| Labor force |  |  |  |  |  |  |  |  |  |
| Employed** | 17.3 | 23.6 | −15.8 | 16.1 | *22.8* | −19.2 | 26.3 | 23.8 | 4.2 |
| Unemployed | *27.9 | *39.3 | −18.7 | *26.0 | *30.5 | −10.2 | *38.2 | *31.6 | 8.3 |
| Not in LF | 16.6 | *18.1 | *−7.5 | 16.5 | 18.1 | *−5.8 | 26.7 | 21.1 | 10.1 |

* Statistically significantly different from comparison row at $p < 0.01$
** Comparison row
IMR $= \bar{x}$ ((inflow/starting population) *100)
OMR $= \bar{x}$ ((outflow/starting population) *100)
MEI $= \bar{x}$ (((inflow − outflow)/(inflow + outflow)) *100)
Values in italics are NOT significantly different from Destination counties at $p < 0.01$.
*Source*: Authors' calculations from US Census 2000 Gross Migration Flows files.

migration are intensified by the fact that many who out-migrate from rural communities to enroll in colleges and universities gain education and take it elsewhere. For this reason, young adult migration flows represent flows of education (to some degree) as well as flows of workers.

Referring to Table 24.2, it is interesting to note that *in*-migration rates are highest among young adults. Considering that people are more likely to move during young adulthood than at any other time in the life course (Mulder, 1993), this may not be surprising. Still, given the attention to *out*-migration of young adults from rural areas, it is important to recognize that young adults do in-migrate at high rates, they just out-migrate even faster. Net-migration decreased the number of young adults, increased the median age of the population between 1 and 2 years, and increased the proportion of the population age 55 and over by up to 1.2% in all rural county types (Tables 24.2 and 24.3). The aging effect is particularly noteworthy in destination counties, considering that these counties were older than other county types at the start of

**Table 24.3** Migration's impact on population composition, 1990–2000

|  | 1990–2000 | | 1995–2000 | | | | |
|---|---|---|---|---|---|---|---|
|  | Median age | Age 55 plus | College degree | Low income | High income | Employed workers | Not in labor force |
| Destination counties | | | | | | | |
| Expected population | 38.8 | 27.6% | 20.0% | 24.1% | 10.3% | 57.7% | 38.8% |
| Observed population | 40.4 | 28.7% | 21.0% | 23.8% | 10.6% | 56.8% | 39.7% |
| Change due to migration | 1.6 | 1.1% | 1.0% | −0.3% | 0.3% | −1.0% | 0.9% |
| Farming counties | | | | | | | |
| Expected population | 36.3 | 27.8% | 14.3% | 32.3% | 5.3% | 57.1% | 39.5% |
| Observed population | 37.5 | 28.2% | 14.4% | 32.3% | 5.3% | 56.1% | 40.8% |
| Change due to migration | 1.2 | 0.5% | 0.1% | 0.0% | 0.0% | −1.0% | 1.2% |
| Mining counties | | | | | | | |
| Expected population | 35.2 | 23.0% | 12.1% | 35.2% | 5.4% | 51.1% | 44.8% |
| Observed population | 37.0 | 24.2% | 11.9% | 35.6% | 5.2% | 49.7% | 46.0% |
| Change due to migration | 1.9 | 1.2% | −0.1% | 0.4% | −0.2% | −1.3% | 1.3% |
| Other nonmetro | | | | | | | |
| Expected population | 36.2 | 24.7% | 14.0% | 28.9% | 6.6% | 57.3% | 39.1% |
| Observed population | 37.2 | 25.2% | 13.6% | 29.4% | 6.4% | 56.3% | 40.1% |
| Change due to migration | 1.0 | 0.5% | −0.4% | 0.5% | −0.2% | −1.0% | 1.0% |

*Note*: Low income refers to households with 1999 income of less than $25,000 and high income is $100,000 or more.
*Source*: Authors' calculations from US Census 2000 Gross Migration Flows files and Voss et al.'s (2004) net migration estimates by age.

the period and they grew significantly older due to migration.

Figure 24.1 shows MEIs by age and county type. In farming and mining counties, *out*-migration of young adults drives the aging process, as is seen with a large negative MEI value at ages 20–29. In destination counties, both *in*-migration of people at retirement ages (50–74) and *out*-migration of young people drive population aging.

Figure 24.2 shows how migration patterns by age are compounded over time to substantially change the number of working-age residents (also see Fuguitt & Heaton, 1995 for a similar review of the impact of migration on age structure 1960–1990). This chart shows change in the age structure of the population by county type due to net migration by age between 1970 and 2000. These data compare the observed population at Census 2000 to an estimate of what the population would have been had there been no net migration by age since 1970. The counterfactual estimate is generated by taking the 1970 census count and aging the population forward in time, adjusting for births and deaths.[6] Black bars represent a loss of population at those ages (age in 2000, rather than age at which the migration occurred) due to migration. Gray bars represent a gain in population due to migration.

For nonspecified nonmetropolitan counties, migration over this thirty year period resulted in a 2000 population with about 10% fewer prime working-age people (age 20–50) than would have been expected and about 20% more people at age 55 and over. In farming- and mining-dependent counties this pattern is exacerbated – migration reduced the number of people under age 50 by about 30%. Out-migration of young adults, over time, considerably reduced the number of working-age adults (human capital). In

---

[6] This method and the associated data are based on county-specific net migration estimates by age for the 1970s, 1980s, and 1990s generated by White et al. (1987); Fuguitt and Beale (1993); and Voss et al. (2004); and the methods these demographers employed.

# 24 Boom or Bust? Population Dynamics in Natural Resource-Dependent Counties

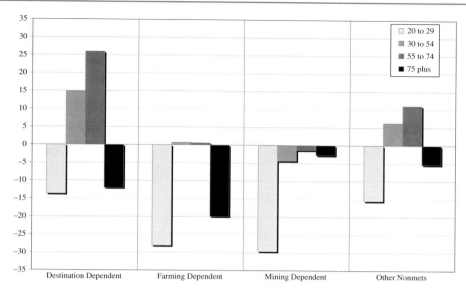

**Fig. 24.1** Migration efficiency index by age

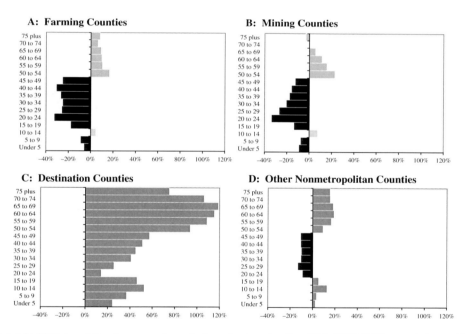

**Fig. 24.2** Change in 2000 population by age and county type due to migration 1970–2000. Difference between 2000 population and expected population with no migration, 1970–2000

destination-dependent counties, migration *increased* the population at all ages. This was especially true at ages 50–74 where the population in 2000 was about double what it would have been had there been no migration, whereas the population of young adults increased by about 20% due to migration. In these counties, migration flows have increased dependency ratios over time by introducing large numbers of older people into the population.

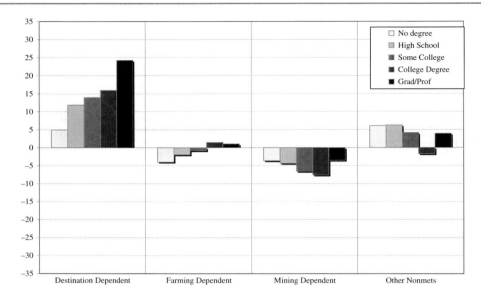

**Fig. 24.3** Migration efficiency index by educational attainment

With regard to the labor force, migration decreased the percent of the working-age population who were employed by about 1% in all rural county types (Table 24.3). In destination counties, this occurred through in-migration of those not in the labor force and the unemployed.[7] In farming- and mining-dependent counties, this occurred due to out-migration of employed residents. Destination county migration is least efficient for the employed population in comparison to any other age, income, or education category examined here. This finding points toward relatively high turnover amongst the employed population in destination counties with little compositional change. Stocks of human capital are strongest when communities experience a stable employed population. In this regard, migration to and from destination counties may diminish human capital (and stimulate increased demand for social services).

At the same time, migration increased the education level of the population in destination counties by 1% in only five years with efficient net inflows of highly educated residents. In farming and mining counties, migration had little change on the proportion college educated. Figure 24.3 illustrates these patterns showing migration efficiency by educational attainment and county type.

Overall, in farming- and mining-dependent counties, migration depleted communities' human capital as young adults and employed residents moved out. Destination counties attracted more highly educated residents, boosting human capital. Still, young adults out-migrated from destination counties at high rates, the employed population experienced high turnover, and those not in the labor force and the unemployed in-migrated. These mixed results complicate interpreting the overall effects of migration on human capital in destination counties.

## Migration and Financial Capital

Households who migrate carry a certain amount of financial capital that contributes to local community well-being by affecting the tax base, consumption patterns, charitable giving, and investment. Household income is one measure of a household's financial capital.[8] Table 24.2 and Fig. 24.4 demonstrate that

---

[7] It is important to note that labor force status is recorded at the end of the migration interval (Census, 2000) and indicates postmigration status.

[8] These data record household income in 1999, which is likely a postmigration measure for most households. While moving may impact household income, the affects of moving should not be

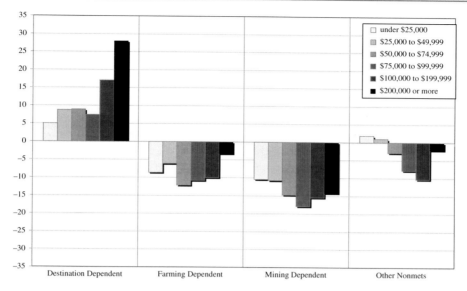

**Fig. 24.4** Migration efficiency index by household income in 1999

farming- and mining-dependent counties experienced net out-migration across income groups. In these counties, more efficient out-migration at higher income levels indicates that migration flows *decreased* income structure in the late 1990s. Mining counties, in particular, experienced declines in financial capital due to migration, while farming counties experienced little change.

As opposed to the extractive resource-dependent counties, destination counties experienced clear gains in financial capital due to migration. Efficient in-migration of high-income households increased the percent of households with incomes greater than $100,000 by 0.3% and decreased the percent of households with incomes less than $25,000 by 0.3%, for a net change in the structure of 0.6% due to migration (Table 24.3).

## Migration and Social Capital

Migration reduces bonding social capital by bringing in new residents who may not have longstanding connections to place and neighbors and/or subtracting residents who have spent time in place and developed relationships. Recent migrants are less likely to be embedded in local social institutions and they have had less time to establish shared local identity, trust, mutual respect, and attachment (Katz, 2000; Ostrom, 1999; Curran, 2002). Flora and Flora explain "when new migrants enter a community, unless they have previous ties, they personally have low levels of community-based social capital. That, in turn, reduces community social capital unless positive action is taken to build trust and reciprocal relationships" (1996, p. 220).

Table 24.4 shows gross migration rates and the proportion of residents who are recent in-migrants by county type. Across the United States, 18.1% of people moved to a different county between 1995 and 2000 (US Census Bureau, 2000). Farming, mining, and other nonmetropolitan counties experienced slightly less population turnover with about 17% of all

**Table 24.4** Population turnover, 1995–2000

|  | Population (1995) | Average inflow | Average outflow | GMR | % New residents |
|---|---|---|---|---|---|
| Destination | 24,132 | 6,434 | 5,171 | 50.0 | 25.0 |
| Farming | 7,146 | 1,292 | 1,481 | 40.2 | 17.5 |
| Mining | 18,274 | 2,771 | 3,406 | 38.2 | 16.5 |
| Other nonmetro | 26,574 | 4,880 | 4,761 | 37.1 | 17.5 |

GMR = $\bar{x}$ (((Inmigrants + Outmigrants)/Starting Population))
*Source*: US Census 2000, SF3 and Gross Migration Flows files

drastic, because household income includes transfer payments from retirement and investments, as well as earned income.

residents having moved in within the five years previous and gross migration rates around 38 per 100. Destination counties, however, were more dramatically affected by in- and out-migration. In 2000, one in every four residents of destination counties was a recent in-migrant. Gross migration rates in destination counties averaged 50 per 100 meaning that on average half of the number of residents in 1995 either moved out of the county or moved into the county from elsewhere during the five year period. High gross migration rates in destination counties persist across age, income, education, and labor force groups, and particularly among young adults and more highly educated people. Overall, our results suggest that outmigration may reduce social capital in farming- and mining-dependent counties and that high population turnover in destination counties may impede the development of social capital.

In total, migration reduced stocks of human capital, financial capital, and social capital in farming- and especially in mining-dependent counties in the 1990s. These counties saw net outflows of young adults, college-educated residents, employed workers, and higher income households. In destination counties, migration supported the accumulation of financial capital by bringing in more wealthy residents. Yet, results are mixed with regards to human and social capitals. Migration increased education levels, supporting human and social capitals, but other migration flows detracted from the accumulation of human and social capitals. Destination counties experienced a net out-migration of young adults, with out-migration rates as high as those in traditional resource-dependent counties, and they attracted unemployed workers and those not in the labor force more efficiently than employed workers. In addition, high turnover in destination counties is likely to have diminished bonding social capital and overall community stability.

## Discussion

One of the most pressing concerns facing rural communities is the out-migration of young adults and more educated people (Lichter et al., 1995; Carr & Kefalas, 2009; Corbett, 2007). Natural-resource-dependent rural communities, in particular, have long experienced out-migration and population loss challenging their very survival. In this context, amenity destination-related development is a key strategy to retain young people, attract more highly educated residents, and build human, financial, and social capitals (Power, 1996; Reeder & Brown, 2005). Do communities dependent on serving as an amenity destination, rather than resource extraction, buck the trend of rural loss of human, financial, and social capitals?

This study reveals that destination counties do attract large numbers of in-migrants who can increase local financial capital, but, the effect of amenity migration on human and social capitals remains less definitive. Migration increases education levels, but if new and educated residents are not in the labor force or are older and have associated health problems, this may pose as many challenges to human capital as it does opportunities. Similarly, new residents are unlikely to have deep social ties in their new destination, and high turnover rates in destination communities suggest that migration may diminish community social capital. Together, these findings call into question the premise that destination-oriented development comprehensively boosts community capitals.

Central to our argument is the importance of young adults for sustaining community capitals over time. Younger adults are often forgotten in discussions of amenity destination development. Policy and research focus on the impacts of retirees, high income, and highly educated migrants or the services they require. Our study reiterates that these groups indeed constitute the most substantial *net* migration change converging on destination communities in the United States. However, our analysis confirms what a large body of research on life course migration (Mulder, 1993; Plane et al., 2005) has long accepted, that young adults are the group with the highest proclivity to migrate. Even in destination counties, we find that young adults in-migrate to destination counties at about twice the rate of people age 50–74, yet they out-migrate at an even higher rate for an overall net out-migration. So, as people age 50–74 flock to rural destinations in large numbers, those same destinations are simultaneously experiencing profound turnover and an ultimate net loss of young adults. The interlinked demographic and social repercussions of this cannot be overstated. While the social capital and civic contributions brought to a community by retirees in the short term should not be discounted (see Brown & Glasgow, 2008), a shortage of rooted young adults can have long-term consequences for community capitals.

The age imbalance resulting from simultaneous out-migration of young people and in-migration of older people suggests from a demographic standpoint that gains in community capitals may be short-lived for destination communities. First, research suggests that young adults who out-migrate from rural areas are most likely to be those of higher socioeconomic status (Carr & Kefalas, 2009; Corbett, 2007; Plane et al., 2005). The exodus of high-status young adults counterbalances the effects of high-status newcomers. Second, with fewer families and children to fill and support schools, these key venues for human capital accumulation may lack political and financial support. Third, even further on the horizon, Rye (2006) finds in Norway that many rural retirement age in-migrants are return migrants who moved away from the same area as young adults. This begs the question of whether or not future retiree cohorts will feel as drawn to rural places as current retirees, who have a higher likelihood of having grown up in rural places. To summarize, the young adults that destination communities are fortunate to attract could prove integral for building enduring stocks of human and social capitals, if it weren't for the fact that so many in their age cohort leave.

Why do destination counties face this paradox? Put simply, even with amenity appeal, young adults experience conspiring pressures to relocate. Evidence suggests that jobs associated with tourism and recreational development tend to be low paying and unstable (Marcouiller, Kim, & Deller, 2004). Although younger adults move to destination counties in search of jobs, we find that many do not stay, perhaps because of this instability. Further, amenity-related development is associated with relatively high housing prices and problems with housing affordability (Reeder & Brown, 2005; Hammer & Winkler, 2006; Hettinger, 2005); suggesting that younger and lower SES residents of destination counties may be displaced due to high housing costs. In addition, communities focused on attracting tourists and retirees may ignore the housing, transportation, and social needs of younger adults further reducing the likelihood that this segment of the population will stay and invest in the community (Winkler, 2009). Overall, destination counties may experience high turnover and net out-migration of young adults because they attract some young workers to take advantage of service industry jobs and repel others who seek more secure and higher paying work, affordable housing, and social opportunities in other places.

The implications of our findings across the industrialized world are varied. Research on population patterns in farming, mining, and destination communities in Canada and Australia suggest that US patterns parallel those in other more developed countries (Alston, 2004; Casado-Diaz et al., 2004; Dahms & McComb, 1999; Gosnell & Abrams, 2009; Hugo, 1988; Champion, 1994). However, as we have discussed, the demographic impact of resource dependence is governed by factors such as affordability and social services, which depend on local and national contexts. For example, in the United States an increasingly suburban populace with poor public transit means that many urban workers devote hours each day to commuting. Thus, American amenity destinations offer permanent respite to people dissatisfied with this lifestyle. Further, US markets for seasonal and permanent housing overlap, which can rapidly escalate housing prices in popular rural places and put home ownership far out of reach of local wage-earners. Finally, social policies and services are generally provided at the local level in the US, meaning that changing rural demographics can reshape civic priorities and thus affect community well-being in more profound ways than in countries with more centralized government and service provision.

Norway presents an alternative example, illustrating important similarities and differences in destination dependency (Van Auken, 2010). Amenity migration in Norway is largely seasonal and nonpermanent. In general, Scandinavian cities are more livable than those in the US, and most urban residents have access to rural seasonal residences but no intention of permanently resettling, even in retirement. In many ways this second-home phenomenon mirrors permanent migration seen in the US, but its social impacts are affected by a few distinct conditions. First, some European countries use zoning or deed restrictions to separate permanent and seasonal housing, which limits the impact of seasonal residences on housing affordability. This means that young people may not feel the same pressure to relocate due to housing costs as in the US. In terms of social capital, however, this separation can stifle the transfer of community capitals between permanent and seasonal residents. Second, while second-home communities may see residual financial benefits from destination development, the extent to which these rural places are economically dependent on their status as destinations is mitigated to some extent by centralized social service and land use policies. Although neoliberalizing national policies are increasingly promoting economic self-sufficiency, Norwegian rural communities continue to benefit from national social policies that promote family creation and funding for public education. Thus, destination communities may be no better or worse equipped to maintain their young adult populations than other rural Scandinavian communities.

Rural areas in developing countries may confront a different set of challenges where migration and resource dependency intersect. They tend to have a younger population structure, considerably less educated and lower income populations, and less industrialized economies. These structural differences likely influence relationships between natural resource dependence and migration patterns that diverge from our US findings. In particular, less developed countries are experiencing dramatic urbanization due to both natural increase and rural to urban migration that mirrors patterns experienced in the US around the turn of the 20th century (Cohen, 2004). For this reason, US migration patterns from earlier time periods may more appropriately represent current patterns in some developing countries than do US patterns in the 1990s.

As nations industrialize, farming-dependent areas tend to experience heightened out-migration, especially of young adults (El Hindi, 2004). Conversely, mining has expanded in many less developed countries (LDCs) over the last several years. This may mean that mining areas of LDCs remain in a population "boom" period and experience considerable in-migration. Little research has been conducted on the effects of amenity migration in developing nations (Glorioso & Moss, 2007), which leaves us to merely hypothesize the likely effects of amenity migration on community capitals. Amenity migrants are even more likely than in more developed countries to have significantly higher incomes and education levels than the longer term population. An influx of high SES residents could substantially boost human and financial capitals; but, the potential challenges of incorporating "outsiders," both foreign and domestic, into the local social fabric (social capital) are numerous. Without the development of inclusive social capital that bridges these divides, gains in human and financial capital may largely be lost.

In conclusion, our analysis confirms that migration brings the potential for both community capital accumulation and loss. It is clear from our results that selective out-migration from farming- and mining-dependent communities produces demographic outcomes that could be detrimental to human, financial, and social capitals. Our findings for destination counties, however, reveal a more complex scenario. Migration flows bring educated and affluent residents into destination communities. If these affluent newcomers are well integrated into local community life, they could strengthen the community fabric by engaging socially and financially. However, high rates of population turnover and continued young adult out-migration compromise the potential for positive impacts to be sustained over time. Thus, it should not be taken for granted that amenity migration will boost community assets. The realization of capital accumulation or loss in destination counties is likely to be closely related to how individual communities integrate new residents and, similar to farming and mining communities, on the ability of communities to retain young adults. Further research on the reasons for young adult out-migration and on the issues and concerns facing young adults in destination communities will be important to understand how communities can retain this population and better integrate the human and social capital resources that they bring.

## References

Alao, A. (2007). *Natural resources and conflict in Africa: The tragedy of endowment*. Rochester, NY: University of Rochester Press.

Albrecht, D. E. (1993). The renewal of population loss in the nonmetropolitan great plains. *Rural Sociology, 58*(2), 233–246.

Alston, M. (2004). 'You don't want to be a check out-chick all your life': The out-migration of youth from Australia's small rural towns. *Australian Journal of Social Issues, 39*(3), 299–313.

Auty, R. M. (1993). *Sustaining development in mineral economies: The resource curse thesis*. London: Routledge.

Auty, R. M. (2001). The political economy of resource-driven growth. *European Economic Review, 45*(4–6), 839–846.

Becker, G. S. (2002). The age of human capital. In E. P. Lazear (Ed.), *Education in the twenty-first century* (pp. 3–8). Hoover Institute: Stanford University.

Birdsall, N., Pinckney, T., & Sabot, R. (2001). Natural resources, human capital, and growth. In R. Auty (Ed.), *Resource abundance and economic development* (pp. 57–75). Oxford: Oxford University Press.

Bowles, G. K., Beale, C. L., & Lee, E. S. (1975). *Net migration of the population, 1960–70, by age, sex and color*. Washington: U.S. Department of Agriculture, Economic Research Service and Athens: University of Georgia.

Bowles, G. K., & Tarver, J. D. (1965). *Net migration of the population, 1950–60, by age, sex and color*. Washington, DC: U.S. Department of Agriculture, Economic Research Service.

Boyle, P., & Halfacree, K. (1998). *Migration into rural areas: Theories and issues*. Chichester: Wiley.

Brown, D. L., & Glasgow, N. (2008). *Rural retirement migration. Springer series on demographic methods and population analysis* (Vol. 24). New York: Springer.

Carr, P., & Kefalas, M. (2009). *Hollowing out the middle: The rural brain drain and what it means for America*. Boston: Beacon Press.

Casado-Diaz, M. A., Kaiser, C., & Warnes, A. M. (2004). Northern European retired residents in nine southern European areas: Characteristics, motivations and adjustment. *Ageing and Society, 24*, 353.

Champion, A. G. (1994). Population change and migration in Britain since 1981: Evidence for continuing deconcentration. *Environment and Planning A, 26*(10), 1501–1520.

Chipeniuk, R. (2004). Planning for amenity migration in Canada: Current capacities of interior British Columbian Mountain communities. *Mountain Research and Development, 24*, 327–335.

Cohen, B. (2004). Urban growth in developing countries: A review of current trends and a caution regarding existing forecasts. *World Development, 32*, 23–51.

Coleman, J. (1988). Social capital in the creation of human capital. *American Journal of Sociology, 94*, 95–S120.

Corbett, M. J. (2007). *Learning to leave: The irony of schooling in a coastal community*. Black Point, NS: Fernwood.

Cromatie, J. & Nelson, P. (2009). *Baby boom migration and its impact on rural America*. Economic Research Report Number 79: U.S. Department of Agriculture Economic Research Service.

Curran, S. (2002). Migration, social capital, and the environment: Considering migrant selectivity and networks in relation to coastal ecosystems. *Population and Development Review, 28*, 89–125.

Dahms, F., & McComb, J. (1999). 'Counterurbanization', interaction and functional change in a rural amenity area—a Canadian example. *Journal of Rural Studies, 15*(2), 129–146.

Dasgupta, P., & Serageldin, I. (1999). *Social capital: Multifaceted perspective*. Washington DC: The World Bank.

Domina, T. (2006). What clean break? Education and nonmetropolitan migration patterns, 1989–2004. *Rural Sociology, 71*, 373–398.

El Hindi, A. (2004). *Agriculture and rural-urban migrations in developing countries: Facts and policy implications*. Proceedings No. 15 of the Agricultural Policy Forum seminar presented in Damascus, 12 December 2004.

Emery, M., & Flora, C. B. (2006). Spiraling-Up: Mapping community transformation with community capitals framework. *Community development: Journal of the Community Development Society, 37*, 19–35.

Fey, S., Bregendahl, C., & Flora, C. B. (2006). The measurement of community capitals through research: A study conducted for the Claude Worthington Benedum Foundation by the North Central Regional Center for Rural Development. *Online Journal of Rural Research and Policy 1*. Retrieved March 8, 2010, from http://www.ojrrp.org/issues/2006/01/index.html

Flora, C. B., & Flora, J. L. (1996). Creating Social Capital: Becoming Native to Place. In W. Vitek (Ed.), *Rooted in the Land: Essays on Community and Place* (pp. 217–225). New Haven, CT: Yale University Press.

Flora, C. B., & Flora, J. L. (2008). *Rural communities: Legacy and change*. Boulder, CO: Westview Press.

Freudenburg, W. R. (1992). Addictive economies: Extractive industries and vulnerable localities in a changing world economy. *Rural Sociology, 57*, 305–332.

Fuguitt, G. V. (1985). The nonmetropolitan population turnaround. *Annual Review of Sociology, 11*(1), 259–280.

Fuguitt, G. V., & Beale, C. L. (1993). The changing concentration of the older nonmetropolitan population, 1960–1990. *Journal of Gerontology: Social Sciences, 8*, 278–288.

Fuguitt, G. V., & Heaton, T. B. (1995). The impact of migration on the nonmetropolitan population age structure, 1960–1990. *Population Research and Policy Review, 14*(2), 215–232.

Fukuyama, F. (2002). Social capital and development: The coming agenda. *SAIS Review, 22*(1), 23–37.

Galston, W. A., & Baehler, K. J. (1995). *Rural development in the United States*. Washington, DC: Island Press.

Gasteyer, S. P. (2009). Agricultural transitions in the context of growing environmental pressure over water. *Journal of Agriculture and Human Values, 25*(4), 469–486.

Glorioso, R. S., & Moss, L. A. G. (2007). Amenity migration to mountain regions: Current knowledge and strategic construct for sustainable management. *Social Change, 37*(1), 137–161.

Gosnell, H., & Abrams, J. (2009). Amenity migration: Diverse conceptualizations of drivers, socioeconomic dimensions, and emerging challenges. *GeoJournal*. doi: 10.1007/s10708-009-9295-4.

Green, G. P. (1991). Rural banking. In C. B. Flora & J. A. Christenson (Eds.), *Rural policies for the 1990s* (pp. 36–46). Boulder, CO: Westview.

Halfacree, K. (1997). Contrasting roles for the post-productivist countryside. In P. Cloke & J. Little (Eds.), *Contested countryside cultures* (pp. 70–93). London: Routledge.

Hammer, R. B., & Winkler, R. L. (2006). Housing affordability and population change in the Upper Midwestern Northwoods. In W. Kandel & D. L. Brown (Eds.), *Population change in rural society in the 21st century. The Springer Series on Demographic Methods and Population Analysis* (Vol. 16). New York: Springer.

Hettinger, W. S. (2005). *Living and working in paradise: Why housing is too expensive and what communities can do about it*. Windham, CT: Thames River Publishing.

Hugo, G. (1988). Counterurbanization in Australia. *Geographical Perspectives, 61*, 43–68.

Humphrey, C. R., Berardi, M. S., Caroll, M. S., Fairfax, S., Fortmann, L., Geisler, C., et al. (1993). Theories in the study of natural resource dependent communities and persistent rural poverty in the United States. In G. Summers (Ed.),

*Persistent poverty in rural America* (pp. 136–172). Boulder, CO: Westview Press.

Jobes, P. (2000). *Moving nearer to heaven: The illusions and disillusions of migrants to scenic rural places*. Westport, CT: Praeger.

Johnson, K. M., & Beale, C. L. (2002). Nonmetro recreation counties: Their identification and rapid growth. *Rural America, 17*, 12–19.

Johnson, T. G., & Stallman, J. (1994). Human capital investment in resource-dominated economies. *Society and Natural Resources, 7*(3), 221–233.

Johnson, K. M., Voss, P. R., Hammer, R. B., Fuguitt, G. V., & McNiven, S. (2005). Temporal and spatial variation in age-specific net migration in the United States. *Demography, 42*(4), 791–812.

Katz, E. (2000). Social capital and natural capital: A comparative analysis of land tenure and natural resource management in Guatemala. *Land Economics, 76*(1), 114–132.

Kuyek, J., & Coumans, C. (2003). *No rock unturned: Revitalizing the economies of mining dependent communities*. Ottawa, ON: MiningWatch Canada.

Larsen, L., Harlan, S. L, Bolin, B., Hackett, E. J., Hope, D., Kirby, A., et al. (2004). Bonding and bridging: Understanding the relationship between social capital and civic action. *Journal of Planning Education and Research, 24*, 64–77.

Lichter, D. T., Heaton, T. B., & Fuguitt, G. V. (1979). Trends in the selectivity of migration between metropolitan and nonmetropolitan areas: 1955–1975. *Rural Sociology, 44*(4), 645–666.

Lichter, D. T., McLaughlin, D. K., & Cornwell, G. T. (1995). Migration and the Loss of Human Resources in Rural America. In L. J. Beaulieu & D. Mulkay (Eds.), *Investing in People: The Human Capital Needs of Rural America* (pp. 235–256). Boulder, CO: Westview Press.

Ma, A., & Chow, N. W. S. (2006). Economic impact of elderly amenity mobility in southern China. *Journal of Applied Gerontology, 25*(4), 275–290.

Marcouiller, D. W., Kim, K. K., & Deller, S. C. (2004). Natural amenities, tourism, and income distribution. *Annals of Tourism Research, 31*, 1031–1050.

Marsden, T. (1998). Economic perspectives. In B. Ilbery (Ed.), *The geography of rural change* (pp. 13–30). London: Longman.

McGranahan, D. A. (1999). *Natural amenities drive rural population change*. Washington, DC: U.S. Department of Agriculture, Economic Research Service.

Moss, L. (2006). *The amenity migrants: Seeking and sustaining mountains and their cultures*. Cambridge, MA: CABI Publishing.

Mulder, C. H. (1993). *Migration dynamics: A life course approach*. Amsterdam: Thela Thesis Publishers.

Ostrom, E. (1999). Social captial: A fad or fundamental concept? In P. DasGupta & I. Seregeldin (Eds.), *Social capital: A multifaceted perspective* (pp. 172–214). Washington, DC: World Bank.

Otero, A., Nakayama, L., Marioni, S., Gallego, E., Lonac, A., Dimitriu, A., et al. (2006). Amenity migration in the Patagonian mountain community of San Martín de los Andes, Neuquén, Argentina. In L. A. G. Moss (Ed.), *The Amenity migrations: Seeking and sustaining mountains and their cultures* (pp. 200–211). Cambridge, MA: CABI Publishing.

Plane, D. A., Henrie, C. J., & Perry, M. J. (2005). Migration up and down the urban hierarchy and across the life course. *Proceedings of the National Academy of Sciences of the United States of America, 102*, 15313–15318.

Portes, A. (1998). Social capital: Its origins and applications in modern sociology. *Annual Review of Sociology, 24*, 1–24.

Power, T. M. (1996). *Lost landscapes and failed economies: The search for a value of place*. Washington, DC: Island Press.

Putnam, R. D. (2000). *Bowling alone: The collapse and revival of American community*. New York: Simon and Schuster.

Reeder, R. J., & Brown, D. M. (2005). *Recreation, tourism, and rural well-being*. Washington, DC: U.S. Department of Agriculture, Economic Research Service.

Rye, J. F. (2006) *Geographic and social mobility: Youth's rural-to-urban migration in Norway*. Doctoral Thesis at the Norwegian University of Science and Technology. Trondheim, Norway.

Sachs, J. D., & Warner, A. M. (2001). The curse of natural resources. *European Economic Review, 45*(4–6), 827–838.

Salamon, S. (2003). *Newcomers to old towns: Suburbanization of the heartland*. Chicago: The University of Chicago Press.

Shin, E. (1978). Effects of migration on the educational levels of the black resident population at the origin and destination, 1955–1960 and 1965–1970. *Demography, 15*(February), 41–56.

Shryock, H. S., Siegel, J. S., & Larmon, E. A. (1980). *The methods and materials of demography*. New York: Academic.

Shumway, J. M., & Otterstrom, S. M. (2001). Spatial patterns of migration and income change in the Mountain West: The dominance of service-based amenity-rich counties. *The Professional Geographer, 53*, 492–502.

Sunil, T., Rojas, V., & Bradley, D. (2007). United States' international retirement migration: The reasons for retiring to the environs of Lake Chapala, Mexico. *Ageing and Society, 27*, 489.

US Census Bureau, Census 2000. County-to-County Migration Flow Files. Summary File 3.

Van Auken, P. (2010). Seeing, not Participating: Viewscape Fetishism in American and Norwegian Rural Amenity Areas. *Human Ecology*. doi: 10.1007/s10745-010-9323-5.

Visser, G. (2004). Second homes: Reflections on an unexplored phenomenon in South Africa. In C. M. Hall & D. K. Müller (Eds.), *Tourism, mobility and second homes: Between elite landscape and common ground* (pp. 196–214). Clevedon, UK: Channel View Publications.

Voss, P. R., McNiven, S., Hammer, R. B., Johnson, K. M., & Fuguitt, G. V. (2004). *County-specific net migration by five-year age groups, Hispanic origin, race and sex 1990–2000*. CDE Working Paper No. 2004-24. Madison, WI: Center for Demography and Ecology, University of Wisconsin—Madison.

White, K. J. C. (2008). Population change and farm dependence: Temporal and spatial variation in the US Great Plains, 1900–2000. *Demography, 45*(2), 363–386.

White, M. J., Mueser, P., & Tierney, J. P. (1987). *Net migration of the population of the United States 1970-80, by age, race and sex*. (Computer file with documentation.) Ann Arbor,

MI: Inter-university Consortium for Political and Social Research.

Winkler, R. L. (2009). *Social capital and concerns facing lower income young adults in the Brainerd Lakes area.* CES4Health.info. 11/10/2009. Product ID#ML6SYW4F.

Winkler, R. L. (2010). *Do natural amenities drive destination development?* Rural destinations and their uneven development across the United States. In *Rural destinations, uneven development, and social exclusion* (pp. 31–74). Diss. University of Wisconsin-Madison, 2010.

# Neoliberal Democratization and Public Health Inequalities in Sub-Saharan Africa: A Proposed Conceptual and Empirical Design

**25**

Moshi Optat Herman

## Introduction

In the late 1980s, the World Bank proclaimed, "underlying the litany of African development problems is a crisis of governance" (World Bank, 1989, p. 60). Shortly afterwards a consensus among the World Bank, the International Monetary Fund (IMF), and the United States Treasury, famously known as the Washington Consensus, decidedly attributed the failure of economic reforms in the region to weak political institutions coupled with dysfunctional governance (Williamson, 1990, 1993). Following these diagnoses, prescriptions such as improving governance, enhancing institutional accountability, and reduction of government interference in the private sector have been a major part of the repertoire of development policies in sub-Saharan Africa (SSA). To achieve these ends, nation-states were advised to liberalize politics by introducing political competition through multi-party elections and to institute economic liberalization through Structural Adjustment Programs (SAP) (Moss, 2007).

The extent of the impact of these structural political-economic transformations on demographic trends in Africa has not been given its due attention. Partly as a result of the unfortunate fact that short-term humanitarian crises are fairly endemic in the continent, researchers in demography have found it incumbent, and justifiably so at times, to focus on "intervention research" to curb theses crises by emphasizing on short-term and medium-term changes. In this chapter I propose a conceptual framework and a concurrent empirical design that can be used to investigate the link between these political-economic transformations and social demographic outcomes in the long term. I underscore spatial inequality between rural and urban areas in infant health after these structural transformations by stressing on rural-urban divide. I then design a template that can be used to make a cross-country comparison between countries with similar sociopolitical trajectories.

As I have hinted already, I focus on two of the most transformative political-economic changes in sub-Saharan Africa in the last three decades, which are economic neoliberalization through structural adjustment programs and political liberalization through introduction of political competition (multipartism). I refer to the concurrent implementation of economic liberalization (neoliberalism) and political liberalization (democratization) as *neoliberal democratization* (henceforth NLD). Specifically, I define neoliberal democratization as the political-economic transition from authoritarian military and/or single-party regimes to competitive politics characterized by multiparty elections that took place concurrently with the implementation of neoliberal economic policies of Structural Adjustment and the "opening" of erstwhile "closed" African economies for Foreign Direct Investment (FDI). Structural Adjustment policies aimed to create conducive conditions for investment and hence economic growth through a set of macroeconomic policies that included privatization of state-owned enterprises, fiscal austerity, and deregulation of capital and

M.O. Herman (✉)
Department of Sociology, Brown University, Providence, RI 02912, USA
e-mail: optat_tengia@brown.edu

financial markets. Such policies have different effects on urban and rural places, and more often than not rural areas may be left behind in economic development.

The conceptual and empirical design suggested by this chapter thus endeavors to link these macrolevel political economic transitions to a microlevel outcome, i.e., differential infant survival rates (infant mortality) across provinces in the selected countries with emphasis on rural-urban divide. The conceptual framework and the corresponding empirical design suggested in this chapter can be used to answer a question such as: to what extent did neoliberal democratization affect substantive social well-being (standard of living) in sub-Saharan Africa in the 1990s? Specifically, what was the impact of neoliberal democratization in sub-Saharan Africa on spatial inequalities in public health outcomes measured by Infant Mortality Rate (IMR) before and after NLD?

There is a loosely defined (and fairly inactive) Political Demography subfield in demography that investigates how governments and public policies influence population structure and the underlying processes of fertility, mortality, and migration (Weiner, 1971). However, very few empirical studies—by demographers—have endeavored to directly include political-economic variables into demographic models of the three main population processes of fertility, mortality, and migration. In one of the rare existing cases, Weinreb (2001a, 2001b) links ethnic differences in the prevalence of contraceptive use in Kenya to differential access to political capital. Few dated studies that have explored the effect of political-economic changes on mortality, such Alberto Palloni and Associates' research on the impact of economic transformations and economic recession on infant mortality in Latin America, have typically focused on economic variables (Palloni & Hill, 1992, 1995; Palloni, Hill, & Aguire, 1996).

Also, without calling themselves political demographers per se, political scientists and researchers from allied fields such as comparative political economy, government, and public policy have also been interested in the relationship between population structures, such as its size, age distribution, and ethnic composition, on political variables such as electoral outcomes (Teitelbaum, 2005). Scholars of the political economy of development have also long been interested in evaluating how policies affect health outcomes. James McGuires' comparative studies of the effect of social policy on mortality trends in Latin America and Asia are such examples (McGuire, 2001, 2010). In the same vein, in his most recent book, Evans Lieberman explores how ethnic politics have influenced government responses to the AIDS epidemic in India, South Africa, and Brazil (Lieberman, 2009).

Conversely, studies of political transitions in SSA mainly focus on the *processes* and the *outcomes* within the political sphere (e.g., van de Walle, 2001; Bratton & van de Walle, 1997; Joseph, 1997, 1998; Diamond, 2002; Karl, 1995; Howard & Roessler, 2006; Levitsky & Way, 2002) without paying much attention to substantive socioeconomic outcomes outside the political sphere. We must bear in mind that political attitude surveys show that sub-Saharan Africans view democracy as an instrument that can be used to improve their socioeconomic well-being in addition to celebrating it as a tool for improving access to political goods such as civil liberties and political freedoms (Bratton, 2007; Bratton & Mattes, 2001). There are indeed a few studies in comparative politics that have explored the relationship between democratization efforts and developmental outcomes (for example Przeworski, Alvarez, Cheibub, & Limongi, 2000). However, most of these studies take comprehensive cross-sectional data covering numerous countries across several continents, which makes them unable to highlight how local institutional context and how specific dynamics of political contestation between local and external actors in a given place mediate the effect between democracy and social well-being. In addition, most of these studies use data dating to pre-1990, a point at which most African nations had not undergone the transitions to competitive democracies.

Lastly, the available research on democratic transitions to competitive politics in SSA has not paid substantial attention to the interaction between democratization efforts and the aforementioned related policy, economic neoliberalism, which was instituted in the same period through Structural Adjustment Programs. In many African states these political transformations happened immediately after or concurrently with neoliberal economic reforms. The available literature continues to explore democratization in SSA and implementation of neoliberal policies through SAP separately. Coupled with the lack of systematic investigation of the concurrence and sequencing of economic liberalism and political liberalism, there is a lack of systematic theorization and empirical case studies that expound upon the role of "global forces" related to a given country's participation in the global economy on the success or failure of the third wave of democratization in Africa. Typically, studies of democracy in Africa put too much emphasis on how local conditions that existed and the emerged institutional arrangement (e.g., patrimonial, clientistic relations, semiauthoritarian etc) affected the meanings and outcomes of the democratization initiatives in Africa. In lieu of putting all the emphasis on local factors, in this chapter I urge us to also give priority to "global forces" as a key variable. Studies that have paid attention to the role extranational factors in political transformations in Africa have for the most part explored the location of a given state in the "world system" (i.e., whether the given state is in the core, semiperiphery, or in the periphery), and the impact of the spatial proximity of a given state with other democratic or undemocratic states (for example, Wejnert, 2005). Even though such studies take into consideration "external factors," they rarely include "external actors" as active strategic players in democratization and de-democratization within the countries of interest. And most importantly how these multitudes of external actors impinge on or facilitate the ability of Africans to improve their standard of life through political-economic institutions. Therefore, since external exigencies (e.g., foreign capital/FDI and foreign donors) were crucial players during the third wave of democratization in Africa, I suggest that when exploring the process and the eventual social outcomes of democratization in sub-Saharan Africa such global political-economic connection must be taken into consideration.

To sum up, this chapter argues that a full picture of development trajectory and spatial inequality between rural and urban areas in sub-Saharan Africa in the last three decades can only be understood through the lens of concurrence and sequencing of economic liberalization and political liberalization initiatives in the continent. In doing so microlevel well-being outcomes such as infant survival rates must systematically be linked not just to their proximate determinants, but also to their distal political-economic determinants. And, in the context of the African continent where external actors such as international Financial Institutions and foreign capital (FDI and foreign trade) are also fairly important determinants of economic and social policies, such "global economic forces" must also be viewed as a crucial part of the equation.

## Theories and Background Literature

### Why were Neoliberalism/Structural Adjustment Programs Implemented in Africa?

Neoliberalism can be viewed as a political-economic ideology, as a discourse, or as a form of "political discipline" dictated by International Financial Institutions (Harrison, 2010). In this dissertation, I focus on neoliberalism as an economic policy, and consequently as a "development discourse" that created a specific political-economic practice. As a political-economic practice, neoliberalism altered class relations within countries that eventually transformed the nature of political contestation within these countries; notably by facilitating concentration of economic and political power into the hands of the richest strata of the population (Harvey, 2006).

Neoliberal economic policies through SAP aimed at creating "structural" conditions conducive to investment; that is, conditions that create a "good business climate," with the idea that increased investment at the aggregate-level stimulates economic growth leading to a trickle-down effect, i.e., an improved welfare for the majority. The neoliberal policy repertoire includes: (i) deregulation of business practices, for example, through relaxed environmental and labor protection laws, (ii) privatization of state enterprises, (iii) tax cuts for the upper income brackets, (iv) fiscal discipline through budget cuts that typically lead to reduction in state-run welfare programs and other social provisions, (v) the use of monetarism as a macroeconomic policy tool (supply-side economics) in lieu of Keynesianism (demand-side), (vi) elimination of protectionist policies, and (vii) liberalization of financial and foreign exchange markets.

In most of SSA, neoliberal policies were implemented under advice from external actors, mostly International Financial Institutions (IFIs). These policies were implemented through SAP as part of conditions attached to loans (Harrison, 2010; Moss, 2007; Rapley, 2002; Leys, 1996). SAP and the "Washington Consensus," which is a subset of the neoliberal principles, were the seminal breakdown of the exact policies that Africans were instructed to implement by IFIs in order to overcome the aforementioned perceived structural barriers to investment and economic growth (Williamson, 1990, 1993, 2003). As such, the implementation of neoliberalism in Africa was mostly top-down: top from international funding agencies and down to state actors, such as finance ministers and planning ministers. In a few cases of middle-income nations such as Mexico, local actors (economists, lawyers, and the business elite) were instrumental in the eventual institutionalization of the policies (Babb, 2001), which was not the case in SSA.

## Transition to Competitive Politics in SSA in the 1990s: A Failed Program?

In the 1990s many African countries went through political transitions from authoritarian regimes ranging from military, dictatorial, and one-party regimes, to pluralistic democracies characterized by competitive multiparty elections. The "democracies" that emerged in Africa and elsewhere following the collapse of the Soviet Union have famously been dubbed the *third-wave democracies* (Huntington, 1991). By the late 1990s, multiparty systems became a political norm in SSA with the majority of countries in the region introducing competitive elections (Adejumobi, 2000; Diamond, 1996; Bratton & Van de Walle, 1997).

Following Huber, Rueschemeyer, and Stephens (1997), there are three broad types of democracies. These include *formal democracies*, which are characterized by regular free and fair elections, universal suffrage, accountability of a state's administrative organs to elected representatives, and guaranteed freedom of expression and association; *participatory democracies*, which have the four dimensions of a formal democracy coupled with discernible improvements in levels of political participation across all social categories such as class, ethnicity, or gender; and *social/substantive democracies* that are characterized by the five features of a participatory democracy in addition to increased equality in social and economic outcomes (Huber et al., 1997).

For all intents and purposes, the transitions from forms of authoritarianism to multiparty regimes in SSA intended to institute formal democracies. The question of whether the necessary social, political, and economic preconditions existed to enable the democratic transitions to take root in such political transformations and whether the transitions led to viable changes in the social and economic sphere has inspired a growing body of theoretical and empirical studies (see for example Acemoglu & Robinson, 2006; Przeworski et al., 2000; Diamond, 1999).

So far, the assertion that the continent lacked necessary preconditions for democratization is the most cited explanation of the slow progress in democratic deepening and durability in the continent. Democratization theory that existed before the transition (Lipset, 1959, 1960, 1994; Moore, 1966) would have predicted such a dire scenario. Partly, Africa was regarded as an infertile ground for democracy because of its homogenous class structure, which typically consists of a majority of peasant/subsistence farmers. A strong middle class fosters democratization in the Global South (Heller, 2000; Sandbrook, Edelman, Heller, & Teichman, 2006). The role of the middle class in mobilizing and organizing for democracy is summarized by Barrington Moore's famous maxim: "*No bourgeoisie, no democracy*" (Moore, 1966, p. 418). In addition, two of the crucial variables for effective democratic deepening, an active civil society and viable state capacity (Heller, 2000) are typically limited in sub-Saharan Africa.

Some critics have associated the lack of viable progress towards deeper democracy in Africa to the shortcomings of the "liberal democratic model" that was instituted in the continent through pluralist politics. At times, this model is seen as a mere attempt to reproduce advanced capitalist societies' path-dependent political trajectories, which are largely incongruent with social realities on the ground in Africa (Ayers, 2006). As a consequence, illiberal democracies, such as neopatrimonial and clientilistic ones have emerged in Africa (van de Walle, 2001; Bratton & van de Walle, 1997). Prebendalism, a system in which elected officials see their "offices" as nothing but "prebends" (i.e., a form of entitlements) in service of their material interests and those of their kinship (Joseph, 1997, 1998), is also prevalent in the continent. It has also been argued that the political transitions in the 1990s in Africa merely led to hybrid regimes, regimes that are neither authoritarian nor democratic (Diamond, 2002; Karl, 1995). For example, variations of competitive-authoritarian and electoral-authoritarian regimes are said to have emerged in the continent (Howard & Roessler, 2006; Levitsky & Way, 2002; Diamond, 2002). In such regimes, regular elections, which are questionably fair and free, take place merely to justify the dominance of authoritarian regimes or to replace them with similar ones.

Regardless of the seemingly ambiguous nature of democratic processes and outcomes in Africa, signs of progress towards expansion of civil and political liberties have been observed. The mere fact of competitive elections leads to "liberalizing electoral outcomes," that is, they lead to a formation of governments that are relatively less authoritarian compared to the previous one (Howard & Roessler, 2006; Lindberg, 2006). However, in spite of the observed signs of an increased supply of political goods, the durability of such transitions towards deeper democracies (participatory and substantive) is often contingent upon substantive changes in the social and economic spheres (Bratton, 2007). That is, without improved quality of life and social equality, such basic democratic transitions are unlikely to be sustainable in the long run. As a consequence, for example, almost 20 years after the highly celebrated democratic transitions, the proportion of Africans who perceive that real democratic progress has taken place has been declining overtime, with only 46% agreeing that they are satisfied with democracy in 2005 compared to 58% in 2002; similarly a decline in support of democracy is observed in the same period (Bratton, 2007; Afrobarometer, 2010).

## Health Costs of Neoliberalism and Rural-Urban Inequality: Did Democratization Help?

In order to disentangle social costs of "economic neoliberalism" in Africa, one must distinguish two arms of the neoliberal era. The first arm is the top-down neoliberalism through adjustment programs; top from International Financial Institutions, such as the IMF and the World Bank, down to African institutional planners, such as ministers of finance. The second manifestation of economic neoliberalism in Africa, albeit also related to the former, was simply an artifact of African economies participating in the global economy in what has been termed the post-1980 "neoliberal globalization" era. Partly due to stipulations from SAP, and partly due to unavoidable vicissitudes of the post-1980s neoliberal globalization, many sub-Saharan Africa countries fashioned themselves in the manner congruent to the dictates of global capitalism. To that end, national economies which were centralized-cum-socialist after independence became open market-cum-capitalist economies. These changes which were voluntary in some countries, had to be implemented in others as a condition for receiving funds from IFIs. The rationale behind these transformations was to attract FDI and to stimulate foreign trade which was already dwindling due to falling commodity (raw materials) prices, which are the mainstay of sub-Saharan Africa nations' exports.

Proponents of the first type of neoliberalism through adjustment programs argued that even though the adjustment measures were to produce adverse effects in the short-run, in the long-run economies will be stabilized and will create an attractive space for investment and hence economic growth with an anticipation that such changes would also translate to improvements in standard of living (Ndulu & O'Connell, 1999; Sahn, Dorosh, & Younger, 1997). However, neoliberal policies failed to deliver the intended results. For the most part even when the policies resulted in short-term improvements in economic growth, quality of life as measured by social indicators (such as education and health) deteriorated in many countries (Harrison, 2010; Moss, 2007; Rapley, 2002; Mkandawire & Soludo, 1999; Leys, 1996). In some countries, institutional commitment to a full implementation of the policies simply did not occur (van de Walle, 2001) and therefore the benefits were only partially or never realized. Specific stipulations of SAP such as privatization of the health sector and introduction of user fees also intended to increase efficiency and better access, however just the opposite has been observed. Detailed anthropological accounts, for example, have provided extensive narratives of worsening health outcomes after SAP (for example Kim, Millen, Irwin, & Gershman, 2000; Castro & Singer, 2004). Similarly, Lugala (1995) provides an account of SAPs adverse impact on children and women's health in Tanzania. Research has also shown that IMF programs in post-Communist Europe and Soviet Russia directly exacerbated tuberculosis incidences in the region (Stuckler, King, & Basu, 2008).

As I mentioned, the other component of economic neoliberalism stems from countries' involvement in global capitalism in the post-1980 neoliberal globalization era. Research has shown that global economic linkages through exports, FDI, and IFIs are associated with higher rates of infant mortality—and this is especially so in countries with "lower levels of democracy"

(Shandra, Nobles, London, & Williamson, 2003). In addition, neoliberal globalization led to higher inequality as it increases returns to owners of capital and high-skill labor relative to owners of low-skill labor (Rodrik, 1997), and may concentrate political bargaining power in the hands of the richer strata of the society (Harvey, 2006). Notably economic inequality grew substantially after SAP, which made the initial justification for allowing a tradeoff of social equity for the sake of economic efficiency untenable. Empirical studies have shown that high inequality leads to worse health outcome as measured by infant mortality (Rodgers, 2002).

One of the most noticeable worldwide outcomes of neoliberalism (stemming from both SAP and participation in neoliberal globalization) has been marginalization of rural areas which has led to massive migration into urban areas characterized by sprawling informal settlements (slumification) in urban areas which are frequently characterized by acute poverty (Davis, 2007). There are different ways through which neoliberalism led to rural marginalization and associated unsustainable urban migration. First, SAP dictated fiscal austerity which led to cuts in rural development initiatives. Fiscal austerity measures and privatization of state-owned enterprises led to massive unemployment in urban areas forcing laid-off urban civil servants to move back to already struggling rural locales which exacerbated the rural immiseration. Finally, neoliberal globalization with its focus on FDI through multinational corporations tends to be mostly based in urban areas especially given the remoteness of rural areas in Africa.

An active body of research has delineated the systematic relationship between political variables and population health variables (see for example Navarro et al., 2003; Navarro & Shi, 2001). For instance, the type of political arrangements in Organization for Economic Cooperation and Development (OECD) countries, for example whether a given nation is liberal, social democratic, Christian democratic etc., has been found to be associated with different levels of health outcomes (Navarro & Shi, 2001). Other studies have also found a positive effect of democracy (e.g., through electoral competition) on health outcomes such as infant mortality (McGuire, 2010, 2001; Przeworski et al., 2000; Navia and Zweifel 2003). A positive correlation between democracy and life expectancy has also been observed (Besley & Kudamatsu, 2006).

Conclusive research on whether democratization initiatives have led to improvements in population health in Africa remains scarce. In one such rare study, Kudamatsu (2007) using retrospective fertility data finds a positive effect of democratization on infant survival. However, given the confluence of multitudes of other development outcomes that are simultaneously affected by democratization, it is hard to isolate the effects of the transition to democracy on health using pooled data from such a group of diverse countries as is done in such studies. A detailed comparative study using a few selected countries with similar sociopolitical context, as suggested in this chapter, may yield more conclusive results. In addition, the social impact of the democratization initiatives in Africa must be explored in relation to neoliberal initiatives which took place at the same time.

## Contradictions of Neoliberal Democratization

Democratization initiatives that began in SSA concurrently with neoliberal economic reforms (structural adjustment) in the 1990s, which I call *neoliberal democratization*, were fraught with contradictions. First, neoliberal economic reforms in SSA aimed at creating what decades earlier Karl Polanyi referred to as "markets-without-states" (Polanyi, 2001). The major tenet of neoliberal reforms as stipulated by Structural Adjustment Programs was to limit the reach of the state not just in the market through deregulation, but also in the provision of social welfare through requirements of fiscal austerity by cutting government spending (World Bank, 1981). Neoliberalism aimed to foster markets' freedom, not political freedoms (Harvey, 2006, p. 11). A *"Neoliberal State,"* which SAP programs envisaged, has one raison d'être, which is to create a good business climate (Prassad, 2006; Harvey, 2006). As such, neoliberal democratization aimed to empower the people by creating state institutions that are accountable to the people while at the same time economic prescriptions from the International Financial Institutions were dictating that for the sake of market efficiency governments had to be tamed, which subsequently rendered the institution through which the population was supposed to be empowered impotent. In fact, as James Ferguson argues in *The Anti-politics Machine*, even before neoliberalism attained its current ubiquity, IFIs, such as the World Bank, had already facilitated depoliticization by creating a development discourse that was entirely centered on technocratic expertise that often overlooked historical and sociopolitical contexts (Ferguson, 1994).

Furthermore, as an institutional project, neoliberalism has an effect of shifting the axis of political authority to the international level (Chorev, 2005, 2010), which ultimately affects adversely the influence of actors at the national level. Given the importance of Foreign Direct Investment in the age of neoliberal globalization, governments have an incentive to placate the demands of foreign capital in fear of *capital flight*, at times to the detriment of local actors (Rodrik, 1997). Neoliberalism is especially likely to produce impotent governments in the sub-Saharan Africa region since the region depends heavily on FDI and foreign aid. In such places, policies are often determined by external agencies creating an institutional structure that undermines the legitimacy of elected governments (Sandbrook, 1999), thus creating "choice-less democracies" (Mkandawire, 1999).

To sum up: the purported contradictions therefore stem from the fact that neoliberal democratization paradoxically attempted to empower people by making the government more accountable to them while at the same time favoring the ability of markets to act "freely" at the expense of "legitimate" governmental institutions through which the people were originally supposed to be empowered. To what extent, then, was the capability of local actors to exert demands on social provisions also weakened? Was the ability of the people to use elected institutions as a vehicle to improve their quality of life adversely affected? And therefore, have there been *real* improvements in substantive social outcomes, such as infant survival, following neoliberal democratization in SSA in the 1990s? These are motivating empirical questions that remain unanswered.

## Case Study: A Sample Empirical Research Design for Exploring the Impact of Neoliberal Democratization on Infant Mortality in Four Eastern African Countries

The postcolonial improvements in economic development and quality of life took a dramatic turn for the worse in many sub-Saharan Africa countries starting from the mid-1980s. The postindependence optimism of economic and social development was met by disappointment when many SSA countries experienced declines and stagnations in economic growth coupled with similarly discouraging statistics on social well-being. Regardless of the massive initiatives (through SAP, for example) that aimed to transform economic and political structures, which were seen as the major hindrances to development, social well-being indicators continued to remain stagnant and in some countries deteriorated in SSA in the 1990s. The underlying causes of this trend are still a puzzle.

As Fig. 25.1 shows, for example, quite a few SSA countries experienced stagnation in IMR decline. It must be noted that in addition to the stalled declines, and the occasional increases in infant mortality, the rates of infant morbidity and mortality are still very high in SSA compared to global averages. The average IMR in SSA is around 100 per thousand, meaning that almost 10% of infants die before their first birthday (Population Reference Bureau, 2008). In a high-income country with average public health outcomes, such as the United States, IMR is around six per thousand (Population Reference Bureau, 2008).

Now, what role did economic neoliberalism combined with democratization transitions to competitive politics play on this observed differential decline and spatial inequalities in public health in these countries? I proceed to design an empirical study that can be applied to answer this question using infant mortality as a proxy of population health (and development) in Kenya, Malawi, Tanzania, and Zambia.

## Conceptualization and Operationalization of Neoliberal Democratization

Following the existing literature I propose three hypothetical pathways through which the NLD affects

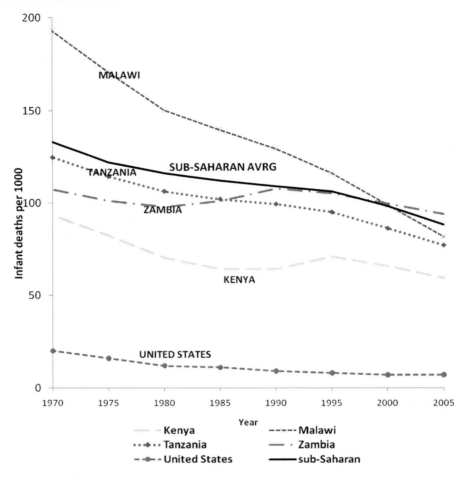

**Fig. 25.1** Infant mortality decline and stagnations in Eastern Africa, 1970–2005

infant survival rates: pre-post effect/increased institutional accountability hypothesis; reward or punish/political patronage hypothesis; and contact with neoliberal policies hypothesis.

As the rationale behind the political reforms would have it (World Bank, 1981, 1989), multiparty democracy increased institutional accountability, which should have led to an overall improvement in access to health services and hence improved infant/child health everywhere in the four countries. Democratic societies have better quality of life outcomes because citizens in such societies are more able to exert demands for better social conditions through public action (Drèze & Sen, 1991; Sen, 1999; Grindle & Thomas, 1991). Also political competition coupled with marketization should have reduced inefficiencies in distribution of state and development resources (Berry, 1989; Bates, 1981; Herbst, 2000; Birdsall & James, 1993; Mbaku, 1999), and should have improved institutional accountability (Mbaku, 1999) leading to an overall improvement in social welfare measured by infant mortality rates. Thus, starting at the macro (country) level, I posit that we should observe differentially lower rates of infant mortality after the transition to multiparty systems in all four countries if indeed the expected positive effects of democratization were manifested. We could refer to this as hypothesis 1.

Hypothesis 1: The period after the transition to a multiparty system is associated with differentially lower infant mortality risk compared to the period prior to the transition

As stated in the theory and background section, some critics of democratization efforts in Africa have pointed out that since sufficient social and political prerequisites were not in place, illiberal democracies may have emerged as a result of introducing multiparty systems (van de Walle, 2001; Bratton & van de Walle, 1997; Joseph, 1997, 1998). Such illiberal practices are likely to emerge especially when political allegiance is organized by essentialized identities such as ethnicity (regionalism), tribal connections, or religion. In such instances where patrimonial, clientistic, and prebendal systems are prevalent, allocation of social welfare resources is thus affected by ethnicity (region), tribe, or religion. I hypothesize differential allocation of primary health-care resources (e.g., by ethnicity or tribe) as the link between provinces' party affiliation (voting behavior) and differential rates of infant survival across provinces of a given country. The election winner, which maintained control of the government in a given country, used the provinces voting outcome as a signal for whether they should channel more resources to the region to maintain control of the region (if the region supported them), or to punish the region so that they may regain control (if the region voted for the opposition).

> Hypothesis 2: Following the transition to a multiparty system, provinces which voted for the winning party had lower risk of infant mortality than provinces which opposed the winning party or were neutral towards them.

Neoliberal policies through structural adjustment required privatization of state-owned enterprises which led to massive unemployment; and reduction of provinces' operating budget due to requirements of fiscal austerity which reduced public health funding. Also, implementation of neoliberal policies redefines class structure and class power (Harvey, 2005) which has an effect of concentrating political power in the hands of a few wealthy individuals, thus disempowering the bargaining power of the majority (middle class and the poor). Neoliberalism also shifts the locus of political authority to the international level (Chorev, 2005, 2010), meaning that elected officials are more likely to give precedence to the demands of foreign investors over the needs of local actors. Second, the extent of neoliberal globalization as measured by a country's degree of economic openness, inflows of FDI, and degree of trade openness has ramifications on a country's social and institutional arrangements and subsequently on provision of healthcare. Thus, we should expect the degree by which a given country was exposed to neoliberal policies to mediate the positive impact of democratization on public health outcomes.

> Hypothesis 3: The risk of infant mortality in a given province of a given country is positively correlated with the degree of contact with neoliberal policies of a given country.

Figure 25.2 presents a heuristic schema of the proposed hypotheses and the corresponding mechanisms.

## Why Infant Mortality as the Outcome Variable of Interest?

Infant health is among the key "human development" indicators (Sen, 1999). Health and life longevity are crucial capabilities; that is, they are essential *ends* of social development (Sen, 1999; Nussbaum, 1999, 2003). In addition, infant mortality correlates fairly well with other social indicators, which may not be easily measurable, such as nutrition and health-care access (Sen, 1999; Lipton & Ravallion, 1995). The known biomedical determinants of infant health and survival, such as birth weight and gestational age, are often related to social factors such as the mother's ability to adhere to nutritional standards, which depend on her education level. Thus, in general infant mortality is among the most reliable proxies of general socioeconomic development as well. Furthermore, as a social indicator, IMR of a given country is highly responsive to short-term institutional and public health interventions, such as control of infectious disease and immunization programs. Changes in IMR are highly sensitive to exogenous shocks that may affect access to and quality of primary healthcare such as political-economic transformations.

In addition to infant mortality rates having such a high association with other accepted indicators of social well-being, there is a fairly well-tested predictive model of infant survival both at the individual level and at the society level, which makes it more practical to use infant mortality as an outcome variable upon which the influence of political-economic variables will be explored.

Infant mortality rates are thus fairly discernible empirically using survey data. Mosley and Chen (1984) designed the classic demographical model of child survival that links such social determinants of infant survival to their respective biomedical

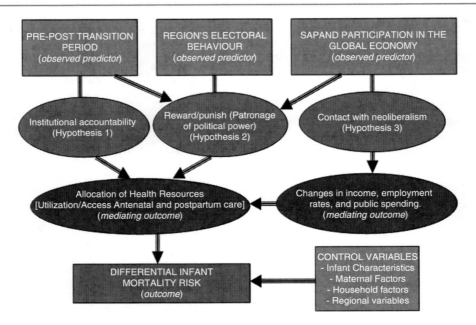

**Fig. 25.2** A heuristic schema of hypotheses and mechanism

proximate causes of infant survival. The socioeconomic determinants of child mortality operate through a set of biological pathways known as the *proximate determinants* (Mosley & Chen, 1984). The proximate determinants of infant survival are: (i) maternal characteristics, such as age, number of previous births, and the interval between recent and last births; (ii) exposure to contamination and pathogens through air, water, and food; (iii) nutrient deficiency, injury, infanticide; and (iv) personal illness controls such as personal hygiene, disease preventive measures, and availability of medical treatment. According to Mosley and Chen (1984), these proximate factors operate through socioeconomic determinants, which are individual-level variables such as mother's and father's productivity (which are functions of mother's and father's level of education and occupation) and traditions/norms/attitudes of child-rearing, household-level variables such as income and wealth, and community-level variables, such as ecological and climatic factors, *political economy, and health systems*. Figure 25.3 summarizes the Mosley and Chen (1984) framework.

Regardless of the reported urban growth in the SSA region in recent decades, the percent of the population in developing sub-Saharan Africa countries that live in rural areas is estimated to be on average about 63% (World Bank, 2009). The difference in access to crucial resources is typically stark between urban and rural areas in the region, which translate to a wide divergence in standard of living as well. As Table 25.1 shows, infant mortality rates, for example, differ greatly between rural and urban areas. The extent of rural-urban spatial inequality when measured by other indicators such as assets ownership, educational attainment, and nutrition also show a wide divide between rural and urban areas (Sahn & Stifel, 2003).

## Country Selection: Why Kenya, Malawi, Tanzania, and Zambia?

The framework suggested in this chapter is contingent on having countries with similar sociopolitical structure. Kenya, Malawi, mainland Tanzania, and Zambia are thus chosen as examples since they have structural similarities in their history and their sociopolitical context while at the same time have sufficient differences in the extent of their contact with neoliberalism. Also, all four countries had first multiparty elections that were categorized as either "free" or "partly free" by *Freedom House* (2004). In that way, the transitions to competitive politics were not affected by civil unrest that has been symptomatic of such transitions in other countries in SSA. Furthermore, two of the countries, Malawi and Zambia had a switch in power after their first multiparty elections as the opposition won,

**Fig. 25.3** A summary of Mosley and Chen's (1984) determinants of infant mortality model

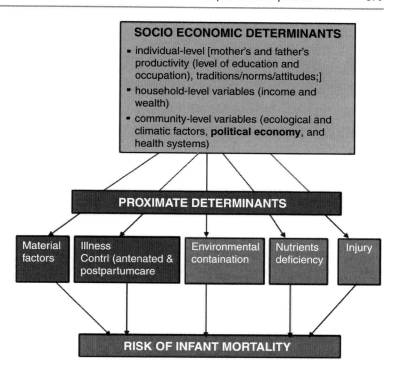

**Table 25.1** Differences between rural and urban infant mortality rates[a] in Eastern Africa, 1980–2008

| DHS survey country and year | Urban | Rural |
|---|---|---|
| Kenya 2008–2009 | 62.8 | 58.5 |
| Kenya 2003 | 61.1 | 78.7 |
| Kenya 1998 | 55.4 | 73.8 |
| Kenya 1993 | 45.5 | 64.9 |
| Kenya 1989 | 56.7 | 59.2 |
| Malawi 2004 | 60.2 | 97.5 |
| Malawi 2000 | 82.5 | 116.7 |
| Malawi 1992 | 118.1 | 138.4 |
| Tanzania 2004–2005 | 72.5 | 84.9 |
| Tanzania 1999 | 87.3 | 113 |
| Tanzania 1996 | 81.7 | 96.8 |
| Tanzania 1991–1992 | 108.3 | 97.1 |
| Zambia 2007 | 80.4 | 82 |
| Zambia 2001–2002 | 76.7 | 102.6 |
| Zambia 1996 | 91.9 | 117.9 |
| Zambia 1992 | 78 | 116 |

[a] The infant mortality rates are computed average of 10 years preceding a given survey. *DHS Demographic and Health Surveys.*
*Source*: Macro International Inc, 2011.

whereas in Kenya and Tanzania the incumbents stayed in power.

Kenya, Malawi, Tanzania, and Zambia share a similar historical and sociopolitical structure because they are all former British colonies which means that they have inherited a somewhat similar legal and constitutional framework from the colonial era. All four countries have presidential systems, which are systems of government where an executive branch exists and presides separately from the legislature. Kenya, Malawi, Tanzania, and Zambia are Representative Democracies, a form of government founded on the principle of elected individuals representing the people; and they are Republics in a sense that at least a part of its people have some element of formal control over its government, and in which the head of state is not a monarch. Finally, all four are unitary states, as opposed to Federations, which are sovereign state governed as one single unit in which the central government is supreme and any administrative divisions (subnational units) exercise only powers that the central government chooses to delegate.[1]

---

[1] Kenya changed its constitution early this year to create a Federal system. This study covers the period before this change.

**Table 25.2** Similarities and differences among the four Eastern Africa countries in the key comparative variables

| Country | Year of 1st multiparty election | Outcome of the 1st multiparty presidential elections | Political-economic system before and after transition | Participation to the global economy in mid-1990s relative to other SSA countries | Available DHS rounds of data |
|---|---|---|---|---|---|
| Kenya | 1992 | Incumbents (KANU) won | Before: open market After: open market | Moderate | 1989, 1993, 1998, 2003, 2008 |
| Malawi | 1994 | Incumbents (MCP) lost | Before: mixed After: open market | Low | 1992, 1996, 2000, 2004 |
| Tanzania | 1995 | Incumbents (CCM) won | Before: state-controlled After: open market | Low | 1991/1992, 1996, 1999, 2004, 2007/2008 |
| Zambia | 1991 | Incumbents (UNIP) lost | Before: mixed After: open market | Moderate | 1992, 1996, 2001, 2007 |

In addition, there are practical advantages for choosing these four cases. These nations went through the political transition to competitive politics around the same time between 1991 and 1995, and they all hold general elections every five years. Also, all four countries have sufficient quantitative data from which the quality of life indicators measured by public health inequalities will be derived. The data is from the nationally representative Demographic and Health Survey (DHS), and all four countries have data rounds covering the period before the political transition and after the transition which makes it possible to do a cross-country comparison.

However, these four countries also have crucial differences in their postcolonial political economies and their degrees of global engagement. Tanzania, for example, was a well-known case in which the economy had a very limited private sector as most of it was under the control of the state, in what has been dubbed African Socialism. Conversely, Kenya adopted open-market capitalism well before Tanzania and Zambia followed suit. Zambia, conversely, rich in copper ore, which was a prized commodity before the discovery of artificial fibers, had fairly high rates of foreign trade compared to Malawi and Tanzania. Table 25.2 summarizes these practical considerations and the crucial similarities and differences which allows for a comparison.

## Research Design

The empirical strategy would require a mixed-methods approach combining both qualitative and quantitative analysis. For example, one could roughly follow a variation of the Nested Analysis Approach (NAP) (Lieberman, 2005). The Nested Analysis Approach can be used to combine large-N statistical analysis with small-N qualitative analysis to shed light on causal mechanism and generate theory. The large-N analysis identifies country-level trends, which provides guidance on key variables and mechanism to be explored in nested qualitative study of selected cases (small-N). The small-N analysis would thus be used to isolate mechanisms connecting neoliberal democratization to public health outcomes and to generate theoretical insights to explain anomalous cases. Such a variant of NAP would involve three levels of analysis: Level I would be a statistical (large-N) study of the four selected countries. Level II is a combined statistical and qualitative analysis of two countries with systematic differences in the outcome variable (infant mortality). Level III is a detailed statistical and qualitative study of one country.

### NAP Step 1: Country-Level Analysis

In this step differential risk of infant mortality would be computed across the four countries to compare values before and after NLD to test the three hypothesized pathways. A comparison of rates of infant mortality between provinces of a given country and between countries can be carried out in the following manner: (i) by before and after transition period in order to test changes in the institutional accountability pathway; (ii) by differences across provinces in a given country conditioned on a given provinces' level of support of the first multiparty election winner in order to test changes in patronage and of political power (punish or reward pathway), and (iii) by a country's degree of contact with neoliberalism.

The applicable demographic data could be obtained from Demographic and Health Surveys. Census data could also be used to enhance data representativeness at subnational levels of analysis but with the shortcoming of having fewer socioeconomic indicators. Election results data is available from the websites of the national electoral commission in each respective country. And, data on extent of implementation of Structural Adjustment Programs can be obtained from IMF and World Bank reports and statistics on trade and international finance, such as FDI flows, is available from national statistics and the IMF and the World Trade Organization (WTO).

In order to capture the macro-micro linkages, predictor variables should include individual-, household-, regional-, and country-level covariates. The selection of the *control* variables loosely follows Mosley and Chen's (1984) "proximate determinants" of the IMR model. For individual-level and household-level variables, the empirically established correlates of infant mortality can be used. At the individual-level, these predictors are mother's age, mother's level of education, infant's birth order, and birth interval. At the household-level the predictors are: household socioeconomic status, which can be measured by a household wealth index, head of household's level of education, household's access to healthcare, and household place of residence depending on whether the household is located in an urban or rural area.

To highlight the transitional effect before and after the transition, *temporal variables* (pre/post transition) and the province voting behavior variables should be the point of focus. The temporal variable is defined as pre-transition and post transition. The post-transition period is defined as the period starting two years after the multiparty elections in a given country to allow for the hypothesized mechanisms linking the political transition and infant survival to take effect. Changes in intermediate variables linking these two processes, such as delivery of primary healthcare and access to antenatal and postpartum care must also be explored. The main province-level variable of interest is the *province's voting pattern* measured by the proportion of the region's residents who voted for the party that won the first multiparty elections. The variable for the percent of votes garnered by the winning party can be divided into *pro-winner*, *neutral*, and *anti-winner provinces* to separate provinces by their relative degrees of support of the winner in the first elections.

Finally, three country-level covariates measuring contact with neoliberalism would be added. These include: a dummy variable indicating whether a given country was an open-market economy at the time of the transition, degree of trade openness, and level of FDI. Also measures of degree of implementation of specific SAP programs would have to be included. The focus here could be on readily available SAP indicators such as changes in primary care budgets due to fiscal austerity measures and number of privatized state enterprises.

Statistical analysis would include appropriate modeling techniques suitable for exploring differential survival rates conditioned on the aforementioned covariates such as Event History models. For example, discrete-time hazard models can be applied here to estimate the effect of the aforementioned variables on odds of infant mortality in a given province $i$, in country $j$ in year $t$. The risk of infant death during the first year varies monthly. Risk of death is typically higher during the first month of life (neonatal period) than in the preceding months (postneonatal period). In order to account for this time-dependency, a parametric distribution, such as the Weibull distribution can be used to estimate the statistical models. In addition, since several rounds of data are available, fixed effects at the country and province level could be further explored to account for unobserved heterogeneity.

## NAP Step 2: Qualitative Comparison of Two Countries: Different Process of Neoliberal Democratization, Different Substantive Outcomes?

This step gives a qualitative explanation of the difference in IMR trends between countries. This qualitative comparison should draw from the statistical study in Step 1. For example, let us say Tanzania and Zambia were the selected countries according to the statistical results. Qualitative explanations of the differences may include explainer variables such as: (i) strength of local political actors before transition, (ii) strength of foreign economic actors, and (iii) type of political-economic regime which emerged. Such comparative qualitative data can be accessed from secondary sources including media archives and published case studies.

### NAP Step 3: Identifying Dimensions of Spatial Inequality with Emphasis on Rural-Urban Divide

This last step of the Nested Analysis Approach would identify mechanisms and contextualize intervening variables of the causal link between the political transformation and infant mortality in order to shed light on within-country inequality in infant health after neoliberal democratization.

Here one of the four countries would be chosen for detailed qualitative study though field work in the selected country. The aim of qualitative analysis is to create *historical narratives* of changing access to health resources after the political transition, which can be gathered through *semistructured interviews* with public health officials from various provinces in a given country (again the selection of provinces should be gauged by the statistical results from Step 1).

In addition, *archival data* from media outlets, government documents (such as ministry of health budgets), political manifestoes, parliamentary negotiations, and province health budget documents can be used to shed light on province- and district-level political economy and the nature of contestation of health resources. In addition, campaign documents from political party offices and the media, for example, can be used to attest whether primary healthcare was indeed a policy focus area that political actors used to lobby for votes. *Open-ended interviews* with officials of the political parties that existed at the time of transition can also be used to ascertain in which parts of the country child health was emphasized as a campaign issue.

### Conclusions

In the last few decades Africa has been a notable laboratory of development experiments. The implication of such highly transformative development initiatives to the well-being of Africans in the long-run has yet to be fully appreciated in the available literature in demography. Even though countless surveys with fairly comprehensive social, economic, and demographic indicators continue to be collected everyday in the continent, such as the highly reliable Demographic and Health Surveys, such data are rarely used to explore complex causal factors behind the observed demographic trends of fertility, mortality, migration, and urbanization.

In sub-Saharan Africa, like elsewhere on the globe, demographic processes and structures are a product of a multitude of complex social, political, and economic factors. If the complexities of these sociodemographic processes are not taken seriously, development trajectories of SSA nations will remain elusive to social scientists for many years to come. If this trend of ignoring underlying structural causes continues rural areas will especially become more prone to immiseration. Only such research would highlight, for example, the implications of the fact that benefits of neoliberal globalization accrue to urban dwellers who are either skilled enough to find employment in the growing sectors that are of interest to multinational corporations or have access to the necessary technologies such as the internet that have become so crucial in the information age. In addition, such research would highlight the fact of how rural areas which in most African countries were the focus of postindependence "community development" initiatives had to be abandoned as states were required to minimize crowding-out private investment at the onset of neoliberalism.

In this chapter, I therefore propose a conceptual framework and a concurrent empirical design that can be used to investigate the link between political-economic transformations and social demographic outcomes with a focus on spatial inequality in child survival. I design a template that can be used to make a cross-country comparison between countries with similar sociopolitical trajectories in South-eastern Africa, i.e., Kenya, Malawi, Tanzania, and Zambia. Using such analyses will shed light on the ever-growing disparity between urban and rural areas in Africa. Policies advocating national growth may achieve different levels of success across the urban-rural continuum, further exacerbating urban-rural inequalities. Most importantly, tracing political-economic origins of these inequalities would put into sharper relief the real causes behind some of these disconcerting trends instead of just looking for quick temporary fixes.

# References

Acemoglu, D., & Robinson, J. A. (2006). *Economic origins of dictatorship and democracy*. New York and Cambridge: Cambridge University Press.

Adejumobi, S. (2000). Elections in Africa: A fading shadow of democracy? *International Political Science Review, 2*(1), 59–73.

Afrobarometer. (2010). *A comparative series of national public attitude surveys on democracy, markets, and civil society in Africa*. Retrieved from http://www.afrobarometer.org/index.html. Accessed 20 October 2010.

Ayers, A. (2006). Demystifying democratization: The global constitution of (neo-)liberal polities in Africa. *Third World Quarterly, 27*(2), 331–338.

Babb, S. (2001). *Managing Mexico: Economists from nationalism to neoliberalism*. Princeton, NJ: Princeton University Press.

Bates, R. H. (1981). *Markets and states in tropical Africa: The political basis of agricultural policies*. Berkeley, CA: University of California Press.

Berry, S. (1989). Social institutions and access to resources. *Africa: Journal of the International African Institute, 59*(1), 41–55.

Besley, T., & Kudamatsu, M. (2006). Health and democracy. *American Economic Review Papers and Proceedings, 96*(2006), 313–318.

Birdsall, N., & James, E. (1993). Efficiency and equity in social spending: How and why governments misbehave. In M. Lipton & J. van der Gaag (Eds.), *Including the poor* (pp. 335–358). New York: Oxford University Press for the World Bank.

Bratton, M. (2007). The durability of political goods? Evidence from Nigeria's new democracy. *Commonwealth and Comparative Politics, 45*(1), 1–33.

Bratton, M., & Mattes, R. (2001). "Support for democracy in Africa: Intrinsic or instrumental?" *British Journal of Political Science, 31*(3), 447–474.

Bratton, M., & van de Walle, N. (1997). *Democratic experiments in Africa: Regime transitions in comparative perspective*. Cambridge, UK: Cambridge University Press.

Castro, A., & Singer, M. (Eds.). (2004). *Unhealthy health policy: A critical anthropological examination*. Walnut Creek, CA: AltaMira Press.

Chorev, N. (2005). The institutional project of neoliberal globalism: The case of WTO. *Theory and Society, 34*, 317–355.

Chorev, N. (2010). Fixing globalization institutionally: U.S. domestic politics of international trade. *International Sociology, 25*(1), 54–74.

Davis, M. (2007). *Planet of slums*. London and New York: Verso.

Diamond, L. (1996). Is the third wave of democracy over? *Journal of Democracy, 7*(3), 20–27.

Diamond, L. (1999). *Developing democracy: Toward consolidation*. Baltimore: Johns Hopkins University Press.

Diamond, L. (2002). Thinking about hybrid regimes. *Journal of Democracy, 13*(2), 21–35.

Drèze, J., & Sen, A. (1991). *Hunger and public action*. Oxford: Oxford University Press.

Ferguson, J. (1994). *The anti-politics machine: Development, depoliticization, and bureaucratic power in Lesotho*. Minneapolis Mn, USA: University of Minnesota Press.

Grindle, M. S., & Thomas, J. W. (1991). *Public choices and policy change: The political economy of reform in developing countries*. Baltimore: Johns Hopkins University Press.

Harrison, G. (2010). *Neoliberal Africa: The impact of global social engineering*. New York: Zed Books.

Harvey, D. (2005). *A brief history of neoliberalism*. New York: Oxford University Press.

Harvey, H. (2006). *Spaces of global capitalism: Towards a theory of uneven geographical development*. London and New York: Verso.

Heller, P. (2000). Degrees of democracy: Some comparative lessons from India. *World Politics, 52*, 484–519.

Herbst, J. (2000) *States and power in Africa: Comparative lessons in authority and control*. Princeton, NJ: Princeton University Press.

Hill, K., & Palloni, A. (1992). Demographic Responses to Economic Shocks: The case of Latin America. The Peopling of the Americas (Vol. 3, pp. 411–438). Liege, Belgium: International Union for the Statistical Study of Population.

Howard, M. M., & Roessler, P. G. (2006). Liberalizing electoral outcomes in competitive authoritarian regimes. *American Journal of Political Science, 50*(2), 365–381.

Huber, E., Rueschemeyer, D., & Stephens, J. D. (1997). The paradoxes of contemporary democracy. Formal, participatory, and social dimensions. *Comparative Politics, 29*(3), 323–341.

Huntington, S. P. (1991). Democracy's third wave. *The Journal of Democracy, 2*(2), 12–34.

Joseph, R. (1997). Democratization in Africa after 1989: Comparative and theoretical perspectives. *Comparative Politics, 29*, 363–382.

Joseph, R. (1998). Africa, 1990–97: From Abertura to closure. *Journal of Democracy, 2*, 3–17.

Karl, T. L. (1995). The hybrid regimes of Central America. *Journal of Democracy, 6*(3), 72–87.

Kim, J. Y., Millen, J. V., Irwin, A., & Gershman, J. (2000). *Dying for growth: Global inequality and the health of the poor*. Monroe, ME: Common Courage Press.

Kudamatsu, M. (2007). Has Democratization Reduced Infant Mortality in Sub-Saharan Africa? Evidence from Micro Data (December 15, 2006). ISER Discussion Paper No. 685. Available at SSRN: http://ideas.repec.org/p/dpr/wpaper/0685.html

Levitsky, S., & Way, L. A. (2002). The rise of competitive authoritarianism. *Journal of Democracy, 13*(2), 51–65.

Leys, C. (1996). *The rise and fall of development theory*. London: James Currey.

Lieberman, E. (2005). Nested analysis as a mixed-method strategy for comparative research. *American Political Science Review, 99*(3), 435–452.

Lieberman, E. (2009). *Boundaries of contagion: How ethnic politics have shaped government responses to AIDS*. Princeton, New Jersey: Princeton University Press.

Lindberg, S. I. (2006). *Democracy and elections in Africa*. Baltimore, MD: The John Hopkins University Press.

Lipset, M. S. (1959). Some social requisites of democracy: Economic development and political legitimacy. *American Political Science Review, 53*(1), 69–105.

Lipset, M. S. (1960). *Political man: The social bases of politics*. Garden City, NY: Doubleday.

Lipset, M. S. (1994). The social requisites of democracy revisited. *American Sociological Review, 59*(1), 1–22.

Lipton, M., & Ravallion, M. (1995). Poverty and policy. In J. Behrman & T. N. Srinivasan (Eds.), *Handbook of development economics* (pp. 2551–2657). New York: Elsevier.

Lugala, J. L. P. (1995). The impact of structural adjustment policies on women's and children's health in Tanzania. *Review of African Political Economy, 22*(63), 43–53.

Macro International Inc. (2011). *MEASURE DHS STATcompiler*. Retrieved March 8, 2011, from http://www.measuredhs.com

Mbaku, J. M. (1999). Democratization and the crisis of policy reform in developing countries. In M. D. Kimenyi & J. M. Mbaku (Eds.), *Institutions and collective choice in developing countries: Applications of the theory of public choice* (pp. 327–354). Aldershot: Ashgate.

McGuire, J. (2001). Social policy and mortality decline in East Asia and Latin America. *World Development, 29*(10), 1673–1697.

McGuire, J. (2010). *Politics, policy, and mortality decline in East Asia and Latin America*. Cambridge: Cambridge University Press.

Mkandawire, T. (1999). Crisis management and the making of "Choiceless Democracies" in Africa. In R. Joseph (Ed.), *The state, democracy and crisis in Africa*. Boulder, CO: Lynne Rienne.

Mkandawire, T., & Soludo, C. C. (1999). *Our continent, our future: African perspectives on structural adjustment*. Dakar: CODESRIA.

Moore, B. (1966). *Social origins of dictatorship and democracy: Lord and peasant in the making of the modern world*. Boston, MA: Beacon.

Mosley, W. H., & Chen, L. C. (1984). An analytical framework for the study of child survival in developing countries. *Population and Development Review, 10*(Suppl), 25–45.

Moss, T. J. (2007). *African development: Making sense of the issues and actors*. London: Lynnne Rienner Publishers.

Navarro, V., Borrell, C., Benach, J., Muntaner, C., Quiroga, A., & Rodriguez-Sanz, M. (2003). The importance of the political and the social in explaining mortality differentials among the countries of the OECD, 1950–1998. *International Journal of Health Services, 33*(3), 419–494.

Navarro, V., & Shi, L. (2001). The political context of social inequalities and health. *Social Science & Medicine, 52*(3), 481–491.

Navia, P., & Zweifel, T. D. (2003). Democracy, dictatorship, and infant mortality revisited. *Journal of Democracy, 14*(3), 90–103.

Ndulu, B., & O'Connell, S. A. (1999). Governance and growth in sub-Saharan Africa. *Journal of Economic Perspectives, 13*(3), 41–66.

Nussbaum, M. K. (1999). *Women and human development*. Cambridge, UK: Cambridge University Press.

Nussbaum, M. K. (2003). Capabilities as fundamental entitlement: Sen and social justice. *Feminist Economics, 9*(2–3), 35–59.

Palloni, A., & Hill, K. (1995). Demographic responses to economic shocks: The case of Latin America. *Human Capital and Development, 8*, 197–223.

Palloni, A., Hill, K., & Aguire, P. (1996). Economic swings and demographic changes in the history of Latin America. *Population Studies, 50*(1), 105–132.

Polanyi, K. (2001). *The great transformation: The political and economic origins of our time*. Boston: Beacon Press.

Population Reference Bureau. (2008). *Country statistics: Tanzania*. Retrieved February 9, 2009, from http://www.prb.org/Datafinder/Geography/Summary.aspx?region=49&region_type=2

Prassad, M. (2006). *The politics of free markets: The rise of neoliberal economic policies in Britain, France, Germany, and the United States*. Chicago: University of Chicago Press.

Przeworski, A., Alvarez, M. E., Cheibub, J. A., & Limongi, F. (2000). *Democracy and development*. Cambridge: Cambridge University Press.

Rapley, J. (2002). *Understanding development*. Boulder, CO: Lynne Rienner.

Rodgers, G. B. (2002) Income and inequality as determinants of mortality: An international cross-section analysis. 1979. *International Journal of Epidemiology, 31*, 533–538.

Rodrik, D. (1997). *Has globalization gone too far?* Washington, DC: Institute of International Economics.

Sahn, D., & Stifel, D. (2003). Urban–rural inequality in living standards in Africa. *Journal of African Economies, 12*(4), 564–597.

Sahn, D. E., Dorosh, P. A., & Younger, S. E. (1997). *Structural adjustment reconsidered: Economic policy and poverty in Africa*. Cambridge: Cambridge University Press.

Sandbrook, R. (1999). The contradictions of neo-liberal democracy. *Cambridge Review of International Affairs, 13*(1), 41–54.

Sandbrook, R., Edelman, M., Heller, P., & Teichman, J. (2006). *Social democracies in the global periphery*. Cambridge: Cambridge University Press.

Sen, A. (1999). *Development as freedom*. New York: Alfred A. Knopf.

Shandra, J. M., Nobles, J., London, B., & Williamson, J. B. (2003). Dependency, democracy, and infant mortality: A quantitative, cross-national analysis of less developed countries. *Social Science & Medicine, 3*(59), 321–333.

Stuckler, D., King, L. P., & Basu, S. (2008). International monetary fund programs and tuberculosis outcomes in post-communist countries. *PLoS Med, 5*(7), e143.

Teitelbaum, M. S. (2005). Political demography. In H. B. Kaplan, D. Poston, & M. Micklin (Eds.), *Handbook of the population* (pp. 719–730). New York: Kluwer-Plenum.

van de Walle, N. (2001). *African economies and the politics of permanent crisis, 1979–99*. Cambridge: Cambridge University Press.

Weiner, M. (1971). Political demography: An inquiry into the political consequences of population change. In National Academy of Sciences, *Rapid population growth: Consequences and policy implications* (Chapter XV). Baltimore, MD: Johns Hopkins University Press.

Weinreb, A. A. (2001a). First politics, then culture: Accounting for ethnic differences in demographic behavior in Kenya. *Population and Development Review, 27*(3), 437–467.

Weinreb, A. A. (2001b). A state-centered political capital approach to the explanation of demographic differences: With special reference to regional/ethnic inequality in sub-Saharan Africa. In *Proceedings of the general conference of the International Union for the Scientific Study of Population (IUSSP)*, 18–24 August, Salvador, Brazil.

Wejnert, B. (2005). Diffusion, development, and democracy, 1800–1999. *American Sociological Review, 70*(53), 53–81.

Williamson, J. (1990). What Washington means by policy reform. In J. Williamson (Ed.), *Latin American adjustment: How much has happened?* (pp. 5–20). Washington, DC: Institute for International Economics.

Williamson, J. (1993). Democracy and the "Washington consensus". *World Development, 21*(8), 1329–1336.

Williamson, J. (2003). From reform agenda to damaged brand name: A short history of the Washington Consensus and suggestions for what to do next. *Finance and Development, 40*(3), 10–13.

World Bank. (1981). *Accelerated development in sub-Saharan Africa: An agenda to action*. Washington, DC: World Bank.

World Bank. (1989). *Sub-Saharan Africa: From crisis to sustainable growth*. Washington, DC: World Bank.

World Bank. (2009). *World Bank Development Indicators*. Washington DC.

# Diverse Ruralities in the 21st Century: From Effacement to (Re-)Invention

Keith Halfacree

*It is back again: the recurrent onset of academic rural doubt in the US. It [has] been 20 years or so since the last onset... when Bill Friedland [1982] engaged a debate about the end of rural society and the future of rural sociology. But recent discussions indicate that US rural scholars are once more in the midst of this uncertain mood (Bell, 2007, p. 402)*

*In short, morbid thoughts about the rural abound (Bell, 2008, p. 6)*

## Introduction: Banishing Morbid Thoughts

Rural demographers reading this final chapter of the *International Handbook of Rural Demography* and seeking a clear understanding of rurality in the 21st century may initially be rather alarmed to discover that the two recent interventions by eminent US rural sociologist Michael Mayerfield Bell quoted from above are by no means anomalies. (From either end of a 38 year period in the journal *Rural Sociology*, for example, see interventions by Copp [1972] and Krannich [2008]; also note numerous other contributions in the intervening years). Furthermore, this tone is not confined to the US (Bell, 2008; Cruickshank, 2009; Woods, 2005), even if it may be felt more acutely there as the academic status of rural scholarship in Europe and the Antipodes appears relatively more secure (Bell, 2007). From the United Kingdom, Woods (2009, p. 849) senses a current "introspective mood in rural geography," for example. Indeed, Bell's "morbid thoughts" are part of a longer tradition that has seen rurality as a significant social scientific concept repeatedly and frequently written off since at least the mid-19th century. Modern times, it seems, have no place for rurality.

Yet, and providing more hope for the *Handbook* reader, in spite of these valedictions, this very tradition also exists **because** rurality equally strongly retains a stubborn social scientific presence and simply does not go away. Notwithstanding often "detectable nervousness" (Cloke, 2006, p. 18) and consequent defensiveness when using the term – "thinking critically about rurality" but nonetheless still thinking about it – rurality is an issue that will not die (Woods, 2009); the matter is never finally "put to bed." Or, as Whatmore (1993, p. 605) reflected:

> For a subject repeatedly dismissed as a figment of our analytical imagination..., the **rural** world has an unruly and intractable popular significance and remains a tenaciously active research domain.

This chapter will draw on recent rural scholarship, mostly from the UK and North America, rooted within these corresponding debates in order to introduce some lines of reasoning as to how "rurality" is (to be) interpreted in the early 21st century, at least within the countries of the global North, and to suggest some of the demographic implications that emerge from these interpretations. It begins by outlining briefly why rurality has often been seen as an anachronistic concept, not least by critical scholars keen to separate the conceptual wood from the trees, to distinguish robust "rational

K. Halfacree (✉)
Department of Geography, School of the Environment and Society, Swansea University, Swansea SA2 8PP, UK
e-mail: k.h.halfacree@swansea.ac.uk

abstraction" from obfuscatory "chaotic conception" (Sayer, 1984). However, not least from the perspective of how we all go on within everyday life, any idea of rurality as simply having been almost completely effaced is inadequate, not least when rurality's status as a taxonomic "in(ter)vention" is proposed. Such an interpretation leads to the next section's presentation of rurality, first, as "representation" and then, second, following some continued desire to ground this interpretation a little more, also as "practice." The next and most substantial section then interrogates the representational interpretation and the idea of rurality as invented further through first developing the idea of "rurality beyond the rural" but then, drawing upon recent interest within social sciences on the more-than-representational, presenting a final interpretation of rurality as still being at least partly embodied and grounded. In conclusion, the chapter argues that all of these interpretations of rurality in the 21st century are often intellectually worthwhile in their own right but each have their own demographic implications. The chapter ends by reflecting overall on some of the implications of accepting inherently diverse interpretations of rurality for demographic practice in the 21st century.

## Effacing Rurality: The Dynamic Spatiality of Capitalism

Within academic literature, as Bell's interventions articulate, and in particular reflecting the influence of political economy perspectives (Cloke, 1989), there is a strong argument that with all that was once seen as solid and timeless instead being recognized as often highly vulnerable to "melt[ing] into air" (Marx & Engels, 1848, p. 6), the spatiality of contemporary capitalism has progressively done away with formerly significant geographical demarcations and borders, including any clear distinction between rural and urban. In Lobao's (1996, p. 89) felicitous phrase, there has been a "spatial loosening of the elements once considered indicative of… rural and urban," as the scales of operations within capitalist society are constantly re-written and elaborated, with the societal significance of any "rural" scale incessantly and plurally undermined.

Moreover, this effacement of the rural is not just the result of economic "logics," reflected at the discursive level through ideas such as Frouws' (1998, p. 61) "utilitarian discourse." For example, Cruickshank argues that within a "modernization discourse" the "governmentality" disposition of the modern state has politically all but eliminated rurality through restructuring "from the local towards the national" (Cruickshank, 2009, p. 100). Although this national level of state power is itself now under threat from more internationally scaled governance, on the one hand, and a regional turn, on the other (Jones, 2001), neither of these trends return political authority to any rural scale.

From both economic and political directions, therefore, and through global, national and even local perspectives, talk of "rurality" can soon appear at best a quaint anachronism, with any urban-rural delineation regarded at most as having only a bit-part role in scaling 21st century society. Thus, for example, reviews of the social construction of scale, such as Marston (2000), typically fail even to acknowledge the rural scale, let alone to give it any significance.

As already flagged up, this apparent conceptual irrelevance today of erstwhile rural space was famously and powerfully outlined by James Copp in a Presidential address to the US Rural Sociological Society as far back as 1972. Copp (1972, p. 519) argued that:

> There is no rural and there is no rural economy. It is merely our analytic distinction, our rhetorical device. Unfortunately we tend to be victims of our own terminological duplicity. We tend to ignore the import of what happens in the total economy and society as it affects the rural sector. We tend to think of the rural sector as a separate entity.

His argument has been reiterated many times over the past four decades, as Bell suggested above, but one final illustration comes from British geographer Keith Hoggart (1990), who argued for the need to "do away with rural" for theoretical progress. Indeed, retaining belief in any town versus country divide can be seen as ideological, since it both denies and confuses understanding of the spatiality of contemporary capitalism. It promotes, in Sayer's (1984, after Marx) terminology, "chaotic conceptions" within our conceptual thinking rather than the desired "rational abstractions."

The implication from these accusations of rurality as now largely effaced ontologically is that the only way to sustain rurality would be to show that there remain **significant** societal processes in operation that are delineated at a local spatial scale **and** that their resulting spatial inscriptions enable us to distinguish "rural" from one or more "nonrural" environments (Halfacree, 1993). In summary, we would need to pinpoint spaces distinguished strongly enough by their own causal forces that we can label "rural." Certainly from the perspective of the global North, Hoggart (1990) strongly doubted this two decades ago and, with subsequent intensification and scaling implications of what can loosely be termed "globalization," such an argument is likely to be reinforced today.

This quest to discover whether rurality retains theoretical salience can be illustrated briefly with respect to agriculture, not least since this industry and the landscapes of farming are usually seen as bedrock elements of rurality (see any rural textbook, for example). Such a task has a long pedigree, not least since Kautsky (1899) famously raised the "agrarian question" at the end of the 19th century. Taking a cue from work in the US, the challenge was taken up by the political economy influenced work on British agriculture that blossomed in the 1980s (for example, Marsden, Munton, Whatmore, & Little, 1986). Indeed, it was in many ways from a desire to challenge the "exceptionalism" of understanding agriculture as somehow "different" from other branches of the capitalist economy that spurred on this approach within rural studies (Cloke, 1989). The result was that agriculture was shown, on the one hand, to resemble other industries in very many ways, through the increasing roles played by commodities, capitalist labor relations, class, and profit. On the other hand, the industry was also seen to express a number of more distinctive features, such as a continued heavy reliance on and a resilience of family labor and an inability to shake off some degree of dependence upon the growth rhythms and seasons of the natural world.

The present chapter must leave this particular debate here, however, and consider briefly the demographic consequences of the rurality as effaced hypothesis. In short, if the rural no longer designates a socially significant spatial scale or demarcation then retaining such a category merely works to reinforce its obfuscatory existence as a chaotic conception. Clearly, such a stark conclusion would have major negative implications for the present *Handbook*. However, the chapter now turns to consider more epistemologically led interpretations of rurality that lead to very different conclusions about the significance of rurality today. As the introductory section suggested, in spite of the powerful contributions of Copp, Hoggart and others, as well as a desire to unpick strong (pro-)rural "ideologies" in countries such as the US and the UK (Bunce, 1994; Hadden & Barton, 1973; Short, 1991), whilst capitalist/urban/industrial society may have effaced rurality as a key scale of everyday life in very many respects, this is neither a finished task nor, indeed, one with a definite, if more or less anticipated, teleology of rurality-as-eliminated. To consider this lack of resolution further we turn to perspectives that present rurality more as malleable social construct/concept than as relatively distinct object. Specifically, we must consider rurality as representation.

## Inventing Rurality: Representations and Practices

As Cruickshank (2009, p. 101) observes, a rurality as effaced argument hinges on accepting a "fixed version of the rural" that is additionally "reduced to the traditional," an unduly static perspective not least in the context of the urban as being generally seen as fundamentally fluid and dynamic. In contrast, interpreting rurality as representation takes its lead from two main intertwined directions. First, it engages epistemological questions of "knowing" rurality before ontological considerations of rural being. Second, it extends ideas of the social construction of scale – such as the rural – from an emphasis on capitalist production and/or governmental regulation to the spheres of consumption and social reproduction (Marston, 2000). Combining these directions – and taking further cues from acknowledgement of rurality's "intractable popular significance" (Whatmore, 1993, p. 605) or its status as "analytic distinction.... [or] rhetorical device" (Copp, 1972, p. 519) – we can interpret rurality as something known through the taxonomic practices of classification, categorization, and codification that are integral to the functioning of everyday life (Billig, 1985; Potter & Wetherell, 1987).

Looking more closely at one example of this way of interpreting rurality, Moscovici (1984) proposed that we use "social representations" in order to deal with the world's complexity. He defined these as, in summary:

> organizational mental constructs which guide us towards what is 'visible' and must be responded to, relate appearance and reality, and even define reality itself. The world

is organized, understood and mediated through these basic cognitive units. Social representations consist of both concrete images and abstract concepts, organized around 'figurative nuclei' (Halfacree, 1993, p. 29).

Rurality can be seen as something "constructed" (Halfacree, 2001) – invented socially rather than an object to be discovered – as a "social representation of space" (Halfacree, 1993). Or put slightly differently, a representational interpretation of rurality presents it as a powerful "lay narrative" (Sayer, 1989) or "conversational reality" (Shotter, 1993). Even if such representations may be regarded as corresponding poorly to practices "on the ground" and even to operate ideologically as already suggested, this negates neither their existence nor their subsequent study.

Understanding rurality as representation is commonplace in rural studies, especially within Europe (for just three recent specific examples, see Baylina & Berg, 2010; Cruickshank, 2009; Mahon, 2007). They are integral to what Cloke (2006) termed the social construction perspective that has predominated within rural studies since the early 1990s. This comes through strongly in the majority of contributions to key edited collections, such as Cloke and Little (1997), Milbourne (1997), Cloke (2003a) and Cloke, Marsden, and Mooney (2006). As Bell (2007); also Cloke (1996, 2006) credits, it was an approach pioneered by Belgian sociologist Marc Mormont, not least by his sharp depiction of the rural as "a category of thought... that each society takes and reconstructs" (Mormont, 1990, pp. 40–41), although outside of rural social science the continuously (re)constructed character of linguistic terms such as "town" and "country" was much earlier illustrated by Welsh polymath Raymond Williams (1973), for example.

Eagerness to embrace rurality as representation can be explained in a number of ways, such as its fit with postmodern or poststructural deconstructions of fixed boundaries and the consequent embracing of more fluid readings of social phenomena (Bell, 2007; see next section). However, its vibrancy is also not least because besides the value of studying representations in their own right and/or in order to critique them, the **popular** resilience of rurality (and related representations such as "countryside") has very real **material** geographical and sociopolitical consequences. In short, and following one of the main functions of our taxonomic operations, people act on or through their representations of rurality in their everyday practices,

and both the rural world and its demographic structures are consequently (partly) produced thus (Halfacree, 2001, 2006). A good way to illustrate this is with reference to migration, although other consumption practices, notably forms of rural leisure and tourism, could equally be considered (Crouch, 2006; Lowe, Murdoch, & Cox, 1995).

Net migration of people to more rural areas, or counterurbanization, is now recognized as a central, if geographically, historically and socially uneven, demographic feature of most countries in the global North, having been first identified as a mass phenomenon in the US in the mid-1970s (Beale, 1975; Champion, 1998). Much academic effort has subsequently been spent seeking the causes of this demographic "turnaround" (from previous urbanization) (for example, Brown & Wardwell, 1980). On the one hand, there are strong economic explanations rooted in the uneven spatial dynamics of the capitalist production process. This explanation has rurality feature mostly in a secondary capacity, primary attention given to the capitalist restructuring that, as already noted, has little respect for rural/urban distinctions. On the other hand, more agency-centered explanations of counterurbanization emphasize what the previous explanation downplays, namely how little of the precise location of the counterurbanizer's new home is really explained by these particular economic factors. Especially given the prevalence of often quite long-distance commuting, counterurbanizers usually have some leeway in deciding exactly where to live and their representations of rurality can feature strongly in guiding their moves. Such representations are even more significant for retired migrants and others unencumbered by job considerations. Thus, in short, how people "know" rurality is pivotal to a key modern demographic phenomenon (Gosnell & Abrams, 2009).

In terms of the content of these seemingly demographically alluring representations of rurality, of central significance is what Cloke (2003b, p. 2) termed the powerful "centripetal force" of various forms of the "rural idyll," which emphasize the attraction of the category "rural" or "countryside" in the discourses of everyday life. These representations, of which Bell (2006, p. 150) recognizes three ideal types – "the pastoral ('farmscapes'), the natural ('wildscapes') and the sporting ('adventurescapes')" – vary considerably geographically (including intranationally; Cloke, Goodwin, & Milbourne, 1998), culturally and socially, but have very strong historical roots (Short, 2006). In general, they position rurality as somewhere more relaxed and relaxing, scenic yet human scale, organic and natural, authentic and rooted, and somehow external to or otherwise distanced from (the negative features of) modern society (for example, Bunce, 1994; Mingay, 1989; Short, 1991). Bunce (2003, p. 14) succinctly suggests the resource potential of these idyllic representations of rurality through reference to a Canadian newspaper story:

> **Picturesque, farming, community, recreational, bucolic**: these are the words of the conventional rural idyll, of the aesthetics of pastoral landscapes, of humans working in harmony with nature and the land and with each other, of a whole scene of contentment and plenty.

The demographic significance of a representational interpretation of rurality in terms of the key element of migration, especially internal migration within the global North, has already been made clear. However, with rurality "moving" from a grounded set of relationships and practices to the more cognitive realm of representation, analytical complexity for the demographer is added. In researching counterurbanization for example, the "rural" category used by the analyst needs to be defined at least in part with reference to elements of the migrants' rural representations that are implicated in the migration decision-making process. For example, rurality defined by the landscape of agribusiness is likely to have much less relevance to or association with counterurbanization than rurality defined by scenic amenity. In short, and as will be returned to in the conclusion, the definition of rurality used by the demographer needs to be appropriate to the task to hand as we move away from any singular or fixed sense of rurality and towards more plural interpretations.

Moreover, the demographic significance of a representational interpretation of rurality does not end with migration. This is because representations such as the rural idyll contain within their everyday imaginaries strong assumptions about domestic life (Little & Austin, 1996). They are generally seen to reinforce the conventional heterosexual nuclear family household (Little, 2003), promoting fertility within this institutional set-up and, at least implicitly, denigrating fertility taking place outside of it. In summary:

> the rural idyll has traditionally included very conventional images and expectations of women's place in rural society; at the heart of the family, the centre of the community. There can be no doubt that the woman of the rural idyll is the wife and mother, not the high-flying professional, the single childless business entrepreneur (Little & Austin, 1996, p. 106).

Rural idyllic life can also be seen as, broadly, pronatalist. In other words, from a fertility perspective the predominant rural representation is likely to promote childbearing but also to reinforce its position within the conventional nuclear household. Finally, although saying little about mortality directly, the same emphasis on the nuclear family as the basis of rural community also indicates the circumscribing of care relationships of the aged and sick within the immediate family (Hughes, 1997).

Finally in this section, interpretation of rurality as representation does not end with ultimately acknowledging the potential everyday and very diverse fecundity of these representations, not least in terms of their potential demographic consequences. Consider Table 26.1, which sketches some of the key features of the English rural idyll. Even from a quick perusal of this table and with limited knowledge of English history, it is clear that this representation of rurality may well be "a product of the bourgeois imaginary" (Bell, 2006, p. 158), even tagged a "hedonist discourse" (Frouws, 1998, p. 62), but that it is also not constructed **solely** along the lines of some utopian castle plucked from thin air. Instead, it clearly speaks of or alludes to **some** connection with what supposedly is thought to exist, thought to have once existed, or thought normatively to exist, in "actual" rural places. In other words,

**Table 26.1** Some "physical" and "social" elements of the English rural idyll

| "Physical" elements | "Social" elements |
| --- | --- |
| Small villages | Timelessness |
| Small farms and fields | Stability and social harmony |
| Narrow lanes | Community and closely knit |
| Tranquility | Knowing one's neighbors |
| Scenic beauty | Strong sense of tradition |
| Attractive vernacular housing | Relaxing environment |
| Village core (village green, pond, benches, etc.) | Little crime or trouble |
| Pub(s), shop(s), school | Mutual support |

*Source*: Halfacree (2009a), Table 3.

we might well accept much of the rural-as-effaced thesis but we are still almost forced to consider potential rural practices as they are enacted today through places when we interpret rurality as largely representational. This is not least because, as Bunce (2003, p. 15) goes on to suggest: "values that sustain the rural idyll speak of a profound and human need for connection with land, nature and community," all of which can be seen to have some dimension of material reality. Thus, when finding variables through which to express rurality within demographic analyses — such as for studying counterurbanization — we can seek out empirical manifestations of elements of rural representations that may indicate the relevant rurality of the location to the potential in-migrants, *etcetera*. Interesting research questions are of course also posed around the extent to which rural representations correspond to ongoing practices within generally regarded "rural" places. The significance of this still-embedded sense of rurality will eventually be returned to at the end of the next section but prior to this a yet more dis-embedded interpretation is considered.

## (Re)inventing Rurality: Post-Rurality and the More-Than-Representational

By this midpoint in the chapter, the ways in which rurality can be interpreted today have already become quite diverse and complex, even confusing, as we shift from seeing it as effaced, to recognizing its strong representational presence, to then somewhat laterally observing that representations also still speak of material "heritage." However, the tale gets still more convoluted when, first, we return to develop further the interpretation of a geographically disembedded or liberated rurality that the representational interpretation heralds and then, second, when this disembedding is again knocked a little off balance through bringing in lived experiences of more-than-representational rurality.

### Post-Rurality

Reflecting on Mormont's (1990) contribution to our understanding of rurality, Cloke (1996, p. 435) observed that his "conclusion... that rurality can no longer be represented as a single rural space, but rather as a multiplicity of social spaces which overlap the same geographic area... affirms rurality as a social construct, reflecting and constituting a world of social, moral, and cultural values." This enabled him (Cloke, 1996, p. 435) to suggest an extended rurality as representation interpretation in line with the strong emphasis on "deconstruction and difference within postmodern and poststructural thinking." For example, we can take our cue from Baudrillard's (1988) age of simulations, where the map no longer follows on from the territory, seeking to represent it, but instead "precedes" and "engenders" it. Consequently, we have a three-way divergence or breaking of bonds between rurality as sign, the meanings of "rurality" (signification) and the rural space which is the supposed referent. Such an opening-up comes through in Murdoch and Pratt's (1993, p. 425) "post-rural," whereby rurality is no longer seen as fixed but as inherently open and "reflexively deployed": rurality becomes something very fundamentally to be thought of, molded and changed, experienced, lived. Instead of searching for any "essence" of (post-)rurality, we can instead focus on how rurality is constructed and practiced to bring about multiple and diverse ruralities, since "the point is there is not one but there are many" (Murdoch & Pratt, 1993, p. 425). Indeed, and competing with the strong idyllic legacy, such inherent mutability, mobility, and flexibility also helps to explain rurality's present fecundity.

A post-rural interpretation opens the way for an appreciation of how representations of rurality are now freed up to be performed and staged in extremely diverse ways (Edensor, 2006; Woods, 2010). They can be deployed culturally, socially, and economically to shape existing rural spaces in myriad ways, and even to corral the components of "networks of rurality" (Halfacree & Boyle, 1998) in places conventionally seen as being "beyond" the rural referent. First, we can again look at the consequences of and for counterurbanization when identifying how rurality is reshaping existing rural spaces. Excellent examples come from a major research project that examined the restructuring of the Aylesbury Vale district of Buckinghamshire, southern England (Murdoch & Marsden, 1994; also Marsden, Murdoch, Lowe, Munton, & Flynn, 1993). Of particular illustrative note was a private developer's construction of a new settlement of 800 houses on a largely self-contained site just outside Aylesbury town (Murdoch & Marsden, 1994, pp. 75–83). This settlement, given the rustic name Watermead, on the one hand, comprised substantial amounts of prestige executive housing, two lakes designed for water sports and an artificial ski slope, none of which are particularly indicative of English "idyllic rurality" and would be unlikely to feature in any rural measure used in demographic analysis, for example. However, on the other hand, Watermead was also meant to comprise a "traditional English village." Publicity and marketing material spoke of accessing "all the warmth and charm of a traditional Edwardian village" and the "distinctive village square, with its pink and cream-painted pub, restaurant and shopping mall, set around an attractive piazza" (Murdoch & Marsden, 1994, pp. 79–80). Overall, the developers strove to construct a particular quality of life infused heavily with clearly idyllic representations of rurality in this corner of "village England." Such a representation was clearly intended to promote the in-migration of people seeking such a place in which to live.

England is far from alone in deploying representations that draw heavily upon idyllic rurality to shape rural space and thus rural demography. Of particular note is the so-called New Urbanism (Katz, 1994; Knox & Pinch, 2010) that has gained popularity in the US as not least a counter to the long-standing demographic trends towards suburbanization and more general urban sprawl which have been accused by some critics of facilitating the fragmentation and destruction of both place and place-based communities. New Urbanism calls for a move back towards "livable communities," whereby functional integration rather than fragmentation allows people to work, shop, live, and play within these communities, also encouraging and empowering them to walk or cycle rather than drive. A pioneering example is the settlement of Seaside in Florida, begun in 1981, but the most famous example is Celebration (Ross, 2000), also in Florida, started in 1996 and aiming for around 20,000 residents. Both projects are sponsored and highly regulated by the Disney Corporation, leading into an initial critique of where the real power within these highly s(t)imulated "communities" lies.

Of key interest to the present chapter is how New Urbanism draws strongly upon a *Gemeinschaft* blueprint of people-in-place, which in turn has clear and strong affiliations with idyllic representations of rurality (Halfacree, 2009b). Thus, for Bell (2006, p. 154), Celebration is depicted as an attempt at "retrofitting small-town life on reclaimed swampland." Consequently, critics also accuse New Urbanism of offering little more than a nostalgic version of late 19th century US society, rooted in an underlying environmental determinism that can only ideologically bring about any reconciliation of people and (local) place (for example, Al-Hindi & Staddon, 1997; Knox & Pinch, 2010; Phillips, 2002) in our globalized era of ever heightened mobilities (Urry, 2007). Be that as it may, the demographic consequences of developments such as this are, again, the promotion of certain forms of in-migration and, if widespread enough, adding at least a degree of empirical "noise" to the long-established suburbanization/counterurbanization trend that has been reorganizing populations within physical space for decades. Indeed, it is unlikely to be captured through any conventional urban-rural classification, suggesting the near irrelevance of such constructions for the study of the demography of developments such as those with New Urbanism underpinnings. In addition, New Urbanism also brings to the fore the fertility implications of the rural idyllic representation, namely the primacy of child rearing within the conventional nuclear family.

A second dimension of post-rurality in practice is more subtle than either Watermead or Celebration and refers to how actually existing rurality can be reconstituted and tidied up to resemble more closely what rurality is "supposed" to look like – the normative ideal/idyll. What results is a "retrofitting" of rurality, whereby "a new social (and spatial) contract [is imprinted] on an existing village" (Bell, 2006, p. 152). Such re-working tends to be driven by the changing and enhanced consumption demands and corresponding expectations increasingly being placed upon rural areas. This tendency was again expressed in Aylesbury Vale by the "rustification" of village centers to cater for in-migrant expectations (Murdoch & Marsden, 1994). However, it is the growing presence and demands of rural tourism that is most strongly implicated in rural retrofitting. For example, the settlement of Cavendish on Prince Edward Island in Canada was the setting (*Avonlea*) of L.M. Montgomery's popular 1908 novel *Anne of Green Gables*. Today, the *Green Gables* site is very much managed for heritage tourism, including being reconstructed in the style of the imagined Edwardian idyll, which includes unambiguously fictive elements becoming material, created so that the "real" place resembles the literary place more closely, thus not disappointing its expectant visitors (Squire, 1992; see other examples in Woods, 2005).

Cavendish's fate is mirrored in an increasing array of other rural places that have been or still are sites of popular television series or feature films, in particular, and reflects the growing popularity and importance of explicitly mediated ruralities (Phillips, Fish, & Agg, 2001). A growing body of scholarship on "film tourism" (Beeton, 2010) stresses, amongst other things, the importance of a strong place image (Croy, 2010; O'Connor, Flanagan, & Gilbert, 2008). One aspect of this is illustrated in Yorkshire, England, where "some destinations within the county have been altered after the increase in tourism" (O'Connor et al., 2008, p. 432). A prime example is the village of Goathland, the setting (*Aidensfield*) of the successful *Heartbeat* television series that centers on the life of a rural police officer. As *Heartbeat* is set in the 1960s, many aspects of the village have not only been reshaped to fit an ideal village but also one from this same period (Mordue, 1999).

Demographically, the consequences of this form of post-rural (re)construction may seem less strong. Whilst people may wish also to reconstruct the Victorian or 1960s household in terms of family size, for example, the major demographic outcome is once again likely to be enhanced levels of selected in-migration, albeit of course with the inevitable counter-flow of those for whom living on a near film set is perhaps too much to endure.

In a third form of post-rural enactment, more or less explicit references to and uses of representations of rurality are being deployed to assemble elements of the rural even beyond what most people would acknowledge as the rural domain; rurality beyond the rural (Halfacree, 2009a). Again, housing development is immediately instructive of this seemingly ruralist pseudo-revanchist intent, with urban developments badged and marketed using associations typically seen as hallmarks of rurality, such as on the urban fringe (Mahon, 2007). More generally, we see associational elements of rurality increasingly brought into the city. We have already noted this with respect to New Urbanism but other examples include the introduction of "nature" into otherwise sterile, super-urban retail environments, such as Canada's prominent West Edmonton Mall (Hopkins, 1990; Shields, 1989), and the general aim of planners to make rural "values" such as community, local place, and identity integral to urban (re)development. For example, on the edge of the city of Pamplona in Spain, the development of *Chantrea* – marketed as Chantrea Vive (*Chantrea Lives*) – involves, according to its marketing publicity, building a neighborhood that is "alive," so as to make the town more "human." To facilitate this process, developers have included explicitly pseudo-rural trees and gardens.[1]

Demographically, revanchist ruralism is likely to confuse the seemingly well-established empirical and geographical picture in a similar manner to that of New Urbanism. How we capture these "urban" rural places in our classification schemes is a major challenge as, once again, conventional urban-rural classifications are unlikely to be flexible, responsive, or subtle enough. Revanchist ruralism promotes what externally appears to be pro-urban forms of migration, in particular, but such migration is likely to be underpinned at least in part by more "rural" representational elements and so is likely to differ from more usual forms of urban in-migration with their typically predominantly economic underpinnings.

The revanchist, at times seemingly almost belligerent, stance of ruralizing the urban demonstrates clearly not only how the urban has been pathologized (Thrift, 2005) but also how rurality speaks strongly and deeply to many different people within many different societies today. In short, rurality certainly has not been effaced culturally even if conceptually its health is often the subject of the previously noted "morbid thoughts." One reason for this vitality comes from the spatial freedom accompanying post-rurality that we have just noted; the intense, frequent and diverse performances of rurality that are occurring (Edensor, 2006), such that one might even suggest that the "hyper-performance of idyllic rurality keeps 'country life' alive" (Bell, 2006, p. 152), the implication being that "the rural remains real only because of widespread efforts to remind ourselves about it" (Lawrence, 2003, p. 103); and the linking of discourses, such as those of rurality, to expressions of power (Frouws, 1998). However, a further reason for this vitality again takes us away from representations and alludes to more embodied, even grounded, considerations.

---

[1] Thanks to Dr. María Jesús Rivera Escribano for this example.

## Rurality Re-Materialized and Experienced

In a recent review of rural geographical work, Mike Woods (2009, p. 850) observes "the creeping back into discussions of questions about the definition and conceptualization of rurality." A key reason for this, Woods argues, is renewed desire to re-materialize rurality. Thus, after acknowledging rurality as performed (Edensor, 2006), Woods (2010) goes on to emphasize how these performances take place in more or less staged ways (as covered above) but with those towards the latter pole inevitably leading to an interest in how rurality is engaged with and experienced within everyday life. From this perspective, interpreting rurality can engage with the increased interest paid within social science to what has been termed nonrepresentational theory (Thrift, 2007).

Within nonrepresentational theory, a core concept is that of affect, or the feelings, emotions and even actions brought about through our engagement with the materiality of the world (Blackman & Venn, 2010; Thien, 2005). Thinking affectively about rurality, we leave the detached concentration on rurality's expression through representation to refocus on what it is like existentially and sensuously to be "in" the rural. The intention is to take rurality's own, often uneven, confusing and unruly, forces seriously – including the diverse agencies of nonhumans, notably other animals (Jones, 2003) and plants such as trees (Jones & Cloke, 2002), but also inanimate objects and physical forces such as the weather – thereby coming to recognize rurality as a hybrid co-construction of humans and nonhumans (Murdoch, 2003). In summary, thinking affectively takes us from "viewing" rurality as a finished (human) landscape to "experiencing" it in all of its multifarious processual and thus always incomplete (human and nonhuman) diversity.

Building on a still limited range of related work, such as Jones and Cloke's (2002) exploration of how the nonhuman agency of trees is co-constitutive of both urban and rural places (also Cloke, 2003b), the need for a much more affectively sensitive understanding of rurality has recently been made forcefully by US sociologist Michael Carolan (2008, 2009). He argues that rurality[2] should not be "treated as [a] mere discursive construct...; [a] product... of a mind devoid of corporeality... [since this] is untenable for one reason: we think, and thus we socially construct, with our bodies" (Carolan, 2008, p. 408). Or, more generally, "Something... must be wrong somewhere, if the only way to understand our own creative role in the world is by taking ourselves out of it" (Ingold, 1995, p. 58), thereby making our theories "dead" (Carolan, 2009, p. 1), rather than acknowledging how so much of how we know rurality comes from our sensing bodies being within it. Carolan (2008) goes on briefly to illustrate this by showing how Iowan farmers, from their more embodied everyday engagement with rurality, demonstrated a more sensuous bodily sense of rurality than nonfarmers.

Before further considering the affective aspect of rurality, however, it is crucial to note that nonrepresentational theory does not deny the existence of representations nor their important role within everyday life (Del Casino & Hanna, 2006; Lorimer, 2005). In this respect, it is not productive to set up representations and practices in binary opposition but to give adequate attention both to the representational and to the more-than-representational. A further key qualification to note here in a written **representational** output such as this chapter is to acknowledge that:

> It is not that we cannot represent sensuous, corporeal, lived experience but that the moment we do so we immediately lose something. Representations [no matter how carefully and subtly constructed] tell only part of the story (Carolan, 2008, p. 412).

With Carolan's cautionary words ringing in our ears, as well as the limiting construction of rurality as landscape being noted, the chapter will now use two visual cues to attempt to engage the reader very briefly with the idea of an affective rurality (see also Halfacree, 2009a). These cues are given in Fig. 26.1 and comprise examples of two relatively distinctive species of what can, fairly noncontentiously (it is hoped) be presented as rurality from the global North today: the US Prairies and village England.

Through both using the imagination and drawing upon past experiences, the reader is invited temporarily to suspend reading this chapter and instead to consider the affective dimensions of the places shown in Fig. 26.1. Imagine, within each place:

- How you would **feel** if sitting, standing, or walking in these environments;

---

[2] Carolan actually refers to "conceptions of the countryside" rather than rurality.

**Fig. 26.1** Examples of rurality today
*Source*: Holly Barcus and the author, respectively.

- What would **strike** you most forcefully in and about these places;
- What would you "get" **existentially** from these place encounters;
- And, since affect should not be seen as inherently subjective, what such places **mean** in their own terms.

Answers to all of the latter questions, which will likely vary considerably both between individuals and between these two types of rurality, will nonetheless almost inevitably pull in the seemingly indelible association that rurality has with **nature**. One might say that it is the "nature of rurality" that holds the key to its affective power, thereby demonstrating clearly how "nature… adds value to culture" (Cruickshank, 2009, p. 104) or how experiential affect adds to "armchair countryside" (Bunce, 1994, p. 37). There is not space here to explore the many issues around either the definition of nature or its association with rurality. However, perhaps key is the sensual manifestation of the physical world – notably its sights, smells, and feelings but also an enchanted sense of the mystical and unexplained. Through nature, therefore, soil, rocks, water, animals, plants, insects, weather, temperature, even supernatural forces – "the mystery, spirituality and ghostliness of rural places" (Cloke, 2003b, p. 6) – are brought (back) directly into human understanding of rurality's re-invention.

Bringing out more-than-representational aspects of rurality suggests, therefore, that post-rurality is not as materially free-standing or unencumbered with ties as any quasi-Baudrillardian perspective might lead us to expect. In summary, we can thus see how what Bell (2007, p. 408) terms "second rural" – "the epistemology of rural as place, as unconfined to lower density space, as (at times) consumption, as socionature, as meanings which we may never unambiguously see – the **ideal moment**" – which is far from culturally weak or disappearing, is still entangled to some extent with "first rural" – "the epistemology of rural as space, as lower population density, as (at times) primary production, as nature, as the non-urban which is so plain to see – the **material moment**" (Bell, 2007, p. 408) – even if the latter often seems to display the clear "victim narrative" (Bell, 2007, p.407) of decline and effacement with which this chapter began. In order to interpret rurality today, we require a "rural plural" of the "idea-real" **and** the "mater-real" together (Bell, 2007, p. 412), discourses grounded and linked, at least to some extent, rather than engaged in some disembedded struggle for singular, if ultimately unduly one-sided, authority (Halfacree, 1993; cf. Frouws, 1998).

What, then, are the demographic consequences of acknowledging more fully the more-than-representational rural? First, we can perhaps begin to appreciate in a more rounded way why people migrate to rural areas and, even when such areas do not match their imagined ideal, remain there. Rural affect, therefore, may be another of the diverse forces that underpin migration behavior. However, the more-than-representational rural is not only significant with respect to migration. Bringing the body center-stage also brings forward the other two key demographic elements. On the one hand, fertility, both socially and biologically, may be affected by a person's rural emplacing as "rural nature" promotes human reproduction in diverse ways. On the other hand, mortality may also be subject to rural affect, although how this may be is still unclear. Indeed, although these last observations may seem somewhat vague, a degree of insight into their likely significance may be gleaned through the now considerable "therapeutic landscapes" (Conradson, 2005; Gesler, 1992; Lea, 2008) literature. This work shows how landscapes and especially rural landscapes can have beneficial impacts on mental and physical health and well-being, not through places having intrinsically therapeutic properties but through therapeutic outcomes emerging from persons' encounters with specific places (Conradson, 2005).

Overall, therefore, the growing tendency in the rural literature to interpret rurality as neither fully effaced nor as completely representational but as at least retaining some sense of grounded reality thus also has some interesting and important implications for demography. Specifically, it sustains the observation that demography does not take place on the metaphorical head of a pin but remains at least partly entangled with the places that the people it involves both pass through and stay within. In this respect, **rural** demography still seems a very worthy subcategory to focus upon. In addition, sensing a still-to-some-extent grounded rural also makes the relevant empirical classification of places for subsequent analysis a little less challenging. Rural classifications retain potential demographic relevance.

## Conclusion: Recognizing Inherent Diversity

This chapter's discussion of how rurality is to be interpreted today[3] has covered three broad perspectives: rurality's status as a sociospatially distinctive set of **practices**; rurality's existence and operation as a powerful **representational** resource; and rurality's existence as a more affective set of everyday **experiences**. It is immediately important to note the intrinsic value of all three interpretations. In terms of practices, we are left with the important and still unresolved question of whether or not rurality can (still) be mapped through the presence of distinctive practices that are constantly writing rural space. A representational perspective, in contrast, makes us realize how rurality (and other spatial taxonomies) can exist more or less independently of physical spatial referent. And rurality as affective everyday experience returns us from the lofty realms of academic abstraction to re-value the embodied material encounters of daily life. Moving through these three interpretations, in addition, with their differing emphases on the ontological and epistemological, demonstrates rurality shifting from an "object," potentially at least relatively amenable to clear statistical measurement and expression, to rurality as a more virtual and thus less mappable on/from the ground concept, to rurality being seen as something with sustained material traces that may well still facilitate empirical capture and measurement.

Overall, one can attempt to combine these three interpretations of rurality within a single model (for example, Halfacree, 2006), but this will not be done here as it is intended that the *Handbook* reader is left with the predominant idea of the rural as inherently diverse or, as Bell (2007) expressed it, plural. Thus, throughout the chapter attention has been given to some of the **different** likely demographic consequences of the **different** interpretations of rurality that have been presented, rurality being one of "the factors that affect [fertility, mortality and migration]" (Poston

---

[3] At least in the global North, although much of what has been argued conceptually here, if not the specific illustrative cases, is equally applicable within the global South. Generally, in the latter rurality has been less totally effaced and rural localities (Halfacree, 2006) remain more strongly defined, at least in remoter locations. However, the appropriateness of our classifications for demographic analysis still require careful thought.

& Bouvier, 2010, p. 3). However, clearly defined rural places – the neat, bounded, distinct kind of spaces that demographic analysis is inevitably likely to prefer – are no longer synonymous with or equivalent to either rural representations or rural experiences. In other words, places which may seem to exhibit a range of characteristic or hallmark rural practices – farming, low population densities, self-reliance – may not be represented so unambiguously and certainly may not be experienced so distinctively. And probably more commonly and significantly given the constructive and even revanchist designs of post-rurality, for example, places may be represented and/or lived as rural but neither express nor contain many of the same characteristic rural practices. Thus, and this is of importance to all of the social sciences, we need to be especially careful when using unexamined and/or blanket classifications of rural if we are to relate demographic measures with place. It is agreed that "space continues to matter in demography" (Champion & Hugo, 2004, p. 7) but also that simple classifications such as rural versus urban can be little more than a crude starting point. Clearly, assigning places to categories remains a central task for the demographer so as to facilitate analysis but exactly how this is done needs always to be thought through carefully, not least with an eye on the task or the topic to hand. Thus, for a migration study the aspects of rurality that are seen as especially relevant to migration need to be given prominence in any classification, whilst if the focus is on health issues then key measurable aspects of the therapeutic landscape merit primary consideration.

In summary, even if across at least the global North the rural world often seems increasingly effaced, rurality and demography remain closely connected through much more than superficial description of the components of the latter as expressed within the former. Rurality does underpin some forms of migration, largely through its representational dimension (which can absorb for example, people's previous experiences of rural places); it also has possible impacts on fertility, both through how representations portray the "normal" practices of everyday life and possibly through more affective influences; and it may well also impact upon mortality and certainly health, especially through its more affective aspects. However, how these connections arise and play themselves out and how they are then to be represented requires careful, nuanced analysis not simplistic reduction to rural equals X and urban equals Y. Thus, we can appreciate some of the considerable tasks presented to all social scientists when we seek to interpret rurality in the 21st century.

**Acknowledgements** The author extends special thanks to László Kulcsár for his initial invitation to write this chapter and for his unwavering support over its subsequent gestation, especially during the times that the author's written progress was not always as rapid as he would have wished!

# References

Al-Hindi, K., & Staddon, C. (1997). The hidden histories and geographies of neotraditional town planning: The case of Seaside, Florida. *Environment and Planning D: Society and Space, 15*, 349–372.

Baudrillard, J. (1988). *Selected writings*. Stanford, CA: Stanford University Press.

Baylina, M., & Berg, N. (2010). Selling the countryside: Representations of rurality in Norway and Spain. *European Urban and Regional Studies, 17*, 277–292.

Beale, C. (1975). *The revival of population growth in non-metropolitan America*. United States Department of Agriculture, Economic Research Service, ERS 605.

Beeton, S. (2010). The advance of film tourism. *Tourism and Hospitality Planning and Development, 7*, 1–6.

Bell, D. (2006). Variations on the rural idyll. In P. Cloke, T. Marsden, & P. Mooney (Eds.), *Handbook of rural studies* (pp. 149–160). London: Sage.

Bell, M. M. (2007). The two-ness of rural life and the ends of rural scholarship. *Journal of Rural Studies, 23*, 402–415.

Bell, M. M. (2008). *Mobilizing the countryside: Rural power and the power of the rural*. Paper presented at Agrarian Studies Seminar, March. Retrieved March 2010, from http://Www.Yale.Edu/Agrarianstudies/Papers/22bell.Pdf.

Billig, M. (1985). Prejudice, categorization and particularization: From a perceptual to a rhetorical approach. *European Journal of Social Psychology, 15*, 79–103.

Blackman, L., & Venn, C. (2010). Affect. *Body and Society, 16*, 7–28.

Brown, D., & Wardwell, J. (Eds.). (1980). *New directions in urban-rural migration: The population turnaround in rural America*. New York: Academic.

Bunce, M. (1994). *The countryside ideal. Anglo-American images of landscape*. London: Routledge.

Bunce, M. (2003). Reproducing rural idylls. In P. Cloke (Ed.), *Country visions* (pp. 14–30). Harlow: Pearson.

Carolan, M. (2008). More-than-representational knowledge/s of the countryside: How we think as bodies. *Sociologia Ruralis, 48*, 408–422.

Carolan, M. (2009). 'I do therefore there is': Enlivening socio-environmental theory. *Environmental Politics, 18*, 1–17.

Champion A. (1998). Studying counterurbanisation and the rural population turnaround. In P. Boyle & K. Halfacree (Eds.), *Migration into rural areas. Theories and issues* (pp. 21–40). Chichester: Wiley.

Champion, T., & Hugo, G. (2004). Introduction: Moving beyond the urban-rural dichotomy. In T. Champion & G. Hugo (Eds.), *New forms of urbanization. Beyond the urban-rural dichotomy* (pp. 3–24). Aldershot: Ashgate.

Cloke, P. (1989). Rural geography and political economy. In R. Peet & N. Thrift (Eds.), *New models in geography* (Vol. 1, pp. 164–197). London: Unwin Hyman.

Cloke, P. (1996). Rural life-styles: Material opportunity, cultural experience, and how theory can undermine policy. *Economic Geography, 72*, 433–449.

Cloke, P. (Ed.). (2003a). *Country visions*. Harlow: Pearson.

Cloke, P. (2003b). Knowing ruralities? In P. Cloke (Ed.), *Country visions* (pp. 1–13). Harlow: Pearson.

Cloke, P. (2006). Conceptualizing rurality. In P. Cloke, T. Marsden, & P. Mooney (Eds.), *Handbook of rural studies* (pp. 18–28). London: Sage.

Cloke, P., Goodwin, M., & Milbourne, P. (1998). Inside looking out; outside looking in. Different experiences of cultural competence in rural lifestyles. In P. Boyle & K. Halfacree (Eds.), *Migration into rural areas: Theories and issues* (pp. 134–150). Chichester: Wiley.

Cloke, P., & Little, J. (Eds.). (1997). *Contested countryside cultures*. London: Routledge.

Cloke, P., Marsden, T., & Mooney, P. (Eds.). (2006). *Handbook of rural studies*. London: Sage.

Conradson, D. (2005). Landscape, care and the relational self: Therapeutic encounters in rural England. *Health and Place, 11*, 337–348.

Copp, J. (1972). Rural sociology and rural development. *Rural Sociology, 37*, 515–533.

Crouch, D. (2006). Tourism, consumption and rurality. In P. Cloke, T. Marsden, & P. Mooney (Eds.), *Handbook of rural studies* (pp. 355–364). London: Sage.

Croy, W. (2010). Planning for film tourism: Active destination image management. *Tourism and Hospitality Planning and Development, 7*, 21–30.

Cruickshank, J. (2009). A play for rurality – modernization versus local autonomy. *Journal of Rural Studies, 25*, 98–107.

Del Casino, V., & Hanna, S. (2006). Beyond the 'binaries': A methodological intervention for interrogating maps as representational practices. *ACME, 4*, 34–56.

Edensor, T. (2006). Performing rurality. In P. Cloke, T. Marsden, & P. Mooney (Eds.), *Handbook of rural studies* (pp. 484–495). London: Sage.

Friedland, W. (1982). The end of rural society and the future of rural sociology. *Rural Sociology, 47*, 589–608.

Frouws, J. (1998). The contested redefinition of the countryside. An analysis of rural discourses in the Netherlands. *Sociologia Ruralis, 38*, 54–68.

Gesler, W. (1992). Therapeutic landscapes: Medical issues in light of the new cultural geography. *Social Science and Medicine, 34*, 735–746.

Gosnell, H., & Abrams, J. (2009). Amenity migration: Diverse conceptualizations of drivers, socioeconomic dimensions, and emerging challenges. *GeoJournal online*. Retrieved march 2010, from http://Www.Springerlink.Com/Content/9l40n2843572mm05/Fulltext.Pdf

Hadden, J., & Barton, J. (1973). An image that will not die: Thoughts on the history of anti-urban ideology. *Urban Affairs Annual Review, 7*, 79–116.

Halfacree, K. (1993). Locality and social representation: Space, discourse and alternative definitions of the rural. *Journal of Rural Studies, 9*, 23–37.

Halfacree, K. (2001). Constructing the object: Taxonomic practices, 'counterurbanisation' and positioning marginal rural settlement. *International Journal of Population Geography, 7*, 395–411.

Halfacree, K. (2006). Rural space: Constructing a three-fold architecture. In P. Cloke, T. Marsden, & P. Mooney (Eds.), *Handbook of rural studies* (pp. 44–62). London: Sage.

Halfacree, K. (2009a). Rurality and post-rurality. In R. Kitchin & N. Thrift (Eds.), *International encyclopedia of human geography* (Vol. 9, pp. 449–456). Oxford: Elsevier.

Halfacree, K. (2009b). Urban-rural continuum. In R. Kitchin & N. Thrift (Eds.), *International encyclopedia of human geography* (Vol. 1, pp. 119–124). Oxford: Elsevier.

Halfacree, K., & Boyle, P. (1998). Migration, rurality and the post-productivist countryside. In P. Boyle & K. Halfacree (Eds.), *Migration into rural areas: Theories and issues* (pp. 1–12). Chichester: Wiley.

Hoggart, K. (1990). Let's do away with rural. *Journal of Rural Studies, 6*, 245–257.

Hopkins, J. (1990). West Edmonton Mall: Landscape of myths and elsewhereness. *Canadian Geographer/Le Géographe Canadien, 34*, 2–17.

Hughes, A. (1997). Rurality and 'cultures of womanhood'. Domestic identities and moral orders in village life. In P. Cloke & J. Little (Eds.), *Contested countryside cultures* (pp. 123–137). London: Routledge.

Ingold, T. (1995). Building, dwelling, living: How people and animals make themselves at home in the world. In M. Strathern (Ed.), *Shifting contexts: Transformations in anthropological knowledge* (pp. 57–80). London: Routledge.

Jones, M. (2001). The rise of the regional state in economic governance: 'partnerships for prosperity' or new scales of state power? *Environment and Planning A, 33*, 1185–1211.

Jones, O. (2003). 'The restraint of beasts': Rurality, animality, Actor Network Theory and dwelling. In P. Cloke (Ed.), *Country visions* (pp. 283–307). Harlow: Pearson.

Jones, O., & Cloke, P. (2002). *Tree cultures*. Oxford: Berg.

Katz, P. (1994). *The New Urbanism: Toward an architecture of community*. New York: Mcgraw Hill.

Kautsky, K. (1899/1988). *The agrarian question*. Winchester, MA: Zwan Publications.

Knox, P., & Pinch, S. (2010). *Urban social geography. An introduction* (6th ed.). Harlow: Pearson.

Krannich, R. (2008). Rural sociology at the crossroads. *Rural Sociology, 73*, 1–21.

Lawrence, M. (2003). The view from Cobb Gate: Falling into liminal geography. In P. Cloke (Ed.), *Country visions* (pp. 93–115). Harlow: Pearson.

Lea, J. (2008). Retreating to nature: Rethinking 'therapeutic landscapes'. *Area, 40*, 90–8.

Little, J. (2003). 'Riding the Rural Love Train': Heterosexuality and the rural community. *Sociologia Ruralis, 43*, 401–417.

Little, J., & Austin, P. (1996). Women and the rural idyll. *Journal of Rural Studies, 12*, 101–111.

Lobao, L. (1996). A sociology of the periphery versus a peripheral sociology: Rural sociology and the dimension of space. *Rural Sociology, 61*, 77–102.

Lorimer, H. (2005). Cultural geography: The busyness of being 'more-than-representational'. *Progress in Human Geography, 29*, 83–94.

Lowe, P., Murdoch, J., & Cox, G. (1995). A civilised retreat? Anti-urbanism, rurality and the making of an Anglo-centric culture. In P. Healey, S. Cameron, S. Davoudi, S. Graham, & A. Madani-Pour (Eds.), *Managing cities* (pp. 63–82). Chichester: Wiley.

Mahon, M. (2007). New populations, shifting expectations: The changing experience of rural space and place. *Journal of Rural Studies, 23*, 345–356.

Marsden, T., Munton, R., Whatmore, S., & Little, J. (1986). Towards a political economy of agriculture: A British perspective. *International Journal of Urban and Regional Research, 11*, 498–521.

Marsden, T., Murdoch, J., Lowe, P., Munton, R., & Flynn, A. (1993). *Constructing the countryside*. London: UCL Press.

Marston, S. (2000). The social construction of scale. *Progress in Human Geography, 24*, 219–242.

Marx, K., & Engels, F. (1848/1998). *The communist manifesto*. Oxford: Oxford University Press.

Milbourne, P. (Ed.). (1997). *Revealing rural 'others'*. London: Pinter.

Mingay, G. (Ed.). (1989). *The rural idyll*. London: Routledge.

Mordue, T. (1999). Heartbeat country: Conflicting values, coinciding visions. *Environment and Planning A, 31*, 629–646.

Mormont, M. (1990). Who is rural? Or, how to be rural: Towards a sociology of the rural. In T. Marsden, P. Lowe, & S. Whatmore (Eds.), *Rural restructuring* (pp. 21–44). London: David Fulton.

Moscovici, S. (1984). The phenomenon of social representations. In R. Farr & S. Moscovici (Eds.), *Social representations* (pp. 3–69). Cambridge: Cambridge University Press.

Murdoch, J. (2003). Co-constructing the countryside: Hybrid networks and the extensive self. In P. Cloke (Ed.), *Country visions* (pp. 263–282). Harlow: Pearson.

Murdoch, J., & Marsden, T. (1994). *Reconstituting rurality*. London: UCL Press.

Murdoch, J., & Pratt, A. (1993). Rural studies: Modernism, postmodernism and the 'post-rural'. *Journal of Rural Studies, 9*, 411–427.

O'Connor, N., Flanagan, S., & Gilbert, D. (2008). The integration of film-induced tourism and destination branding in Yorkshire, UK. *International Journal of Tourism Research, 10*, 423–437.

Phillips, D. (2002). Consuming the West. *Space and Culture, 5*, 29–41.

Phillips, M., Fish, R., & Agg, J. (2001). Putting together ruralities: Towards a symbolic analysis of rurality in the British mass media. *Journal of Rural Studies, 17*, 1–28.

Poston, D., & Bouvier, L. (2010). *Population and society. An introduction to demography*. Cambridge: Cambridge University Press.

Potter, J., & Wetherell, M. (1987). *Discourse and social psychology*. London: Sage.

Ross, A. (2000). *Celebration chronicles*. London: Verso.

Sayer, A. (1984). *Method in social science*. London: Hutchinson.

Sayer, A. (1989). The 'new' regional geography and problems of narrative. *Environment and Planning D: Society and Space, 7*, 253–276.

Shields, R. (1989). Social spatialization and the built environment: The West Edmonton Mall. *Environment and Planning D: Society and Space, 7*, 147–164.

Short, B. (2006). Idyllic ruralities. In P. Cloke, T. Marsden, & P. Mooney (Eds.), *Handbook of rural studies* (pp. 133–148). London: Sage.

Short, J. (1991). *Imagined country*. London: Routledge.

Shotter, J. (1993). *Cultural politics of everyday life*. Buckingham: Open University Press.

Squire, S. (1992). Ways of seeing, ways of being: Literature, place and tourism in L.M. Montgomery's Prince Edward Island. In P. Simpson-Housley & G. Norcliffe (Eds.), *A few acres of snow: Literary and artistic images of Canada* (pp. 137–147). Toronto, ON: Dundurn Press.

Thien, D. (2005). After or beyond feeling? A consideration of affect and emotion in geography. *Area, 37*, 350–356.

Thrift, N. (2005). But malice aforethought: Cities and the natural history of hatred. *Transactions of the Institute of British Geographers, 30*, 133–150.

Thrift, N. (2007). *Non-representational theory: Space, politics, affect*. London: Routledge.

Urry, J. (2007). *Mobilities*. Cambridge: Polity.

Whatmore, S. (1993). On doing rural research (or breaking the boundaries). *Environment and Planning A, 25*, 605–607.

Williams, R. (1973). *The country and the city*. London: Chatto and Windus.

Woods, M. (2005). *Rural geography*. London: Sage.

Woods, M. (2009). Rural geography: Blurring boundaries and making connections. *Progress in Human Geography, 33*, 849–858.

Woods, M. (2010). Performing rurality and practicing rural geography. *Progress in Human Geography, 34*, 835–846.

# Index

**A**
Aboriginality, 191–193
Aboriginal languages, 198–199, 203
Aboriginal peoples, 191–205
Africa, 2–5, 29, 38, 57, 59, 61, 68, 70–72, 76–77, 82, 89, 96, 125–133, 140, 307–308, 334, 337, 353, 364, 369–382
Age
   65 and over, 67, 144–145
   dependency, 67, 69, 76, 90, 96, 98, 125, 131, 133, 144, 146, 152
   at marriage, 177, 186
   -sex structures, 196
   -specific fertility rate, 26, 70
   structure, 18, 26–27, 67, 82, 90, 96, 100, 108, 116, 126–131, 133, 144, 149, 157, 161, 196, 204, 240, 296, 338, 354, 358
Aging, 2, 5, 17–18, 26–27, 31–32, 42, 67–77, 98, 108, 130, 157, 207, 209, 213, 240–241, 244, 250, 257, 260, 267, 284–285, 288, 315, 339, 349, 356–358
Agrarian subjects, 161–163
Agricultural employment, 76, 119–121, 140
Agriculture, 2, 7–8, 25, 36, 44, 49–50, 52–53, 73, 75, 89, 96, 99, 103–104, 108–109, 116, 119–122, 142, 149, 159, 163, 166, 169, 187, 204, 207–208, 210–211, 216, 248, 274, 276, 278, 283, 285, 287, 294–296, 300–302, 307–308, 339, 343–344, 352, 389
American Indian, 194, 199, 203–204, 211, 257
Argentina, 59, 61, 95, 97, 109, 353
Arranged marriage, 178
Asia, 3–5, 17, 38, 51, 57, 59–61, 81–82, 96, 111–123, 129, 138, 191, 259, 276, 307–308, 334, 370
Australia, 59, 82, 140, 194, 203–204, 259, 351–352, 363

**B**
Behavioral Risk Factor Surveillance System (BRFSS), 261–263, 265
Boundary, 9, 19, 36, 39–40, 49, 52, 63, 81, 89, 122, 131, 150, 192, 194, 203, 228, 320, 326, 330, 335–337, 340, 344, 390
Brazil, 95, 151, 276, 370
Brea, J.A., 95–96, 98

**C**
Career ladders, 315
Caretaking, 75–77
Caribbean, 82, 95, 97, 109
Caste, 169, 171, 173, 177
Census, 8–9, 11, 13, 19–21, 23, 26, 39–40, 42–43, 54, 68, 70, 81, 98, 109, 113, 117, 119–122, 139–140, 143, 146, 149–150, 156, 160, 169, 171–176, 179, 182–183, 187, 191–204, 208, 211, 213, 229, 240, 244–245, 276, 283–284, 294, 298–299, 301–302, 308, 322, 325, 337, 340–341, 350, 354–358, 360–361, 381
Census of India, 169, 171–173, 175–176, 179, 182–183, 187
Central America, 207, 209, 218, 295
Changing demographics, 239, 242
Chaotic conception, 388–389
Chicago, IL, 319–324
Child care, 179, 231–233, 235–236, 250–251, 315
Child health, 109, 123, 129, 181–182, 260, 376, 382
Chile, 59, 95–109
Chilean Ministry of Planning and Cooperation (MIDEPLAN), 98, 100, 102–107
China, 2, 5, 38, 51, 59–61, 63, 71, 75–77, 111–113, 119, 137–153, 180, 260, 312, 316, 329, 338, 353
Cold War, 96
Community capitals, 350–352, 362–364
Commuting, 8–9, 19, 45–46, 119, 121–123, 229, 232, 280, 286, 288, 319–330, 363, 390
Complementarity, 320–321
Compositional effects, 356
Contextual effects, 330
Contraception, 130, 173, 180–181, 260
Counterurbanization, 2, 36, 57, 63, 83, 90, 111, 352, 390–393
Coupled human-nature systems, 334, 342
Cuba, 97
Culture, 7, 73, 76, 87, 117, 138–139, 183, 195, 198, 202, 225, 227, 310, 349, 396
   and fertility, 87, 116, 183–186, 226, 349, 396–398

**D**
Daughter discrimination, 181, 183–184
Dayshift, 226, 231, 233, 235
Deconcentration, 5, 40–42, 45–46, 319–330
Demand-side policies, 313

Demographic transition, 17–32, 36, 38, 69, 72, 77, 90, 96–98, 107, 109, 125–126, 129, 133, 146–148, 183, 333, 349
Demography, 1–5, 7–13, 81–91, 95–109, 111–123, 127, 133, 137–153, 169–188, 195, 204, 207, 255, 284–285, 333–344, 369–370, 382, 393, 397–398
  of rural health, 12, 255
Development
  place-based economic, 246, 248
  workforce, 307, 312–313, 315
District level household and facility survey, 173
Disturbance, 337–339, 342
Divorce, 17, 99–100, 109, 146, 211, 239–240, 242–244, 246, 248, 250, 261
Dominance, 54, 61–62, 81, 372
Dowry, 177–178, 185–186
Dowry Prohibition Act, 178

## E
Ecuador, 95
Education, 1, 8, 37, 52, 54, 86–87, 102–106, 108, 112, 116–118, 123, 126–129, 131–132, 139, 149, 169, 174, 177–179, 181, 184–187, 197, 199–204, 208–210, 212, 218–219, 221, 227–229, 232, 235, 239, 243, 245–246, 255–257, 260–262, 267, 277–278, 283–285, 288, 297, 300–302, 307, 309, 311–312, 315, 320, 324, 330, 350–351, 356–357, 360, 362, 364, 373, 377–378, 381
Educational outcomes, 200–201
Ehrlich, P. R., 333–334, 339
Eisenhower, Dwight D., 95–96
Employment
  and unemployment rates, 202
  women/men, 188, 228, 232–233, 235–236, 239–240, 245, 248–250
Environment, 4–5, 9, 12–13, 39, 42, 285, 288, 313–314, 333–335, 338–343, 349
Ethnic affiliation, 192–194
Ethnic identity, 192–193
Ethnic mobility, 192–194, 196, 204
EU accession states, 89
Europe, 3–5, 17, 31–32, 35, 37–38, 50, 54, 59, 61, 69, 71, 75–77, 81–91, 140, 151, 227, 307–308, 320, 329, 339, 373, 387, 390
European Union (EU), 41, 75, 81, 83, 86–87, 89–91
Everyday life, 388–390, 395, 398

## F
Family change, 248
Family decision making, 173, 187
Family planning, 129, 149, 170, 174, 177, 180–181, 183
Family well-being, 246, 250
Female feticide, 170, 185
Fertility
  decline, 26, 36, 125, 129, 149, 174, 177, 179–180, 183–186
  differentials, 174
  rates, 17–18, 26–27, 29–30, 32, 38, 49, 67, 69–70, 71, 73–74, 77, 87, 97, 116, 120, 129, 143, 152, 155–157, 179, 226, 240–241, 244
  transition, 125, 129–130, 133
Financial capital, 308, 311, 349–353, 356, 360–362, 364

First Nations, 191, 193–196, 198–202, 204
Fosterage, 126, 128, 131–133

## G
Gender inequality, 186, 227
Gender roles, 225, 227, 239
Geographically weighted regression, 319, 324
Germany, 69, 75, 87, 89
Girl child schemes, 186
Globalization, 22, 126–127, 133, 160, 173, 178, 274–279, 288, 373–375, 377, 382, 389
Green jobs, 313–315
Guadeloupe, 97

## H
Health, 12, 116–118, 181, 217–218, 255–267, 369–382
  disparities, 255–267, 273
Highest level of eduction, 200–201, 203, 261
High school, 129, 131, 200–201, 203, 210, 216, 218, 227, 235, 239, 241, 261, 285, 300–302, 312
Hinduism, 173, 177
Hindu-Muslim fertility, 174, 179
HIV/AIDS, 76, 129, 256, 260
Home language, 13, 198
Honduras, 96, 295
Household
  amenities, 105, 176
  size, 101, 333–334
  type, 173
Housing, 8–9, 11–12, 38, 41, 75, 87–88, 100, 127, 156, 163, 198, 256–257, 277, 282, 288, 295, 315, 324–326, 328, 330, 339–344, 354, 363, 393–394
  growth, 340–342
Human capital, 75, 102, 106, 108, 127, 186, 221, 226, 228, 232, 235–236, 242, 248, 273–274, 277–278, 281, 283–285, 288, 295–297, 299, 302, 350–352, 356–360, 362–364
Human Development Index, 55, 97
Hungary, 38–40, 45–47

## I
Ideology (gender role ideology), 225–228, 232–233, 235–236, 371
Illiteracy, 102, 108, 174
Immigration, 17, 19–20, 26, 28, 30–32, 41, 44, 74, 77, 85–86, 89, 95–96, 196, 221, 288, 295
Import substitution industrialization, 96
Income, 8, 41–42, 50, 54–55, 57, 59, 73, 87–88, 97, 101–102, 108, 116, 118–123, 125, 127, 142–143, 150, 152, 158–159, 164–166, 179, 181, 186, 188, 210, 212, 217–218, 221, 225–226, 229–231, 239–240, 242, 246, 249–251, 255–258, 260–262, 267, 273, 275, 277, 279, 285, 288, 293, 295, 302, 304
  inequality, 127, 239–240, 249–250, 293, 295, 308
India, 5, 59, 111–113, 151, 169–188, 260, 370
Indian Act, 192, 194
Indian
  reserves, 192, 194–195, 204
  youth, 174
Indigenous groups, 96, 101

Indonesia, 61, 111–113, 115–123, 151
Industrialization, 1, 38, 41, 50, 59, 74, 89, 96–97, 120, 142, 156, 295–296, 304
Industry, 38, 103–104, 113, 116, 119–120, 123, 142, 160, 207, 209–210, 227, 229, 282, 297, 309–311, 324, 352, 363, 389
Inequality, 118, 125–133, 142, 152, 163, 186, 207, 209–210, 221, 227, 239–240, 249–250, 256, 293–295, 308, 352, 369, 371, 373–374, 378, 382
Infant mortality rate, 97, 117–118, 156, 256–257, 260, 370, 376–379
Internal migration, 11, 38–39, 44, 46, 105, 108, 150, 157, 391
International labour migration, 90
Inuit, 191, 193–196, 198–202, 204
IPAT, 333
Italy, 69, 72, 75, 87, 89–90, 96

### J
Japan, 17, 49–51, 68–69, 71–72, 74–75, 112–115, 119–120, 122, 138, 140, 151, 259
Java, 112, 115–116, 119–122
Joint family, 173

### K
Kenya, 76, 129, 370, 375, 378–380, 382

### L
Labor force participation (wives/husbands), 103, 108, 143, 160, 226, 228, 232, 239–340, 350
  rate, 202
Labor markets, 5, 40, 103–104, 120–121, 131, 133, 156, 159, 164, 166, 199–204, 210, 225–228, 232, 235–236, 246, 248–250, 273–283, 285–288, 295, 304, 307, 310–313, 315–316, 350
Land cover change, 343
Landscape
  change, 340–341
  ecology, 334
Land use change, 329, 338
Language retention, 198–199
Latin America, 3–5, 28, 38, 57, 61, 71, 75–76, 82, 95–99, 101, 103, 105, 107–109, 116, 123, 129, 160, 307, 334, 370
Latin American and Caribbean Demographic Centre (CELADE), 97–98
Life expectancy, 50, 55, 68–74, 89, 97, 131, 179, 196, 217, 240, 258, 339, 374
  at birth, 69–71, 73, 97
Lifespan, 69–70
Literacy, 102–103, 108, 112, 169, 174, 182
  level, 174

### M
Malthus, T. R, 4, 333
Manufacturing, 8, 22–23, 41–42, 49, 53–54, 57, 89, 96, 104, 116, 120–121, 152, 166, 208, 216, 228, 240, 248, 274–276, 278, 281–284, 295–297, 300–303, 308–312, 314–315, 354
Marital status, 137, 146, 212, 218, 221, 243, 245, 249, 261
Marriage, 17, 73, 96, 99–101, 108–109, 116, 146, 149–150, 170, 175, 177–179, 185–186, 192, 199, 229, 239, 242–245, 248, 250, 338
Massachusetts, 226, 228, 234, 341, 344
Maternal health, 256–257
Mate selection, 177–178
Median age, 29, 67–71, 90, 177, 196, 203–204, 213–214, 244, 357
Megacities, 60–63, 321, 325
Métis, 191, 193–196, 198–200, 202, 204
Metropolitan Statistical Areas, 8, 69, 261
Mexican rural population, 155–167
Mexico, 5, 37–38, 44, 95, 151, 155–167, 203, 207–210, 218, 293, 295, 312, 372
Micropolitan Areas, 8, 71–72, 279, 285
Migration
  rural-rural, 115
  rural-urban, 38, 42, 99, 101, 112–116, 121, 128, 156–157, 208
Minority
  groups, 20, 26, 151–152, 207, 209–211, 216–218, 221, 294
  nationalities, 137, 151
  population, 18, 20, 27–31, 149, 151–152, 210, 221, 250, 295–296
Missing girls, 181
Morbidity, 96, 256, 258, 260–262, 266, 375
More-than-representational, 392, 395–396
Mortality, 10–11, 13, 17–19, 24–26, 29, 32, 36, 38, 49–52, 59, 69, 86, 96–97, 118, 127, 133, 137, 146, 149, 152, 156, 166, 169, 173, 179, 181, 183–184, 186, 192, 211, 216–217, 255–260, 266, 349, 370, 373–382, 396–397
Mother tongue, 192, 198–199

### N
National family health survey, 173, 177, 180–181, 186
National Socioeconomic Characterization Survey (CASEN), 98–107, 109
Natural amenities, 22
Natural change, 82–86, 89
Natural increase, 17–32, 36, 38, 41–42, 45, 86, 90, 96–98, 112–113, 139, 196, 364
Natural resources, 2, 4–5, 18, 54, 169, 201, 274, 282, 288, 314, 333, 339, 342, 349–350, 352
New Zealand, 59, 82, 203–204
Non-agricultural employment, 120–121
Nonmetropolitan, 8–9, 13, 18–22, 24–32, 39–40, 43–44, 46, 54, 67–68, 71–72, 76–77, 211, 226–229, 240, 242–244, 249–250, 258, 261, 273, 279–287, 307–311, 321–322, 329–330, 353–355, 358–359, 361
Nonmetropolitan America, 18–19, 22, 26, 32, 228, 244, 250
Nonstandard work arrangements, 229, 231
North America, 3, 38, 50, 59, 69, 71, 140, 191, 204, 307, 387
North American Indians, 199, 204
Northwest Territories, 195–196
Nuclear family, 76–77, 391, 393
Nunavut, 195–196

## O

Occupational sex segregation, 234
Off-farm employment, 120, 122
Old-age dependency ratio, 67, 69, 90
Old age support, 185
Ovenbird, 341–342, 344

## P

Percent age 60 and over, 68, 75
Pinochet, Augusto, 97, 101
PNDT (Regulation and Prevention of Misuse) Act, 185
Policy options, 90
Population
    aging, 2, 17, 31–32, 42, 67–71, 74–75, 87, 90, 98, 257, 267, 358
    growth, 3–4, 18, 20, 22, 24, 27–28, 32, 35–38, 40–46, 50, 52, 54, 58–59, 61, 82–85, 88, 96–98, 112, 128, 137–139, 160, 171, 177–178, 194, 196, 209, 249, 281, 295–296, 319, 321–322, 329–330, 333, 339–340, 344, 349, 353
    momentum, 96, 112
    projections, 180
    pyramid, 143, 166, 240–241
    redistribution, 35–40, 45–47
Population Reference Bureau, 72, 74, 95, 97–98, 375
Portugal, 72, 75, 84, 89–90, 96
Post-secondary education, 200
Poverty, 118–119, 285–287, 293–304
Primacy, 61–62, 97, 393
Primary schools, 118, 123

## R

Racial and ethnic relations, 12, 20, 30, 32, 72, 207–209, 211–213, 216–218, 221, 293–294
Recession, 12, 46, 75, 77, 91, 245–246, 250, 273, 282, 287–288, 293, 370
    2008, 54, 83, 85, 288
Regional growth policies, 329
Regional transportation planning, 329
Registered Indian, 191–194
Religion, 169, 173–174, 181, 377
Religious composition, 173–174
Renewable energy, 314–316
Representation, 3, 37–38, 128, 143, 151, 157, 241–242, 297, 340, 388–398
Reproductive and child health, 181–182
Restructuring, 18, 36, 87, 207, 225, 240, 242, 246, 248–249, 274–277, 307, 319–321, 323–324, 326, 329, 388, 390, 392
Retention ratio, 198–199
Retirement
    age, 41, 67, 69–70, 145, 240, 339, 349–350, 353, 358, 363
    migration, 18, 75, 88–90
Rural
    definitions of
        international, 89, 256, 259–260, 267
        United States, 10
    demography, 1–5, 7–13, 81–91, 96, 107, 109, 111–123, 137, 169–188, 204, 255, 285, 334, 387, 393, 397
        integration of, 13
    density analyses, 10, 13
    diversity, 3
    families, 128, 226, 230, 235–236, 239–251
    households, 101, 108, 112, 118–119, 121, 126, 131, 143, 158–163, 166, 175, 177, 228, 236, 244, 307
    infrastructure, 105, 174–175
    labor markets, 273–275, 277–283, 285, 287–288, 307, 313, 316
        in developing countries, 316
    myth (rural ideology) (gemeinschaft), 225–236
    population estimates/projections, 19, 21, 23, 180
    to urban migration, 38, 52, 86, 96–98, 107–109, 128, 175, 308, 316, 364
    -urban population, 36, 38, 137, 139–142
    USDA codes, 44
Rural areas, demographic processes, 10–11
Rurality, 1–5, 8–10, 13, 85, 111–112, 137, 139–142, 160, 387–398

## S

Santiago, Chile, 98–99
Scale, 3, 24, 32, 36–37, 39, 50, 67, 75, 88, 91, 127, 139, 158, 179, 181, 204, 209, 226, 274, 279–280, 307, 312, 324, 335, 337, 340–344, 354, 388–389, 391
Scenario planning, 330
Secondary school diploma, 200
*Seiurus aurocapillus*, 341
Selective migration, 18, 364
Self-rated health, 258, 260–264, 266
Sequential scheduling of work, 226, 235–236
Service sector, 73, 122, 248, 276, 280–283, 307–309, 312
Sex
    composition of children, 184
    ratio, 73–74, 144–145, 170, 176, 181–186, 213–214, 216, 218, 338
    selection, 183, 185–186
    selective abortion, 184–186
Social capital, 234, 236, 248, 330, 350–353, 356, 361–364
Social impact analyses, 363, 374
Sonography, 181
Son preference, 144, 181, 183–186
South Africa, 76, 353, 370
South America, 77, 95, 97
Spain, 84, 90, 96, 394
Spatial heterogeneity, 319–330
Sprawl, 98, 334, 374, 393
Spread urbanization, 52–54
Sri Lanka, 113–115, 118, 120
Standard work arrangements (full-time, year-round employment), 229, 231, 233–234
Status of women, 173, 177, 179, 181–182, 186–187
Sterilization, 180
Sub-Saharan Africa, 68, 71, 76, 125–133, 140, 260, 369–382
Substitution, 9, 11–12, 96, 120, 320–321
Suburbanization, 2, 53, 83, 319, 327, 393
Supply-side policies, 313
Sustainability, 2, 4, 256, 273, 314, 351, 354
Sweden, 72, 75, 84, 87, 89
Switzerland, 37, 75, 81, 83

# Index

**T**
Thailand, 51, 76, 111–118, 120, 123
Thin labor markets, 311, 313
Total dependency ratio, 69
Total fertility rate (TFR), 17, 26, 38, 69–71, 73–74, 97, 125, 129, 152, 179–180, 182
Treaty Indian, 191

**U**
UK (United Kingdom), *see* United Kingdom (UK)
Ultrasound, 181, 186
Unemployment, 87–88, 103, 128, 131, 150, 174, 202–203, 217–218, 221, 229, 243, 246, 248, 273, 280, 285–288, 374, 377
United Kingdom (UK), 41, 75, 84–86, 88–89, 227, 259, 352, 387, 389
United States (U.S.), 2–5, 7–13, 17, 24–25, 31, 49–50, 52, 57, 59–61, 76, 137, 144, 150–151, 194, 203–204, 207, 209, 221, 227, 240, 255–257, 259–260, 262, 266, 273, 287, 293–295, 299, 302–303, 319–320, 329, 350, 352, 354, 361–363, 369, 375
University of Chile, 98
Unwanted daughters, 181, 183
Urbanization, 1–5, 35–44, 46, 49–63, 76, 81–82, 84–89, 95–98, 107–108, 111, 113, 116, 119, 128, 139, 141, 155, 166, 209, 280, 307, 334, 337, 364, 382, 390
Urban-rural dichotomy, 35, 111

Urban transition, 82
Uruguay, 95, 97
U.S. (United States), *see* United States (U.S.)

**V**
Valparaiso, Chile, 99
Value-added, 308
Value of children, 181, 183, 185–186

**W**
Wages/earnings/income, 8, 41–42, 44, 50, 54–55, 57, 59, 73, 87–88, 97, 101–102, 108, 116, 118–123, 125–127, 131, 142–143, 150, 152, 158–159, 164–166, 179, 181, 186, 188, 207, 209–212, 217–218, 221, 225–226, 228–231, 235–236, 239–240, 242, 245–246, 248–251, 255–258, 260–262, 267, 273, 275, 277, 279, 282–286, 288, 293, 295, 297, 303–304, 307–312, 315, 324, 326, 328
Washington Consensus, 96–97, 369, 371
Wisconsin, 225–226, 228–231, 235–236, 314, 321
Women's employment, 228, 232–233, 235–236, 239–240, 245, 248–250
Work force, 75, 278

**Y**
Youth exodus, 87
Yukon, 195–196